A TEXTBOOK ON
EU LAW

A Textbook on
EU LAW

Andrew Evans

HART PUBLISHING – OXFORD
1998

Hart Publishing
Oxford
UK

Distributed in the United States by
Northwestern University Press
625 Colfax
Evanston
Illinois
60208-4210 USA

Distributed in Australia and New Zealand by
Federation Press Pty Ltd
PO Box 45
Annandale, NSW 2038
Australia

Distributed in Netherlands, Belgium and Luxembourg by
Intersentia, Churchillaan 108
B2900 Schoten
Antwerpen
Belgium

Hart Publishing is a specialist legal publisher based in Oxford, England. To order further
copies of this book or to request a list of other publications please write to:

Hart Publishing, 19 Whitehouse Road, Oxford, OX1 4PA
Telephone: +44 (0)1865 434459 Fax: +44 (0) 1865 794882
email: hartpub@janep.demon.co.uk

British Library Cataloguing in Publication Data
Data Available

ISBN   1-901362-36-1(cloth)
1-901362-37-X (paper)

Typeset in Minion
by John Saunders Design & Production, Reading
Printed in Great Britain on acid-free paper
by Biddles Ltd, Guildford and Kings Lynn.

Preface

This book examines the "core" principles of European Union law. The main sources on which reliance has been placed, apart from the EC Treaty, the Treaty on European Union, and the Amsterdam Treaty themselves, are judgments of the European Courts, legislative enactments of the Council of the Union, administrative decisions of the European Commission, and official publications of national and Union institutions. Reference is also made to legal and, occasionally, to social scientific literature. Reference to literature of the latter kind is felt to be justified by the insights into law which can be gained by taking account of its social context.

The scope and detail of the book are designed to make it suitable for EU law courses generally as well as for those courses which concentrate on the institutional or "substantive" economic aspects of Union law. At the same time, the book should also be useful for courses on subjects such as Consumer Law, Environmental Law, or Labour Law, which necessarily have an EU law component.

More fundamentally, this is the first textbook which provides a systematic basis for studying EU law against the background of globalisation. Globalisation is a complicated process, which is particularly manifest in the diminishing significance of national frontiers. Its relationship with European integration is controversial. On the one hand, Member States may seek to reacquire at Union level powers lost at national level. On the other hand, the reality of the process may be such that it is problematic for the Union to base its activities on the premise that its frontiers have taken on the significance lost by national frontiers. Equally, the tendency of more traditional textbooks to treat the law governing relations between Member States separately from the law governing relations between the Union and third states may be problematic both for students and practitioners. It is hoped that, by challenging the tendency, this textbook will make a modest contribution to developing more outward-looking approaches to the study and practice of EU law.

ANDREW EVANS
January 1998

Contents

Part Two
LAW OF THE COMMON MARKET

Part Three
LAW OF HARMONISATION AND COMMON POLICIES

List of Abbreviations

AELE	Association Européenne de Libre Echange
AiH	Aktuellt i Handelspolitiken
ANSI	American National Standards Institute
Benelux	Belgium, The Netherlands, and Luxembourg
Bull. EC	Bulletin of the European Communities
Bull. EU	Bulletin of the European Union
CAP	Common Agricultural Policy
CCT	Common Customs Tariff
CEAB	Commission Européenne Archives Bruxelles
CECA	Communauté Européenne du Charbon et de l'Acier
CEN	Comité Européen de Normalisation
CENELEC	Comité Européen de Normalisation Electronique
CEPT	Conférence Européenne des Administration des Postes et Télécommunications
CFI	Court of First Instance
CFSP	Common Foreign and Security Policy
CMLR	Common Market Law Reports
Cmnd	Command Paper (British Government Publication)
CoCom	Coordinating Committee for Multilateral Export Controls
CoCor	Coordinating Committee
COM	Communication from the European Commission
COR	Committee of the Regions
COREPER	Comité des Représentants Permanents
CREST	Scientific and Technical Research Committee
CSF	Community Support Framework
Débs PE	Débats du Parlement Européen
DN	Dagens Nyheter
Ds	Departementsserien
EAGGF	European Agricultural Guidance and Guarantee Fund
EC	European Community
ECJ	European Court of Justice
ECLR	European Competition Law Review
ECR	European Court Reports
ECSC	European Coal and Steel Community
ECU	European Currency Unit
EEC	European Economic Community

EEA	European Economic Area
EES	European Economic Space
EFTA	European Free Trade Association
EFTA Bull.	Bulletin of the European Free Trade Association
EG	Europeiska Gemenskaperna
EIB	European Investment Bank
EMU	European Monetary Union
EOTC	European Organisation for Testing and Certification
EP Debs	European Parliament Debates
EP Doc.	European Parliament Working Document
EPC	European Political Cooperation
ERDF	European Regional Development Fund
ESA	EFTA Surveillance Authority
ESC	Economic and Social Committee
ESF	European Social Fund
ETSI	European Telecommunications Standards Institute
ETUC	European Trade Union Confederation
Euratom	European Atomic Energy Community
Eurostat	Statistical Office of the European Communities
GATT	General Agreement on Tariffs and Trade
GDP	Gross Domestic Product
GNP	Gross National Product
GRUR Int.	Gewerblicher Rechtsschutz und Urheberrecht: Internationaler Teil
HC	House of Commons
HL	House of Lords
ILM	International Legal Materials
JO	Journal Officiel des Communautés Européennes
LO	Landsorganisationen
MEPs	Members of the European Parliament
MT	Merger Treaty
NATO	North Atlantic Treaty Organisation
NJA	Nytt Juridisk Archiv
NU	Nordisk Utredningsserie (Nordic Report Series)
OCT	Overseas Countries and Territories
OECD	Organisation for Economic Cooperation and Development
OGTLR	Oil and Gas Law and Taxation Review
OJ	Official Journal of the European Communities
Prop.	Regeringens Proposition (Swedish Government Bill)
R & D	Research and Development
Rec.	Recueil de la Cour de Justice des Communautés Européennes
SAF	Svenska Arbetsgivareföreningen (Swedish Employers' Association)

SEC	Internal Document from the Secretariat-General of the European Commission
SEW	Sociaal-Economische Wetgeving
SFS	Svensk Författningssamling (Swedish Official Journal)
SG	Secretariat-General of the European Commission
SLT	Scots Law Times
SMEs	Small and Medium-sized Enterprises
SOU	Sveriges Offentliga Utredningar (Sweden's Official Reports)
SPD	Single Programming Document
SvD	Svenska Dagbladet
TCN	Third country national
TSN	Third state national
TEU	Treaty on European Union
UNICE	Union des Industries de la Communauté Européenne
UU	Utrikesutskottets Betänkande (Reports of the Swedish Foreign Affairs Committee)
VAT	Value Added Tax
VER	Voluntary Export Restraints
WEU	Western European Union
WQ	Written Question (European Parliament)
WTO	World Trade Organisation

Tables

Numbering of the Treaty on European Union and the EC Treaty before and after entry into Force of the Amsterdam Treaty

A. Treaty on European Union

Before	After	Before	After
TITLE I	TITLE I	Article J.15	Article 25
		Article J.16	Article 26
Article A	Article 1	Article J.17	Article 27
Article B	Article 2	Article J.18	Article 28
Article C	Article 3		
Article D	Article 4	TITLE VI (***)	TITLE VI*
Article E	Article 5		
Article F	Article 6	Article K.1	Article 29
Article F.1 (*)	Article 7	Article K.2	Article 30
		Article K.3	Article 31
TITLE II	TITLE II	Article K.4	Article 32
		Article K.5	Article 33
Article G	Article 8	Article K.6	Article 34
		Article K.7	Article 35
TITLE III	TITLE III	Article K.8	Article 36
		Article K.9	Article 37
Article H	Article 9	Article K.10	Article 38
		Article K.11	Article 39
TITLE IV	TITLE IV	Article K.12	Article 40
		Article K.13	Article 41
Article I	Article 10	Article K.14	Article 42
TITLE V (***)	TITLE V	TITLE VIa (**)	TITLE VII
Article J.1	Article 11	Article K.15(*)	Article 43
Article J.2	Article 12	Article K.16(*)	Article 44
Article J.3	Article 13	Article K.17(*)	Article 45
Article J.4	Article 14		
Article J.5	Article 15	TITLE VII	TITLE VIII
Article J.6	Article 16		
Article J.7	Article 17	Article L	Article 46
Article J.8	Article 18	Article M	Article 47
Article J.9	Article 19	Article N	Article 48
Article J.10	Article 20	Article O	Article 49
Article J.11	Article 21	Article P	Article 50
Article J.12	Article 22	Article Q	Article 51
Article J.13	Article 23	Article R	Article 52
Article J.14	Article 24	Article S	Article 53

B. Treaty establishing the European Community

Before	*After*	*Before*	*After*
PART ONE	PART ONE	Article 17 (repealed)	—
Article 1	Article 1	Section 2 (deleted)	—
Article 2	Article 2	Article 18 (repealed)	—
Article 3	Article 3	Article 19 (repealed)	—
Article 3a	Article 4	Article 20 (repealed)	—
Article 3b	Article 5	Article 21 (repealed)	—
Article 3c (*)	Article 6	Article 22 (repealed)	—
Article 4	Article 7	Article 23 (repealed)	—
Article 4a	Article 8	Article 24 (repealed)	—
Article 4b	Article 9	Article 25 (repealed)	—
Article 5	Article 10	Article 26 (repealed)	—
Article 5a (*)	Article 11	Article 27 (repealed)	—
Article 6	Article 12	Article 28	Article 26
Article 6a	Article 13	Article 29	Article 27
Article 7 (repealed)	—		
Article 7a	Article 14	CHAPTER 2	CHAPTER 2
Article 7b (repealed)	—	Article 30	Article 28
Article 7c	Article 15	Article 31 (repealed)	—
Article 7d (*)	Article 16	Article 32 (repealed)	—
		Article 33 (repealed)	—
PART TWO	PART TWO	Article 34	Article 29
Article 8	Article 17	Article 35 (repealed)	—
Article 8a	Article 18	Article 36	Article 30
Article 8b	Article 19	Article 37	Article 31
Article 8c	Article 20		
Article 8d	Article 21	TITLE II	TITLE II
Article 8e	Article 22	Article 38	Article 32
		Article 39	Article 33
PART THREE	PART THREE	Article 40	Article 34
TITLE I	TITLE I	Article 41	Article 35
Article 9	Article 23	Article 42	Article 36
Article 10	Article 24	Article 43	Article 37
Article 11 (repealed)	—	Article 44 (repealed)	—
		Article 45 (repealed)	—
CHAPTER 1	CHAPTER 1	Article 46	Article 38
Section 1 (deleted)	—	Article 47 (repealed)	—
Article 12	Article 25		
Article 13 (repealed)	—	TITLE III	TITLE III
Article 14 (repealed)	—	CHAPTER 1	CHAPTER 1
Article 15 (repealed)	—	Article 48	Article 39
Article 16 (repealed)	—		

Before	After
Article 49	Article 40
Article 50	Article 41
Article 51	Article 42
CHAPTER 2	**CHAPTER 2**
Article 52	Article 43
Article 53 (repealed)	—
Article 54	Article 44
Article 55	Article 45
Article 56	Article 46
Article 57	Article 47
Article 58	Article 48
CHAPTER 3	**CHAPTER 3**
Article 59	Article 49
Article 60	Article 50
Article 61	Article 51
Article 60	Article 50
Article 62 (repealed)	—
Article 63	Article 52
Article 64	Article 53
Article 65	Article 54
Article 66	Article 55
CHAPTER 4	**CHAPTER 4**
Article 67 (repealed)	—
Article 68 (repealed)	—
Article 69 (repealed)	—
Article 70 (repealed)	—
Article 71 (repealed)	—
Article 72 (repealed)	—
Article 73 (repealed)	—
Article 73a (repealed)	—
Article 73b	Article 56
Article 73c	Article 57
Article 73d	Article 58
Article 73e (repealed)	—
Article 73f	Article 59
Article 73g	Article 60
Article 73h (repealed)	—
TITLE IIIa (**)	**TITLE IV**
Article 73i (*)	Article 61
Article 73j (*)	Article 62

Before	After
Article 73k (*)	Article 63
Article 73l (*)	Article 64
Article 73m (*)	Article 65
Article 73n (*)	Article 66
Article 73o (*)	Article 67
Article 73p (*)	Article 68
Article 73q (*)	Article 69
TITLE IV (**)	**TITLE V**
Article 74	Article 70
Article 75	Article 71
Article 76	Article 72
Article 77	Article 73
Article 78	Article 74
Article 79	Article 75
Article 80	Article 76
Article 81	Article 77
Article 82	Article 78
Article 83	Article 79
Article 84	Article 80
TITLE V	**TITLE VI**
CHAPTER 1	**CHAPTER 1**
SECTION 1	**SECTION 1**
Article 85	Article 81
Article 86	Article 82
Article 87	Article 83
Article 88	Article 84
Article 89	Article 85
Article 90	Article 86
Section 2 (deleted)	—
Article 91 (repealed)	—
SECTION 3	**SECTION 2**
Article 92	Article 87
Article 93	Article 88
Article 94	Article 89
CHAPTER 2	**CHAPTER 2**
Article 95	Article 90
Article 96	Article 91
Article 97 (repealed)	—
Article 98	Article 92

Before	After
Article 99	Article 93
CHAPTER 3	CHAPTER 3
Article 100	Article 94
Article 100a	Article 95
Article 100b (repealed)	—
Article 100c (repealed)	—
Article 100d (repealed)	—
Article 101	Article 96
Article 102	Article 97
TITLE VI	TITLE VII
CHAPTER 1	CHAPTER 1
Article 102a	Article 98
Article 103	Article 99
Article 103a	Article 100
Article 104	Article 101
Article 104a	Article 102
Article 104b	Article 103
Article 104c	Article 104
CHAPTER 2	CHAPTER 2
Article 105	Article 105
Article 105a	Article 106
Article 106	Article 107
Article 107	Article 108
Article 108	Article 109
Article 108a	Article 110
Article 109	Article 111
CHAPTER 3	CHAPTER 3
Article 109a	Article 112
Article 109b	Article 113
Article 109c	Article 114
Article 109d	Article 115
CHAPTER 4	CHAPTER 4
Article 109e	Article 116
Article 109f	Article 117
Article 109g	Article 118
Article 109h	Article 119
Article 109i	Article 120
Article 109j	Article 121

Before	After
Article 109k	Article 122
Article 109l	Article 123
Article 109m	Article 124
TITLE VIa (**)	TITLE VIII
Article 109n (*)	Article 125
Article 109o (*)	Article 126
Article 109p (*)	Article 127
Article 109q (*)	Article 128
Article 109r (*)	Article 129
Article 109s (*)	Article 130
TITLE VII	TITLE IX
Article 110	Article 131
Article 111 (repealed)	—
Article 112	Article 132
Article 113	Article 133
Article 114 (repealed)	—
Article 115	Article 134
TITLE VIIa	TITLE X
Article 116 (*)	Article 135
TITLE VIII	TITLE XI
CHAPTER 1 (***)	CHAPTER 1
Article 117	Article 136
Article 118	Article 137
Article 118a	Article 138
Article 118b	Article 139
Article 118c	Article 140
Article 119	Article 141
Article 119a	Article 142
Article 120	Article 143
Article 121	Article 144
Article 122	Article 145
CHAPTER 2	CHAPTER 2
Article 123	Article 146
Article 124	Article 147
Article 125	Article 148
CHAPTER 3	CHAPTER 3
Article 126	Article 149

Before	After	Before	After
Article 127	Article 150	Article 130s	Article 175
		Article 130t	Article 176
TITLE IX	TITLE XII		
Article 128	Article 151	TITLE XVII	TITLE XX
		Article 130u	Article 177
TITLE X	TITLE XIII	Article 130v	Article 178
Article 129	Article 152	Article 130w	Article 179
		Article 130x	Article 180
TITLE XI	TITLE XIV	Article 130y	Article 181
Article 129a	Article 153	PART FOUR	PART FOUR
TITLE XII	TITLE XV	Article 131	Article 182
		Article 132	Article 183
Article 129b	Article 154	Article 133	Article 184
Article 129c	Article 155	Article 134	Article 185
Article 129d	Article 156	Article 135	Article 186
		Article 136	Article 187
TITLE XIII	TITLE XVI	Article 136a	Article 188
Article 130	Article 157	PART FIVE	PART FIVE
TITLE XIV	TITLE XVII	TITLE I	TITLE I
Article 130a	Article 158	CHAPTER 1	CHAPTER 1
Article 130b	Article 159	SECTION 1	SECTION 1
Article 130c	Article 160		
Article 130d	Article 161	Article 137	Article 189
Article 130e	Article 162	Article 138	Article 190
		Article 138a	Article 191
TITLE XV	TITLE XVIII	Article 138b	Article 192
Article 130f	Article 163	Article 138c	Article 193
Article 130g	Article 164	Article 138d	Article 194
Article 130h	Article 165	Article 138e	Article 195
Article 130i	Article 166	Article 139	Article 196
Article 130j	Article 167	Article 140	Article 197
Article 130k	Article 168	Article 141	Article 198
Article 130l	Article 169	Article 142	Article 199
Article 130m	Article 170	Article 143	Article 200
Article 130n	Article 171	Article 144	Article 201
Article 130o	Article 172		
Article 130p	Article 173	SECTION 2	SECTION 2
Article 130q (repealed)	—	Article 145	Article 202
		Article 146	Article 203
TITLE XVI	TITLE XIX	Article 147	Article 204
Article 130r	Article 174	Article 148	Article 205
		Article 149 (repealed)	—

Before	After	Before	After
Article 150	Article 206	SECTION 5	SECTION 5
Article 151	Article 207		
Article 152	Article 208	Article 188a	Article 246
Article 153	Article 209	Article 188b	Article 247
Article 154	Article 210	Article 188c	Article 248
SECTION 3	SECTION 3	CHAPTER 2	CHAPTER 2
Article 155	Article 211	Article 189	Article 249
Article 156	Article 212	Article 189a	Article 250
Article 157	Article 213	Article 189b	Article 251
Article 158	Article 214	Article 189c	Article 252
Article 159	Article 215	Article 190	Article 253
Article 160	Article 216	Article 191	Article 254
Article 161	Article 217	Article 191a (*)	Article 255
Article 162	Article 218	Article 192	Article 256
Article 163	Article 219		
		CHAPTER 3	CHAPTER 3
SECTION 4	SECTION 4	Article 193	Article 257
		Article 194	Article 258
Article 164	Article 220	Article 195	Article 259
Article 165	Article 221	Article 196	Article 260
Article 166	Article 222	Article 197	Article 261
Article 167	Article 223	Article 198	Article 262
Article 168	Article 224		
Article 168a	Article 225	CHAPTER 4	CHAPTER 4
Article 169	Article 226		
Article 170	Article 227	Article 198a	Article 263
Article 171	Article 228	Article 198b	Article 264
Article 172	Article 229	Article 198c	Article 265
Article 173	Article 230		
Article 174	Article 231	CHAPTER 5	CHAPTER 5
Article 175	Article 232		
Article 176	Article 233	Article 198d	Article 266
Article 177	Article 234	Article 198e	Article 267
Article 178	Article 235		
Article 179	Article 236	TITLE II	TITLE II
Article 180	Article 237	Article 199	Article 268
Article 181	Article 238	Article 200 (repealed)	—
Article 182	Article 239	Article 201	Article 269
Article 183	Article 240	Article 201a	Article 270
Article 184	Article 241	Article 202	Article 271
Article 185	Article 242	Article 203	Article 272
Article 186	Article 243	Article 204	Article 273
Article 187	Article 244	Article 205	Article 274
Article 188	Article 245	Article 205a	Article 275
		Article 206	Article 276

Before	After	Before	After
Article 206a (repealed)	—	Article 227	Article 299
Article 207	Article 277	Article 228	Article 300
Article 208	Article 278	Article 228a	Article 301
Article 209	Article 279	Article 229	Article 302
Article 209a	Article 280	Article 230	Article 303
		Article 231	Article 304
PART SIX	PART SIX	Article 232	Article 305
		Article 233	Article 306
Article 210	Article 281	Article 234	Article 307
Article 211	Article 282	Article 235	Article 308
Article 212 (*)	Article 283	Article 236 (*)	Article 309
Article 213	Article 284	Article 237 (repealed)	—
Article 213a (*)	Article 285	Article 238	Article 310
Article 213b (*)	Article 286	Article 239	Article 311
Article 214	Article 287	Article 240	Article 312
Article 215	Article 288	Article 241 (repealed)	—
Article 216	Article 289	Article 242 (repealed)	—
Article 217	Article 290	Article 243 (repealed)	—
Article 218 (*)	Article 291	Article 244 (repealed)	—
Article 219	Article 292	Article 245 (repealed)	—
Article 220	Article 293	Article 246 (repealed)	—
Article 221	Article 294		
Article 222	Article 295	FINAL	FINAL
Article 223	Article 296	PROVISIONS	PROVISIONS
Article 224	Article 297		
Article 225	Article 298	Article 247	Article 313
Article 226 (repealed)	—	Article 248	Article 314

(*)   New Article introduced by the Treaty of Amsterdam.
(**) New Title introduced by the Treaty of Amsterdam.
(***) Chapter 1 restructured by the Treaty of Amsterdam.

Legislation

NOTE: for the sake of clarity, this Table of Legislation is confined to major international treaties, the various European treaties and EC legislation of general application. Omitted, in particular, are the various Free Trade and Association agreements and EC Decisions, which are usually directed at single undertakings or small economic areas. All legislation is tabled in chronological/numerical order.

INTERNATIONAL CONVENTIONS

NATIONAL LEGISLATION

Cases

NOTE: in this Table the cases are given their more familiar shortened names. Readers are reminded that they can obtain the full names from the footnotes to the text.

1

Introduction: Fundamental Principles of EU Law

This book examines the law of the European Union. Strictly speaking, the Union is composed of three Communities, each with its own constituent Treaty and its own legal personality.[1]

1.1 History of the Treaties

The first Community to be established was the European Coal and Steel Community (ECSC), under the ECSC Treaty, which came into force in 1952. This Treaty provided for the introduction of a common market in coal and steel and for detailed regulation of these industries.[2] In other words, the Treaty provided for replacement of the national markets for these industries with an enlarged European market. It also provided for market regulation to be transferred from the national to the European level. The Treaty establishing the European Atomic Energy Community (Euratom), which came into force in 1958 and is concerned with the development of the nuclear industry,[3] contains similarly detailed provisions.

The Treaty establishing the European Economic Community (EEC), which also came into force in 1958, had a much broader scope. According to Article 2 of the Treaty, this Community had as its task the establishment of a common market (for goods generally) and the progressive approximation of the economic policies of Member States. By these means, the Community was to promote a harmonious development of economic activities, a continuous and balanced expansion, an increase in stability, an accelerated raising of the standard of living, and closer relations between the Member States. Although the task of this Community was so broad, the Treaty originally contained only 248 provisions. Hence, these provisions were inevitably couched in general terms and tended merely to lay down a framework to be given detailed application by the Community institutions.

---

[1] Art. 6(1) ECSC; Art. 210 EC; and Art. 184 Euratom. See also, regarding legal capacity, Art. 6(2) & (3) ECSC; Art. 211 EC; and Art. 185 Euratom.
[2] Art. 2 ECSC.   [3] Art. 1 Euratom.

All three Treaties were originally concluded by France, Germany, Italy, and the Benelux countries (Belgium, the Netherlands, and Luxembourg). Denmark, Ireland, and the United Kingdom joined the Communities in 1973. Subsequent accessions have involved Greece; Portugal and Spain; and Austria, Finland, and Sweden. As a result, there are now fifteen Member States. Further enlargements to include countries of Central and Eastern Europe as well as countries such as Cyprus and Malta are planned.[4]

The three Communities have always shared the same court (the European Court of Justice) and parliament[5] (which has become known as the European Parliament[6]). Moreover, the Treaty establishing a Single Council and a Single Commission of the European Communities (the "Merger Treaty") of 1965 replaced the old ECSC High Authority, EEC Commission, and Euratom Commission with a single Commission. It also replaced the old ECSC Special Council of Ministers, EEC Council of Ministers, and Euratom Council of Ministers with a single Council of Ministers. As a result, the same major institutions were now shared by the three Communities.

The role of these institutions and relations between them were modified by the Single European Act of 1987,[7] which was a further agreement between Member States. Not only was provision made for increased use of majority decision making in the Council,[8] but also introduction of a "co-operation procedure"[9] enhanced the legislative role of the European Parliament. The same Act also amended the EEC Treaty, to provide for completion of the "internal market" by the end of 1992 as well as the strengthening of "accompanying policies". The internal market was defined in Article 8a of the EEC Treaty[10] as an area without internal frontiers in which the free movement of goods, persons, services and capital was to be ensured in accordance with the provisions of this Treaty.

Article A of the Treaty on European Union, or "Maastricht Treaty", which came into force in 1993, has now established a European Union. The Union is founded on the three European Communities, supplemented by the policies and forms of co-operation, also established by this Treaty. These are

---

[4] See, e.g., *Agenda 2000*, Bull. EC, Supp. 5/97.

[5] Convention on Certain Institutions common to the European Communities.

[6] It was called the Common Assembly in the ECSC Treaty, and the Assembly in the EEC Treaty. It declared itself the European Parliamentary Assembly (Resolution of 20 Mar. 1958 (JO 1958 6) on the denomination of the Assembly) and, later, the European Parliament (Resolution of 30 Mar. 1962 (JO 1962 1045) concerning the denomination of the Assembly). The Council was reluctant to depart from the terms of the Treaties. See, e.g., the Reply to WQ 55/62 (JO 1962 2102) by Mr Poher. However, the denomination European Parliament was implicitly accepted by the ECJ in Case 230/81 *Luxembourg* v. *European Parliament: seat and working place of the Parliament* [1983] ECR 255 and, later, in Art. 3(1) SEA (OJ 1987 L169/1). This denomination is now used in the TEU and in EC Treaty provisions amended by the TEU and the Treaty of Amsterdam (OJ 1997 C340/1).

[7] OJ 1987 L169/1.   [8] Sect. 4.2.4 below.   [9] Sect. 3.1.1 below.

[10] It is now Art. 14 EC, as amended by the Amsterdam Treaty.

the common foreign and security policy (CFSP)[11] and co-operation in the fields of justice and home affairs.[12] The three Communities or, more particularly, the European Community, may be regarded as the "first pillar" of the Union, foreign and security policy as the "second pillar", and justice and home affairs as the "third pillar". The task of the Union is to organise, in a manner demonstrating consistency and solidarity, relations between the Member States and between their peoples.[13] The Union is served by a single institutional framework.[14] Hence, the above institutions may now be termed "Union institutions", and the Council of Ministers has officially changed its denomination to "Council of the Union".[15] An important characteristic of these institutions is their capacity to adopt legal acts entailing rights and obligations for individuals.

The Treaty on European Union also renamed the EEC as the European Community (EC) and introduced wide-ranging amendments to what now became the EC Treaty.[16] Both Treaties are now to be amended by the Treaty of Amsterdam,[17] which was signed in October 1997 and is currently undergoing ratification by the Member States. The Treaty of Amsterdam envisages the future renumbering of provisions of the EC Treaty and Treaty on European Union. This book uses the present numbering system throughout. However, a conversion table is provided,[18] so that the reader can find the number which any given provision will have when the Amsterdam Treaty comes into force.

1.2 Scope of Union Law

According to Article 2 of the EC Treaty, the European Community has as its task the establishment of a common market and the implementation of common policies and activities. By these means, a harmonious, balanced, and sustainable development of economic activities throughout the Union, a high level of employment and social protection, equality between men and women, sustainable and non-inflationary growth, a high degree of competitiveness and convergence of economic performance, a high level of protection and improvement of the quality of the environment, the raising of the standard of living and quality of life, and economic and social cohesion[19] and solidarity among Member States are to be promoted.

The "activities" to be undertaken for these purposes are outlined in Article

---

[11] Arts J.1–18 TEU.   [12] Arts K.1–17 TEU.   [13] Art. A TEU.   [14] Art. C TEU.
[15] Dec. 93/591 (OJ 1993 L281/18) concerning the name to be given to the Council following the entry into force of the TEU.
[16] Art. G TEU.   [17] OJ 1997 C340/1.   [18] At xvii–xxiii.
[19] "Cohesion" is not defined in the EC Treaty, but Art. 130a EC indicates that it includes "reducing disparities between the levels of development of the various regions [of the Union] and the backwardness of the least favoured regions or islands, including rural areas".

3(1) of the EC Treaty. This provision makes clear that the common market entails: the elimination, as between Member States, of customs duties and of quantitative restrictions on the import and export of goods, and of all other measures having equivalent effect;[20] an internal market characterized by the abolition, as between Member States, of obstacles to the freedom of movement for persons, services, and capital;[21] and a system to ensure that competition in the internal market is not distorted.[22]

In addition, the approximation of the laws of the Member States to the extent required for the proper functioning of the common market – "legislative harmonization" – is to take place.[23] In other words, differences between the laws of the various Member States are to be reduced, where these differences jeopardise the functioning of the common market. At the same time, the pursuit of a range of social and economic policies is envisaged. Their pursuit is to be based on both legislative harmonisation and harmonisation through financial instruments. They are to include: common policies in the sphere of agriculture and fishing[24] and for transport;[25] co-ordination between employment policies of Member States;[26] a policy in the social sphere comprising a European Social Fund;[27] the strengthening of economic and social cohesion;[28] environmental policy;[29] the strengthening of the competitiveness of Union industry;[30] the promotion of research and technological development;[31] encouragement for the establishment and development of trans-European networks (for transport and communications);[32] a contribution to the attainment of a high level of health protection;[33] a contribution to education and training of quality and to the flowering of the cultures of the Member States;[34] a contribution to the strengthening of consumer protection;[35] and measures in the spheres of energy, civil protection, and tourism.[36]

In all these activities the Union shall aim to eliminate inequalities, and to promote equality, between men and women.[37] At the same time, environmental protection requirements must be integrated into the definition and implementation of these policies and activities. This integration is to be designed, in particular, to promote sustainable development.[38]

Moreover, Article 3a of the EC Treaty states that the activities of the Union and the Member States shall also include the adoption of an economic policy. This policy is to be based on the close co-ordination of Member States' economic policies, on the internal market, and on the definition of common objectives. It is to be conducted in accordance with the principle of an open market economy with free competition.[39] At the same time,

---

[20] Art. 3(1)(a) EC.   [21] Art. 3(1)(c) EC.   [22] Art. 3(1)(g) EC.   [23] Art. 3(1)(h) EC.
[24] Art. 3(1)(e) EC.   [25] Art. 3(1)(f) EC.   [26] Art. 3(1)(i) EC.   [27] Art. 3(1)(j) EC.
[28] Art. 3(1)(k) EC.   [29] Art. 3(1)(l) EC.   [30] Art. 3(1)(m) EC.   [31] Art. 3(1)(n) EC.
[32] Art. 3(1)(o) EC.   [33] Art. 3(1)(p) EC.   [34] Art. 3(1)(q) EC.   [35] Art. 3(1)(t) EC.
[36] Art. 3(1)(u) EC.   [37] Art. 3(2) EC.   [38] Art. 3c EC.   [39] Art.3a(1) EC.

exchange rates are to be irrevocably fixed, leading to the introduction of a single currency, the "Euro".[40] A single monetary policy and exchange-rate policy are also to be defined and conducted. The primary objective of these last two policies is to maintain price stability. Without prejudice to this objective, they are to support the general economic policies in the Union, in accordance with the principle of an open market economy with free competition.[41] These activities shall all comply with the following guiding principles: stable prices, sound public finances and monetary conditions, and a sustainable balance of payments.[42]

The establishment of a common customs tariff[43] and a common commercial policy for trade with third states (that is, non-Member States of the Union) is considered a necessary corollary to these activities.[44] Their establishment is needed to ensure that one Member State cannot distort competition in the common market by granting more favourable conditions to third states than do other Member States. Analogously, it is felt that the removal of frontier controls on persons moving between Member States necessitates the adoption of harmonized rules on entry and movement in the Union by nationals of third states.[45] Development co-operation[46] and, more particularly, the association of the overseas countries and territories of Member States,[47] to increase trade and jointly to promote economic and social development,[48] are also envisaged.

The Union institutions with responsibility for these activities are, according to Article 4(1) of the EC Treaty, the European Parliament, the Council, the Commission, the Court of Justice, and the Court of Auditors. According to Article 4(2) of the Treaty, the Council and Commission are to be assisted by the Economic and Social Committee and the Committee of the Regions, acting in an advisory capacity. In addition, Article 4a refers to the European System of Central Banks and the European Central Bank itself, and Article 8b to the European Investment Bank.

1.3 Fundamental Principles

Fundamental principles or "*Grundsätze*",[49] to be respected by the Union institutions and the Member States in the establishment and development of

---

[40] Reg. 1103/97 (OJ 1997 L162/1) on certain provisions relating to the introduction of the Euro. See also Practical aspects of the introduction of the Euro, COM(97)491.

[41] Art. 3a(2) EC. [42] Art. 3a EC.

[43] Its establishment means that the same customs duties are levied on goods imported from third states into the Union, irrespective of the Member State through which they enter the Union.

[44] Art. 3(1)(b) EC. [45] Art. 3(1)(d) EC. [46] Art. 3(1)(r) EC.

[47] The OCT are listed in Annex IV to the EC Treaty. [48] Art. 3(1)(s) EC.

[49] Part One of the EC Treaty is headed "Principles" in the English version and "*Grundsätze*" in the German version.

the common market and the common policies, are laid down in the Treaty on European Union and in Part One (Articles 1 to 7d) of the EC Treaty. These may be regarded as constitutional principles.

In particular, the principle of the rule of law is embodied in Article 4(1) of the EC Treaty. It states that each Union institution shall act within the limits of the powers conferred upon it by this Treaty. Moreover, Article A of the Treaty on European Union provides that Union decisions are to be "taken as openly as possible and as closely as possible to the citizen". Far-reaching implications may be drawn from this provision. For example, it is asserted that the existence of "autonomous regional bodies endowed with sufficient powers and resources"[50] is a condition for achievement of Union objectives. It may further be asserted that fulfilment of this condition is required by the Treaties.[51]

However, the normative effect of the principle in Article A of the Treaty on European Union seems to be dependent on the operation of Article 3b of the EC Treaty.[52] The latter provision only refers to relations between the European Community and Member States.[53] It states: "The Community shall act within the limits of the powers conferred upon it by this Treaty and of the objectives assigned to it therein. In areas which do not fall within its exclusive competence, the Community shall take action, in accordance with the principle of subsidiarity, only if and in so far as the objectives of the proposed action cannot be sufficiently achieved by the Member States and can therefore, by reason of the scale or effects of the proposed action, be better achieved by the Community. Any action by the Community shall not go beyond what is necessary to achieve the objectives of this Treaty."[54]

The freedom of Member States to choose internally to centralise or decentralise seems unaffected by these provisions.[55] Indeed, it has been argued that the "subsidiarity" principle embodied therein will lead to increased use of "soft law"[56] by the Commission and, hence, to reduced transparency in

---

[50] Resolution of the European Parliament of 18 Nov. 1993 (OJ 1993 C329/279) on the participation and representation of the regions in the process of European integration: the Committee of the Regions, para. E of the preamble.

[51] Opinion of the Committee of the Regions of 17 May 1994 (OJ 1994 C217/10) on the draft notice from the Commission laying down guidelines for operational programmes which Member States are invited to establish in the framework of a Community initiative concerning urban areas, para. 5 of the preamble.

[52] Cf., in the particular field of environmental policy, Art. 130r(4) EEC.

[53] Cf. the 10th Amendment to the US Constitution, which provides that "the powers not delegated to the US by the Constitution, nor prohibited by it to the states, are reserved to the states respectively, or to the people".

[54] Cf. the distinction between "substantive" and "procedural" subsidiarity in A. Scott, J. Peterson and D. Millar, "Subsidiarity: A Europe of the Regions v. the British Constitution" [1994] *JCMS* 47–68. See also K. Neunreither, "Subsidiarity as a Guiding Principle for European Community Activities" [1993] *Government and Opposition* 206–20.

[55] Cf. the Declaration by Germany, Austria, and Belgium on subsidiarity, adopted with the Amsterdam Treaty (OJ 1997 C340/1).

[56] I.e. rules introduced without recourse to formal legislative procedures. See sect. 2.3.1 below.

Union decision making.[57] Reduced transparency will, presumably, entail a reduction in the accessibility of such decision making to citizens and regional institutions within Member States.[58]

Certainly, Article 3b of the EC Treaty does not reflect the German proposal,[59] that the subsidiarity principle should apply generally in relations between Union, national and regional institutions.[60] Nor does it reflect the demands to similar effect made by the European Parliament.[61] It seems more consistent with the statement of the European Council in December 1992 that "Community measures should leave as much scope for national decision as possible".[62] Indeed, account may be taken of the principle in Article F.1 of the Treaty on European Union that the Union "shall respect the national identities of its Member States".[63] Account may also be taken of the reference to fundamental rights in Article F.1 and 2 of the same Treaty.[64] Both are said to require respect for the internal institutional arrangements established by the constitution of each Member State.

According to Article F.2, the Union shall respect fundamental rights, as guaranteed by the European Convention on Human Rights and as they result from the constitutional traditions common to the Member States. The Union shall respect them, as general principles of Union law.[65] The concern underlying this recognition of a fundamental rights dimension to Union activities seems to be to contain encroachment on fundamental rights by the Union institutions.[66] There seems to be less concern to develop Union law as an instrument for promoting such rights.

Only in the event of systematic violations of fundamental rights by

[57] F. Snyder, "Soft Law and Institutional Practice in the European Community" in S. Martin (ed.), *The Construction of Europe: Essays in Honour of Emile Noel* (Kluwer, Deventer, 1994), 197–225.

[58] See, generally, regarding the importance of accessibility in relation to decision-making, H. Smith, *The Power Game* (Ballantine, New Jersey, 1993), 70–83.

[59] Cf. Council Reply to WQ E–3100/93 (OJ 1994 C147/1) by Mr Victor Arbeloa Muru.

[60] "Beteiligung der Bundesländer an Regierungskonferenz zur Revision der Gemeinschaftsverträge" [1990] *Europäische Zeitschrift für Wirtschaftsrecht* 431.

[61] Resolution of 18 Nov. 1993 (OJ 1993 C329/279) on the participation and representation of the regions in the process of European integration: the Committee of the Regions, para. 4.

[62] Conclusions of the Presidency, Annex 1 to Part A, Bull. EC 12–1992, I.19.

[63] U. Everling, "Reflections on the Structure of the European Union"(1992) 29 *CMLRev.* 1053–77, 1071.

[64] R. Rivello, "Il Ruolo delle regioni nel diritto comunitario e nel diritto internazionale: considerazioni sulla normativa vigente e sui progetti di revisione costituzionale" [1995] *Diritto Comunitario e degli Scambi Internazionali* 255–308, 290, n. 110.

[65] According to Art. M TEU, this provision does not, in principle, affect the EC Treaty. However, "respect for fundamental rights forms an integral part of the general principles of law protected by the Court of Justice" (Case 11/70 *Internationale Handelsgesellschaft mbH* v. *Einfuhr-und Vorratsstelle für Getreide und Futtermittel* [1970] ECR 1125, 1134). Such rights are inspired by "the constitutional traditions common to the Member States" and "international treaties for the protection of fundamental rights" (ibid.).

[66] See Art. L(d) TEU. See, more particularly, regarding data privacy and Union institutions and bodies, Art. 213b EC. But cf. Dir. 97/66 (OJ 1998 L24/1) concerning the processing of personal data and the protection of privacy in the telecommunications sector.

Member States may Union law constitute such an instrument.[67] Systematic violations of these rights may, according to Article F.1 of the Treaty on European Union, lead to the suspension of the rights of the Member State concerned under the Treaties.[68]

A more general duty of "loyalty" to the Union derives for Member States from Article 5 of the EC Treaty. According to this provision, Member States shall take all appropriate measures, whether general or particular, to ensure fulfilment of the obligations arising out of this Treaty or resulting from action taken by the Union institutions. They shall facilitate the achievement of the tasks established by the Treaty and shall abstain from any measure that could jeopardise the attainment of the objectives of this Treaty.

Article 5a of the same Treaty introduces "flexibility" into the duty of Member States to the Union. It allows for certain Member States to be authorised to undertake more demanding obligations amongst themselves and thus to engage in closer integration than the remaining Member States.[69]

Article 6 of the Treaty concerns both the Union institutions and the Member States. It provides that within the scope of application of this Treaty, and without prejudice to any special provisions contained therein, any discrimination on grounds of nationality shall be prohibited.[70] This provision exemplifies a more general principle of equality in Union law.[71] The principle means, for example, that differentiation between different categories of consumers will only be permissible where there is an objective justification.[72]

The equality principle is developed in Part Two of the EC Treaty, which is headed "Citizenship of the Union". It includes Article 8(1), which "establishes" Union Citizenship for nationals of Member States and stipulates that this Citizenship complements rather than replaces national citizenship. It also includes Articles 8a to 8d, which set out a non-exhaustive list[73] of the rights to be enjoyed by holders of this Citizenship.

In particular, Article 8a provides that Union Citizens have the right to move and reside freely within the territory of Member States. However, it stipulates

[67] Fundamental rights may also be protected against Member States as a consequence of the requirements of the "four freedoms". See, in connection with the free movement of workers, sect. 9.8 below. But cf., regarding the limitations of the underlying approach to protection of fundamental rights, sect. 7.2.4 below.

[68] See also Art. 236 EC.

[69] See also Arts. K.12 and K.15–17 TEU; and, more particularly, Art. 5(1) of the Protocol integrating the Schengen *acquis* into the framework of the EU.

[70] See, e.g., regarding the requirement of a security for judicial costs, Case C–122/96 *Stephen Austin Saldanha and MTS Securities Corpn.* v. *Hiross Holding AG*, 20 Oct. 1997.

[71] See, regarding action to combat discrimination based on sex, racial or ethnic origin, religion or belief, disability, age or sexual orientation, Art. 6a EC.

[72] Case 8/57 *Groupement des Hauts Fourneaux et Aciéries Belges* v. *ECSC High Authority* [1957-8] ECR 245, 258; and Case 9/57 *Chambre Syndicale de la Sidérurgie Française* v. *ECSC High Authority* [1957–8] ECR 319, 330.

[73] Art. 8e EC allows for adoption of "provisions to strengthen or to add to the rights laid down".

that this right is subject to the limitations and conditions laid down in this Treaty and by the measures adopted to give it effect. Article 8b(1) grants the right to vote and stand as a candidate in local government elections to Union Citizens resident in a Member State other than their own under the same conditions as nationals of that Member State. Article 8b(2) grants corresponding rights in relation to elections to the European Parliament. Again, under Article 8c a Union Citizen is entitled, in the territory of a third state in which the Member State of which he is a national lacks representation, to protection by the diplomatic or consular authorities of any other Member State. The latter Member State is to afford him protection on the same conditions as it affords protection to its own nationals. Finally, Article 8d provides for Union Citizens to have the right to petition the European Parliament and to apply to the European Ombudsman. Moreover, every Union Citizen may write to a Union institution in one of the official languages of the Union[74] and have an answer in the same language. According to the European Commission, these rights have "constitutional status".[75]

These provisions highlight the challenge that the establishment of the European Union poses for the legal system created by the Treaties. The challenge is for this system to evolve from one that has treated individuals essentially as economic actors in the common market. The system now needs to give meaning to their status as Union Citizens faced with globalisation.

1.4 Structure of the Book and its Special Features

Problems involved in the evolution of Union law will be taken into account in the following chapters. Throughout the examination the expressions "Union law" and "Union institutions" will be used to denote the law and institutions created by or under the above Treaties, except when attention is drawn to specific features of one of the three Communities. The examination is divided into three parts.

The first part of the book concerns institutional law. It examines, in turn, the principal institutions of the Union (the Commission, European Parliament, Council of the Union, and European Courts[76]) as well as various other bodies established by or under the Treaties. It also examines the relationship between Union law and the national law of the Member States and of third states.

The second part of the book looks at the law of the common market. It covers the "four freedoms", that is, the free movement of goods, persons,[77]

---

[74] Art. 248 EC.

[75] Citizenship of the Union, COM(93)702, 2.

[76] I.e., the ECJ and the CFI.

[77] The EC Treaty deals separately with free movement for employed persons and free movement for the self-employed.

services, and capital, and competition law. Competition law relates to restrictive practices by undertakings, the operation of public undertakings, state aid and taxation of goods.

The third part of the book turns to the law of harmonisation and common policies. In particular, Chapter 19 examines legislative harmonisation. Such harmonisation may be regarded as harmonisation proper, though as the "new approach"[78] highlights, the dynamics and effects of harmonisation may go beyond the formal requirements of legislative procedures and enactments. Chapter 20 concerns harmonisation through financial instruments. It explores the role of the Structural Funds and the other financial instruments of the Union in securing harmonisation of state practice and the conduct of undertakings. Chapter 21 looks at the implementation of common policies, based on these two kinds of harmonisation, for which specific provision is made in the EC Treaty or the Treaty on European Union.

In examining the evolution of this law, each chapter systematically examines both its "internal" and "external" aspects. The former aspects are those concerning matters within the Union, and the latter aspects are those concerning relations between the Union and third states. The chapters consider problems involved in separation of the two aspects of Union law as well as the growing recognition of these problems in Union practice. In other words, they consider not only the law of the internal market but also its interactions with the law concerning the role of the Union in the world.

These chapters, therefore, depart from the pattern set by other textbooks in their treatment of the law governing relations between the Union and third states. Other textbooks tend to confine consideration of the law governing these relations to special chapters or, indeed, to ignore it altogether. These tendencies may reflect the early emphasis of EEC law and practice on the establishment of a common market between Member States and the more recent emphasis on completion of the internal market. They do not reflect current Union practice or the realities of globalisation. In practice, all the Union institutions have tasks extending to relations between the Union and third states; the "four freedoms" and competition law have implications, or at least raise difficult issues, for relations with third states; and the implementation of common policies is seen by the EC Treaty and the Treaty on European Union as partly dependent on agreements with third states.

The realities of globalisation may be more readily recognised in Union practice than by legal doctrine. For example, according to the Commission, the evolution of "internal Community legislation is not independent from the actions of the EU in the external sphere".[79] Similarly, the Court of Justice insists that in the implementation of internal policies the Union institutions

---

[78] I.e., an approach that seeks minimum harmonisation and places reliance on the work of standards bodies. See sect. 19.4 below.

[79] Impact and effectiveness of the single market, COM(96)520, 21.

may not disregard obligations in agreements concluded by the Union.[80]

Certainly, the EC Treaty provides for the Union to co-operate with international organisations, including the organs of the United Nations and of its specialised agencies,[81] the Council of Europe,[82] and the Organisation for Economic Co-operation and Development.[83] The Union is also to "foster co-operation" with third states and international organisations in specified fields, including vocational training,[84] culture,[85] public health,[86] research and technological development,[87] environmental protection,[88] and development.[89] It may also decide to co-operate with third states to promote transport projects of mutual interest and to ensure the "interoperability" of networks.[90]

Such co-operation may often be seen as implying the need to conclude agreements with third states. The EC Treaty provides for the Union to develop its relations with third states through agreements concerning various specific matters. The Court of Justice has ruled that the Union is also competent to conclude agreements with third states in fields, such as agriculture[91] and transport,[92] in which it is competent to enact internal measures.[93] The latter are to be interpreted consistently with such agreements.[94]

General rules concerning procedures for the conclusion of such agreements are laid down in Article 228 of the EC Treaty. More particularly, Article 113(3) provides for the conclusion of free trade agreements pursuant to the common commercial policy with one or more third states or international organisations.[95] These agreements seek essentially to eliminate tariffs and quantitative restrictions on industrial products traded between the parties. The Union institutions have exclusive competence to conclude such agreements.[96] In fields other than that of commercial policy their competence may be shared with that of the Member States.[97]

If agreements are intended to go beyond the field of commercial policy,

---

[80] Case C–280/93 *Germany* v. *EU Council: bananas* [1996] ECR I–4973, I–5060.

[81] Art. 229 EC.   [82] Art. 230 EC.   [83] Art. 231 EC.   [84] Art. 127(3) EC.

[85] Art. 128(3) EC.   [86] Art. 129(3) EC.   [87] Art. 130m EC.   [88] Art. 130h(4) EC.

[89] Art. 130y EC.   [90] Art. 129c(3) EC.

[91] Joined Cases 3, 4 & 6/76 *Cornelis Kramer* [1976] ECR 1279.

[92] Case 22/70 *EC Commission* v. *EC Council: ERTA* [1971] ECR 263.

[93] *Ibid.*, 274. At the same time, the Union must under Art. 234 EC respect agreements concluded by Member States before entry into force of the EC Treaty. See, e.g., Case C–324/93 *Evans Medical and Macfarlan Smith* [1995] ECR I–563, I–606; and Case C–124/95 *R.* v. *HM Treasury and the Bank of England, ex p. Centro-Com srl* [1997] ECR I–81, I–130.

[94] Case C–61/94 *EC Commission* v. *Germany: International Dairy Agreement* [1996] ECR I–3989, I–4021.

[95] See, recently, the Free Trade Agreement with the Faroe Islands (OJ 1997 L53/2).

[96] See, regarding the scope of their competence under Art. 113 EC, *Opinion 1/78, International Agreement on Natural Rubber* [1978] ECR 2871; and Case 45/87 *EC Commission* v. *EC Council* [1987] ECR 1493.

[97] See, e.g., *Opinion 1/94 International Agreements on Services and the Protection of Industrial Property* [1994] ECR I–5267.

they may be based on Article 235 as well as Article 113.[98] The former provision allows for the adoption of acts necessary in the operation of the common market for the attainment of Treaty objectives.

Moreover, Article 238 of the EC Treaty provides for the conclusion of association agreements with third states or international organisations. These agreements establish an association involving reciprocal rights and obligations, common action and special procedures. They thus provide for closer and broader co-operation than that entailed by free trade agreements. Association agreements may, in the case of developing states, be concluded for the purposes of development co-operation.[99] They may also be concluded with states whose future accession to the Union[100] is envisaged. Thus association agreements were concluded with Cyprus,[101] Greece,[102] and Turkey.[103] Similarly, "Europe Agreements" have been concluded with Central European States. The most sophisticated association agreement is the European Economic Area (EEA) Agreement[104] with three EFTA[105] States (Iceland, Liechtenstein, and Norway). Since association agreements may extend to matters in relation to which Member States retain competence, they are usually concluded as "joint agreements" by the Union and the Member States themselves.[106]

The agreements may reproduce trade liberalisation provisions contained in the EC Treaty. Such reproduction has taken place, for example, in free trade agreements; association agreements (including the Europe Agreements); and the EEA Agreement. Free trade agreements concern liberalisation of trade in goods.[107] The Europe Agreements concern not only goods[108] but also the movement of persons,[109] services,[110] and capital.[111] The EEA Agreement goes further and seeks to establish a "homogeneous" European Economic Area.[112]

Article 1 of the EEA Agreement provides that the aim of this Agreement is to promote a continuous and balanced strengthening of trade and economic relations between the Contracting Parties with equal conditions of competition and respect for the same rules, with a view to creating a homogeneous European Economic Area. EEA law is designed to be "identical in substance" to much of the law contained in the EC Treaty and implementing measures, though not that relating to tax harmonisation, the common agricultural

---

[98] See, e.g., the Co-operation Agreement with Slovenia (OJ 1993 L189/2).

[99] See, currently, the Fourth ACP–EEC Convention (OJ 1991 L229/3).

[100] See Art. O TEU, regarding accession agreements.

[101] OJ 1973 L133/2.   [102] JO 1963 26.   [103] JO 1964 368.   [104] OJ 1994 L1/3.

[105] European Free Trade Association.

[106] See, e.g., *Opinion 1/91 Draft Agreement between the Community and the EFTA Countries relating to the Creation of the EEA* [1991] ECR 6079.

[107] See, e.g., Art. 2 of the Free Trade Agreement with the Faroe Islands (OJ 1997 L53/2).

[108] See, e.g., Art. 7 of the Europe Agreement with Poland (OJ 1993 L348/2).

[109] *Ibid.*, Arts. 37–54.   [110] *Ibid.*, Arts. 55–57.   [111] *Ibid.*, Arts. 59–62.

[112] Arts. 28–45 EEA.

policy, the common customs tariff, or the common commercial policy. Identity in substance is sought through including in the Agreement many provisions corresponding to EC Treaty provisions and by "referring" to Union implementing measures in annexes to the Agreement.[113] This Agreement, therefore, highlights the problems of "traditional" tendencies to treat Union law governing relations between Member States separately from Union law governing relations between the Union and third states.

---

[113] According to Art. 119 EEA, the annexes and the acts referred to therein, as adapted for the purposes of this Agreement, form an integral part of this Agreement.

Part One
LAW OF THE INSTITUTIONS

2

European Commission

The European Commission originally had largely technical functions associated with establishment of the common market. It now performs functions more generally associated with a government. It draws up legislative proposals and is responsible for supervising application of the resulting legislation and for implementation of the Union Budget. In practice, it also engages in further activities associated with a government. However, performance of these functions may be rendered problematic by efforts in the Treaties, presumably in the light of the largely technical nature of its original functions, to "depoliticise" this institution.

2.1 Composition

Originally, the EEC Commission,[1] like the ECSC High Authority,[2] had nine members. The Euratom Commission, in contrast, had only five.[3] However, Article 133 of the Euratom Treaty provided that the Council, acting unanimously, could agree that the government of a Member State[4] might accredit to the Commission a qualified representative to undertake permanent liaison duties. Under the Merger Treaty the new single Commission had fourteen members,[5] but this number was to be reduced to nine within three years.[6] However, successive enlargements have led to the number of Commissioners being increased to the current figure of twenty.[7] The number may be altered by the Council, acting unanimously.[8]

There must, according to Article 157(1) of the Treaty, be at least one Commissioner having the nationality of each of the Member States. However, there must be not more than two Commissioners having the nationality of the same Member State. Only nationals of Member States may be Commissioners.

To some extent, then, the Treaty allows for compromise of the principle of the sovereign equality of states. The compromise is designed to permit some

---

[1] Art. 157 EEC.   [2] Art. 10 ECSC.   [3] Art. 126 Euratom.
[4] In practice, Luxembourg.   [5] Art. 32 MT.   [6] Art. 10(1) MT.
[7] Art. 157(1) EC.   [8] *Ibid.*

account to be taken of differences in population sizes as between the various Member States. In practice, each of the "big four" Member States (France, Germany, Italy, and the United Kingdom) and Spain have two Commissioners, and the others have one each. In the case of the United Kingdom, the representative character of its nominations is developed to the extent that one nominee is drawn from the Conservative Party and one from the Labour Party. Similar arrangements have been made in the case of the Spanish Commissioners, and the Benelux countries have agreed among themselves that their nominees will include a Christian Democrat, a Liberal, and a Socialist.

2.1.1 Appointment Procedure

Commissioners are, according to Article 157(1) of the EC Treaty, chosen on the grounds of their general competence. More particularly, according to Article 158(2), the governments of the Member States nominate the President by common accord. The nomination must be approved by the European Parliament, which requests the nominee to make a statement to the House.[9] Then, by common accord with the Presidential nominee, the governments nominate the other persons whom they intend to appoint as Commissioners. The nominees are subject as a body to a vote of approval by the Parliament,[10] which interviews each nominee.[11] After such approval the President and the other Commissioners are appointed by common accord of the governments of the Member States.[12]

The requirement of common accord[13] is treated as meaning that all governments must vote in favour of the Presidential nomination and in favour of the appointment of the President and other Commissioners. This arrangement is presumably designed to prevent a Member State from nominating a Commissioner without regard to the views and interests of other Member States or, indeed, the Union interest. In practice, however, a Member State may feel compelled to approve the nominations of the others in order to secure the necessary approval of its own nominations. Effectively, then, each Member State may choose its "own" Commissioner or

---

[9] Art. 32 of the Rules of Procedure of the Parliament (OJ 1997 L49/1).

[10] Decision approving the nominated Commission (OJ 1995 C43/34).

[11] Art. 33 of the Rules of Procedure of the Parliament (OJ 1997 L49/1).

[12] The present Commission was appointed by Dec. 95/12 (OJ 1995 L19/51).

[13] Cf. the reference in Art. 215(2) EC to "principles common to the laws of the Member States", where the term "common" does not mean that the principle must be present in the laws of all the Member States (see, e.g., Lagrange AG in Case 14/61 *Koninklijke Nederlandsche Hoogovens en Staalfabrieken NV* v. *ECSC High Authority* [1962] ECR 253, 283). However, other language versions of the Treaty may not be disregarded (Case 283/81 *CILFIT Srl* v. *Ministry of Health* [1982] ECR 3415, 3430), and the German version uses "*gegenseitig*" in Art. 158(2) EC and "*gemeinsam*" in Art. 215(2) EC. Apparently, the use of the term "common" in Art. 158(2) EC of the English version has a function different from that in Art. 215(2) EC. Its use in the former provision may be explained by concern to oust the general rule in Art. 148(3) EC that unanimity is not affected by abstentions.

Commissioners.[14] The European Parliament may not be well placed to challenge this practice. Except in the case of the Presidential nominee, the Parliament only votes on the nominees as a body.

As a result, a politically homogeneous Commission is unlikely to emerge,[15] but the selection of such a body is not the objective of the relevant Treaty provisions. Rather, these provisions seek to ensure that the Commission will be in a position to fulfil its essential function – enshrined in Article 157(2) of the Treaty – of promoting "the general interest of the Community". They recognise that this function can only be fulfilled if account is taken of the interests of each Member State. Accordingly, they ensure that there is at least one Commissioner for each Member State.

2.1.2 Independence of Commissioners

Although the individual Commissioners may have a certain representative function,[16] the Treaty seeks to safeguard their independence, in both the active and the passive senses. Thus they must be persons whose independence is beyond doubt.[17] They must also act with complete independence in the performance of their duties, neither seeking nor taking instructions from any government or any other body.[18] Participation in scholarly or educational activities or activities within the framework of political, cultural, or similar organisations serving the public interest is considered compatible with these obligations. Moreover, Commissioners retain their political rights, including the right to seek public office, during their term of appointment.[19] However, they must not engage in any other occupation, paid or unpaid.

On taking up their appointment, Commissioners must make a solemn declaration to the effect that they accept these obligations. In particular, they must accept the duty to "behave with integrity and discretion" as regards acceptance, even after leaving office, of certain appointments or benefits. They are also bound by obligations of professional secrecy.[20] At the same

[14] According to Art. 10 ECSC, 8 members of the High Authority were appointed by a 5/6 majority of the Member States. The 9th member was co-opted by a majority of the 8 already appointed. A national veto could be exercised, though excessive use of the veto could be challenged before the ECJ. However, there is no evidence that the arrangements were ever used to overrule a Member State. See R. Pryce, *The Political Future of the European Community* (Marshbank, London, 1973), 34, n.1.

[15] House of Lords Select Committee on the European Communities, European Union, HL (1984–5) 226, xxiv.

[16] D. Sidjanski, 'L'Originalité des Communautés européennes et la répartition de leurs pouvoirs' [1961] *RGDIP* 40–61, 58.

[17] Art. 157(1) EC.

[18] Art. 157(2) EC. They may, however, participate in meetings of sub-committees of national government cabinets (Reply by Mr Santer to WQ E–2837/96 (OJ 1997 C72/83) by Jan Wiebenga).

[19] Commission Replies to WQ 34/60 (JO 1960 1109) by Mr Vals and to WQ 734/73 (OJ 1974 C53/32) by Lord O'Hagan.

[20] Art. 214 EC.

time, each Member State undertakes not to seek to influence them in the performance of their tasks.[21]

The same concern for formal independence is demonstrated in Commission practice. For example, a Commissioner who stands as a candidate in national elections refrains from exercising his Commission functions during the electoral campaign.[22] Again, when Lord Cockfield was appointed to the Commission, it was accepted that he might retain his membership of the British House of Lords. However, he had to take leave of absence from the House for the duration of his service as a Commissioner.[23]

Termination of Appointments

The appointments of Commissioners normally last for five years,[24] in line with the life of the European Parliament, and are renewable.[25] They may be terminated prematurely only by death, compulsory retirement, or resignation.[26] The Council was once empowered to dismiss and replace a Commissioner or to suspend him temporarily.[27] However, this power has been abolished. Consequently, an individual Commissioner may now only be compelled to retire where he ceases to fulfil the conditions required for performance of his duties[28] or has been found guilty of serious misconduct. Application may be made by the Council or the Commission itself,[29] and the Court of Justice may make the necessary order. In addition, the whole Commission may be compelled to resign following the passage of a censure motion in the European Parliament.[30] So far, these powers of compulsory retirement and censure have not been employed, though censure has been threatened.[31]

Portfolio Allocation

Doubts as to the real independence of Commissioners are raised by government efforts to ensure that their nationals have portfolios considered most closely to affect their particular concerns.[32] The implication is that

---

[21]   Art. 157(2) EC.

[22]   See the statement of Commissioner Malfatti to the European Parliament (Débs PE No. 148, 11, 14 Mar. 1972). See also Commission Reply to WQ 193/77 (OJ 1977 C206/12) by Mr Clerfayt.

[23]   European Parliament Resolution of 13 Dec. 1984 (OJ 1985 C12/97) on the appointment of Lord Cockfield as Member of the Commission and on the interpretation and application of Art. 10 MT, para. 6, though a minority view was advanced in the Parliament that it would be insufficient merely for him to take leave of absence.

[24]   Under the ECSC Treaty (Art. 10) it was originally 6 years, while under the EEC (Art. 158), Euratom (Art. 127), and Merger (Art. 11) Treaties it was 4 years.

[25]   Art. 158(1) EC.

[26]   Art. 159 EC. If a vacancy occurs, the Council may decide not to fill it (ibid.).

[27]   Art. 160 EEC. It was replaced by Arts 13 and 19 MT.

[28]   See Dec. 76/619 (OJ 1976 L201/31) appointing a member of the EC Commission.

[29]   Art. 160 EC. In theory, the European Parliament could bring Art. 175 EC proceedings for an order requiring the Commission or Council to make such an application.

[30]   Art. 144 EC.   [31]   Sect. 3.3.3 below.   [32]   See, e.g., *The Times*, 10 Dec. 1984.

Commissioners are not expected, at least by the governments of their respective Member States, to be fully independent.[33] This implication finds some confirmation in the failure of various Commissioners, such as Ivor Richard[34] and Lord Cockfield,[35] to secure reappointment after having clashed with their national governments.[36]

Questions may arise whether Member States are complying with their obligation in Article 157(2) of the Treaty to respect the independence of Commissioners. Questions may also arise whether they are complying with their obligation in Article 5 to abstain from any measure jeopardizing attainment of Treaty objectives taken together with the requirement in Article 158(2) that Commissioners be appointed by common accord.[37] However, the sensitivity of the issues raised as well as the evidential difficulties likely to be encountered mean that default proceedings against Member States under Article 169[38] may not be realistically expected.

2.2 Organisation

The Commission is a collegiate institution, on which the EC Treaty confers considerable freedom of internal organisation. Article 162(2) of the Treaty entails that questions of internal organisation are to be determined by the Commission itself. Its freedom to determine such questions is limited only by the requirements that both the college and its departments operate according to the Treaty and that the Rules of Procedure[39] are published.

2.2.1 Presidency

A significant role in the organisation of the Commission may be played by its President. According to Article 163 of the EC Treaty, the Commission shall work under the political guidance of its President. The President presides over Commission meetings and performs ceremonial functions, such as the accreditation of ambassadors. Under paragraph (a)3 of the Luxembourg Accords,[40] this function is shared with the President of the Council. A Vice-

---

[33] Cf. K. van Miert, "The Appointment of the President and Members of the European Commission" (1973) 10 *CMLRev.* 257–73, 259.

[34] *The Times*, 15 Dec. 1985.   [35] *The Times*, 2 Apr. 1988.

[36] Reform is envisaged. See the Declaration on the organisation and functioning of the Commission, adopted with the Treaty of Amsterdam (OJ 1997 C340/1).

[37] Cf. P. Hay, *Federalism and Supranational Organizations* (University of Illinois Press, Chicago, Ill., 1966), 200.

[38] See, regarding such proceedings, sects. 2.3.3 below.

[39] Dec. 93/492 (OJ 1993 L230/15). A violation of these Rules only entails the invalidity of the resulting act if there is an "objective irregularity". See Case 15/85 *Consorzio d'Abruzzo v. EC Commission* [1987] ECR 1005, 1035–6; and Joined Cases T–79, 84–86, 89, 91–92, 94, 96, 98, 102 & 104/89 *BASF AG v. EC Commission* [1992] ECR II–315, II–357.

[40] Bull. EC 3–1966, 9.

President[41] succeeds to the functions of the President, when the latter is unavailable.

2.2.2 Collegiality

Treaty references to the Commission as a whole rather than to individual Commissioners[42] and, more particularly, the references to "meetings of the Commission"[43] imply that the Commission should act as a collegiate body. This basic principle is expressly stated in Article 1 of the Rules of Procedure.[44] Such collegiality is intended to strengthen Commission independence. It entails that the Commission itself, rather than individual Commissioners has responsibility for Commission acts,[45] these acts being taken by majority vote.[46] To preserve such collegiality in practice, Article 7 of the Rules of Procedure[47] stipulates that Commission discussions are confidential.

2.2.3 Internal Structure

Effective collegiality may not be easily maintained, particularly given the internal structure of the Commission.

Cabinets

Each Commissioner is assisted by a *cabinet* of "personal staff",[48] who tend to possess the same nationality as the Commissioner whom they serve. These *cabinets* are headed by *chefs de cabinets*, who may deputise for the relevant Commissioner at Commission meetings. The *chefs* meet weekly under the *chef* of the President, to prepare the weekly meetings of the Commission. Drafts prepared by the *chefs* may be voted on by Commissioners and adopted without discussion.[49]

---

[41] According to Art. 161 EC, the Commission may appoint 1 or 2 Vice-Presidents from its members.

[42] In Commission Reply to WQ 83/60 (JO 1961 2) by Mr Vredeling the implication of collegiality was drawn from the requirement in Art. 23 ECSC that "the High Authority" was to reply to Parliamentary Questions. See, similarly, the 3rd para. of Art. 140 EC, though the 2nd para. refers to Commissioners being "heard on behalf of the Commission".

[43] See, e.g., Art. 163 EC.   [44] OJ 1993 L230/15.

[45] Case 5/85 *AKZO Chemie BV and AKZO Chemie UK Ltd* v. *EC Commission* [1986] ECR 2585, 2614.

[46] Art. 163 EC, though Art. 10 of the Rules of Procedure (OJ 1993 L230/15), provides for adoption of proposals by written procedure and Art. 11 (*ibid.*) provides for the Commission to delegate powers to one of its members. Cf., regarding delegation to a Director General, Joined Cases 8–11/66 *Société Anonyme Cimenteries CBR Cementbedrijven NV* v. *EC Commission* [1967] ECR 75. Cf. also, regarding delegation to other bodies, Case 9/56 *Meroni & Co., Industrie Metallurgiche, SpA* v. *ECSC High Authority* [1957–8] ECR 133, 151–4; and Joined Cases 32 & 33/58 *Société Nouvelle des Usines de Pontlieue Aciéries du Temple (SNUPAT)* v. *ECSC High Authority* [1959] ECR 127, 137–8.

[47] OJ 1993 L230/15.   [48] Art. 14 of the Rules of Procedure (*ibid.*).

[49] H.G. Krenzler, "Die Rolle der Kabinette in der Kommission der Europäischen Gemeinschaften" [1974] *EuR* 75–9, 79.

Directorates General

The Commission is divided into Directorates General, whose tasks include ensuring the application of Union law in their particular field.[50] They are themselves divided into various directorates and units[51] and are presided over by a Director General. The latter is responsible to the particular Commissioner whose portfolio covers that Directorate General.

The Director General is always of a different nationality from the Commissioner responsible for the Directorate General concerned. However, informal quotas have apparently developed regarding the allocation of senior posts among the various Member States.[52] At the lower levels of the administrative hierarchy there are around 19,000 posts. At these levels a balanced representation of all Union nationalities is sought, though the question whether a satisfactory balance is really achieved often proves controversial.[53] Officially, no posts may be reserved for nationals of a specific Member State. However, "in recruiting over the widest possible geographical basis, the Commission takes into account the relative importance of the Member States".[54]

Such arrangements recognise the need for national representation. Indeed, in staff recruitment the Commission relies partly on secondment from national civil services and in screening applicants for posts seeks information from national authorities.[55] Hence, persons unacceptable to national governments are unlikely to be appointed. At the same time, the arrangements apparently seek to reconcile national representation with the preservation of Commission independence from national governments.[56]

However, efforts are made to satisfy the demands of Member States and to allocate to each Commissioner, except the President, a portfolio of roughly equal size.[57] The result has been a proliferation of Directorates General and ancillary services, between which there is limited staff movement. Preparatory work for Commission proposals may be entrusted to open groups of Commissioners, and interdepartmental groups may be established.[58] Even so, co-ordination of the various policies pursued by the

---

[50] H.A.H. Audretsch, *Supervision in European Community Law: Observance by the Member States of their Treaty Obligations* (2nd edn., North-Holland, Amsterdam,1986), 292.

[51] Art. 18 of the Rules of Procedure (OJ 1993 L230/15).   [52] *The Independent,* 4 Jan. 1990.

[53] See, e.g., Case T–58/91 *Dierk Booss and Robert Caspar Fischer* v. *EC Commission* [1993] ECR II–147.

[54] Reply by Mr Liikanen to WQ E–3017/96 (OJ 1997 C83/109) by Jean-Antoine Giansily.

[55] See, e.g., the statement of Commission Vice-President Vredeling to the European Parliament (EP Debs No. 230, 28, 8 May 1978).

[56] According to Art. 11 of the Staff Regulations (JO 1962 1385), the duty of officials is "to the Community interest".

[57] Cf. the suggestion in the European Parliament Resolution of 17 Apr. 1980 (OJ 1980 C117/53) on relations between the European Parliament and the Commission, para. 5, that a Commission Vice-President should have special responsibility for assisting the President in co-ordination of Commission activity.

[58] Art. 13 of the Rules of Procedure (OJ 1993 L230/15). See also Art. 20 (*ibid.*).

Commission may be inadequate.[59] Indeed, the Commission is said to be divided into "watertight compartments which do not communicate with each other".[60]

Ancillary Services

The Commission has various ancillary services. They include the Legal Service, the Joint Interpreting and Conference Service, the Statistical Office, the Customs Union Service, the Security Office, the Spokesman's Group, the Joint Research Centre, the Euratom Supply Agency, and the Publications Office. The Legal Service gives legal advice to the Commission, represents the Commission before the European Courts, and gives its opinion on draft proposals. It is entitled to be present at all Commission meetings.

Secretariat General

The Secretariat General is responsible for the preparation of the agenda and administration of the Commission and has overall responsibility for relations between the Commission and other Union institutions and the Member States. The Secretariat General is entitled to be present at all Commission meetings.

2.2.4 Number of Commissioners

Reduction of the number of Commissioners has often been advocated as a means of tackling organisational problems of the Commission. For example, the anticipated increase in the membership of the Commission entailed by the first enlargement of the Union in 1973 was criticised. It was argued that increased membership would render the Commission an unwieldy and less effective institution.[61]

Moreover, both the Spierenberg Report[62] and the Report of the Three Wise Men[63] referred to the increased size of the Commission and the difficulty of allocating equally meaningful portfolios to each Commissioner. They considered that these factors had contributed to a loss of effective collegiality. More particularly, the desirability of the "big four" each having two Commissioners possessing their nationality was questioned. This arrangement was said to run counter to the idea of Commission independence. At the same time, national interests were considered to be adequately protected by the system of

[59] See, e.g., A. Evans, *EC Law of State Aid* (Oxford Series in EC Law, Clarendon Press, Oxford, 1997).

[60] The future of rural society, House of Lords Select Committee on the European Communities, HL (1989-90) 80-I, 33.

[61] Action Committee for the United States of Europe, *Problems of British Entry into the EEC* (Political and Economic Planning, London, 1969), 101.

[62] D. Spierenberg, *Proposals for Reform of the Commission of the European Communities and its Services* (EC Commission, Brussels, 1979).

[63] Committee of Three, *Report on the European Institutions* (EC Commission, Brussels, 1979).

weighted voting in the Council[64] and the distribution of seats in the European Parliament.[65] Both reports, therefore, like the later Dooge Report,[66] favoured a smaller Commission containing one member from each Member State. Such reform was calculated not only to strengthen the Commission but also to assist re-establishment of its image as that of a team.

The importance of such reform was recognised when the Treaty on European Union was adopted. In particular, a Declaration on the number of members of the Commission and the European Parliament was adopted along with this Treaty. According to this Declaration, the Member States would examine "the questions relating to the number of members of the Commission" before the end of 1992. The only concrete result is a Protocol, on the institutions with the prospects of Union enlargement, adopted with the Amsterdam Treaty.[67] According to this Protocol, it is agreed that, on the next enlargement of the Union, the Commission will have one national of each Member State. This agreement is subject to the proviso that by then the weighting of Council votes,[68] "whether by reweighting of votes or by a dual majority", will have been modified in a manner acceptable to all Member States.[69]

2.3 Functions

The functions of the Commission may be broadly divided into the legislative, the budgetary, and the administrative, though the distinction between these categories of functions may be imperfect.

2.3.1 Legislation

A formal basis for Commission performance of legislative functions is provided by Article 155 of the EC Treaty. In practice, however, the Commission may go beyond the formal terms of this provision in its performance of legislative functions.

Policy Documents

The Commission is required by the second indent of Article 155 of the EC Treaty to formulate recommendations or deliver opinions[70] on matters dealt with in the Treaty, if the Treaty expressly so provides or the Commission considers it necessary.[71] Recommendations or opinions may have to be

---

[64] Sect. 4.2.4 below.   [65] Sect. 3.1.1 below.   [66] Bull. EC 11–1984, 3.5.1.

[67] OJ 1997 C340/1. The Protocol is annexed to the founding Treaties.   [68] Sect. 4.2.4 below.

[69] Art. 1 of the Protocol. See also the Declaration on the organisation and functioning of the Commission, adopted with the Amsterdam Treaty (OJ 1997 C340/1).

[70] Cf. the requirement of consultation of the Commission in Art. 195(2) EC and Art. N TEU; and, regarding reports from the Commission, Art. 8e EC.

[71] See, e.g., Commission Rec. 87/63 (OJ 1987 L33/16) concerning the introduction of deposit-guarantee schemes in the Community.

addressed to the Council[72] or to the Member States.[73] Such instruments lack binding force,[74] though they may envisage legislative action by the Union or the Member States.[75]

Policy documents may also take the form of a memorandum or communication, forms not expressly mentioned in the Treaty. Such documents may envisage the co-ordination of national action or the introduction of legislative measures by the Union itself. They too lack binding force.[76]

"Shaping" of Legislation

The Commission is required by the third indent of Article 155 of the EC Treaty to participate in the shaping of measures to be adopted by the Council.[77] Even where the Treaty does not expressly provide for the Commission to make proposals to the Council, the Commission may still be invited to do so. Apparently, the Council values a statement of the common interest at least as a starting point for its deliberations.

In compliance with the Luxembourg Accords,[78] the Commission consults the Member States through COREPER[79] before submitting proposals to the Council itself.[80] Moreover, except in cases of particular urgency or confidentiality, the Commission must "consult widely" before submitting such proposals.[81]

In practice, a proposal is drafted by the responsible Directorate General under the authority of its Commissioner and in consultation with other services. There may also be contacts with bodies such as the Union of Industrial and Employers' Confederations of Europe (UNICE) and the European Trade Union Confederation (ETUC) and with other interest groups.[82] When the draft proposal is ready, it is submitted for approval to the Commission as a body. Drafts must be accompanied by a statement as to their budgetary implications;[83] a statement as to their impact on small and medium-sized enterprises;[84] and a justification in terms of subsidiarity.[85]

---

[72] See, e.g., Arts. 113(3) and 109(3) EC.   [73] See, e.g., Art. 102(1) EC.   [74] Art. 189(5) EC.

[75] Cf. regarding reports on economic and social cohesion, which may be accompanied by appropriate proposals, Art. 130b EC.

[76] Case C–325/91 *France* v. *EC Commission: transparency communication* [1993] ECR II–3283.

[77] See, generally, C.W.A. Timmermans, "How Can One Improve the Quality of Community Legislation" (1997) 34 *CMLRev.* 1229–57.

[78] Bull. EC 3–1966, 9.   [79] Sect. 4.2.3 below.

[80] Bull. EC 3–1966, 9, para. (a)1. This clause embodied pre-existing practice. See, under the ECSC Treaty, I. Davidson, "Sovereignty in the European Economic Community: the Case of France" [1975] *The Round Table* 235–42, 237.

[81] Para. 9 of the Protocol on the application of the principles of subsidiarity and proportionality, annexed to the EC Treaty.

[82] Sect. 6.1.6 below.   [83] Cf. Art. 201a EC.

[84] Cf. the declaration on environmental impact assessments, adopted with the Treaty of Amsterdam (OJ 1997 C340/1).

[85] Para. 4 of the Protocol on the application of the principles of subsidiarity and proportionality, annexed to the EC Treaty. The need for such a justification has received judicial recognition. See Case C–233/94 *Germany* v. *European Parliament and EU Council* (13 May 1997).

Original Legislation

Article 155 of the EC Treaty states in the third indent that the Commission has its own power of decision,[86] where the Treaty so provides. This power includes the adoption of legislation. For example, Article 48(3)(d) empowers the Commission to enact regulations laying down the conditions under which nationals of Member States may remain permanently in a Member State other than their own after having worked there.[87] Again, under Article 90(3) the Commission may, where necessary, enact directives concerning the operation of public undertakings by Member States.[88] The Court of Justice has rejected arguments drawn from the structure of the Treaty to the effect that Article 90(3) only empowers the Commission to enact measures dealing with specific situations.[89]

Delegated Legislation

The fourth indent of Article 155 of the EC Treaty envisages the enactment of delegated legislation by the Commission. It provides for the Commission to exercise the powers conferred on it by the Council for the implementation of rules laid down by the Council.[90] Article 145 of the Treaty requires the Council to confer such powers on the Commission. In connection with the conferment of such powers, the concept of implementation is to be given a broad interpretation.[91] The powers are particularly prominent in the fields of agriculture and competition.

However, according to the Court of Justice, the essential elements of matters to be dealt with by the Commission pursuant to such powers must be determined by a Council act directly based on the Treaty.[92] Moreover, "certain requirements" may be imposed on the exercise of the powers, and the Council may reserve the right in specific cases to exercise directly the powers itself. In practice, the exercise of the powers is usually limited by a committee system.[93] The validity of such a limitation has been upheld by

[86] For the purposes of this provision, "decision" is not limited to its technical meaning in Art. 189(4) EC. See Joined Cases 188–190/80 *France, Italy, and the UK* v. *EC Commission: transparency directive* [1982] ECR 2545, 2565.

[87] Reg. 1251/70 (JO 1970 L142/24) on the right of workers to remain in the territory of a Member State after having been employed in that state.

[88] Dir. 80/723 (OJ 1980 L195/35) on the transparency of financial relations between Member States and public undertakings.

[89] Joined Cases 188–190/80 *France, Italy, and the UK* v. *EC Commission: transparency directive* [1982] ECR 2545, 2573.

[90] A broad interpretation is to be given to this indent. See Case 57/72 *Westzucker GmbH* v. *Einfuhr-und Vorratsstelle für Zucker* [1973] ECR 321, 338; and Case T–70/94 *Comafrica SpA and Dole Fresh Fruit Europe Ltd & Co.* v. *EC Commission* [1996] ECR II–1741, II–1765.

[91] See, e.g., Case 23/75 *Rey Soda* v. *Cassa Conguaglio Zucchero* [1975] ECR 1279, 1301; and Lenz AG in Case 61/86 *UK* v. *EC Commission: sheepmeat and goatmeat* [1988] ECR 431, 452–4.

[92] Case 25/70 *Einfuhr-und Vorratsstelle für Getreide und Futtermittel* v. *Köster, Berodt & Co.* [1970] ECR 1161, 1170.

[93] Dec. 87/373 (OJ 1987 L197/33) laying down the procedures for the exercise of implementing powers conferred on the Commission.

the Court,[94] even where the measures concern budgetary expenditure.[95]

"Default Legislation"

The Commission maintains that it may adopt measures to prevent a Council failure to act from endangering the functioning of the common market. This view is not entirely without the support of the Court of Justice.[96]

In particular, regard may be had to the case law concerning matters covered by the common agricultural policy. In relation to such matters, unilateral action by Member States is prohibited. Hence, Member States must, in the event of Council inaction, act only in co-operation with the Commission.[97] Such co-operation may enable the Commission to play an important role in the elaboration of what amount to legislative rules. However, in the absence of co-operation, the Commission alone may not adopt such rules simply because of Council inaction.

"Soft Legislation"

"Soft legislation" may be defined as "rules of conduct which, in principle, have no legally binding force but which nevertheless may have practical effect".[98] A possible problem with this definition is that rules having practical effect may not be readily distinguishable from those having binding legal force.[99] The expression "soft legislation" may more appropriately be used to indicate instruments that may have effects of legislation without being adopted according to formal legislative procedures.

The instruments concerned are systematic rather than piecemeal and thus resemble legislation rather than litigation. They enable the Commission, without securing the consent of the Union legislature or the European Courts, to present its interpretation and seek to develop its policy. They circumscribe the arena for debate and define the agenda for negotiation and, if necessary, litigation.[100] At the same time, they may be perceived by the Commission as entailing greater flexibility for continued negotiation and elaboration and for adaptation to market changes[101] than formal legis-

---

[94] See, e.g., Case 25/70 *Einfuhr-und Vorratsstelle für Getreide und Futtermittel* v. *Köster, Berodt & Co.* [1970] ECR 1161, 1171; and Case 16/88 *EC Commission* v. *EC Council: fisheries expenditure* [1989] ECR 3457, 3486.

[95] *Ibid.*, 3487.

[96] Case 325/85 *Ireland* v. *EC Commission: fishery conservation* [1987] ECR 5041, 5087–8.

[97] It is a more general principle that a Council failure to perform its obligations cannot justify a breach of the Treaty by a Member State. See, e.g., Joined Cases 90 & 91/63 *EEC Commission* v. *Luxembourg and Belgium: duty on milk imports* [1964] ECR 625, 631.

[98] F. Snyder, "The Effectiveness of European Community Law: Institutions, Processes, Tools, and Techniques" (1993) 56 *MLR* 19–54, 32.

[99] See, generally, K.C. Wellens and G.M. Borchardt, "Soft Law in European Community Law" [1989] *ELR* 267–321.

[100] M. Melchior, "Les Communications de la Commission" in *Mélanges en honneur de Fernand Dehousse* (Labor, Brussels, 1979), ii, 243–58, 250.

[101] See, e.g., Code on aid to the synthetic fibres industry (JO 1992 C346/2).

lation. Thus they may assist Commission efforts to become "head of the river".[102]

The Commission usually describes such soft legislation as "co-ordination principles", "guidelines", "codes", or "frameworks". It plays an important role in the work of the Commission, particularly in relation to state aid control within the Union.[103] It may also serve "as a reference when establishing the Union's position on state aid cases in countries with whom the Community has entered into free trade agreements".[104]

Various forms may be taken. Even policy statements in the annual reports on competition policy are sometimes classified as soft legislation.[105] Certainly, it is said that "guidelines as to the Commissions policy may be deduced from those reports".[106] The Commission itself considers that such statements promote transparency,[107] and may "assist" national courts in examining individual cases.[108]

Commission officials apparently believe that it makes no practical difference whether rules are embodied in formal legislation or in "simple notices or statements by the Commission which may or may not be immediately published".[109] However, the Commission may prefer embodiment of its principles in forms expressly approved by Member States. Indeed, the Commission secured approval of its original "co-ordination principles" for regional aid in a Resolution of the Representatives of the Governments of the Member States meeting in the Council.[110]

A legal basis for the adoption of such soft legislation may sometimes seem to be provided by particular Treaty provisions. For example, according to Article 93(1), the Commission shall, in co-operation with Member States, keep under constant review all systems of aid existing in those Member States. It shall also propose "appropriate measures" to the Member States. However, if such proposals only constitute recommendations for the

---

[102] F. Andriessen, "The Role of Anti-Trust in the Face of Economic Recession: State Aids in the EEC" [1983] *ECLR* 340–50, 350.

[103] Cf. Draft Commission interpretative communication: freedom to provide services and the general good in the insurance sector (OJ 1997 C365/7).

[104] European automobile industry, COM(94)49, 15.

[105] C. Blumann, "Régime des aides d'état: jurisprudence récente de la Cour de justice" [1992] *RMC* 721–39, 731.

[106] VerLoren van Themaat AG in Case 323/82 *SA Intermills* v. *EC Commission* [1984] ECR 3809, 3835.

[107] *Twenty-Third Report on Competition Policy* (EC Commission, Brussels, 1994), 255.

[108] Notice on co-operation between national courts and the Commission in applying Arts. 85 and 86 EC (OJ 1993 C39/6), para. 36. Cf., however, M.G. Santiago, "Las 'Comunicaciones interpretativas' de la Comision: concepto y valor normativo" [1992] *Revista de Instituciones Europeas* 933–49, 936, regarding the inadequate details usually provided in such statements.

[109] F. Rawlinson, "The Role of Policy Frameworks, Codes and Guidelines in the Control of State Aid" in I. Harden (ed.), *State Aid: Community Law and Policy* (Bundesanzeiger, Trier, 1993), 52–60, 59.

[110] Of 20 Oct. 1971 (JO 1971 C111/1) on general systems of regional aid.

purposes of Article 189(5) of the Treaty,[111] they need not be followed by Member States.[112] Hence, the Commission seeks to obtain the consent of Member States to proposals under Article 93(1).[113]

The need for such consent is confirmed by the case law. According to the Court of Justice, this provision "involves an obligation of regular, periodic co-operation on the part of the Commission and the Member States, from which neither the Commission nor a Member State can release itself for an indefinite period depending on the unilateral will of either of them".[114] Obligations on the Commission to obtain acceptance from the Member States of measures proposed under this provision, periodically to review them,[115] and to amend them only with such acceptance[116] are implied.

In fact, the creation of soft legislation, like more formal legislation,[117] may be regarded by the Commission as conditional on information to, and negotiation with, Member States. There may also be more formal similarities with legislation, in that soft legislation may be reasoned and published in the Official Journal.[118] In particular, it is argued that, to be binding, the instruments concerned must be reasoned according to Article 190 of the Treaty.[119] However, reasoning requirements in the instruments themselves may be reduced, if Member States have already been informed.[120] More fundamentally, institutions such as the European Parliament do not play the same role in adoption of soft legislation as in adoption of formal legislation.

The emphasis on negotiation with Member States may reflect Commission fears that, if "strongly opposed" by Member States, soft legislation may be unworkable. The emphasis may also reflect Commission fears that implementation of such legislation may be delayed by proceedings before the Court of Justice.[121] Thus, for example, the framework for aid to the motor industry "took into account the principal observations made by the representatives of the Member States at a multilateral meeting on 27 October 1988".[122] On the other hand, since the reactions of Member States to the

---

[111] Lenz AG in Case C–135/93 *Spain v. EC Commission: framework for aid to the automobile industry* [1995] ECR I–1651, I–1661.

[112] According to Art. 189(5) EC, recommendations lack binding force. See also Mayras AG in Case 70/72 *EC Commission v. Germany: investment grants for mining* [1973] ECR 813, 834.

[113] Case C–292/95 *Spain v. EC Commission: framework for aid to the automobile industry* [1997] ECR I–1931.

[114] Case C–135/93 *Spain v. EC Commission: framework for aid to the automobile industry* [1995] ECR I–1651, I–1686.

[115] *Ibid.*, I–1683.   [116] Lenz AG (*ibid.*, I–1668).

[117] J. Biancarelli, "Le Contrôle de la Cour de justice des Communautés européennes en matière d'aides publiques" [1993] *AJDA* 412–36, 423 refers to the Commission as exercising a *"quasi normatif"* power.

[118] M. Melchior, n. 100 above, 252.

[119] Lenz AG in Case C–135/93 *Spain v. EC Commission: framework for aid to the automobile industry* [1995] ECR I–1651, I–1669–70.

[120] *Ibid.*, I–1670.   [121] F. Rawlinson, n. 109 above, 60.

[122] Case C–135/93 *Spain v. EC Commission: framework for aid to the automobile industry* [1995] ECR I–1651, I–1675.

draft principles regarding export aid were "mixed", the Commission favoured leaving the matter to a Council directive under Article 113 of the Treaty.[123] Planned frameworks may also be abandoned because of opposition within the Commission.[124] In other cases, however, disagreements may merely lead to the postponed introduction of the guidelines concerned. For example, such disagreements led to the postponed introduction of new guidelines for environmental aid[125] and aid to undertakings in difficulty because of a recession or restructuring.[126] In other words, procedures for the adoption of soft legislation are problematic.

Where such legislation is adopted, it is considered by the Commission to have the advantage of being comparatively easy to amend. For example, the Commission stated that it would follow its guidelines on environmental aid[127] until the end of 1999. Before the end of 1996 it would review their operation. It might amend them at any time, should it prove appropriate to make changes for reasons connected with competition policy, environmental policy, or regional policy. Equally, amendment might be needed to take account of other Union policies and of international commitments.[128] The apparent implication is that the need for flexibility may lead to unilateral amendment or, in other words, may be perceived to override the need to obtain consent.

This implication may be supported by Commission practice in the field of regional aid. In May 1973 the Commission organised a multilateral meeting with senior national officials responsible for aid to discuss implementing the principles regarding regional aid in the three new Member States (Denmark, Ireland, and the United Kingdom). However, "no general agreement was to be found",[129] and so the Commission unilaterally extended the principles to these Member States.[130] In 1981 the Commission also discussed with Member States the possibility of lowering the aid ceiling set for the central regions by the principles. However, the majority of Member States where such regions were located was opposed.[131] The response of the Commission was unilaterally to impose lower ceilings.[132]

Such practice may be problematic. The European Courts do not accept

[123] *Twenty-Second Report on Competition Policy* (EC Commission, Brussels, 1993), 207–8.

[124] See F. Rawlinson, n. 109 above, 55, regarding aid to the audio-visual industry.

[125] *Twenty-Second Report on Competition Policy* (EC Commission, Brussels, 1993), 208.

[126] *European Report* 1837 (20 Feb. 1993). Guidelines on state aid for rescuing and restructuring firms in difficulty (OJ 1994 C368/12; OJ 1997 C283/2) were later adopted.

[127] Community guidelines on state aid for environmental purposes (OJ 1994 C72/3).

[128] *Ibid.*, para 4.3. See, similarly, regarding "amplification" or "modification" of the Guidelines for the examination of state aid to fisheries and aquaculture (OJ 1994 C260/3) "in the light of the gradual development of the common fisheries policy", para. 1.7 thereof. See also Application of Arts. 92 and 93 EC and Art. 61 EEA to state aids in the aviation sector (OJ 1994 C350/5), para. 51.

[129] *Third Report on Competition Policy* (EC Commission, Brussels, 1974), 76.

[130] COM(73)1110, para. III.

[131] *Twelfth Report on Competition Policy* (EC Commission, Brussels, 1983), 139.

[132] *Ibid.*, 143–5.

that Article 93(1) supports examination of aid according to "rules established or agreed . . . depending on the unilateral will of either the Commission or the Member States".[133] These Courts maintain that instruments which only apply by virtue of the consent of the Member States cannot be amended unilaterally by the Commission.[134] For example, the Commission decided, on 23 December 1992, that the framework for aid to the motor industry, originally adopted for a limited period, should remain in force until the situation was reviewed.[135] Spain challenged this decision before the Court of Justice, which annulled the decision.[136]

Such problems in the procedures for adoption and amendment of soft legislation are matched by problems regarding its legal effects. The Commission considers that the instruments concerned promote consistency in its application and interpretation of Union law.[137] Even if not binding in the strict sense, they have authority, in that they publicly set out the policy that the Commission intends to follow. Member States and all the others concerned are entitled to expect,[138] because of the principles of legal certainty and legitimate expectations,[139] that the policy will be followed.[140] True, the possibility is not excluded that individual Commission decisions may depart from, though "without prejudice to", such soft legislation.[141] However, in the absence of "completely new and unforeseen circumstances",[142] such departures may entail violation of the equality principle.[143] In contrast, where there is no soft legislation, inconsistency as between Commission decisions may be treated simply as indicating an "irregularity" in a previous decision that does not affect the validity of a later, inconsistent decision.[144]

Equally, soft legislation is said to produce improved levels of compliance and discipline on the part of the Member States,[145] though it may be argued

---

[133] Case C–135/93 *Spain* v. *EC Commission: framework for aid to the automobile industry* [1995] ECR I–1651, I–1683.

[134] Lenz AG in Case C–313/90 *Comité International de la Rayonne et des Fibres Synthétiques (Cirfs)* v. *EC Commission* [1993] ECR I–1125, I–1175.

[135] OJ 1993 C36/17.

[136] Case C–135/93 *Spain* v. *EC Commission: framework for aid to the automobile industry* [1995] ECR I–1651.

[137] *Twenty-Third Report on Competition Policy* (EC Commission, Brussels, 1994), 239–40.

[138] See, regarding a presumption to this effect, C. Blumann, n. 105 above, 731.

[139] Cf., regarding estoppel, M. Melchior, n. 100 above, 254.

[140] See the submission of the Commission in Joined Cases 166 & 220/86 *Irish Cement Limited* v. *EC Commission* [1988] ECR 6473, 6482.

[141] Dec. 94/266 (OJ 1994 L114/21) on the proposal to award aid to SST–Garngesellschaft mbH, Thüringen.

[142] M.G. Santiago, n. 108 above, 945.

[143] Cf., regarding the need to give reasons for departures from internal guidelines of the Commission, Case 148/73 *Raymond Louwage and Marie-Thérèse Louwage, née Moriame* v. *EC Commission* [1974] ECR 81, 89.

[144] Darmon AG in Joined Cases C–324 & 342/90 *Germany and Pleuger Worthington GmbH* v. *EC Commission* [1994] ECR I–1173, I–1191.

[145] Reply by Mr Van Miert to WQ 365/93 (OJ 1993 C288/5) by Mrs Christine Oddy.

that the importance of legal certainty implies the need for formal legislation.[146] Indeed, with soft legislation rendering Commission policy increasingly well known, it is anticipated that Member States will modify and structure their practice, to bring it into line with the policy.[147] At the same time, soft legislation allows the Commission to pursue a "flexible approach". As a result, a contribution to implementation of the subsidiarity principle in Article 3b of the Treaty is said to be involved.[148]

The Court of Justice accepts that soft legislation has "legal effects" for the purposes of judicial review of its legality and has called it "secondary Community law".[149] However, the requirements of legal certainty may set limits to the formal legal effects of the instruments concerned. They may "constitute a frame of reference, but they cannot be regarded as legally binding and thus capable of forming the basis of a . . . decision."[150]

According to the Court, binding legal force may only arise from Union acts which expressly indicate their legal basis in a provision of Union law. That provision must, in turn, prescribe the legal form which the act must take.[151] The implication, it may be imagined, is that the prescribed legal form must be that of a binding act. Thus although the Commission may derive powers under Articles 5 and 155 of the Treaty, these provisions cannot be used to create new obligations.[152] In particular, Article 5 does not entail that Commission "memoranda" have binding force,[153] and the power in Article 155 to formulate recommendations or opinions does not provide a basis for the adoption of binding measures.[154] An extreme position is that even a "negotiated act" must have a formal legal basis.[155]

It appears, however, that binding force may arise from acceptance by the Member State concerned of an otherwise non-binding act,[156] though mere

---

[146] K. Hellingman, "State Participation as State Aid under Article 92 of the EEC Treaty: the Commission Guidelines" (1986) 23 *CMLRev.* 111–31, 127–8.

[147] *Seventeenth Report on Competition Policy* (EC Commission, Brussels, 1988), 141.

[148] Application of the subsidiarity principle 1994, COM(94)533, 22–3.

[149] Case C–135/93 *Spain* v. *EC Commission: framework for aid to the automobile industry* [1995] ECR I–1651, I–1683.

[150] Darmon AG in Case 310/85 *Deufil GmbH & Co. KG* v. *EC Commission* [1987] ECR 901, 914.

[151] Case C–325/91 *France* v. *EC Commission: communication on aid to public undertakings* [1993] ECR I–3283, I–3311–12. See also, regarding a Commission communication on opening up of cross-border investment in pension funds, Tesauro AG in Case C–57/95 *France* v. *EC Commission: internal market for pension funds* (22 Jan. 1997).

[152] See, however, H. Morch, "Summary of the Most Important Recent Developments" (1995) 5 *Competition Policy Newsletter* 43–9, 47.

[153] Case 229/86 *Brother Industries* v. *EC Commission* [1987] ECR 3757, 3763.

[154] Case C–303/90 *France* v. *EC Commission: code of conduct on the use of the Structural Funds* [1991] ECR I–5315, I–5348. However, in Case C–135/93 *Spain* v. *EC Commission: framework for aid to the automobile industry* [1995] ECR I–1651, I–1666 Lenz AG did not apparently rule out the possibility that Art. 115 EC could play a role in relation to binding principles.

[155] Case C–325/91 *France* v. *EC Commission: communication on aid to public undertakings* [1993] ECR I–3283, I–3312.

[156] Lenz AG in Case C–313/90 *Comité International de la Rayonne et des Fibres Synthétiques (Cirfs)* v. *EC Commission* [1993] ECR I–1125, I-1154–6.

acquiescence may be insufficient for this purpose.[157] In other words, the relevant instruments may not have original binding force, but the possibility cannot be excluded that they subsequently acquire such force. Indeed, Article 154 of the first Accession Act provided that the principles for regional aid would apply to the new Member States, as "*acquis communautaire*", from 1 July 1973.[158] They may also acquire binding legal force by agreement with third states,[159] and there may be calls for their incorporation in the domestic law of Member States.[160]

Whether or not binding force is formally acquired, soft legislation may be of interpretative significance.[161] Certainly, the Court of Justice holds that national courts must take account of recommendations designed to "supplement" binding Union provisions.[162] In practice, however, it may be difficult to maintain a distinction between instruments which "make more explicit" a binding rule and those which "add to the text" of the provision containing that rule[163] or "add new obligations".[164] In other words, the distinction between the interpretation and modification of a rule may be difficult to maintain.[165] As a result, soft legislation may effectively have binding force as an interpretation of Treaty provisions.[166]

For example, the Commission may simply refer to "objective criteria" in soft legislation, without having to set out its assessment of the compatibility of state aid with the Treaty. Hence, the burden of the reasoning requirements otherwise imposed on the Commission may be eased.[167] Moreover, since the

[157] Lenz AG (*ibid.*, I–1175) and in Case C–135/93 *Spain* v. *EC Commission: framework for aid to the automobile industry* [1995] ECR I–1651, I–1660.

[158] Cf. the requirements in annexes to the EEA Agreement (OJ 1994 L1/3), including Annex XIV, on state aid, that "due account" is taken of such principles.

[159] See, e.g., Art. 39 of Dec. 1/95 of the EC–Turkey Association Council (OJ 1996 L35/1).

[160] C. Pourre, "Le Cumul d'aides" [1993] AJDA 444–50, 451. See, earlier, regarding Belgian incorporation, M. Melchior, n. 100 above, 256.

[161] Cf., regarding "position statements of the Commission", *R.* v. *Secretary of State for the Home Dept, ex p. Donald Walter Flynn* [1995] 3 CMLR 397, 409. Cf. also, regarding the interpretative function of declarations, Case C–292/89 *R.* v. *Immigration Appeal Tribunal, ex p. Gustaff Desiderius Antonissen* [1991] ECR I–745, I–778.

[162] Case C–322/88 *Salvatore Grimaldi* v. *Fonds des Maladies Professionnelles* [1989] ECR I–4407, I–4421. At the same time, soft legislation must be "understood in a manner consistent with the Treaty provision it is intended to implement". See Case C–135/93 *Spain* v. *EC Commission: framework for aid to the automobile industry* [1995] ECR I–1651, I–1683.

[163] Case C–366/88 *France* v. *EC Commission: internal instructions on use of the EAGGF* [1990] ECR I–3571, I–3601.

[164] Case C–325/91 *France* v. *EC Commission: communication on aid to public undertakings* [1993] ECR I–3283, I–3311.

[165] Cf. the objections of Warner AG to resort to unpublished documents for interpretation of binding measures in Case 28/76 *Milac GmbH Groß-und Aussenhandel* v. *Hauptzollamt Freibourg* [1976] ECR 1639, 1664. But cf. also where a binding measure itself is not published, Case 299/82 *Horst W. Steinfort* v. *EC Commission* [1983] ECR 3141, 3146.

[166] Case C–313/90 *Comité International de la Rayonne et des Fibres Synthétiques (Cirfs)* v. *EC Commission* [1993] ECR I–1125, I–1186.

[167] Darmon AG in Joined Cases C–324 & 342/90 *Germany and Pleuger Worthington GmbH* v. *EC Commission* [1994] ECR I–1173, I–1189.

processing of aid schemes covered by soft legislation is simplified, the Commission is enabled to concentrate its limited resources[168] on cases that involve the most serious distortions of competition.[169]

The convenience entailed may be of substantive as well as procedural significance. For example, the Commission may find state aid to be prohibited merely because it is contrary to soft legislation.[170] Moreover, inconsistency of aid with such legislation may be decisive for a finding by the Court of Justice that aid is prohibited.[171] Equally, if a Commission decision is found to have been taken on the basis of a misinterpretation of such legislation, the decision may be annulled by the Court.[172] The Commission may also be obliged to comply with procedures laid down in such legislation.[173]

Where soft legislation goes beyond mere "interpretation" of Treaty provisions, however, its effects may depend on the consensus of Member States not to challenge it. If such a challenge takes the form of proceedings before the Court of Justice, the result may be that the relevant instrument is annulled.[174] The Commission may respond to,[175] or possibly seek to preempt, such proceedings by embodying its principles in a more formal legal act. The latter has been done, for example, in relation to the framework for aid to automobiles,[176] the "rules" regarding aid cumulation,[177] and, more particularly, following failure of the Belgian authorities to comply with an "informal agreement" previously reached with the Commission.[178]

These various problems of soft legislation have led to claims that the Commission enjoys too much discretionary power. The conclusion drawn is

---

[168] *Twenty-Third Report on Competition Policy* (EC Commission, Brussels, 1994), 239–40.

[169] Reply by Mr Van Miert to WQ 365/93 (OJ 1993 C288/5) by Mrs Christine Oddy.

[170] See, e.g., Dec. 83/245 (OJ 1983 L137/24) on an aid scheme in favour of the textile and clothing industry in France.

[171] Case C–301/87 *France* v. *EC Commission: Boussac* [1990] ECR I–307, I–364-5; and Case C–303/88 *Italy* v. *EC Commission: Lanerossi* [1991] ECR I–1433, I–1480.

[172] Case C–313/90 *Comité International de la Rayonne et des Fibres Synthétiques (Cirfs)* v. *EC Commission* [1993] ECR I–1125, I–1189.

[173] Lenz AG in Case C–135/93 *Spain* v. *EC Commission: framework for aid to the automobile industry* [1995] ECR I–1651, I–1664.

[174] See, e.g., regarding a communication on the sampling and analysis of products to benefit from aid from the EAGGF, Case C–366/88 *France* v. *EC Commission: internal instructions on use of the EAGGF* [1990] ECR I–3571.

[175] Following annulment by the ECJ in Case C–325/91 *France* v. *EC Commission: communication on aid to public undertakings* [1993] ECR I–3283 of the communication concerning the application of Arts. 92 and 93 EEC and of Art. 5 of Dir. 80/723 to public undertakings in the manufacturing sector, the Commission embodied in Dir. 93/84 (OJ 1993 L254/16) amending Dir. 80/723 the obligation for Member States to provide the Commission with financial data on an annual basis.

[176] Dec. 90/381 (OJ 1990 L188/55) amending German aid schemes for the motor vehicle industry.

[177] Notice regarding cumulation of aids for different purposes in France and Greece (OJ 1987 C300/4).

[178] Dec. 75/397 (OJ 1975 L177/13) on the aids granted by the Belgian Government pursuant to the Law of 17 July 1959 introducing and co-ordinating measures to encourage economic expansion and the creation of new industries.

that adoption of formal legislation is preferable.[179] However, it is not clear that the implementation problems which have arisen would necessarily be any more amenable to resolution through formal legislation[180] than through soft legislation.[181]

2.3.2 Budget

All items of Union revenue and expenditure are to be shown in the budget.[182] However, borrowing and lending operations, operational expenditure of the ECSC, loans and grants from the European Investment Bank, Euratom borrowing and loans, and the expenditure of the European Development Fund are not included.

The revenue and expenditure shown in the budget must be in balance.[183] Revenue derives from duties under the common customs tariff, levies on agricultural imports, a proportion of national value-added tax receipts up to 1.4 per cent,[184] and an annual amount based on gross domestic product.[185] Fraud against the Union is to be countered pursuant to Article 209a of the Treaty, with the Commission making annual reports to the European Parliament.[186]

The budgetary role of the Commission is laid down in Article 203 of the EC Treaty. The Commission is responsible for the preparation of the preliminary draft of the budget.[187] This draft is based on a consolidation of the estimates of its expenditure by each Union institution. These estimates are to be submitted to the Commission before 1 July of each year.[188] The draft must, in turn, be placed before the Council not later than 1 September of the year preceding that in which the budget is to be implemented.[189] The financial year runs from 1 January to 31 December.[190]

The preparation of the budget and the drafting of legislation may be interdependent activities. On the one hand, budgetary resources may often be necessary for legislation to be feasible. On the other hand, budgetary proposals may provide an impetus to legislative action.[191]

---

[179] Report of the Committee on Economic and Monetary Affairs and Industrial Policy on the Twentieth Report on Competition Policy, EP Doc. A3–0338/91, 16.

[180] See, now, the Commission proposal for a reg. on the application of Arts. 92 and 93 EC to certain categories of horizontal state aid (OJ 1997 C262/6).

[181] In Joined Cases 188–190/80 *France, Italy, and the UK* v. *EC Commission: transparency directive* [1982] ECR 2545, 2565 the Commission maintained that the "institutional balance" within the Union would alter if it were to "adopt rules on the application of Articles 92 and 93".

[182] Art. 199 EC.

[183] *Ibid.* However, no item of revenue can be designated for a specific item of expenditure. See Art. 3(1) of the Financial Reg. of 21 Dec. 1977 (OJ 1977 L356/1).

[184] 1% in 1999.

[185] Art. 2(1) of Dec. 94/728 (OJ 1994 L293/9) on the system of the European Communities' own resources. It is calculated so as to reach the budgetary ceiling of 1.27% in 1999.

[186] Art. 209a(5) EC.

[187] Basic principles regarding its arrangement are laid down by Art. 202 EC.

[188] Art. 203(2) EC.   [189] Art. 203(3) EC.   [190] Art. 203(1) EC.   [191] Sect. 3.3.2 below.

2.3.3 Administration

Commission administration may take the form of individual decisions, contracts, or the initiation of proceedings before the Court of Justice.

Individual Decisions

Article 155 of the EC treaty states in the third indent that the Commission has its own power of decision, where the Treaty so provides. This power includes that of taking individual decisions. For example, the Commission takes such decisions regarding the application of certain safeguard clauses,[192] the prohibition of anti-competitive conduct by undertakings in Articles 85 and 86 of the Treaty,[193] and the prohibition of state aid in Article 92 of the Treaty.[194]

Moreover, in the financial field the Commission takes individual decisions implementing the budget under Article 205 of the EC Treaty.[195] Under the ECSC Treaty the Commission also receives the levy imposed on coal and steel undertakings and disburses the levy obtained.[196] Moreover, the Commission enjoys borrowing and lending powers under the ECSC Treaty,[197] under the New Community Instrument,[198] and under the Euratom Treaty.[199] The Commission is also responsible for the operation of the Structural Funds (the European Regional Development Fund, the European Agricultural Guidance and Guarantee Fund, and the European Social Fund) and other financial instruments.[200]

The relevant Commission decisions must, according to Article 191(3) of the EC Treaty, be notified to those to whom they are addressed. However, there is no requirement that they be published. In practice, they are rarely published in full, if at all. For example, in the case of the Cohesion Fund, only the "key details" of Commission decisions granting assistance are to be published in the Official Journal.[201] The Commission itself decided in 1989

---

[192] E.g., Art. 115 EC, concerning commercial policy measures. See, regarding the delegation of powers to the Commission, Art. 3 of Dir. 87/373 (OJ 1987 L197/33) laying down the procedures for the exercise of implementing powers conferred on the Commission.

[193] Reg. 17 (JO 1962 204) First Reg. implementing Arts. 85 and 86 EEC. See also, in connection with competition in transport, Arts. 75(4) and 76(2) EC.

[194] Art. 88 EC. See, generally, J.A. Winter, "Supervision of State Aid: Article 93 in the Court of Justice" (1993) 30 *CMLRev.* 311–29.

[195] Commission autonomy in this field was stressed by the ECJ in Case 93/85 *EC Commission* v. *United Kingdom: own resources* [1986] ECR 4011, 4033.

[196] Arts. 49–53 ECSC.

[197] *Ibid.*

[198] Dec. 78/870 (OJ 1978 L298/9) empowering the Commission to contract loans for the purpose of promoting investment within the Community.

[199] Art. 172 Euratom.

[200] See Chap. 20.

[201] Art. 10(7) of Reg. 1164/94 (OJ 1994 L130/1) establishing a Cohesion Fund. See, e.g., Publication of main points of decisions to grant financial assistance under Reg. 1164/94 (OJ 1996 C325/1).

to amend its practice concerning decisions to grant Union assistance for the improvement of agricultural structures. These decisions, which took effect on notification to the respective Member States, would no longer be published in full, "except in exceptional cases".[202]

While in principle the decisions merely entail application of pre-existing rules, in reality they may modify such rules or even generate new ones. Certainly, to the extent that actors can deduce "general principles" from such decisions, they may "spontaneously" modify their conduct accordingly.[203] Moreover, according to the Commission, national courts "can always be guided . . . by the existing decisions of the Commission"[204] or by "its customary practice".[205] In practice, the Commission may seek to formulate "criteria" for its decision-making;[206] to follow "constant practice"[207] or a single precedent,[208] though attempts by Member States to invoke such precedents in proceedings before the Commission may be cursorily rejected;[209] to implement a "global sectoral approach";[210] or to develop a "consistent policy", which has been applied in previous decisions.[211]

For example, Decision 87/194[212] concerned planned aid to a Belgian producer of mineral water. Here the Commission noted that aid planned by the Belgian Government for similar investments in this sector had previously been found incompatible with the common market and, hence, had been prohibited.[213] As the situation in the sector had not changed, the Commission felt that it had to be guided by the same considerations.

---

[202] Communication of agricultural structure decisions (OJ 1989 L174/31).

[203] M. Melchior, n. 100 above, 246.

[204] Notice on co-operation between national courts and the Commission in applying Arts. 85 and 86 EC (OJ 1993 C39/6), para. 21.

[205] Notice regarding co-operation between national courts and the Commission in the state aid field (OJ 1995 C312/8), para. 29.

[206] Notice C48/94 (NN104/94 (ex N514/92)) (OJ 1995 C161/5) regarding aid which the French Government had decided to grant to "Institut Français du Pétrole".

[207] Notice C45/91 (ex N255/91) (OJ 1993 C37/15) regarding the proposal of the Italian authorities to provide state aid to the Fiat Group in support of its Mezzogiorno investment plan.

[208] Dec. 88/468 (OJ 1988 L229/37) on aids granted by the French Government to a farm machinery manufacturer at St Dizier, Angers, and Croix; and Notice C66/91 (NN154/91) (OJ 1992 C48/3) regarding aid which Germany had decided to grant to Sony GmbH.

[209] Notice C7/95 (N412/94) (OJ 1995 C262/16) concerning aid the German Government intended to grant to Maschinenfabrik Sangerhausen, GmbH, Sachsen-Anhalt.

[210] Dec. 88/174 (OJ 1988 L79/29) concerning aid which Baden-Württemberg had provided to BUG-Alutechnik GmbH, an undertaking producing semi-finished and finished aluminium products.

[211] Dec. 89/373 (OJ 1989 L166/60) on aid decided by the Italian Government for investments at the public flat-glass industry (Veneziana Vetro).

[212] On a FIM loan to a mineral-water and glass-bottle manufacturer (OJ 1987 L77/43).

[213] Dec. 82/774 (OJ 1982 L323/31) on a Belgian Government aid scheme concerning the setting-up of a new factory by a soft drinks manufacturer; Dec. 82/775 (OJ 1982 L323/34) on a Belgian Government aid scheme concerning the expansion of the production capacity of an undertaking manufacturing mineral water and soft drinks; and Dec. 82/776 (OJ 1982 L323/37) on a Belgian Government aid scheme concerning the expansion of the production capacity of an undertaking manufacturing mineral water, hot spring water, and soft drinks.

Only where the facts are sufficiently different to exclude "parallelism", may the Commission be willing to depart from an earlier decision.[214] The principle of equal treatment may be invoked by the Commission as the legal basis for such practice,[215] and consistency of Commission decisions may be expected by the European Courts.[216]

Contracts

Contracts have sometimes been seen as a suitable legal form for giving content to individual Commission decisions. The parties to such contracts may be regions and individuals as well as the Commission and Member States. However, their enforcement through proceedings under Article 215(1) of the Treaty[217] may be precluded, to the extent that Commission operations are characterized as "unilateral acts falling within the province of public law".[218]

Examples were provided by Community programmes or national programmes of Community interest. Such programmes were to be agreed between the Commission and the Member State or Member States concerned and were to be adopted by the Commission after consultation of the Committee for the European Regional Development Fund. They then constituted "programme agreements" for the purposes of use of Fund aid under Regulation 1787/84.[219]

Again, implementation of Integrated Mediterranean Programmes was, according to Article 9 of Regulation 2088/85,[220] to be regulated by programme contracts. These contracts were to be concluded between the parties concerned (the Commission, Member States, regional authority, or any other authority designated by the Member States). They were to set out the respective commitments of these parties. The standard contents of the contracts were specified in Annex IV to the Regulation.[221]

Enforcement Decisions

The first indent of Article 155 of the EC Treaty requires the Commission to

---

[214] Dec. 93/627 (OJ 1993 L309/21) concerning aid granted by the Spanish authorities on the occasion of the sale by Cenemesa/Cadmesa/Conelec of certain selected assets to Asea-Brown Boveri.

[215] Case C–313/90 *Comité International de la Rayonne et des Fibres Synthétiques (Cirfs)* v. *EC Commission* [1993] ECR I–1125, I–1187.

[216] Case T–459/93 *Siemens SA* v. *EC Commission* [1995] ECR II–1675, II–1714–15. See, similarly, regarding "internal directives", Case 148/73 *Raymond Louwage and Marie-Thérèse Louwage, née Moriame* v. *EC Commission* [1974] ECR 81, 89.

[217] It provides that the contractual liability of the European Community shall be governed by the law applicable to the contract in question.

[218] Verloren van Themaat AG in Case 44/81 *Germany* v. *EC Commission: deadline for claiming payment of ESF aid* [1982] ECR 1855, 1881.

[219] Art. 13(1) of Reg. 1787/84 (OJ 1984 L169/1) on the ERDF.

[220] Concerning the IMPs (OJ 1985 L197/1).

[221] See, e.g., Dec. 88/62 (OJ 1988 L32/23) approving an IMP for Corsica.

ensure that Union law is applied.[222] More particularly, Regulation 17[223] empowers the Commission to take action, including imposition of fines and penalties,[224] against undertakings in violation of the prohibition of restrictive practices in Articles 85 and 86 of the Treaty. Article 93(2) of the Treaty also provides for the Commission to take proceedings before the Court of Justice against a Member State. It may do so where the Member State fails to comply with a Commission decision that state aid incompatible with the common market has been granted and that, accordingly, this aid should be altered or abolished.[225]

Moreover, proceedings may be brought under Article 225 against a Member State considered to be abusing its right to take measures necessary for the protection of its security which are connected with the production of or trade in arms, munitions, and war material.[226] Similar proceedings may be brought against a Member State considered to be abusing its right to take measures necessary in the face of serious internal disturbances affecting the maintenance of law and order, war, or serious international tension constituting a threat of war or in order to carry out obligations it has accepted for the purpose of maintaining international peace and security.[227] Finally, where the Commission considers that a Member State is making improper use of a derogation from harmonisation measures, the Commission may bring the matter before the Court.[228]

The procedure generally used against Member States is that contained in Article 169 of the Treaty.[229] This provision states that where the Commission considers that a Member State has failed to fulfil an obligation under this Treaty,[230] it shall deliver a reasoned opinion on the matter after giving the Member State concerned the opportunity to submit its observations.[231] The

---

[222] Problems in this area led to the Declaration on the Implementation of Community Law, which was adopted with the TEU.

[223] First Regulation implementing Arts 85 and 86 EEC (JO 1962 204).

[224] *Ibid.*, Arts. 15 and 16. In so acting, the Commission acts as an administrative authority rather than as a judicial or quasi-judicial tribunal. See Joined Cases 209–215 & 218/78 *Heintz van Landewyck Sàrl* v. *EC Commission* [1980] ECR 3125, 3248.

[225] A corresponding procedure is contained in Art. 6(4) of Dec. 2496/96 (OJ 1996 L338/42) establishing Community rules for state aid to the steel industry and Art. 8 of Dec. 3632/93 (OJ 1993 L329/12) establishing Community rules for state aid to the coal industry

[226] Art. 223(1)(b) EC.   [227] Art. 224 EC.   [228] Art. 100a(9) EC.

[229] Cf. Art. 88 ECSC. The *lex specialis* principle may require resort to Art. 93(2) EC rather than Art. 169 EC where the grant of state aid is involved. The latter procedure may only be employed in relation to elements of an aid scheme that violate Union law rules other than those in Art. 92 (Case C–35/88 *EC Commission* v. *Greece: Kydep* [1990] ECR I–3125, I–3154) and that are not necessary for the operation of that scheme (see Mancini AG in Case 290/83 *EC Commission* v. *France: aid to poor farmers* [1985] ECR 439, 443).

[230] Failure by a Member State to co-operate with a Commission investigation may constitute a breach of Art. 5 EC. See Case 240/86 *EC Commission* v. *Greece: cereal imports* [1988] ECR 1835, 1858.

[231] This opportunity is an essential requirement of the Art. 169 EC procedure. See Case 211/81 *EC Commission* v. *Denmark: energy meters* [1982] ECR 4547, 4557-8. Thus the Commission may not add further issues in the reasoned opinion (Case 15/83 *EC Commission* v. *Italy: additives* [1984] ECR

opinion must enable the alleged violation to be identified.[232] It must also specify the desired remedial measures and the period, usually fixed at one month, within which these measures are to be taken.[233] If these measures are not taken within the period specified, the Commission may refer the matter to the Court of Justice. No time limit for the reference is stipulated.[234] If the Court finds that there has been a breach of Union law, the Member State concerned is required by Article 171(1) of the Treaty to remedy the breach. Article 171(2) provides for the imposition of sanctions on a Member State failing to comply with such a judgment.[235] This procedure reflects the idea that a violation of Union law affects the common interest and cannot, therefore, be treated simply as contrary to the terms of a contractual relationship between Member States.[236]

At the same time, the Article 169 procedure may offer the Commission an opportunity to circumvent failure by the Council to adopt measures implementing Treaty requirements. In particular, the Commission may use this procedure to secure a judgment from the Court of Justice providing the definition of these requirements that has not been forthcoming in Council measures.[237]

Discretion regarding resort to the procedure may be necessary, so that the Commission may take account of policy implications.[238] The necessity for such discretion may implicitly derive from the Commission obligation in the first indent of Article 155.[239] This obligation entails that the Commission should choose the means of effectively ensuring application of Union law. By the same token, however, the obligation in Article 155 may

---

2793, 2804) or in proceedings before the ECJ (Case 232/78 *EC Commission* v. *France: mutton and lamb* [1979] ECR 2729, 2737).

[232] It must provide "a coherent statement of the reasons which led the Commission to believe that the State in question has failed to fulfil an obligation under the Treaty". See Case 7/61 *EEC Commission* v. *Italy: pigmeat* [1961] ECR 317, 327.

[233] Even if the Member State adopts the measures specified in the reasoned opinion, other parties may still claim that the Member State is in breach of Union law. See Joined Cases 142 & 143/80 *Amministrazione delle Finanze dello Stato* v. *Essevi and Salengo* [1981] ECR 1413, 1433.

[234] Case 288/83 *EC Commission* v. *Ireland: potato imports* [1985] ECR 1761, 1774; and Case 174/84 *Bulk Oil (Zug) AG* v. *Sun International Ltd* [1986] ECR 559, 595.

[235] Commission Communication on Art. 171 (OJ 1996 C242/6). Cf. the sanctions that the Council may, according to Art. 104c(11) EC and the Protocol to the EC Treaty on the excessive deficit procedure, impose on a Member State that fails to reduce an "excessive government deficit" according to remedial measures decided upon by the Council pursuant to the same provision.

[236] Joined Cases 90 & 91/63 *EEC Commission* v. *Luxembourg and Belgium: duty on milk imports* [1964] ECR 625, 631; and Case 39/72 *EC Commission* v. *Italy: premiums for slaughtering cows* [1973] ECR 101, 115.

[237] A. Evans, "Fishery Conservation and EEC Law", 1982 *SLT* 109–11.

[238] A. Evans, "Institutions of the European Communities Other Than The Court of Justice" in *Stair Memorial Encyclopaedia of the Laws of Scotland*, vol. x, 132–262 (Butterworths, London, 1990), 175.

[239] This obligation was recognised in Joined Cases 2 & 3/62 *EEC Commission* v. *Luxembourg and Belgium: gingerbread* [1962] ECR 425, 430.

imply that Commission discretion regarding resort to the procedure is not unlimited.[240]

2.4 The Commission and Third States

The performance of Commission functions, legislative, budgetary, and administrative, may concern relations with third states.[241] Hence, the Commission has delegations in most third states, and many such states have delegations in Brussels. However, nationals of third states may not be Commissioners.[242] As a result, the Commission may not be ideally equipped to appreciate "international" aspects of its work. The implied difficulties may be exacerbated by the organisation of the Commission and by policy frameworks.

2.4.1 Organisation

The importance of relations with third states for the work of the Commission has been recognised in the establishment of Directorate General I. It is responsible for trade relations with third states. However, the existence of a special Directorate General tends towards separation of the treatment of such relations from the treatment of relations between Member States. To address the problems entailed, it is considered "desirable" to bring external relations under the responsibility of a Vice-President.[243]

A more particular tendency is for essentially the same issues to be the responsibility of different Directorates General, depending on whether their "internal" or "external" aspects are tackled. For example, environmental issues arising in relations with third states may be treated as trade issues by Directorate General I. In contrast, within the Union the same issues may be addressed by the Directorate General responsible for environmental policy.

In other words, organisational problems of the Commission may be exaggerated in the context of relations with third states.

2.4.2 Policy Frameworks

The policy frameworks established by Union law may reduce the legislative role of the Commission in the context of relations with third states by

---

[240] Commission submission in Case 7/68 *EC Commission* v. *Italy: art treasures* [1968] ECR 423, 426; Case 7/71 *EC Commission* v. *France: supply agency* [1971] ECR 1003, 1016 and (Roemer AG) 1026; and Trabucchi AG in Case 2/73 *Riseria Luigi Geddo* v. *Ente Nazionale Risi* [1973] ECR 865, 885–7. See, generally, A. Evans, n. 238 above, 176–8; and A. Evans, "The Enforcement Procedure of Article 169 EEC: Commission Discretion" [1979] *ELR* 442–56.

[241] See also Chaps. 20 and 21 below.   [242] Art. 157(1) EC.

[243] Declaration on the organisation and functioning of the Commission, adopted with the Treaty of Amsterdam (OJ 1997 C340/1).

rendering this institution more than usually dependent on the Council. This dependence is clear in relation to the conclusion of agreements with third states pursuant to the commercial policy.[244] It is even more clear in the case of the common foreign and security policy, which is essentially concerned with relations with third states,[245] and police and judicial co-operation in criminal matters, which often concerns third states or their nationals.[246] In these two fields the Commission lacks the guaranteed role in the "shaping" of legislation which it usually enjoys. Article J.12(1) of the Treaty on European Union merely provides that the Commission, like a Member State, may submit proposals to the Council regarding the common foreign and security policy. Again, Article K.6(2) of the same Treaty merely provides for Commission or Member State "initiatives" in relation to co-operation in the fields of justice and home affairs.[247] In neither case does the Commission have an exclusive right of initiative.

2.5 Agreements with Third States

The Commission may be involved in both the conclusion and the implementation of agreements with third states.

2.5.1 Conclusion of Agreements

Agreements with third states or international organisations are usually negotiated by the Commission[248] and concluded by the Council or by the Council and the Member States.[249] A few agreements are concluded by the Commission.

Negotiation by the Commission

When agreements with third states are envisaged, the Commission usually makes recommendations to the Council. The latter then authorizes the Commission to open negotiations.[250] The Commission conducts the negotiations in consultation with special committees appointed by the Council and within the framework of directives issued by the Council.[251] In the case of accession agreements, only consultation of the Commission is formally

---

[244] Sect. 2.5.1 below.   [245] Sect. 21.14 below.   [246] Sect. 21.15 below.

[247] Cf., regarding initiatives from a Member State, Art. 73o(1) EC.

[248] CFSP agreements are negotiated by the Council Presidency, assisted by the Commission as appropriate. See Art. J.14 TEU.

[249] Art. 109 EC makes special arrangements for agreements on an exchange rate system for the Euro in relation to third states and on foreign-exchange regime matters.

[250] Art. 228(1) EC.

[251] See, more particularly, in the case of commercial policy agreements, Art. 113(3) EC. See, regarding the advisory status of the committees, Case C–61/94 *EC Commission* v. *Germany: International Dairy Agreement* [1996] ECR I–3989, I–4011.

required by Article O of the Treaty on European Union. In practice, however, a role in negotiation of such agreements has been acquired by the Commission.

Conclusion by the Commission

The Commission has only limited powers to conclude agreements.[252] In particular, Article 101 of the Euratom Treaty envisages the conclusion of certain types of international agreements by the Commission with the consent of the Council. Moreover, Article 7(1) of the Protocol on the Privileges and Immunities of the European Communities provides for the Commission alone to conclude agreements with third states regarding the recognition of *laissez-passer* issued to members and servants of the Union institutions.

2.5.2 Implementation

The Commission may be involved in the implementation of agreements with third states. The involvement may take the form of Commission participation in joint bodies established by such agreements. New competences in relation to Union undertakings and Member States may also be entailed for the Commission.

Joint Bodies

When concluding an agreement, the Council may authorise the Commission to approve modifications on behalf of the Union where the agreement provides for them to be adopted by a body set up by the agreement.[253] Thus the Commission may participate in joint committees established by free trade agreements[254] and association committees established by association agreements. In particular, the Commission may adopt the "Community position" in such bodies, where a simple transposition of Union acts or assessment of anti-competitive behaviour is made.[255] In other circumstances, the position may be adopted by the Council on the basis of a Commission proposal.[256] Such committees are discussed in Chapter 4.

---

[252] Case C–327/91 *France* v. *EC Commission: EC-US competition law agreement* [1994] ECR I–3641, I–3675–8.

[253] Art. 228(4) EC.

[254] Cf. the co-operation committees established by the Co-operation Agreement with Slovenia (OJ 1993 L189/2), Arts. 38 and 41 and by the Partnership and Co-operation Agreement with Kazakhstan (OJ 1994 C319/6), Arts. 77 and 79.

[255] See, e.g., Art. 2 of Dec. 97/833 (OJ 1997 L345/52) laying down the procedure for adopting the Community's position in the Customs Union Joint Committee set up by Dec. 1/95 of the EC–Turkey Association Council in implementation of the final phase of the customs union.

[256] *Ibid.*, Art. 1.

EDF

Under the Fourth Lomé Convention[257] the Commission is responsible for the European Development Fund. From this Fund grants and loans are made to the overseas countries and territories of Member States and to African, Caribbean, and Pacific countries associated with the Union.

EEA Agreement

The Commission may, as in the case of the EEA Agreement,[258] acquire new competences in relation to Union undertakings and Member States under agreements with third states. For example, the EEA Agreement provides for the Commission to act against restrictive practices by Union undertakings which distort competition in EU–EFTA trade.[259] The same Agreement empowers the Commission to act against aid granted by Member States which distorts such trade.[260]

---

[257] OJ 1991 L229/1.   [258] OJ 1994 L1/3. See Chap. 1.   [259] Arts. 56 and 57 EEA.
[260] Art. 61 EEA.

3

European Parliament

The need for establishment of such an institution as the European Parliament was given little apparent consideration in the original version of the Schuman Plan,[1] which led to conclusion of the ECSC Treaty. However, the negotiators of this Treaty, partly in response to British criticism,[2] accepted the need for inclusion of a parliamentary-type body within the institutional system of the European Coal and Steel Community.[3] Their approach was broadly followed in the EEC and Euratom Treaties. Apparently, therefore, the origins of the Parliament owed more to concern with constitutional form than to popular demands for participation in Union decision making.

The role of the European Parliament has developed considerably both in its own practice and through successive Treaty amendments. As a result, it increasingly performs functions associated with parliaments generally. Even so, the "very redefinition of the European polity" is said to entail a "democratic deficit", which may not easily be removed by this Parliament alone.[4]

3.1 Composition

The European Parliament is, according to Article 137 of the EC Treaty, to represent the "peoples of the states brought together in the Community".[5] However, the task of securing this representative character for the Parliament is complicated by the fact that the Treaties regard the Union as the creation of the Member States.[6]

[1] Instead, a report twice a year to the UN was envisaged (Schuman Plan, Cmnd 7970).

[2] 476 HC Debs. 5s. c. 216, 27 June 1950. On the influence of the criticism, see P. Reuter, "Le Plan Schuman" (1952) 81 *RDC* 523–629, 564–5. A parliamentary body may also have been seen as a means of meeting Belgian and Dutch demands for control of the ECSC High Authority (*New York Times*, 4 July 1950).

[3] A. Evans, "Institutions of the European Communities other than the Court of Justice" in *Stair Memorial Encyclopaedia of the Laws of Scotland*, vol. x, 132–262 (Butterworths, London, 1990), 179, n. 3.

[4] J. Weiler, "The Transformation of Europe" (1991) 100 *Yale Law Journal* 2403–83, 2473.

[5] The French *Conseil Constitutionnel* preferred "de chacun des peuples de ces Etats", judgment of 30 Dec. 1976, Dall. (1977) J. 201.

[6] Art. 1 EC and Art. A TEU.

3.1.1 Allocation of Seats

There are currently 626 Members of the European Parliament (MEPs),[7] and Article 137 of the EC Treaty stipulates that their number may not exceed 700. They are divided between the Member States as follows: ninety-nine for Germany; eighty-seven each for France, Italy, and the United Kingdom; sixty-four for Spain; thirty-one for the Netherlands; twenty-five each for Belgium, Greece, and Portugal; twenty-two for Sweden; twenty-one for Austria; sixteen each for Denmark and Finland; fifteen for Ireland; and six for Luxembourg.[8]

This division gives some recognition to differences in the relative population sizes of the various Member States. Indeed, the number of representatives elected in each Member State is supposed to ensure "appropriate representation" of the peoples of the Member States.[9] However, the populations of the various Member States range from less than half a million in the case of Luxembourg to more than fifty millions in the case of each of the big four. Hence, a division of seats based on strict mathematical proportionality would have been problematic. It would have meant that in a Parliament of anything like the size of the present one the smaller Member States would have enjoyed only negligible representation or would have been denied representation altogether.[10] At the same time, according to the Parliament itself, "the development of a federal type of European Union has not yet reached a sufficiently advanced stage for proportional representation in the European Parliament to be introduced".[11]

For these reasons, strict mathematical proportionality in the allocation of seats to Member States has been compromised. This compromise is less pronounced than in the case of the Common Assembly created by the ECSC Treaty.[12] Even so, it means that there is a considerable disparity in the number of MEPs per head of population within the various Member States.[13] However, the Treaty often stipulates[14] that a simple majority of MEPs is insufficient for exercise of Parliamentary powers. It thereby seeks to ensure that important decisions cannot be taken by coalitions of MEPs unrepresentative of the Union population generally.

---

[7] The ECSC Common Assembly only had 78 members (Art. 21 ECSC).

[8] Art. 138(2) EC.

[9] Art. 2 of the Act on Direct Elections, as amended by the Amsterdam Treaty (OJ 1997 C340/1).

[10] Cf. F.L. Kirgis, *International Organisations in their Legal Setting* (West Publishing, St. Paul, Minn., 1977), 686

[11] Resolution on a uniform electoral procedure: a scheme for allocating the seats of MEPs (OJ 1992 C176/72), para. 2.

[12] Germany had 18 seats and Luxembourg 4 (Art. 21 ECSC).

[13] As a result, Luxembourg has been described as a "rotten borough" (T.C. Hartley, *The Foundations of Community Law* (1st edn, Clarendon Press, 1981), 16).

[14] See, e.g., Arts. 144 and 203(8) EC. The general rule is stated in Art. 141 EC.

3.1.2 Elections

Since 1979[15] MEPs have been elected by direct universal suffrage,[16] for a term of five years.[17] Some rudimentary requirements of electoral procedure are laid down in the Act concerning the election of the representatives of the Assembly by direct universal suffrage[18] and in legislation regarding the electoral rights of Union citizens resident in a Member State other than their own.[19] Apart from these requirements, the electoral procedure is left to be governed in each Member State by its national provisions.[20]

However, this situation may not be sustainable. Article 138(4) of the EC Treaty provides for the Council to lay down further provisions on the matter. These provisions are to require that elections to the European Parliament be held according to a uniform procedure in all Member States or according to principles common to all Member States.

3.1.3 Privileges and Immunities of MEPs

Individual MEPs benefit from the Protocol on the Privileges and Immunities of the European Communities, annexed to the Merger Treaty. In particular, they enjoy freedom of movement to and from meetings of the Parliament.[21] As evidence of their entitlement to this freedom they are issued with a *laissez-passer*.[22] In relation to customs and exchange controls, they are to be accorded by their own government the same facilities as those accorded to senior officials travelling abroad on temporary official missions. They are to be accorded by the governments of other Member States the same facilities as those accorded to representatives of foreign governments engaged in such missions.[23]

In addition, MEPs may not be subject to any form of inquiry, detention, or legal proceedings in respect of opinions expressed or votes cast by them in the performance of their duties.[24] Moreover, during Parliamentary sessions[25] and when travelling to and from meetings of the Parliament, they are entitled in their own Member State to the immunities accorded to members

---

[15] MEPs were previously selected by each national parliament from amongst its members under Art. 138(1) EEC.

[16] Art. 1 of the Act concerning the election of the representatives of the Assembly by direct universal suffrage (OJ 1976 L278/5).

[17] *Ibid.*, Art. 3(1).   [18] *Ibid.*

[19] Sect. 9.3.2 below.

[20] Art. 7(2) of the Act (OJ 1976 L278/5).

[21] Art. 8 of the Protocol on the Privileges and Immunities of the European Communities.

[22] *Ibid.*, Art. 7.

[23] *Ibid.*, Art. 8.

[24] *Ibid.*, Art. 9.

[25] The Parliament is treated as being in session throughout the year. See Case 101/63 *Albert Wagner* v. *Jean Fohrmann and Antoine Krier* [1964] ECR 195, 201; and Case 149/85 *Roger Wybot* v. *Edgar Faure* [1988] ECR 2391, 2409.

of the parliament of that Member State. They are entitled in other Member States to immunity from any measure of detention or legal proceedings. However, immunity cannot be claimed where an MEP is found in the act of committing an offence, and the European Parliament may waive the immunity.[26]

A consequence may be that the treatment accorded to an MEP in a particular Member State depends on whether he is a national of that Member State. If he is, his treatment may ultimately be determined by the treatment accorded members of the parliament of that Member State under domestic law. This situation presumably reflects reluctance on the part of members of national parliaments to accept that their compatriots who become MEPs should have a more privileged legal status than they themselves enjoy in their own Member State. It means, however, that the legal capacity of MEPs to perform their functions may vary. This variation is rendered potentially all the more anomalous by the possibility that nationals of a Member State may exercise their right to stand as candidates in elections to the European Parliament in a Member State other than their own.[27] If their candidature is successful, their legal status in that Member State will differ from the legal status of nationals of that Member State who are also successful in elections to the Parliament held there.

Nevertheless, the above arrangements do much to assimilate the legal position of individual MEPs to that of parliamentarians generally. Further assimilation may take place under Article 138(5) of the EC Treaty. It provides that the Parliament, after seeking an opinion from the Commission and with the unanimous approval of the Council, shall lay down the regulations and general conditions governing the performance of the duties of its Members.[28]

3.2 Organisation

The Parliament enjoys freedom of internal organisation. Such freedom, the importance of which is stressed by the European Court of Justice,[29] is associated with parliaments generally. It may be noted, however, that the seat of the Parliament is left to be determined by common accord of the Member States under Article 216 of the EC Treaty. Since the Member States have failed to agree on a single place of work for the Parliament, this work is divided between Brussels, Luxembourg, and Strasbourg. It holds the

---

[26] Art. 10 of the Protocol. [27] Sect. 9.3.2 below.
[28] Cf. the Resolution of the European Parliament of 10 Dec. 1996 (OJ 1997 C20/31) on participation of citizens and social players in the EU's institutional system and the IGC, para. 34, regarding the need for a common statute for MEPs.
[29] Case 208/80 *Lord Bruce of Donnington* v. *Eric Gordon Aspden* [1981] ECR 2205, 2219; and Case 78/85 *Group of the European Right* v. *European Parliament* [1986] ECR 1753, 1757. Cf., however, Case 358/85 *France* v. *European Parliament: intervention rights* [1986] ECR 2149.

monthly plenary sessions in Strasbourg. Additional plenary sessions are held in Brussels, where its committees meet. The Secretariat and departments must remain in Luxembourg.[30] This division is controversial.[31] It may also be noted that the Parliament needs the approval of the Council to lay down regulations and general conditions governing the performance of the duties of its members[32] and of the Ombudsman.[33]

3.2.1 Sessions

The European Parliament convenes itself and holds an annual session under Article 139 of the EC Treaty. In practice, the annual session is divided into part-sessions, which are usually held for one week in every month except August. In addition, extraordinary sessions may be held on the initiative of a majority of MEPs or at the request of the Council or Commission.[34] Debates may be held and resolutions adopted on "any question concerning the Communities"[35] or on any "matter falling within the sphere of activities of the European Union".[36] Such questions may include those concerning relations with third states and violations of fundamental rights by such states.

These sessions take place according to the Rules of Procedure,[37] which the Parliament is to adopt under Article 142 of the Treaty. These Rules are to be adopted by a majority of MEPs rather than simply by a majority of the votes cast. They are required to specify the quorum[38] and the manner of publication of Parliamentary proceedings.[39] Apart from these two requirements, the content of the Rules is left to be determined by the Parliament itself, though they may not authorise any violation of Union law.[40]

---

[30] Protocol to the founding Treaties on the location of the seats of the institutions and of certain bodies and departments of the European Communities and of Europol, para. (a). See, earlier, the Decision taken by common agreement between the Representatives of the Governments of the Member States on the location of the seats of the institutions and certain bodies and departments of the European Communities (OJ 1992 C341/1).

[31] See, e.g., Joined Cases C–213/88 & 39/89 *Luxembourg* v. *European Parliament: seat of the Parliament* [1991] ECR I–5643, regarding offices outside Luxembourg; Case 108/83 *Luxembourg* v. *European Parliament: Secretariat* [1984] ECR 1945, regarding the maintenance of the bulk of the Secretariat in Luxembourg; and Joined Cases 258/85 & 51/86 *France* v. *European Parliament: plenary sessions* [1988] ECR 4821, regarding the possibility of exceptional plenary sessions being held outside Strasbourg.

[32] Art. 138(5) EC.   [33] Art. 138e(4) EC.   [34] Art. 139 EC.

[35] Case 230/81 *Luxembourg* v. *European Parliament: seat and working place of the European Parliament* [1983] ECR 255, 287.

[36] Rule 45(1) of the Rules of Procedure (OJ 1997 L49/1).

[37] OJ 1997 L49/1.   [38] Art. 141(2) EC.   [39] Art. 142(2) EC.

[40] See, e.g., Case 1/55 *Antoine Kergall* v. *Common Assembly* [1954–6] ECR 151, 158; and Case 230/81 *Luxembourg* v. *European Parliament: seat and working place of the European Parliament* [1983] ECR 255, 287. Cf. Case 294/83 *Parti Ecologiste "Les Verts"* v. *European Parliament: information campaign for elections* [1986] ECR 1339, 1370, where the matter concerned was found to fall outside the scope of internal organisation.

3.2.2 Officers

The Parliament is to elect its President and officers from among its members.[41] The President, the fourteen Vice-Presidents and, in an advisory capacity, the five Quaestors, who are administrative managers,[42] constitute the Bureau.[43] The Bureau is responsible for administrative questions.

The President and the chairmen of the political groups[44] constitute the Conference of the Presidents.[45] It drafts agenda for plenary sessions of the Parliament and is responsible for the composition of committees[46] of the Parliament.[47]

Such arrangements may be controversial. For example, there is an informal arrangement whereby the Presidency is held for two-and-a-half-year periods[48] alternately by a member of the European Socialists Party and a member of the European People's Party. This arrangement has been criticised.[49]

3.2.3 Committees

The Rules of Procedure,[50] following a precedent set by the ECSC Common Assembly,[51] provide for establishment of standing committees.[52] These committees each specialise in a particular field of Union activity, which broadly corresponds to that of a Commission Directorate General or group of Directorates General. There are currently twenty committees, including a Committee on External Economic Relations.[53] Their existence is recognised by the EC Treaty.[54]

When a Commission proposal is received by the Parliament, it is referred to the relevant committee, which draws up a report. The report is then presented to a plenary session by a *rapporteur* appointed by the committee from among its members.[55] Any debate considered necessary takes place on the basis of the report.

The role of such committees is not solely to enhance the technical competence of Parliamentary consideration of Commission proposals. The committees have also developed the practice of submitting "own initiative" reports to plenary sessions. On the basis of these reports, the Parliament may decide to call on the Commission to propose Union action. Moreover, the

---

[41] Art. 140 EC.   [42] Rule 25 of the Rules of Procedure (OJ 1997 L49/1).   [43] *Ibid.*, Rule 21.

[44] Sect. 3.2.4 below.   [45] Rule 23 of the Rules of Procedure (OJ 1997 L49/1).

[46] Sect. 3.2.3 below.   [47] Rule 24 of the Rules of Procedure (OJ 1997 L49/1).

[48] *Ibid.*, Rule 17.   [49] See, e.g., *The European*, 16–22 Jan. 1997.

[50] OJ 1997 L49/1.   [51] 7 committees were established in 1953 (JOCECA 1953 1/8).

[52] Chap. XVII of the Rules of Procedure (OJ 1997 L49/1).

[53] Dec. of 15 Jan. 1997 (OJ 1997 C33/32) on the number and numerical composition of parliamentary committees. Subcommittees may also be established under Rule 141 (OJ 1997 L49/1).

[54] Arts. 103(4) and 109b(3) EC.

[55] He is effectively chosen by agreement between the political groups. See, e.g., M. Palmer, *The European Parliament* (Pergamon Press, Oxford, 1981), 86.

committees meet at least once between plenary sessions and whenever requested to do so by their chairman or the President of the Parliament itself. Hence, they may add continuity to the work of the Parliament. Again, the fact that the committees may sit in camera means that they may receive information concerning, for example, the common foreign and security policy, which might not otherwise be made available to the Parliament.[56]

3.2.4 Political Groups

As early as 1952 the Christian Democrats, Liberals, and Socialists in the ECSC Common Assembly began to sit in political groups rather than in national groups or in alphabetical order.[57] Provision for such groups was first inserted in the Rules of Procedure of the following year.[58] Under the present Rules[59] there must be at least twenty-nine MEPs from one Member State, twenty-three from two Member States, eighteen from three Member States, or fourteen from four or more Member States to form such a group.[60] The stipulation of these minimum numbers is designed to promote the development of Union-wide groupings. It is also designed to prevent national blocs under the guise of political affinity from obtaining the advantages conferred on political groups by the Rules of Procedure. Besides the Socialists, who constitute the largest political group, the European People's Party, which is composed of Christian Democrats and, since 1992, the British Conservatives, and various other groups have been formed. The latest one to be established is the Group of Independents for a Europe of Nations.[61]

These groups may be viewed as constituting the nuclei of European political parties.[62] Hence, the European Parliament may be thought politically as well as legally comparable to parliaments generally. As Article 138a of the EC Treaty recognises, political parties at European level are important as a factor for integration within the Union. They contribute to forming a European awareness and to expressing the political will of Union citizens.[63]

However, such groups lack the popular base of domestic parties. In this connection, the introduction of direct elections may have had ambiguous effects. These elections involved abolition of the compulsory "dual mandate"[64] and, hence, may have been expected to lessen the control over

---

[56] B. Cocks, *The European Parliament* (HMSO, London, 1973), 20.

[57] Note from the Secretariat of the Common Assembly to the High Authority (CEAB 1, 591).

[58] JOCECA 1953 155.   [59] OJ 1997 L49/1.   [60] *Ibid.*, Rule 29(2).   [61] OJ 1997 C33/1.

[62] D. Lasok and J.W. Bridge, *Law and Institutions of the European Communities* (5th edn., Butterworths, London, 1991), 251.

[63] See also the Resolution of the European Parliament of 10 Dec. 1996 (OJ 1997 C20/29) on the constitutional status of European political parties.

[64] Before the first direct elections in 1979 only members of the national parliaments could become MEPs (Art. 138(1) EEC).

political groups exercised by domestic parties.[65] More particularly, the elections have enabled these groups to offer common programmes to a Union-wide electorate. Even so, little impact has been made on the underlying isolation of these groups from the electorate generally. Indeed, abolition of the compulsory dual mandate may have reduced opportunities for political groups to seek popular support for their policies through the activities of their members in national parliaments.[66]

A solution to these problems may be sought through arrangements for the European Parliament and the national parliaments to meet as a Conference of the Parliaments.[67] The President of the European Council and the President of the Commission report to each session of the conference on the state of the Union.[68] Moreover, before the Union exceeds twenty Member States, the national governments are to come together to decide on the role of national parliaments in the Union.[69] These arrangements may be expected to promote networking between MEPs and national parliamentarians. They may be rendered all the more important by future enlargements of the Union. These enlargements and compliance with the above-mentioned limit to the total number of MEPs[70] will logically lead to fewer seats in the European Parliament for each Member State.

3.2.5 Secretariat

There is a General Secretariat,[71] including interpreters, translators, and technical services. More particularly, there are a Legal Service and seven Directorates General. In addition, each political group has a secretariat, and individual MEPs may employ personal assistants.[72]

3.3 Functions

Article 20 of the ECSC Treaty provided for the old Common Assembly to fulfil a supervisory function. The Assembly was thus to control High Authority administration of policy already formulated in the Treaty itself, though the Assembly considered its powers inadequate for this purpose.[73] It was only under Article 95, which allowed for enactment of measures necessary to attain

---

[65] Though efforts may still be made to exercise such control. See, e.g., in the case of British MEPs in the European Socialists Party, *Daily Telegraph*, 23 Oct. 1997.

[66] Cf. the Protocol to the founding Treaties on the role of national parliaments in the EU.

[67] See also *ibid.*, regarding the Conference of European Affairs Committees.

[68] Declaration on the Conference of the Parliaments, adopted along with the TEU.

[69] Art. 2 of the Protocol on the institutions and with the prospects of EU enlargement, annexed to the founding Treaties.

[70] Sect. 3.1.1 above.

[71] Rule 164 of the Rules of Procedure (OJ 1997 L49/1).

[72] Rule 9(2) and Annex IX (*ibid.*)

[73] See, e.g., the Resolution of 13 Feb. 1957 (JOCECA 1957 100) on the relaunch of Europe, para. 2.

ECSC objectives and not otherwise provided for in the Treaty, that the Assembly was expressly allocated any legislative function.

The EEC Treaty left the institutions much broader scope for policy-making. Hence, it was apparently thought appropriate in this Treaty to allocate the European Parliament both kinds of functions on a more general basis.[74] Accordingly, Article 137 of this Treaty provided that the Parliament would exercise the "advisory and supervisory" powers conferred on it by the Treaty.

This qualification to the powers conferred on the Parliament has now been removed in Article 137 of the EC Treaty. This removal reflects the development of its legislative function and its acquisition of a budgetary function. In essence, the Parliament is not only responsible for supervising the work of the other institutions but also participates in the development of Union policies.

3.3.1 Legislation

According to Article 138b(1) of the EC Treaty, the Parliament shall participate in the process leading up to the adoption of Union acts. It is to do so by exercising its powers under the procedures laid down in Articles 189b and 189c of the Treaty and by giving its assent or delivering advisory opinions. In addition, the Parliament enjoys a right of initiative under Article 138b(2). In some cases, however, the Parliament only has to be informed of action taken by the Commission or Council.[75] In some other cases no reference at all may be made to participation in legislative decision making by the Parliament.[76]

The role of the Parliament depends on the provision under which the Council acts. If there may be a choice of provisions, the exercise of the choice may affect the role of the Parliament.[77] However, the Council may not choose the basis with a view to limiting the participation of the Parliament.[78]

Conciliation Procedure

Within the ECSC the Common Assembly demanded greater powers than those formally conferred by the ECSC Treaty, and the High Authority sought to enlist the political support of the Assembly for its activity. As a result, a practice developed whereby the High Authority would voluntarily consult the Assembly on various matters.[79]

---

[74] Though the proposed powers were considered inadequate (Resolution of 11 May 1956 (JOCECA 1956 144) on the common market and Euratom, para. 3).

[75] Arts 73g(2), 103(2) and (4), 103d(2), 104c(11), 109(1), 109b(3), and 109c(3) EC; and Art. J.11 TEU.

[76] See, e.g., Art. 7a(3) EC.

[77] See, e.g., Case 242/87 *EC Commission* v. *EC Council: Erasmus* [1989] ECR 1425.

[78] Case C–70/88 *European Parliament* v. *EC Council: capacity of the European Parliament to bring an action for annulment* [1990] ECR I–2041. The legal basis must be stated, if there would otherwise be uncertainty about the basis of the act concerned. See Case 45/86 *EC Commission* v. *EC Council: general system of preferences* [1987] ECR 1493, I–1519–20.

[79] See, e.g., the Report on the Common Assembly produced by the Fifth Joint Meeting of the Common Assembly and the Consultative Assembly of the Council of Europe, Official Report, 19 Oct. 1957, 33–4.

This practice was given tacit approval by the EEC Treaty. Thus most provisions of the EEC Treaty required Council consultation of the Parliament before the enactment of regulations or directives thereunder. Even where a provision, such as Article 49 of the Treaty, merely provided for consultation of the Economic and Social Committee, the Parliament might also, in practice, be consulted.[80] As the Court of Justice has ruled, the Council is always entitled to consult the Parliament.[81]

On the other hand, the Parliament objects that it is not consulted regarding delegated legislation.[82] According to the Court of Justice, such legislation may lawfully be adopted without consultation of the Parliament. However, the provisions and essential elements of the empowering legislation, on which the Parliament will have been consulted, must be respected.[83]

Under the EC Treaty the consultation procedure continues to apply in several important areas, including agriculture,[84] indirect taxation,[85] and certain environmental protection matters.[86] It also applies in new areas, such as procedures for dealing with excessive deficits.[87]

When this procedure applies, the relevant Commission proposal is referred to the appropriate Parliamentary committee. The committee examines the proposal and then produces a report containing a draft legislative resolution. Unless the committee recommends that a vote is unnecessary or a second reading in committee is favoured, the report is debated in the House on the basis of the draft resolution. If the resolution is passed, it is then forwarded as an opinion to the Council and Commission.[88] According to Article 190 of the EC Treaty, the resulting enactments must refer to the opinion where the Treaty required the latter to be obtained. In practice, all opinions are also published in the Information and Notices section of the Official Journal, though in the case of voluntarily requested opinions the Council may unanimously decide against publication.[89]

---

[80] See, e.g., the Resolution on the proposal under Art. 49 EEC for a reg. on freedom of movement for workers within the Community (JO 1967 268/9). Provisions such as Art. 103a EC require consultation of neither body. Voluntary consultation is inadequate where the correct legal basis for a Council act would have made consultation compulsory. See Case C–316/91 *European Parliament* v. *EC Council* [1994] ECR I–625.

[81] Case 165/87 *EC Commission* v. *EC Council* [1988] ECR 5545, 5562.

[82] See, e.g., the Resolution of 9 July 1986 (OJ 1986 C227/54) on the proposal for a regulation laying down the procedures for the exercise of implementing powers conferred on the Commission.

[83] Case C–156/93 *European Parliament* v. *EU Council: organic production of agricultural products* [1995] ECR I–2019, I–2047; and Case C-303/94 *European Parliament* v. *EU Council: plant protection products* [1996] ECR I–2943, I–2969.

[84] Art. 43 EC.   [85] Art. 99 EC.   [86] Art. 130(2) EC.

[87] Art. 104c(14) EC. It also applies under Arts. 8b, 8e, 75(2), 87, 94, 100, 106(6), 109(1), 1st sentence, 109a(2)(b), 109f(1), (6) & (7), 109j(2) and (4), 109k(2), 130(3), 130b, 130i(4), 201, 209, and 228(3), 1st para. EC; and Art. K.11(1) TEU.

[88] Rule 58(3) of the Rules of Procedure (OJ 1997 L49/1). According to Art. 109j(2) EC, the Parliament is to forward its opinion to the Council, meeting in the composition of the heads of state or government. See, similarly, Art. 109j(4) EC.

[89] *Seventh Survey of the Activities of the Council* (EEC Council, Luxembourg, 1962), 336.

Problems may occur, where a proposal is amended after an opinion has been delivered. Where the amendment is a substantial[90] and not in line with the opinion,[91] the amendment "affects the whole of the planned arrangements",[92] or the amendment means that the proposal differs in essence from that on which the Parliament was consulted,[93] the Court of Justice has ruled that the "prerogatives" of the Parliament entail the need for renewed consultation. The Commission has also agreed to withdraw proposals from the Council where their "nature" is changed.[94]

The opinions are not legally binding on the Council or Commission, and the Council is not apparently required to spend much time considering the opinion obtained.[95] In practice, the Council may reach a "political agreement" on a proposal without waiting for the opinion of the Parliament.[96] However, the consultation procedure is not without significance. In *SA Roquette Frères and Maizena* v. *EC Council* the Council had enacted a regulation[97] under a Treaty provision[98] that required consultation of the Parliament without obtaining an opinion from the Parliament. The Court of Justice ruled that the Council had to give the Parliament an adequate opportunity to consider and deliver an opinion on proposals submitted to it.[99] The Council was found to have adopted the regulation without having given such an opportunity to the Parliament. Consequently, the regulation was annulled under Article 173 of the Treaty[100] for breach of an essential procedural requirement.

The Court did not venture a definition of what constituted an adequate opportunity for such purposes. However, reference was made to the failure of the Council, in view of the urgency of the matter, to request the holding of an extraordinary session of the Parliament under Article 139 of the Treaty.[101] The implication may be drawn that, if the Council makes a request of this kind in relation to an urgent matter and an opinion is still not forthcoming, the Council may lawfully go ahead and enact the necessary measure without

---

[90] Case 41/69 *ACF Chemiefarma NV* v. *EC Commission* [1970] ECR 661, 702; and Case C–65/90 *European Parliament* v. *EC Council: road haulage* [1992] ECR I–4593, I–4621–2.

[91] Case 1253/79 *Dino Battaglia* v. *EC Commission* [1982] ECR 297, 318–19; and Case C–21/94 *European Parliament* v. *EC Council: road tax* [1995] ECR I–1827, I–1852.

[92] Case C–392/95 *European Parliament* v. *EU Council: visas for TSNs* (10 June 1997).

[93] Case C–280/93 *Germany* v. *EC Council: bananas* [1994] ECR I–4973, I–5054–6.

[94] Statement of Commission President Delors to the Parliament (EP Debs. No. 3–386, 29–30, 13 Feb. 1990).

[95] E.g., in Case 114/81 *Tunnel Refineries* v. *EC Council* [1982] ECR 3189 the ECJ did not find a regulation enacted a day after the opinion had been delivered to be void for inadequate consideration.

[96] OJ 1990 C324/125.

[97] Reg. 1293/79 (OJ 1979 L162/10) amending Reg. 1111/77 laying down common provisions for isoglucose.

[98] Art. 43(2) EEC.   [99] Case 138/79 [1980] ECR 3333.   [100] See sect. 5.3.1 below.

[101] [1980] ECR 3333, 3361. See also Case 817/79 *Buyl* v. *EC Commission* [1982] ECR 245, 262. Concern for the effectiveness rather than simply the form of consultation was already well established. See Case 6/54 *Netherlands* v. *ECSC High Authority: coal prices* [1954–6] ECR 103, 134.

having obtained an opinion.[102] According to internal Council "arrange-ments", such a request must be genuinely exceptional in nature and supported by reasons.[103]

In non-urgent cases the above ruling implies that the Council may not impose a deadline for receipt of an opinion without regard to the impor-tance of the consultation procedure. In effect, therefore, the Parliament may enjoy a suspensive veto, which is of uncertain duration but which is unlikely to exceed three months. This is the basic duration of the period allowed for a second Parliamentary reading according to the co-operation and co-decision procedures, discussed below.

It has been objected that the Parliament cannot delay giving its opinion simply in an attempt to block what it regards as an undesirable enactment.[104] However, the Parliament assumes that it possesses a delaying power. Thus Rule 58(2) of the Rules of Procedure[105] states that the consultation of the Parliament is completed once a draft legislative resolution has been adopted. Under Rule 59(3), if the Parliament opposes the proposal in question and the Commission declines to withdraw it, the Parliament may decide not to take a vote on the draft resolution and to refer it back to the committee.

Such arrangements are designed, more particularly, to enable the Parliament to take advantage of the possibilities offered by Article 189a(2) of the Treaty. According to this provision, as long as the Council has not acted on a proposal from the Commission, the latter may amend the proposal. The Council, in contrast, may only amend the proposal unanimously.[106] Therefore, to the extent that the Commission is persuaded to amend its proposal so as to incor-porate the substance of a Parliamentary opinion, the Council will only be able unanimously to adopt a measure lacking Parliamentary approval.

Conciliation Procedure

Provision is made in the 1975 Joint Declaration on Budgetary Procedure[107] for resort to a conciliation procedure. This procedure concerns proposals that have general application as well as appreciable financial implications and are not required to be adopted by existing Union measures. The proce-dure may, according to the Declaration, be invoked by the Council or the

---

[102] See, e.g., Reg. 1992/83 (OJ 1983 L196/1) laying down the implementing rules for 1983 for Reg. 3331/82 concerning food-aid policy and food-aid management, 14th and 15th recitals in the preamble. See also Case C-65/93 *European Parliament* v. *EU Council: GSP* [1995] ECR I–643.

[103] Council Reply to WQ E–2153/96 (OJ 1997 C72/16) by Ian White.

[104] Cf. External competence of the European Communities, House of Lords Select Committee on the European Communities, HL (1984–5) 236, 23.

[105] OJ 1997 L49/1.

[106] Exceptions are provided for in Art. 189b(4) and (5) EC, in the case of the co-decision proce-dure (see p. 60 below).

[107] OJ 1975 C88/1. This declaration was agreed by way of settlement of a dispute between the Council and the Parliament that had been referred to, but not decided by, the ECJ in Case 72/82 *EC Council* v. *European Parliament: budgetary procedure* (OJ 1983 C72/7; OJ 1983 C204/4).

Parliament, whenever the former intends to depart from a Parliamentary opinion on such a proposal. If the procedure is invoked, a conciliation committee, composed of Council members and MEPs, is established. This committee, with the assistance of the Commission, seeks to reach agreement normally within three months, though a shortened period may be fixed in cases of urgency.

Thus the opportunity for the Parliament to express its position and to seek to influence the Council is enhanced. However, the opportunity is only available within a limited sphere. Moreover, Council members of the committee only have limited room for manœuvre in the course of the procedure. Consequently, the Parliament has been consistently critical of the limitations of this procedure.[108]

Co-operation Procedure

Article 7 of the Single European Act[109] provided that a co-operation procedure was to apply in relation to Council action under several amended EEC Treaty provisions.[110] This procedure has now been embodied in Article 189c of the EC Treaty. It applies in relation to matters of economic[111] and monetary policy.[112]

According to this procedure, the Council, acting by a qualified majority, adopts a common position on a Commission proposal after obtaining an opinion from the Parliament.[113] The common position is then communicated to the Parliament together with the reasons of the Council. The Commission also states its own position.[114] Thus an informed tripartite discussion of the proposal is apparently facilitated.

If the outcome is that the Parliament approves the common position or fails to take a decision within three months, the Council is to act definitively according to its common position.[115] If, however, within the same three-month period the Parliament rejects the common position by an absolute majority of its component members, the Council may only adopt the proposal unanimously and has three months to do so.[116] Thus the position of the Parliament is formally strengthened not only in relation to the Council but also the Commission. In effect, the Parliament needs only one ally in the Council to prevent adoption of a Commission proposal of which it disapproves.[117]

---

[108] See, e.g., the Resolution of 14 Dec. 1983 (OJ 1984 C10/34) on the draft second joint declaration of the European Parliament, the Council, and the Commission on the conciliation procedure.

[109] OJ 1987 L169/1.   [110] Art. 6 SEA   [111] Arts. 104a(2) and 104b(2) EC.

[112] Art. 105a(2) EC.   [113] Art. 189c(a) EC.   [114] Art. 189c(b) EC.   [115] *Ibid.*

[116] Art. 189c(c) EC.

[117] However, the Commission will not undertake always to withdraw a proposal following a Parliamentary rejection of a common position. It may, indeed, be argued that adoption of a common position by the Council means that the latter has "acted" for the purposes of Art. 189a(2) EC and, hence, that the Commission may not withdraw its proposal. See the statement of Commission President Delors to the Parliament (EP Debs. No. 3–386, 30, 13 Feb. 1990).

The Parliament may also, within the same three-month period, propose amendments to the common position of the Council by an absolute majority of its component members.[118] The Commission must then re-examine its original proposal within one month, forward the re-examined version to the Council, and express its opinion on any Parliamentary amendments that it does not accept.[119] Thus the Commission has a formal legal obligation and not merely a "political obligation" to take account of the views of the Parliament. The Commission may be expected to attach particular importance to such amendments so as to provide the Parliament with an incentive to vote for amendment rather than outright rejection of a common position.[120] However, the imposition of the one-month deadline means that the Commission has very limited time to seek to reconcile the attitudes of the Council and the Parliament. Within a further three months the Council may adopt the re-examined proposal by a qualified majority or amend it unanimously.[121]

Except where the Council is left free to act definitively by a qualified majority according to its common position, failure to meet any of the above deadlines means that the Commission proposal will be deemed not to have been adopted.[122] The deadlines may only be extended for one month by common accord of the Council and Parliament.[123]

Co-decision Procedure

The co-decision procedure applies, when the Council acts under an EC Treaty provision referring to Article 189b of this Treaty.[124] This procedure applies to internal market legislation[125] and such areas as transport,[126] vocational training,[127] culture,[128] consumer protection,[129] environmental protection,[130] trans-European networks,[131] development co-operation,[132] and multiannual research programmes.[133]

According to this procedure, the Commission submits its proposal to the Parliament and the Council.[134] The Council is to obtain the opinion of the Parliament. Acting by a qualified majority, the Council may approve all amendments proposed by the Parliament and adopt the proposed act as

---

[118] Art. 189c(c) EC.   [119] Art. 189c(d) EC.

[120] The capacity of the Commission to do so is presumably enhanced by arrangements in internal Commission practice designed to ensure that the same consideration is given to the views of Parliamentary committees as to those of COREPER committees (Fifth report concerning the implementation of the white paper on the completion of the internal market, COM(90)90, 9).

[121] Art. 189c(e) EC.   [122] Art. 189c(f) EC.   [123] Art. 189c(g) EC.

[124] Art. 189b(1) EC.

[125] Including that under Art. 100a EC. See also Arts. 49, 54, 56(2), and 57 EC.

[126] Art. 75(1) EC.   [127] Art. 127(4) EC.

[128] Art. 128(5) EC. The Council must act unanimously under this provision.

[129] Art. 129a EC.   [130] Art. 130n(1) EC.   [131] Art. 129d EC.   [132] Art. 130w(1) EC.

[133] Art. 130i EC. See also Arts. 8a, 126, and 129 EC.

[134] See, in the case of Commission implementing measures, the *modus vivendi* of Dec. 1994 (Bull. EC 12–1994, 1.7.1).

amended. Similarly, if the Parliament does not propose any amendments, the Council may adopt the act.

Otherwise, the Council is to adopt a common position and communicate it to the Parliament. The Council shall inform the Parliament fully of the reasons which led it to adopt its common position. The Commission shall also inform the Parliament fully of its position.[135]

If the Parliament approves the common position or fails to take a decision within three months, the act is deemed to have been adopted in accordance with that common position. The Parliament may, however, reject the common position by an absolute majority of its component members. If the Parliament does so, the act is deemed not to have been adopted. This procedure thus formally confers on the Parliament a right of veto.[136]

The Parliament may also propose amendments by an absolute majority of its component members. The amended text is forwarded to the Council and the Commission, which delivers an opinion on the proposed amendments.[137] The Council may then adopt by a qualified majority the act in line with the amendments proposed by the Parliament within three months. However, the Council must act unanimously on the amendments on which the Commission has delivered a negative opinion. If the Council does not approve all the amendments, a conciliation committee, composed of Council members or their representatives and an equal number of MEPs, is convened within six weeks.[138]

If a joint text is agreed by the conciliation committee within a period of six weeks, it must be approved by the Parliament, by an absolute majority of the votes cast within a further period of six weeks. It must also be approved by the Council by qualified majority within the same period. If the deadline[139] is not met by either institution, the act is deemed not to have been adopted.[140] If the conciliation committee fails to approve a joint text, the proposed act shall also be deemed not to have been adopted.[141]

Assent Procedure

The assent procedure means that Parliamentary approval of a Union act is necessary. This procedure covers introduction of a uniform procedure or common principles for direct elections;[142] amendment of certain provisions of the Statute of the European System of Central Banks;[143] conferment on

---

[135] Art. 189b(2) EC.   [136] *Ibid.*

[137] The Commission may decide to take none of the proposed amendments into account, in the hope that a compromise will emerge between the Parliament and the Council. See, e.g., the Opinion regarding the proposal for a decision adapting for the second time Dec. 1110/94 concerning the Fourth Framework Programme on RTD (1994–8), COM(97)155.

[138] Art. 189b(3) and (4) EC.

[139] Art. 189b(7) EC provides for limited extension of the deadlines by common accord of the Parliament and the Council. Note also the Declaration on respect for time limits under the co-decision procedure, adopted with the Treaty of Amsterdam (OJ 1997 C340/1).

[140] Art. 189b(5) EC.   [141] Art. 189b(6) EC.   [142] Art. 138(4) EC.   [143] Art. 106(5) EC.

the European Central Bank of specific tasks concerning policies relating to the prudential supervision of credit institutions and other financial institutions, except insurance companies;[144] and definition of the tasks and priority objectives and organisation of the Structural Funds.[145] It also applies in relation to the conclusion of certain agreements with third states[146] and decisions on applications for Union membership.[147]

This procedure does not simply entail a right of veto for the Parliament, but makes adoption of an act dependent on Parliamentary assent. Such assent usually requires a majority of the votes cast. However, an absolute majority of MEPs is required for decisions on applications for Union membership[148] and for introduction of a uniform procedure or common principles for direct elections.[149]

Right of Initiative

Article 138b of the EC Treaty confers a right of initiative on the Parliament, acting by a majority of its members. It provides that the Parliament may request the Commission to submit any appropriate proposal on matters on which it considers that an act is required to implement the Treaty.

3.3.2 Budget

The budgetary role of the Parliament is based on Article 203 of the EC Treaty.

Preliminary Draft

In March or April the Parliament passes a resolution on the guidelines for its own budget for the following year. Like the other institutions, it has to draw up, before 1 July, its expenditure estimates. The Commission consolidates these estimates in a preliminary draft budget and attaches an opinion, which may contain different estimates. The preliminary draft budget shall contain an estimate of revenue and an estimate of revenue.[150] In July the consolidated estimates of the Commission are debated, and a Parliamentary delegation meets the Council.

The Commission places the preliminary draft budget before the Council by 1 September of the year preceding that in which the budget is to be implemented. The Council is to consult the Commission and, where appropriate, the other institutions concerned, whenever it intends to depart from the preliminary draft budget. The Council, acting by a qualified majority, shall establish the draft budget and forward it to the Parliament[151] before 5 October for a first reading.[152]

---

[144] Art. 105(6) EC.   [145] Art. 130d EC.   [146] Sect. 3.5 below.   [147] Art. O TEU.
[148] *Ibid.*   [149] Art. 138(4) EC.   [150] Art. 203(2) EC.   [151] Art. 203(3) EC.
[152] Art. 203(4) EC.

First Reading

Once received by the Parliament, the draft budget is passed to its various committees, which report to the Committee on Budgets. This Committee, before which the Commission and Council are represented, produces for debate a report incorporating the views of the individual committees. The President or another member of the Council is present at this debate. Following the debate, the Parliament may adopt the draft budget as its stands.[153]

Alternatively, the Parliament may propose modifications to "compulsory" items by a majority of votes cast. Compulsory expenditure is defined as "expenditure necessarily resulting from this Treaty or from acts adopted in accordance therewith".[154] The Parliament may also make amendments by a majority of MEPs to "non-compulsory" expenditure items. Any increase in non-compulsory expenditure is subject to a ceiling calculated by reference to the maximum rate of increase set by the Commission.[155] The maximum rate of increase is to be fixed on the basis of the trend, in volume terms, of the gross domestic products within the Union; the average variation in the budgets of the Member States; and the trend in the cost of living during the preceding financial years.[156]

However, a new maximum rate may be agreed between the Parliament and the Council.[157] Moreover, where the Council intends to increase non-compulsory expenditure by more than half the maximum rate, the Parliament may increase such expenditure by up to half the maximum rate.[158] An inter-institutional agreement between the Parliament, Council, and Commission,[159] according to which annual ceilings are agreed among the three, has sought to resolve potential conflicts implicit in these arrangements. This form of resolution has been found by the Court of Justice not to entail breaches of rules of law or exercise of discretion in a manifestly wrong or arbitrary manner.[160]

If, within forty-five days, the Parliament has given its approval, the budget stands as finally adopted. If, within the same period, the Parliament has not

---

[153] *Ibid.*   [154] *Ibid.*   [155] Art. 203(9) EC.

[156] An "agriculture guideline" has been introduced, to ensure that annual increases in agriculture spending are kept below increases in GDP. See, currently, Dec. 94/729 (OJ 1994 L293/14) on budgetary discipline.

[157] Art. 203(9) EC. See also Case 34/86 *EC Council* v. *European Parliament: non-compulsory expenditure* [1986] ECR 2155.

[158] Art. 203(9) EC.

[159] On budgetary discipline and improvement of the budgetary procedure (OJ 1988 L185/33 and OJ 1993 C331/1).

[160] Case 204/86 *Greece* v. *EC Council: special aid for Turkey* [1988] ECR 5323, 5359. Cf. Case C–25/94 *EC Commission* v. *EU Council: FAO Agreement* [1996] ECR I–1469, I–1510. See, most recently, the interinstitutional agreement between the European Parliament, the Council, and the European Commission on provisions regarding the financing of the CFSP (OJ 1997 C286/80). See, regarding the CFSP, sect. 21.14

amended the draft budget or proposed any modifications, it shall be deemed to be finally adopted. Otherwise, it is to be returned to the Council,[161] which discusses the draft with the Commission.

The Council, acting by a qualified majority, may then modify any amendments to non-compulsory items. By the same majority it may accept or reject proposed modifications to compulsory items. Those proposed modifications which would have the effect of re-allocating sums of expenditure within the overall sum established in the draft budget stand in the absence of a Council decision to reject them. Those proposed modifications, which would have the effect of increasing that overall sum, fall in the absence of a Council decision to accept them. Thus the Council needs sufficient votes to constitute a qualified majority in order to prevent the former category of proposed modifications as well as amendments from taking effect. If within fifteen days the Council accepts all the modifications and modifies none of the amendments, the budget is deemed to be finally adopted. Otherwise, the draft must be returned to the Parliament within fifteen days for a second reading.[162]

Second Reading

The second reading by the Parliament must be completed within fifteen days of the draft being returned to it. At this stage, the Parliament possesses no powers in relation to compulsory items of expenditure. However, it does enjoy the "final word" in relation to non-compulsory items. Thus the Parliament may, acting by a majority of its Members and three-fifths of the votes cast, amend or reject modifications to its amendments made by the Council.

When the procedure has been completed, the President of the Parliament shall declare that the budget has been finally adopted.[163] If the Parliament has not acted within the period allowed, the budget shall be deemed to be finally adopted.[164]

However, "if there are important reasons", the Parliament may reject the whole draft budget and ask for a new draft budget to be submitted. The Parliament must do so by a majority of its members and two-thirds of the votes cast.[165] When this power is exercised and no budget is adopted by the beginning of the next financial year, the Union is financed through monthly expenditure. The expenditure must be equivalent to one twelfth of the previous year's budget or the rejected draft budget, whichever is the lower.[166] This power has been exercised on two occasions so far.[167]

Clearly, the budgetary powers of the Parliament are not without significance. However, the distinction between compulsory and non-compulsory expenditure is controversial. Indeed, even the meaning of compulsory

---

[161] Art. 203(4) EC. [162] Art. 203(5) EC. [163] Art. 203(7) EC [164] Art. 203(6) EC.
[165] Art. 203(8) EC. [166] Art. 204 EC. [167] OJ 1980 C4/36 and OJ 1985 C12/91.

expenditure remained in dispute until the Joint Declaration on Budgetary Procedure of the Commission, Council, and Parliament was adopted in 1982.[168] According to this declaration, compulsory expenditure is "such expenditure as the budgetary authority is obliged to enter in the budget to enable the Community to meet its obligations, both internally and externally, under the Treaties and acts adopted in accordance therewith". Thus, for example, expenditure of the Guarantee Section of the European Agricultural Guidance and Guarantee Fund in the form of price support measures is compulsory. In contrast, expenditure of the European Regional Development Fund is non-compulsory.

In relation to non-compulsory items, the Parliament has the final word. However, the Parliament remains largely dependent on Council approval of legislative proposals to render effective its powers in relation to such items. According to the Court of Justice, inclusion of an item in the budget confers authority to incur the relevant expenditure but does not impose an obligation to do so.[169]

The budgetary powers of the Parliament may also have been prejudiced by limitations to the role of the Parliament in relation to treaty-making.[170] However, this problem may have been ameliorated by extension of the assent procedure to "agreements having important budgetary implications for the Community".[171]

3.3.3 Supervision of Administration

The supervisory role of the Parliament may vary, depending on whether the Commission or the Council is discharging the relevant administrative functions.

Commission Responsibility

Article 140 of the EC Treaty requires the Commission to reply orally or in writing to questions put by the Parliament or its Members. In theory, difficulties may be expected to arise from the fact that, in recognition of Commission collegiality, this provision only requires the Commission as a whole to answer oral questions.[172] In practice, however, MEPs, being aware

---

[168] OJ 1982 C194/1. It was accepted by the ECJ in Case 34/86 *EC Council* v. *European Parliament: non-compulsory expenditure* [1986] ECR 2155, 2212. See now the Joint Declaration of 11 Nov. 1987 (OJ 1987 C345/48).

[169] VerLoren van Themaat AG in Joined Cases 87 & 130/77, 22/83 & 10/84 *Vittorio Salerno* v. *EC Commission and EC Council* [1985] ECR 2523, 2432; and Case 16/88 *EC Commission* v. *EC Council: waste* [1989] ECR 3457, 3487.

[170] Resolution of 18 Feb. 1982 (OJ 1982 C66/68) on the role of the European Parliament in the negotiation and ratification of treaties of accession and of other treaties and agreements between the EC and third countries.

[171] Art. 228(3) EC.

[172] Commission Reply to WQ 120/61 (JO 1961 485) by Mr Vredeling.

of the particular responsibilities entrusted to each Commissioner, will be able to direct their questions to the most appropriate Commissioner. Moreover, one week's notice of oral questions must be given.[173] Hence, arrangements may be made to ensure the presence in the House of the appropriate Commissioner when questions are put.

Oral questioning of the Commission developed significantly in 1973, when British MEPs were admitted to the Parliament and regular Question Times were introduced at each plenary session of the Parliament.[174] At such Question Times short, pointed questions may be put to the Commission and followed by supplementary questions. On other occasions during plenary sessions questions may be put and followed by a short debate. Commissioners are also questioned during committee meetings.

In the case of written questions, the adequacy of replies[175] and delays[176] in their production have often been criticised. The Commission considers that greater recourse to computerisation may alleviate such problems. Even so, certain delays are an inevitable consequence of the fact that, with the increasing range and complexity of the issues raised, involvement of more Directorates General and co-ordination of their views are necessary. They are also a consequence of the fact that detailed investigations and contacts with national authorities may be required.[177]

Nevertheless, the mere knowledge that it may be faced with Parliamentary questions means that the Commission must constantly take account of Parliamentary views when performing its functions. The need for the Commission to do so presumably increased after the holding of the first direct elections in 1979. The associated increase in the number[178] of MEPs and abolition of the compulsory dual mandate allowed Members more time to devote to questioning the Commission and to improve their technical effectiveness in this regard. Moreover, the significance of such questioning does not lie solely in its impact on the relations between the two institutions. Replies to oral questions are published in the reports of Parliamentary proceedings, and those to written questions are published in the Information and Notices section of the Official Journal. They thus provide the public with a valuable source of information concerning Union activity.

Discussion and airing of longer-term policy issues are envisaged in Article 143 of the Treaty. According to this provision, the Parliament is to discuss in open session the annual general report submitted to it by the

---

[173] Rule 40(2) of the Rules of Procedure (OJ 1997 L49/1).

[174] Resolution of 18 Jan. 1973 (OJ 1973 C4/17) on the addition of Rule 47A to the Rules of Procedure introducing a Question Time in the European Parliament followed by a debate, if requested.

[175] See, e.g., WQ 739/76 (OJ 1977 C50/39) by Mr Lagorce.

[176] See, e.g., WQ 77/66 (JO 1966 3108) by Mr Apel and WQ 86/73 (OJ 1974 C67/67) by Lord O'Hagan.

[177] Reply to WQ 1457/84 (OJ 1985 C93/39) by Lord O'Hagan.

[178] From 198 to 410.

Commission.[179] Moreover, the President of the Commission and Commissioners attend plenary sessions, participate in debates, and give a monthly account of action taken or not taken on Parliamentary resolutions. The Parliament also debates the annual legislative programme of the Commission.[180]

The implication in these procedures is that the Commission is responsible to the Parliament. This implication is confirmed by Article 144 of the Treaty. According to this provision, a censure motion on Commission activities may be tabled before the Parliament. With a view to preventing excessive recourse to this procedure, the Rules of Procedure stipulate that such a motion may only be tabled by at least one tenth of the MEPs.[181] Once tabled, a vote may take place after a delay of at least three days and must be open. If the motion is passed by a two-thirds majority of the votes cast, representing a majority of MEPs, the Commission must resign as a body. By prescribing this special majority,[182] the Treaty authors presumably sought to ensure that the Commission could not be censured without there being general dissatisfaction amongst MEPs with its work.[183]

The procedure has been threatened under both the ECSC[184] and EC Treaties,[185] but no censure motion has yet been carried. The inference may be drawn that the Parliament does not regard the procedure as an important means of rendering effective its supervision of the Commission. Certainly, criticism has been levied against the procedure on the ground that an individual Commissioner cannot be censured.[186] It has also been criticised on the ground that Member States would be free to nominate a new Commission composed of precisely the same persons as its censured predecessor.[187]

The first difficulty with the procedure may be regarded as a necessary

---

[179] Art. 156 EC requires the Commission to publish this report not later than 1 month before the opening of the session of the Parliament.

[180] Rule 49 of the Rules of Procedure (OJ 1997 L49/1).

[181] *Ibid.*, Rule 34(1).

[182] Though in Case 294/83 *Parti Ecologiste "Les Verts"* v. *European Parliament: information campaign for elections* [1986] ECR 1339, 1351 Mancini AG doubted whether the procedural legality of a censure motion could be challenged before the ECJ.

[183] A similar end may have been sought by the stipulation in the original version of Art. 24 ECSC that a censure motion could only be tabled following presentation of the annual report. However, EC Treaty arrangements go further and seek to ensure that the bias in favour of smaller Member States in the allocation of seats cannot lead to the passage of a censure motion supported by MEPs representing only a minority of the Union population.

[184] Art. 24 ECSC

[185] A motion was first tabled (though withdrawn) in Dec. 1972 (EP Debs. No. 156, 51, 12 Dec. 1972) and was first voted on in June 1976 (EP Debs. No. 204, 18*ff*, 15 June 1976 and 106, 16 June 1976). See, most recently, the proceedings of 20 Feb. 1997 (OJ 1997 C85/103).

[186] See, e.g., M. Palmer, n. 55 above, 124. However, proposed amendment 71 to the Draft Treaty establishing a European Union (OJ 1984 C77/33) providing for the censure of individual Commissioners was rejected by a majority of the House.

[187] M. Palmer, n. 55 above, 158. Cf. the suggestion in European Union, House of Lords Select Committee on the European Communities, HL (1984-5) 226, xxiv, that approval of the European Parliament should be necessary for reappointment of a Commissioner.

consequence of Commission collegiality.[188] Even so, where an individual Commissioner has seriously failed in his allotted functions within the Commission, it is possible for MEPs during debate to make clear that he has been particularly at fault. It is also possible for them to recommend that the Commissioners except him be reappointed.[189] As for the second difficulty, insofar as an effective case is made out by the Parliament against one or more Commissioners, Member States may feel politically inhibited from nominating them for reappointment.[190] Indeed, their reappointment could constitute a violation of the Treaty. In particular, it could violate the requirement in Article 157(1) of the Treaty that Commissioners be chosen "on the grounds of their general competence", taken together with the requirements of Article 5 of the Treaty. According to the latter provision, Member States must collaborate in achievement of Treaty objectives and abstain from any measure that could jeopardize their achievement.

Therefore, the potential effectiveness of the censure procedure should not be underestimated.[191] True, Commission perception of the likelihood of its use may be important. Even so, the very existence of the procedure and the clear statement of the principle of Commission responsibility contained in Article 144 may have a significance that cannot be gauged simply by the frequency of its use.

There is also some indication that the Article 144 procedure is supplemented by a convention. According to the supposed convention, where the Parliament refuses to give the Commission a discharge in respect of its implementation of the budget under Article 206, the latter must resign.[192] However, the problem arises that the special majority stipulated in Article 201 is not required for a decision refusing a discharge under Article 206. Hence, there may be a risk of abuse of the discharge procedure. Certainly, in 1984 the Commission declined to resign following adoption of such a decision. In so declining, the Commission argued that the Parliament was abusing the procedure by basing its decision on general dissatisfaction with general Commission activity rather than alleged budgetary failings.[193]

Council Responsibility

No statement of Council responsibility to the European Parliament is

---

[188] See Commission Reply by Mr Santer to WQ E–0685/97 (OJ 1997 C321/26).

[189] Cf. the Dec. of 14 Nov. 1984 (OJ 1984 C337/23) refusing to grant a discharge to the Commission in respect of the Budget for 1982, para. 6, where the Parliament singled out Commissioner Tugendhat and President Thorn for criticism.

[190] M. Catalano, "I Poteri dell'Assemblea parlamentare europea" [1971] RDE 31–47, 45.

[191] M. Palmer, n. 55 above, 43.

[192] See the statement of Commissioner Tugendhat (EP Debs. No. 219, 303, 7 July 1977).

[193] EP Debs. No. 2–319, 121*ff*, 14 Nov. 1984. Ultimately, this procedure suffers from the same problem as the censure procedure, namely that administration is not a function exclusively reserved for the Commission. Rather, it is a function shared with the Council. Cf. R. Quadri, R. Monaco, and A. Trabucchi, *Trattato istitutivo della Comunità economica europea* (Giuffré, Milan, 1965), 1080.

embodied in the EC Treaty. Such an omission may be viewed as the consequence of uncritical reluctance on the part of the authors of this Treaty to
depart from precedents set in the ECSC Treaty. In the latter Treaty the
Common Assembly was primarily an institution intended to subject High
Authority exercise of direct powers over the coal and steel industries to
democratic control. However, the nature of the powers of the Council in all
three founding Treaties is similar, and it is only the scope of these powers
that is broadened in the EC Treaty. Hence, the above view begs the question
why the ECSC Treaty itself did not contain such a statement.

The usual explanation advanced is that control of the Council by the
European Parliament is unnecessary for the safeguarding of democratic
principles.[194] It is said to be unnecessary because of the responsibility of
Council members to national parliaments. In reality, however, their responsibility to national parliaments may be so inadequately secured[195] that it is
doubtful whether such principles can realistically be said to be satisfied.
Rather, a democratic deficit may be entailed.

The true explanation is not that Council responsibility to the European
Parliament is unnecessary as much as that its effectiveness would inevitably
be limited. Council members are, according to Article 146 of the EC Treaty,
representatives of Member States. Hence, the censuring and dismissal of the
Council by the Parliament would lead simply to its replacement by persons
similarly representative and thus expected to conduct themselves in the same
manner as their predecessors.

Such a conclusion does not, however, completely preclude any responsi-
bility of the Council to the European Parliament. Certainly, the availability of
Article 175 proceedings[196] against the Council indicates that this institution
has a legal responsibility at the Union level. For example, in *European
Parliament* v. *EC Council*[197] the Parliament challenged the failure of the
Council to introduce a transport policy and, more particularly, to enact
legislation securing freedom of establishment in the transport sector. The
Court of Justice ruled that the Council had unlawfully failed to enact
measures securing this freedom in the transport sector. This ruling
amounted effectively to a finding that the Council had failed to discharge its
legal responsibility at Union level.

There is no apparent reason why the Council should not, as a Union institution, also have a political responsibility at the Union level, while its members
remain individually responsible to their respective national parliaments.[198]

---

[194] Such principles are referred to in the 3rd recital in the Preamble to the TEU and in Art. F(1) TEU.

[195] See, e.g., A. Evans, "Participation of National Parliaments in the European Community
Legislative Process" (1981) *Public Law* 388–400.

[196] Sect. 5.3.2 below.   [197] Case 13/83 [1985] ECR 1513.

[198] Cf. recognition by Dutheillet de Lamothe AG of the Council as a "Community institution
where government ministers meet" in Case 22/70 *EC Commission* v. *EC Council: ERTA* [1971] ECR
263, 288–9.

The European Parliament may have a role to play in ensuring Council discharge of this responsibility at the Union level. Certainly, according to the Court of Justice, it is the task of the Parliament to "exercise a political review of Commission activities and to a certain extent those of the Council".[199]

True, Article 140 of the EC Treaty merely provides that the Council shall be heard by the Parliament according to the conditions laid down by the former in its rules of procedure. Again, Article 23 of the ECSC Treaty simply authorises members of the Council to attend all meetings of the Parliament. These provisions cannot be said to impose obligations on the Council in relation to the Parliament. However, they do appear to envisage co-operation between the two institutions and to imply that the Council may perceive a need to explain its position to the Parliament. At the very least, contacts between the two may be expected to confer a degree of legitimacy on the Council as a Union institution.

In practice, the Council has proved ready, though maintaining that it does so voluntarily, to answer written questions from MEPs. Through its President, the Council also answers oral questions put during Question Time or on other occasions during plenary sessions or in committee.[200] In the case of oral questions in the whole House, three weeks' notice must be given.[201] This requirement reflects the fact that while the President may add a personal statement indicating his own view, his principal task is to answer on behalf of the Council itself. He must, therefore, seek to achieve consensus amongst Council members in advance. For this reason, replies tend to be somewhat vague and generalised.

Besides replying to specific questions, at the beginning of his term of office each Council President gives to the Parliament a statement about what he regards as the prospects and problems of his term. In addition, preliminary versions of the agenda which the Council expects to have before it during the coming six months are circulated. The President of the European Council also gives an account of the European Council meeting over which he has presided, and the President of the Foreign Affairs Council gives a report on his country's presidency. Moreover, at least once during each presidency, the president of each "specialised" Council[202] attends a meeting of the relevant Parliamentary committee.

Petitions

The supervisory role of the Parliament, in relation to both the Council and the Commission, has apparently been strengthened by EC Treaty provisions introduced by the Treaty on European Union. In particular, Article 138d of the EC Treaty benefits any Union citizen and any natural or legal person

---

[199] Case 13/83 *European Parliament* v. *EC Council: transport policy* [1985] ECR 1513, 1588.
[200] Solemn Declaration on European Union, pt. 2.3.3 (Bull. EC 6–1983, 24).
[201] Rule 40(2) of the Rules of Procedure (OJ 1997 L49/1).
[202] Sect. 4.1.1 below.

residing or having his registered office in a Member State. It recognises his right to address, individually or in association with other citizens or persons, a petition to the Parliament. The petition may concern any matter that comes within the European Community's fields of activity and which affects him directly.[203]

Committees of Inquiry

Article 138c of the EC Treaty provides that the Parliament may, in the course of its duties and at the request of a quarter of its members, set up temporary committees of inquiry. Such committees are to investigate alleged contraventions or maladministration in the implementation of Union law.[204] For example, a committee of inquiry into the handling of "mad cow disease" problems was established in July 1996.[205]

Ombudsman

Article 138e of the EC Treaty provides for the Parliament to appoint an Ombudsman. The latter is empowered to receive complaints from any Union citizen or any natural or legal person residing or having his registered office in a Member State. Such complaints may concern maladministration in the activities of the Union institutions or bodies. The complaints may not, however, concern the Court of Justice and the Court of First Instance acting in their judicial role.[206]

3.4 The European Parliament and Third States

The European Parliament may take an interest in relations with third states partly as an element of its work supervising the activities of other Union institutions. The Parliament may also make special organisational arrangements relevant to relations with third states and takes a special interest in human rights issues arising in such relations. However, the relevant policy frameworks may not necessarily be favourable to Parliamentary control. As a result, general problems of the "democratic deficit" may be exaggerated in the context of Union relations with third states.

---

[203] See, earlier, the interinstitutional agreement (OJ 1989 C120/361).

[204] See also Dec. 95/167 (OJ 1997 L113/2) on the detailed provisions governing the exercise of the European Parliament's right of inquiry.

[205] The resulting report was published as EP Doc. A4/0020/97. See also the Resolution of 19 Feb. 1997 (OJ 1997 C 85/61) on the results of the temporary committee of inquiry into BSE, which noted the problems of lack of co-operation with the inquiry from Union institutions and Member States.

[206] See also the Dec. of 9 Mar. 1994 (OJ 1994 C113/15) on the regulations and general conditions governing the performance of the Ombudsman's duties, as approved by Council Dec. 94/114 (OJ 1994 L54/25).

3.4.1 Organisation

The European Parliament has a Committee on External Relations. Moreover, there are interparliamentary delegations of MEPs, which participate in joint meetings with parliamentarians from third states.[207] Such meetings may be designed to exercise some democratic control over relations with the third states concerned and, more particularly, over decision making pursuant to any agreement with these states.

3.4.2 Policy Frameworks

The policy framework for relations with third states, as established by Union law, may not necessarily be favourable to Parliamentary control of Union participation in such relations. In particular, Article J.11 of the Treaty on European Union requires the Council Presidency to consult the Parliament on the main aspects of the basic choices of the common foreign and security policy. The Council Presidency and the Commission are also to keep the Parliament regularly informed of the development of this security policy.[208] The Council Presidency is required to ensure that the views of the Parliament are duly considered. Corresponding requirements in relation to police and judicial cooperation in criminal matters are imposed by Article K.11 of the same Treaty. However, no procedures equivalent to those of co-operation or co-decision are provided for in this Treaty. In practice, the Parliament is said to have only a "minimal influence"[209] in these fields.

3.5 Agreements with Third States

Article 228(3) of the EC Treaty provides in its first paragraph that the Council must consult the European Parliament before concluding agreements with third states or international organisations. This provision applies even where an agreement covers a field for which the co-operation or co-decision procedure is required for the adoption of "internal rules".[210] The Council may lay down a time-limit, according to the urgency of the matter, for delivery of an opinion by the Parliament. In the absence of an opinion within that time-limit, the Council may not act.

---

[207] Chap. XVIII of the Rules of Procedure (OJ 1997 L49/1); and Dec. of 12 Dec. 1996 (OJ 1997 C20/99) on the number and membership of delegations to joint parliamentary committees and interparliamentary delegations.

[208] Cf., earlier, regarding reports on political co-operation, Bull. EC 10–1979, 129.

[209] B. Meyring, "Intergovernmentalism and Supranationality: Two Stereotypes for a Complex Reality" [1997] ELR 221–47, 237.

[210] Note the concern of the ECJ that the Council and Commission should not be able through concluding agreements with third states to deny Parliament the participation it enjoys in the adoption of "internal" measures in Opinion 1/94, *International Agreements on Services and the Protection of Industrial Property* [1994] ECR I–5267, I–5406.

However, in relation to accession agreements[211] and association agreements,[212] the assent procedure was introduced into the EEC Treaty by the Single European Act.[213] The introduction of this procedure meant that Parliamentary approval of such agreements became necessary.

Moreover, according to the second paragraph of Article 228(3), the assent procedure now also applies to conclusion of other agreements establishing a specific institutional framework by organising co-operation procedures; agreements having important budgetary implications for the Union; and agreements entailing amendment of an act adopted under the co-decision procedure. In an urgent situation the Council and the Parliament may agree upon a time limit for the assent to conclusion of such agreements.[214]

However, even where the assent procedure applies to the conclusion of an agreement with a third state, challenges to the democratic control exercised by the European Parliament may still be posed by decision making under that agreement.

3.5.1 Free Trade Agreements

Free trade agreements may make no express arrangements for democratic control.[215] In practice, limited arrangements may develop between parties to such agreements.[216] Thus MEPs[217] and, more particularly, the Committee for External Trade Relations of the European Parliament[218] may hold meetings with parliamentarians from the third states concerned.

However, such arrangements may be inadequate to the needs of democratic control. For example, Article 4 of the Rules of Procedure of the Swedish–EC Joint Committee[219] stated that meetings of the Committee were not public except insofar as a decision was adopted. This language was interpreted as meaning that only formal decisions should be published. The implication may be that the Committee was expected to engage in consideration of sufficiently important and sensitive issues as to demand such

---

[211] Art. 237 EEC.   [212] Art. 238 EEC.

[213] Arts. 8 and 9 SEA (OJ 1987 L169/1) respectively amended Arts. 237 and 238 EEC to this effect. There was no amendment of corresponding provisions in the ECSC and Euratom Treaties.

[214] Art. 228(3) EC.

[215] Cf., regarding Art. 38 of the Co-operation Agreement with Jordan (OJ 1978 L268/2), the Report of the Committee on External Relations on the draft regulations concluding Co-operation Agreements between the EEC and Egypt, Jordan, and Syria, EP Doc. 99/77.

[216] Cf. Arts. 82–84 of the Partnership and Co-operation Agreement with Kazakhstan (OJ 1994 C319/6), regarding the Parliamentary Co-operation Committee.

[217] EFTA Bull. 5/1981, 16. See, generally, A. Teschl, "EFTA–EG och framtiden: ur en EFTA-parlamentarikers synvinkel", EFTA Bull. 3/1985, 1–2. Representatives of political parties in EFTA states also attended meetings of the relevant political groups within the European Parliament as observers. See *Sverige och den västeuropeiska integrationen*, 1990/91:UU8, 26.

[218] *Sverige–EFTA–EG 1988* (Utrikesdepartementets handelsavdelning, Stockholm, 1989), 14–15.

[219] Dec. 1/73 of Feb. 1973. See *Sverige–EG 1973* (Utrikes-och handelsdepartementen, Stockholm, 1974), bil. 5.

secrecy.[220] On the other hand, this provision exemplifies the secrecy which generally surrounds decision-making under free trade agreements and which may seriously impede democratic control of such decision-making.[221]

3.5.2 Association Agreements

Association agreements may go further than free trade agreements in arranging for democratic control. Thus the Europe Agreements have established Association Parliamentary Committees, composed of MEPs and members of the national parliament of the third country concerned. For example, an Association Parliamentary Committee is established by the Europe Agreement with Poland.[222] It comprises MEPs and Members of the Polish Parliament.[223]

Article 110 of the Polish Agreement provides that the Association Council, also established by this Agreement, must supply the Association Parliamentary Committee with any information requested regarding implementation of the Agreement. In addition, the Committee is to be informed of decisions of the Association Council and may make recommendations to the latter.[224] However, the Association Council has established various committees,[225] which may not be effectively subject to the supervision of the Association Parliamentary Committee or the European Parliament.

3.5.3 EEA Agreement

The EEA Agreement[226] provides for establishment of a Joint Parliamentary Committee, containing MEPs and EFTA Parliamentarians. In addition, limited arrangements are made for the European Parliament itself to supervise Union participation in decision making under the Agreement.

EEA Joint Parliamentary Committee

Article 95(1) of the EEA Agreement and the Agreement on a Committee of Members of Parliament of the EFTA states[227] established the EEA Joint Parliamentary Committee. It is composed of twelve MEPs[228] and an equal number[229] of members of the parliaments of the EFTA states.[230]

---

[220] The ECJ may also be reluctant to review the legality of decision-making by such bodies. See Van Gerven AG in Case C–188/91 *Deutsche Shell AG* v. *Hauptzollamt Hamburg-Harburg* [1993] ECR I–363, I–380.

[221] Cf. the criticism of the work of the Integration Office within the Swedish Government by the Constitutional Committee of the Swedish Parliament (1989/90: KU30).

[222] OJ 1993 L348/2, Art. 108.   [223] *Ibid.*, Art. 106(1).

[224] Cf. Art. 27 of the Association Agreement with Turkey (JO 1964 3865).

[225] Sect. 6.5.2 below.   [226] OJ 1994 L1/3.

[227] European economic co-operation area, prop. 1991/92:170.

[228] Dec. of 12 Dec. 1996 (OJ 1997 C20/99).

[229] The European Parliament considered that the number of members of the Committee should be determined with account being taken of the Committee's ability to function and its wide-ranging tasks. See the Resolution of 14 Feb. 1992 (OJ 1992 C67/196) on the EEA, para. 10.

[230] Rule 7 of the Rules of Procedure of the EEA Joint Parliamentary Committee (OJ 1994

This Committee is intended to contribute, through dialogue and debate, to a better understanding between the Union and EFTA states in the fields covered by the EEA Agreement.[231] It is to meet at least twice a year,[232] with the Presidency being held for one year alternately by an MEP and a member of a parliament of an EFTA state. It shall adopt its Rules of Procedure[233] and may express its views in the form of reports or resolutions, as appropriate.

It shall examine the annual report of the EEA Joint Committee.[234] The President of the EEA Council may appear before the Joint Parliamentary Committee in order to be heard by it.[235] Rule 10 of the Rules of Procedure of the Committee[236] goes further. It provides that the President of the Council and representatives of the EEA Joint Committee will be invited to participate actively in its work. Under Rule 16 its members have the right to put oral and written questions to the representatives of the EEA Council and the EEA Joint Committee.

However, no specific provision is made in the EEA Agreement for consultation of the Joint Parliamentary Committee before the adoption of acts by the EEA Joint Committee. The official explanation is that since the EEA Agreement entails no transfer of legislative powers,[237] the national parliaments of the EFTA states retain their legislative powers. Even so, the European Parliament has objected[238] that the absence of any such provision is incompatible with the democratic principles outlined in the Preamble to the EEA Agreement.[239] Rule 10 of the Rules of Procedure[240] of the Joint Parliamentary Committee merely states that all Union legislation applying to the EEA as well as its implementation shall be subject to "scrutiny" by this Committee.

European Parliament Powers

Where a proposal for Union legislation on a matter covered by the EEA Agreement is sent to the European Parliament, the Parliament is simultane-

---

L247/34) provides that any parliament of an EFTA state that does not "take part in the EEA Agreement" may obtain observer status during sessions of this Committee.

[231] Art. 95(3) EEA.

[232] The European Parliament considered that the Committee should itself determine its calendar of sittings in the light of actual requirements. See the Resolution of 14 Feb. 1992 (OJ 1992 C67/196) on the EEA, para. 10. According to Rule 6 of the Rules of Procedure of the Committee (OJ 1994 L247/34), it shall hold a general session twice a year and extraordinary sessions on its own initiative or upon a written request of at least one third of its members.

[233] Art. 95(6) EEA.   [234] Art. 95(4) EEA.   [235] Art. 95(5) EEA.   [236] OJ 1994 L247/34.

[237] Prot. 35 to the EEA Agreement, on the implementation of EEA rules.

[238] See the observations of the Parliament in Opinion 1/92, *Draft Agreement between the Community and the EFTA Countries relating to the Creation of the EEA* [1992] ECR I–2821, I–2837.

[239] 1st recital in the preamble to the EEA Agreement. Cf., regarding constitutional problems in the budgetary field, the Report of the Committee on Foreign Affairs and Security on the conclusion of the EEA Agreement, EP Doc. A3–0316/92, 10.

[240] OJ 1994 L247/34.

ously requested to deliver an opinion on its extension to the EEA.[241] Thus consultation of the European Parliament takes place before an act is adopted by the EEA Joint Committee.

However, the European Parliament has a purely advisory role regarding such extensions. More fundamentally, in the preparation of such proposals the Commission is required by the EEA Agreement to consult experts of EFTA states.[242] Hence, effective agreement may be reached with these states before the proposal reaches the Parliament.[243] In other words, the Parliament may be presented with *faits accomplis.*[244]

To address this problem, the Commission has undertaken to keep the competent bodies of the Parliament informed of the adoption of all proposals and measures relating to the EEA. The Commission has also undertaken, if necessary, to introduce new procedures for keeping Parliament abreast of negotiations with the EFTA states in the light of the practical experience of implementing the EEA Agreement.[245]

---

[241] Art. 3(1) of Reg. 2894/94 (OJ 1994 L305/6) concerning arrangements for implementing the EEA Agreement. Cf. the Resolution of 30 Oct. 1992 (OJ 1992 C305/586) on economic and trade relations between the EC and the EFTA countries in the EEA, para. 20.

[242] Sect. 6.5.3 below.

[243] Cf. the Resolution of the European Parliament of 16 Dec. 1993 (OJ 1994 C20/174) on the role of national experts and the Commission's right of initiative, para. 6.

[244] Resolution of 14 Feb. 1992 (OJ 1992 C67/196) on the EEA, para. 8.

[245] Report of the Committee on Foreign Affairs and Security on the conclusion of the EEA Agreement, EP Doc. A3–316/92, 14.

4

Council of the Union

The Council is included within the list of institutions in Article 4(1) of the EC Treaty, though its members represent their respective Member States. It originated, as the ECSC Special Council of Ministers, in Benelux concern that the ECSC High Authority would be unduly influenced by France and Germany.[1] Under Article 2 of the Merger Treaty the Council of Ministers replaced the ECSC Special Council of Ministers, the EEC Council of Ministers, and the Euratom Council of Ministers.[2] The Council, which is now known as the "Council of the Union",[3] plays a central role in the enactment of Union legislation. It also performs budgetary and administrative functions.

4.1 Composition

Article 146 of the EEC Treaty provided that the Council should consist of representatives of the Member States. Each government was to delegate to it one of its members. Article 146 of the EC Treaty now recognises decentralising tendencies in several Member States. It provides that the Council shall consist of a representative of each Member State at ministerial level, authorised to commit the government of that Member State.

4.1.1 Variations in Composition

Subject to the requirements of Article 146 of the EC Treaty, the composition of the Council is left to be determined by the individual Member States. In practice, a basic distinction has emerged between general and specialised Council meetings. The former meetings are attended by Foreign Ministers. They discuss not only "external relations" but also matters of general Union concern, such as institutional reform. In addition, they seek to co-ordinate

---

[1] *New York Times*, 3 and 26 July 1950.
[2] There had been a *de facto* merger since 1958.
[3] Dec. 93/591 (OJ 1993 L281/18) concerning the name to be given to the Council following the entry into force of the TEU.

the work of specialised Council meetings.[4] The latter meetings are attended by those ministers whose national portfolios relate most closely to the specific subject matter for discussion. Their proliferation is a notable feature of the developments in Council practice. The co-ordination problems posed by this proliferation may be seen as detrimental to Council efficiency.[5]

On the other hand, variations in Council composition may have certain advantages. In particular, the utilisation of ministerial expertise most relevant to the subjects under discussion at Council meetings is facilitated. Problems may arise from the fact that the issues raised by a particular subject may range beyond the scope of any single national portfolio. However, these problems are presumably mitigated by the possibility that where the subject demands, a Member State may be represented by two ministers jointly. For example, "Ecofin" meetings of Economics Ministers and Financial Affairs Ministers take place, in principle, each month except August.

4.1.2 Regional Representation

Article 146 of the EC Treaty allows for regional representatives from a Member State to participate in the Council. However, it requires that representatives of a Member State within the Council must be empowered to commit their government. The necessary implication of this requirement is that they must be so empowered by national law.

The European Parliament has called on Member States which, because of their constitutional provisions, have regions with exclusive legislative powers to facilitate the participation of representatives of these regions in meetings of the Council when matters falling within their competence are being considered.[6] However, as the Parliament implicitly acknowledges, Union law leaves possibilities for such participation dependent on internal arrangements for distribution of power within Member States. These arrangements are, in turn, left to be determined by the national law of the individual Member State concerned, provided only that such arrangements do not prevent the Member State from fulfilling its Treaty obligations. Thus Member States are free to "delegate" responsibility for implementation of Union measures to regional institutions, but they must ensure that the responsibility is discharged.[7] Subject to this proviso, the Treaty entails that

---

[4] Cf. the idea of "representations" of Member States, each representation being chaired by a minister permanently and specifically responsible for Union affairs in the Draft Treaty establishing a European Union (OJ 1984 C77/33), Art. 20.

[5] See, e.g., House of Lords Select Committee on the European Communities, European Union, HL (1984–5) 226, xxxi.

[6] Resolution of 18 Nov. 1993 (OJ 1993 C329/279) on the participation and representation of the regions in the process of European integration: the Committee of the Regions, para. 11.

[7] See, e.g., Capotorti AG in Case 73/81 *EC Commission* v. *Belgium: waste from the titanium nitrate industry* [1982] ECR 153, 162; and Joined Cases 227–230/85 *EC Commission* v. *Belgium: failure to comply with judgments of the Court* [1988] ECR 1, 11.

national law may restrict or enlarge opportunities for the regional institutions of the Member State concerned to participate in Council decision making. In other words, the Treaty formally applies a "neutrality" principle, which embodies the question-begging idea that Member States have only transferred to the Union the sovereignty[8] necessary for fulfilment of Treaty obligations.

National law principles, such as the "localisation principle"[9] in Sweden or the "speciality principle"[10] in France, may imply limitations to participation by regional institutions in the Council.[11] These limitations may be reinforced by the practical tendency of Member States to treat "European matters" as foreign policy matters. They may also be reinforced by the tendency of Member States to adopt "realist"[12] conclusions as to the need for national positions in Council decision-making to be unified.[13] In Sweden, for example, local authorities may not interfere with state "foreign policy"[14] and cannot undertake commitments binding on the state without special authority or transfer public powers to foreign authorities.[15] In the case of such Member States, participation of regional representatives in the Council may be precluded by national law.

4.1.3 European Council

Since February 1961 summit conferences of Heads of State or Government have taken place with increasing frequency. The conferences are now known as meetings of the European Council and are held at least twice a year.[16]

Article D of the Treaty on European Union provides that the European Council "shall bring together" the Heads of State or Government of the Member States and the President of the Commission. They "shall be assisted by" the Ministers for Foreign Affairs of the Member States and by a Member

---

[8] Sects. 7.2 and 7.5.3 below.

[9] According to this principle, regional institutions may not deal with matters within the responsibility of central institutions. See Communal involvement in international questions, Ds C 1986:10.

[10] According to this principle, regional institutions may only deal with matters of specifically regional interest. See R. Letteron, "Les Aides des collectivités territoriales aux services publics" [1993] *AJDA* 437–43.

[11] See, similarly, in the case of Italy, I. Techini, "Il Contributo delle regioni al processo d'integrazione europea" [1990] *RDE* 267–77, 272.

[12] See, e.g., J.M. Grieco, *Co-operation among Nations* (Cornell University Press, Ithaca, N.Y., 1990).

[13] According to F. Snyder, "Ideologies of Competition in European Community Law" (1989) 52 *MLR* 149–78, 172, different, conflicting, and often contradictory interests may be expressed as "unified" national interests in the Council.

[14] Communal involvement in international questions, Ds C 1986:10. Cf. the significance for German regions of the importance attached to "imperative reasons of foreign and integration policy" in *Bayerische Staatsregierung* v. *Bundesregierung* [1990] 1 CMLR 649, 651.

[15] Bill to approve an agreement between Denmark, Finland, Norway, and Sweden on communal co-operation over Nordic frontiers, prop. 1977/78:44.

[16] Art. D TEU.

of the Commission. The President of the European Council shall also invite the economics and finance ministers to participate in meetings when matters relating to economic and monetary union are discussed.[17] The outcomes of the meetings are usually published as "conclusions of the Presidency",[18] though the Heads of State or Government can also meet as the Council of the Union[19] and adopt more formal acts.[20] When the European Council deals with matters of "Community competence", it conforms to Treaty procedures.[21]

The European Council is to provide the Union with the necessary impetus for its development and to define the general political guidelines thereof.[22] More particularly, it is to produce conclusions on broad guidelines for economic policy[23] and to define the principles of and general guidelines for the common foreign and security policy.[24]

4.2 Organisation

The EC Treaty itself lays down only rudimentary rules governing the organisation of the Council of the Union, and Article 151(3) of this Treaty provides for the Council to adopt its Rules of Procedure.[25]

4.2.1 Presidency

The EC Treaty contains rules concerning the rotation of the Presidency between Member States and concerning the powers of the Presidency.

Rotation

Article 146 of the EC Treaty provides that the Presidency is to be held in turn by each Member State in the Council for a term of six months in the order decided by the Council acting unanimously. A particularly complicated demonstration of concern for the sovereign equality of Member States was provided before the latest enlargement by the creation of six sub-divisions of Member States. The order in which each Member State within each sub-division held the Presidency was reversed every other

---

[17] Declaration on Part Three, Title VI, of the EC Treaty, adopted with the TEU.

[18] Cf. the conclusions concerning the employment situation envisaged in Art. 128 EC.

[19] Solemn Declaration on European Union, Bull. EC 6–1983, 24, point 2.1.3. See, generally, A. Evans, "Institutions of the European Communities Other Than The Court of Justice" in *Stair Memorial Encyclopaedia of the Laws of Scotland*, vol. x, 132–262 (Butterworths, London, 1990), 220–1. Cf. the refusal of the ECJ in Case 38/69 *EC Commission* v. *Italy: duty on metals* [1970] ECR 47, 58 to treat the "acceleration decision" as an international agreement.

[20] See, e.g., Art. 109j(3) and (4) EC.

[21] Bull. EC 6–1977, 2.3.1. See also Lenz AG in Joined Cases 31 & 35/86 *Levantina Agricola Industria SA and CPC España SA* v. *EC Council* [1988] ECR 2285, 2309–10.

[22] Art. D TEU.   [23] Art. 103(2) EC.   [24] Art. J.3 TEU.

[25] Dec. 93/662 (OJ 1993 L304/1) adopting the Council's Rules of Procedure.

cycle, so that the part of the year in which each Member State held the Presidency alternated.[26]

In the case of the ECSC Special Council of Ministers, there was a three-monthly rotation.[27] In the case of the Council of the Union, there is a six-monthly rotation. This departure from precedent is presumably designed to promote the continuity of Council activity.[28] In reality, however, even the extended term may be too short, particularly in view of the proliferation of specialised Council meetings, for the Presidency to realise its full potential for influencing Council activity. On the other hand, conferment of the Presidency for a longer period would strain the resources of the relevant national administrations, particularly where the Presidency was held by a smaller Member State. It would also mean, in a Union of fifteen or more Member States, that the period between relinquishment and re-acquisition of the Presidency by each Member State would become unacceptably protracted. Such a situation could become a highly controversial matter, given the political prestige attaching to the Presidency of any body in which fifteen states are represented. This prestige is all the greater because of synchronisation of the rotation of this office as between the Council of the Union and the European Council. To extend the period for which the Presidency is held but to reserve it for the larger Member States or for such Member States and groups of smaller Member States could be even more controversial.[29]

In short, therefore, the composition of the Council is such as to demand a major organisational role for the Presidency. At the same time, however, its composition may also be such as to preclude the Presidency from being held for a sufficient time for the potential of its role to be fully realised.[30]

Powers

Many of the powers conferred on the Presidency have little to do with the organisational problems of the Council. The President is to be passed any letters of resignation written by members of the European Courts.[31] He is also to be notified of any decision of the Court depriving one of its members of his office.[32]

Moreover, paragraph (a)I of the Luxembourg Accords[33] concerns the credentials of Head of Missions of third states accredited to the Union. It

[26] Art. 146 EEC. These arrangements were important, when the number of Member States was even. See, now, Art. 146 EC; and Dec. 95/2 (OJ 1995 L1/220) determining the order in which the office of President of the Council shall be held.

[27] Art. 27 ECSC.

[28] *Tindemans Report* (Bull. EC, Supp. 1/76, 31) favoured a 12-monthly rotation.

[29] See, e.g., *Europe* 5727 (11/12 May 1992).

[30] Cf. the arrangements for "rolling" Presidency programmes, approved by the European Council in June 1986 (Bull. EC 6–1986, 1.1.7).

[31] Arts 5(2) and 44 of the Statute of the ECJ.

[32] *Ibid.*, Art. 6(2).   [33] Bull. EC 3–1966, 9.

requires that they be submitted jointly to the President of the Council and the President of the Commission. The two Presidents meet together for this purpose.

On the other hand, Article N of the Treaty on European Union provides for the President of the Council to convene conferences of representatives of the governments of the Member States for the purposes of determining by common accord amendments to be made to the Treaties. More generally, under Article 147 of the EC Treaty it is the President who convenes the Council on his own initiative or at the request of one of the members or the Commission.[34] In practice, the Presidency may play a critical role in seeking compromises at Council meetings.

Moreover, the Presidency speaks for the Council of the Union in the European Parliament. Twice a year the President of the European Council also addresses the Parliament.

4.2.2 Sessions

Provided that the President does not decide otherwise, Council sessions may be attended by national officials other than ministers. Formal functions, however, such as presiding, voting, and calling into session, may only be exercised by a minister.[35] Article 150 of the EC Treaty does permit proxy voting, but this provision also seeks to curb excessive absenteeism. It stipulates that a minister may not vote on behalf of more than one Member State additional to his own.

The proceedings of these sessions take place according to an agenda fixed by the President in consultation with the Member States and the Commission.[36] Article 7(1) of the Rules of Procedure[37] states that the President may call for a vote on his initiative. Moreover, the President must start the voting procedure at the request of a member of the Council or of the Commission, provided that a majority of members approve. To facilitate this arrangement, the provisional agenda for each session are to be sent to the other members of the Council and the Commission at least fourteen days before the beginning of the meeting. According to Article 2 of the Rules, the provisional agenda must indicate the items on which the Presidency, a Council member, or the Commission can request a vote.[38]

---

[34] The Treaty itself does not specify the frequency of such meetings, and Art. 1(1) of the Rules of Procedure (OJ 1993 L304/1) simply follows Art. 147 EC in this regard.

[35] See, e.g., Art. 7(3) of the Rules of Procedure (OJ 1993 L304/1). See also the Reply to WQ 681/74 (OJ 1975 C86/62) by Mr Broeckz, regarding the practice of representation by officials.

[36] Art. 2 of the Rules of Procedure (OJ 1993 L304/1).

[37] *Ibid.*

[38] The European Parliament would have preferred a stipulation requiring a vote when requested by the Commission or 3 Member States (Resolution of 16 Jan. 1986 (OJ 1986 C36/144) on the position of the European Parliament on the SEA, para. 2).

"*Items*"

Council agenda are divided into "A items" and "B items".[39] The former items are those on which provisional agreement has been reached within COREPER.[40] Formal Council approval of such items is still required,[41] though such approval is rarely delayed. Thus the preparatory work for which COREPER has responsibility is capable of compensating for the relative infrequency of Council meetings and thereby of expediting decision-making by the latter. Indeed, if all the Council members agree[42] and, where the decision is to be taken on the basis of a Commission proposal, the Commission gives its consent, urgent matters may be decided by a written procedure.[43] Resort to this procedure is particularly frequent where a Council meeting is not scheduled early enough for an A item decision to be taken by the date required. As for B items, these relate to matters on which, despite the preparatory work, disagreement persists. Protracted discussion of such matters in the Council may be necessary.

Secrecy

In the absence of a unanimous vote to the contrary[44] and except for policy debates on the six-monthly work programmes,[45] the sessions are held in camera.[46] The secrecy thus surrounding Council debates[47] and even Council minutes,[48] except in the case of a resolution, apparently renders the Council an institution less sensitive to public opinion.[49] By way of justification of this degree of secrecy, an analogy is often drawn with national cabinet meetings.[50] Insofar as Council sessions provide ministers with an opportunity to be decisively involved in legislative action, such an analogy cannot easily be rejected.

However, "leaks" may occur[51] and Council members may have to make

---

[39] Art. 2(6) of the Rules of Procedure (OJ 1993 L304/1).   [40] Sect. 4.2.4 below.

[41] Art. 2(6) of the Rules of Procedure (OJ 1993 L304/1). Cf. Case 131/86 *UK* v. *EC Council: battery hens* [1988] ECR 905, 934; and Case C–25/94 *EC Commission* v. *EU Council: FAO Agreement* [1996] ECR I–1469, I–1505.

[42] According to Lenz AG, in Case 68/86 *UK* v. *EC Council: hormones* [1988] ECR 855, 885, where the matter has been extensively discussed, unanimity is unnecessary for resort to the procedure. The ECJ did not follow him on this point.

[43] Art. 8 of the Rules of Procedure (OJ 1993 L304/1).

[44] *Ibid.*, Art. 6(2).   [45] *Ibid.*, Art. 6(1).

[46] *Ibid.*, Art. 4(1). Hence, the Commission may not answer questions regarding Council deliberations (Commission Reply to WQ 1152/84 (OJ 1985 C93/15) by Ms Tongue).

[47] Secrecy is not required by the EC Treaty itself, except in relation to professional secrecy. See Art. 214 EC. See also Art. 5 of the Rules of Procedure (OJ 1993 L304/1).

[48] See, regarding Council statements in the minutes, the Council Reply to WQ 2385/96 (OJ 1997 C72/38) by Jens-Peter Bonde.

[49] According to the European Ombudsman, other Union institutions are also less than open (*The European*, 30 Jan.–5 Feb. 1997).

[50] Cf. the Reply to OQ 10/73 by Lord Gladwyn, EP Debs. No. 161, 54, 5 Apr. 1973.

[51] See, e.g., WQ 429/74 by Lord O'Hagan (OJ 1975 C19/8). The Council will not confirm any information thus provided. See the Reply to WQ 407/69 (JO 1970 L33/7) by Mr Vredeling.

certain information available to their respective national parliaments. Moreover, a Declaration on the Right of Access to Information was adopted along with the Treaty on European Union, and a public right of access to Council,[52] Commission,[53] European Parliament,[54] and Economic and Social Committee[55] documents has been introduced. This right is confirmed by Article 191a of the Treaty.[56] More particularly, at the December 1992 meeting of the European Council it was agreed that formal votes taken in the Council would be recorded in press *communiqués*, along with any explanations of a vote. In addition, certain Council debates would be televised live to the press room in the Council building.[57]

The Council is now to elaborate in its Rules of Procedure[58] on the conditions under which the public shall have access to Council documents. Greater openness is required where the Council acts in a legislative capacity. In any event, when the Council acts in this capacity, the results of votes and explanations as well as statements in the minutes shall be made public.[59]

4.2.3 Voting

Article 148(1) of the EC Treaty provides that, save as otherwise provided therein, the Council is to act by a majority of its members.[60] However, most Treaty provisions require unanimity or at least a qualified majority[61] in the Council before a measure may be enacted thereunder.[62] Hence, the significance of Article 148(1) is mainly confined to Council consideration of decisions to be taken under existing Council measures.

---

[52] Council Dec. 93/731 (OJ 1993 L340/43) on public access to Council documents. See also Case T–194/94 *John Carvel and Guardian Newspapers Ltd* v. *EU Council* [1995] ECR II–2765 and Case T–105/95 *WWF UK (World Wide Fund for Nature)* v. *EC Commission* [1997] ECR II–313.

[53] Commission Dec. 94/90 (OJ 1994 L46/58) on public access to Commission documents.

[54] European Parliament Dec. 97/632 (OJ 1997 L263/27) on public access to European Parliament documents.

[55] ESC Decision on public access to ESC documents (OJ 1997 L339/18).

[56] But see, in relation to documents originating from a Member States, the Declaration on Art. 191a EC, adopted with the Treaty of Amsterdam (OJ 1997 C340/1).

[57] Conclusions of the Presidency, Bull. EC 12–1992, I.24. The Draft Treaty establishing a European Union (OJ 1984 C77/33), Art. 24 envisaged that where the Council was acting as a legislative or budgetary authority, its meetings should be open to the press and public.

[58] OJ 1993 L304/1.   [59] Art. 151(3) EC.

[60] Under the ECSC Treaty the Council acts by an absolute majority (Arts. 55(2)(c) and 56(1)(b)); a 2/3 majority (Arts. 50(2), 56(2), and 88(3)); a 5/6 majority (Art. 95(4)); or unanimously (Arts. 53(b) and 54(2)). No vote is necessary under Art. 28 ECSC in the case of mere consultation of the Council.

[61] Cf. the requirement of a 2/3 majority in Art. 104c(11) EC.

[62] Cf. Art. J.13(3) TEU; Arts. 151(3), 152, 153, and 162 EC; Arts. 128 EEC and 228 EEC; and, before its amendment by the SEA (OJ 1987 L169/1), Art. 49 EEC. See, regarding Art. 128 EEC, Case 56/88 *UK* v. *EC Council: vocational training* [1989] ECR 1615.

Qualified Majority

When a qualified majority is required, a system of weighted voting, which is provided for in Article 148(2) of the Treaty, comes into operation. According to this system, each of the "big four" has ten votes, Spain has eight; Belgium, Greece, the Netherlands, and Portugal have five each; Austria and Sweden four each; Denmark, Finland, and Ireland three each; and Luxembourg two. Sixty-two votes are required for a qualified majority.[63] Where the Council is not acting on a Commission proposal, these votes must also be cast by at least ten Member States.[64]

More particularly, Article 109k(5) provides that, for certain decisions relating to monetary union, a qualified majority shall be two-thirds of the votes of representatives of Member States participating in the third stage of monetary union.[65] Participating Member States are those that are found to have met the convergence criteria. Exceptional arrangements are made in the Protocol on Certain Provisions relating to the United Kingdom. Paragraph 7 of the Protocol provides that unless the United Kingdom decides to move to the third stage, its votes shall be excluded from any calculation of the qualified majority for the purposes of Article 109k(5). Similarly, certain decisions concerning a Member State with an excessive government deficit are to be taken under Article 104c with the votes of that Member State excluded.[66]

In other cases, where not all Member States are "concerned", a qualified majority may be defined differently. It may be defined as the same proportion of the weighted votes of the members of the Council concerned as laid down in Article 148(2).[67]

This system of weighted voting does not achieve strict mathematical proportionality. However, the system does secure a greater degree of proportionality between voting strength and population size[68] than would result from rigid adherence to the principle of the sovereign equality of states. At the same time, the minimum number of votes stipulated for a qualified

---

[63] Though the Council seeks to avoid acting on a "bare" qualified majority. See the "Ioannina Compromise" (OJ 1994 C105/1; OJ 1995 C1/1).

[64] Cf., in the case of measures adopted pursuant to the Protocol to the EC Treaty on Social Policy, when the UK was not a party, para. 2 of the Protocol.

[65] I.e., when national currencies are replaced by the Euro. See Art. 109d(4) EC.

[66] Art. 104c(11) EC.

[67] See, in connection with abolition of frontier controls on the movement of persons, the Protocol on the position of the UK and Ireland; and the protocol on the Position of Denmark. See, in connection with a Member State suspended for violations of fundamental rights, Art. F.1(4) TEU and Art. 236(4) EC.

[68] There is more proportionality than in the original EEC Treaty (where France, Germany, and Italy each had 4 votes; Belgium and the Netherlands 2 each; and Luxembourg 1). On the other hand, a qualified majority was 12, which meant that the Luxembourg vote could never be decisive. Moreover, a qualified majority could be achieved by the "big three" alone. Hence, the Benelux countries were dependent on the Commission. A special majority was required in Art. 44(6) EEC, regarding agricultural prices, and is required in Art. 28(2) ECSC, where some proportionality of voting power to share in ECSC coal and steel production is sought.

majority is designed to protect the smaller Member States against domination by the larger ones. The Treaty authors apparently treated as a mathematical task the devising of arrangements reconciling respect for the "popular vote" with respect for the individuality of each Member State. Thus the system of weighted voting meant that, before the fourth enlargement of the Union, a measure might only be adopted with the support of Council members who represented approximately two-thirds of the Union population.

Unanimity

Article 148(3) of the Treaty provides that abstentions by members present in person or represented in the Council shall not prevent adoption by the Council of measures which must be reached unanimously.[69] Since abstentions reduce the possibility of the sixty votes necessary for a qualified majority being obtained, such a majority may occasionally turn out to be more difficult to achieve than that of unanimity.

On the other hand, a requirement of unanimity does have the consequence that a single Member State will be able to prevent adoption of a proposal supported by all the other Member States.[70] In the case of Treaty provisions conferring broad powers on the Council, this consequence was apparently acceptable to Member States. Hence, the unanimity requirement in these provisions was to be permanent.[71] In the case of provisions conferring more narrowly defined powers, the unanimity requirement was replaced with one of qualified majority by the end of the transitional period for establishment of the common market.[72] Apparently, the thinking was that, at least after the end of this period, the acceptability of decision-making by qualified majority would be in direct proportion to the degree of circumscription of Council powers in any given provision. Such thinking, however, may lack the sophistication necessary to ensure that the Council takes adequate account of the special interests of each Member State.[73]

For example, Article 56(2) of the EEC Treaty provided for the Council, on the basis of Commission proposals, to enact directives co-ordinating national public policy rules governing the exclusion or expulsion of aliens.

---

[69] This is contrary to the general rule in Art. 28(3) ECSC.

[70] Cf. the Declaration on Voting in the Field of the CFSP, which was adopted along with the TEU. According to this Declaration, "with regard to Council decisions requiring unanimity, Member States will, to the extent possible, avoid preventing a unanimous decision where a qualified majority exists in favour of that decision". Cf., earlier, the Draft Act on European Union (Bull. EC 11–1981, 87), II.8(2); and the Solemn Declaration on European Union, (Bull. EC 6–1983, 24, II, 2.2.2). Cf. also the embodiment of the estoppel principle in Art. 8(3) EEC. See, now, the arrangements for "constructive abstention" in Art. J.13(1) TEU.

[71] See, e.g., Art. 235 EEC.   [72] See, e.g., Art. 56(2) EEC.

[73] Art. 23(3) of the Draft Treaty establishing a European Union (OJ 1984 C77/33) envisaged preservation of the unanimity requirement where certain, serious interests of a Member State were at stake.

They were to be enacted by qualified majority after the end of the first transitional stage. However, the Court of Justice recognises that the requirements of public policy vary in time and place. Hence, Union law can only set certain limits within which precise determination of these requirements has to be left to the particular Member State concerned.[74] The implication is that a single Member State wishing to block adoption of an Article 56(2) proposal because the proposal failed to take adequate account of its particular public policy requirements might have found some basis for doing so in the Treaty structure. Certainly, Article 100a(4)[75] tacitly accepts that a majority vote may not override the "major needs" of a single Member State.

Luxembourg Accords

The difficulties of moving from unanimity to decision-making by qualified majority were reflected in the Luxembourg Accords.[76] These Accords were adopted at an extraordinary Council session in January 1966 by way of resolution of the constitutional crisis of 1965–6. The crisis had revolved around the "empty chair" policy pursued by France. This policy constituted a protest against Commission plans to introduce agricultural and budgetary reforms through securing adoption of the necessary measures by qualified majority voting in the Council. The Accords represented a resolution of the crisis, though they only dealt imperfectly with the underlying constitutional issues.

In particular, Paragraph (b)I of the Accords dealt with decisions that might be taken by a majority vote on a Commission proposal. It stated that where very important interests of one or more Member States were at stake, the members of the Council would endeavour within a reasonable time to reach solutions which could be adopted by all Council members. Their mutual interests and those of the Community were to be respected according to Article 2 of the EEC Treaty. France further expressed the view in Paragraph (b)II that where such interests were at stake, the Council discussion should be continued until unanimous agreement was reached.

Therefore, the then six Member States all apparently recognised that the transition to majority voting should not be allowed to lead to disregard of the "very important interests" of a Member State. However, only France expressly drew the conclusion that protection of such interests might necessitate recognition of a right to a veto for the Member State concerned.

Quite apart from the fact that France alone expressed this conclusion, these Accords cannot be regarded as having amended the EEC Treaty so as to confer such a right where unanimity was not required by the existing terms of a particular provision.[77] They cannot be so regarded, because Treaty

---

[74] Case 41/74 *Yvonne Van Duyn* v. *Home Office* [1974] ECR 1337, 1350.

[75] Sect. 19.4.1 below.   [76] Bull. EC 3–1966, 9.

[77] The Council alone cannot change voting rules contained in the Treaties. See Case 68/86 *UK* v. *EC Council: hormones* [1988] ECR 855, 902. As regards Council resolutions, see Joined Cases 90 & 91/63 *EEC Commission* v. *Luxembourg and Belgium: duty on milk imports* [1964] ECR 625, 631.

provisions might only be amended according to Article 236.[78] Thus the Commission refused to accept that the Accords amended the Treaty.[79] True, some of the requirements laid down in Article 236 may be thought to have been substantially satisfied. However, the same cannot easily be said of the requirement in this provision that the European Parliament be consulted or that the relevant amendments be ratified by all Member States according to their respective constitutional requirements.

At most, the Accords may be regarded as "conventional",[80] in that Council members respect them insofar as they feel politically obliged to do so. Consequently, these Accords cannot in themselves constitute a defence in the event of Article 175 proceedings[81] being brought against the Council for failure, in the face of its "very important interests" being invoked by a Member State, to adopt a proposal under a Treaty provision envisaging majority voting.[82]

However, the reference to Article 2 of the EEC Treaty in Paragraph (b)I of the Accords may be noted. According to this provision, the Community task included the promotion of a *harmonious* development of economic activities and the achievement of a *balanced* economic expansion. The implication in this language is that in the performance of its task the Community was to take account of the particular interests of each Member State. This view finds some support in the willingness of the Court of Justice, apparently on the basis of the Treaty structure, to find national measures otherwise prohibited by specific Treaty provisions to be lawful, as being necessary to satisfy "mandatory requirements".[83] Therefore, the Luxembourg Accords may be regarded as consistent with underlying principles of Union law,[84] which may, perhaps, offer a basis for a defence to Article 175 proceedings.

According to the current position of the Council itself, the Accords do not prevent the Council from taking its decisions according to the EC Treaty. At the same time, the fact that the Treaty provides in many cases for decision making by majority does not preclude members of the Council from endeavouring, as a general rule, to narrow their differences before the Council votes.[85]

In practice, reduced willingness in the Council to allow individual Member States to prevent adoption of proposals may be implied by the increased tendency towards adoption of legislative proposals by qualified

[78] See now Art. N TEU. Nor can they easily be regarded as a Treaty interpretation, because under Art. 219 EEC interpretation was exclusively a matter for the ECJ.

[79] Débs PE No. 105, 125, 3 July 1969.

[80] In the British constitutional law sense.   [81] Sect. 5.3.2 below.

[82] Cf. Lenz AG in Case 13/83 *European Parliament* v. *EC Council: transport policy* [1985] ECR 1513, 1549.

[83] Sect. 8.5.4 below.

[84] Cf. the Council argument in Case 13/83 *European Parliament* v. *EC Council: transport policy* [1985] ECR 1513, 1578.

[85] Council Reply to WQ E–0317/96 (OJ 1996 C217/22) by James Moorhouse.

majority since the early 1980s. This tendency, however, may be attributable partly to the "new approach" to harmonisation pursued by the Commission.[86] It may also be partly attributable to the fact that since the early 1980s France favoured limiting availability of a veto to proposals for the introduction of "new policies". That attempts by Germany, Greece, and the United Kingdom to veto decisions concerning farm prices were rejected may not be decisive. Neither "new policies" nor, indeed, vital national interests were directly at stake.[87] Equally, the fact that the Single European Act[88] introduced new opportunities for majority voting and that these opportunities were used in the Council is not decisive. The reforms excluded fiscal policy, the movement of persons, and the rights and interests of employees.[89] At the same time, they were accompanied by new arrangements to permit exceptions subsequently to be invoked from the requirements of directives adopted by qualified majority.[90] The Single European Act also left unaffected the unanimity requirement in Articles 28 (common customs tariff), 59 (services), 70(1) (exchange restrictions on the movement of capital), 84 (transport) and 99 (taxation) of the EEC Treaty, as did the Treaty on European Union.[91] Moreover, in respect of controversial proposals, the Council may still tend to continue to seek unanimity, even though unanimity may not be required by the relevant Treaty provision.

More particularly, account may be taken of Treaty provisions regarding "flexibility".[92] According to Article 5a(2), a member of the Council may declare that for important and stated reasons of national policy, it intends to oppose the granting of an authorisation of flexibility by qualified majority. If a member does so, a vote shall not be taken. However, the Council may, acting by a qualified majority, request that the matter be referred to the European Council, meeting in the composition of Heads of State or Government, for decision by unanimity.[93]

4.2.4 COREPER

Questions concerning the preparation of Council meetings were not specifically addressed in the ECSC Treaty. However, in February 1953 the Special Council of Ministers established a Co-ordinating Committee (CoCor) under Article 10 of its Rules of Procedure, which provided for establishment of

---

[86] Sect. 19.4 below.   [87] A. Evans, "The 'Veto' in EEC Law" [1982] *Public Law* 366–9.

[88] OJ 1987 L169/1, Art. 18.   [89] Art. 100a(2) EEC.   [90] Art. 100a(4) EEC.

[91] The unanimity requirement in Art. 99 EC, has been preserved by the Amsterdam Treaty (OJ 1997 C340/1) also. See also Arts 5a(2), 8a, 8b, 8e, 51, 57(2), 73c(2), 73o, 75(2), 99, 101(14), 105(6), 108(5), 109(1), 109b(7), 109l(4) and (5), 113(5), 118(3), 118b(2), 121, 128(5), 130(3), 130b, 130d, 130n(2) and (3), 136, 138(4) and (5), 145, 146, 151(2), 166, 168a(2) and (4), 188, 188b(3), 184, 188a, 201, 209, 217, 223(2), 228(2), and 235 EC. The Amsterdam Treaty removed the unanimity requirement from Arts. 130c and 130o EC. A qualified majority was stipulated in the following new provisions: Arts. 5a(2), 109g(2), 116, 119(3), 209a(4), 213a, 213b, and 227(2) EC.

[92] Chap. 1.   [93] See, similarly, in connection with the CFSP, Art. J.13(2) TEU.

committees. This Committee was composed of senior officials drawn from the national administrations of the Member States and met about once a month to carry out the preparatory work for Council meetings.

This precedent was followed in the EEC and Euratom Treaties. They provided that the Rules of Procedure of the two new Councils might "provide for the setting up of a committee consisting of representatives of the Member States, the powers and tasks of which [were] to be determined by the Council".[94] Accordingly, a Committee of Permanent Representatives (COREPER) was established for the EEC and Euratom. This development was implicitly approved in Article 4 of the Merger Treaty. It provided that a committee consisting of the Permanent Representatives of the Member States should be responsible for preparing the work of the Council. The Committee should also be responsible for carrying out the tasks assigned to it by the Council.[95] Consequently, CoCor was abolished, and a single Committee of Permanent Representatives took over such responsibilities under all three Treaties.[96]

It meets at least once a week and maintains close contacts with the Council Presidency. Indeed, the latter and the COREPER Presidency rotate simultaneously. The meetings are attended by representatives of the General Secretariat of the Council and the Commission. Presumably, the effectiveness of its work benefits from the comparative frequency of its meetings and the comparative degree of permanence of its members. However, since it lacks powers of its own, it is classified as an "auxiliary body" rather than as an institution.[97] The Committee may merely adopt procedural decisions in cases provided for in the Rules of Procedure of the Council.[98]

"Parts"

COREPER is divided into two "Parts". The First Part is composed of Deputy Permanent Representatives and deals with what are regarded as technical matters. The Second Part is composed of the Permanent Representatives themselves and deals with more controversial matters.

Working Groups

The detailed work of COREPER is devolved to working groups covering each field of Union activity as well as to *ad hoc* groups that may be created.[99] There are around one hundred and fifty of these bodies. Their work is co-ordinated by COREPER, they are composed of national officials as well as a

---

[94] Art. 151 EEC and Art. 121 Euratom.   [95] See now Art. 151(1) EC.

[96] In the agricultural sector the Special Committee on Agriculture performs functions that would otherwise have been the responsibility of COREPER. See Art. 5(4) of the Dec. of 12 May 1960 (JO 1960 1217) of the Representatives of the Governments of the Member States meeting within the Council concerning the acceleration of the implementation of Community objectives. See also, regarding the role of the Economic and Financial Committee, Art. 109c(2) EC.

[97] Case C–25/94 *EC Commission* v. *EU Council: FAO Agreement* [1996] ECR I–1469, I–1505.

[98] Art. 151(1) EC.   [99] Art. 19(2) of the Rules of Procedure (OJ 1993 L304/1).

Commission representative, and they are chaired by the Member State holding the Council Presidency. Their work may be valuable not only in a technical sense but also, more generally, in promoting mutual understanding between the Commission and national governments.[100] In other words, networking may be facilitated.

4.2.5 Secretariat

The Council shall be assisted by a General Secretariat.[101] The Secretary-General and a Deputy Secretary-General are appointed by the Council, acting unanimously. The Council decides the organisation of the Secretariat-General. However, since heavy reliance is placed on the work of national officials in COREPER and its working groups, the Secretariat is comparatively small.[102] It comprises around two thousand persons.

Its functions are limited and technical. It may, for example, correct the grammar and spelling of a text agreed by the Council, but may not alter its content.[103]

4.3 Functions

Despite the impression that may be given by its composition and organisation, the Council is legally a collegiate institution. It is required by Article 4 of the EC Treaty, as are other Union institutions, to collaborate in achievement of Treaty objectives. More particularly, according to Article 145 of the Treaty, the functions of the Council involve the co-ordination of national economic policies and the power to take decisions. In substance, legislative, budgetary, and administrative functions are entailed.

4.3.1 Legislation

Under Article 26 of the ECSC Treaty the Council is to harmonise Commission action with that of national governments, which "are responsible for the general economic policies of their countries". This provision recognises that while the ECSC Treaty is concerned only with the coal and steel sectors, these sectors cannot be isolated from the national economies generally. Hence, the Council is to ensure that due account of this inter-relationship is taken in Union action as well as in the action of the national governments. It is essentially for this purpose that under the ECSC Treaty the Council is to be involved in legislative activity.

---

[100] See, generally, *Council and Commission Committees*, Bull. EC, Supp. 2/80.
[101] Art. 151(2) EC.
[102] Art. 21 of the Rules of Procedure (OJ 1993 L304/1).
[103] Case 131/86 *UK* v. *EC Council: battery hens* [1988] ECR 905, 934.

Under the EC Treaty, however, such involvement is not simply a necessary consequence of European Community action in specific sectors. As Article 2 of this Treaty makes clear, such involvement also reflects an essential element of the Community's task. More extensive involvement of the Council in legislative activity is implied. This implication underlies the more specific attention paid by this Treaty to the relationship between the Council and the Commission. In particular, Article 162(1) imposes an obligation on these two institutions to consult each other and to settle by common accord their methods of co-operation. In practice, the Commission is invited to take part in Council meetings.[104] These arrangements highlight the absence of a strict doctrine of the separation of powers in Union law.[105]

Co-operation with the Commission

Council co-operation with the Commission occurs in relation to the co-ordination of national economic policies envisaged in Article 145.[106] Thus the Commission regularly presents the Council with reports and other documents. On the basis of these, the Council is to seek to formulate an agreed policy to be pursued by the Member States in the sector concerned. More particularly, according to Article 152, the Council may request[107] the Commission to undertake any studies that the Council considers desirable for the attainment of "the common objectives". The Council may, according to the same provision, request the Commission to submit to it any appropriate proposals. More particularly, Article 109d confers on the Council or a Member State the power to request proposals from the Commission regarding amendment of the Protocol of the Excessive Deficit Procedure.[108] Thus the Council is apparently allocated a role in relation to the earliest stages of Union legislation. However, fulfilment of its functions requires the Council to go beyond the generalisations involved in policy formulation and to adopt legislative measures.

Consideration of Commission Proposals

Where legislation is to be introduced, the Council usually has to act on the basis of a Commission proposal. The Council may, in principle, only amend the proposal unanimously under Article 189a(1) of the Treaty, agree a text

---

[104] Art. 4(2) of the Rules of Procedure of the Council (OJ 1993 L304/1).

[105] Cf., K. Lenaerts, "Some Reflections on the Separation of Powers in the European Community" (1991) 28 *CMLRev.* 11–28.

[106] Cf. Art. 118c EC, which requires the Commission to "encourage co-operation between the Member States" in the social field.

[107] "*Demander*"; "*chiedere*"; but in German, "*auffördern*". Cf. Council dir. regarding Commission negotiation of trade agreements with third states or international organisations under Art. 113(3) EC. Cf. also Art. 121 EC, regarding Council assignment of tasks to the Commission in connection with the implementation of common measures, particularly as regards social security for migrant workers covered by Arts. 48–51 EC.

[108] Cf., regarding requests from a Member State, Art. 73o(2) EC.

with the European Parliament under Article 189b(4) and (5), or by a majority request the submission of a fresh proposal under Article 152. Subject to these exceptions, all the Council may do is adopt or reject the Commission proposal. Hence, the conclusion may be drawn that the Council is primarily intended to provide a safeguard that Commission policy cannot be implemented through adoption of a proposal lacking the support of a qualified, or at least a simple, majority of its members or, in certain circumstances, where one member is opposed to its adoption.

National Interests

In practice, each Council member may seek to ensure that adoption of a proposal can be justified solely in terms of the national interests of his Member State. The result is that the Council tends to enlarge its role and to participate in detailed consideration of legislative proposals. Proposals that can satisfy the particular national interests of each Member State will inevitably be limited both in their number and their substance.[109] "New approach" directives[110] may have been adopted more readily by the Council, but their provisions are rarely of such a kind as to cause controversy. In controversial areas, such as harmonisation of indirect tax levels in the Member States and the abolition of systematic frontier checks on individuals moving between Member States, agreement has proved difficult to attain.[111]

4.3.2 Budget

Where budgetary decisions are taken, the Council acts on the basis of the draft preliminary budget prepared by the Commission. The Council may not raise the maximum rate of increase fixed by the Commission for non-compulsory expenditure without the agreement of the European Parliament.[112] Moreover, the latter may overrule Council decisions in relation to items of such expenditure.[113] Compulsory expenditure, in relation to which the Council cannot be so overruled, is that which necessarily results from the Treaties or acts adopted thereunder.[114] Determination of the level of the latter kind of expenditure may be thought to be an exercise allowing little scope for policy decisions.

In practice, however, while the Commission regards its preliminary draft budget as a detailed policy document, the Council may seek to make the necessary policy decisions itself. The Council is not well organised to take

---

[109] The need for "a certain flexibility necessary for achieving a convergence of views between the institutions" is recognised by the ECJ. See Case C–280/93 *Germany* v. *EU Council: bananas* [1994] ECR I–4973, I–5054.

[110] Sect. 19.4 below.

[111] Seventh report concerning the implementation of the White Paper on the completion of the internal market, COM(92)383.

[112] Art. 203(9) EC.   [113] Art. 203(6) EC.   [114] Sect. 3.3.2 above.

such decisions. Not only may national interest considerations predominate in Council deliberations. The varying composition of this institution also means that the draft budget established by the Council[115] may represent little more than the sum of inadequately coordinated decisions by individual groups of ministers.[116] There may even be a lack of consistency between budgetary and legislative decision making.[117]

4.3.3 Administration

The Council alone is empowered to adopt certain individual decisions,[118] though sometimes a recommendation[119] or opinion[120] may be necessary from the Commission.

For example, the Council may authorise particular aid measures on application by the Member State concerned under Article 93(2) of the EC Treaty.[121] This procedure has been employed in relation to French aid to the paper industry,[122] following a political commitment made during intergovernmental tariff negotiations; British aid for sugar refining[123] and for beef farmers;[124] French and Italian aid to wine producers faced with market surpluses;[125] and Danish aid for the slaughter of hens, also in the context of a market surplus.[126] It reflects the Council function in Article 145 of the Treaty of ensuring co-ordination of the general economic policies of the Member States. However, such an authorisation must be "justified by exceptional circumstances". Thus when German farmers were already recovering under Union legislation[127] 80 per cent. of their loss of income due to the dismantling of positive monetary compensatory amounts, the discovery of the

---

[115] Art. 203(3) EC.

[116] The Council failed to approve the draft budget for 1988, and the Commission (Bull. EC 10–1987, 2.3.2 and 2.4.5) and the European Parliament (OJ 1987 C305/126) initiated proceedings under Art. 175 EEC. The Budget was finally adopted on 1 June 1988 (OJ 1988 L226/1).

[117] Report of the Court of Auditors for 1986 (OJ 1987 C336/1), paras 1.24–7.

[118] See, e.g., Art. 73(1) EEC and Arts. 76, 93(2), and 104c(7)–(9) and (11) EC. See also, regarding decisions concerning other institutions, Arts. 188, 188b(3), and 217 EC, Art. 6 MT and, during the transitional period, Art. 44(3) EEC.

[119] Arts. 103(2) and (4), 104c(6), 109j(2), 109k(1), and 113(3) EC.   [120] Art. 106(5) EC.

[121] Case C–122/94 *EC Commission v. EU Council: aid to wine producers* [1996] ECR I–881.

[122] Dec. of 19 Dec. 1960 (JO 1960 1972) on the aid system in France for certain categories of paper pulp.

[123] Dec. 73/209 (OJ 1973 L207/47) concerning the present system of aid in the UK for the refining of raw sugar.

[124] Dec. 75/142 (OJ 1975 L52/35) concerning the system of aid in the UK for the slaughter of certain adult bovine animals intended for slaughter.

[125] Dec. 76/306 (OJ 1976 L72/15) on the system of aid to be applied in France for certain wine-growers; and Dec. 85/213 (OJ 1985 L96/34) on the granting of aid for the distillation of wines obtained from table grapes in Sicily.

[126] Dec. 76/556 (OJ 1976 L168/12) on the system of aid applicable to the slaughter of hens in Denmark.

[127] Reg. 855/84 (OJ 1984 L90/1) on the calculation and the dismantlement of the monetary compensatory amounts applying to certain agricultural products.

shortfall did not constitute an exceptional circumstance such as to justify an aid authorisation[128] under Article 93(2).[129] Therefore, this provision does not empower the Council to develop its own "aid policy".[130]

4.4 The Council and Third States

The role of the Council in relations with third states may be problematic. This institution has, by virtue of the common foreign and security policy and the conclusion of agreements with third states, a more central role in relations with third states than in connection with internal Union matters. As a result, problems of the predominance of national-interest considerations in the work of the Council may be exaggerated.

4.4.1 Council Composition

Article 146 of the EC Treaty provides for the Council to be composed of a representative of each Member State. This provision embodies a general principle that participation in Union decision making implies membership of the Union,[131] and so by definition third states are excluded from such participation. This principle reflects the ideas that the Union institutions exercise decision-making powers transferred to them by the Member States and that these institutions thus have no authority to share the powers with third states.[132]

4.4.2 Council Organisation

The "duty of loyalty" imposed on Member States by Article 5 of the EC Treaty[133] may affect the working of the Council. This duty means that a Member State must not undertake formal or informal commitments to third states which may have the effect of limiting its freedom to vote in the Council[134] or of prejudicing the possibility of the Council reaching a

---

[128] Dec. 84/361 (OJ 1984 L185/41) concerning an aid granted to farmers in Germany; and Dec. 88/402 (OJ 1988 L195/70).

[129] Slynn AG in Case 253/84 *Groupement Agricole d'Exploitation en Commun (GAEC) de la Ségaude* v. *EC Council and EC Commission* [1987] ECR 123, 147.

[130] E. Grabitz, *Kommentar zum Europäische Union* (Beck, Munich, 1992), Art. 93, para. 36.

[131] Commission President Delors (EP Debs. No. 3–385, 111, 17 Jan. 1990). According to an earlier formulation of the principle, only Member States could "exert an effective influence on the life of the Community". See *Opinion on Problems Raised by Applications for Membership from the United Kingdom, Ireland, Denmark and Norway*, Bull. EC, Supp. 4/68, 9.

[132] Cf. Opinion 1/76, *European Laying-up Fund for Inland Waterway Vessels* [1977] ECR 741, 759.

[133] Chap. 1.

[134] At the same time, "unity in the international representation of the Community" is sought. See Opinion 2/91, *ILO Convention 170 concerning Safety in the Use of Chemicals at Work* [1993] ECR I–1061, I–1083.

decision relating to the subject matter of such commitments.[135] In other words Member States must not make commitments to third states which disturb the "internal constitution" of the Union.[136]

4.4.3 CFSP

Ministers may meet to discuss matters going beyond the scope of the EC Treaty.[137] In particular, following an agreement of November 1959, Foreign Ministers came to hold regular quarterly meetings to discuss European political co-operation.[138] Such co-operation is now called the common foreign and security policy and is governed by the Treaty on European Union.[139]

Article J.3(1) of this Treaty provides for the European Council to define the principles of, and general guidelines for, this policy. The Council of the Union is to take the decisions necessary for defining and implementing the policy on the basis of such guidelines.[140]

Presidency

The Presidency is to represent the Union in matters coming within the common foreign and security policy.[141] The Presidency is also responsible for the implementation of common measures. In that capacity it shall, in principle, express the position of the Union in international organisations and at international conferences.[142] In these tasks the Presidency shall be assisted, if need be, by the previous and next Member States to hold the Presidency. The Commission shall be fully associated in these tasks.[143] The Presidency is also assisted by the Secretary-General of the Council, who exercises the function of a High Representative for this policy.[144]

Voting

In principle, common foreign and security policy decisions must be taken unanimously by the Council,[145] the Commission being "fully associated" with such work.[146] However, only a qualified majority is required when the

---

[135] Relations between the Community and EFTA, House of Lords Select Committee on the European Communities, HL (1989-90) 55–2, 144. According to Case 208/80 *Rt Hon. Lord Bruce of Donington* v. *Eric Gordon Aspden* [1981] ECR 2205, 2219, Art. 5 EC entails for Member States a "duty not to take measures which are likely to interfere with the internal functioning of the institutions of the Community".

[136] Opinion 1/76 *European Laying-up Fund for Inland Waterway Vessels* [1977] ECR 741, 758.

[137] Cf., regarding the distinction between a Council act and "an act taken by the Member States collectively", Joined Cases C–181 & 248/91 *European Parliament* v. *EC Council and EC Commission: emergency aid* [1993] ECR I–3685, I–3717–19.

[138] See the Hague Summit Conference of 1 Dec. 1969 (Bull. EC 2–1970, 38).

[139] Sect. 21.14.   [140] Art. J.3(3) TEU.   [141] Art. J.8(1) TEU.   [142] Art. J.8(2) TEU.   [143] Art. J.8(4) TEU.

[144] Arts. J.8(3) and J.16 TEU. The Council may also, whenever deemed necessary, appoint a special representative with a mandate in relation to particular policy issues (Art. J.8(5) TEU).

[145] Art. J.3(1) TEU.   [146] Art. J.17 TEU.

Council adopts joint actions or common positions, takes any other decision on the basis of a common strategy, or adopts a decision implementing a joint action or a common position, unless there are military or defence implications.[147] Moreover, for procedural questions, the Council acts by a majority of its members.[148]

Political Committee

Article J.15 of the Treaty on European Union provides for a Political Committee, consisting of political directors from the Member States, for the common foreign and security policy.[149] It is to monitor the international situation and contribute to the definition of policies by delivering opinions to the Council at the request of the Council or on its own initiative. It shall also monitor the implementation of agreed policies, without prejudice to the responsibility of the Presidency and the Commission.[150]

4.5 Agreements with Third States

Agreements with third states are usually concluded by the Council. The agreements may establish bodies composed of Union representatives and representatives of the third states concerned. Such bodies are responsible for joint decision-making by the parties. In other words, they are supposed to reconcile the Union position with that of the third states concerned. However, the Union position expressed in such bodies is the result of "internal" Union negotiations and compromises and thus may not easily be modified to accommodate the needs of such reconciliation. Therefore, the work of such bodies may be problematic.[151]

4.5.1 Free Trade Agreements

Free trade agreements establish joint committees,[152] composed of representatives of the Union and the third state concerned. Article 29(1) of the Swedish Free Trade Agreement,[153] for example, established a Joint

---

[147] Art. J.13(2) TEU.   [148] Art. J.13(3) TEU.

[149] See also, regarding Council working groups on security matters, the Council Reply to WQ E–4093/96 by Peter Crampton (OJ 1997 C319/14).

[150] A Co-ordinating Committee of senior officials is also established by Art. K.8 TEU to prepare meetings regarding police and judicial co-operation in criminal matters.

[151] However, Art. 238 EC, which concerns association agreements, envisages partial participation by third states in Union decision-making. See Darmon AG in Case 12/86 *Meryem Demirel* v. *Stadt Schwäbisch Gmünd* [1987] ECR 3719, 3741 and the ECJ itself (*ibid.*, 3751).

[152] The importance of such bodies was stressed in the Report of the Committee on External Economic Relations on the agreements negotiated with the EFTA Member and Associated States which had not applied to join the Community, EP Doc. 322/72, 7.

[153] JO 1972 L300/96.

Committee, which was to consist of representatives of the Union and representatives of Sweden.[154] The Union was to be represented by the Commission, assisted by representatives of the Member States.[155] There was no requirement that the representatives be of ministerial rank and authorised to commit the Party concerned.

In practice, the Committee was composed only of officials.[156] They lacked the competence formally to bind their respective parties as to matters of any significance. Moreover, the Union position in the Committee was determined according to the "Article 113 procedure".[157] In other words, it was determined according to the procedure employed for negotiation of agreements under Article 113(3) of the EC Treaty.[158] As a result, real discussions might necessarily take place outside the Joint Committee.

It may have been for this reason that from 1981 the summer meeting of the Committee was replaced by a bilateral meeting between Swedish Ministers and the Commission.[159] The initiative for this change apparently came from the Union, which did not consider the work of the Joint Committee sufficiently important to justify the amount of "red tape" involved.[160] Questions are begged why the Parties favoured informal contacts of this kind[161] rather than higher-level representation in the Joint Committee.

The explanation may be that the only important function recognised for such bodies concerns control of resort to safeguard measures.[162] Such measures can only be adopted "in specific circumstances and as a general

---

[154] *Ibid.*, Art. 30.

[155] Art. 3 of Reg. 2838/72 (JO 1972 L300/96) concluding an agreement with Sweden and adopting provisions for its implementation.

[156] H. Lidgard, "Sverige–EEG och konkurrensregler" [1974] SvJt 18–33, 30. The Swedish representatives were led by the Head of the Swedish Delegation to the Union and the Union representatives by the Director General for External Relations. See AiH 4/1990, 20.

[157] J. Mégret, J.V. Louis, D. Vignes, M. Waelbroeck, J-L. Dewost, P. Brueckner, and A. Sacchettini, *Le Droit de la Communauté économique européenne* (University of Brussels, Brussels, 1980), i, 152.

[158] Sect. 2.5 above.

[159] The EU/US Transnational Declaration of 22 Nov. 1990 (Bull. EC 11–1990, 1.5.3) goes further in providing for informal contacts. It provides for biannual consultations between the US President and the Presidents of the Council and Commission. In addition, biannual meetings between the Foreign Ministers of the Member States, the Commission, and the US Secretary of State are foreseen as well as biannual Commission–US consultations at cabinet level and *ad hoc* consultations at ministerial level. See also the Reply by Mr Andriessen to WQ 1900/91 (OJ 1992 C112/20) by Mr Miguel Arias Canete *et al.*

[160] P. Luif, "Decision Structures and Decision-Making Processes in the European Communities' Relations to the EFTA Countries: A Case Study of Austria" [1983] *Österreichisches Zeitschrift für Aussenpolitik* 139–60, 154.

[161] Cf. the argument that formalisation of institutional relations between the Union and the US will increase internal bureaucratic struggles and (undesirable) litigation, at least in the US, in B.E. Carter, "A Code of Conduct for EC–US Relations" in J. Schwarze (ed.), *The External Relations of the European Community, in Particular EC–US Relations* (Nomos, Baden-Baden, 1989), 131–39, 132.

[162] Rozès AG in Case 270/80 *Polydor Ltd and RSC Records Inc.* v. *Harlequin Record Shops and Simon Records Ltd* [1982] ECR 329, 354.

rule after consideration within the joint committee in the presence of both parties".[163] In reality, however, practice concerning adoption of anti-dumping measures and anti-trust measures suggests that the above function may not be effectively performed by such bodies.[164]

Bilateralism

It may be thought that problems arising in trade between parties to a free trade agreement are often not such as to be capable of a purely bilateral solution between the two. For example, the Commission acted against Finnish wood producers involved in restrictive practices without first consulting the Joint Committee established by the Free Trade Agreement with Finland.[165] This failure to consult the Joint Committee was challenged before the Court of Justice in the *Wood Pulp* case.[166] However, the Court pointed out that Canadian and United States producers as well as Finnish producers were involved in the restrictive practices to which the Commission objected. In these circumstances, bilateral action through the Joint Committee could not alone have provided a solution.[167]

Certainly, there has been a general tendency for multilateral solutions to be sought. Even before entry into force of the EEA Agreement,[168] problems arising under free trade agreements with EFTA states were tackled in multilateral bodies. For example, in 1974 problems concerning rules of origin began to be referred to informal meetings between representatives of the Commission and EFTA states.[169] Moreover, in 1980 informal multilateral meetings of customs experts from EFTA states and Member States began to be held in association with meetings of the customs committees established by the joint committees.[170] More generally, because the free trade agreements with EFTA states were virtually identical and matters discussed in the joint committees usually concerned all the agreements, co-ordination of the positions of these states took place before meetings of these committees.[171] Such practice resulted in the creation of the High Level Contact Group, within the framework of the "Luxembourg process",[172] to provide a forum

[163] Case 104/81 *Hauptzollamt Mainz* v. *C.A. Kupferberg & Cie KG* [1982] ECR 3641, 3664.

[164] A. Evans, *The Integration of the European Community and Third States in Europe: a Legal Analysis* (Clarendon Press, Oxford, 1996).

[165] OJ 1973 L328/2, Art. 29.

[166] Joined Cases 89, 104, 114, 116, 117 & 125–129/85 A. *Åhlström Osakeyhtiö* v. *EC Commission* [1988] ECR 5193.

[167] *Ibid.*, 5246.   [168] OJ 1994 L1/3.

[169] *Sverige–EG 1974* (Utrikes-och handelsdepartementen, Stockholm, 1975), 11.

[170] *Sverige–EG 1980* (Utrikes-och handelsdepartementen, Stockholm, 1981), 13.

[171] An EFTA Committee of Origin and Customs Experts was established by EFTA Council Dec. No. 8 of 1974. See also F. Weiss, "The European Free Trade Association After Twenty-five Years" [1985] *YBEL* 287–323.

[172] I.e., developments in EC–EFTA relations following the Luxembourg Declaration of Apr. 1984 (Bull. EC 4–1984, 1.2.1).

for multilateral contacts.[173] The joint committees then played the purely formal role of implementing agreed solutions in the form of decisions.[174]

Moreover, multilateral meetings came to be held each year between EFTA Ministers and the Commissioner for External Relations and might also be held between EFTA Ministers and Ministers from Member States. However, practical considerations, such as the difficulties of adequate preparation of such meetings associated with the overloaded agenda of the Council, may have limited the usefulness of these multilateral meetings. More fundamentally, an internal decision-making process that might leave the Union little room for manœuvre in such meetings may have further limited their usefulness.[175]

More formal developments of a multilateral kind also occurred. For example, a Joint Committee was established by the Convention on the Simplification of Formalities in Trade in Goods,[176] concluded with EFTA states multilaterally. Each Contracting Party was represented in the Committee, which acted by mutual agreement.[177]

It cannot be assumed, however, that the bilateral character of joint committees is the only reason for their limited impact. For example, in 1985 the Commission imposed provisional anti-dumping duties on Swedish clogs[178] imported into the Union without prior consultation taking place in the Joint Committee established by the Free Trade Agreement with Sweden.[179] It is not immediately apparent why the bilateral character of the Committee should have rendered it an unsuitable body for consultation in such a case.

"Politicisation"

The real problem with joint committees may be thought to be that they are "political"[180] rather than "legal" bodies. A distinction may also be made between "diplomatic settlement" and "legal or judicial settlement".[181] Thus a "political procedure"[182] is said to have been allocated to the Joint Committee

---

[173] EFTA Bull. 3/1984, 17.

[174] To this extent, the joint committees implemented coordinated regulation of trade with EFTA States. See EFTA Secretariat, *The European Free Trade Association* (EFTA, Geneva, 1980), 90.

[175] Cf. A. von Stechow, "The Council of Ministers: the Constraint on Action" in G. Edwards and E. Regelsberger (eds.), *Europe's Global Links* (Pinter, London, 1990), 161–8. Cf. also G. Edwards, "The Relevance of Theory to Group-to-Group Dialogue" (*ibid.*), 201–18, 212–13.

[176] OJ 1987 L134/2.   [177] *Ibid.*, Art. 10.

[178] Reg. 2823/85 (OJ 1985 L268/11) imposing a provisional anti-dumping duty on imports of certain clogs originating in Sweden.

[179] *Sverige–EG 1985* (Utrikesdepartementets handelsavdelning, Stockholm, 1985), 25.

[180] *Redovisning av det svenska integrationsarbetet våren 1988–mars 1989* (Utrikesdepartementets handelsavdelning, Stockholm, 1989), 132; and U. Bernitz, "Sveriges EG–Anknuting i rättsligt perspektiv" [1989/90] *JT* 47–69, 54.

[181] EFTA/GLE 3/87.

[182] Rozès AG in Case 104/81 *Hauptzollamt Mainz* v. *C.A. Kupferberg & Cie KG* [1982] ECR 3641, 3674.

established by the Free Trade Agreement with Portugal.[183] Such bodies are, it is said, "a forum for discussion between the contracting parties . . . in which the experiences gained [in the application of the agreement concerned] are compared".[184] The conclusion may be drawn that dispute-solving procedures of a more legal character are needed.[185]

Clear-cut distinctions of this kind may not be easy to make,[186] let alone to apply to joint committees.[187] Apparently much may depend on whether such a body is involved in a dispute before the parties have reached a political *impasse*, which may affect its proceedings.[188] In the absence of such a situation, the committees may exercise what amounts to legislative power at the international level.[189]

However, the fact that to describe joint committees as "political bodies" may be an oversimplification does not in itself mean that the committees can provide a legal means of settling disputes. In view of the limited liberalisation secured by free trade agreements,[190] such agreements may rarely be treated as providing a satisfactory legal framework for tackling trade problems arising between the parties. In fact, GATT successes in securing tariff reductions mean that the elimination of tariffs secured by free trade agreements has lost much of its significance. A further consequence is that non-tariff barriers to trade, which are largely unaffected by the liberalisation requirements in the latter agreements, have become more important.[191] Consequently, the limitations to the liberalisation requirements entailed by the agreements and reliance on joint decision-making to secure satisfactory operation of these requirements throughout the territories of the parties may

---

[183] JO 1972 L301/2.

[184] Van Gerven AG in Case C–188/91 *Deutsche Shell AG* v. *Hauptzollamt Hamburg-Harburg* [1993] ECR I–363, I–377–8.

[185] *Sverige–EFTA–EG 1988* (Utrikesdepartementets handelsavdelning, Stockholm, 1989), 126.

[186] Cf., regarding dispute-settlement within the GATT framework, M. Hilf, "Settlement of Disputes in International Economic Organizations: Comparative Analysis and Proposals for Strengthening the GATT Dispute Settlement Procedures" in E-U. Petersmann and M. Hilf (eds.), *The New GATT Round of Multilateral Trade Negotiations* (Kluwer, Deventer, 1991), 285–322, 289–90.

[187] Cf., regarding the reluctance of the ECJ to interfere with decision-making by such bodies, Van Gerven AG in Case C–188/91 *Deutsche Shell AG* v. *Hauptzollamt Hamburg-Harburg* [1993] ECR I–363, I–380.

[188] Cf. J.H. Bello, "Midterm Report on Binational Dispute Settlement Under the United States–Canada Free-Trade Agreement" [1991] *The International Lawyer* 489–516.

[189] A. Evans, *The Integration of the European Community and Third States in Europe: A Legal Analysis* (Clarendon Press, Oxford, 1996). Cf. the view expressed in relation to the joint committees established by trade and commercial and economic co-operation agreements, such as that with Poland (OJ 1989 L339/2), that "the Committee's nature as a recommending body, and its duty to reach consensus prior to any further act, deprives it of effective and binding legal powers" (D. Horovitz, "EC–Central/East European Relations: New Principles for a New Era" (1990) 27 *CMLRev.* 259–84, 271).

[190] Sect. 8.8.1 below.

[191] See, e.g., Trade policy conditions for Swedish exports during the 1980s, SOU 1984:6, bil. 6.

tend to be mutually reinforcing in impeding effective joint committee involvement in tackling trading problems between the parties.

4.5.2 Association Agreements

Institutional arrangements in association agreements may be more elaborate than those in free trade agreements. The Europe Agreements are typical. For example, an Association Council and an Association Committee are established by the Europe Agreement with Poland.[192]

Association Councils

The Association Council established by the Europe Agreement with Poland consists of the members of the Council of the Union, members of the Commission, and members of Polish Government.[193] Members of the Association Council may arrange to be represented, according to arrangements to be laid down in its Rules of Procedure.[194]

The Association Council is to meet at ministerial level once a year and when circumstances require.[195] The Presidency of the Association Council is to be held in turn by a member[196] of the Council of the Union and a member of the Polish Government, according to the provisions to be laid down in its Rules of Procedure.[197] These Rules are to be drawn up by the Association Council itself.

The Association Council is to supervise the implementation of the Agreement.[198] Its powers, which may be delegated to the Association Committee,[199] are to be exercised for the purposes of attaining the objectives of the Agreement.[200] The Association Council is also to examine any major issues arising within the framework of the Agreement and any other bilateral or international issues of mutual interest.[201]

In their performance of these functions such bodies are apparently entitled to assistance from the parties to the relevant agreement.[202] Certainly, each party has a duty to take account of the legitimate interests of the other party to the agreement and a contractual obligation to refrain from jeopardizing achievement of the aims of the agreement.[203]

---

[192] OJ 1993 L348/2   [193] *Ibid.*, Art. 103(1).   [194] *Ibid.*, Art. 103(2).   [195] *Ibid.*, Art. 102.

[196] Art. 1 of the Hungarian–EC Association Council Dec. 1/94 (OJ 1994 L242/23) on its Rules of Procedure refers to a representative of the Council of the Union and a representative of the Hungarian Government.

[197] Art. 103(4) of the Polish Agreement (OJ 1993 L348/2).

[198] *Ibid.*, Art. 102.   [199] *Ibid.*, Art. 106(2).   [200] *Ibid.*, Art. 104.

[201] *Ibid.*, Art. 102. With regard to political dialogue, the Association Council shall have general responsibility for any matters the Parties may wish to put to it (*ibid.*, Art. 3(2)).

[202] See Case C–432/92 *R.* v. *Minister of Agriculture, Fisheries, and Food, ex p. S.P. Anastasiou (Pissouri) Ltd* [1994] ECR I–3087, I–3133, regarding the Association Agreement with Cyprus (OJ 1973 L133/2).

[203] E.g., Art. 115(1) of the Polish Agreement (OJ 1993 L348/2) requires the Parties to take any general or specific measures required to fulfil their obligations under the Agreement. They must see to it that the objectives set out in the Agreement are attained.

The composition of the Association Council[204] and the importance attached by the Agreement to political dialogue[205] may be thought to confirm its capacity to play an effective role. There may, however, be an element of unreality in the work of bodies where fifteen Member States, on the one hand, and a single third state, on the other, are equally represented. More fundamentally, the supposed benefits of "inter-organisational co-operation"– the tendency for the edge to be taken off national ambitions[206] and for the actions of a greater number of participants to become more transparent and calculable[207] – may be secured in a one-sided way at most. Possibly in recognition of such problems, the European Council agreed in December 1994 that there would be annual summit conferences with the Parties to the Europe Agreements. There would also be two meetings each year at the level of foreign ministers.[208]

Association Committees

The Association Committee established by the Europe Agreement with Poland is composed of representatives of the Council of the Union, members of the Commission, and representatives of the Polish Government, normally at senior civil servant level.[209] The Rules of Procedure of the Association Council are also to determine the duties of the Association Committee.[210] These duties include the preparation of the meetings of the Association Council, and how the Committee shall function.[211] The fact that the Association Committee is to include Commissioners may imply a more effective role for this Committee than that played by joint committees under free trade agreements.

---

[204] Cf. Art. 3 (*ibid.*), which provides for consultations to take place, as appropriate, between the President of the European Council, the President of the Commission, and the President of Poland.

[205] Title I of the Polish Agreement (*ibid.*).

[206] S. Nuttall, "The Commission: Protagonists of Inter-regional Co-operation" in G. Edwards and E. Regelsberger (eds.) n. 175 above, 143–57, 156.

[207] E. Regelsberger, "The Dialogue of the EC/Twelve with Other Regional Groups: A New European Identity in the International System" in G. Edwards and E. Regelsberger (eds.), n. 175 above, 3–26, 9. "Third parties" to negotiations, such as traders, may also welcome the relative ease with which they can discover which commitments have been made by which state. See S. Peers, "An Ever Closer Waiting Room? The Case for Eastern European Accession to the European Economic Area" (1995) 32 *CMLRev.* 187–213, 204.

[208] Conclusions of the Presidency, Annex IV (Bull. EU 12–1994, I.40).

[209] Art. 106(1) of the Polish Agreement (OJ 1993 L348/2).

[210] The Hungarian Association Committee is to meet when circumstances require and with the agreement of both Parties. See Art. 2 of the Rules of Procedure of the Committee, annexed to the Hungarian–EC Association Council Dec. 1/94 (OJ 1994 L242/23).

[211] Art. 106 of the Polish Agreement (OJ 1993 L348/2). Art. 13(2) of the Rules of Procedure of the Hungarian–EC Association Council (OJ 1994 L242/23) provides that the Committee shall consider any matter referred to it by the Association Council as well as any other matter which may arise in the day-to-day implementation of the Agreement.

4.5.3 EEA Agreement

The EEA Agreement[212] provides for the establishment of multilateral rather than bilateral institutions. In particular, Article 89 of the Agreement establishes an EEA Council. It is composed of members of the Council of the Union, members of the European Commission, and one member of the government of each of the EFTA States.[213] An EEA Joint Committee is also established.[214] The precise composition of the Joint Committee and its relationship with the EEA Council are not specified in the Agreement.

EEA Council

The Presidency of the EEA Council is held alternately, for six months, by a member of the Council of the Union and a member of the Government of an EFTA state.[215] The EEA Council has adopted its Rules of Procedure under Article 89(3) of the EEA Agreement.[216]

The EEA Council is to be convened twice a year by its President.[217] It shall also meet whenever circumstances so require, according to the Rules of Procedure.[218] The Rules make it clear that such circumstances include those where a Party makes use of its *"droit d'évocation"*. This is the right of a Party to raise "any issue giving rise to a difficulty"[219] under Article 89(2) of the Agreement.[220]

The EEA Council may only act unanimously, though the Agreement seeks to adapt unanimity requirements to the needs of a "twin-pillar" construction. According to this construction, the Union is the one pillar and the EFTA states the other. Thus Article 90(2) of the Agreement provides that decisions of the EEA Council shall be taken by agreement between the Union, on the one hand, and the EFTA states, on the other. The Union's position in the EEA Council is to be adopted by the Council of the Union.[221] Likewise, when taking decisions, EFTA Ministers are to "speak with one voice".[222]

The EEA Council is responsible for laying down general guidelines and giving the political impetus in the implementation of the Agreement.[223] No formal power to take decisions is conferred on this Council. In this sense, therefore, it has more in common with the European Council than with the Council of the Union.

---

[212] OJ 1994 L1/3.   [213] Art. 90(1) EEA.   [214] Art. 92 EEA.   [215] Art. 91(1) EEA.

[216] Dec. 1/94 (OJ 1994 L138/39) adopting the Rules of Procedure of the EEA Council.

[217] Art. 91(2) EEA.   [218] OJ 1994 L138/39.

[219] Cf. Art. 5 EEA, which refers to a "matter of concern", and Art. 92(2) EEA, which refers to "any point of relevance to the Agreement giving rise to a difficulty".

[220] Agreed Minute *ad* Art. 91(2) EEA. See now Art. 1(2) of Dec. 1/94 (OJ 1994 L138/39).

[221] Art. 2 of Reg. 2894/94 (OJ 1994 L305/6) concerning arrangements for implementing the EEA Agreement.

[222] Art. 4 of the Rules of Procedure (OJ 1994 L138/39). The official Swedish position was that EFTA states would decide *"gemensamt"*. This expression is reminiscent of that of "common accord" in Art. 158(2) EC.

[223] Art. 89(1) EEA.

EEA Joint Committee

The Presidency of the EEA Joint Committee shall be held alternately, for six months, by the "representative of the Community", that is, the Commission, and the representative of one of the EFTA states.[224] The Committee has adopted its Rules of Procedure under Article 92(3) of the EEA Agreement.[225]

The EEA Joint Committee shall meet, in principle, at least once a month.[226] It shall also meet on the initiative of its President or at the request of one of the Parties according to its Rules of Procedure. That frequent meetings are envisaged for the EEA Joint Committee may be expected to contribute to securing for this Committee an active role in relations between the Parties.

The Joint Committee may only act unanimously, though the EEA Agreement seeks to adapt unanimity requirements to the needs of the twin-pillar construction. Thus Article 93(2) provides that the Committee shall take decisions by agreement between the Union, on the one hand, and the EFTA states "speaking with one voice" on the other. The apparent consequence is that while EFTA states may agree to veto EEA decisions, individual EFTA states will lack an "opting-out" right.

The Committee is to be responsible for the implementation and operation of the Agreement.[227] In particular, according to Article 92(1), the Committee shall take decisions in the cases provided for in this Agreement.[228]

In practice, the Commission alone states the Union position in the Committee where a simple extension of a Union act to the EEA is envisaged. The Commission also does so where it is responsible for adopting the Union act in question.[229] Where more than technical changes to the act are involved and in cases other than those where a simple extension of an act is involved, the Union position in the Committee is to be established by the Council of the Union. The Council is to establish this position according to the procedures laid down in the corresponding Treaty provisions.[230] In other words, the Union position is to be determined in advance. Possibilities of the modification of this position in the Committee may be expected, in practice, to be limited.

---

[224] Art. 94(1) EEA.
[225] Dec. 1/94 (OJ 1994 L85/60) adopting the rules of procedure of the EEA Joint Committee.
[226] Art. 94(2) EEA.   [227] Art. 92(1) EEA.
[228] See, e.g., Arts. 61(3)(d), 82(1)(b) and (c), 83, 86, and 102(1) and (5) EEA.
[229] Art. 1(2) of Reg. 2894/94 (OJ 1994 L305/6).
[230] *Ibid.*, Art. 1(3).

5

European Courts

The European Court of Justice is included among the institutions listed in Article 4 of the EC Treaty. According to Article 4, these institutions are to carry out the tasks outlined in the Treaty. In effect, the Court is called upon to collaborate in the integration process. On the other hand, according to Article 164, the Court is to ensure that in the interpretation and application of this Treaty the law is observed. "The law" includes not only provisions of the Treaties and implementing legislation. It also includes general principles which "contribute to forming that philosophical, political and legal substratum common to the Member States from which through the case law an unwritten Community law emerges".[1]

It may be imagined that some contradictions can arise between the duty in Article 4 and that of doing justice in individual cases. The latter duty may not only be regarded as inherent in the judicial function. It is also implicit in Article 164. In reality, however, Article 4 may simply entail that the Court of Justice should take account of the underlying values particular to the legal system within which it operates. Courts in any legal system are likely to do the same.

5.1 Composition

There are two European Courts: the Court of Justice and the Court of First Instance. Different rules govern the composition of each.

5.1.1 Court of Justice

The EEC Treaty originally provided for a Court of Justice composed of seven judges and two Advocates General. As a result of successive enlargements of the Union, there are now fifteen judges.[2] There will also be nine Advocates General until 6 October 2000, and eight thereafter.[3]

---

[1] Dutheillet de Lamothe AG in Case 11/70 *Internationale Handelsgesellschaft* v. *Einfuhr- und Vorratsstelle für Getreide* [1970] ECR 1125, 1146.

[2] Art. 165 EC.   [3] Art. 166 EC.

Conditions for Appointment

Judges and Advocates General, that is, members of the Court, are to be chosen from persons whose independence is beyond doubt. They must possess the qualifications required for appointment to the highest judicial offices in their respective countries or be jurisconsults of recognised competence. There is no requirement that a member of the Court possess the nationality of a Member State or have previously held judicial office. In practice, there is a judge having the nationality of each Member State. Moreover, the "big four" and Spain each nominate an Advocate General. The other Advocates General are nominated by smaller Member States according to a system of rotation. Appointment is made by common accord[4] of the Member States.[5]

Independence

While holding office, a member of the Court may not occupy any political or administrative office or engage in any other occupation, whether gainful or not, without the permission of the Council. A member may only be deprived of his office, pension, or other benefits by a unanimous decision of the Court (including the Advocates General), if he no longer fulfils the requisite conditions or no longer meets the obligations arising from his office. Moreover, members enjoy immunity from legal proceedings. They continue to enjoy immunity after ceasing to hold office in respect of acts performed by them in their judicial capacity, including words spoken or written. This immunity may be waived, but only by the Court sitting in plenary session.[6]

However, the normal term of appointment is only six years,[7] with the possibility of renewal for a further term or terms. The implication is that a member of the Court wishing to retain his membership for more than six years may need to avoid offending his national government.

5.1.2 Court of First Instance

Article 168a of the EEC Treaty, introduced by the Single European Act,[8] provided for the creation by the Council of a Court of First Instance, to be attached to the Court of Justice. This provision was implemented by Decision 88/591,[9] in order to reduce the time taken to produce judgments and to improve fact-finding procedures. It has now been replaced by Article 168a of the EC Treaty.

The Court of First Instance has fifteen members.[10] They must be persons whose independence is beyond doubt and must possess the ability required for appointment to judicial office. They are appointed by common accord of

---

[4] See, sect. 2.1.1 above, regarding the meaning of "common accord".
[5] Art. 167 EC.   [6] Art. 3 of the Protocol on the Statute of the ECJ.   [7] *Ibid.*
[8] OJ 1987 L169/1.   [9] Establishing a CFI (OJ 1988 L319/1).
[10] Art. 10 of Dec. 95/1 (OJ 1995 L1/1) adjusting the instruments concerning the accession of new Member States to the EU.

the governments of the Member States every six years. The membership is partly renewed every three years, though retiring members are eligible for reappointment.[11] While this Court does not have Advocates General as such, any member may be called upon to perform the tasks of an Advocate General in any particular case.

5.2 Organisation

Certain rules governing the organisation of the European Courts are contained in the EC Treaty and the Protocol on the Statute of the Court of Justice. Others are contained in rules of procedure adopted by the European Courts themselves.

5.2.1 Chambers

Article 165 of the EC Treaty provides that the Court of Justice is to sit in plenary session, but it may form chambers of three or five judges.[12] A chamber may undertake certain preparatory inquiries or adjudicate on particular classes of cases according to rules laid down for these purposes. A case is assigned to a plenary session or to a chamber by the President. A Member State or a Union institution which is a party to the proceedings may insist on the case going before a plenary session.

5.2.2 Presidents

The President of the Court of Justice is elected by the judges for a renewable term of three years.[13] The President presides at hearings and deliberations of the Court[14] and fixes the dates of sittings.[15] He is also normally responsible for hearing applications for interim measures.[16]

Each chamber also elects its own president. The latter exercises the functions of the President of the Court in cases assigned to his chamber. The President appoints a *juge-rapporteur* for each case, who takes the lead in the deliberations.

5.2.3 Registrar

The Registrar is appointed by the Court of Justice.[17] He is responsible for the registrary. Thus he is responsible for seeing that the file in each case is

---

[11] Art. 168a(3) EC.
[12] See also Art. 95(1) of the Rules of Procedure of the ECJ (OJ 1991 L176/7).
[13] Art. 167(5) EC.   [14] Art. 8 of the Rules of Procedure of the ECJ (OJ 1991 L176/7).
[15] *Ibid.*, Art. 25.   [16] Art. 36 of the Protocol on the Statute of the ECJ.
[17] Art. 12(1) of the Rules of Procedure of the ECJ (OJ 1991 L176/7).

properly maintained. He is also responsible for effecting service of writs and other documents on parties to the case, on the Member States, and on the other Union institutions. He or an assistant acts as clerk at sittings of the Court.[18] He is responsible under the authority of the President for the general administration of the Court.

5.2.4 Cabinets

Each member of the Court of Justice has his own *cabinet*. The staff of a *cabinet* includes two or three *référendaires*. The latter are legal assistants whose functions include general administration and provision of legal advice and assistance to the member by way of preliminary drafting of reports, judgments, or opinions.

5.2.5 Majority Decision-Making

The Court of Justice may reach its decisions by a simple majority.[19] In contrast to the Anglo-American system, there is no procedure for the delivery of dissenting judgments. The absence of such a procedure may have originated in concern that judgments of the Court of Justice would have had less weight, if the Court had appeared less than united. More particularly, it may have been thought that collegiality of decision-making would protect the independence of individual judges.

On the other hand, the absence of such a procedure may partly explain the tendency for judgments of the Court to give the impression of being compromises. It may also partly explain why the wording of the judgments often makes them difficult to interpret.

5.2.6 Precedent

The Court of Justice does not recognise a strict doctrine of precedents of the common-law type. Accordingly, the Court may feel able expressly to depart from previous rulings.[20] In general, however, the Court follows previous rulings. Indeed, the Court may sometimes reproduce *verbatim* passages from earlier rulings. It may also formally cite its previous rulings.

5.2.7 Advocates General

Impediments to the development of case law entailed by the absence of dissenting opinions may, to some extent, be offset by the work of the Advocates General. According to Article 166 of the EC Treaty, it is their duty,

---

[18] See, regarding the languages used, *ibid.*, Art. 29.
[19] *Ibid.*, Art. 27(5).
[20] See, e.g., Joined Cases C–267 & 268/91 *Bernard Keck and Daniel Mithouard* [1993] ECR I–6097.

acting with complete impartiality and independence, to make reasoned submissions on cases brought before the Court of Justice, in order to assist the latter in fulfilling its task under the Treaty. These submissions, known as opinions, are usually much longer than the judgment itself. They may offer a detailed interpretation of the law, particularly the case law, relevant to the issues before the Court.

The opinions are not binding on the Court itself. However, judgments may refer with approval to them.

5.2.8 Court of First Instance

The Court of First Instance normally sits in Chambers of three or five judges.[21] However, in cases where the legal difficulty or the factual complexity of the case so requires, it may sit in plenary session.[22] When it does so, it must be assisted by an Advocate General.[23] It has its own Registrar and Rules of Procedure.[24]

5.3 Jurisdiction

The function of the Court of Justice, according to Article 164 of the EC Treaty, is to ensure that in the interpretation and application of this Treaty the law is observed. The expression "the law" may be an inadequate English translation of expressions found in other language versions of the Treaty. If nothing more than written law were meant, then the language of Article 164 would seem tautologous. Moreover, Article 215(2), regarding the non-contractual liability of the European Community, refers to general principles of law. This reference indicates that the law to be upheld by the Court is not solely written but also unwritten. Accordingly, the French version of Article 164 requires the Court to ensure observance of *droit* rather than *loi*. Similarly, the German version requires the Court to ensure observance of *recht* rather than *gesetz*. In other words, the Court is to "do justice" in cases brought before it. Thus, for example, the Court applies various principles, such as unjust enrichment,[25] and protects fundamental rights,[26] notably those enshrined in the European Convention on Human Rights.[27]

More particularly, in relation to the other Union institutions, the Court is to uphold the "rule of law" enshrined in Article 4 of the Treaty. According to

---

[21] Art. 10 of the Rules of Procedure of the CFI (OJ 1991 L136/1).   [22] *Ibid.*, Art. 14.

[23] *Ibid.*, Art. 17.   [24] *Ibid.*

[25] Joined Cases C–192–218/95 *Société Comateb* v. *Directeur Général des Douanes et Droits Indirects* [1997] ECR I–165.

[26] Case 4/73 *J. Nold, Kohlen-und Baustoffgroßhandlung* v. *EC Commission* [1974] ECR 491, 507.

[27] Case C–260/89 *Elliniki Radiophonia Tileorassi AE* v. *Dimitoki Etairia Pliroforissis and Sotirios Kouvelas* [1991] ECR I–2925, I–2963–4.

this provision, each Union institution is to act within the limits of the powers conferred upon it by the Treaty. Thus the Court has jurisdiction to ensure that these institutions do not act or fail to act in breach of Union law.[28] It also has jurisdiction to order compensation in favour of individuals whose interests are adversely and unlawfully affected by the Union institutions.[29] More particularly, Article 172 provides for unlimited jurisdiction to be conferred on the Court in relation to penalties imposed pursuant to a Council regulation, such as Regulation 17.[30] At the same time, it has jurisdiction in relation to complaints that Member States are failing to respect Union law and in relation to preliminary rulings requested by national courts.[31]

The jurisdiction of the Court extends to disputes concerning the European Investment Bank, national central banks, and the European Central Bank[32] and to disputes between the Union and its servants.[33]

Suspensory orders may be made by the Court under Article 185. Interim measures may be prescribed under Article 186.

According to Article 219, the Member States undertake not to submit a dispute concerning the interpretation or application of the Treaty to any method of settlement other than those provided for therein. Moreover, under Article 182 disputes between Member States related to the subject matter of the Treaty may be submitted to the Court under a special agreement between the parties.

In addition, jurisdiction may be conferred on the Court by conventions. For example, the Court has jurisdiction under the Protocol on the Interpretation by the Court of Justice[34] of the Convention on Jurisdiction and the Enforcement of Judgments in Civil and Commercial Matters.[35] Similarly, it has jurisdiction under the Protocol on the Interpretation by the Court of Justice[36] of the Convention on the Mutual Recognition of Companies and Legal Persons.[37]

In exercising its jurisdiction, the Court must act according to the provisions of the particular Treaty relevant to the matter before it.[38] Hence, jurisdiction may vary according to whether the matter falls under the EC, ECSC, or Euratom Treaty. However, if the matter is one affecting all three Treaties, it is sufficient that the Court has jurisdiction under one of them.[39]

---

[28] This jurisdiction may go beyond that specifically conferred by the Treaties. See Case C-2/88 *J.J. Zwartveld* [1990] ECR I-3365, I-3372-3.

[29] Sects. 5.3.1–3.

[30] First Regulation implementing Arts. 85 and 86 EEC (JO 1962 204), Art. 17. See also Art. 24 of Reg. 1017/68 (JO 1968 L175/1) applying rules of competition to transport by rail, road, and inland waterway; and Art. 20 of Reg. 4064/89 (OJ 1989 L395/1, as corrected by OJ 1990 L257/13) on the control of concentrations between undertakings.

[31] Sects 5.3.4–5.   [32] Art. 180 EC.   [33] Art. 179 EC.   [34] OJ 1978 L304/36.

[35] OJ 1978 L304/97.   [36] Bull. EC, Supp. 4/71.   [37] Bull. EC, Supp. 2/69.

[38] Arts. 3 and 4 of the Convention on Certain Institutions Common to the European Communities.

[39] Case 230/81 *Luxembourg* v. *European Parliament: seat and working place of the European Parliament* [1983] ECR 255, 282–3.

5.3.1 Annulment Proceedings

According to Article 173 of the EC Treaty,[40] the Court of Justice may review the legality of acts adopted jointly by the European Parliament and the Council,[41] acts of the Council, acts of the Commission, and acts of the European Central Bank other than recommendations or opinions as well as acts of the Parliament intended to produce legal effects *vis-à-vis* third parties.[42]

Such acts are those which affect the interests of an applicant by bringing about a distinct change in his legal position.[43] The form of the act is immaterial.[44] Sometimes an act is arrived at by a procedure which involves several stages. It is the final stage, whereby the position of the institution is definitively laid down, which must be reviewed rather than the preliminary stages leading thereto.[45]

Such review is to be exercised on grounds taken from the case law of the French *Conseil d'Etat.*[46] They comprise: lack of competence (*incompétence*), infringement of an essential procedural requirement (*vice de forme*), infringement of the Treaty or of any rule of law relating to its application (*violation de loi*), and misuse of powers (*détournement de pouvoir*). The review takes place on the basis of the facts and the law as they stood at the time when the act was adopted.[47]

Locus Standi

Proceedings may be brought by a Member State, the Council, or Commission. They may also be brought by the European Parliament, the Court of Auditors, or the European Central Bank to protect their prerogatives.[48] In addition, proceedings may be brought by private persons. However, such persons must proceed before the Court of First Instance and must satisfy special *locus standi* requirements.

An individual has standing to challenge the legality of a decision addressed to him. He also has standing to challenge an act which, although in the form

---

[40] Cf. Arts. 33 and 38 ECSC.

[41] I.e. acts adopted under Art. 189b EC.

[42] Case 22/70 *EC Commission* v. *EC Council: ERTA* [1971] ECR 263, 277.

[43] Case 60/81 *International Business Machines Corporation* v. *EC Commission* [1981] ECR 2639, 2651; and Case T–541/93 *James Connaughton* v. *EU Council* [1997] ECR II–549, II–559.

[44] Case 22/70 *EC Commission* v. *EC Council: ERTA* [1971] ECR 263, 277.

[45] Case 60/81 *International Business Machines Corporation* v. *EC Commission* [1981] ECR 2639, 2652.

[46] The Council of State (i.e. the supreme administrative court).

[47] Case T–115/94 *Opel Austria GmbH* v. *EC Commission* [1997] ECR II–39, II–69.

[48] Under Art. 173 EEC the Parliament had implied standing to bring such proceedings to protect its prerogatives. See Case C–70/88 *European Parliament* v. *EC Council: Chernobyl* [1991] ECR I–2041. It had no general standing to bring such proceedings. See Case 302/87 *European Parliament: capacity of the Parliament to bring an action for annulment* v. *EC Council* [1988] ECR 5615.

of a regulation or decision[49] addressed to another person, is of direct and individual concern to him.[50]

To be of direct concern to an individual, a measure must have an immediate effect on his legal position. An act may leave the national authorities such a margin of discretion regarding the manner of its implementation that this condition is not met.[51] However, an act may be of direct concern to an individual, if at the time the act was taken it was known that the discretion would certainly be exercised against him[52] or the possibility that it would not be so exercised was purely theoretical.[53] For example, a Commission decision reducing aid from the European Social Fund,[54] though addressed to a Member State, is of direct concern to the recipient. It is of direct concern to the recipient, because it deprives him of part of the aid originally granted to him, the Member State not having any discretion of its own in that respect.[55]

The requirement of individual concern means that proceedings will only be admissible against an act not addressed to the applicant where the act affects him by reason of certain attributes peculiar to him or by reason of circumstances differentiating him from all other persons and distinguishing him individually just as in the case of the person addressed.[56] The rationale is that the Union institutions should not be able, merely by choosing the form of a regulation, to exclude an application by an individual against an act which concerns him directly and individually.[57] Indeed, it is recognised that an act may be of a legislative nature and, at the same time, *vis-à-vis* some of the persons concerned in the nature of a decision.[58]

An act may be of individual concern to a person where he is specifically mentioned in it;[59] where he is a member of a class which was closed when

---

[49] See sect. 7.1.2 below, regarding the formal classification of regulations and decisions.

[50] "The EC Treaty does not grant individuals the same capacity to act as national law" (Roemer AG in Joined Cases 10 & 18/68 *Società "Eridania" Zuccherifici Nazionali* v. *EC Commission* [1969] ECR 459, 493).

[51] Case 69/69 *SA Alcan Aluminium Raeren* v. *EC Commission* [1970] ECR 385; and Case C–181/90 *Consorgan* v. *EC Commission* [1992] ECR I–3557, I–3568.

[52] Joined Cases 106 & 107/63 *Alfred Toepfer and Getreide-Import Gesellschaft* v. *EEC Commission* [1965] ECR 405, 411; and Case 62/70 *Werner A. Bock* v. *EC Commission* [1971] ECR 897, 908.

[53] Case T–380/94 *Association Internationale des Utilisateurs de Fils de Filaments Artificiels et Synthétiques et de Soie Naturelle and Apparel, Knitting and Textiles Alliance* v. *EC Commission* [1996] ECR II–2169, II–2187.

[54] Sect. 20.5 below.

[55] Case T–85/94 *EC Commission* v. *Eugenio Branca* [1995] ECR II–45, II–55.

[56] Case 25/62 *Plaumann* v. *EEC Commission* [1963] ECR 95, 107; and Joined Cases T–447–449/93 *Associazione Italiana Tecnico Economica del Cemento* v. *EC Commission* [1995] ECR II–1971, II–1988.

[57] Joined Cases 789 & 790/79 *Calpak SA and Società Emiliana Lavorazione Frutta SpA* v. *EC Commission* [1980] ECR 1949, 1961.

[58] Joined Cases T–481 & 484/93 *Vereiniging van Exporteurs in Levande Varkens* v. *EC Commission* [1995] ECR II–2941, II–2961; and Case T–60/96 *Merck & Co. Inc. NV Organon, Glaxo Wellcome* v. *EC Commission* (3 June 1997).

[59] Case 113/77 *NTN Toyo Bearing Co. Ltd* v. *EC Commission* [1979] ECR 1185, 1205; and Case 138/79 *Roquette Frères SA* v. *EC Council* [1980] ECR 3333, 3356.

the act was adopted;[60] or where he is a member of a limited class of traders identified by the act or identifiable by the Commission and particularly affected by the act.[61] Thus, for example, in the agricultural field a regulation prohibiting the implementation of contracts of sale already concluded between a national intervention agency and certain traders may be of individual concern to those traders.[62]

In the fields of competition law and anti-dumping law Commission procedures may have particular relevance to questions of standing. Where the Commission carries out an inquiry prior to adopting an act in these fields, a person whose original complaint to the Commission led to the holding of the inquiry, who has participated in the conduct of the inquiry, and whose commercial position is affected by its outcome, may be individually concerned.[63] That is particularly so where Union law lays down, in regard to the conduct of the inquiry, express provisions intended to safeguard the interests of complainants.[64]

Competitors of the addressee of an act may challenge its legality, where their market position has been "significantly affected" by the act.[65] However, the mere fact that an act may affect the competitive relationships existing on the market in question cannot suffice to allow any trader in any competitive relationship whatever with the addressee to be regarded as directly and individually concerned by that act. Only the existence of specific circumstances gives standing under Article 173.[66] Thus a competitor must be concerned in a particular manner,[67] as for example where he is in the same region as the addressee.[68] Account may be taken of such factors as the number of competitors in the market concerned[69] and whether the competitor has participated in the proceedings leading to the adoption of the contested decision.[70]

A competitor may more easily fulfil *locus standi* requirements under Article 33 of the ECSC Treaty. According to this provision, undertakings may

---

[60] Joined Cases 106 & 107/63 *Alfred Toepfer and Getreide-Import Gesellschaft* v. *EEC Commission* [1965] ECR 405, 411.

[61] Case 11/82 AE *Piraiki-Patraiki* v. *EC Commission* [1985] ECR 207, 246.

[62] Case 232/81 *Agricola Commerciale Olio srl* v. *EC Commission* [1984] ECR 3881, 3895–6.

[63] Case 264/82 *Timex Corporation* v. *EC Council and EC Commission* [1985] ECR 849, 865–6.

[64] Case 26/76 *Metro SB-Großmärkte GmbH & Co. KG* v. *EC Commission* [1977] ECR 1875, 1901; and Case 210/81 *Demo-Studio Schmidt* v. *EC Commission* [1983] ECR 3045, 3063.

[65] Cf. Case 169/84 *Cie Française de l'Azote (COFAZ) SA* v. *EC Commission* [1986] ECR 391, 415; and Joined Cases T–447–449/93 *Associazione Italiana Tecnico Economica del Cemento* v. *EC Commission* [1995] ECR II–1971, II–1994–6 and II–2002.

[66] Joined Cases 10 & 18/68 *Società "Eridania" Zuccherifici Nazionali* v. *EC Commission* [1969] ECR 459, 481.

[67] Roemer AG (*ibid.*, 491).   [68] *Ibid.*, 492.

[69] Case T–435/93 *Association of Sorbitol Producers in the EC (ASPEC)* v. *EC Commission* [1995] ECR II–1281, II–1309.

[70] Submission of the Commission in Joined Cases 10 & 18/68 *Società "Eridania" Zuccherifici Nazionali* v. *EC Commission* [1969] ECR 459, 473.

challenge "decisions . . . concerning them which are individual in character". Hence, an undertaking may challenge an act which entails benefits for one or more undertakings in competition with it.[71] Undertakings may also challenge general decisions which they consider to involve a misuse of powers affecting them.

Trade associations may, given the "valuable role" they may play in administrative procedures, also be entitled to bring proceedings under Article 173 of the EC Treaty. It is recognised, for example, that they may be in a better position than their individual members to put the sector's case to the Commission.[72] However, trade associations must have a "personal" interest in bringing proceedings.[73] Thus the interests of the association must be shown to be distinct from the interests of the industrial policy of the Member State concerned.[74] Moreover, an association cannot be considered to be individually concerned by an act that has consequences affecting the general interests of the category of persons it represents.[75] Hence, an association is only entitled to bring an action for annulment where its members may also bring an action individually.[76] Such thinking may be appropriate in the case of trade associations representing the market interests of their members. If the latter interests are not affected, it may be argued that the association itself is not affected.

However, the underlying thinking is problematic. According to the case law, for example, a distinction may be made between a decision declaring state aid compatible with the common market and a decision declaring it incompatible. Persons who consider themselves adversely affected by a decision of the former type are fully entitled to judicial protection, because the EC Treaty guarantees them protection against aid which distorts competition. It is not so with persons complaining of a decision of the latter type, because the Treaty does not guarantee, but at most tolerates, state aid. In other words, the aid has its source not in the Treaty but in the will of the Member State concerned. Where the Commission decides that it is unlawful, the Member

---

[71] Joined Cases 24 & 34/58 *Chambre Syndicale de la Sidérurgie de l'Est de la France* v. *ECSC High Authority* [1960] ECR 281, 292; and Joined Cases 172 & 226/83 *Hoogovens Groep BV* v. *EC Commission* [1985] ECR 2831, 2847.

[72] Slynn AG in Joined Cases 67, 68 & 70/85 *Kwekereij Gebroeders van der Kooy* [1988] ECR 219, 246. Cf. the view of the EFTA Court in Case E–2/94 *Scottish Salmon Growers Association Ltd* v. *ESA* [1995] 1 CMLR 851, 862.

[73] Roemer AG in Joined Cases 10 & 18/68 *Società "Eridania" Zuccherifici Nazionali* v. *EC Commission* [1969] ECR 459, 493.

[74] Case 282/85 *Comité de Développement et de Promotion du Textile et de l'Habillement* v. *EC Commission* [1986] ECR 2469, 2481.

[75] Joined Cases 16 & 17/62 *Confédération Nationale des Producteurs de Fruits et Légumes* v. *EEC Council* [1962] ECR 471, 479–80; and Case T–117/94 *Associazione Agricoltori della Provincia di Rovigo* v. *EC Commission* [1995] ECR II–455, II–466.

[76] Case T–585/93 *Stichting Greenpeace Council (Greenpeace International)* v. *EC Commission* [1995] ECR II-2205, II-2230-1; and Case T-197/95 *Sveriges Betodlares Centralförening and Sven Åke Henrikson* v. *EC Commission* [1996] ECR II–1283, II–1296.

State may or may not challenge the decision. If it brings a challenge, the interests of the recipients are indirectly protected by this challenge. If the Member State does not bring a challenge, either because it considers the decision well founded or because its policy has changed, no one can remedy its *"volonté défaillante"* (lack of will). Such thinking concentrates on the right to free competition. It does not recognise the possibility that a right to aid, particularly from the Union, may derive from the establishment of economic and social cohesion as a Union objective.[77] In short, market-based conceptions may imply limitations to recognition of *locus standi*,[78] which may be difficult to reconcile with the more general evolution of Union law.[79]

The significance of these limitations was exemplified in *Stichting Greenpeace Council (Greenpeace International)* v. *EC Commission*.[80] Here the grant of aid from the European Regional Development Fund[81] for the building of two power-stations in the Canary Islands was challenged on environmental grounds. The Court of First Instance was urged by the challengers to go beyond consideration of "purely economic interests" in determining question of standing.[82] According to the Court, however, by limiting *locus standi* to those whose competitive position was significantly affected by Union aid, the case law merely sought, in accordance with Article 173, to limit standing to those who were individually concerned by the contested act. The applicant had to be affected in a manner which differentiated him from all other persons.[83] Thus it was not enough to be a resident, fisherman, farmer, or tourist in a region where Union aid assisted the construction of a power-station to have standing to challenge the grant of aid on environmental grounds.[84]

Such thinking may be particularly problematic for interest groups other than trade associations. In the same case Greenpeace was found to have no standing, because the interests of its members were not individually affected.[85] However, the credibility and campaigning capacity of Greenpeace may be adversely affected by the denial of standing in such cases. Nor was it enough for Greenpeace to have complained to the Commission about the grant of aid. It was not enough, because the legislation governing the Structural Funds did not provide specific procedures for associating such bodies with decisions granting aid from the European Regional Development Fund.[86] Apparently, therefore, limitations to judicial intervention are thought to be justified by perceived limitations to the relevant Union legislation.

---

[77] Art. B TEU and Art. 2 EC.
[78] Cf. Lenz AG in Case C–309/89 *Cordoniu SA* v. *EU Council* [1994] ECR I–1853, I–1868, regarding the criterion of "economic repercussions".
[79] But cf. sect. 7.3 below, regarding damages before national courts.
[80] Case T–585/93 [1995] ECR II–2205.   [81] Sect. 20.1 below.
[82] [1995] ECR II–2205, II–2220.   [83] *Ibid.*, II–2227.   [84] *Ibid.*, II–2229.
[85] But cf. Lenz AG in Case 297/86 *Confederazione Italiana Dirigenti di Azienda (CIDA)* v. *EC Council* [1988] ECR 3531, 3543.
[86] [1995] ECR II–2205, II–2229

Similar problems may arise for regional institutions. Cohesion implies that the relationship between regions is to be based on more than the market alone.[87] The implication is that standing should derive for regional representatives from the possibility that the aid may significantly affect their cohesion prospects. Aid for building a power-station may affect such prospects through damaging tourism and fishing.[88]

The Court of Justice has not ruled out the possibility that a decision addressed to a Member State may leave the latter with so little discretion, that it may be of direct concern to regional institutions affected by it.[89] However, a wide circle of persons in the region, including employers, customers, suppliers, and businessmen, may also be affected. Hence, the decision may not easily be regarded as of individual concern to a regional institution.[90]

The argument has also been made that a regional institution would have standing to challenge a measure affecting its prerogatives.[91] However, the Court of Justice apparently infers from cohesion requirements no need to discourage centralisation within Member States. For example, according to the Court, "the Member State is the sole interlocutor of the [European Social] Fund"[92] or at least has a "central role" in the operations of this Fund.[93] Therefore, while regional institutions may have a vital role to play in the articulation of cohesion requirements, the European Courts are uncertain about securing such a role for them in judicial proceedings.

Opportunities to intervene in proceedings before the European Courts[94] may be more generally available to such persons as consumer groups,[95] trades unions,[96] and regional authorities.[97] They only have to establish an interest in the result of the proceedings. However, they cannot intervene in cases between Union institutions and Member States. Moreover, an intervener must accept the case as he finds it at the time of his intervention.[98]

---

[87] Cohesion is not defined in the EC Treaty, though under Art. 130a it includes the reduction of regional disparities.

[88] Note the link made between environmental policy and regional policy in Art. 130r(3) EC.

[89] Cf. Case 222/83 *Municipality of Differdange* v. *EC Commission* [1984] ECR 2889.

[90] Lenz AG (*ibid.*, 2905).

[91] M. Vellano, "Coesione economica e sociale e ripartizione di competenze: le nuove iniziative comunitarie" [1995] *RDE* 193–208, 194.

[92] Case C–291/89 *Interhotel* v. *EC Commission* [1991] ECR I–2257, I–2280. Cf., earlier, Case 310/81 *Ente Italiano di Servizio Sociale* v. *EC Commission* [1984] ECR 1341, 1353.

[93] Case C–304/89 *Establecimentos Isodoro M. Oliveira SA* v. *EC Commission* [1991] ECR I–2283, I–2313.

[94] See, generally, Joined Cases C–151 & 157/97P(I) *National Power plc and PowerGen plc* (17 June 1997).

[95] Joined Cases 41, 43–48, 50, 111, 113 & 114/73 *Société Anonyme Générale Sucrerie* v. *EC Commission* [1973] ECR 1465.

[96] Case 22/74 *Union Syndicale* v. *EC Council* [1975] ECR 401, 410.

[97] Case T–194/95Intv I *Area Cova SA* [1996] ECR II–591.

[98] Art. 93(4) of the Rules of Procedure of the ECJ (OJ 1991 L176/7).

Consequently, he may be precluded from raising arguments of specific relevance to his interests.

Substantive Illegality

Union acts may be annulled on three substantive grounds. First, they may be annulled on grounds of lack of competence.[99] For example, Commission departments are only competent to exercise delegated powers, in the name of the Commission and, subject to its control, to take clearly defined measures of management or administration. If they adopt a decision which goes beyond such limits, the decision may be annulled for lack of competence.[100]

Secondly, Union acts may be annulled for infringement of the Treaty or of any rule of law relating to its application. Such rules include general principles of law. Thus decisions may be annulled for breach of the principles of proportionality,[101] *non bis in idem*,[102] non-retroactivity of penal measures,[103] the prohibition of *reformatio in pejus*,[104] equality of treatment,[105] legitimate expectations,[106] and legal certainty.[107] In the application of these principles fundamental rights may be safeguarded.[108]

In the case of the grant of Union aid, for example, the rationale for application of the principle of legal certainty is that foreseeability as to the payment of aid is necessary to enable the recipients to commit themselves to expenditure free of the risk of ultimately having themselves to bear the burden of it.[109] Consistently with this rationale, the principle may be more demanding where expenditure has been incurred than when only an aid application has been made.[110] By the same token, the principle does not apply in the case of unapproved expenditure or expenditure above the amount approved by the Union institutions.[111]

[99] Case 9/56 *Meroni & Co., Industrie Metallurgiche, SpA* v. *ECSC High Authority* [1957–8] ECR 133, 151; and Case C–327/91 *France* v. *EC Commission: EC–US competition law agreement* [1994] ECR I–3641, I–3675–8. See also, in connection with Dec. 85/381 (OJ 1985 L217/25), sect. 21.4.1 below.

[100] Case T–450/93 *Lisrestal–Organizacaõ Gestaõ de Restaurantes Colectivos Lda* v. *EC Commission* [1994] ECR II–1177, II–1191–2.

[101] Case 62/70 *Werner A. Bock* v. *EC Commission* [1971] ECR 897.

[102] Joined Cases 18 & 35/65 *Max Gutmann* v. *EAEC Commission* [1966] ECR 103, 119.

[103] Case 63/83 *R.* v. *Kent Kirk* [1984] ECR 2689, 2718.

[104] Case T–73/95 *Isodoro M. Oliveira SA* v. *EC Commission* [1997] ECR II–381.

[105] Joined Cases 103 & 145/77 *Royal Scholten-Honig (Holdings) Ltd* v. *Intervention Board for Agricultural Produce* [1978] ECR 2037, 2072-3. See also Capotorti AG in Case 107/80 *Giacomo Cattaneo Adorno* v. *EC Commission* [1981] ECR 1469, 1497–8.

[106] Case 120/86 *J. Mulder* v. *Minister van Landbouw en Visserij* [1988] ECR 2321.

[107] Case 15/85 *Consorzio Cooperative d'Abruzzo* v. *EC Commission* [1987] ECR 1005, 1037; and Case T–478/93 *Wafer Zoo Srl* v. *EC Commission* [1995] ECR II–1479, II–1497.

[108] Case 63/83 *R.* v. *Kent Kirk* [1984] ECR 2689, 2718.

[109] Darmon AG in Case C–157/90 *Infortec Projectos & Consultadoria, Lda* v. *EC Commission* [1992] ECR I–3525, I–3354. See, earlier, Case C–291/89 *Interhotel* v. *EC Commission* [1991] ECR I–2257, I–2267.

[110] Case 44/81 *Germany* v. *EC Commission: deadline for claiming payment of ESF aid* [1982] ECR 1855, 1877.

[111] Darmon AG in Case C–304/89 *Isodoro M. Oliveira SA* v. *EC Commission* [1991] ECR I–2283, I–2298.

However, in the case of a decision withdrawing unlawfully granted aid, the requirements of the principle of legality and the principle of legal certainty may be contradictory.[112] In particular, the former principle may have priority over the latter, where the equality principle would otherwise be violated.[113] In other words, there may be conflict between the "public interest in legality and the sound management of public funds" and "the private interest" of the aid recipient.[114]

More generally, judicial review must be circumspect where the exercise of sovereign power in respect of economic policy is questioned; where the Commission is judging economic circumstances of fact which also involve elements of economic and structural policy;[115] or where several Union objectives are relevant and the Commission must make the necessary reconciliation as best it can between the interests entrusted to it. In such circumstances, "considerable, although not unlimited, discretion" is available to the Commission.[116] The same idea is expressed in Article 33 of the ECSC Treaty. It states that the Court may not usually examine the evaluation of the situation, resulting from economic facts or circumstances, in the light of which the Commission took its decision or made its recommendation. The Court may only do so, where the Commission is alleged to have misused its powers or to have manifestly failed to observe the provisions of this Treaty or of any rule relating to its application.

For example, the Commission enjoys discretion in assessing the existence of conditions justifying the grant of Union aid and the "overriding requirements of the proper administration of Community finances".[117] Similarly, the Commission enjoys discretion in determining whether expenditure has been properly incurred by the recipient.[118] Hence, the European Courts cannot undertake a detailed re-examination of an aid application during proceedings before it.[119] Even less is it the function of the Courts to undertake investigations of the kind performed by the Court of Auditors.[120]

---

[112] Mischo AG in Case 15/85 *Consorzio Cooperative d'Abruzzo* v. *EC Commission* [1987] ECR 1005, 1025.

[113] Joined Cases T–551/93 & 231-234/94 *Industrias Pesqueras Campos SA* v. *EC Commission* [1996] ECR II-247, II-293–4.

[114] Submission of the Commission in Case C–200/89 *Funoc* v. *EC Commission* [1990] ECR I–3669, I–3679.

[115] Joined Cases 10 & 18/68 *Società "Eridania" Zuccherifici Nazionali* v. *EC Commission* [1969] ECR 459, 502.

[116] Lagrange AG in Case 13/57 *Wirtschaftsvereinigung Eisen-und Stahlindustrie Gußstahlwerk Carl Bönhoff, Gußstahlwerk Witten, Ruhrstahl, and Eisenwerk Annahütte Alfred Zeller* v. *ECSC High Authority* [1957–8] ECR 265, 301.

[117] Da Cruz Vilaça AG in Case 84/85 *UK* v. *EC Commission: aid for part-time employment* [1987] ECR 3765, 3781.

[118] *Ibid.*, 3797.

[119] Case T–465/93 *Consorzio Gruppo di Azione Locale "Murgia Messapica"* v. *EC Commission* [1994] ECR II–361, II–379; and Case T–109/94 *Windpark Groothusen GmbH & Co. Betriebs KG* v. *EC Commission* [1995] ECR II–3007, II–3026.

[120] Joined Cases T–551/93 & 231–234/94 *Industrias Pesqueras Campos SA* v. *EC Commission* [1996] ECR II–247, II–307. See, regarding the Court of Auditors, sect. 6.3.1 below.

Again, in deciding to authorise state aid under Article 92(3),[121] the Commission may reasonably take account of regional disparities which investment faces and for which aid is designed to compensate.[122] More generally, as a body which supervises compliance with the competition rules and has specialised departments for that purpose, the Commission has many years of experience. For this reason, its findings carry a degree of authority.[123] At the same time, the Commission is responsible for the implementation and orientation of competition policy. The performance of this task necessarily entails complex economic assessments.[124] The European Courts will only question such assessments in extreme cases.[125]

Nevertheless, a Commission assessment may be overturned where there is found to have been an *erreur manifeste d'appréciation* (clear error of assessment). For example, where it is clear from the description of a project proposed in an application for Union aid that the project fits in with the policies adopted to meet Union priorities laid down by the Council, the Commission may commit such an error in refusing to grant Union aid.[126] There may also be such an error, if the information on which the Commission decision has been based is not representative and objective.[127]

For example, in *Cook*[128] a competitor had objected to Spanish aid to a producer of machine parts. The Commission had decided not to proceed against the aid because the industrial sector to which the recipient belonged did not suffer from overcapacity. However, the Court of Justice ruled that the Commission had failed to substantiate its finding that the sector was not in a state of overcapacity. Hence, the decision was annulled for manifest error.[129] Again, a Commission finding that there was no aid contrary to Article 92(1) of the Treaty, based on an overestimation of the cost savings associated with a preferential tariff charged by a publicly controlled supplier of natural gas, has been found to be vitiated by such an error.[130]

A Commission decision may also be annulled because an *erreur de droit* (error of law) renders it contrary to the Treaty. Such an error may be present

---

[121] Sect. 17.3.2 below.

[122] Case C–225/91 *Matra SA* v. *EC Commission* [1993] ECR I–3203, I–3257.

[123] Van Gerven AG in Case C–128/92 *HJ Banks & Co. Ltd* v. *British Coal Corpn* [1994] ECR I–1209, I–1265.

[124] Case C–234/89 *Stergios Delimitis* v. *Heninger Bräu AG* [1991] ECR I–935, I–991.

[125] Case 730/79 *Philip Morris Holland BV* v. *EC Commission* [1980] ECR 2671, 2691. See also VerLoren van Themaat AG in Case 169/84 *Cie Française de l'Azote (COFAZ) SA* v. *EC Commission* [1986] ECR 391, 405.

[126] Case C–213/87 *Gemeente Amsterdam and Stichting Vrouwenvakschool voor Informatica Amsterdam (VIA)* v. *EC Commission* [1990] ECR I–221.

[127] Case C–169/95 *Spain* v. *EC Commission: aid to Teruel* [1997] ECR I–135, I–160.

[128] Case C–198/91 *William Cook PLC* v. *EC Commission* [1993] ECR I–2487.

[129] *Ibid.*, I–2531. See also Case 84/82 *Germany* v. *EC Commission: aid to textiles and clothing* [1984] ECR 1451, 1501, where Slynn AG considered that the Commission had wrongly classified a capital injection by the state as aid.

[130] Case C–169/84 *Société CdF Chimie Azote et Fertilisants* v. *EC Commission* [1990] ECR I–3083.

where, for example, the Commission reaches a decision without examining whether aid distorts competition and affects trade between Member States[131] or on the basis of incorrect facts.[132]

Finally, a decision may be annulled for a misuse of powers.[133] A decision may be annulled on this ground where it appears, on the basis of objective, relevant, and consistent factors, to have been taken with the purpose of achieving ends other than those stated[134] or of evading a procedure specifically prescribed by the Treaty for dealing with the circumstances of the case.[135] It may also be annulled on the same ground where it represents a departure, without reasons being given, from "rules of conduct" by which the Commission considers itself to be bound.[136]

Procedural Illegality

The European Courts may annul Union acts for infringement of an essential procedural requirement. Such an infringement may take the form, for example, of a failure by the Commission to consult an advisory committee[137] or a management committee,[138] to grant a fair hearing, or to give adequate reasons for its decisions. Similarly, it may take the form of a failure by the Council to consult the European Parliament.[139]

The right to a fair hearing has particular importance. According to the European Courts, any person who may be directly concerned and adversely affected by a decision[140] must be placed in a position in which he may effectively make known his views on the evidence against him which the Commission has taken as the basis for the decision at issue.[141] For example, "the Member State is the sole interlocutor of the [European Social] Fund". Therefore, the opportunity for it to comment before a definitive decision to

---

[131] Joined Cases T–447–449/93 *Associazione Italiana Tecnico Economica del Cemento* v. *EC Commission* [1995] ECR II–1971, II–2021–2.

[132] Joined Cases T–244 & 486/93 *TWD Textilwerke Deggendorf GmbH* v. *EC Commission* [1995] ECR II–2265, II–2296.

[133] Case T–109/94 *Windpark Groothusen GmbH & Co. Betriebs KG* v. *EC Commission* [1995] ECR II–3007, II–3026.

[134] Mischo AG in Case 15/85 *Consorzio Cooperative d'Abruzzo* v. *EC Commission* [1987] ECR 1005, 1024–5.

[135] Case C–248/89 *Cargill BV* v. *EC Commission* [1991] ECR I–2987, I–3015; and Case C–156/93 *European Parliament* v. *EC Commission: organic products* [1995] ECR I–2019, I–2050.

[136] Case 15/85 *Consorzio Cooperative d'Abruzzo* v. *EC Commission* [1987] ECR 1005, 1016.

[137] Da Cruz Vilaça AG in Case 84/85 *UK* v. *EC Commission: aid for part-time employment* [1987] ECR 3765, 3788–9.

[138] Mischo AG in Case 15/85 *Consorzio Cooperative d'Abruzzo* v. *EC Commission* [1987] ECR 1005, 1019.

[139] Case 138/79 *Roquette Frères SA* v. *EC Council* [1980] ECR 3333.

[140] Case T–450/93 *Lisrestal–Organizacaõ Gestaõ de Restaurantes Colectivos Lda* v. *EC Commission* [1994] ECR II–1177, II–1194–5; and Case C–32/95P *EC Commission* v. *Lisrestal–Organizacaõ Gestaõ de Restaurantes Colectivos Lda* [1996] ECR I–5373, I–5398.

[141] Case T–450/93 *Lisrestal–Organizacaõ Gestaõ de Restaurantes Colectivos Lda* v. *EC Commission* [1994] ECR II–1177, II–1194.

reduce Fund assistance is adopted constitutes an essential procedural requirement.[142]

A private recipient of Union aid must also be placed in a position in which he can effectively make known his views on the evidence relied on against him to justify a decision reducing aid.[143] However, no hearing is required where an applicant has merely been put on a reserve list of possible aid recipients.[144] Where a hearing is required and the recipient has not been afforded the opportunity to comment on the evidence, the Commission may not use this evidence in a decision. However, for such an infringement of the right to a fair hearing to result in annulment of the decision concerned, it must be established that without that infringement, the decision might have been different.[145]

In the case of applicants for Union aid, they need not be given a hearing during a selection procedure conducted on the basis of the documentation submitted by them. At least where hundreds of applications must be evaluated, the denial of a hearing may be considered reasonable.[146] The Commission also considers that notice, let alone a hearing, is unnecessary in the case of those who have an interest contrary to the grant of aid.[147] On the other hand, arguments based on practical grounds cannot justify infringement of a fundamental principle, such as observance of the rights of defence.[148] If such rights are found to be at stake, it seems that denial of a hearing may be more problematic.

The right to be given reasons for a decision also has particular importance. Article 190 of the EC Treaty requires that regulations, directives, and decisions "state the reasons on which they are based". This requirement is a matter of "public policy".[149] Hence, the European Courts are entitled to review, even of their own motion, the statement of reasons for Commission decisions challenged before them.[150]

---

[142] Case 310/81 *Ente Italiano di Servizio Sociale* v. *EC Commission* [1984] ECR 1341, 1353; and Case C–291/89 *Interhotel* v. *EC Commission* [1991] ECR I–2257, I–2280. Cf. Case C–304/89 *Establecementos Isodoro M. Oliveira SA* v. *EC Commission* [1991] ECR I–2283, I–2313.

[143] Case T–450/93 *Lisrestal–Organizacaõ Gestaõ de Restaurantes Colectivos Lda* v. *EC Commission* [1994] ECR II–1177, II–1194.

[144] Case T–109/94 *Windpark Groothusen GmbH & Co. Betriebs KG* v. *EC Commission* [1995] ECR II–3007, II–3024.

[145] Case 259/85 *France* v. *EC Commission: aid to textiles and clothing* [1987] ECR 4393, 4415; and Case C–142/87 *Belgium* v. *EC Commission: Tubemeuse* [1990] ECR I–959, I–1016.

[146] Case T–109/94 *Windpark Groothusen GmbH & Co. Betriebs KG* v. *EC Commission* [1995] ECR II–3007, II–3023.

[147] Joined Cases 10 & 18/68 *Società "Eridania" Zuccherifici Nazionali* v. *EC Commission* [1969] ECR 459, 476.

[148] Case T–450/93 *Lisrestal–Organizacaõ Gestaõ de Restaurantes Colectivos Lda* v. *EC Commission* [1994] ECR II–1177, II–1194; and Case C–32/95P *EC Commission* v. *Lisrestal–Organizacaõ Gestaõ de Restaurantes Colectivos Lda* [1996] ECR I–5373, I–5373.

[149] Case T–106/95 *Fédération Française des Sociétés d'Assurances* v. *EC Commission* [1997] ECR II–229, II–253.

[150] Case C–304/89 *Establecementos Isodoro M. Oliveira SA* v. *EC Commission* [1991] ECR I–2283, I–2312.

The statement must be appropriate to the decision at issue and must not be contradictory.[151] It must also disclose in a clear[152] and unequivocal fashion the reasoning of the Commission. It must do so in such a way as to enable the persons concerned to ascertain the reasons for the decision and to enable the European Courts to carry out their review.[153]

The duty of confidentiality imposed on the Commission by Article 214 of the Treaty[154] may offer no defence to a failure to meet these requirements. This provision cannot be interpreted so broadly that the duty to give reasons is "deprived of its essential content". For example, recipients of state aid, their competitors, and others may not be denied the information needed to ascertain whether a Commission decision on the legality of the aid concerned is well founded and whether they have an interest in starting legal proceedings.[155] In any case, some relevant facts may manifestly be of a non-confidential nature. At the same time, the entry into force of the decision is not dependent on its publication in the Official Journal pursuant to Article 191 of the Treaty. Hence, information which is confidential can be omitted from the published text.[156]

The statement of reasons need not, however, go into all the relevant facts and points of law. The question whether it meets the requirements of Article 190 must be assessed with regard not only to its wording. Regard must also be had to the nature of the measure,[157] to its context, and to all the rules governing the matter in question.[158] For example, the reduction of Union aid may have been proposed by the national authorities, which have given an explanation to the recipient. In these circumstances, it may be sufficient for the Commission to refer with sufficient clarity to the national measure containing that explanation.[159] Again, reasoning requirements may be less

---

[151] Mischo AG in Case 15/85 *Consorzio Cooperative d'Abruzzo* v. *EC Commission* [1987] ECR 1005, 1023; and Joined Cases T–447–449/93 *Associazione Italiana Tecnico Economica del Cemento* v. *EC Commission* [1995] ECR II–1971, II–2020. Cf., regarding reasoning requirements under the EEA Agreement, Case E–2/94 *Scottish Salmon Growers Association Ltd* v. *ESA* [1995] 1 CMLR 851.

[152] Case C–181/90 *Consorgan* v. *EC Commission* [1992] ECR I–3557, I–3569; and Case T–85/94 *EC Commission* v. *Eugenio Branca* [1995] ECR II–45, II–57.

[153] Case 24/62 *Germany* v. *EEC Commission: wine from third countries* [1963] ECR 63, 69; and Darmon AG in Case 157/90 *Infortec Projectos & Consultadoria, Lda* v. *EC Commission* [1992] ECR I–3525, I–3541.

[154] According to this provision, the Commission must not "disclose information of the kind covered by the obligation of professional secrecy, in particular, information about undertakings, their business relations, or their cost components".

[155] Roemer AG in Joined Cases 10 & 18/68 *Società "Eridania" Zuccherifici Nazionali* v. *EC Commission* [1969] ECR 459, 488.

[156] Joined Cases 296 & 318/82 *Netherlands and Leeuwarder Papierwarenfabriek BV* v. *EC Commission* [1985] ECR 809, 826.

[157] Case 181/90 *Consorgan* v. *EC Commission* [1992] ECR I–3557, I–3569.

[158] Case C–213/87 *Gemeente Amsterdam and Stichting Vrouwenvakschool voor Informatica Amsterdam (VIA)* v. *EC Commission* [1990] ECR I–221, I–222; and Case C–56/93 *Belgium* v. *EC Commission: natural gas tariffs* [1996] ECR I–723, I–792.

[159] Case T–85/94 *EC Commission* v. *Eugenio Branca* [1995] ECR II–45, II–58.

demanding in the case of an unsuccessful applicant for Union aid who has incurred no expenditure on the project for which aid is sought.[160]

More generally, the reasoning need not go beyond what is necessary, regard being had to the requirements and constraints inherent in the functioning of the Union institutions.[161] Accordingly, account may be taken of whether the person concerned is in a position to defend sufficiently his own point of view before the European Courts. Equally, account may be taken of whether the ability of these courts to review the lawfulness of the decision has been diminished or impaired.[162] For example, where the addressee of a decision has taken part in the preparation of the decision, a limited statement of reasons may be found to satisfy Article 190. The statement must, however, contain the indispensable elements which permit the addressee to determine whether the decision is vitiated by a defect.[163] Again, a summary of the reasons for rejecting an application for Union aid may be regarded as "an inevitable consequence of the computerised handling of several thousands of applications for [Union financial] assistance on which the Commission is required to give a decision rapidly". In such a situation a more detailed statement of reasons in support of each decision would be likely to jeopardise the rational and efficient allocation of the Union aid.[164]

More fundamentally, the Commission argues that a distinction should be made between the performance of its public service duties (*Leistungsverwaltung*) and the exercise of its prerogatives as a public authority (*Eingriffverwaltung*). According to the Commission, its duty to give reasons should be less demanding in relation to the former than in relation to the latter. This is because only the exercise of such prerogatives limits the rights of those subject to its administration. For example, since there is no right to Union aid, its refusal causes no damage to applicants and reasoning requirements should be limited.[165] Thinking of this kind may be reflected in the literature. According to the latter, where action is to benefit individuals in the framework of a largely discretionary policy, judicial review has less of a role than where the action takes place through coercive measures.[166] The underlying idea is that such review is concerned with protecting market interests. Such thinking may not be well adapted to Union pursuit of an

---

[160] Darmon AG in Case 157/90 *Infortec Projectos & Consultadoria, Lda* v. *EC Commission* [1992] ECR I–3525, I–3541–2.

[161] Darmon AG (*ibid.*), I–3541.

[162] Capotorti AG in Case 107/80 *Giacomo Cattaneo Adorno* v. *EC Commission* [1981] ECR 1469, 1496.

[163] Darmon AG in Case C–157/90 *Infortec Projectos & Consultadoria, Lda* v. *EC Commission* [1992] ECR I–3525, I–3542.

[164] Case C–213/87 *Gemeente Amsterdam and Stichting Vrouwenvakschool voor Informatica Amsterdam (VIA)* v. *EC Commission* [1990] ECR I–221, I–222.

[165] Cf. Case T–109/94 *Windpark Groothusen GmbH & Co. Betriebs KG* v. *EC Commission* [1995] ECR II–3007, II–3024.

[166] R. Priebe, "Le Droit communautaire des structures agricoles" [1988] *CDE* 3–38, 5.

objective such as cohesion[167] or to making a reality of the establishment of Union citizenship. Both imply that Union citizens have rights going beyond those which are market-based.[168]

In practice, therefore, the effect of reasoning requirements may not be greatly different from a review of the grounds for a decision which examines the *exactitude* (accuracy) and *qualification* (relevance) of the facts but otherwise avoids consideration of the *opportunité* (reasonableness) of the decision. Thus "provided that they are supported by a logical and adequate statement of reasons, decisions taken by the Commission cannot be challenged from the point of view of expediency".[169]

More particularly, reasoning requirements may be limited because of information available to a Member State through its involvement in administrative proceedings leading to a Commission decision.[170] For example, *Intermills* concerned a Commission decision prohibiting Belgian aid to a paper-manufacturing firm. Here Advocate General VerLoren van Themaat noted that the disputed decision made no reference to the position of Intermills in trade between Member States. However, in his view this position was sufficiently known to the government addressee and to the applicant.[171]

Such views seem questionable. It may be that the Commission is not obliged "to adopt a position on all the arguments relied on by the parties concerned".[172] Even so, provisions such as Article 92(3)(c)[173] are concerned with action by Member States favourable to attainment of Union objectives. The Commission is obliged to seek to promote the same objectives in accordance with the principles in Articles 4 and 155 of the Treaty. A possible implication is that the Commission must not simply give reasons for rejecting claims made by the Member State concerned. The Commission must also ensure that its reasons show why the aid is not justified by reference to such objectives. More particularly, if such views are followed, aid recipients, their competitors, and others may be denied the information needed to ascertain whether the decision is well founded. Such considerations may underlie the position of the Court of First Instance that Article 190 implicitly requires an opportunity for "all interested parties of ascertaining the circumstances in which the Commission has applied the Treaty".[174] If this requirement is developed, it may have the effect of opening up Commission

---

[167] Art. 158 EC.

[168] Cf. A. Evans, "Union Citizenship and the Constitutionalization of Equality in European Union Law" in M. La Torre, *European Citizenship: An Institutional Challenge* (Kluwer, Deventer, 1997).

[169] Mancini AG in Case 259/85 *France* v. *EC Commission: aid to textiles and clothing* [1987] ECR 4393, 4440.

[170] Case 102/87 *France* v. *EC Commission: a brewery loan* [1988] ECR 4067, 4090.

[171] Case 323/82 *Intermills SA* v. *EC Commission* [1984] ECR 3809, 3843.

[172] Case T–459/93 *Siemens SA* v. *EC Commission* [1995] ECR II–1675, II–1691.

[173] Sect. 17.3.2 below.

[174] Case T–459/93 *Siemens SA* v. *EC Commission* [1995] ECR II–1675, II–1690.

decision making and lead to increased pluralism in such decision-making.

Commission practice, particularly its use of reports from consultants,[175] already seems to have been affected by such case law. For example, the Commission no longer feels able simply to cite its previous decisions[176] or simply to refer to the general difficulties of beneficiary industries[177] as sufficient to show that trade between Member States is likely to be affected and competition distorted by aid contrary to Article 92(1). Commission decisions now routinely contain market and trade statistics to support conclusions concerning the impact of aid on competition and on trade between Member States. In particular, they may contain statistics, such as those regarding the proportion of the production of an aided undertaking which is exported to other Member States as well as the share in Union production of the Member State where the undertaking is based.[178]

Limitation Period

Proceedings for annulment must be instituted within two months[179] of the publication of the act concerned or of its notification to the applicant[180] or, in the absence thereof, of the day on which the applicant had precise knowledge of the content and grounds of the act in question.[181] However, this limitation period does not apply where the alleged defect in the decision is so serious that, if substantiated, the decision "would lack any legal foundation in the context of the Community".[182] Moreover, it may be extended because of "unforeseeable circumstances or *force majeure*".[183]

Consequences of Illegality

If an annulment action is well founded, the Court must, under Article 174(1)

---

[175] Compare the annulment of the Commission decision in Case C–198/91 *William Cook PLC* v. *EC Commission* [1993] ECR I–2487 for lack of supporting figures or statistics with the acceptance of the decision in Case C–225/91 *Matra SA* v. *EC Commission* [1993] ECR I–3203, where such a report had been obtained.

[176] Dec. 82/829 (OJ 1982 L350/36) on a proposed aid by the Belgian Government in respect of certain investments carried out by an oil company at its Antwerp refinery.

[177] Dec. 80/932 (OJ 1980 L264/28) concerning the partial taking-over by the state of employers' contributions to sickness insurance schemes in Italy.

[178] *Ibid.*

[179] 1 month under Art. 33 ECSC. Cf., regarding unforeseeable circumstances, Joined Cases 25 & 26/65 *Società Industriale Metallurgica di Napoli (Simet) and Accaierie e Ferriere di Roma (Feram)* v. *ECSC High Authority* [1967] ECR 33, 42–3.

[180] Where it has been notified to the person concerned, time begins to run from the day after receipt by him; where it has been published in the Official Journal, time begins to run from the 15th day after the date of publication (Rules of Procedure of the ECJ (OJ 1991 L176/7), Art. 81(1)). Moreover, the time limit is extended to take account of distance from Luxembourg (*ibid.*, Annex II).

[181] Case T–109/94 *Windpark Groothusen GmbH & Co. Betriebs KG* v. *EC Commission* [1995] ECR II–3007, II–3017.

[182] Joined Cases 6 & 11/69 *EC Commission* v. *France: export aid* [1969] ECR 523, 539; and Joined Cases T–79, 84–86, 89, 91–92, 94, 96, 98, 102, 104/89 *BASF AG* v. *EC Commission* [1992] ECR II–315, II–364.

[183] Case 352/87 *Fazoo and Kortmann* v. *EC Commission* [1988] ECR 2281, 2284.

of the Treaty, declare the act concerned to be void. However, under Article 174(2) the Court may declare certain effects of a regulation to be definitive, if it considers this necessary.[184] For example, the Court may maintain the validity of the act up to the date of the judgment, declaring it void only for the future,[185] or until the Council adopts new legislation on the matter. In the latter case the Council must act within a reasonable period.[186] Although Article 174(2) expressly refers only to regulations, the Court may, in practice, exercise a similar power in relation to other acts.[187] However, the Court may only substitute its own decision for that of the institution whose act has been challenged, where Council legislation confers on the Court unlimited jurisdiction in relation to penalties provided for in the regulations.[188]

The institution or institutions[189] whose act has been declared void shall, according to Article 176, take the necessary measures to comply with the judgment of the Court. This obligation shall not affect any obligation which may result from the application of Article 215(2) of the Treaty,[190] which concerns non-contractual liability.[191]

Exception d'Illegalité

According to Article 184 of the Treaty, where a regulation is at issue in proceedings before the Court, any party[192] may, despite expiry of the limitation period in Article 173, plead the grounds specified in Article 173 in order to invoke the inapplicability of that regulation. This is known as the *exception d'illégalité* in French administrative law. Article 184 does not entail any independent cause of action.[193]

Thus a party to proceedings before the Court has the right to challenge, for the purposes of obtaining the annulment of a decision of direct and individual concern to him, the applicability of a previous Union regulation which forms the legal basis of the decision being attacked.[194] The fact that the party may never have been entitled to seek annulment of the regulation does not affect his right to plead its inapplicability.[195] However, resort may

---

[184] Case 45/86 *EC Commission* v. *EC Council: generalized tariff preferences* [1987] ECR 1493, 1522.
[185] Case 4/79 *Société Coopérative "Providence Agricole de la Champagne"* v. *Office National Interprofessionnel des Céréales (ONIC)* [1980] ECR 2823, 2853–4.
[186] Case C–392/95 *European Parliament* v. *EU Council: visas for TSNs* (10 June 1997).
[187] Case 17/74 *Transocean Marine Paint Association* v. *EC Commission* [1974] ECR 1063, 1081; and Case 34/86 *EC Council* v. *European Parliament: non-compulsory expenditure* [1986] ECR 2155, 2212.
[188] Art. 172 EC.   [189] Including the ECB.   [190] Art. 176(2) EC.   [191] Sect. 5.3.3 below.
[192] Cf., regarding a Member State, Case 156/77 *EC Commission* v. *Belgium: aid for railway transport* [1978] ECR 1881, 1896–7.
[193] Joined Cases 31 & 33/62 *Milchwerke Heinz Wöhrmann & Sohn KG and Alfons Lütticke GmbH* v. *EC Commission* [1962] ECR 501, 506–7.
[194] *Ibid.*, 507. See also Joined Cases 87, 130/77, 22/83, 9 & 10/84 *Vittorio Salerno* v. *EC Commission and EC Council* [1985] ECR 2523, 2536.
[195] See, e.g., Case 15/57 *Compagnie des Hauts Fournaux de Chasse* v. *ECSC High Authority* [1957–8] ECR 211, 224–5.

not be had to a plea of illegality where the party seeking to invoke the plea could have challenged the regulation directly by means of an action for annulment but failed to do so timeously.[196] Although Article 184 only refers expressly to regulations, the procedure may also be used against other Union acts which "produce similar effects".[197]

If the plea is successful, the regulation is rendered inapplicable to the person concerned, and the decision based on the regulation is deprived of its legal basis and annulled.[198] The same end may be achieved by a judgment of a national court which has obtained a preliminary ruling from the Court of Justice on the validity of a Union regulation.[199]

5.3.2 Proceedings for Failure to Act

Proceedings for unlawful inaction may be brought under Article 175 of the EC Treaty. These proceedings may be brought where the European Parliament, the Council, or the Commission fails, in infringement of the Treaty, to act. In addition, the Court has jurisdiction, under the same conditions, in proceedings brought against the European Central Bank in the areas falling within field of competence of this Bank.

Such proceedings must concern a breach of a sufficiently defined duty to act.[200] The wording of Article 175, especially in the German[201] and Dutch versions,[202] seems to call for an interpretation which presupposes the existence of a failure to adopt a specific act. However, the other language versions are so worded as to allow the inclusion of a less clearly circumscribed failure. Moreover, the purpose of Article 175 would be frustrated if an applicant were not able to refer to the Court the failure of an institution to adopt several decisions, or a series of decisions, where the adoption of such decisions is an obligation which the Treaty imposes on that institution.[203]

Locus Standi

Article 175(1) provides that proceedings may be brought by the Member States and the other institutions of the Union. Since "other institutions" may bring such actions, the European Parliament may also make use of this procedure, as in *Parliament* v. *EC Council: transport policy*.[204] In addition, the

---

[196] Case 156/77 *EC Commission* v. *Belgium: aid for railway transport* [1978] ECR 1881, 1897; and Case 348/82 *Industrie Riunite Odelesi SpA* v. *EC Commission* [1984] ECR 1409, 1415.

[197] Case 92/78 *Simmenthal SpA* v. *EC Commission* [1979] ECR 777, 800.

[198] Joined Cases 31 & 33/62 *Milchwerke Heinz Wöhrmann & Sohn KG and Alfons Lütticke GmbH* v. *EC Commission* [1962] ECR 501, 507.

[199] Sect. 5.3.5 below.

[200] Case 13/83 *European Parliament* v. *EC Council: transport policy* [1985] ECR 1513, 1592. Under Art. 35 ECSC proceedings may be brought against failure to exercise a power, provided the failure constitutes a misuse of power.

[201] "*Beschluß*". [202] "*Besluit*".

[203] Case 13/83 *European Parliament* v. *EC Council: transport policy* [1985] ECR 1513, 1592.

[204] Case 13/83 [1985] ECR 1513, 1588.

Court has jurisdiction, under the same conditions, in proceedings brought by the European Central Bank in the areas falling within the field of competence of this Bank.

Private persons may bring actions under Article 175(3). However, this provision stipulates that they may only do so on the ground that a Union institution has failed to address to them any act other than a recommendation or an opinion.[205] Hence, individuals have no standing to challenge a failure to do something which could only be done by a regulation or other legislative act.[206] Moreover, they cannot complain about acts which should be addressed to third parties. Thus, for example, provided that the Commission has defined its position, an individual may not bring proceedings against that institution for failure to act against a Member State in breach of Union law.[207] On the other hand, in exceptional situations an individual may have standing to bring proceedings against a refusal by the Commission to adopt a decision pursuant to its supervisory functions under Article 90(1) and (3),[208] which concern state measures relating to public undertakings.[209] This possibility does not, however, arise in the case of a failure by the Commission to act against state measures of general application.[210]

Limitation Period

Actions under Article 175 are only admissible where the applicant has first called upon the institution concerned to act. No time limit is laid down for the period within which the applicant may call upon the institution to act, but his unreasonable delay in doing so may bar proceedings.[211] Within two months of being so called upon, the institution concerned must define its position under Article 175(2). A reply which neither denies nor confirms the alleged failure to act nor gives any indication of the institution's views as to the measures to be taken cannot be regarded as a definition of position within the meaning of Article 175(2).[212] If there is no definition, the action must be brought within a further period of two months. If the definition is forthcoming, proceedings may be instituted under Article 173 for annulment of the act constituting the definition.

---

[205] See, e.g., Case 15/71 *C. Mackprang Jr.* v. *EC Commission* [1971] ECR 797, 804.

[206] Case 90/78 *Granaria BV* v. *EC Council and EC Commission* [1979] ECR 1081, 1092–3.

[207] See, e.g., Case 246/81 *Nicholas William, Lord Bethell* v. *EC Commission* [1982] ECR 2277, 2291.

[208] Case C–107/95P *Bundesverband der Bilanzbuchhalter eV* v. *EC Commission* [1997] ECR I–947, I–964.

[209] Chap. 16.

[210] Case C–107/95P *Bundesverband der Bilanzbuchhalter eV* v. *EC Commission* [1997] ECR I–947, I–965.

[211] Case 59/70 *Netherlands* v. *EC Commission: aid to the iron and steel industry* [1971] ECR 639, 653.

[212] Case 13/83 *European Parliament* v. *EC Council: transport policy* [1985] ECR 1513, 1590.

Consequences of an Unlawful Failure to Act

According to Article 176, an institution or institutions[213] whose failure to act has been declared contrary to the Treaty shall be required to take the necessary measures to comply with the judgment of the Court. This requirement shall not affect any obligation which may result from the application of Article 215(2) of the Treaty.[214]

5.3.3 Proceedings for Compensation

Article 215(2) of the EC Treaty concerns non-contractual liability. It provides that the Union must, in accordance with the general principles common to the laws of the Member States, make good any damage caused by its institutions or its servants in the performance of their duties. The same obligation applies to damage caused by the European Central Bank or its servants. However, there is only liability for acts of servants which are "the necessary extension of the tasks entrusted to the institutions".[215] Part of the compensation claimed under Article 215(2) may be awarded as an interim measure under Article 186.[216]

Such proceedings may provide a means whereby a person lacking standing to bring annulment proceedings or proceedings for failure to act may challenge the action or inaction of Union institutions.[217] However, a person who was in a position entitling him to bring an action for annulment of the act complained of but who has omitted timeously to start annulment proceedings may not be allowed to repair the omission by bringing an action for damages.[218]

Whereas proceedings under Article 173 seek annulment of an act *erga omnes*, proceedings under Article 215(2) seek simply to obtain compensation for an individual who has suffered damage. Proceedings for compensation constitute an abuse of procedure, if their real purpose is to secure the withdrawal of a measure which has become definitive.[219] Conversely, the annulment of measure does not necessarily mean that compensation is payable.[220]

For compensation to be awarded, there must be illegality, damage, and a causal link between the two.[221] Provided damage is caused by action or inaction incompatible with general principles of law, compensation may be

---

[213] Including the European Central Bank (ECB).

[214] Art. 176(2) EC.

[215] Case 9/69 *Claude Sayag* v. *Jean-Pierre Leduc* [1969] ECR 329, 336. Cf. Art. 40 ECSC.

[216] Case C–393/96 P(R) *J. Antonissen* v. *EU Council and EC Commission* [1997] ECR I–441.

[217] Case 4/69 *Alfons Lütticke GmbH* v. *EC Commission* [1971] ECR 325, 336; and Case T–185/94 *Geotronics SA* v. *EC Commission* [1995] ECR II–2795, II–2809.

[218] Case 4/67 *Anne Muller (née Collignon)* v. *EC Commission* [1967] ECR 365, 373–4.

[219] Case T–514/93 *Cobrecaf* v. *EC Commission* [1995] ECR II–621, II–641.

[220] Case T–478/93 *Wafer Zoo Srl* v. *EC Commission* [1995] ECR II–1479, II–1500.

[221] Case C–200/89 *Funoc* v. *EC Commission* [1990] ECR I–3669, I–3695.

payable.[222] However, fault on the part of the complainant may break the causal link.[223]

Illegality

Unlike Article 40 of the ECSC Treaty,[224] Article 215(2) of the EC Treaty does not expressly limit liability to fault situations. Even so, the Court seems reluctant to embrace the idea of "no-fault liability".[225] For example, it may not be enough to constitute illegality that an institution has made an error. Rather, the error must be one which would not have been committed by a normally prudent administrative body exercising reasonable care. For example, the giving of erroneous advice on Union law may not give rise to liability. However, failure to warn the recipient of the advice of its erroneous nature, once that has been discovered, may render the Union liable for damage resulting therefrom.[226] Similarly, where an institution has delegated an administrative task to another body, the Union will be liable for a failure to supervise that other body with reasonable care.[227] Again, failure to take any steps to see that a Member State performs its obligations may constitute fault on the part of the Commission.[228] However, if steps which may reasonably have been expected are taken by the Commission, liability will not arise.[229]

Damage

The applicant must be able to show that he has suffered damage[230] or that damage is foreseeable with sufficient certainty, even if the damage cannot yet be precisely assessed.[231] The damage must relate to loss suffered rather than the opportunity to make profits.[232] The nature and extent of the damage must be specified in the pleadings.[233]

---

[222] See, e.g., Case 145/83 *Stanley George Adams* v. *EC Commission* [1985] ECR 3539; and Case C–358/90 *Compagnie Italiana Alcool* v. *EC Commission* [1990] ECR I–4887.

[223] Case 169/73 *Compagnie Continentale France* v. *EC Commission* [1975] ECR 117, 135–6. But cf. Case 145/83 *Stanley George Adams* v. *EC Commission* [1985] ECR 3539, 3592, where the compensation was reduced by half because of the applicant's negligence.

[224] Art. 40 ECSC provides for "reparation . . . to make good any injury caused . . . by a wrongful act or omission" by the ECSC.

[225] Cf. Case 59/83 *SA Biovilac NV* v. *EEC* [1984] ECR 4057, 4081.

[226] Joined Cases 19, 20, 25 & 30/69 *Richez-Parise* v. *EC Commission* [1970] ECR 325, 339–40. Cf. Case 145/83 *Stanley George Adams* v. *EC Commission* [1985] ECR 3539, 3590.

[227] Contrast Joined Case 19 & 21/60, 2 & 3/61 *Société Fives Lille Cail* v. *ECSC High Authority* [1961] ECR 281, 296–7 with Case 23/59 *Accaieria Ferriera di Roma SpA* v. *ECSC High Authority* [1959] ECR 245, 251–2.

[228] Joined Cases 9 & 12/60 *Société Commerciale Antoine Vloeberghs SA* v. *ECSC High Authority* [1961] ECR 197, 216–17.

[229] Case 4/69 *Alfons Lütticke GmbH* v. *EC Commission* [1971] ECR 325, 338.

[230] Case 49/79 *Richard Pool* v. *EC Council* [1980] ECR 569.

[231] Case 59/83 *SA Biovilac NV* v. *EEC* [1984] ECR 4057, 4075

[232] Case 74/74 *Comptoir National Technique Agricole SA* v. *EC Commission* [1975] ECR 533, 550; and Case 238/78 *Ireks-Arkady GmbH* v. *EC Council and EC Commission* [1979] ECR 2955, 2974.

[233] Case 5/71 *Aktion-Zuckerfabriek Schoppenstedt* v. *EC Council* [1971] ECR 975, 984. Cf. Case 90/78 *Granaria BV* v. *EC Council and EC Commission* [1979] ECR 1081, 1090.

The amount of compensation may be reduced because of the speculative nature of the damage.[234] Moreover, there is a duty to mitigate losses. For example, an applicant must undertake alternative forms of business when Union action renders his original business uneconomic.[235]

Strictly speaking, no claim for payment of aid from Union funds may be brought.[236] Indeed, the Commission once maintained that claims for compensation under Article 215(2) had to be distinguished from "actions for the provision of benefits" and that the latter were not admissible under this provision.[237] However, the Court of Justice accepts that compensation may be claimed for damage resulting from non-payment of Union aid.[238]

Remedies before National Courts

Most Union legislation is administered by the national authorities, and individuals may have to pursue their rights under Union law against those authorities. Thus claims for payment of sums of money, such as export refunds, to which the claimant is entitled under Union law but which fall to be made by the national authority administering the relevant scheme should be directed against that authority.[239] Further, if the basis of the claim is that the national authority wrongly applied Union law, that authority is the proper defendant.[240]

In relation to damage caused by a wrongful act of a Union institution which is implemented by a national authority, the view of the Court of Justice has evolved. At one time the view was taken by the Court that any remedy by way of damages against the national authority should be pursued first, before recourse was had against the Union.[241] The position now seems to be that a claim for loss suffered as a result of a wrongful act or omission of the Union may be pursued in the Court of Justice, irrespective of whether remedies may also be available against the action or inaction of the national authority in the national courts.[242] In particular, the existence in the national

---

[234] Joined Cases 5, 7 & 13–24/66 *Firma E. Kampffmeyer* v. *EEC Commission* [1967] ECR 245, 266.

[235] Joined Cases 104/89 & 37/90 *Mulder* v. *EC Commission and EC Council* [1992] ECR I–3602, I–3136–7.

[236] Case 44/81 *Germany* v. *EC Commission: deadline for claiming payment of ESF aid* [1982] ECR 1855, 1874–5.

[237] Joined Cases 261 & 262/78 *Interquell Starke GmbH & Co. KG and Diamalt AG* v. *EC Council and EC Commission* [1979] ECR 3045, 3050.

[238] *Ibid.*, 3062.

[239] Case 99/74 *Société des Grands Moulins des Antilles* v. *EC Commission* [1975] ECR 1531, 1540.

[240] Case 12/79 *Hans-Otto Wagner GmbH Agrarhandel KG* v. *EC Commission* [1979] ECR 3657, 3671–2; and Case 133/79 *Sucrimex SA and Westzucker GmbH* v. *EC Commission* [1980] ECR 1299, 1310–11.

[241] Joined Cases 5, 7 & 13–24/66 *Firma E. Kampffmeyer* v. *EEC Commission* [1967] ECR 245, 264; and Joined Cases 67–85/75 *Lesieur Cotelle et Associés SA* v. *EC Commission* [1976] ECR 391, 406.

[242] Case 126/76 *Firma Gebrüder Dietz* v. *EC Commission* [1976] ECR 2431, 2441; and Joined Cases 64, 113/76, 167 & 239/78, 27, 28 & 45/79 *P. Dumortier Frères SA* v. *EC Council* [1978] ECR 3091, 3113. Cf. Case 43/72 *Merkur- Aussenhandels-GmbH* v. *EC Commission* [1973] ECR 1055, 1069; and Joined Cases 106–127/87 *Asteris* v. *Greece* [1988] ECR 5515, 5541.

courts of a remedy other than damages, such as the annulment of a national measure implementing the Union act, will not prevent the Court of Justice from having jurisdiction.[243]

Legislative Measures

In the case of legislative measures, compensation will only be awarded where there has been a serious breach of an important principle designed to protect private interests,[244] such as equality of treatment[245] or proportionality.[246] Thus, for example, liability does not arise from a breach of a provision governing the powers of the Union institutions,[247] failure to give reasons for a legislative measure[248] or from a breach of a principle which is insufficiently serious to be regarded as "verging on the arbitrary".[249]

A breach is sufficiently serious where the circumstances are exceptional and where the institution concerned has manifestly[250] and gravely disregarded the limits on the exercise of its powers.[251] Individuals may be required to accept within reasonable limits certain harmful effects on their commercial interests inherent in the trade or sector concerned.[252] Thus the damage must exceed the limits of the economic risks inherent in operating in the sector concerned.[253]

The same requirement applies whether the complaint is of a failure to adopt new, or to amend existing, legislation rather than about legislation actually enacted.[254] The rationale is that Union institutions should not be deterred by the prospect of actions for damages from adopting legislative measures in the public interest which may adversely affect individual interests.[255] Thus even when the conditions for liability are otherwise met,

---

[243] Case 281/82 *Unifrex Sàrl* v. *EC Commission and EC Council* [1984] ECR 1969, 1982–3.

[244] See, e.g., Case 5/71 *Aktion-Zuckerfabriek Schöppenstedt* v. *EC Council* [1971] ECR 975, 984; and Case 153/73 *Holtz and Willemsen GmbH* v. *EC Council* [1974] ECR 675, 693.

[245] Joined Cases 64 & 113/76, 167, 239/78, 27, 28, 45/79 *P. Dumortier Frères SA* v. *EC Council* [1978] ECR 3091, 3114.

[246] Joined Cases 83 & 94/76, 4, 15, 40/77 *Bayerische HNL Vermehrungsbetriebe GmbH & Co KG* v. *EC Council and EC Commission* [1978] ECR 1209, 1224.

[247] Case C–282/90 *Industrie-en Handelsonderneming Vreugdenhil BV* v. *EC Commission* [1992] ECR I–1937, I–1968.

[248] Case 106/81 *Julius Kind KG* v. *EEC* [1982] ECR 2885, 2918.

[249] Joined Cases 116 & 124/77 *GR Amylum NV and Tunnel Refineries Ltd* v. *EC Council and EC Commission* [1979] ECR 3497, 3561.

[250] Joined Cases T–481 & 484/93 *Vereiniging van Exporteurs in Levande Varkens* v. *EC Commission* [1995] ECR 2941, 2970.

[251] Joined Cases 83 & 94/76, 4, 15, 40/77 *Bayerische HNL Vermehrungsbetriebe GmbH & Co KG* v. *EC Council and EC Commission* [1978] ECR 1209, 1224; and Case 143/77 *Koninklijke Scholten-Honig NV* v. *EC Council and EC Commission* [1979] ECR 3583, 3626.

[252] [1978] ECR 1209, 1224.

[253] Case 59/83 *SA Biovilac NV* v. *EEC* [1984] ECR 4057, 4080–1.

[254] Case 50/86 *Les Grands Moulins de Paris* v. *EEC* [1987] ECR 4833, 4857.

[255] Joined Cases 83 & 94/76, 4, 15 & 40/77 *Bayerische HNL Vermehrungsbetriebe GmbH & Co KG* v. *EC Council and EC Commission* [1978] ECR 1209, 1224; and Case T–390/94 *Aloys Schröder* v. *EC Commission* [1997] ECR II–501, II–521.

an institution may escape liability because of an overriding public interest.[256]

Limitation Period

Proceedings are, according to the Protocol on the Statute of the Court of Justice, barred after a period of five years from the event giving rise to liability.[257] This period does not begin to run before all the requirements governing an obligation to provide compensation are satisfied. In particular, it does not begin to run before the damage has materialised[258] and the applicant is, or could reasonably be expected to be, aware of the event giving rise to liability.[259] The period may be interrupted either by the institution of proceedings under Article 173 or 175 or by an application to the relevant Union institution for compensation. If the application is unsuccessful, time does not begin to run again until expiry of the period of two months prescribed by Article 173 or four months prescribed by Article 175.[260]

5.3.4 Contractual Liability

Article 215(1) of the EC Treaty concerns the jurisdiction of the Court of Justice in relation to the contractual liability of the Union. The Court has jurisdiction to entertain a direct action based on a contract concluded by the Union, but it has to apply whatever is the proper, national law of the contract.[261]

Again, Article 181 of the Treaty concerns the jurisdiction of the Court of Justice pursuant to arbitration clauses in contracts concluded by Union.[262] According to this provision, the Court has jurisdiction to give judgment pursuant to any such clause, whether the contract is governed by public or private law.

Save where jurisdiction is conferred on the Court of Justice by the Treaty, disputes to which the Union is a party shall not on that ground be excluded from the jurisdiction of the courts or tribunals of the Member States.[263]

---

[256] Case 152/88 *Sofrimport SARL* v. *EC Commission* [1990] ECR I–2477, I–2511; and Joined Cases 104/89 & 37/90 *Mulder* v. *EC Commission and EC Council* [1992] ECR I–3061, I–3133.

[257] Art. 43 of the Protocol on the Statute of the ECJ.

[258] Joined Cases 256, 257, 265 & 267/80 & 5/81 *Birra Wührer SpA* v. *EC Council and EC Commission* [1982] ECR 85, 106.

[259] Case 145/83 *Stanley George Adams* v. *EC Commission* [1985] ECR 3539, 3591–2.

[260] Joined Cases 5, 7 & 13–24/66 *Firma E. Kampffmeyer* v. *EEC Commission* [1967] ECR 245, 260.

[261] See, e.g., Case 23/76 *Luigi Pellegrini & C. Sas and Flexon Italia SpA* v. *EC Commission* [1976] ECR 1807; and Case 109/81 *Teresita Pace, née Porta* v. *EC Commission* [1982] ECR 2469.

[262] See, similarly, Art. 42 ECSC.

[263] Art. 183 EC. Art. 35.2 of the Protocol on the Statute of the ESCB and of the ECB, annexed to the EC Treaty, is less ambiguous.

5.3.5 Default Proceedings

The Court of Justice has jurisdiction in proceedings brought by the Commission against Member States under Article 169 of the EC Treaty for failure to respect Union law.[264] This procedure is complemented by more traditional arrangements in Article 170(1).[265] This provision enables a Member State to institute proceedings against another Member State for violation of Union law,[266] though Article 170(2) provides that the Commission must be given the opportunity to take over the proceedings. Interim measures may be ordered under Article 186,[267] where the case discloses a *prima facie* breach of Union law and the situation is of sufficient urgency to warrant an order being pronounced.[268] Moreover, "accelerated procedures" are provided for in Articles 93(2), 100a(9), and 225.[269] These provisions do not require the Commission to issue a reasoned opinion to the Member State concerned before referring the matter to the Court. In relation to excessive budget deficits, the possibility of such proceedings being brought is limited by Article 104c(10).

A Member State is required by Article 171(1) to take the necessary measures to comply with a judgment to the effect that it has failed to respect Union law. If the Member State does not do so, Article 171(2) provides for the Court to impose a lump sum or penalty payment on it.[270]

Moreover, a judgment finding that a Member State has defaulted prohibits the competent national authorities from applying any national rule recognised as incompatible with the Treaty. The judgment also obliges them to take all appropriate measures to enable Union law to be fully applied.[271] Even if the legislative or administrative authorities of the Member State concerned fail to take appropriate action, its courts are bound if possible to enforce the judgment and not the offending national rule.[272] At the same time, the judgment may render the Member State concerned liable to pay compensation to anyone who has suffered from the breach of Union law.[273]

[264] Cf. Art. 88 ECSC.

[265] Case 141/78 *France* v. *UK: sea fisheries* [1979] ECR 2923.

[266] A Member State may not respond to a Treaty breach of another Member State by adopting unilateral counter measures. Rather, proceedings must be taken under Art. 170 EC. See Joined Cases 90 & 91/63 *EEC Commission* v. *Luxembourg and Belgium* [1964] EC 625, 631; and Case C–14/96 *Paul Denuit* (29 May 1997).

[267] Case 61/77R *EC Commission* v. *Ireland: fishery conservation* [1977] ECR 937.

[268] Joined Cases 31 & 53/77R *EC Commission* v. *UK: aid to pig producers* [1977] ECR 921; and Case 293/85R *EC Commission* v. *Belgium: vocational training* [1985] ECR 3521.

[269] See also the Proposal for a regulation creating a mechanism whereby the Commission can intervene in order to remove certain obstacles to trade, COM(97)619.

[270] See the Commission Communication on Art. 171 (OJ 1996 C242/6). Sanctions provided for under Art. 88 ECSC have never been imposed.

[271] Case 48/71 *EC Commission* v. *Italy: art treasures* [1972] ECR 527, 532

[272] Joined Cases 314–316/81 & 83/82 *Procureur de la République and Comité National de Défense contre l'Alcolisme* v. *Alex Waterkeyn* [1982] ECR 4337, 4360.

[273] See Joined Cases C–6 & 9/90 *Andrea Francovich* v. *Italy* [1991] ECR I–5357, regarding a failure to implement a directive.

5.3.6 Preliminary Rulings

Under Article 177 of the EC Treaty the Court of Justice has jurisdiction to deliver preliminary rulings requested by national courts. According to Article 177(1), the Court may deliver such rulings on the interpretation of the Treaty; on the validity and interpretation of acts[274] of the Union institutions[275] and of the European Central Bank. It may also deliver such rulings on the interpretation of the statutes of bodies established by an act of the Council where those statutes so provide.

Nature of the Procedure

Article 177 does not establish the Court of Justice as a court to which judgments of national courts may be appealed. It simply recognises that questions of Union law may arise in disputes between individuals or between individuals and a Member State. They may arise where an individual invokes Union law either as a basis of his claim or as a defence to a civil action or criminal prosecution. Such disputes cannot be brought before the European Courts by means of a direct action. This is because individuals may not be sued in direct actions before these Courts and because the Member State may not be sued by individuals before the same Courts. Rather, the dispute must be the subject of appropriate proceedings before a national court, which must apply the relevant Union law. To ensure that in such circumstances Union law is interpreted and applied uniformly in the Member States,[276] preliminary rulings on the interpretation of Union law may be delivered by the Court of Justice.

For example, the management of the common agricultural policy in conditions of equality between traders in the Member States requires that the national authorities of a Member State should not, by the expedient of a wide interpretation of a Union law provision regarding aid from the European Agricultural Guidance and Guarantee Fund,[277] favour traders in that Member State to the detriment of those in other Member States where a stricter interpretation is applied.[278] With the assistance of preliminary rulings such divergent interpretations may be prevented.

Interpretation

Article 177(2) provides that where a question of Union law is raised before a national "court or tribunal", that court may, if it considers that a decision on

---

[274] They need not be directly applicable. See, e.g., Case 113/75 *Giordano Frecassetti* v. *Amministrazione delle Finanze dello Stato* [1976] ECR 983.

[275] Including the European Parliament. See Case 208/80 *Lord Bruce of Donnington* v. *Eric Gordon Aspden* [1981] ECR 2205.

[276] See, e.g., Case 166/73 *Rheinmühlen-Düsseldorf* v. *Einfuhr-und Vorratstelle für Getreide und Futtermittel* [1974] ECR 33, 38.

[277] Sect. 20.4 below.

[278] Case 11/76 *Netherlands* v. *EC Commission: EAGGF* [1979] ECR 245, 279.

the question is necessary to enable it to give judgment, request a preliminary ruling from the Court of Justice.

The expression "court or tribunal" is broadly interpreted.[279] It is interpreted having regard to the nature, powers, and functions of a body rather than the name or description given to the body under national law. The body must have been established by law, have a permanent existence, exercise binding jurisdiction, be bound by rules of adversary procedure, apply the rule of law, and be independent.[280] However, an arbitrator called upon to resolve a contractual dispute between parties under an arbitration clause in a contract may not be so treated.[281]

It is for the national court to determine the need for a preliminary ruling and the relevance of the questions referred to the Court of Justice.[282] The discretion thus conferred on a national court by Union law[283] may not be restricted by provisions of national law.[284]

In exercising their discretion, national courts must show caution in concluding that Union law is clear and free of all difficulty. They must show caution for various reasons. In particular, Union legislation is drafted in several, equally authentic languages.[285] Concepts and terminology may also have a different meaning in Union law than do they do in a national context.[286] In addition, every provision of Union law must be placed in its context and interpreted in the light of the provisions of Union law as a whole.[287]

Under Article 177(3) a national court of last resort[288] is obliged to request a preliminary ruling when a question of Union law is raised. However, there

---

[279] See, e.g., Case 246/80 *C. Broekmeulen* v. *Huisarts Registratie Commissie* [1981] ECR 2311, 2328. Cf. Case 138/80 *Jules Borker* [1980] ECR 1975, 1977.

[280] Case C–393/92 *Municipality of Almelo* v. *Energiebedrijff IJsellmij NV* [1994] ECR I–1477, I–1515. See also Case C–24/92 *Pierre Corbiau* v. *Administration des Contributions du Grand-Duché de Luxembourg* [1993] ECR I–1227.

[281] Case 102/81 *Nordsee Deutsche Hochseefischerei GmbH* v. *Reederei Mond Hochseefischerei Nordstern AG & Co. KG and Reederei Friedrich Busse Hochseefischerei* [1982] ECR 1095. Cf. Case 61/65 *Vaassen (née Göbbels)* v. *Management of the Beambtenfonds voor het Mijnbedrijf* [1966] ECR 261, 273 and Case 109/88 *Handels-og Kontorfunktionærernes Forbund i Danmark* v. *Dansk Arbejdsgiverforening (acting on behalf of Danfoss)* [1989] ECR 3199, 3224–5.

[282] Case 6/64 *Flaminio Costa* v. *ENEL* [1964] ECR 585, 593; and Case 338/85 *Fratelli Pardine SpA* v. *Ministero del Commercio con l'Estero* [1988] ECR 2041, 2074.

[283] See, regarding the way such discretion should be exercised by English courts, *H.P. Bulmer* v. *J. Bollinger* [1974] Ch. 401.

[284] Case 166/73 *Rheinmühlen-Düsseldorf* v. *Einfuhr-und Vorratstelle für Getreide und Futtermittel* [1974] ECR 33, 38–9.

[285] See, e.g., Case 122/87 *EC Commission* v. *Italy: veterinary services* [1988] ECR 2685.

[286] See, e.g., regarding "consideration", Case 102/86 *Apple and Pear Development Council* v. *Commissioners of Customs and Excise* [1988] ECR 1443.

[287] Case 238/81 *Srl CILFIT and Lanificio di Gararado SpA* v. *Ministry of Health* [1982] ECR 3415, 3430.

[288] A national court against whose interim or interlocutory decisions no appeal exists is not bound to refer, if the question of Union law may be reviewed at a subsequent stage of the proceedings. See Case 107/76 *Hoffmann-La Roche* v. *Centrafarm Vertriebsgesellschaft Pharmazeutischer Erzeugnisse mbH* [1977] ECR 957, 973.

is some margin of appreciation whether a point of Union law is sufficiently unclear as to constitute a "question".[289] There is also some margin of appreciation whether a question is of sufficient relevance to the proceedings before the national court for it to be said to be "raised" in such proceedings.[290] Besides, while the Commission could, in theory, bring Article 169 proceedings against a Member State whose supreme court had violated Article 177(3),[291] the Commission is unlikely to take such a step. Concern to avoid appearing to threaten judicial independence and jeopardising continuation of the co-operative attitude generally demonstrated by national courts in the development of Union law has apparently influenced the Commission. Thus the Commission has limited itself to informal contacts with the governments of Member States whose courts commit such apparent violations of the Treaty.

Validity

Preliminary rulings on the validity of Union acts may do much to compensate for the limitations to the standing of private persons to bring proceedings for annulment.[292] There is no requirement in this provision that the Union act be of direct and individual concern to the litigant.[293] In such proceedings Treaty provisions which lack direct effects and general principles of Union law, such as equality of treatment and proportionality,[294] may be applied by the Court of Justice.[295] However, where an individual has had actual knowledge of a Commission decision and of the possibility to take action against that decision under Article 173 but has failed to do so within the prescribed period, he is precluded from bringing an indirect challenge under Article 177.[296]

Such rulings may be delivered where a national measure, purportedly based on a Union act, is challenged in a national court on the ground that

---

[289] Cf., where the point has been dealt with in a previous ruling of the ECJ, Case 238/81 *Srl CILFIT and Lanificio di Garardo SpA* v. *Ministry of Health* [1982] ECR 3415, 3429.

[290] *Ibid.*, 3428–30.

[291] The liability of a Member State under Art. 169 EC arises whatever the state agency whose action or inaction is the cause of the failure to fulfil its obligations, even in the case of a constitutionally independent institution. See Case 77/69 *EC Commission* v. *Belgium: wood duties* [1970] ECR 237, 243.

[292] See, e.g., Joined Cases 21–24/72 *International Fruit Company NV, Kooy Rotterdam NV, Velleman en Tas NV and Jan Van den Brink's Im-en Exporthandel NV* v. *Produktschap voor Groenten en Fruit* [1972] ECR 1219.

[293] Case T–271/94 *Eugenio Branca Lda* v. *EC Commission* [1996] ECR II–749, II–766.

[294] Case C–27/95 *Woodspring District Council* v. *Bakers of Nailsea Ltd* [1997] ECR I–1847.

[295] However, in the case of agreements with third states, only provisions conferring rights on individuals can be relied on before national courts to contest the validity of a Union act. See Joined Cases 21–24/72 *International Fruit Company NV, Kooy Rotterdam NV, Velleman en Tas NV and Jan Van den Brink's Im-en Exporthandel NV* v. *Produktschap voor Groenten en Fruit* [1972] ECR 1219, 1226–7.

[296] Case 52/84 *EC Commission* v. *Belgium: Boch* [1986] ECR 89, 104; and Case C–188/92 *TWD Textilwerke Deggendorf GmbH* v. *Germany* [1994] ECR I–833, I–855.

the Union act itself is invalid. National courts may not declare the Union act invalid. Rather, they must make a reference to the Court of Justice.[297]

A ruling declaring a Union act to be void is sufficient for any other national court to regard that act as void for the purpose of any judgment it has to give.[298] However, other national courts may decide that it is necessary to request a further ruling.[299] A ruling that a Union act is void means that the act is void from the start, but in exceptional circumstances the Court may limit the retrospective effect of its ruling.[300]

Division of Responsibilities

Formally, a division of responsibilities between national courts and the Court of Justice is envisaged in Article 177.[301] The former are responsible for application of Union law to the issues before them,[302] while the Court of Justice merely interprets the meaning of the relevant provisions of Union law. Thus the Court of Justice has no power to interpret national law,[303] to apply Union law to a specific case, or to declare that a provision of national law is incompatible with Union law and invalid. Nevertheless, the fact that the question referred may be couched by the national court in terms which relate to the application of Union law or to the interpretation or validity of national law does not prevent the Court of Justice from effectively reformulating the question so as to extract from the case the true issues of interpretation of Union law arising.[304] Thus the Court may provide the national court with all criteria for the interpretation of Union law which may enable it to determine the issue of compatibility of a national measure for the purposes of the decision in the case before it.[305] In practice, the preliminary ruling may frequently be worded in such a way as to leave no option to the national court but to declare the provisions of national law in question to be incompatible with Union law.[306]

[297] Case 314/85 *Fotofrost* v. *Hauptzollamt Lübeck-Ost* [1987] ECR 4199, 4230–2, though this rule may be qualified in the case of an application for interim measures (*ibid.*).
[298] Case 66/80 *SpA International Chemical Corporation* v. *Amministrazione delle Finanze dello Stato* [1981] ECR 1191, 1215.
[299] *Ibid.*
[300] Case 4/79 *Société Coopérative "Providence Agricole de la Champagne"* v. *Office National Interprofessionnel des Céréales (ONIC)* [1980] ECR 2823, 2853; and Case 112/83 *Société de Produits de Maïs SA* v. *Administration des Douanes et Droits Indirects* [1985] ECR 719, 748.
[301] Case 6/64 *Flaminio Costa* v. *ENEL* [1964] ECR 585, 593.
[302] Joined Cases 91 & 127/83 *Heineken Brouwereijen BV* v. *Inspecteurs der Vennootschapsbelasting, Amsterdam, and Utrecht* [1984] ECR 3435, 3451.
[303] Case 93/75 *Jacob Adlerblum* v. *Caisse Nationale d'Assurance Vieillesse des Travailleurs Salariés* [1975] ECR 2147.
[304] Case 6/64 *Flaminio Costa* v. *ENEL* [1964] ECR 585, 593.
[305] Case C–438/92 *Rustica Semences* v. *Finanzamt Kehl* [1994] ECR I–3519, I–3533; and Case C–63/94 *Groupement National des Négociants en Pommes de Terre de Belgique* v. *ITM Belgium SA and Vocarex SA* [1995] ECR I–2467, I–2489.
[306] See, e.g., Case 31/74 *Mr Filippo Galli* [1975] ECR 47; and Case 177/78 *Pigs and Bacon Commission* v. *McCarren & Co Ltd* [1979] ECR 2161.

On the other hand, the Court of Justice will not normally go beyond the general scope of the questions referred to it. For example, it will not allow parties to raise issues of validity when only questions of interpretation of a provision of Union law have been referred.[307] The Court may also decline to deliver a ruling on the ground that there is no "genuine dispute" between the parties to the national court proceedings,[308] inadequate information is provided by the national court about the factual and legal background,[309] or the question "quite obviously" bears no relationship to the subject matter of the main action[310] or its purpose.[311] To assist national courts in determining what references are appropriate, the Court of Justice has produced a Note for Guidance on References by National Courts for Preliminary Rulings.[312]

Effects of a Preliminary Ruling

If a preliminary ruling is delivered, it states what the law is, and always has been. Only in exceptional cases may the Court of Justice be prepared to limit the retroactive effect of its ruling.[313] The ruling given by the Court of Justice is binding on the national court in respect of the case in which the ruling was requested.[314] The same court may, however, request a further ruling on the same question, if it arises in a subsequent case.[315]

This procedure has played a central role in the application and development of Union law. However, in the *Fifth Annual Report to the European Parliament on its Monitoring of the Application of Community Law*[316] the Commission noted that problems could arise in the operation of the Article 177 procedure, because rules regarding costs for the parties varied between

---

[307] Case 44/65 *Hessissche Knappschaft* v. *Maison Singer & Fils* [1965] ECR 965, 970–1. But cf. Case 16/65 *Firma C. Schwarz* v. *Einfuhr-und Vorratsstelle für Getreide und Futtermittel* [1965] ECR 877, 886.

[308] Case 104/79 *Pasquale Foglia* v. *Maria Novello* [1980] ECR 745, 760; and Case 244/80 *Pasquale Foglia* v. *Maria Novello* [1981] ECR 3045, 3066.

[309] Case C–458/93 *Mostafa Saddik* [1995] ECR I–511, I–518.

[310] Case C–286/88 *Falciola Angelo SpA* v. *Comune di Pavia* [1990] ECR I–191, I–195; and Case C–368/89 *Antonio Crispoltoni* v. *Fattoria Autonoma Tabacchi di Città di Castello* [1991] ECR I–3695, I–3718–19.

[311] Case C–415/93 *Union Royal Belge des Sociétés de Football Association ASBL* v. *Jean-Marc Bosman* [1995] ECR I–4921, I–5059–60; and Case C–134/95 *Unità Socio-Sanitaria Locale No 47 di Biella (USSL)* v. *Istituto Nazionale per l'Assicurazione contro gli Infortuni sul Lavoro (INAIL)* [1997] ECR I–195, I–208–9.

[312] [1997] 1 CMLR 78. See, generally, C. Barnard and E. Sharpston, "The Changing Face of Article 177 References" (1997) 34 *CMLRev.* 1113–37.

[313] Case 43/75 *Defrenne* v. *SABENA* [1976] ECR 455, 480–1; and Case 24/86 *Vincent Blaizot* v. *University of Liège* [1988] ECR 379, 406–7.

[314] Case 29/68 *Milch-, Fett- und Eierkontor GmbH* v. *Hauptzollamt Saarbrücken* [1969] ECR 165, 180.

[315] Joined Cases 28–30/62 *Da Costa en Schaake NV, Jacob Meijer NV and Hoechst-Holland NV* v. *Nederlandse Belastingadministratie* [1963] ECR 31, 38; and Case 24/86 *Vincent Blaizot* v. *University of Liège* [1988] ECR 379, 406–7.

[316] COM(88)425.

Member States.[317] More fundamentally, the Commission asserted that misuse by national courts of last resort of the *acte clair* doctrine,[318] according to which rulings need not be sought from the Court of Justice on questions of Union law where the answer is clear, tended to weaken the procedure.

5.3.7 Appellate Jurisdiction

There is a right of appeal from the Court of First Instance to the Court of Justice on points of law.[319] Appeals may be made against: final decisions; decisions disposing of the substantive issues in part only; decisions disposing of a procedural issue concerning a plea of lack of competence or inadmissibility; refusal of an application to intervene; and a decision granting or refusing interim measures.[320] If an appeal is successful, the Court of Justice quashes the judgment of the Court of First Instance. The former may then either decide the case itself or remit it to the Court of First Instance for rehearing.[321]

5.3.8 Jurisdiction of the Court of First Instance

The jurisdiction of the Court of First Instance has been expanded since its creation, though the expansion does not go as far as is allowed by the EC Treaty.

When it was established by Decision 88/59,[322] the Court of First Instance was to hear three categories of cases at first instance. These were: staff cases brought by Union servants under Article 179 of the EEC Treaty;[323] cases by natural or legal persons against Union institutions in connection with the implementation of competition rules applicable to undertakings;[324] and cases brought by undertakings or associations of undertakings under the ECSC Treaty in connection with levies, steel production quotas, pricing practices and competition matters, and related claims for compensation.

Article 168a of the EC Treaty now allows for much broader jurisdiction to be conferred, only jurisdiction to deliver preliminary rulings being expressly excluded. Hence, jurisdiction may be conferred in relation to actions brought by natural or legal persons generally and to actions brought by Member States or Union institutions.

---

[317] The real effectiveness of the procedure may also vary depending on the delays arising in judicial procedures in the different Member States. See, regarding the variations that may arise, the *Financial Times*, 13 Jan. 1992.

[318] See, generally, M. Lagrange, "The Theory of the *Acte Clair*: a Bone of Contention or a Source of Unity?" (1971) 8 *CMLRev.* 313–24.

[319] Art. 49 of the Protocol on the Statute of the ECJ.

[320] Dec. 88/591 (OJ 1988 L319/1).

[321] Art. 47 of the Protocol on the Statute of the ECJ.

[322] OJ 1988 L319/1.   [323] Now Art. 179 EC.

[324] Proceedings might be split where, e.g., Arts. 30 EEC and 85 EEC were involved. See Case C–72/90 *Asia Motor France* v. *EC Commission* [1990] ECR I–2181.

Decision 93/350[325] does not go so far. It provides that the jurisdiction of the Court of First Instance now covers proceedings brought by private persons generally under Articles 173 and 175 of the EC Treaty. This reform is designed, particularly in respect of actions requiring close examination of complex facts, to improve the judicial protection of individual rights.[326] It is also designed to maintain the quality and effectiveness of judicial review in the Union legal order by enabling the Court of Justice to concentrate on its fundamental task of ensuring the uniform interpretation of Union law.[327] However, the Court of Justice retains jurisdiction in relation to actions brought by Member States and Union institutions as well as in relation to references for preliminary rulings.

Generally, the position of private persons is said to have been improved by these arrangements, and it is anticipated that a more critical appraisal of Commission practice may be stimulated.[328] For example, in *Sytraval*[329] the Court of First Instance annulled a Commission decision rejecting a complaint of alleged state aid in favour of Securipost, a subsidiary of the French Post Office. According to the Court, the Commission had to examine impartially and exhaustively all allegations by complainants and could not impose on the complainant the burden of proof concerning the existence and incompatibility of aid. Otherwise, complainants would be required to obtain information in support of their allegations which in most cases they would be unable to obtain without the Commission as an intermediary. Therefore, the Commission could not justify the lack of sufficient reasoning by referring to the scarce information provided by the complainant.[330]

However, the primary weakness of judicial control lies in the definition of standing. This definition takes no apparent account of, for example, the "establishment" of Union Citizenship by Article 8 of the EC Treaty, subsidiarity and decision-making close to the individual,[331] or the "constitutionalisation" of cohesion objectives in Article 130b.[332] This weakness is not directly affected by the creation of the Court of First Instance and extension of its jurisdiction. On the other hand, the tendency of the Court of Justice

---

[325] Amending Dec. 88/59 (OJ 1993 L144/21).

[326] Provision is made for the CFI to encourage an amicable settlement between the parties in Art. 64 of the Rules of Procedure of the CFI (OJ 1991 L136/1).

[327] 8th recital in the preamble to Dec. 93/350 (OJ 1993 L144/21).

[328] See, e.g., L. Hancher, T. Ottervanger, and P.J. Slot, *EC State Aids* (Chancery Publishing, London, 1993), 15; and F. Y. Jenny, "Competition and State Aid Policy in the European Community" (1994) 18 *Fordham Int. Law J* 525–54.

[329] Case T–95/94 *Chambre Nationale des Entreprises de Transport de Fonds et Valeurs (Sytraval) and Brink's France SARL* v. *EC Commission* [1995] ECR II–2651.

[330] See also Case T–49/93 *Société Internationale de Diffusion et de l'Edition* v. *EC Commission* [1995] ECR II–2501, II–2527–8.

[331] Art. A TEU.

[332] See, regarding the "constitutionalisation" of these objectives, A. Valle Galvez, "La Cohesion economica y social como objetivo de la Union europea: analisis e perspectivas" [1994] *Revista de Instituciones Europeas* 341–78.

narrowly to define standing may, at least partly, have reflected a fear of being overloaded with applications. It is possible that the work of the Court of First Instance will lessen this fear and thus lead to a broader definition of standing.

Moreover, complications may arise where actions brought by individuals and actions brought by Member States against the same decision may be pending before different courts. In such circumstances, the Court of First Instance may decline jurisdiction and refer the matter to the Court of Justice under Article 47(3) of the Statute of the Court of Justice, to enable the individuals to put their case to the latter court.[333]

5.4 The European Courts and Third States

Rules governing the European Courts seem primarily concerned with the uniform interpretation of Union law within the common market and with "representation" of Member States in judicial decision-making.

5.4.1 Composition

There is no requirement that members of the European Courts possess the nationality of a Member State, but in practice only Union Citizens are appointed. Hence, these Courts may not be ideally equipped to learn from the law of third states. Their need to do so may be of particular importance where, for example, competition law issues are involved.

5.4.2 Locus Standi

Third states have no standing to take proceedings before the European Courts under provisions such as Articles 173 and 175 of the EC Treaty. Their nationals may, however, have standing.[334]

5.4.3 Intervention Rights

Third states are entitled to intervene in plenary proceedings before the Court of Justice, provided that the necessary interest in the result of the case can be established under Article 37 of the Statute of the Court of Justice.[335]

---

[333] Case T–490/93 *Bremer Vulkan Verbund AG* v. *EC Commission* [1995] ECR II–477.

[334] See, e.g., Case C–49/88 *Al-Jubail Fertilizer Co and Saudi Arabian Fertilizer Co.* v. *EC Council* [1991] ECR I–3187.

[335] Joined Cases 91 & 100/82 *Chris International Foods Ltd* v. *EC Commission* [1983] ECR 417. Moreover, in Case 266/81 *Società Italiana per l'Oleodotto Transalpino (SIOT)* v. *Ministero delle Finanze Ministero, Ministero della Marina Mercantile, Circoscrizione Doganale di Trieste and Ente Autonomo del Ponte di Trieste* [1983] ECR 731, 769 Germany referred the ECJ to a memorandum and a letter from the Austrian Embassy to the German Government.

However, this provision stipulates that the entitlement does not apply to cases between Member States, between Union institutions, or between Member States and Union institutions.[336] The rights of third states to intervene are limited to proceedings brought by private persons against Union institutions. Hence, limitations to the possibilities for private persons to take advantage of the plenary jurisdiction of the European Courts indirectly limit the significance of the intervention rights of third states.

In the case of preliminary rulings, Member States and the Commission are to be notified of references for such rulings under Article 20 of the Statute. Where the validity or interpretation of a Council act is involved, the Council is also to be notified. Moreover, the parties, the Member States and, where appropriate, the Council are entitled to submit statements of case or written observations to the Court. However, no such entitlement is conferred on third states,[337] and this provision has been strictly interpreted by the Court.[338] As a result, third states may be excluded from Court of Justice proceedings leading to the delivery of preliminary rulings.

5.4.4 Jurisdictional Exclusions

Care may be taken to limit the jurisdiction of the Court of Justice in relation to matters of special relevance to third states and their nationals. Thus, according to Article L of the Treaty on European Union, the Court does not have jurisdiction in relation to the common foreign and security policy and only has limited jurisdiction in relation to police and judicial co-operation in criminal matters.[339] Similarly, the jurisdiction of the Court under Title IV of the EC Treaty, which concerns visas, asylum, immigration, and other policies related to free movement of persons, is limited.[340] In particular, the Court has no jurisdiction in relation to measures which Member States may take concerning nationals of third states to maintain law and order and to safeguard internal security.[341]

5.4.5 Conventions

The jurisdiction conferred on the Court of Justice by various conventions may be of relevance to third states or their nationals. For example, conventions may, as in the case of computerisation of customs arrangements,[342]

---

[336] The stipulation has been relaxed in favour of EFTA states. See sect. 5.5.3 below.

[337] See, however, sect. 5.5.3 below, in the case of EFTA states.

[338] Case 19/68 *Giovanni De Cicco* v. *Landesversicherungsanstalt Schwaben* [1968] ECR 473, 479.

[339] See also Art. K.7 TEU.   [340] Art. 73p EC.

[341] Art. 73p(2) EC; and Art. 2 of the Protocol integrating the Schengen *acquis* into the framework of the EU.

[342] Protocol on the interpretation, by way of preliminary rulings, by the ECJ of the convention on the use of information technology for customs purposes (OJ 1997 C151/15). Cf. the Protocol on the interpretation, by way of preliminary rulings, by the ECJ of the convention for the protection of the European Communities' financial interests (OJ 1997 C151/1).

confer jurisdiction on the Court in relation to police and judicial co-operation in criminal matters. In addition, the Court has jurisdiction in relation to the European Patent Convention[343] pursuant to a convention on this matter.[344]

5.5 Agreements with Third States

Article 228(6) of the EC Treaty provides for the Court of Justice to give advisory opinions on the compatibility of agreements with third states or international organisations with the Treaty. The Court also has jurisdiction under Article 177 of the Treaty to deliver preliminary rulings on such agreements as "Community acts",[345] at least insofar as the relevant provision of an agreement concerns a Union commitment falling within Union powers.[346] Default proceedings may also be brought under Article 169 against a Member State in violation of an agreement between the Union and a third state.[347]

Further jurisdiction may be conferred by agreements with third states.

5.5.1 Free Trade Agreements

Free trade agreements do not specifically provide for judicial involvement in development of the integration sought by these agreements, though the possibility of establishing arbitration bodies to resolve disputes between the parties has been discussed. At the same time, however, the agreements do not preclude such involvement.

Proposed Arbitration Bodies

During the negotiations for the Swedish Free Trade Agreement[348] the Swedish Government indicated willingness to explore all possible arrangements to ensure uniform application of this Agreement. In particular, the introduction of some system of arbitration for settling disputes was envisaged. In a memorandum of 6 September 1971 Swedish willingness was even

---

[343] OJ 1976 L17/1.

[344] Protocol on the interpretation, by way of preliminary rulings, by the ECJ of the Convention on the establishment of a European Patent Office (OJ 1996 C299/1).

[345] Opinion 1/91 *Draft Agreement between the Community and the EFTA Countries relating to the Creation of the EEA* [1991] ECR I–6079, I–6105. In relation to GATT, where the Union assumed the obligations originally undertaken by the Member States, see Joined Cases 267–269/81 *Amministrazione delle Finanze dello Stato* v. *Società Petrolifera Italiana SpA (SPI) and SpA Michelin Italiana (SAMI)* [1983] ECR 801. But in relation to agreements concluded by Member States, where the Union has not assumed their obligations, see Case 44/84 *Derrick Guy Hurd* v. *Kenneth Jones (HM Inspector of Taxes)* [1986] ECR 29, 76–7 and Case C–379/92 *Matteo Peralta* [1994] ECR I–3453, I–3494–5.

[346] Case 12/86 *Meryem Demirel* v. *Stadt Schwäbisch Gmünd* [1987] ECR 3719, 3751.

[347] Case 241/85 *EC Commission* v. *Greece: ACP* [1988] ECR 1037.

[348] JO 1972 L300/96.

expressed to accept that any such arbitration body would take account of the case law of the Court of Justice. Apparently, the prospect of decision-making by a court in which there was no Swedish judge was preferable to the prospect of the economic pressure which could otherwise be exercised by the Union, particularly pursuant to safeguard clauses in the Agreement.[349]

The Union, however, was opposed to such an arrangement because of possible interference with its own decision-making processes. In particular, it was feared that introduction of an arbitration system might result in divergences between decisions of arbitrators and the case law of the Court of Justice.[350] Establishment of a separate arbitration body under other free trade agreements would have rendered such divergences all the more likely.

Union thinking in this regard has not proved easy to change. Hence, although inclusion of "an impartial legal disposition" in the Swiss Free Trade Agreement[351] was discussed in the early 1980s, the Commission apparently considered such an arrangement not to be possible.[352] On the other hand, the Union was willing to accept arrangements for arbitration in relation to more specialist agreements,[353] such as a research agreement with Switzerland of 1976[354] and a fishing agreement with Sweden of 1980.[355]

Court of Justice

The Court of Justice recognises that the operation of provisions of free trade agreements within the Union cannot be allowed to vary from Member State to Member State. Hence, the Court claims jurisdiction to interpret such provisions, with a view to ensuring their uniform interpretation throughout the Union.[356]

However, the Court interprets liberalisation requirements in these agreements so narrowly[357] that their provisions may have little relevance to the real issues of trade relations between the parties. Such interpretation may explain

---

[349] Cf. Commission Reply by Sir Leon Brittan to WQ E–1148/94 (OJ 1994 C362/57) by Cristiana Muscardini, regarding Union "pressure" on Poland to relax restrictions on exports of raw and semi-finished hides to the Union.

[350] *Commission Opinion to the Council on Relations of the Enlarged Community with the EFTA Member and Associated Countries which have not Asked to Join the EEC*, Bull. EC, Supp. 3/71, 11 and the Swedish memorandum of 6 Sept. 1971, which is reproduced in Annex 3 to D. Viklund, *Spelet om Frihandelsavtalet* (Rabén & Sjögren, Stockholm, 1977).

[351] JO 1972 L300/189.

[352] Relations between the Community and EFTA, House of Lords Select Committee on the European Communities, HL (1989–90) 55–2, 43. The matter remained "very delicate". See P.J. Kuyper, "The European Communities and Arbitration" in A.H.A. Soons (ed.), *International Arbitration: Past and Prospects* (Kluwer, Dordrecht, 1989), 181–8, 187.

[353] Though no such arrangements were made in the Civil Aviation Agreement between Norway, Sweden, and the EEC (OJ 1992 L200/21).

[354] Co-operation agreement with Switzerland in the field of controlled thermo-nuclear fusion and plasma physics (OJ 1978 L242/2), Art. 17.

[355] Art. 7(2) of the Agreement on fisheries with Sweden (OJ 1980 L226/2).

[356] Case 104/81 *Hauptzollamt Mainz* v. *C. A. Kupferberg & Cie KG* [1982] ECR 3641, 3662.

[357] Sect. 8.8.1 below.

why traders have shown less interest in invoking provisions of free trade agreements[358] than EC Treaty provisions in proceedings before the Court.[359]

5.5.2 Association Agreements

Association agreements may go further than free trade agreements in providing for judicial involvement in the integration sought thereby.[360]

Arbitration Bodies

Arbitration may be more acceptable as a means of resolving disputes between parties to association agreements[361] than between parties to free trade agreements.[362] In the case of the Greek Association Agreement,[363] the Union originally suggested that such disputes should be submitted to the Court of Justice, augmented by a Greek judge, but this arrangement was rejected by Greece.[364] The solution adopted was to provide in Article 67 of the Agreement that disputes concerning the interpretation or application of the Agreement should go to arbitration.

The Europe Agreements follow this precedent. For example, Article 105 of the Polish Agreement[365] provides that if a dispute between the Parties cannot be settled within the Association Council, either Party may notify the other of the appointment of an arbitrator. The other Party must then also appoint an arbitrator within two months. The Association Council is to appoint a third arbitrator. These arbitrators are to decide the dispute by majority vote. Each Party to the dispute must take the steps required to implement the decision of the arbitrators.

The willingness of the Union to accept such arrangements for arbitration in association agreements is comparable with Union attitudes within the World Trade Organisation. These attitudes are said to reflect Union concern regarding GATT-inconsistent actions by the United States.[366] More funda-

[358] In Joined Cases 89, 104, 114, 116–117 & 125–129/85 *A. Åhlström Osakeyhtiö* v. *EC Commission* [1988] ECR 5193 the Finnish Free Trade Agreement (OJ 1973 L328/2) was invoked as part of a procedural argument.

[359] See, e.g., Case 22/78 *Hugin Kassaregister AB and Hugin Cash Registers Ltd* v. *EC Commission* [1979] ECR 1869; and Case 86/82 *Hasselblad (GB) Ltd* v. *EC Commission* [1984] ECR 883.

[360] See, regarding the need to avoid divergent interpretations of association agreements, H.G. Schermers, "Case C–192/89 *S.Z. Sevince* v. *Staatssecretaris van Justitie*" (1991) 28 CMLRev. 183–9, 185.

[361] Cf. the arbitration arrangements in the Yaoundé Convention (JO 1970 L282/2), Art. 53.

[362] Cf., in connection with relations with the US, B.E. Carter, "A Code of Conduct for EC–US Relations" in J. Schwarze (ed.), *The External Relations of the European Community, in Particular EC–US Relations* (Nomos, Baden-Baden, 1989), 131–9, 135.

[363] JO 1963 294.

[364] H. Smit and P. Herzog, *The Law of the European Economic Community: A Commentary on the EEC Treaty* (Matthew Bender, New York, 1976), vi, 417.

[365] OJ 1993 L348/2.

[366] J.H. Jackson, "EC 92 and Beyond: Comments from a US Perspective" [1991] *Aussenwirtschaft* 341–8, 347.

mentally, it may reflect recognition of the difficulties of reconciling a "legal" regime for completion of the internal market with a "political" regime for liberalisation of trade with third states.[367]

Court of Justice

In connection with the Turkish Association Agreement,[368] the Court has claimed jurisdiction to give preliminary rulings on the interpretation of an association agreement "in so far as it is an act adopted by one of the institutions of the Community".[369] In contrast to the earlier position of the Court, adopted in relation to the Greek Association Agreement,[370] its jurisdiction is no longer expressed as being limited by the framework of the Union legal system.[371] Likewise, the Court will deliver preliminary rulings on the interpretation of acts of bodies created by such agreements.[372]

5.5.3 EEA Agreement

The EEA Agreement[373] contains more developed provisions for judicial decision making than other agreements with third states.

Arbitration Bodies

Article 111(4) of the EEA Agreement refers to disputes concerning the scope or duration of safeguard measures taken according to Article 111(3) or Article 112. It also refers to disputes concerning the proportionality of "rebalancing measures" taken according to Article 114. If the EEA Joint Committee fails to resolve any such dispute within three months, any Contracting Party may refer the dispute to binding arbitration under procedures laid down in Protocol 33 to the Agreement.[374] However, no question of interpretation of the provisions of this Agreement referred to in Article 111(3), that is, provisions which are substantially identical[375] to corresponding provisions of Union law, may be dealt with in such procedures.

---

[367] Cf. the conclusions drawn from "the changes which had occurred in the international economy in recent years" by Tesauro AG in Case C–327/91 *France* v. *EC Commission: EC/US agreement on competition* [1994] ECR I–3641, I–3644.

[368] JO 1964 3687.

[369] Case C–192/89 *S.Z. Sevince* v. *Staatssecretaris van Justitie* [1990] ECR I–3461, I–3501.

[370] JO 1963 294.

[371] Case 181/73 *R. & V. Haegeman* v. *Belgium* [1974] ECR 449, 460.

[372] Case C–192/89 *S.Z. Sevince* v. *Staatssecretaris van Justitie* [1990] ECR I–3461, I–3501–2. See, most recently, Darmon AG in Case C–355/93 *Hayriye Eroglu* v. *Land Baden-Württemberg* [1994] ECR I–5113, I–5117. The same reasoning implies that the ECJ also has jurisdiction to deliver rulings on the "validity" of such acts under Art. 177(1)(b) EC.

[373] OJ 1994 L1/3.

[374] On arbitration procedures.

[375] The terminology "textually identical", which was employed by the ECJ in Opinion 1/92 *Draft Agreement between the Community and the EFTA Countries relating to the Creation of the EEA* [1992] ECR I–2821, I–2844, may be preferable, in that it does not have the same question-begging character.

Thus the Court of Justice apparently remains free to determine the require-ments of these provisions. As the Court puts it, such arbitration "is not liable adversely to affect the autonomy of the Community legal order".[376]

Preliminary Rulings

Article 1 of Protocol 34[377] to the EEA Agreement refers to questions of inter-pretation of provisions of the Agreement, which are identical in substance to provisions of Union law. Where such a question arises in a case pending before a court or tribunal of an EFTA state, the court or tribunal may, if it considers this necessary, ask the Court of Justice to decide on the question. However, according to Article 2 of the Protocol, it is for each EFTA state to decide whether and how the Protocol will apply to its courts or tribunals.

"Homogeneity Proceedings"

Article 111(3) of the EEA Agreement deals with disputes concerning case law regarding provisions of this Agreement which are identical in substance to corresponding rules of the EC Treaty, ECSC Treaty, or acts adopted in appli-cation of these Treaties. If such a dispute has not been settled within three months after it has been brought before the EEA Joint Committee, the Contracting Parties to the dispute may agree to request the Court of Justice to give a ruling (*se prononcer*) on the interpretation of the relevant rules.[378] Since the ruling is to be binding, the nature of the function of the Court as conceived in the EC Treaty is not changed.[379] At the same time, since the agreement of EFTA states is necessary for a matter to be referred, they are protected against compulsory jurisdiction of a Court on which none of their nationals sits. This reconciliation of the integrity of the Court of Justice and the sovereignty of EFTA states is achieved, however, at the expense of denial of judicial protection to private persons. Such persons cannot invoke this procedure.

Annulment Proceedings

Article 6(2) of Protocol 24[380] to the EEA Agreement confers a right on EFTA states to challenge Commission decisions regarding reference of a notified concentration to an EFTA state whose distinct market may be affected. In such cases any EFTA state may "appeal" to the Court of Justice on the same grounds and conditions as a Member State under Article 173 of the EC Treaty. In particular, an EFTA state may request the application of interim measures, for the purpose of applying its national law. In this respect, EFTA

---

[376] *Ibid.,* I–2844.

[377] On the possibility for courts and tribunals of EFTA states to request the ECJ to decide on the interpretation of EEA rules corresponding to EC rules.

[378] It has apparently been agreed that in such circumstances the Commission will request the ECJ to deliver an Art. 228(6) EC opinion ([1992] ECR I–2821, I–2834).

[379] *Ibid.,* I–2844.

[380] On co-operation in the field of control of concentrations.

states are to have the same rights as Member States under Article 9(9) of Regulation 4064/89[381] to take proceedings before the Court of Justice.[382]

Intervention Rights for EFTA States

A Declaration by the Union, attached to the EEA Agreement, sought to reinforce legal homogeneity within the EEA through the opening of intervention possibilities for EFTA states and the EFTA Surveillance Authority before the Court of Justice. In accordance with this Declaration, Articles 20 and 37 of the Statute of the Court of Justice[383] were amended.[384] As a result, EFTA states, like Member States, have a general entitlement to intervene in proceedings before the European Courts.

EEA Information System

Article 6 of the EEA Agreement deals, without prejudice to future developments of case law, with the provisions of this Agreement which are identical in substance to corresponding rules of the EC Treaty, the ECSC Treaty, or acts adopted in application of these two Treaties. Such provisions shall in their implementation and application be interpreted in conformity with the relevant rulings of the Court of Justice given before the date of signature of this Agreement.[385]

For the future, to ensure as uniform an interpretation as possible of the EEA Agreement,[386] in full deference to the independence of courts, an information system has been established under Article 106 of the Agreement. This system concerns judgments of the EFTA Court,[387] the Court of Justice, the Court of First Instance, and the courts of last instance of the EFTA states. This system involves, in particular, transmission to the Registrar of the Court of Justice of judgments delivered by such courts on the interpretation and application of this Agreement or the EC or ECSC Treaty, as amended or supplemented, as well as the acts adopted in pursuance thereof, in so far as they concern provisions which are identical in substance to those of this Agreement.[388]

---

[381] On the control of concentrations between undertakings (OJ 1989 L395/1, as corrected by OJ 1990 L257/13). See Chap. 15 below.

[382] Para. 2 of the Declaration by the EC on the Rights for the EFTA states before the ECJ. The grant of these rights reflects the exceptional powers in relation to mergers conferred on the Commission by Art. 57(2)(a) EEA.

[383] See also the Declaration by the EC on the Rights of Lawyers of the EFTA States under Community law, concerning rights of lawyers before the ECJ and CFI and legal privilege.

[384] Dec. 94/993 (OJ 1994 L379/1) amending the Protocol on the Statute of the ECJ.

[385] See, more particularly, Art. 2(1) of Prot. 28, on intellectual property, concerning the exhaustion of rights doctrine developed in the case law of the ECJ, and the adaptation in Annex XVI of Art. 2(8) of Dir. 89/665 (OJ 1989 L395/33) on review procedures relating to the award of public supply and public works contracts.

[386] See also the 15th recital in the preamble to the EEA Agreement.

[387] Established under Art. 108(2) EEA and the EFTA Agreement on the establishment of a Surveillance Authority and a Court of Justice (OJ 1994 L344/1).

[388] This arrangement is reminiscent of the Lugano Convention on jurisdiction and the enforcement of judgments in civil and commercial matters (OJ 1988 L319/9).

Moreover, Article 105(2) requires the Joint Committee to keep under constant review the development of the case law of the Court of Justice and the EFTA Court. To this end, judgments of these Courts shall be transmitted to the Committee. If the Committee after two months from the date when a difference in the case law of the two courts has been brought before it, has not succeeded in preserving the homogeneous interpretation of the Agreement,[389] the procedures laid down in Article 111 may be applied.[390]

This system may not be not purely "one way", in the sense that the EFTA Court simply follows judgments of the European Courts. The Court of First Instance at least may cite judgments of the EFTA Court.[391]

---

[389] The European Parliament has argued that a Joint Committee cannot work effectively to interpret judgments of the ECJ or resolve differences caused by diverse judicial decisions. See the observations of the Parliament in Opinion 1/92 *Draft Agreement between the Community and the EFTA Countries relating to the Creation of the EEA* [1992] ECR I–2821, I–2837.

[390] Art. 105(3) EEA. These procedures may involve resort to safeguard measures or suspension of EEA law affected.

[391] Case T–115/94 *Opel Austria GmbH* v. *EC Commission* [1997] ECR II–39, II–61 and II–76.

6

Other Bodies

Besides the institutions already discussed, a variety of other bodies participates in the work of the Union. The bodies concerned may increase the technical expertise available to the Union and broaden the range of participants in its work. At the same time, however, their proliferation may be criticised, as leading to reduced efficiency and transparency.[1] Indeed, insofar as they may not easily be subjected to control by the European Parliament, they may often be seen as exacerbating the "democratic deficit".

Some have been established by the Union Treaties or agreements with third states, others by the Union institutions[2] or by Member States,[3] and others "privately". The role of privately established bodies in the work of the Union highlights the extent to which, at the Union level as at the national level, state and market are intertwined. The Court of Auditors[4] is the only one of these bodies which is included in the list of institutions in Article 4(1) of the EC Treaty.[5]

They may variously be termed "bodies",[6] "Community bodies",[7] "advisory bodies",[8] "organs",[9] or "administrative organisms".[10] Freedom of internal

---

[1] See, e.g., the European Parliament Resolution of 16 Sept. 1983 (OJ 1983 C277/195) on the cost to the EC budget and effectiveness of committees of a management, advisory, and consultative nature. Cf. the requirement in Art. 5 ECSC that administrative machinery should be kept to a minimum.

[2] A list of committees is contained in Part A, Annex II to the 1997 Budget (OJ 1997 L44/3).

[3] Cf., regarding the European Schools, which have been established by international agreements concluded between Member States and whose staff receive salary supplements from the budget (Item A–3270 of the 1997 Budget (OJ 1997 L44/3)), Case 44/84 *Derrick Guy Hurd* v. *Kenneth Jones (HM Inspector of Taxes)* [1986] ECR 29.

[4] The Court of Auditors was added to the list of institutions in Art. 4(1) EC by the TEU.

[5] The EIB participates in the fulfilment of Union tasks, though it is formally separate from the Union.

[6] Arts 8d and 213b EC; and the Protocol on the location of the seats of the institutions and of certain bodies and departments of the European Communities and of Europol.

[7] Decision of the Representatives of the Governments of the Member States on the provisional location of certain institutions and departments of the Communities of 8 Apr. 1965 (JO 1967 152/18), Art. 10.

[8] Protocol on the Privileges and Immunities of the European Communities, Art. 11(2). See also the Financial Reg. of 21 Dec. 1977 (OJ 1977 L356/1), Art. 12(4)(c).

[9] Draft Treaty establishing a European Union (OJ 1984 C77/33), Art. 33, though this provision came within the Chapter headed "Institutions of the Union".

[10] *Ibid.*, Art. 61.

organisation[11] and, more particularly, budgetary autonomy[12] may be stressed as decisive criteria for distinguishing between "institutions" and such bodies. In practice, however, the distinction may often be less than perfect.[13]

They may have advisory functions, primarily in connection with the enactment of Union legislation, administrative functions, or supervisory functions.

6.1 Advisory Bodies

Advisory bodies may be established by the Treaties themselves or by the Union institutions.[14] Other such bodies may be established "privately".

6.1.1 ECSC Consultative Committee

Article 18 of the ECSC Treaty provides for establishment of a Consultative Committee.

Composition

The ECSC Consultative Committee, which is attached to the Commission, is to contain between eighty-four and 108 members.[15] It is to accord equal representation to producers, workers, consumers, and dealers in the coal and steel industries. The members are all appointed by the Council, though in the case of producers and workers special arrangements are made. In their case the Council designates those representative organisations[16] which are to be allocated the relevant seats. Each organisation then draws up a list nominating twice as many candidates as there are seats allocated to it, and from these lists the Council makes the appointments.

---

[11] See, e.g., Joined Cases 161 & 162/80 *Maria Grazia Carbognani and Marisa Coda Zabetta* v. *EC Commission* [1981] ECR 543, 563.

[12] Under Art. 11 of the Financial Reg. of 21 Dec. 1977 (OJ 1977 L356/1) the Court of Auditors submitted an estimate of its expenditure directly to the Commission, whereas the Economic and Social Committee passed it to the Council. But see, regarding the Court of Auditors, Reg. 2333/95 (OJ 1995 L240/1) amending the Financial Reg. See, regarding the Economic and Social Committee and the Committee of the Regions, Reg. 1923/94 (OJ 1994 L198/4) amending the Financial Reg.

[13] The Court of Auditors, e.g., once described itself as having "semi-institutional status" (Annual report for 1977 (OJ 1978 C313/1), para. 15). According to Case 828/79 *Adam* v. *EC Commission* [1982] ECR 269, 291 and Case 1253/79 *Dino Battaglia* v. *EC Commission* [1982] ECR 297, 319, the Court of Auditors and the Economic and Social Committee were institutions for certain purposes.

[14] Cf., regarding objections to the allocation of judicial functions to such bodies, Gand AG in Case 19/67 *Bestuur der Sociale Verzekeringsbank* v. *Van der Vecht* [1967] ECR 345, 361.

[15] Dec. 95/1 (OJ 1995 L1/1) adjusting the instruments concerning the accession of new Member States to the EU, Art. 16.

[16] In the case of consumers and traders, Art. 4 of the Convention on Transitional Provisions, adopted with the ECSC Treaty, envisaged the provision of information regarding their organisations.

Members of the Committee are appointed in their personal capacity. They may not be bound by any mandate or instructions from the organisations which nominated them.

Organisation

The Consultative Committee has established standing committees on general objectives, markets and prices, labour, and research and development as well as various *ad hoc* committees.[17] The standing committees promote continuity in the work of the Committee between plenary sessions and facilitate concentration of the expertise of its members on relevant issues. Hence, their establishment may enhance the technical effectiveness with which the Committee performs its functions.

Committee sessions are not held in public.[18] However, the ECSC Treaty requires the minutes of the proceedings of the Committee to be forwarded to the Commission and the Council at the same time as its opinions.[19] In practice, its reports, opinions, and resolutions are sent to the Presidents of the Commission and Council.[20] Moreover, its proceedings *may* be published in the Official Journal.

The lack of any obligation to publish the proceedings may reflect the fact that the Treaty confers no immunity on Committee members in respect of views expressed in the course of such proceedings. Possibly, conferment of immunity would have constituted too close an assimilation to parliamentary practice to have been acceptable to opponents of formal institutionalised representation of socio-economic interest groups. In these circumstances, the confidentiality of such proceedings may have been thought necessary to protect the independence of members from the organisations which nominated them. However, a consequence is that public expression can only be given to the range of views within the Committee through a watering-down of its opinions to accommodate an often diverse range of views or through the delivery of minority opinions. In either case, the political weight attached to its opinions may be diminished. A further consequence is that the public and even some Union bodies may lack awareness of the work of the Committee.

Functions

Article 19(1) of the ECSC Treaty provides that the Commission must consult the Consultative Committee when such consultation is prescribed by particular Treaty provisions.[21] The Commission may also consult the Committee in other cases where consultation is thought appropriate.[22]

---

[17] Art. 4 of the Internal Regulations of the Committee (OJ 1986 C149/4).
[18] *Ibid.*, Art. 12.   [19] Art. 19(5) ECSC.
[20] Art. 13 of the Internal Regulations of the Committee (OJ 1986 C149/4).
[21] Arts. 53, 55, 58, 59, 60, 61, 62, 67, 68, and 95 ECSC.
[22] Cf. Art. 46 ECSC, which empowers the Commission to consult concerned parties directly.

When consulted, the Committee must be informed of all the elements of the problem but need not be given the text of a proposal. This is because its function is to advise on economic problems rather than to provide opinions on drafts.[23]

The difficulties likely to be experienced in reaching consensus among representatives of diverse, and even possibly antagonistic, interest groups may be implicitly recognised in Article 19(3) of the Treaty. It empowers the Commission to set a time limit for receipt of an opinion from the Committee.[24] The period allowed must not be less than ten days from the date when the Chairman of the Committee is notified of the deadline.

However, the role of the Committee is not apparently intended to be merely reactive. Article 19(4) provides that the Committee may be convened, either at the request of the Commission or of a majority of its members, to discuss a specific question. In effect, the Committee is empowered to deliver opinions on its own initiative.

Moreover, Article 19(2) requires the Commission to submit to the Committee its general objectives and programmes drawn up under Article 46 concerning economic and social developments in the coal and steel industries. It is only after such submission that these general objectives and programmes may be published. The Commission is also to keep the Committee informed of the broad lines of its action under Article 54, which deals with the promotion and regulation of investment in these industries, and Articles 65 and 66, which deal with anti-competitive conduct.

In practice, the Commission makes both oral and written statements on such matters and answers questions put to it during plenary sessions of the Committee. Hence, while such a role may not be expressly envisaged in Article 19, the Committee has apparently acquired a position in which it may exercise a degree of supervision over more detailed administration.

6.1.2 Economic and Social Committee

The EEC[25] and Euratom[26] Treaties each provided for establishment of an Economic and Social Committee. However, Article 5(1) of the Convention on Certain Institutions Common to the European Communities made clear that there was to be a single such body for the two Communities.[27]

---

[23] Lagrange AG in Case 2/54 *Italy* v. *ECSC High Authority: steel prices* [1954–6] ECR 37, 60; and Roemer AG in Case 6/54 *Netherlands* v. *ECSC High Authority: coal prices* [1954–6] ECR 103, 134.

[24] The earlier Internal Regs. (JOCECA 1955 596) provided for sessions to be held to comply with such deadlines (Art. 12). The present Internal Regs. (OJ 1986 C149/4) provide for written consultation (Art. 7).[25] Art. 193(1) EEC.   [26] Art. 165(1) Euratom.

[27] See, now, Art. 9(2) of the Amsterdam Treaty (OJ 1997 C340/1).

Composition

According to Article 193(2) of the EC Treaty, the Economic and Social Committee is to consist of representatives of the various categories of economic and social activity. In particular, it is to contain representatives of producers, farmers, carriers, workers, dealers, craftsmen, professional occupations, and the general public. France, Germany, Italy, and the United Kingdom are entitled to twenty-four members each; Spain to twenty-one; Austria, Belgium, Greece, the Netherlands, Portugal, and Sweden to twelve each; Denmark, Finland, and Ireland to nine each; and Luxembourg to six.[28] This bias in favour of smaller Member States is more pronounced than in the allocation of seats in the European Parliament.[29]

The members of the Economic and Social Committee are appointed, for renewable four-year terms, by the Council acting unanimously.[30] In making these appointments, the Council acts on the basis of lists provided by each Member State and containing twice as many names as there are seats allocated to it. It is stipulated in Article 195(1) that the composition of the Committee should take account of the need to ensure adequate representation of the various categories of economic and social activity. Moreover, under Article 195(2) the Council must consult the Commission. The Council may also obtain the opinion of European bodies which are representative of the various economic and social sectors to which the activities of the Union are of concern. The European Parliament, however, is denied any formal role in the appointment process.

Members of the Committee may not be bound by any mandatory instructions. They shall be completely independent in the performance of their duties, in "the general interest of the Community".[31]

Organisation

The Committee is to elect its Chairman and officers from among its members.[32] The Chairman, two Vice-Chairmen, and thirty-three elected members form the Bureau, which is responsible for organising the Committee's work.[33]

The Rules of Procedure of the Committee[34] originally had to be submitted for the approval of the Council, acting unanimously.[35] The Committee thus lacked the freedom of the ECSC Consultative Committee to adopt its own Rules. Article 196(2) of the EC Treaty now empowers the Committee to

---

[28] Art. 194(1) EC.   [29] Sect. 3.1.1 above.   [30] Art. 194(2) EC.
[31] Art. 194(3) EC.   [32] Art. 196 EC.
[33] Rule 5 of the Rules of Procedure of the Committee (Dec. 96/235 (OJ 1996 L82/1)).
[34] *Ibid.*
[35] Art. 196(3) EEC. This procedure diverged from the general rule in Art. 153 EEC that the Council was to act by majority in determining rules governing committees provided for in the Treaty on the basis of a Commission opinion.

adopt these Rules itself, though the Treaty still regulates matters of its internal organisation in some detail.

Article 197(1) of the Treaty provides that the Committee shall include specialised sections for the principal fields covered by the Treaties.[36] In particular, references are made to an agricultural section[37] and a transport section.[38] These specialised sections must, according to Article 197(2), operate within the general terms of reference of the Committee itself and may not be consulted independently of the latter. This stipulation is designed to protect the integrity of the Committee.[39] The methods of composition and terms of reference of the specialised sections are, according to Article 197(4), to be laid down in the Rules of Procedure.[40] Sections have also been established for economic affairs, social affairs, environment, industry, regional development, energy, and external relations. The sections each appoint a *rapporteur*, whose report and draft opinion are debated and voted on by the Committee at its monthly meetings.

At the same time, tacit approval is given to ECSC Consultative Committee practice in Article 197(3). It provides for establishment of sub-committees to prepare, on specific questions or in specific fields, draft opinions to be submitted to the Economic and Social Committee for its consideration.

In practice, however, the activity of the Committee revolves not so much around these bodies as around three groups, the Employers' Group, the Workers' Group, and the General Interests' Group. Although these groups are not mentioned in the Treaty, their importance is recognised in the Rules of Procedure.[41] Thus, for example, the Chairman of the Committee is to be chosen in rotation from each of these groups.[42]

Functions

The substance of Committee activity is, according to express statement in Articles 4(2) and 193(1) of the EC Treaty, to be directed towards performance of advisory functions. In particular, the Committee must be consulted by the

---

[36] Art. 5(2) of the Convention on Common Institutions also required establishment of a section for nuclear energy.

[37] See also Art. 47 EEC.

[38] According to Art. 83 EC, an Advisory Transport Committee, consisting of experts designated by the governments of Member States, shall be attached to the Commission. The Commission, whenever it considers consultation desirable, shall consult the Committee on transport matters without prejudice to the powers of the transport section of the Economic and Social Committee.

[39] Chambre des Députés, *Projets de loi portant approbation du Traité instituant la Communauté économique européenne: exposé des motifs* (Luxembourg, 1957), 40.

[40] OJ 1996 L82/1, Chap. IV.   [41] *Ibid.*, Art. 22.   [42] *Ibid.*, Art. 5(1).

Council[43] or Commission[44] where the Treaty so provides. Consultation may also take place in all other cases considered appropriate. A time limit of not less than one month may be imposed on the consultation procedure.[45]

On the other hand, Article 196(3) of the EEC Treaty provided that the Committee was to be convened by its chairman at the request of the Council or Commission. The implication was that the Committee, unlike the ECSC Consultative Committee, could not convene itself. The conclusion was drawn that it could not deliver opinions on its own initiative. However, in 1974 the Council approved an amendment to the Rules of Procedure[46] so as to entitle the Committee to deliver "own initiative" opinions.

Article 196(3) of the EC Treaty now provides that the Committee may meet on its own initiative. Article 198 also provides that the Committee may issue an opinion on its own initiative in cases in which it considers such action appropriate.

Further enhancement of the role of the Committee has resulted from developments in practice,[47] though the European Parliament considers that there remains a need for greater consultation of the Committee.[48] Thus the Commission regularly consults the Committee, even where such consultation is not required by the Treaty. In fact, where a draft is adopted by the Commission, it will usually be sent to the Committee at the same time as it is sent to the European Parliament. Where a draft is amended in the light of a Committee opinion, the amended version will generally be returned to the Committee at the same time as it is sent to the Council. More generally, senior Commission officials assist the Committee in its work, and Commissioners often attend plenary sessions, at which they may answer questions. Moreover, the Commission submits its quarterly schedule unofficially and confidentially to the Committee and informs the Committee each Thursday of the main decisions taken at its weekly meetings.

Notable developments have also taken place in relations between the Council and the Committee. Thus the President of the Council attends one plenary session of the Committee each year. At this session the President

[43] Arts. 43(2), 49, 54(1), 63, 75, 79(3), 99, 100, 100a(1), 109q(2), 109r, 118(2) and (3), 119(3), 121, 125, 126(4), 127(4), 129(4), 129a(4), 129d, 130(3), 130b, 130d, 130e, 130i(1) and (4), 130o, and 130s EC.

[44] Art. 118c EC; Arts. 9(1), 31(1), 40(2), 41(2), 96(2), and 98(2) Euratom. Under Art. 7(5) EEC the Commission was merely to inform the Committee. Under Arts. 120 and 130b EC the Commission reports to the Committee.

[45] Art. 198(2) EC.

[46] Dec. 74/428 (OJ 1974 L228/1).

[47] See, generally, Economic and Social Committee, *The Right of Initiative of the Economic and Social Committee* (ESC, Brussels, 1972), 45.

[48] Resolution of 10 Dec. 1996 (OJ 1997 C20/31) on participation of citizens and social players in the EU's institutional system and the IGC, para. 37.

presents to the Committee a general statement concerning the work of the Council. In addition, COREPER and the General Secretariat send observers to plenary sessions. Even so, the technical rather than political significance of the work of the Committee tends to be stressed.[49]

6.1.3 Committee of the Regions

Article 4(2) of the EC Treaty provides for a Committee of the Regions to assist the Council and Commission in an advisory capacity. This Committee, consisting of representatives of regional and local bodies,[50] is established by Article 198a of the Treaty.

Composition

According to Article 198a of the Treaty, the members of the Committee are appointed for four years by the Council, acting unanimously on proposals from the respective Member States. Their term of office is renewable. Members of the Committee may not be bound by any mandatory instructions. They shall be completely independent in the performance of their duties, in the general interest of the Union.

In its contributions to the intergovernmental conference which adopted the Treaty on European Union the Commission favoured a stipulation that, as in the case of the earlier Consultative Council of Regional and Local Authorities,[51] membership of the Committee should be limited to those holding elective office at regional or local level.[52] The European Parliament also considers that Committee members should be "elected representatives at immediate sub-central government level and/or that they should derive direct democratic legitimacy from a regional or local assembly".[53] However, no such stipulation is included in Article 198a of the Treaty. Hence, each Member State is free, but not obliged, to propose elected representatives as members of the Committee.[54] This arrangement is designed to allow for the fact that "the Member States have very different institutional structures which are exclusively within their purview".[55]

As a result, even if centralised representation through such a body were

[49] Joined Cases 281, 283–285 & 287/85 *Germany* v. *EC Commission: migration policy* [1987] ECR 3203, 3256.

[50] It is not apparently necessary that these bodies constitute local or regional "authorities" or "government".

[51] Art. 3(1) of Dec. 88/487 (OJ 1988 L247/23) setting up a Consultative Council of Regional and Local Authorities.

[52] Art. 198a(2) of the Commission draft (Bull. EC, Supp. 2/91, 178).

[53] Resolution of 18 Nov. 1993 (OJ 1993 C329/279) on the participation and representation of the regions in the process of European integration: the Committee of the Regions, para. 9. See also the Resolution of 23 Apr. 1993 (OJ 1993 C150/329) on the Committee of the Regions, para. 4.

[54] Reply by Mr Millan to WQ 1206/92 (OJ 1993 C6/10) by Mr Jaak Vandemeulebroucke.

[55] Reply by Mr Millan to WQ 1405/92 (OJ 1993 C16/15) by Mr Sotiris Kostopoulos.

an appropriate mechanism for regional participation in Union decision making, the Treaty fails to ensure that such participation may take place. In fact, the inadequacy of this form of representation is implicitly recognised by the Committee of the Regions itself. According to the Committee, it should be represented on various committees consulted by the Commission, to ensure that views of *individual regions* affected by Union decisions will be heard.[56]

Organisation

The Committee elects its chairman and officers from its members for a term of two years. It shall adopt its Rules of Procedure[57] and submit them for approval to the Council acting unanimously. It shall be convened by its chairman at the request of the Council of Commission. It may also meet on its own initiative.[58]

Functions

According to Article 198c of the EC Treaty, the Committee shall be consulted by the Council or Commission where the Treaty so provides.[59] It is to be consulted in all other cases, particularly those concerning cross-border co-operation, in which one of these institutions considers such consultation to be appropriate. It may also be consulted by the European Parliament. Moreover, the Committee may take the initiative and issue an opinion in cases in which it considers such action appropriate. The opinions, together with a record of the proceedings, are to be forwarded to the Council and Commission.

Hence, this Committee is described as "an institution through which regional and local bodies can officially be involved in drawing up and implementing Community policies".[60] According to the Committee itself, its establishment "enables regional and local bodies to participate, via the Committee of the Regions, in the decision-making process of the European Union".[61] Indeed, the "inclusion" of such bodies in the legislative process is said to be entailed by its establishment.[62] However, it is questionable whether the rules governing the composition of the Committee are such as to ensure that this role can satisfactorily be played.

[56] Opinion of 17 May 1994 (OJ 1994 C217/26) on the proposal for a decision laying down a series of guidelines on trans-European energy networks, para. A.5.1.

[57] OJ 1994 L132/49.   [58] Art. 198c EC.

[59] Arts. 109q(2), 109r, 118, 125, 126(4), 127(4), 128(5), 129(4), 129d, 130b, 130d, 130e, and 130s EC.

[60] Preamble to Dec. 94/209 (OJ 1994 L103/28) winding up the Consultative Council of Regional and Local Authorities, 3rd recital.

[61] Opinion of 17 May 1994 (OJ 1994 C217/10) on the draft notice laying down guidelines for operational programmes which Member States are invited to establish in the framework of a Community initiative concerning urban areas, para. 4 of the preamble.

[62] Resolution of the European Parliament of 18 Nov. 1993 (OJ 1993 C329/279) on the participation and representation of the regions in the process of European integration: the Committee of the Regions, recital G in the preamble.

6.1.4 Expert Groups

According to Paragraph (a)I of the Luxembourg Accords,[63] the Commission seeks advice from experts of the Member States in elaborating its proposals for legislative enactments. For this purpose, the Commission establishes working groups of experts.[64] Although these experts are expected to act independently, they include civil servants, who will be in a position to advise the Commission of the acceptability of its proposal to their respective national governments.

6.1.5 Other Advisory Committees

Various other committees have been established by the Treaties or the Union institutions, to advise the Commission. While their functions are advisory, the Commission is to take "utmost account" of their opinions.[65]

For example, there is an Advisory Committee on the Development and Conversion of Regions. According to the legislation establishing this body, the Commission must "take utmost account of the opinions of the Committee".[66]

Again, an Advisory Committee for the European Social Fund was provided for in Article 124 of the EEC Treaty[67] and was established in 1960.[68] This committee delivers opinions on draft Commission decisions. The Commission is to inform the committee of the manner in which it has taken account of these opinions.[69]

Arrangements regarding the Advisory Committee on Integrated Mediterranean Programmes went further. This Committee, consisting of representatives of the Member States and chaired by the Commission, was established by Article 7(1) of Regulation 2088/85.[70] According to Article 7(2) of the same Regulation, the Committee was to consider draft programmes submitted by the Commission. If the Committee delivered a negative opinion on a draft programme presented by the Commission, the latter had to amend its original draft taking into consideration the Committee's opinion and to resubmit the amended draft. Within a month of the second submission the Commission was required finally to decide on implementation of the

---

[63] Bull. EC 3–1966, 9.

[64] See, generally, M. Ayral, "Essai de classification des groupes et comités" [1975] *RMC* 330–42. See, regarding the origins of these arrangements under the ECSC Treaty, D. Vignes, *Communauté européenne de la charbon et de l'acier* (Thone, Liège, 1956), 24.

[65] Art. 2 of Dir. 87/373 (OJ 1987 L197/33) laying down the procedures for the exercise of implementing powers conferred on the Commission.

[66] Art. 27 of Reg. 2082/93 (OJ 1993 L193/20) amending Reg. 4253/88 laying down provisions for implementing Reg. 2052/88 as regards co-ordination of the activities of the different Structural Funds between themselves and with the operations of the EIB and the other existing financial instruments.

[67] See now Art. 147 EC. Cf., regarding the Employment Committee, Art. 109s EC.

[68] Reg. 9/60 on the ESF (JO 1960 1189), Arts. 27–30.

[69] Art. 28 of Reg. 2082/93 (OJ 1993 L193/20).

[70] Concerning the IMPs (OJ 1985 L197/1).

programme.

The relevant committees may be mainly intended to provide a link between the representatives of the Member States and the Commission. Their work may, however, be criticised on the ground that they do not aim specifically to ensure efficient administration.[71]

6.1.6 Lobbying Bodies

Lobbying may appear to be rendered a constitutional right by recognition of the right to petition the European Parliament in Article 138d of the EC Treaty.[72] More particularly, Article 118a of the Treaty requires the Commission to promote "the consultation of management and labour at Community level" and to "facilitate their dialogue". Limited progress has been made in formalising this dialogue. However, lobbying of the Union institutions is well established through bodies such as the Union of Industrial and Employers' Confederations of Europe (UNICE) and the European Trade Union Confederation (ETUC).[73]

Lobbying, as a response to trading problems, and the operation of Union law may be interrelated processes. In particular, lobbying constitutes a response on the political market as an alternative to an exit response on the economic market. In other words, economic actors may lobby for more satisfactory legislation rather than leaving the market because they consider existing regulation unsatisfactory. Lobbying may thus affect the extent to which the operation of four-freedom provisions leads to "regulatory competition" between Member States.[74] At the same time, in so far as "integration management" leads the Union to adopt harmonisation acts, lobbying may be regarded as an instrument of "participatory democracy", according to which those more directly affected by such an act should have a proportionally greater input in its preparation than others.[75] The implication is that the content of such acts may be affected by lobbying.

However, lobbying may be both controversial,[76] because of fears that decision making may be "distorted" thereby,[77] and of variable effectiveness.[78]

---

[71] Special Report 3/92 of the Court of Auditors (OJ 1992 C245/1), para. 2.8.

[72] Sect. 3.3.3 above.

[73] The European Parliament has adopted a code of conduct on the matter. See Rule 9 of, and Annexes I and IX to, the Rules of Procedure of the Parliament (OJ 1997 L49/1).

[74] J.-M. Sun and J. Pelkmans, "Regulatory Competition in the Single Market" [1995] *JCMS* 567–89. See sect. 8.3.4 below, regarding regulatory competition and the free movement of goods.

[75] K. Lenaerts, "Regulating the Regulatory Process: 'Delegation of Powers' in the European Community" [1993] *ELR* 23–49, 24.

[76] See, regarding plans for a register of interests of assistants of MEPs, *The European*, 10–16 Feb. 1995 and 31 Mar.–6 Apr. 1995.

[77] Cf. the application of the idea of comparative advantage to situations where a Member State has nationals well placed in committees of the European Parliament in J.-M. Sun and J. Pelkmans, n. 74 above, 80, n. 11.

[78] See, generally, C. Harlow, "A Community of Interests? Making the Most of European Law" (1992) 55 *MLR* 331–50.

6.2 Administrative Bodies

Various bodies have responsibilities relating to the administration of Union policies. Besides the bodies examined below, they include, for example, the European Centre for the Development of Vocational Training[79] and the European Foundation for the Improvement of Living and Working Conditions.[80]

6.2.1 European Investment Bank

The European Investment Bank is an autonomous body with its own power of decision. The Bank is established by the EC Treaty,[81] which also confers legal personality on it.[82] However, the Protocol on the Privileges and Immunities of the European Communities applies to the Bank.[83] Moreover, the details of its tasks, composition, organisation, and functioning are laid down in the Treaty, together with the Protocol on the Statute of the European Investment Bank annexed thereto. Therefore, despite having its own legal personality, the Bank has been described as a "Community institution"[84] or a "Community organ".[85]

Composition

Article 198d of the EC Treaty designates the Member States as members of the European Investment Bank. According to the Protocol on the Statute of the Bank, its work is to be directed by a Board of Governors, a Board of Directors, and a Management Committee.[86]

Organisation

The Board of Governors consists of the finance ministers of each Member State.[87] In substance, this body may thus be indistinguishable from a Council meeting to discuss financial affairs. However, the organisation and work of the Board are largely governed by the special rules of Statute of the Bank rather than the general Treaty rules governing the Council. Under the Statute its role is essentially to lay down general directives for the credit policy of the Bank and to ensure that these directives are implemented.[88] Save as otherwise provided in the Statute, the Board acts by a majority of its members,

---

[79] Reg. 337/75 (OJ 1975 L39/1).

[80] Reg. 1365/75 (OJ 1975 L139/1). See also the European Parliament Resolution of 13 Mar. 1987 (OJ 1987 C99/199) on the proposal for a regulation amending Reg. 1365/75, para. 8.

[81] Art. 4b EC. See, originally, Art. 129 EEC.

[82] See also Art. 28(1) of the Protocol on the Statute of the EIB.

[83] *Ibid.*, Art. 22.

[84] Case 110/75 *Mills* v. *EIB* [1976] ECR 955, 968.

[85] Warner AG (*ibid.*, 974).

[86] Arts. 8 and 9 of the Protocol on the Statute of the EIB.

[87] *Ibid.*, Art. 9(1).   [88] *Ibid.*, Art. 9(2).

though it is stipulated that a majority must represent at least 45 per cent of the subscribed capital.[89] Apart from this stipulation, voting takes place according to the general provisions of the Treaty.[90]

The Board of Directors consists of twenty-five directors with thirteen alternates, all of whom are appointed for five-year renewable terms by the Board of Governors on the basis of nominations made by the Member States. Each of the "big four" nominates three directors, Spain nominates two, and the other Member States and the Commission nominate one each. Each of the "big four" also nominates two alternates, while the Benelux countries by common accord, Denmark, Greece, and Ireland, by common accord, Spain and Portugal by common accord, Finland and Sweden by common accord, and the Commission nominate one.[91] The task of this Board is to manage the Bank according to the Treaty, the Statute, and the general directives of the Board of Governors. Thus the former Board may grant loans and guarantees, raise loans, and fix the interest rates charged on loans.[92] Save as otherwise provided in the Statute, the Board takes its decisions by a simple majority of its members. However, where a qualified majority is stipulated, seventeen affirmative votes are required.[93]

The Management Committee is composed of a President and six Vice-Presidents, who are all appointed for six-year renewable terms by the Board of Governors on a proposal from the Board of Directors.[94] This Committee has responsibility for the current business of the Bank.[95] It acts under the authority of the President and the supervision of the Board of Directors. It prepares the Board's decisions, particularly those regarding the raising of loans and the granting of loans and guarantees, and ensures the implementation of these decisions.[96] The President of the Committee or, in his absence, a Vice-President also acts as a non-voting Chairman of the Board of Directors.[97]

Functions

The Bank is required by Article 198e of the Treaty to contribute to the balanced and steady development of the common market in the "Community interest". To this end, the Bank is to grant loans or guarantees, on a non-profit-making basis, which facilitate the financing of: projects benefiting the less developed regions of the Union; projects modernising or converting undertakings called for by the progressive establishment of the common market, provided that the projects are of such a size or nature that they cannot be financed entirely by the various means available within the individual Member States; and, subject to the same proviso, projects of common interest to several Member States. According to the Protocol on

---

[89] *Ibid.*, Art. 10.   [90] I.e., Art. 148 EC.
[91] Art. 11(2) of the Protocol on the Statute of the EIB.   [92] *Ibid.*, Art. 11(1).
[93] *Ibid.*, Art. 12(2).   [94] *Ibid.*, Art. 13(1).   [95] *Ibid.*, Art. 13(3), 1st para.
[96] *Ibid.*, Art. 13(3), 2nd para.   [97] *Ibid.*, Art. 22.

Economic and Social Cohesion,[98] annexed to the Treaty, the Bank will continue to devote the majority of its resources to the promotion of economic and social cohesion.

Democratic Control

Although performance of its tasks may raise serious issues in the economic and even political fields,[99] the Bank is not responsible to the European Parliament. The most that may be said is that the Commission is responsible to the Parliament for the actions of its representative on the Board of Directors.[100] Protection from undue political pressures may be thought essential for the effective fulfilment by the Bank of its functions. In reality, however, it is only protection against pressure from the Parliament which is enjoyed. There is little guarantee that the Bank may not be employed by the finance ministers or the Commission to secure ends in respect of which a greater degree of democratic control may usually be exercised.[101]

6.2.2 European Central Bank

Article 4a of the EC Treaty provides for the establishment of the European Central Bank, which is to have legal personality[102] and to enjoy decision-making powers.[103] It is to be established immediately after a decision on the date for the beginning of the third stage of monetary union by the Council under Article 109j(3) of the Treaty or at the latest by 1 July 1998.[104] It is thus to replace the European Monetary Institute,[105] which was established at the start of the second stage.[106]

Composition

The capital of the European Central Bank is, in principle, subscribed by Member States participating in the third stage of monetary union,[107] that is when the Euro replaces the national currencies in these Member States. It is these Member States which appoint the Executive Board of the Bank.[108] The

[98] Para. 13.

[99] See, e.g., regarding the freezing of loans following the military *coup* in Greece, Commission Reply to WQ 108/67 (JO 1967 243/3) by Mr Seifriz.

[100] Note the concerns of the Court of Auditors in its annual report for 1986 (OJ 1987 C336/1), especially in Chap. 14. See, generally, A. Evans, "Institutions of the European Communities other than the Court of Justice" in *Stair Memorial Encyclopaedia of the Laws of Scotland*, vol. x, 132–262 (Butterworths, London, 1990), 257–8.

[101] But see now Art. 188c(3) EC.

[102] Art. 106(2) EC.   [103] Art. 108a(1) EC.   [104] Art. 109d(1) EC.

[105] Art. 109d(2) EC.

[106] Art. 109f(1) EC. There is also a Monetary Committee with advisory status (Art. 109c EC), which will be replaced by an Economic and Finance Committee at the start of the 3rd stage of monetary union (Art. 109c(2) EC).

[107] Art. 48 of the Protocol on the Statute of the ESCB and of the ECB.

[108] *Ibid.*, Arts. 11(2) and 43(3).

European Central Bank and the national central banks constitute the European System of Central Banks.[109] This System shall be governed by the decision-making bodies of the European Central Bank, which are the Executive Board and the Governing Council.[110]

In performing its tasks, the Bank[111] shall neither seek nor take instructions from Union institutions or bodies, from any government of a Member State, or from any other body. The Union institutions and bodies and the governments of the Member States undertake to respect this principle and not to seek to influence the members of the decision-making bodies of the Bank in their work.[112]

Organisation

The Executive Board has responsibility for the current business of the Bank.[113] It is composed of a President, Vice-President, and four other members. They must be nationals of Member States[114] and have recognised standing and professional experience in monetary or banking matters. They are appointed by common accord of the governments of Member States participating in monetary union at the level of Heads of State or Government, on a recommendation from the Council, after it has consulted the European Parliament and the Governing Council of the Bank. Their term of office is eight years and is not renewable. They may be compulsorily retired, if they no longer fulfil the conditions required for the fulfilment of their duties or have been guilty of serious misconduct.[115]

The Governing Council comprises the members of the Executive Board and the governors of the national central banks.[116] It is to formulate the monetary policy of the Union. The Executive Board is to implement the policy according to the guidelines and decisions laid down by this Council.[117]

Functions

The European Central Bank shall have the exclusive right to authorise the issue of banknotes within the Member States participating in monetary

---

[109] Art. 106(1) EC.   [110] Art. 106(3) EC.

[111] Like the ESCB and the national central banks.   [112] Art. 107 EC.

[113] Art. 11(6) of the Protocol on the Statute of the ESCB and of the ECB.

[114] Art. 109a(2) EC.

[115] Art. 11(4) of the Protocol on the Statute of the ESCB and of the ECB. See, similarly, regarding governors of national central banks, Art. 14(2) (*ibid.*).

[116] Art. 109a(1) EC. There is also to be a General Council, which is to be similarly composed, but the ordinary members of the ECB will have no voting rights (Art. 45(2) of the Protocol on the Statute of the ESCB and of the ECB). It is to be established for as long as there are Member States with a derogation under Art. 109k(1) EC, i.e., Member States which do not meet the necessary conditions for adoption of the single currency (Art. 109l(3) EC). These conditions are set out in Art. 109j(1) EC and the Protocol on the Convergence Criteria, annexed to the EC Treaty.

[117] Art. 12(1) of the Protocol on the Statute of the ESCB and of the ECB.

union.[118] This Bank and the national central banks may issue such notes, which shall be the only such notes to have the status of legal tender within these Member States. The Bank is also empowered to make regulations, take decisions, and deliver recommendations and opinions.[119] It is to lay down general principles for open market and credit operations carried out by itself or national central banks.[120] It must also approve operations in foreign reserve assets remaining with national central banks, in order to ensure consistency with the exchange and monetary policies of the Union.[121]

Democratic Control

The European Central Bank is to draw up and publish reports on the activities of the European System of Central Banks at least quarterly.[122] Moreover, the President of the Bank and the other members of the Executive Board may, at the request of the European Parliament or on their own initiative, be heard by the competent committees of the Parliament. The Bank shall also address an annual report on the activities of the European System of Central Banks and on the monetary policy of both the previous and current years to the Parliament, the Commission, the Council of the Union, and the European Council. The President of the Bank shall present this report to the Council and the Parliament, which may hold a general debate on the basis of the report.[123]

At the same time, the President of the Council and a Commissioner may participate, without having the right to vote, in meetings of the Governing Council of the Bank. Moreover, the President of the Council may submit a matter for deliberation to the Governing Council.[124] Conversely, the President of the Bank shall be invited to participate in Council meetings when the Council is discussing matters relating to the objectives and tasks of the European System of Central Banks.[125]

6.2.3 Programme Committees

Various committees are involved with the Commission in the implementation of Union programmes, such as those for science and technology and for education and training. For example, the Committee for the European Development of Science and Technology was established by Decision 82/835.[126] Its task was to assist the Commission in the preparation and

---

[118] Art. 107(1) EC.   [119] Art. 108a(1) EC.
[120] Art. 18(2) of the Protocol on the Statute of the ESCB and of the ECB.
[121] *Ibid.*, Art. 31(2). Art. 23 (*ibid.*) governs the external operations of the ECB and national central banks; relations with central banks and financial institutions in other states and international organisations; foreign exchange operations; and borrowing and lending operations.
[122] *Ibid.*, Art. 14(1).   [123] Art. 109b(3) EC.   [124] Art. 109b(1) EC.
[125] Art. 109b(2) EC.
[126] On the creation of the Committee for the European Development of Science and Technology (OJ 1982 L350/45).

implementation of its policy regarding the stimulation of the Community's science and technical potential.[127] It has been replaced by the European Science and Technology Assembly.[128] The latter is composed of "high-level" persons in European organisations representing exact and natural sciences.[129]

For the implementation of Comett II (the Community Action Programme on Education and Training), Article 5(2) of Decision 89/27[130] provided for the Commission to be assisted by a committee consisting of two representatives from each Member State and chaired by a Commission representative. In relation to general guidelines regarding the programme, general guidelines regarding Union financial assistance and questions regarding the general balance of the programme,[131] the committee acted a management committee.[132] If Commission proposals regarding such guidelines or questions were not approved by the committee, the Council might take a different decision.[133] In the case of measures governing the procedure for selecting the various types of projects to be supported,[134] the Commission was to "take utmost account" of committee opinions.[135] In addition, Article 5(8) of the same Decision provided for a group of experts to advise the Commission and the committee.

6.2.4 "Partnership"

While the work of the European Investment Bank and the European Central Bank may tend towards centralisation of decision making, partnership seeks decentralisation.

Definition

"Partnership" is the process whereby a range of public and private bodies from the Member States may participate in the administrative work of the Union. In particular, operations of the Union funds[136] are, according to Article 4 of Regulation 2081/93,[137] to be conducted on the basis of partnership. The latter

---

[127] *Ibid.*, Art. 2(1).

[128] Dec. 94/204 1994 (OJ 1994 L98/34) on the creation of the European Science and Technology Assembly.

[129] *Ibid.*, Art. 3(2).

[130] Adopting the second phase of the programme on co-operation between universities and industry regarding training in the field of technology (COMETT II 1990–4) (OJ 1989 L13/28).

[131] *Ibid.*, Art. 5(3)(a).

[132] See, regarding management committees, sect. 6.3.3 below.

[133] OJ 1989 L13/28, Art. 5(4).   [134] *Ibid.*, Art. 5(3)(b).   [135] *Ibid.*, Art. 5(5).

[136] See Chap. 20.

[137] Amending Reg. 2052/88 (OJ 1993 L193/5) on the tasks of the Structural Funds and their effectiveness and on the co-ordination of their activities between themselves and with the operations of the EIB and the other existing financial instruments. See, regarding the ERDF and "regional partnership", Art. 9 of Reg. 2083/93 (OJ 1993 L193/34) amending Reg. 4254/88 laying down provisions for implementing Reg. 2052/88 as regards the ERDF.

is defined therein as "close consultations between the Commission, the Member State concerned, and the competent authorities and bodies, including within the framework of each Member State's national rules and current practices, the economic and social partners, designated by the Member States at national, regional, local, or other levels, with all parties acting as partners in pursuit of a common goal".[138] This definition leaves designation of the relevant bodies to Member States. However, the Commission is concerned to ensure that partnership arrangements involve all authorities and bodies which are competent for the areas and sectors in which the operations are to be performed.[139]

Partnership has been judicially defined as "a kind of dialogue ... between the Commission and the Member State concerned".[140] Within this dialogue the Commission is presumably expected to perform its duty to "take steps and implementing measures to ensure that Community operations are in support of the objectives of the Structural Funds and impart an added value to national initiatives".[141] However, the formal legal status of dialogue outcomes may be problematic. According to the Court of Justice "negotiated acts", if not provided for in Union legislation, cannot affect the legal position of Member States under the relevant legislation.[142]

Bodies Involved

In practice, according to the Commission, partnership means ensuring that decisions on regional economic development are taken collectively by all those involved, notably the Commission, the Member States, and the local or regional authorities concerned. Ideally, the partnership should incorporate other relevant economic actors, such as chambers of commerce, employers, and trades unions, all of whom have a valuable role to play in the success of a region's economy.[143] The Commission, however, considers that the legislation does not fully meet these needs. Rather, the Commission criticised the Council for watering down its proposals for greater involvement of the social partners.[144] In particular, the Commission criticised the stipulation that the involvement of the social partners must take place "within the framework of each Member State's national rules and current practices"[145] and "in full

---

[138] "Verification" arrangements are not covered. See Case C–303/90 *France v. EC Commission: code of conduct* [1991] ECR I–5315, I–5348.

[139] Community Structural Funds 1994–9, COM(93)67, 21.

[140] Tesauro AG in Case C–303/90 *France v. EC Commission: code of conduct* [1991] ECR I–5315, I–5338.

[141] Art. 4(2) of Reg. 2081/93 (OJ 1993 L193/5).

[142] Case C–303/90 *France v. EC Commission: code of conduct* [1991] ECR I–5315, I–5349.

[143] Address by Bruce Millan at the European League for Economic Co-operation's Conference on "Developing Europe's Regions after 1992: New Ideas for the New Europe", Cleveland, 10 July 1992 (IP92/563).

[144] Explanatory memorandum to the re-examined proposals for legislation on the Structural Funds, COM(93)379, 2.

[145] Art. 4(1) of Reg. 2081/93 (OJ 1993 L193/5).

compliance with the respective institutional, legal, and financial powers of each of the partners".[146] The result is said to be that the mobilisation of regional authorities, social partners, and non-profit-making organisations is often inadequate and always too formal.[147]

The Commission may still take account of participation by regional bodies in assessing applications for Union aid.[148] The Commission may take particular account of the involvement of regional and local authorities and the social partners in the preparation of programmes and their implementation in a way appropriate to each Member State.[149] For example, according to the Notice to the Member States laying down guidelines for the initiative concerning the modernisation of the Portuguese textile and clothing industry,[150] the "regional and local authorities and the social partners must be involved in the most appropriate manner in the preparation and implementation of the operational programmes".[151] Priority may also be given to applications made in cooperation with regional and local authorities which include the creation and development of shared institutional or administrative structures.[152]

The European Parliament wishes to go further.[153] In particular, the Parliament favours "Community framework agreements" with each region.[154] Moreover, the "Recite model",[155] according to which applications for Union assistance were to be made to the Commission by groups of regional authorities or by international associations representing such authorities at Union level, is favoured by the Parliament.[156]

---

[146] *Ibid.* Plans for Objectives 3 and 4 of the Structural Funds are to indicate the way in which the association of economic and social partners will be secured "within the procedures available under each Member State's institutional rules and existing practices". See Art. 4(3) of Reg. 2084/93 (OJ 1993 L193/39) amending Reg. 4255/88 laying down provisions for implementing Reg. 2052/88 as regards the ESF.

[147] Community structural assistance and employment, COM(96)109, 26.

[148] See, e.g., Notice laying down guidelines for global grants or integrated operational programmes for which Member States are invited to submit applications for assistance within the framework of a Community initiative concerning the restructuring of the fisheries sector (OJ 1994 C180/1), para. VII.17.

[149] Notice laying down guidelines for operational programmes in the framework of a Community initiative concerning the most remote regions, which Member States are invited to establish (OJ 1994 C180/44), para. 14.

[150] OJ 1994 C180/15. [151] *Ibid.*, para. V.6

[152] Para. 11 of the Communic. laying down guidelines for operational programmes which Member States are invited to establish in the framework of a Community Interreg initiative concerning transnational co-operation on spatial planning (OJ 1996 C200/23).

[153] See the amendments proposed to legislation on the Structural Funds on 20 May 1988 (OJ 1988 C167/443).

[154] Resolution of 22 Jan. 1993 (OJ 1993 C42/211) on Community structural policies: assessment and outlook ("mid-term review"), para. 15.

[155] Call for network proposals from regional and local authorities wishing to carry out joint economic projects pursuant to Art. 10 of the ERDF Reg. – Regions and cities for Europe (OJ 1991 C198/8).

[156] Resolution of 22 Jan. 1993 (OJ 1993 C42/211) on Community structural policies: assessment and outlook ("mid-term review"), para. 32.

The Committee of the Regions, in turn, argues that projects supported by the European Regional Development Fund[157] should be directly administered by regional authorities. It also considers that the final selection of such projects should be made by the Commission and these authorities.[158] According to this Committee, the Commission should refuse to accept programmes which have not been endorsed by regional partnerships.[159] Such demands are partly met by the legislation governing the Poseidom Programme.[160] It requires a guarantee of the active involvement of local, regional, and national authorities.[161]

National Constitutional Constraints

National constitutional arrangements may allow the central governments of Member States to "exercise authority" over regional institutions and thereby undermine the partnership principle.[162] The ultimate result may be that regional institutions have difficulty implementing development strategies inspired by the Union.[163]

On the other hand, in some Member States constitutional guarantees may have positive effects for the role of regional institutions.[164] Thus partnership is said to operate particularly well in the framework of the "regional structure" of Germany.[165]

The effects of differences in national constitutional arrangements may be complicated by the impact of Union aid on resource interdependencies within Member States. On the one hand, administrative burdens are placed on national officials. These burdens can render the officials more dependent on regional institutions, whose co-operation, information, and organisational capabilities are required to assemble acceptable development plans

---

[157] See sect. 20.1 below.

[158] Opinion of 15 Mar. 1994 (OJ 1994 C217/10) on the draft notice laying down guidelines for operational programmes which Member States are invited to establish in the framework of a Community initiative concerning urban areas, para. 4.

[159] Opinion of 21 Mar. 1996 (OJ 1996 C182/7) on the Commission communication on the new regional programmes under Objectives 1 and 2, para. 20.

[160] Dec. 89/487 (OJ 1989 L239/23) establishing a programme of options specific to the remote and insular nature of the French overseas departments.

[161] *Ibid.*, 24th recital in the preamble.

[162] Economic and Social Committee Opinion of 25 Mar. 1992 (CES(92)363) on the annual report on the implementation of the reform of the structural funds (1990), 3.

[163] K. Dyson, "Introduction" in K. Dyson (ed.), *Local Authorities and New Technologies: The European Dimension* (Croom Helm, London, 1988), 1–23.

[164] J.J. Hesse and L.J. Sharpe, "Local Government in International Perspective: Some Comparative Perspectives" in J.J. Hesse (ed.), *Local Government and Urban Affairs in International Perspective* (Nomos, Baden-Baden, 1991), 603–20, 612. See, regarding subsidiarity and the German *Länder*, H. Wilke and H. Wallace, *Subsidiarity: Approaches to Power-Sharing in the European Community* (RIIA Discussion Paper 27, London, 1990).

[165] Resolution of the European Parliament of 22 Jan. 1993 (OJ 1993 C42/228) on the regional and social redevelopment plan and the CSF for the areas of the Germany included in Objective 2, para. 8.

and Community Support Frameworks.[166] On the other hand, resource deficiencies at the regional level, such as the lack of administrative capacity to develop joint projects suitable for Union assistance, may be exposed. The result may be that regional institutions become even more dependent on national officials.[167]

The Commission, like the European Parliament,[168] recognises problems of resource deficiencies at regional level. For example, the Commission considers that the implementation of the Integrated Mediterranean Programmes would have been facilitated by the "strengthening of public administration structures, centrally and regionally, through improved management training, technical support, and information processing".[169]

"Technical Assistance"

Union legislation does little to address the above problems. Article 4(3) of Regulation 2081/93[170] merely provides that the Commission may contribute to the preparation, implementation, and adjustment of operations by financing preparatory studies and technical assistance operations locally in agreement with the Member State concerned and, where appropriate, the authorities and bodies designated by Member States. However, it is stipulated that such contributions must be made within the framework of the partnership. The implication is that the position of central institutions of Member States under national constitutional law is not to be prejudiced.

Programmes of technical assistance and support for the social partners at regional level have been suggested,[171] and the Union may already provide financial support for the activities of various bodies. For example, aid under Article B4–306 of the budget[172] may be provided to representative organisations operating in the environmental field. It is recognised that these organisations may play a fundamental role in fostering awareness of environmental problems.[173] In particular, checks on the use of Union aid may be carried out by local authorities as the result of local public opinion being aroused by

---

[166] Such frameworks, agreed with Member States, are supposed to programme development efforts assisted by the Union.

[167] J.J. Anderson, "Skeptical Reflections on a Europe of Regions: Britain, Germany, and the ERDF" [1990] *Journal of Public Policy* 417–45.

[168] Resolution of 16 Dec. 1993 (OJ 1994 C20/179) on the conclusions of the mission of inquiry of the Committee on Budgetary Control into the management and monitoring of the Structural Funds in Italy, para. 4.

[169] Annual report on the implementation of the IMPs 1991–2, COM(93)485, 19–20.

[170] OJ 1993 L193/5.

[171] Opinion of the Economic and Social Committee of 10 July 1996 (OJ 1996 C295/47) on the sixth annual report on the Structural Funds for 1994 and the new regional programmes under Objectives 1 and 2, para. 4.7.

[172] See, for 1997, OJ 1997 L44/3.

[173] Special report 3/92 of the Court of Auditors (OJ 1992 C245/1) concerning the environment, para. 2.15.

such organisations.[174] However, the Commission considers that it has no basis in the legislation for demanding their involvement in decision-making.[175]

6.2.5 Standards Bodies

The significance for Union activity of international standards bodies, which draw up standards to be met by products, is highlighted by Union adoption of "the new approach" to harmonisation.[176] According to this approach, Union directives harmonising national law seek simply to lay down objectives. The technical specifications needed to meet these objectives are, as for example in the case of Directive 88/378 on toy safety,[177] left to be agreed by the relevant standards bodies.[178] The legality of such an approach has been accepted by the Court of Justice.[179]

However, judicial control problems may arise from the work of such bodies. For example, an agreement reached by bodies which are "governed by private law and act within the framework of the functions attributed to them by their statutes and the national legislation to which they are subject" cannot be considered an act of a Union institution for the purposes of review of its legality by the European Courts. Such an agreement cannot be so considered, since no Union institutions have taken part in its conclusion. The fact that the conclusion of the agreement may be a precondition for the entry into force of a Council enactment and that the length of time for which the enactment applies may be determined by the duration of the agreement does not affect the nature of the agreement as a measure adopted by private bodies.[180]

6.3 Supervisory Bodies

Various bodies are responsible for supervising the work of the Union institutions.[181]

---

[174] *Ibid.*, para. 4.2.

[175] *Ibid.*, para. 3.1–5 (Commission reply).

[176] Sect. 19.4 below.

[177] On the approximation of the laws of the Member States concerning the safety of toys (OJ 1988 L187/1), Art. 5(1).

[178] Dir. 83/189 (OJ 1983 L109/8) laying down a procedure for the provision of information in the field of technical standards and regulations.

[179] Case 815/79 *Gaetano Cremonini and Maria Luisa Vrankovich* [1980] ECR 3583.

[180] Case 152/83 *Marcel Demouche* v. *Fonds de Garantie Automobile and Bureau Central Français* [1987] ECR 3833, 3852–3. Cf. Joined Cases 87, 130/77, 22/83, 9 & 10/84 *Vittorio Salerno* v. *EC Commission and EC Council* [1985] ECR 2523.

[181] A supervisory body for data protection is also to be established by 1 Jan. 1999 (Art. 213b EC).

6.3.1 Court of Auditors

The Court of Auditors was established by Article 206(1) of the EEC Treaty,[182] as amended by Article 15 of the Treaty amending Certain Financial Provisions of the EEC Treaty.[183]

Composition

The Court of Auditors is composed of fifteen members[184] enjoying renewable six-year terms of office.[185] In practice, there is one member for each Member State. When the first appointments were made, four members, chosen by lot, were appointed for only three years.[186] This exceptional arrangement was necessary to permit implementation of a system which entailed that four or six members alternatively should be reappointed or replaced every three years. This system was designed to promote continuity in the work of this Court.

Members are appointed by the Council, acting unanimously and after consulting the European Parliament.[187] Thus the Parliament only has a consultative role in their appointment,[188] even though the preamble to the Treaty amending Certain Financial Provisions of the EEC Treaty[189] stressed the importance of strengthening the budgetary powers of the Parliament.[190] Appointees must be persons who belong, or have belonged, in their respective countries to external audit bodies, who are especially qualified for office, and whose independence is beyond doubt.[191]

They must, "in the general interest of the Community", be completely independent in the performance of their duties. Like Commissioners, they must neither seek nor take instructions from any government or any other body,[192] and they must give a solemn undertaking to respect the duties of their office.[193] In contrast to the provisions governing the Commission, no express undertaking by Member States to respect the independence of members of the Court of Auditors is required. However, Member States are obliged by the general provisions of the EC Treaty to respect that independence.[194] Such independence is safeguarded, more particularly, by the

---

[182] Art. 78e(1) ECSC and Art. 180(1) Euratom. It thus replaced the old Audit Board and ECSC Auditor.

[183] OJ 1977 L359/1. See now Arts. 188a–188c EC; and the Rules of Procedure of the Court of Auditors (OJ 1991 L176/1).

[184] Art. 188b(1) EC.   [185] Art. 188b(3) EC.   [186] Art. 188b(3) EEC.   [187] *Ibid.*

[188] On the role sought by the Parliament, see the Resolution of 5 Oct. 1973 (OJ 1973 C87/8) on the strengthening of the budgetary powers of the European Parliament, para. 23. The Draft Treaty establishing a European Union (OJ 1984 C77/33) envisaged that half the members would be appointed by the Parliament and half by the Council (Art. 33(2)).

[189] OJ 1977 L359/1, 5th recital.

[190] Cf. the earlier call for such a body in the European Parliament Resolution of 24 Sept. 1964 (OJ 1964 2447) on budgetary and administrative problems posed by the merger of the executives and eventually the Communities, para. 15.

[191] Art. 188b(2) EC.   [192] Art. 188b(4) EC.   [193] Art. 188b(5) EC.

[194] Art. 5 EC read with Art. 188b(4) EC.

extension of the provisions of the Protocol on the Privileges and Immunities of the European Communities applicable to members of the Court of Justice, to cover members of the Court of Auditors.[195] Moreover, they may only be removed from office prematurely where the Court of Justice finds that they no longer fulfil the requisite conditions for the holding of their office or no longer meet the obligations arising therefrom.[196]

Organisation

The members of the Court of Auditors elect their President from among their number for a term of three years. The President may be re-elected.[197] The Court adopts its annual reports, special reports, and opinions by a majority of its members.[198]

Functions

The principal function of the Court of Auditors is to examine the accounts of all Union revenue and expenditure. It is also to examine the accounts of all bodies set up by the Union, in so far as the relevant constituent instrument does not preclude such examination.[199] The Court of Auditors is to determine not only whether all revenue has been received and all expenditure incurred in a lawful and regular manner[200] but also whether the financial management has been sound.[201] Since the soundness of the financial management is to be assessed, the Court of Auditors may question policy decisions involved. The necessary investigations may extend to activity undertaken in and by Member States on behalf of the Union, such as agricultural expenditure and the collection of customs duties. The investigations may also extend to use of Union aid by third states.[202]

   The other Union institutions, any bodies managing revenue or expenditure on behalf of the Union, any person in receipt of payments from the budget, and national authorities must cooperate with the Court of Auditors. Thus they must, at the request of the Court, forward to it any document or information necessary for it to carry out its task. More particularly, the European Investment Bank must provide the Court with access to information necessary for the audit of Union expenditure and revenue managed by the Bank.[203]

   On the basis of its work the Court of Auditors is required to draw up an annual report. The report is to be forwarded to the Union institutions and published, together with the replies of these institutions to the observations of this Court, in the Official Journal. In addition, the Court of Auditors may at any time submit observations on specific questions and deliver opinions at the request of a Union institution.[204] In practice, the Court of Auditors is

---

[195] Art. 188b(9) EC.   [196] Art. 188b(7) EC.   [197] Art. 188b(3) EC.
[198] Art. 188c(4) EC.   [199] Art. 188c(1) EC.
[200] Case 69/83 *Luxembourg* v. *Court of Auditors* [1984] ECR 2447, 2464.
[201] Art. 188c(2) EC.   [202] Sect. 20.7.1 below.   [203] Art. 188c(3) EC.
[204] Art. 188c(4) EC. See also Art. 209a(4) EC.

regularly consulted regarding legislative proposals which have budgetary or financial implications. More generally, it is required to assist the European Parliament and the Council in exercising their powers of control over implementation of the budget.[205] The Parliament has been particularly keen to make use of such assistance,[206] and members of the Court of Auditors attend and speak at meetings of Parliamentary committees discussing budgetary or financial matters.

6.3.2 Monitoring Committees

Monitoring Committees, which were originally introduced for each Integrated Mediterranean Programme,[207] are now established for Structural Fund[208] operations generally. Their establishment is based on agreement between the Member State concerned and the Commission within the "partnership"[209] framework. The Commission and, where appropriate, the European Investment Bank may delegate representatives to these committees.[210]

The legislation governing the Cohesion Fund apparently does more to ensure decentralisation. According to this legislation, where regional and local authorities are competent for the execution of a project supported by the Cohesion Fund and where they are directly concerned by a project, they are to be represented on the relevant monitoring committee.[211]

The committees may, subject to confirmation by the Commission and Member State concerned, adjust both the procedure for granting Union aid as initially approved and the financing plan envisaged.[212]

6.3.3 Management Committees

To ensure attainment of Treaty objectives, the Council is required by Article 145 of the EC Treaty to confer on the Commission powers to implement Council legislation.[213] However, the Commission may still be required to submit draft measures to a management committee, or occasionally a regulatory committee,[214] composed of national representatives.

---

[205] Art. 188c(4) EC.

[206] See, e.g., the Resolution of 19 Jan. 1988 (OJ 1988 C49/29) on the future financing of the European Communities – aspects concerning budgetary control.

[207] Art. 9 of Reg. 2088/85 (OJ 1985 L197/1) concerning the IMPs.

[208] I.e. the ERDF, the ESF, and the Guidance Section of the EAGGF. See Chap. 20.

[209] Sect. 6.2.4 above.

[210] Art. 25(3) of Reg. 2082/93 (OJ 1993 L193/20).

[211] Art. F.3 of Annex II to Reg. 1164/94 (OJ 1994 L130/1) establishing a Cohesion Fund.

[212] Art. 25(5) of Reg. 2082/93 (OJ 1993 L193/20).

[213] Sect. 2.3.1 above.

[214] See, regarding the distinction, Art. 2 of Dec. 87/373 (OJ 1987 L197/33) laying down the procedures for the exercise of implementing powers conferred on the Commission.

Management committees adopt opinions by a qualified majority, the votes being weighted, as in the Council, according to Article 148(2) of the Treaty. If a Commission decision is not in accordance with such an opinion, the Commission is required to defer application of the decision for up to two months. Within that period the Council may adopt a different decision also by a qualified majority. Therefore, if such a committee objects to the draft concerned, the Council may effectively take back the powers delegated to the Commission.[215]

Such committees favour network building by officials from different Member States. Hence, their creation is said to have done much to overcome bureaucratic resistance within Member States to Union decision making.[216]

Problems of democratic control may arise. Thus the European Parliament has demanded that it should be comprehensively informed and consulted by the Commission about all draft implementing measures to be forwarded to a committee.[217] An agreement has been reached regarding the Structural Funds,[218] and a more general code of conduct has been agreed between the Parliament and the Commission.[219] However, the Parliament considers that these arrangements are still inadequate, and it seeks an equal right to veto draft measures.[220]

6.4 Other Bodies and Third States

Third states may have effective opportunities to participate in Union work through certain of the bodies discussed above.

6.4.1 Advisory Bodies

Advisory bodies may concern relations with third states and may even imply opportunities for third states or their representatives to participate in the work of the Union.

In particular, a section has been established within the Economic and

---

[215] *Ibid.* See also the Declaration attached to the SEA (OJ 1987 L169/1).

[216] H.G. Schermers, "Comment on Weiler's *The Transformation of Europe*" (1991), 100 *Yale Law Journal* 2525–36, 2527.

[217] Resolution of 23 Oct. 1986 (OJ 1986 C297/94) on the proposal for a regulation laying down the procedures for the exercise of implementing powers conferred on the Commission, para. 1.

[218] Code of conduct on the implementation of structural policies by the Commission (OJ 1993 C255/19).

[219] OJ 1995 C89/69, para. 6. See also *Modus vivendi* (OJ 1996 C102/1) between the European Parliament, the Council, and the Commission concerning the implementing measures for acts adopted in accordance with the procedure laid down in Art. 189b EC; and the Declaration by the European Parliament, the Council, and the Commission on the incorporation of financial provisions into legislative acts (OJ 1996 C102/4).

[220] Resolution of 17 May 1995 (OJ 1995 C151/56) on the functioning of the TEU with a view to the 1996 IGC – implementation and development of the Union, para. 32.

Social Committee for external relations. In addition, the Committee may appoint delegations drawn from its members to maintain relations with the socio-occupational organisations of third states.[221]

6.4.2 Administrative Bodies

Administrative bodies may concern relations with third states and may even imply opportunities for third states or their representatives to participate in the work of the Union.

European Investment Bank

The European Investment Bank is, according to Article 130w(2) of the EC Treaty, to contribute to implementation of development co-operation policy. More particularly, it is a member of the European Bank for Reconstruction and Development.[222] It also contributes to the financing of capital development projects under the Europe Agreements,[223] agreements with Latin American and Asian countries,[224] agreements with African, Caribbean, and Pacific countries, overseas countries and territories,[225] and financial protocols with Mediterranean countries.[226] Loans granted for this purpose may carry a guarantee from the Union budget.[227] At the same time, the Bank is involved in the operation of the EFTA Financial Mechanism.[228]

Standards Bodies

Third states may participate in international standards bodies, such as the Comité Européen de Normalisation (CEN), the Comité Européen de Normalisation Electronique (CENELEC), and the European Conference of Postal and Telecommunications Administrations (CEPT).[229]

For example, the first EC–EFTA common mandate was given to CEN in 1982, and a common working group was established within CEN and CENELEC.[230] Framework agreements were also signed with CEN and

---

[221] Art. 21 of the Rules of Procedure of the Committee (OJ 1996 L82/1).

[222] Agreement establishing the EBRD (OJ 1990 L372/4), Art. 3.

[223] See, e.g., Art. 97 of the Polish Agreement (OJ 1993 L348/2).

[224] Dec. 96/723 (OJ 1996 L329/45) granting a Community guarantee to the EIB against losses under loans for projects of mutual interest in Latin American and Asian countries with which the Community has concluded co-operation agreements.

[225] Arts. 233–238 of the Lomé Convention (OJ 1991 L229/2).

[226] Reg. 1763/92 (OJ 1992 L181/5) concerning financial co-operation in respect of all Mediterranean non-member countries.

[227] See, e.g., Dec. 97/256 (OJ 1997 L102/33) granting a Community guarantee to the EIB against losses under loans for projects outside the Community.

[228] Sect. 20.9.3 below.

[229] See, generally, *Europastandardiseringens Betydelse för Sverige och för Integration i Västeuropa* (Fakta Europa 1989:2, Utrikesdepartementet, Stockholm, 1989).

[230] *Sverige–EG 1982* (Utrikesdepartementets handelsavdelning, Stockholm, 1983), 25.

CENELEC in January 1986,[231] which made it possible for EFTA states to take part in an advance information procedure concerning draft standards and standardisation programmes.[232] Moreover, the American National Standards Institute (ANSI) has close contacts with CEN and CENELEC, and United States firms and associations may participate as observers in the work of the European Telecommunications Institute (ETSI).

Third states not represented in bodies of these kinds may face an increased risk that their undertakings will see such bodies and the associated norms "captured" by their competitors.[233] In other words, undertakings from third states may become marginal to partnership strategies between public and private actors designed to create comparative advantage in rapidly-changing and oligopolistic global markets.[234]

6.5 Agreements with Third States

Formal arrangements for participation by third states in various Union bodies may be made in agreements with such states.

6.5.1 Free Trade Agreements

Free trade agreements may make no express reference to bodies of the kind discussed in the present Chapter. However, within the more general context of relations between parties to such agreements arrangements for participation by third states in such bodies may be made.

Third states which are parties to free trade agreements may conclude co-operation agreements providing for their participation in Union programmes and, more particularly, for their representation in the relevant programme committees. For example, a co-operation agreement with Sweden regarding research in the field of wood, including cork, as a renewable raw material[235] provided for the enlargement of the Management, Co-ordination and Advisory Committee on Raw Materials, to include three Swedish representatives.[236] However, those representatives might only attend discussions concerning wood, including cork, as a renewable raw material.

Again, a co-operation agreement with Sweden was designed to increase the international co-operation and the exchange of research scientists between the Parties. According to Article 4 of the agreement,[237] Sweden was

---

[231] EFTA Bull. 1/1986, 19.

[232] A common declaration was also made by EFTA and CEPT in 1985 (*Sverige–EG 1985* (Utrikesdepartementets handelsavdelning, Stockholm, 1986), 38).

[233] Cf. G. Koopman and H-E. Scharrer, *Scenarios of a Common External Trade Policy for the EC after 1992* (Institut für Wirtschaftsforschung, Hamburg, 1990), 30.

[234] W. Wallace, *The Transformation of Western Europe* (Pinter, London, 1990), 89.

[235] OJ 1988 L276/5.   [236] *Ibid.*, Art. 4.

[237] Co-operation agreement with Sweden on a programme to stimulate the international co-operation and interchange needed by European research scientists (Science) (OJ 1990 L50/22).

entitled to send a delegate to the Committee for European Development of Science and Technology. The delegate was to participate in the definition and outline of plans for the stimulation of the international co-operation and interchange needed by European research scientists. He was also to partici- pate in the examination of applications submitted under the stimulation plan.[238] He was not apparently to participate in the more general work of the Committee and was not a member of it.[239]

However, such arrangements may not secure for third states any real say in the operation of the programmes. Even though they may have concluded a co-operation agreement with the Union, these states may not be represented at all in some programme committees.[240] Apparently, the Union considers that their representation may jeopardise its decision-making autonomy.[241]

6.5.2 Association Agreements

Association agreements may go further than free trade agreements in providing for participation by third states in Union bodies.

Expert Groups

Committees of experts from the Union and Central and East European countries are responsible for guiding "voluntary harmonisation" by such countries.[242] Such committees are to be established by the Association Councils, created by the Europe Agreements. For example, Article 107 of the Hungarian Agreement[243] provides that the Association Council may estab- lish subcommittees to assist it. More particularly, according to Article 10 of Protocol 2 to the Agreement, which concerns ECSC products, the Parties agreed that the Association Council should establish a contact group to discuss implementation of this Protocol. Article 33 of Protocol 4 to the Agreement, concerning the definition of the concept of "originating products" and methods of administrative co-operation, also provides for the

---

[238] *Ibid.*, Art. 4.

[239] See also Art. 8 of Dec. 82/835 (OJ 1982 L350/45) on the creation of the Committee for the European Development of Science and Technology.

[240] See, e.g., Dec. 89/27 (OJ 1989 L13/28) adopting the second phase of the programme on co- operation between and industry regarding training in the field of technology. Art. 7 of the Agreement with Sweden establishing co-operation in the field of training in the context of the implementation of COMETT II (1990–4) (OJ 1990 L102/42) established a Joint Committee to represent Sweden in matters relating to this country. Art. 9 (*ibid.*) also required the Commission to ensure that the composition of the expert group (established pursuant to Art. 5(8) of Dec. 89/27) was such as to enable it to give any advice required in regard to the participation of universities and industry from Sweden.

[241] SvDN, 18 Dec. 1989.

[242] Follow up to the Commission Communication on 'The Europe Agreements and beyond: a strategy to prepare the countries of Central and Eastern Europe for accession', COM(94)361, 5. See sect. 19.5.2 below, regarding such harmonisation.

[243] OJ 1993 L347/2.

establishment of a customs co-operation committee. In the event, committees on customs co-operation, transport, agriculture, approximation of legislation, and science and technology, an *ad hoc* group on ECSC matters, and a
working group on implementation of competition rules have been established under the Agreement.[244]

However, the "efficiency" of such bodies is disputed.[245] In any case, they
are designed to assist the third states concerned in implementing Union
decisions rather than to facilitate their involvement in Commission work
leading to the adoption of the decisions.

Standards Bodies

Provision is made in the Europe Agreements for co-operation to encourage
the participation of the third states concerned in international standards
bodies.[246] Such participation is considered important for the preparation of
these states for Union membership.[247]

Management Committees

While the Europe Agreements make no reference to management committees, provision is made under the Association Agreement with Turkey[248] for
Turkish experts to express their country's position, though not to vote, in
certain "technical committees".[249] These committees may include management committees.[250] However, on the initiative of its chairman, such a
committee may meet without the Turkish expert being present.[251] In other
words, like third states which are party to other association agreements,
Turkey lacks the same right as Member States to participate in Union
decision-making through the medium of management committees.

6.5.3 EEA Agreement

The EEA Agreement[252] builds upon pre-existing arrangements for participation by EFTA states in the work of the Union.

---

[244] Annex II to the Hungarian–EC Association Council Dec. 1/94 (OJ 1994 L242/23) on its Rules of Procedure.

[245] Opinion of the Economic and Social Committee of 25 Jan. 1995 (OJ 1995 C102/40) on relations between the EU and Russia, Ukraine, and Belarus, para. 3.25.

[246] See, e.g., Art. 74 of the Polish Agreement (OJ 1993 L348/2).

[247] Preparation of the associated countries of Central and Eastern Europe for integration into the internal market of the Union, COM(95)163, Annex, 13.

[248] JO 1964 368.

[249] Art. 1 of Dec. 5/95 (OJ 1996 L35/49) of the EC–Turkey Association Council on the arrangements for involving Turkish experts in certain technical committees.

[250] Annex to Dec. 1/95 (OJ 1996 L35/1) of the EC–Turkey Association Council implementing the final phase of the customs union.

[251] Art. 3 of Dec. 5/95 (OJ 1996 L35/49).

[252] OJ 1994 L1/3.

EEA Consultative Committee

Article 96(1) of the EEA Agreement seeks to promote relations between members of the Economic and Social Committee and other bodies representing the social partners in the Union[253] and the corresponding bodies in the EFTA states. It requires them to strengthen their contacts and to co-operate in an organised and regular manner. The aim is to enhance the awareness of the economic and social aspects of the growing interdependence of the economies of the Contracting Parties and of their interests within the context of the European Economic Area. Accordingly, an EEA Consultative Committee is established by Article 96(2) of the Agreement. It is composed of equal numbers of members of the Economic and Social Committee and members of the EFTA Consultative Committee.[254]

The EEA Consultative Committee shall adopt its own Rules of Procedure[255] under Article 96(3) of the Agreement. It may express its views in the form of reports or resolutions as appropriate.[256] However, no powers are conferred on this body.

These arrangements formalise established practice, according to which representatives from the Economic and Social Committee and the EFTA Consultative Committee had been meeting regularly since 1975. They may be seen as a model to be adopted in relations between the Union and Central and East European countries.[257] Thus, for example, a Joint Consultative Committee has been established under the Europe Agreement with Hungary. It contains six representatives of the Economic and Social Committee and six representatives of the economic and social interest groups within Hungary's National Council for the Reconciliation of Interests.[258]

Expert Groups

Article 99(1) of the EEA Agreement provides that when new legislation is being drafted by the Commission in a field governed by this Agreement, the Commission shall informally seek advice from experts of the EFTA states. The Commission shall do so in the same way as it seeks advice from experts of the Member States for the elaboration of its proposals. Such arrangements were apparently criticised by the External Relations Committee of the European Parliament.[259] However, the Parliament as a whole considered that

[253] No reference to representation of the ECSC Consultative Committee or the Committee of the Regions is made in Art. 96(2) EEA, though they may qualify for observer status under Art. 4 or 5 of the Rules of Procedure of the EEA Consultative Committee (OJ 1994 L301/10).
[254] This body was originally established by EFTA Council Dec. No. 5 of 1961.
[255] OJ 1994 L301/10. [256] Art. 96(2) EEA.
[257] Opinion of the Economic and Social Committee of 26 Jan. 1995 (OJ 1995 C102/40) on relations between the EU and Russia, Ukraine, and Belarus, para. 3.18.
[258] Dec. 1/96 (OJ 1996 L192/17) amending, through the setting up of a Joint Consultative Committee, Dec. 1/94.
[259] *Europe* 5221, 24 Mar. 1990.

for EFTA experts to give their opinions before the drafting of proposals would be acceptable.[260]

Before the EEA Agreement, EU–EFTA expert meetings might already be held to discuss Commission drafts.[261] Similar meetings were held at least once a year to exchange information on the economic situation in the Union and EFTA states as well as on their respective economic policies. More particular exchanges of information took place regarding, for example, application of indirect taxation to trade across frontiers[262] and the regulation of financial services.[263] Hence, Article 99(1) of the Agreement has merely put pre-existing practice on a more systematic basis. It is not designed to prejudice the "autonomy" of Union decision making.

Programme Committees

Article 81(b) of the EEA Agreement provides that the status of EFTA states in the committees which assist the Commission in the management or development of a Union programme to which these states contribute financially shall take full account of that contribution.[264] More details are provided by Protocol 31 to the Agreement, on Co-operation in Specific Fields Outside the Four Freedoms.[265]

For example, Article 1 of the Protocol deals with co-operation in relation to research and technological development. In particular, Article 1(1)(c) provides for EFTA states to participate fully in all the Union committees which assist the Commission in the management, development, and implementation of the Framework Programme for Research and Development[266] and its specific programmes. Moreover, Article 1(1)(d) provides that, given the particular nature of the co-operation foreseen in this field, representatives of EFTA states shall be associated with the work of the Scientific and Technical Research Committee (Crest) and other Union committees which the Commission consults in this field. They are to be associated to the extent necessary for the good functioning of that co-operation. According to an exchange of letters attached to the EEA Agreement, this "association" entails that EFTA states may send experts to participate in meetings of the

---

[260] Resolution of 5 Apr. 1990 (OJ 1990 C113/172) on relations between the EEC and EFTA, para. 5; and Resolution of 12 June 1990 (OJ 1990 C175/51) on economic and trade relations between the EC and the EFTA countries, para. 10.

[261] See, e.g., *Redovisning av det svenska integrationsarbetet våren 1988–mars 1989* (Utrikesdepartementets handelsavdelning, Stockholm, 1989), 37.

[262] *Sverige–EFTA–EG 1987* (Utrikesdepartementets handelsavdelning, Stockholm, 1988), 24.

[263] *Ibid.*, 35.

[264] There is concern in the European Parliament that its budgetary powers may be prejudiced. See the Opinion of the Committee on Budgets in the Report of the Committee on Foreign Affairs and Security on the conclusion of the EEA Agreement, EP Doc. 3–0316/92, Annex I, 10.

[265] Art. 3(1) of Prot. 31 also provides for the adoption of the necessary decisions to ensure the participation of EFTA states in the European Environmental Agency.

[266] Dec. 94/1110 (OJ 1994 L126/4) concerning the fourth framework programme of the EC activities in the field of research and technological development and demonstration (1994–8).

Committee, when it is advising the Commission on matters relevant to the European Economic Area. However, they may not participate when the Committee is advising the Commission on internal Union matters or is advising the Council.

The meaning of these arrangements is clarified by a Joint Declaration attached to the EEA Agreement.[267] According to this Declaration, the EFTA states shall have the same rights as Member States within such committees. However, this equality of representation does not extend to voting procedures. In reaching its decision on matters with which the committees are concerned, the Commission merely has to take due account of the views expressed by the EFTA states in the same manner as of the views expressed by the Member States before voting.

Management Committees

Article 100 of the EEA Agreement provides that the Commission shall ensure experts of the EFTA states as wide a participation as possible, according to the areas concerned, in the preparatory stage of draft measures to be submitted subsequently to the committees which assist the Commission in the exercise of its executive powers. This provision concerns management committees.[268]

According to the Declaration on the Participation of the EFTA States' Experts in EEA Relevant EC Committees in Application of Article 100 of the Agreement, attached to the Agreement, each EFTA state will designate its own experts. These experts will be involved on an equal footing with experts from the Member States in the preparatory work. The Commission will pursue consultations as long as deemed necessary, until submitting its proposal to a formal meeting of the relevant committee.[269] When submitting its proposal, the Commission is to transmit the views of the experts of the EFTA states.

If the committee opposes the draft concerned, the Council may effectively take back the powers delegated to the Commission and may itself decide the measures to be adopted. Article 100 of the Agreement requires that in such cases the Commission shall transmit to the Council the views of the experts of the EFTA states.

These arrangements mean that EFTA experts have a more limited role than representatives of Member States. The arrangements certainly fail to meet the demands made by EFTA states during negotiation of the

---

[267] Joint declaration on applicable procedures in cases where, by virtue of Art. 76 and Part VI of the Agreement and corresponding protocols, EFTA States participate fully in EC committees.

[268] In addition, Part XXI of Annex II, on Technical regulations, standards, testing, and certification, provides that Art. 100 EEA shall apply to the participation of EFTA states in the work of the European Organisation of Technical Approval.

[269] An exchange of letters, attached to the EEA Agreement (OJ 1994 L1/3), deals, more particularly, with the Banking Advisory Committee.

Agreement. These states had insisted on the close link between the accept-ability of the substance of Union legislation and arrangements for its imple-mentation within the framework of the powers delegated to the Commission.[270] However, the Union considered that to permit EFTA states to vote in management committees, as was sought by these states, would have conflicted with the autonomy of Union decision-making.[271]

---

[270] Para. 2.1 of the Commission Communication to the Council recommending a Council decision authorising the Commission to negotiate an agreement with the EFTA states on the creation of the EEA (unpublished).

[271] Relations between the Community and EFTA, House of Lords Select Committee on the European Communities, HL (1989–90) 55–2, 26.

7

Relationship between EU Law and National Law

Union law not only governs the work of the institutions and bodies already examined. It may also directly concern individuals in proceedings before national courts.

Article 5 of the EC Treaty may be assumed to be relevant to the underlying issues. According to this provision, Member States are to take all appropriate measures, whether general or particular, to ensure fulfilment of the obligations arising out of the Treaty or resulting from action taken by the Union institutions. They shall facilitate the achievement of the tasks outlined in the Treaty and shall abstain from any measure which may jeopardize the attainment of the Treaty objectives. This provision implies an obligation on Member States to ensure that Union law is respected within their territories. Thus, for example, in the United Kingdom the European Communities Act 1972 was enacted. The particular implication may be that the internal legal effects of Union law, including its effects for individuals, and its relationship with national law are to depend on national constitutional rules.

The Court of Justice, however, considers that the direct effectiveness of Union law before national courts and its supremacy in relation to national law are inherent features of the "new legal order" established by the Treaties. As such, these features are not, according to the Court, dependent on national constitutional rules.

7.1 Internal Legal Effects

EC Treaty provisions and acts of the Union institutions may, depending on their characteristics, have internal legal effects within Member States.

7.1.1 Treaty Provisions

Van Gend en Loos[1] concerned a Dutch customs reclassification, which had the result of increasing the duty payable by certain goods imported from

---

[1] Case 26/62 *NV Algemene Transport- en Expeditie Onderneming van Gend en Loos* v. *Nederlandse Administratie der Belastingen* [1963] ECR 1, 12.

other Member States. The Court of Justice was asked, in a request for a preliminary ruling from a Dutch court, whether the reclassification was prohibited by the "standstill" clause in Article 12 of the EEC Treaty. According to this provision, Member States were prohibited from increasing customs duties in trade with other Member States.

"New Legal Order"

The Court of Justice went further in the *Van Gend en Loos* ruling than may have been strictly necessary to answer the question referred to it.[2] According to the Court, the establishment of a common market implied that the EEC Treaty did more than simply create a system of mutual rights and obligations for contracting states. Rather, the participation of individuals in the common market was envisaged. Individuals also had the opportunity to participate in the work of the Union through representation in the European Parliament and the Economic and Social Committee. More particularly, an important implication was drawn from the procedure in Article 177 of the Treaty, whereby national courts might refer questions of Union law to the Court of Justice for a preliminary ruling. This procedure implied that Union law was to be applied to individuals within the Member States. At the same time, the vigilance of individuals interested in protecting their rights under the Treaty constituted an effective control of compliance with the Treaty additional to that entrusted by Article 169 to the diligence of the Commission.[3]

On the basis of these considerations the Court concluded that "a new legal order" had been created and that individuals as well as Member States were the subjects of this order. In their capacity as such individuals might derive rights from Treaty provisions, such as Article 12, which were to be upheld by national courts. Hence, a national court was, at the request of an individual, to hold that a customs reclassification of the kind at issue was prohibited by Article 12 of the Treaty.[4]

Conditions for Direct Effectiveness

As subsequent case law has made clear, a Treaty provision may have direct effects where four conditions are met. First, the provision must be sufficiently clear and precise for judicial application.[5] Secondly, it must establish an unconditional obligation. Thirdly, it must establish a complete and legally perfect obligation. Fourthly, its implementation must not be dependent on measures being subsequently taken by Union institutions or Member States

---

[2] Cf., regarding the political context in which the *Van Gend en Loos* ruling was delivered, A. Evans, "Institutions of the European Communities other than the Court of Justice" in *Stair Memorial Encyclopaedia of the Laws of Scotland*, vol. x, (Butterworths, London, 1990), 132–262, 144, n. 3.

[3] [1963] ECR 1, 13.   [4] Ibid., 14–15.

[5] See, e.g., Case 43/75 *Gabrielle Defrenne* v. *SA Belge de Navigation Aérienne (Sabena)* [1976] ECR 455, 473.

with discretionary power in the matter.[6] This final condition may apparently be met where there is discretion but is exercise is considered sufficiently amenable to judicial control.[7]

Where these conditions are met, the provision concerned must be applied directly by national courts to the situations with which the provision is concerned. Direct effects may arise for individuals in the form of rights or obligations directly enforceable by these courts.[8]

It is not only prohibitions on state action which may entail direct effects. Positive obligations on Member States to remove restrictive measures or to eliminate discrimination may also entail such effects. Thus, for example, provisions such as Articles 52 and 59 of the EC Treaty, which require the abolition of restrictions on freedom of establishment and freedom to provide services respectively, entail rights for individuals against the state.

Article 52 of the EC Treaty also entails obligations for "all the competent public authorities, including legally recognised professional bodies",[9] and Article 119 of the EC Treaty, which concerns equal pay for mean and women, is binding in relation to collective agreements and contracts between employers and employees.[10] Moreover, Articles 85 and 86 of the EC Treaty, which respectively concern cartels and monopolies, entail both rights and obligations for private persons.[11]

Policy Considerations

Complicated issues may arise from findings that some, but not all, Treaty provisions have direct effects. For example, Article 92(1) of the EC Treaty, which prohibits state aid distorting competition in trade between Member states, has been interpreted by the Court of Justice as lacking such effects. Apparently, the Court considers that economic analysis and policy decisions, for which national courts may be ill-suited, are required by this provision. On the other hand, Article 93(3) is directly effective.[12] Hence, national courts may have to determine whether there has been a violation of aid notification requirements imposed on Member States by this provision. To make this determination, such courts must only decide whether aid within

---

[6] Mayras AG in Case 2/74 *Jean Reyners* v. *Belgium* [1974] ECR 631, 659–61.

[7] See, e.g., Case 41/74 *Yvonne van Duyn* v. *Home Office* [1974] ECR 1337, 1347.

[8] See, e.g., regarding Art. 95 EC, Case 57/65 *Alfons Lütticke GmbH* v. *Hauptzollamt Saarlouis* [1966] ECR 205, 210–11.

[9] Case 197/84 *P. Steinhauser* v. *City of Biarritz* [1985] ECR 1819, 1826–7. See also, regarding Art. 30 EC, Joined Cases 266 & 267/87 *R.* v. *Royal Pharmaceutical Society of Great Britain, ex p. Association of Pharmaceutical Importers* [1989] ECR 1295, 1327.

[10] Case 43/75 *Defrenne* v. *SA Belge de Navigation Aérienne (Sabena)* [1976] ECR 455, 476.

[11] Case 127/73 *Belgische Radio en Televisie (BRT) and Société Belge des Auteurs, Compositeurs, et Editeurs* v. *SV SABAM and NV Fonior* [1974] ECR 51.

[12] Case 74/76 *Iannelli and Volpi SpA* v. *Meroni* [1977] ECR 557, 575; and Joined Cases C–78–83/90 *Compagnie Commerciale de l'Ouest E.A.* [1992] ECR I–1847, I–1883.

the meaning of Article 92(1) has been granted without prior notification and not whether it distorts competition and affects trade between Member States.[13] In other words, they are not to decide whether the aid is compatible with the common market.[14]

It has been argued that national courts should only give judgment where they conclude that aid is "clearly" present or absent.[15] For the purposes of such judgment, they may request preliminary rulings from the Court of Justice on the question whether state intervention is "capable of constituting aid within the meaning of" Article 92(1).[16] Complications may still arise, however, where the Commission finds aid to be compatible with the common market and a national court has already ordered its repayment for breach of Article 93(3).[17]

Again, the prohibition of cartels in Article 85(1) of the Treaty is directly effective.[18] Agreements covered by this provision are, according to Article 85(2), void. Article 85(3) provides that certain agreements may be exempted from the prohibition. The latter provision is not directly effective. Apparently, the economic analysis and policy decisions implicit in the application of Article 85(3) are considered to be tasks for which the Commission is more suited than national courts. The problem arises, however, that a national court may hold to be void an agreement which the Commission subsequently exempts under Article 85(3).[19]

7.1.2 Union Acts

According to Article 189(1) of the EC Treaty, the Union institutions may enact regulations, issue directives, take decisions, make recommendations, or deliver opinions. The last two kinds of measures lack binding force,[20] though they may assist interpretation of Union law having such force.[21] A decision is binding in its entirety upon those to whom it is addressed. It may be addressed to Member States or to private persons.[22] Direct effects may arise for the addressee and for other persons affected by a decision.[23]

---

[13] Lenz AG in Case C–44/93 *Namur – Les Assurances du Crédit SA* v. *Office National du Ducroire and Belgium* [1994] ECR I–3829, I–3847–8.

[14] The Court (*ibid.*), I–3871.

[15] Jacobs AG in Case C–39/94 *Syndicat Français de l'Express International (SFEI)* v. *La Poste* [1996] ECR I–3547, I–3565.

[16] Ibid., I–3587.

[17] A. Evans, *EC Law of State Aid* (Oxford Series in EC Law, Clarendon Press, Oxford 1997).

[18] Case 127/73 *Belgische Radio en Televisie (BRT) and Société Belge des Auteurs, Compositeurs, et Editeurs* v. *SV SABAM and NV Fonior* [1974] ECR 51, 62.

[19] Cf. V. Korah, *An Introductory Guide to EC Competition Law and Practice* (Hart Publishing, Oxford, 1997).

[20] Art. 189(5) EC.

[21] Warner AG in Case 113/75 *Giordano Frecassetti* v. *Amministrazione delle Finanze dello Stato* [1976] ECR 983, 996–7; and Case C–322/88 *Salvatore Grimaldi* v. *Fonds des Maladies Professionnelles* [1989] ECR I–4407, I–4421.

[22] Art. 189(4) EC.   [23] Case 9/70 *Franz Grad* v. *Finanzamt Traunstein* [1970] ECR 825, 837.

However, the true nature of any such act depends not on its form but on its content and object.[24] According to the Declaration on the Hierarchy of Community Acts, adopted along with the Treaty on European Union, the intergovernmental conference to be convened in 1996 was to examine to what extent it might be possible to review the classification of such acts with a view to establishing an appropriate hierarchy between the different categories of act.[25] There has so far been no concrete outcome.

Regulations

According to Article 189(2), a regulation "shall have general application. It shall be binding in its entirety and directly applicable in all Member States". Like Treaty provisions, therefore, provisions of regulations which are sufficiently precise must be applied directly by national courts to the situations with which those provisions are concerned. They may not be re-enacted in national legislation.[26]

Direct effects may arise for individuals.[27] For example, such effects may arise from Regulation 1612/68,[28] which requires equal treatment for Union Citizens employed in a Member State other than their own. Similarly, they may arise from Regulation 1408/71,[29] which concerns the social security rights of such persons. Again, in *Omada*[30] the Court of Justice ruled that Article 5 of Regulation 389/82[31] obliged Member States to grant aid to producer groups recognised under Article 2 of this Regulation for investments included in national programmes for the development and rationalisation of cotton production and marketing approved by the Commission. On the other hand, provisions of Regulation 2052/88[32] concerning the objectives of the Structural Funds may be unable to meet the conditions for direct effectiveness.

Directives

According to Article 189(3), a directive shall be binding, as to the result to be achieved, upon each Member State to which it is addressed. It shall leave to the national authorities the choice of form and methods of achieving this

---

[24] Joined Cases 16 & 17/62 *Confédération Nationale des Producteurs de Fruits et Légumes* v. *EEC Council* [1962] ECR 471, 478.

[25] Cf. the Draft Treaty establishing a European Union (OJ 1984 C77/33).

[26] Case 24/73 *Fratelli Variola SpA* v. *Amministrazione Italiana delle Finanze* [1973] ECR 981, 991.

[27] Case 93/71 *Orsolina Leonesio* v. *Italian Ministry for Agriculture and Forestry* [1972] ECR 287, 293. Cf. Case 41/74 *Yvonne van Duyn* v. *Home Office* [1974] ECR 1337, 1348.

[28] On freedom of movement for workers within the Community (JO 1968 L257/2).

[29] On the application of social security schemes to employed persons and their families moving within the Community (JO 1971 L149/2).

[30] Case 8/87 *Omada Paragogon Vamvakiou Andrianou-Gizinou & Co* v. *Greece* [1988] ECR 1001, 1014.

[31] On producer groups and associations thereof in the cotton sector (OJ 1982 L51/1).

[32] On the tasks of the Structural Funds and their effectiveness and on the co-ordination of their activities between themselves and with the operations of the EIB and the other existing financial instruments (OJ 1988 L185/9).

result. However, according to the Court of Justice, after expiry of the period within which national law must be introduced for their implementation, provisions of directives which are sufficiently precise may have direct effects.[33] The rationale is that the Member State should not profit from its failure to meet the deadline for implementation.[34]

Rights for individuals against the Member State may be entailed.[35] However, the availability of these rights depends on what is meant by "the state" for this purpose. According to the Court, they are available against "a body, whatever its legal form, which has been made responsible, pursuant to a measure adopted by the state, for providing a public service under the control of the state and has for that purpose special powers beyond those which result from the normal rules applicable in relations between individuals".[36]

In particular, directly effective provisions of directives are to be applied by national courts, where any such body acts contrary to such provisions. For example, a Union Citizen excluded or expelled from a Member State other than his own may rely on provisions of Directive 64/221[37] to challenge such action before national courts.[38] This Directive limits the conditions under which such action may be taken and lays down procedural safeguards for persons affected.[39] Again, in *Banfi*[40] the Court of Justice ruled that legal persons could not be denied aid for farm modernisation under Directive 72/159[41] solely because they had assumed a specific legal form.

However, no rights which the Member State may invoke against individuals are entailed.[42] Moreover, directives entail no rights or obligations in the context of relations between individuals. Hence, their direct effects are said to be "vertical" but not "horizontal".

On the other hand, "indirect effects" may arise. Thus when a dispute concerns a matter within the sphere of application of a directive,[43] national courts must, as far as possible, interpret national legislation in the light of the wording of the directive.[44]

---

[33] Case 9/70 *Franz Grad* v. *Finanzamt Traunstein* [1970] ECR 825, 838.

[34] Case 148/78 *Pubblico Ministero* v. *Tullio Ratti* [1979] ECR 1629, 1642.

[35] See, e.g., *ibid.*, 1642.

[36] Case C–188/89 *A. Foster* v. *British Gas plc* [1990] ECR 3313, 3349.

[37] On the co-ordination of special measures concerning the movement and residence of foreign nationals which are justified on grounds of public policy, public security, or public health (JO 1964 850).

[38] Case 41/74 *Yvonne van Duyn* v. *Home Office* [1974] ECR 1337, 1348–9.

[39] Sect. 9.2.5 below.

[40] Case 312/85 *SpA Villa Banfi* v. *Regione Toscana* [1986] ECR 4039, 4055.

[41] On the modernisation of farms (JO 1972 L96/1).

[42] See, e.g., Case 152/84 *M.H Marshall* v. *Southampton and South-West Hampshire Area Health Authority (Teaching)* [1986] ECR 723, 749; and Case C–91/92 *Paola Faccini Dori* v. *Recreb Srl* [1994] ECR I–3325, I–3355–6.

[43] But see, in the criminal law field, Case 14/86 *Pretore di Salò* v. *X* [1987] ECR 2545, 2570.

[44] Case C–106/89 *Marleasing SA* v. *La Comercial International de Alimentación SA* [1990] ECR I–4135, I–4159. Cf. the objections of the House of Lords in *Duke* v. *GEC Reliance Ltd* [1988] AC 618 to interpreting earlier UK legislation in the light of a later dir.

7.1.3 European Communities Act

Provision is made in the European Communities Act 1972 to ensure observance of direct effects by British courts. Thus, according to section 2(1) of this Act, such courts must uphold "directly enforceable Community rights". In other words, they must uphold rights which "are without further enactment to be given legal effect or used in the United Kingdom". Respect for indirect effects is, presumably, dependent on section 3(2) of the same Act.[45]

7.2 Supremacy

In *Costa*[46] questions were put to the Court of Justice concerning the compatibility with the EEC Treaty of the nationalisation of the electricity industry in Italy. The Court of Justice interpreted the Treaty as not prohibiting this nationalisation.

However, the Court took the opportunity to rule on more general matters of Union law. According to the Court, the Treaty had created a Union of unlimited duration, having its own institutions, its own personality, its own legal capacity, and its own capacity of representation on the international plane. More particularly, the Union had real powers stemming from a limitation of sovereignty or a transfer of powers from the Member States to the Union. Hence, the Member States had limited their sovereign rights, albeit within limited fields, and had created a body of law which bound both their nationals and themselves.

As the Court has subsequently made clear,[47] a consequence is that national courts must refrain from applying provisions of national law conflicting with directly effective Union law. In this sense, Union law enjoys supremacy over national law.

However, the concept of supremacy may be inadequate to capture and express the variegation of the relationship between Union law and national law.

7.2.1 Competing Legal Orders

Various Treaty provisions may authorise Member States to maintain or introduce national legislation which conflicts with Union legislation. In particular, according to Article 100a(4) of the Treaty, after adoption of a harmonisation measure by the Council a Member State may maintain conflicting national provisions on grounds of major needs referred to in Article 36 or related to protection of the environment or the working

---

[45] Sect. 7.3.2 below.

[46] Case 6/64 *Flaminio Costa* v. *ENEL* [1964] ECR 585, 593.

[47] Case 14/68 *Walt Wilhelm* v. *Bundeskartellamt* [1969] ECR 1, 14–15; and Case 106/77 *Amministrazione delle Finanze dello Stato* v. *Simmenthal SpA* [1978] ECR 629, 644.

environment. Moreover, according to Article 100a(5), a Member State may, in the light of new scientific evidence and because of a problem specific to that Member State arising after the enactment of Union legislation, intro- duce conflicting legislation on the same grounds.[48] The implication is that the Union legislature lacks a legal monopoly to determine the requirements with which harmonisation is concerned.

Similarly, in developing general principles of law, the Court of Justice is "inspired" by national law.[49] In other words, the content of the case law of the Court of Justice may owe much to national law.

7.2.2 Competing Institutions

There may be a dialogue between national supreme courts[50] and the Court of Justice. At least, it seems that the Court of Justice cannot disregard rulings of national supreme courts.[51]

The role of national parliaments in the development of Union law may also be important. Arrangements are made with a view to ensuring that national parliaments have the opportunity to examine Commission proposals before the Council reaches a decision or adopts a common position on them. A more generalised role may also be played by the Conference of European Affairs Committees of the national parliaments.[52] Moreover, before the Union exceeds twenty Member States, the national governments are to come together to decide on the role of national parlia- ments in the Union.[53] These arrangements may be expected to promote networking between MEPs and national parliamentarians. In other words, national legislatures may have an input into Union legislation.

7.2.3 Subsidiarity

The principle of subsidiarity may affect the relationship between Union law and national law. In a sense, it establishes "ground rules" within which competition between legal orders and institutions is to take place. At the same time, it may be seen as anchoring an "autocontrol" system.

According to this principle, "the Community shall act within the limits of the powers conferred upon it by this Treaty and of the objectives assigned to it therein. In areas which do not fall within its exclusive competence, the

---

[48] Cf., in the field of consumer protection, Art. 129a(5) EC, and, in the case of environmental protection, Art. 130t EC.

[49] See, e.g., sect. 7.2.4 below.

[50] See, e.g., *Minister of the Interior* v. *Cohn-Bendit* [1980] 1 CMLR 543; and *Manfred Brunner* v. *The European Union Treaty* [1994] 1 CMLR 57.

[51] See, in the field of fundamental rights, sect. 7.2.4 below.

[52] Protocol to the founding Treaties on the role of national parliaments in the EU.

[53] Art. 2 of the Protocol on the institutions and with the prospects of EU enlargement, annexed to the founding Treaties.

Community shall take action, in accordance with the principle of subsidiarity, only if and in so far as the objectives of the proposed action cannot be sufficiently achieved by the Member States and can therefore, by reason of the scale or effects of the proposed action, be better achieved by the Community. Any action by the Community shall not go beyond what is necessary to achieve the objectives of this Treaty."[54] In effect, then, national law may be supreme where it may deal more satisfactorily with the matter concerned than Union law. Furthermore, the Court of Justice is, in interpreting and applying this principle, to ensure that this supremacy of national law is not endangered by developments in Union law.

On the other hand, a static situation may not be entailed. Article 235 provides for the adoption of acts necessary in the operation of the common market for the attainment of Treaty objectives.[55] Apparently, then, the legitimate scope of Union law may evolve.

7.2.4 Fundamental Rights

Fundamental rights may structure the relationship between Union law and national law. According to the Court of Justice, the supremacy of Union law applies even in relation to fundamental rights provisions of national constitutions.[56] However, concern has been expressed, particularly by the German Federal Constitutional Court,[57] that such rights may be endangered by Union law. In response, the Court of Justice has developed fundamental rights principles within Union law, which are "inspired" by national constitutions and the European Convention on Human Rights.[58]

However, the rights are only protected within the framework of Union law.[59] Thus, for example, they may not benefit third-state nationals excluded or expelled from a Member State.[60]

Moreover, the protection of fundamental rights is subject to the public interest requirements of the Union. Thus, for example, in the context of

---

[54] Art. 3b EC.

[55] See, regarding pre-emption and supremacy, Case 218/85 *Association Comité Agricole Régional Fruits et Légumes de Bretagne* v. *A. Le Campion* [1986] ECR 3513, 3534.

[56] Case 11/70 *Internationale Handelsgesellschaft mbH* v. *Einfuhr- und Vorratsstelle für Getreide und Futtermittel* [1970] ECR 1125, 1134.

[57] *Internationale Handelsgesellschaft mbH* v. *Einfuhr- und Vorratsstelle für Getreide und Futtermittel* [1974] 2 CMLR 540, 550–1.

[58] Case 4/73 *J. Nold, Kohlen-und Baustoffgrosshandlung* v. *EC Commission* [1974] ECR 491, 507. See, e.g., in connection with "due process" and Art. 6 of the Convention, Case 222/84 *Marguerite Johnston* v. *Chief Constable of the Royal Ulster Constabulary* [1986] ECR 1651, 1682–3. See, now, Art. F(2) TEU.

[59] Case C–260/89 *Elliniki Radiphonia Tileorassi AE* v. *Dimotiki Etairia Pliroforissis and Sotiris Kouvelas* [1991] ECR I–2925, I–2964. See also Van Gerven AG in Case C–159/90 *Society for the Protection of Unborn Children Ireland Ltd* v. *Stephen Grogan* [1991] ECR I–4685, I–4723.

[60] Case 12/86 *Meryem Demirel* v. *Stadt Schwäbisch Gmünd* [1987] ECR 3719. The position may be affected by police and judicial co-operation in criminal matters (sect. 21.15 below) or action under Art. 73i EC (sect. 9.2.3 below).

enforcement of competition law the Commission may enjoy "search and seizure powers", which override the right to privacy in Article 8 of the European Convention.[61] However, pursuit of such requirements may not lead to Union action "impairing the very substance" of fundamental rights.[62]

Inevitably, Union and national courts may disagree whether fundamental rights are satisfactorily safeguarded in Union law. From the perspective of national courts, the problems may be approached in terms of the legitimacy of sovereignty transfers. In other words, problems arise as to the extent to which sovereignty transfers are compatible with national constitutions. Certainly, the German Federal Constitutional Court considers that the national constitution may set limits to permissible transfers.[63]

7.2.5 European Communities Act

In the United Kingdom section 2(4) of the European Communities Act provides that "any enactment passed or to be passed must be construed and have effect" subject the requirements of section 2(1) of the Act. In other words, British courts must not apply national law conflicting with directly effective Union law.

Parliamentary Sovereignty

The relationship between section 2(4) of the European Communities Act and the demands of the doctrine of Parliamentary sovereignty is problematic. In essence, the problem concerns the constitutionality of seeking to incorporate the doctrine of the supremacy of Union law into United Kingdom law. More particularly, the problem is whether the sovereignty of the United Kingdom Parliament allows for a statute to limit the effect which courts give to future Parliamentary legislation. The 1972 Act may not be subject to implied repeal by a subsequent statute conflicting with Union law.[64] However, express repeal or amendment of the Act by a subsequent statute conflicting with Union law may remain possible.[65] If so, British courts may apply the subsequent statute rather than the directly effective Union law with which it conflicts.

Pluralism within the UK

A complication may result from the fact that parliamentary sovereignty is a

[61] Case 136/79 *National Panasonic (UK) Ltd* v. *EC Commission* [1980] ECR 2033, 2057. But cf. Case 374/87 *Orkem* v. *EC Commission* [1989] ECR 3283, 3350-1.
[62] Case 5/88 *Hubert Wachauf* v. *Germany* [1989] ECR 2609, 2639.
[63] *Manfred Brunner* v. *The European Union Treaty* [1994] 1 CMLR 57.
[64] *Macarthys* v. *Smith* [1979] ICR 785; *Garland* v. *British Rail Engineering* [1983] 2 AC 751; and *R.* v. *Secretary of State for Transport, ex Parte Factortame Ltd.* [1990] 2 AC 85, 140.
[65] D. Wyatt and A. Dashwood, *European Community Law* (3rd edn. Sweet and Maxwell, London, 1993), 58; and L. Collins, *European Community Law in the United Kingdom* (4th edn., Butterworths, London, 1990), 40.

judicial doctrine and that the Scottish judicial system is separate from that of England and Wales. Hence, problems of the relationship between Union law and national law may not necessarily have an identical resolution throughout the United Kingdom.[66]

7.3 Damages

Union law was once essentially concerned with preventing national interference with the abolition of barriers to economic activity between Member States, the prevention of such interference being necessary for establishment of the common market. This concern might be met simply by the supremacy of Union law requiring freedom of economic activity between Member States. However, now that the Union engages in more general regulatory activity, more developed means of securing compliance with Union law may be required.

According to the case law of the Court of Justice, Member States may be liable in damages for harm caused to private persons by their violations of Union law, including failures to implement directives.[67] National legislation limiting the amount of damages that may be awarded may be inapplicable.[68]

Such case law reduces the practical significance of the lack of horizontal effects of directives. While directives remain unenforceable in relations between individuals, individuals who are harmed by other individuals conducting themselves contrarily to the requirements of a non-implemented directive may obtain damages from national authorities for the harm suffered. Hence, the case law adds to the blurring of the effective distinction between directives and regulations.

More generally, the case law entails that a Member State must compensate individuals for harm caused by breaches of Union law for which it is responsible, if three conditions are met. First, the rule of law infringed must be intended to confer rights on individuals.[69] Secondly, the breach must be sufficiently serious. Thirdly, there must be a direct causal link between the breach of the obligation resting on the Member State and the damage sustained by the injured party.[70]

---

[66] A. Evans, "Treaties and United Kingdom Legislation: the Scottish Dimension" [1984] *Juridical Review* 41–62.

[67] Joined Cases C–6 & 9/90 *Andrea Francovich* v. *Italy* [1992] ECR I–5357, I–5415–16.

[68] Case C–271/91 *M.H. Marshall* v. *Southampton and South West Hampshire Health Authority* [1993] ECR I–4367, I–4409. See also Joined Cases C–46–48/93 *Brasserie de Pêcheur SA* v. *Germany* [1996] ECR I–1029, I–1158.

[69] Reasons must also be given for any measure affecting the exercise of fundamental rights conferred by Union law on individuals. See Case 222/86 *Union Nationale des Entraîneurs et Cadres Techniques Professionnels de Football* v. *Georges Heylens* [1987] ECR 4097, 4117; and Case C–70/95 *Sodemare SA* v. *Regione Lombardia* (17 June 1997).

[70] Case C–66/95 *R.* v. *Secretary of State for Social Security, ex p. Eunice Sutten* [1997] ECR I–2163, I–2191.

However, the role of national courts may be affected by policy considerations. Their role may also be affected by the dependence of such courts on national procedural rules, though Union legislation may be envisaged to develop the role of national courts.[71]

7.3.1 Policy Considerations

A clear distinction between its own role and the role of national courts is sought by the Commission. The Commission describes itself as the administrative authority responsible for the implementation and development of competition policy in the public interest of the Union. National courts, in turn, are said to be responsible for the protection of rights and the enforcement of duties, usually at the behest of private parties.[72]

Thus, for example, it is the Commission which examines the compatibility of aid with the common market under Article 92 of the EC Treaty, even where the Member State has acted in breach of the prohibition on giving effect to aid. The Commission's final decision cannot have the effect of regularising implementing measures which are invalid for having been effected in breach of notification requirements in Article 93(3).[73]

It is for national courts, in turn, to ensure that individuals are able to enforce rights of action in respect of any breach of Article 93(3). All the proper consequences must follow from such a breach, according to national law. Such consequences may concern the validity of acts granting aid and the recovery of aid granted in breach of that provision. National courts are thus to preserve, until the final decision of the Commission, the rights of individuals faced with a possible breach by state authorities of Article 93(3).[74] In particular, such courts may find acts granting aid to be invalid,[75] suspend the

---

[71] See, e.g., the amended proposal of 6 Jan. 1997 (OJ 1997 C80/10) for a dir. on injunctions for the protection of consumer interests.

[72] Notice on co-operation between national courts and the Commission in the state aid field (OJ 1995 C312/8), para. 4. The distinction between policy implementation and the protection of private rights may be more complicated than is suggested by the Commission. Cf. the dismissal by the French *Cour de Cassation* of a negligence action regarding the failure to apply for aid in good time on the ground that the Commission had found the aid to be contrary to Art. 92 EC. The defendant had been negligent, but no reparable loss had been caused to the plaintiff, since the aid was unlawful anyway (*Lener Ignace SA* v. *Beauvois* [1994] 2 CMLR 419).

[73] Case C–354/90 *Fédération Nationale du Commerce Extérieur des Produits Alimentaires and Syndicat National des Négociants et Transformateurs de Saumon* v. *France* [1991] ECR I–5505, I–5528. See also Jacobs AG in Case C–301/87 *France* v. *EC Commission: Boussac* [1990] ECR I–307, I–339. Cf. Wolf J. in *R.* v. *AG, ex p. ICI* [1985] 1 CMLR 588, 608.

[74] Case C–354/90 *Fédération Nationale du Commerce Extérieur des Produits Alimentaires and Syndicat National des Négociants et Transformateurs de Saumon* v. *France* [1991] ECR I–5505, I–5528. A remedy before national courts may remove the need for the grant of counter aid by other Member States. See I. Harden, "State Aids and the Economic Constitution of the Community" in I. Harden (ed.), *State Aid: Community Law and Policy* (Bundesanzeiger, Trier, 1993), 12–18, 17.

[75] Case C–17/91 *Georges Lornoy en Zonen NV* v. *Belgium* [1992] ECR I–6523, I–6545.

implementation of unnotified aid,[76] order its repayment,[77] or award damages against the state to competitors.[78] Similarly, national courts may apparently award damages where undertakings breach anti-trust rules in Article 85[79] or 86 of the Treaty.[80]

However, problems resulting from the lack of direct effectiveness of provisions such as Articles 85(1) and 92 of the Treaty reappear. In particular, decisions of national courts regarding damages may not necessarily be consistent with Commission decisions as to the compatibility of state aid or restrictive practices with the common market.

7.3.2 European Communities Act

In the absence of relevant Union rules, remedies before national courts depend on national procedural law.[81] However, the Court of Justice insists that in the case of claims based on Union law, national procedural law must be no less favourable than in the case of similar claims based on national law. Moreover, such law must not make it virtually impossible or excessively difficult to obtain damages.[82] At the same time, general principles of Union law must be respected. Thus no rule of national law, such as the rule that a British court cannot set aside an Act of Parliament,[83] may affect the availability of remedies. In other words, national law may not prevent the grant of a remedy which is otherwise available, but the creation of a remedy is not required. More particularly, in the grant of legal aid the national authorities must not discriminate or jeopardize the exercise of freedom of movement under Union law.[84]

Section 2 of the European Communities Act may not necessarily be sufficient to ensure respect for these requirements. However, section 3(2) of the same Act provides that questions of Union law are to be resolved by British courts according to the principles laid down in rulings of the Court of Justice

---

[76] M. Dony, "Les Aides aux entreprises et le droit communautaire de la concurrence" (1991) 1316 *Courrier hebdomadaire de la centre de recherche et d'information socio-politiques* 26.

[77] Para. 10 of the Notice on co-operation between national courts and the Commission in the state aid field (OJ 1995 C312/8). See also Case C–354/90 *Fédération Nationale du Commerce Extérieur des Produits Alimentaires et Syndicat National des Négociants et Transformateurs de Saumon* v. *France* [1991] ECR I–5505, I–5528; and Jacobs AG in Case C–39/94 *Syndicat Français de l'Express International (SFEI)* v. *La Poste* [1996] ECR I–3547, I–3571.

[78] Jacobs AG (*ibid.*), I–3573.

[79] Cf., regarding injunctions, *Cutsforth* v. *Mansfield Inns Ltd* [1986] 1 All ER 577.

[80] *Garden Cottage Foods* v. *Milk Marketing Board* [1984] AC 130.

[81] See, generally, C.M.G. Himsworth, "Things Fall Apart: the Harmonization of Community Judicial Procedural Protection Revisited" [1997] *ELR* 291–311.

[82] Case C–66/95 *R.* v. *Secretary of State for Social Security, ex p. Eunice Sutton* [1997] ECR I–2163, I–2191.

[83] Case C–213/89 *R.* v. *Secretary of State for Transport, ex p. Factortame Ltd* [1990] ECR I–2433, I–2474–5.

[84] Reply by Mrs Gradin to WQ E–2866/96 (OJ 1997 C72/84) by Alex Smith.

or are to be referred to the latter under Article 177 of the EC Treaty. Therefore, British courts must either grant remedies according to Union law requirements or request a preliminary ruling as to the meaning of these requirements.

7.4 Union Law and Third States

The effects of Union law in third states may be expected to depend on national constitutional rules in the third state concerned, on whether that state has concluded an agreement with the Union, and, more particularly, on the terms of any such agreement. In practice, however, certain effects may arise independently of such agreements.

Some decisions suggest that courts of third states may be willing to take account of developments in Union law.[85] For example, before Sweden acceded to the Union, in one decision[86] a Swedish court referred to the Directive on product liability.[87] In another decision[88] reference was made to the Convention on the Recognition and Enforcement of Judgments in Civil and Commercial Matters.[89]

At the same time, third states may introduce national provisions designed to ensure that their national legislation is aligned with Union legislation.[90]

7.5 Agreements with Third States

Agreements with third states often contain provisions reminiscent of, though more limited than, Article 5 of the EC Treaty. Moreover, agreements concluded according to Article 228 of the Treaty are binding on the Union institutions and on Member States.[91] Provisions of such agreements and acts adopted by institutions established by the agreements may also have internal legal effects within the Union.[92] They may even apparently enjoy supremacy over both

---

[85] Cf. the argument that, even before the EEA Agreement (OJ 1994 L1/3), the ECJ and national courts were obliged to seek to promote the homogeneity of the then EES in D. Thürer, "The Role of Soft Law in the Actual Process of European Integration" in O. Jacot-Guillarmod (ed.), *L'Avenir du libre-échange en Europe: vers un Espace économique européen* (Schulthess, Zürich, 1990), 131–8.

[86] NJA 1989:66.

[87] Dir. 85/374 (OJ 1985 L210/29) on the approximation of the laws, regulations, and administrative provisions of the Member States concerning liability for defective products.

[88] NJA 1989:10.

[89] Convention on jurisdiction and the enforcement of judgments in civil and commercial matters (OJ 1978 L304/36; OJ 1990 C189/2).

[90] See, sect. 19.5.2, regarding "voluntary harmonisation".

[91] Art. 228(7) EC.

[92] But cf., regarding Art. XI of GATT, Joined Cases 21 & 22/72 *International Fruit Company NV* v. *Produktschap voor Groenten en Fruit* [1972] ECR 1219, 1227–8 and Case 70/87 *Fédération de l'Industrie de l'Huilerie de la CEE (Fediol)* v. *EC Commission* [1989] ECR 1781, 1830–1.

Union law and national law.[93] Their supremacy over national law may affect not only the validity of conflicting agreements concluded by a Member State with a third state. It may also affect the applicability of national law by national courts. At the same time, depending on national constitutional rules, agreements with third states may also have effects within the third states concerned.

7.5.1 Free Trade Agreements

Article 22(1) of the Swiss Free Trade Agreement[94] provides that the parties shall refrain from any measure likely to jeopardize the fulfilment of the objectives of the Agreement. Moreover, according to Article 22(2), they are to take any general or specific measures required to fulfil their obligations under the Agreement. If either party considers that the other party has failed to fulfil an obligation under the Agreement, the former may take appropriate measures.

More particularly, Article 29(1) of the Agreement provides that the Joint Committee established by this Agreement may take decisions in the cases provided for in the Agreement and make recommendations. The former are to "be put into effect by the Contracting Parties in accordance with their own rules".

Internal Legal Effects within Member States

Provisions of a free trade agreement which exhibit the same characteristics as directly effective provisions of the EC Treaty may, given "the object and purpose of the agreement and its context", have direct effects before national courts of Member States.[95] These effects are not precluded by any lack of reciprocity regarding the internal legal effects of such agreements within the third states concerned.[96]

Provided there is a direct connection with a free trade agreement, acts adopted by a joint committee established thereunder may also have direct effects within Member States.[97] Recommendations, on the other hand, are not binding, though national courts of Member States may have to take account of the recommendations of such bodies for interpretative purposes.[98]

However, free trade agreements are not interpreted as requiring the same trade liberalisation as the EC Treaty. Consequently, the direct effects of provisions in such agreements may be of little avail to a party invoking them.[99]

---

[93] Case 22/70 *EC Commission* v. *EC Council: ERTA* [1971] ECR 263, 274–5.

[94] JO 1972 L300/189.

[95] See, regarding Art. 21 of the Portuguese Free Trade Agreement (JO 1972 L301/2), Case 104/81 *Hauptzollamt Mainz* v. *C.A. Kupferberg & Cie KG* [1982] ECR 3641, 3665.

[96] Ibid., 3664.

[97] Case C–188/91 *Deutsche Shell AG* v. *Hauptzollamt Hamburg-Harburg* [1993] ECR I–363, I–388.

[98] Ibid., I–388.

[99] Cf. G. Gaja, "Instruments for Legal Integration in the European Community – A Review" in M. Cappelletti, M. Seccombe, R.M. Buxbaum, K.J. Hopt, T. Daintith, S.F. Williams, T. Bourgoignie, and D. Trubek (eds), *Integration Through Law* (de Gruyter, Berlin, 1986), i, 113–60, 139, n. 82.

In practice, provisions of free trade agreements may sometimes be invoked by traders of the third state concerned before national courts of Member States. However, traders may be more inclined to take proceedings before such courts on the basis of the EC Treaty[100] than on the basis of free trade agreements. Presumably, it is assumed that the requirements contained in the agreements are too limited often to be of assistance in resolving trade disputes. The result of the assumption may be that whatever potential the agreements have for resolving such disputes[101] remains largely unexplored.[102]

Internal Legal Effects within Third States

The question whether a free trade agreement may have direct effects within the third state concerned depends of the national constitutional law of that state. In Sweden, for example, the Swedish Free Trade Agreement[103] was regarded as lacking direct effects.[104] This lack may be thought to provide a straightforward explanation for the failure of Swedish courts to play a significant role in resolving disputes under the Agreement. However, it cannot be assumed that provisions of the Agreement would have been entirely disregarded by Swedish courts.[105] At least, it appears to have been open to the Swedish legislature to provide for national courts to take account of its provisions and the relevant case law of the Court of Justice.[106] Therefore, lack of direct effectiveness in itself may not fully explain the apparent disinterest in free trade agreements shown by parties to proceedings before courts in third states.

7.5.2 Association Agreements

Association agreements may contain the same kind of "loyalty" clause as free trade agreements. For example, according to Article 117(1) of the Europe

---

[100] See, in particular, Case 238/87 *AB Volvo* v. *Erik Veng (UK) Ltd* [1988] ECR 6211. In Case 125/88 *HFM Nijman* [1989] ECR 3533 the Swedish Free Trade Agreement (JO 1972 L300/96) was invoked in conjunction with the EEC Treaty.

[101] Cf. U. Bernitz, "The EEC–EFTA Free Trade Agreements with Special Reference to the Position of Sweden and the Other Scandinavian EFTA Countries" (1986) 23 *CMLRev.* 567–90, 573.

[102] Failure to seek to exploit the potential of an agreement may apparently have extreme consequences. At least in the case of the OCT, association under Arts. 131–136 EC can lapse as a result of the failure of an associated country to use its associated status. See Trabucchi AG in Case 147/73 *Carlheinz Lensing Kaffee-Tee-Import KG* v. *Hauptzollamt Berlin-Packhof* [1973] ECR 1543, 1551.

[103] JO 1972 L300/96.

[104] Bill on the agreement with the EEC, prop. 1972:135, 21. But cf. H. Lidgard, "Sverige-EEG och Konkurrensen" [1974] *SvJT* 18–33, 100.

[105] Cf., earlier, the inconclusive judgment in *Hans Hauenschild Chemische Fabric KG* v. *AB Kemiska Byggnadsprodukter* [1976] 1 CMLR D9. It has been argued that Swiss courts may, in suitable cases, be prepared to go further. See M. Baldi, "Direct Applicability of Free Trade Agreements between the EEC and the EFTA Countries from a Swiss Perspective" [1985] *Swiss Review of International Competition Law* 30–8. Cf. also sect. 7.4 above.

[106] See, e.g., prop. 1990/91:197, on product liability.

Agreement with Hungary,[107] the Parties shall take any general or specific measures required to fulfil their obligations under this Agreement. They shall see to it that the objectives set out in this Agreement are attained. A Party may take "appropriate measures" under Article 117(2), if the other has failed to fulfil an obligation under this Agreement.

Internal Legal Effects within Member States

Provisions of association agreements may have direct effects within Member States.[108] A provision may do so when, regard being had to its wording and the purpose and the nature of the agreement itself, the provision contains a clear and precise obligation which is not subject, in its implementation or effects, to the adoption of any subsequent measure.[109]

On the other hand, provisions which "essentially serve to set out a programme and are not sufficiently precise and unconditional" do not have internal legal effects.[110] Likewise, a provision which "does no more than impose on contracting parties a general obligation to cooperate in order to achieve the aims of the agreement . . . cannot directly confer on individuals rights which are not already vested in them by other provisions of the agreement".[111]

Acts of bodies established by association agreements may also have internal legal effects within Member States. For example, the Europe Agreement with Poland[112] provides that decisions taken by the Association Council[113] and the Association Committee[114] shall be binding on the Parties, which shall take the measures necessary to implement these decisions. Within the Union decisions of such kinds are now "regularly" published in the Official Journal of the European Communities.[115] They may be directly effective before national courts of Member States according to the same criteria as may provisions of the relevant agreement itself.[116]

Internal Legal Effects within Third States

Association agreements may contemplate adoption of arrangements to secure for provisions of such agreements or of acts adopted thereunder internal legal effects within the third states concerned. For example, a Joint Declaration regarding Article 63(3) of the Europe Agreement with Poland,[117]

---

[107] OJ 1993 L347/2.

[108] See, regarding the direct effectiveness of Art. 2(1) of the Yaoundé Convention (JO 1964 1431), Case 87/75 *Conceria Daniele Bresciani* v. *Amministrazione Italiana delle Finanze* [1976] ECR 129, 140–2. See also, in the case of a protocol to the Association Agreement with Cyprus (OJ 1973 L133/2), Case C–432/92 *R.* v. *Minister of Agriculture, Fisheries, and Food, ex p. S.P. Anastasiou (Pissouri) Ltd* [1994] ECR I–3087, I–3128.

[109] Case 12/86 *Meryem Demirel* v. *Stadt Schwäbisch Gmünd* [1987] ECR 3719, 3752.

[110] Ibid., 3753.   [111] Ibid., 3754   [112] OJ 1993 L348/2.   [113] Ibid., Art. 104.

[114] Ibid., Art. 106(2).

[115] Reply by Mr Delors to WQ E–260/93 (OJ 1994 C352/1) by Anita Pollack.

[116] Case C–192/89 *S.Z. Sevince* v. *Staatssecretaris van Justitie* [1990] ECR I–3461, I–3502.

[117] OJ 1993 L348/2.

which concerns competition, was annexed to this Agreement. According to the Declaration, the Parties may request the Association Council at a later stage, and after the adoption of the implementing rules referred to in Article 63(3), to examine to what extent and under which conditions certain competition rules may be directly applicable. Account is to be taken of the progress made in the integration process between the Union and Poland.

7.5.3 EEA Agreement

Article 3 of the EEA Agreement[118] provides that the Contracting Parties shall take all appropriate measures, whether general or particular, to ensure fulfilment of the obligations arising out of this Agreement. They shall abstain from any measure which could jeopardize the attainment of the objectives of this Agreement. These obligations may be reinforced by express requirements regarding the internal legal effects and supremacy of EEA law.

The requirements do not distinguish between provisions of the Agreement itself and acts adopted by the EEA Joint Committee. According to Article 119, such acts are an integral part of the Agreement. Moreover, the requirements do not distinguish between effects within Member States of the Union and within EFTA states.

Thus Article 104 provides that decisions taken by this Committee in the cases provided for in the Agreement shall, unless otherwise provided for therein, upon their entry into force be binding on the Parties. The latter shall take the necessary steps to ensure their implementation and application. If constitutional obstacles prevent ratification of such a decision, the "affected part" of EEA law may be suspended under Article 102(5).[119]

Internal Legal Effects

According to the eighth recital in the Preamble to the EEA Agreement, the Contracting Parties are convinced of the important role that individuals will play in the European Economic Area. It is envisaged that they will play this role through the exercise of the rights conferred on them by this Agreement and through the judicial defence of these rights. Hence, EEA law is designed to create rights for individuals, which are to be protected by national courts.

More particularly, paragraph 7 of Protocol 1 to the Agreement, on horizontal adaptations, states that rights and obligations imposed upon the Member States or their public entities, undertakings, or individuals in relation to each other shall be understood to be conferred or imposed upon Contracting Parties. The latter are understood, as the case may be, as their competent authorities, public entities, undertakings, or individuals.

However, EFTA commitment to preservation of national sovereignty may

---

[118] OJ 1994 L1/3.

[119] Art. 103(2) EEA. According to a Joint Declaration on Art. 103 EEA, there are "no practical implications for internal Community procedures".

limit assimilation of EEA law with other Union law as regards its internal legal effects. Article 7 of the Agreement seems to accept that the internal legal effects of acts adopted thereunder may depend on national law. It requires that acts referred to or contained in the annexes to this Agreement or in decisions of the EEA Joint Committee shall be binding upon the Contracting Parties. They shall also be, or *be made*, part of their internal legal order as follows:

a) an act corresponding to a regulation shall as such *be made* part of the internal legal order of the Contracting Parties;
b) an act corresponding to a directive shall leave to the authorities of the Contracting Parties the choice of form and method of implementation.

This provision seems to treat the internal legal effects of EEA law as dependent on national constitutional rules. In EFTA states with dualist systems,[120] then, EEA law only has internal legal effects where it is made part of the internal legal order. In other words, it only has the effects which are given to it by national constitutional rules.

Supremacy

Protocol 35 to the EEA Agreement, on the implementation of EEA rules, notes that the Agreement aims at achieving a homogeneous European Economic Area, based on common rules, without requiring any Contracting Party to transfer legislative powers to any EEA institution. Consequently, homogeneity will have to be achieved through national procedures.

Article 1 of the Protocol deals with cases of possible conflicts between implemented EEA rules and other statutory provisions. The Contracting Parties undertake to introduce, if necessary, a statutory provision to the effect that EEA rules shall prevail in these cases. According to a Joint Declaration on Protocol 35, this Protocol does not restrict the effects of existing internal rules which provide for direct effect and primacy of international agreements.

The Court of Justice ruled in *Opinion 1/91*[121] that a fundamental difference between the then EEC Treaty and EEA law was entailed. The internal legal effect of the Treaty in Member States and its supremacy over the national law of the Member States were, according to the Court, inherent features of the Union legal system. In contrast, the internal legal effect of EEA law in the EFTA states and its supremacy over the national law of these states were apparently to depend on national legal arrangements made by each EFTA state.[122]

---

[120] I.e. systems which separate treaty law from national law.
[121] Opinion 1/91 *Draft Agreement between the Community and the EFTA countries relating to the Creation of the EEA* [1991] ECR I–6079.
[122] Ibid., I–6102.

Viewed from national constitutional perspectives, this ruling is questionable. From such perspectives, similarities are apparent between the European Communities Act in the United Kingdom and national legal arrangements required by the EEA Agreement. Hence, questions arise whether the Court oversimplified the contrast between the EEC Treaty and EEA law.

Viewed from the perspective preferred by the Court of Justice, however, the context in which the objectives of the Agreement were situated seemed to justify the contrast. According to the Court, this context differed from that in which Union aims were pursued. The European Economic Area was to be established on the basis of an international treaty. In essence, this treaty merely created rights and obligations as between the Contracting Parties. It provided for no transfer of sovereign rights to the intergovernmental institutions which it established. In contrast, the EEC Treaty, albeit concluded in the form of an international agreement, nonetheless constituted "the constitutional charter of a Community based on the rule of law". As the Court had consistently held, this Treaty established a new legal order for the benefit of which the Member States had limited their sovereign rights, in ever wider fields.[123] The subjects of this order comprised not only Member States but also their nationals. The essential characteristics of the legal order which had thus been established were in particular its primacy over the law of the Member States and the direct effect of a whole series of provisions which were applicable to their nationals and to the Member States themselves. It followed that legal homogeneity throughout the European Economic Area was not secured by the fact that the provisions of the Treaty and those of the Agreement were identical in their content or wording.[124]

In effect, the Court may have been concerned that the EEA Agreement did not demonstrate sufficient EFTA acceptance of supranationalism as to render the Agreement capable of effectively securing the same kind of integration as the EEC Treaty.

However, the grounds which the Court discerned in the EEC Treaty for originally asserting the existence of the "new legal order" in *Van Gend en Loos*[125] were far from unambiguous. The lesson to be drawn may be that the attitude of EFTA states and their national courts as well as the EFTA Court, established pursuant to the EEA Agreement,[126] to the development of this Agreement may be more important than the terms of its individual provisions[127] and the "five

---

[123] Cf. Case 26/62 *NV Algemeine Transport- en Expeditie Onderneming Van Gend en Loos* v. *Nederlandse Administratie der Belastingen* [1963] ECR 1, 12, where the ECJ used the wording "albeit within limited fields".

[124] [1991] ECR I–6079, I–6103.   [125] [1963] ECR 1, 13.

[126] Art. 108(2) EEA and the EFTA Agreement on the establishment of a Surveillance Authority and a Court of Justice (OJ 1994 L344/1)

[127] Finnish officials apparently felt that embodiment in EEA law of the same kind of freedom of movement of goods as prevails within the Union might require that "the Cassis de Dijon principle . . . be spelt out more clearly in the EEA context". See L. Sevón, "Legal Issues in the Negotiations on a European Economic Area" [1991] *JFT* 278–87, 281.

years of rather futile talks"[128] preceding the adoption of these provisions. Certainly, the information system established by the EEA Agreement[129] implies that these courts may contribute to a dialogue concerning the relationship between Union law (including EEA law) and national law.

[128] P. Pescatore, "The Dynamics and Homogeneity of the European Economic System" [1991] JFT 295–320, 318.
[129] Sect. 5.5.3 above.

Part Two

LAW OF THE COMMON MARKET

8

Free Movement of Goods

Article 9(1) of the EC Treaty states that the European Community shall be based upon a customs union. This union shall cover all trade in goods and shall involve the prohibition between Member States of customs duties on imports and exports and of all charges having equivalent effect. In addition, provision is made in Articles 30 to 36 of the Treaty for the elimination of quantitative restrictions and measures having equivalent effect on trade between Member States. Moreover, Article 37 provides for the adjustment of state trading monopolies, so as to ensure that no discrimination exists between nationals of Member States regarding the conditions under which goods are procured or marketed.

The free movement sought by these provisions applies not only to goods originating in the Member States[1] but also to goods from third states which are in free circulation in a Member State.[2] According to Article 10 of the Treaty, goods from third states shall be considered to be in free circulation in a Member State if two conditions are met. First, there must have been compliance with import formalities. Secondly, any customs duties or charges having equivalent effect which are payable must have been levied in that Member State, and the goods must not have benefited from a total or partial drawback of such duties or charges.[3]

On the other hand, freedom of movement does not usually apply to goods marketed in the Member State where they are manufactured. In other words, this freedom does not affect restrictions having "purely internal effects" on trade within a Member State.[4]

---

[1] As determined according to Reg. 2913/92 (OJ 1992 L302/1) establishing the Community Customs Code, Arts. 22–27.

[2] Art. 9(2) EC.

[3] See also Arts. 79–83 of Reg. 2913/92 (OJ 1992 L302/1) establishing the Community Customs Code.

[4] A. Evans, *The Integration of the European Community and Third States in Europe: A Legal Analysis* (Clarendon Press, Oxford, 1996), 12–19.

8.1 Goods Covered

The term "goods" is not defined in the EC Treaty.[5] In an early judgment the Court of Justice defined goods for the purposes of Union law as "all products which can be valued in money and which are capable as such of forming the subject of commercial transactions".[6] The definition is not limited to consumer goods, articles of general use, or merchandise. For example, coins may constitute goods, if they do not constitute a means of payment in the Member States.[7] In fact, it now seems that anything which *gives rise to* commercial transactions may be treated as a good. Hence, waste is so treated, apparently because waste disposal undertakings are remunerated.[8]

8.2 Customs Duties and Charges Having Equivalent Effect

Customs duties and charges having equivalent effect on goods traded between Member States are prohibited by Article 12 of the EC Treaty.[9] This prohibition has been broadly interpreted by the Court of Justice. According to the Court, it covers any charge imposed on goods by virtue of their crossing a frontier within the Union, irrespective of whether it has a protectionist purpose or effect.[10] The prohibition thus applies even to charges which are not discriminatory.[11] An inspection fee may, however, be charged where it constitutes "consideration for a service actually rendered to importers and is of an amount commensurate with that service".[12] It may also be charged in respect of checks required by Union law[13] or by international law.[14]

The prohibition of charges having equivalent effect to customs duties[15] and the prohibition of discriminatory internal taxation in Article 95 of the Treaty[16] are distinct. According to the case law, the legality of a charge falls to be decided under Article 95 when it forms an integral part of the internal tax

---

[5] The English version of the EC Treaty sometimes refers to "goods" (e.g. Art. 9(1)) and sometimes to "products" (e.g. Arts. 9(2) and 10). The German text is more consistent in using "*Waren*".

[6] Case 7/68 *EC Commission* v. *Italy: exports of artistic or historic interest* [1968] ECR 423, 428.

[7] Case 7/78 R. v. *Ernest George Thompson, Brian Albert Johnson, and Alex Norman Woodiwiss* [1978] ECR 2247, 2275.

[8] Case C–2/90 *EC Commission* v. *Belgium: prohibition of waste from other Member States* [1990] ECR I–4431, I–4478.

[9] See, earlier, Arts. 12 to 17 EEC.

[10] Joined Cases 2 & 3/69 *Sociaal Fonds voor de Diamantarbeiders* v. *SA Ch. Brachfeld and Sons and Chougal Diamond Co.* [1969] ECR 211, 222.

[11] Case 24/68 *EC Commission* v. *Italy: statistical levy* [1969] ECR 193, 201.

[12] Case 132/82 *EC Commission* v. *Belgium: storage charges* [1983] ECR 1649, 1658–9.

[13] Case 46/76 *W.J.G. Bauhuis* v. *Netherlands* [1977] ECR 5, 18.

[14] Case 89/76 *EC Commission* v. *Netherlands: plant inspections* [1977] ECR 1355, 1365.

[15] Cf. the provision in Art. 4(1) EEA (OJ 1994 L1/3) that the Parties may replace a customs duty of a fiscal nature or the fiscal element of a customs duty by an internal tax

[16] See, regarding Art. 95 EC, Chap. 18.

system.[17] For example, a charge may formally apply both to imported products and national products, but in practice it may apply almost exclusively to imported products, because domestic production is extremely small. However, it does not necessarily constitute a charge having equivalent effect to a customs duty within the meaning of Article 12 of the Treaty. If it is part of a general system of internal dues applied systematically to categories of products according to objective criteria, irrespective of the origin of the product, it constitutes internal taxation within the meaning of Article 95.[18]

8.3 Quantitative Restrictions and Measures Having Equivalent Effect

Articles 30 and 34 of the EC Treaty prohibit quantitative restrictions and measures having equivalent effect on imports and exports respectively between Member States.

Quantitative restrictions are defined by the Court of Justice as "measures which amount to a total or partial restraint of, according to the circumstances, imports, exports, or goods in transit".[19] The concept of measures having equivalent effect is even broader. In *Dassonville*[20] a Belgian requirement of a certificate of authenticity was at issue. This certificate was less easily obtainable by importers into Belgium of an authentic product put into free circulation in another Member State than by persons importing the same product directly from the country of origin. The Court ruled that the requirement was prohibited by Article 30. In so ruling, the Court of Justice introduced the formula that "all trading rules enacted by a Member State which are capable of hindering, directly or indirectly, actually or potentially, intra-Community trade" constitute measures having equivalent effect to quantitative restrictions.[21] Subsequently, in *Rewe-Zentral AG* v. *Bundesmonopolverwaltung für Branntwein*, the Court ruled that German legislation requiring a minimum level of alcohol content for spirit liqueurs marketed in the Federal Republic constituted such a measure.[22] Rulings of this kind imply that any measure which is capable of restricting imports from another Member State is prohibited by Article 30. In particular, the apparent implication is that a measure may be prohibited, irrespective of whether it is discriminatory.

[17] Case 77/72 *Carmine Capolongo* v. *Azienda Agricola Maya* [1973] ECR 611, 623. The position regarding "parafiscal taxes" may be more complicated. See, e.g. Case C–266/91 *Celulose Beira Industrial (CELBI) SA* v. *Fazenda Publica* [1993] ECR I–4337, I–4367.

[18] Case C–343/90 *Manuel José Lourenço Dias* v. *Director da Alfândega do Porto* [1992] ECR I–4673, I–4717.

[19] Case 2/73 *Riseria Luigi Geddo* v. *Ente Nazionale Risi* [1973] ECR 865, 879. See also Case 34/79 *R.* v. *Maurice Donald Henn and Frederick Ernest Darby* [1979] ECR 3795, 3812.

[20] Case 8/74 *Procureur du Roi* v. *Benoît and Gustave Dassonville* [1974] ECR 837.

[21] *Ibid.*, 852.   [22] Case 120/78 [1979] ECR 649.

8.3.1 Discrimination

In practice, discrimination issues in the operation of the free movement of goods may be controversial.

Formal Discrimination

Member States are prohibited from differentiating between their own products and imports from another Member State in such a way that the marketing of the latter becomes more difficult than the marketing of the former. For example, the Court of Justice has ruled that a requirement imposed only on imported souvenirs that they be stamped with the word "foreign" or their country of origin is prohibited by Article 30.[23] In the case of exports, any difference in the treatment of products on the basis of their destination conflicts with the fundamental unity of the common market and is, in principle, prohibited by Article 34.[24] In other words, Member States are prohibited from "formally" discriminating.

Material Discrimination

Directive 70/50[25] was enacted to secure the abolition of national measures having an effect equivalent to quantitative restrictions on imports between Member States. According to Article 3 of this Directive, measures equally applicable to imports and domestic products are prohibited where their restrictive effects exceed those intrinsic to trade rules. The Preamble to the Directive indicates that this condition will be met where imports are precluded or their disposal is made more difficult or more costly than the disposal of domestic products and where the measures are not necessary for attainment of their objective.[26]

The conclusion may be drawn that "material discrimination" as well as "formal discrimination" against products from other Member States is prohibited. The former kind of discrimination is present, for example, where a measure equally applicable to imports and domestic products has the effect of favouring the latter.

However, the view that Article 30 embodies the concept of material discrimination may be controversial. This concept has been said to be unsuitable for application in the context of Union law on the ground that Member States would be obliged to differentiate between products so as to level off competitive advantages within the Union in a manner not

---

[23] Case 113/80 *EC Commission* v. *Ireland: souvenirs* [1981] ECR 1625.

[24] Capotorti AG in Case 53/76 *Procureur de la République, Besançon* v. *Bouhelier* [1977] ECR 197, 210.

[25] Based on the provisions of Art. 33(7) EEC, on the abolition of measures which have an effect equivalent to quantitative restrictions on imports and are not covered by other provisions adopted in pursuance of the EEC Treaty (JO 1970 L13/29).

[26] *Ibid.*, 10 and 11th recitals.

conducive to rationalisation and the optimum utilisation of resources.[27] Such an obligation would entail the nullification of comparative advantages[28] and, hence, the removal of the traditional[29] purpose of trade between states. However, the assumption that the prohibition of material discrimination entails such an obligation is questionable. The assumption seems to confuse the prohibition of such discrimination, which merely means that natural disadvantages of traders must not be reinforced through imposition of restrictions on the traders concerned, with a requirement of "positive discrimination", which means that action must be taken to reduce the effects of natural disadvantages. The free movement of goods sought by the Treaty is not apparently interpreted by the Court of Justice as embodying the latter requirement.[30]

Nevertheless, application of the concept of material discrimination may present serious problems of delimitation. For example, Article 30 may prohibit a Member State from depriving consumers of access to advertising from another Member State.[31] Thus a Member State must not reinforce the obstacles faced by a trader in one Member State who wishes to inform consumers in another Member State of his products. On the other hand, the Treaty may not protect persons in one Member State unrelated to a supplier of goods in another Member State who advertise in the former Member State the availability of the goods in the latter.[32] Apparently, those who seek to offer consumers special information designed to compensate for natural obstacles to their access to information do not benefit from the free movement of goods. However, such distinctions seem too artificial to address the real needs of liberalising trade between Member States.

Again, Article 2(3)(e) of Directive 70/50[33] includes measures fixing the prices of products solely on the basis of the cost price of domestic products at such a level as to create a hindrance to importation in the list of measures "other than those applicable equally to domestic or imported products".

---

[27] A.W.H. Meij and J.A. Winter, "Measures Having an Equivalent Effect to Quantitative Restrictions" (1976) 13 *CMLRev.* 79–104, 87–8.

[28] I.e. advantages in the natural conditions under which production and distribution take place.

[29] Though if trade between states involves differentiated goods with increasing returns to scale and consumer preferences, gains from trade may arise which have nothing to do with comparative advantages. See E. Helpman and P. Krugman, *Market Structure and Foreign Trade* (Wheatsheaf Books, Brighton, 1985) and R.K. Abrams, P.K. Cornelius, P.L. Hedfors, and G. Tersman, *The Impact of the European Community's Internal Market on the EFTA* (IMF, Washington, 1990), 14.

[30] According to Reischl AG in Case 155/73 *Guiseppe Sacchi* [1974] ECR 409, 444, even Art. 7 EEC was probably not to be understood as meaning that having regard to the handicap of foreign undertakings, namely their different needs for advertising, provision should be made in their favour to increase publicity by opening up a private television service.

[31] Case C–362/88 *GB-Inno-BM* v. *Confédération du Commerce Luxembourgeois Asbl* [1990] ECR I–667, I–686.

[32] Cf., regarding services, Case C–159/90 *Society for the Protection of Unborn Children Ireland Ltd* v. *Stephen Grogan* [1991] ECR I–4685, I–4740.

[33] JO 1970 L13/29.

Similar treatment of such measures seems to be favoured by the Court of Justice.[34] Price-fixing measures of such kinds, however, seem to constitute clear examples of equally applicable measures which have discriminatory effects.

More generally, to establish the existence of material discrimination, a detailed and complex examination of economic circumstances may be necessary. As such circumstances vary, a measure may oscillate between being discriminatory and thus prohibited and being non-discriminatory and thus permitted. Even more serious problems may arise where there is no domestic production of the goods concerned in relation to which discrimination against imports can be established.[35]

In practice, the operation of Article 30 of the Treaty does not always seem to depend on formal or material discrimination between domestic products and those from other Member States being established. Indeed, the obligation to adapt a product to legal requirements applicable to all products marketed in the Member State of importation may, as in *Rewe*,[36] be prohibited by Article 30 of the Treaty. However, this obligation may not easily be characterised as involving such discrimination.[37] The implication is that the prohibition goes beyond measures involving such discrimination.

For example, in *Cinéthèque*[38] French legislation banning the distribution of films by means of video-cassettes during the first few months of their release in the cinema was at issue. The Court of Justice noted that, if such a system applied without distinction to both domestic and imported video-cassettes, it did not have the purpose of regulating trade patterns. Moreover, its effect was not to favour national production as against the production of other Member States, but to favour cinematographic works as such. Nevertheless, the application of such a system might create barriers to trade between Member States in video-cassettes. It might do so, because of the disparities between the systems operated in the different Member States and between the conditions for the release of cinematographic works in those Member States.[39] Hence, the system was, in principle, contrary to Article 30.

Such case law apparently reflects conclusions drawn from the Treaty framework. Thus it is said to be because the requirements of the free movement of goods must be interpreted in the light of Treaty objectives that

---

[34] Case 231/83 *Henri Cullet and Chambre Syndicale des Réparations Automobiles et Détaillants de Produits Pétroliers* v. *Centre Leclerc Toulouse and Centre Leclerc Saint-Orens-de-Gameville* [1985] ECR 305, 324.

[35] P. Oliver, "Measures of Equivalent Effect: A Reappraisal" (1982) 19 *CMLRev.* 217–44, 226.

[36] Case 120/78 *Rewe-Zentral AG* v. *Bundesmonopolverwaltung für Branntwein* [1979] ECR 649.

[37] A. Mattera, "De l'Arrêt 'Dassonville' à l'arrêt 'Keck': l'obscure clarté d'une jurisprudence riche en principes novateurs et en contradictions" [1994] *Revue du Marché Unique Européen* 117–60, 149.

[38] Joined Cases 60 & 61/84 *Cinéthèque* v. *Fédération Nationale des Cinémas Français* [1985] ECR 2605.

[39] *Ibid.*, 2626.

discrimination against imports in comparison with domestic products may not be necessary for a national measure to be prohibited by Article 30.[40]

8.3.2 "Dual Burdens"

It may be thought that the prohibition in Article 30 operates analogously to a prohibition of "dual taxation".[41] According to such thinking, in the case of goods traded between Member States, the application of non-discriminatory rules in the Member State of destination may entail compliance costs which cumulate with the costs of complying with rules laid down in the Member State of origin. Such cumulation entails that trade between Member States is restricted more than trade within a Member State because of the dual burden implied for the former trade.

In reality, cumulation seems to entail a sufficient, but not a necessary, condition for operation of Article 30. For example, a trader may not be obliged by the law of the Member State of origin to incur the costs involved in registering a patent in that Member State in order to market his products there. However, provided that he is not prohibited from marketing his products there, he will, in principle, be free under Article 30 to market them in other Member States. Thus the operation of Article 30 is unaffected by the question whether the products concerned are imported from a Member State where they are not patentable.[42] Apparently, therefore, it is not necessary for trading activity within a Member State to be burdened. It is merely necessary that such activity should be permissible in order for its extension to other Member States to be liberalised by this provision.[43]

8.3.3 "Equivalence"

The equivalence doctrine,[44] which is closely associated with the judgment in

---

[40] Gand AG in Joined Cases 2 & 3/69 *Diamentarbeiders* v. *Brachfeld* [1969] ECR 211, 230. Cf., regarding the equality of treatment demanded for persons by the ECSC Treaty, Joined Cases 24 & 34/58 *Chambre Syndicale de la Sidérurgie de l'Est de la France* v. *ECSC High Authority* [1960] ECR 281. According to Roemer AG, the international theory that no discrimination occurred when foreigners received no worse treatment than the worst placed nationals of the state concerned was inapplicable, because "Community inter-relations" differed basically from the usual relations governed by international law (*ibid.*, 319).

[41] See, e.g., VerLoren van Themaat AG in Case 97/83 *CMC Melkunie BV* [1984] ECR 2367, 2390.

[42] Case 434/85 *Allen and Hanburys Ltd* v. *Generics (UK) Ltd* [1988] ECR 1245, 1277; and Joined Cases C–267 & 268/95 *Merck & Co. Inc.* v. *Primecrown Ltd* [1996] ECR I–6285. See, generally, V. Korah, "The Exhaustion of Patents by Sale in a Member State when a Monopoly Profit Could not be Earned" [1997] ECLR 265–72.

[43] See, more generally, Case C–39/90 *Denkavit Futtermittel GmbH* v. *Land Baden-Württemberg* [1991] ECR I–3069, I–3106. Cf., regarding freedom of establishment, Case 79/85 *D.H.M. Segers* v. *Bestuur van de Bedrijfsvereniging voor Bank-en Verzekeringwezen, Groothandel en Vrije Beroepen* [1986] ECR 2375, 2387–8.

[44] See, e.g., P. Oliver, n. 35 above, 234 *ff.*

Rewe,[45] may be thought to offer elucidation of the operation of Article 30. In this judgment the Court of Justice ruled that there was no valid reason, provided that they had been lawfully manufactured and marketed in another Member State, to exclude imported liqueurs containing an alcohol content below the minimum level prescribed by the legislation of the importing Member State.[46] Although the same proviso has been included in subsequent rulings,[47] no explanation for its inclusion is immediately apparent. It is, however, reminiscent of a similarly cryptic reference in *Dassonville*.[48] Here the Court ruled that Article 30 prohibited restrictions on the marketing of products originating from a third state and having been put into free circulation in another Member State "in a regular manner", which is presumably the counterpart in the case of such products to lawful manufacturing and marketing in another Member State in the case of products originating within the Union.

The explanation has been offered for the proviso that the Court applies an equivalence principle in its determination of whether an exception from Article 30 can be permitted on grounds such as the protection of public health or the defence of the consumer.[49] The conclusion has been drawn that domestic legislation protecting such interests cannot be employed as the basis for excluding imports which have been manufactured and marketed in another Member State according to legislation affording equivalent protection to these interests.[50] Indeed, the Commission has interpreted the requirement of lawful production in another Member State as meaning that a product must conform to the rules and processes of manufacture that are customarily and traditionally accepted in the exporting Member State.[51] In other words, Article 30 prohibits restrictions on imports which have been so manufactured.

However, where no such interests as the protection of public health or the defence of the consumer are at stake, the equivalence or otherwise of national law protecting such interests may be irrelevant. In *Rewe* itself the Court considered that the minimum alcohol level requirement was *per se* unnecessary for the protection of such interests,[52] and so no issue of equivalence of protection arose. Consequently, the above explanation for the

---

[45] Case 120/78 *Rewe-Zentral AG* v. *Bundesmonopolverwaltung für Branntwein* [1979] ECR 649.

[46] *Ibid.*, 664.

[47] See, e.g., Case 788/79 *Herbert Gilli and Paul Andres* [1980] ECR 2071, 2079.

[48] Case 8/74 *Procureur du Roi* v. *Benoît and Gustave Dassonville* [1974] ECR 837, 852.

[49] Sect. 8.5.4 below.

[50] See, e.g., P. Oliver, n. 35 above, 234 *ff*. The proviso is even said to fulfil the same function as that of the "fair and traditional practices" test employed in cases such as Case 16/83 *Karl Prantl* [1984] ECR 1299, 1328.

[51] Communication concerning the Consequences of the Judgment given by the ECJ on 20 Feb. 1979 in Case 120/78 (OJ 1980 C256/2).

[52] Case 120/78 *Rewe-Zentral AG* v. *Bundesmonopolverwaltung für Branntwein* [1979] ECR 649, 663–4.

proviso does not account satisfactorily for its inclusion in the grounds, let alone the operative part, of the *Rewe* ruling.

Confirmation of the inadequacy of this explanation was provided by *De Kikvoorsch Groothandel*,[53] which concerned Dutch law prohibiting statements as to the strength of the original wort on the labels of beer bottles. Here the Court ruled that requirements relating to the information to be supplied on the labels of beer bottles, which necessitated an alteration of the label under which imported beer was lawfully marketed in the Member State of exportation,[54] were contrary to Article 30.[55] This ruling was not preceded by consideration of the equivalence of information requirements applied to labels of beer bottles in other Member States.[56]

Apparently, the real explanation for the *Rewe* proviso is that it reflected the facts put to the Court.[57] Certainly, in the same case Advocate General Capotorti considered that the national restrictions were prohibited simply because they created "an obstacle to the importation from other Member States of spirits and liqueurs having a lower alcohol content".[58]

The fact that products may have had to comply with equivalent legal requirements imposed by the Member State of origin seems to be a sufficient condition to render unlawful their subjection to different requirements in the Member State of importation. It does not, however, seem to be a necessary condition to do so. For example, in *Smanor SA*[59] French legislation providing that the designation "yogurt" could be used only to denote fresh fermented milk was at issue. The Court drew a simple conclusion from the fact that deep-frozen yogurts were lawfully manufactured and marketed under that designation in other Member States. The conclusion drawn was that it could not be ruled out that such products might be imported into France and French law applied to them contrary to Article 30.[60]

The Treaty may not, it is true, benefit those who move their production

[53] Case 94/82 *De Kikvoorsch Groothandel-Import-Export BV* [1983] ECR 947. See, earlier, Case 27/80 *Officier van Justitie* v. *Anton Adriaan Fietje* [1980] ECR 3839, 3853–4.

[54] [1983] ECR 947, 958. Cf., regarding a rule which compelled undertakings to give up certain marketing methods or promotional techniques, Case 382/87 *Regina Buet and Educational Business Services (EBS) SARL* v. *Ministère Public* [1989] ECR 1235, 1251.

[55] However, it may not only be the costs of altering the packaging which mean that Article 30 is breached. See Case C–317/92 *EC Commission* v. *Germany: labelling of pharmaceuticals* [1994] ECR I–2039, I–2060.

[56] There may, perhaps, be said to have been a presumption of equivalence in such cases. However, in Case 53/80 *Officier van Justitie* v. *Koninklijke Kaasfabriek Eyssen BV* [1981] ECR 409, 421 it was enough for the addition of nisin to cheese to be permissible in other Member States for the prohibition of this additive in cheese imported into the Netherlands to be contrary to Art. 30.

[57] Lenz AG in Case 94/83 *Albert Heijn BV* [1984] ECR 3263, 3285.

[58] Case 120/78 *Rewe-Zentral AG* v. *Bundesmonopolverwaltung für Branntwein* [1979] ECR 649, 669. In Joined Cases C–401 & 402/92 *Tankstation 't Heukske vof and J.B.E. Boermans* [1994] ECR I–2199, I–2233 the ECJ referred simply to products "from other Member States".

[59] Case 298/87 [1988] ECR 4489.

[60] *Ibid.*, 4510. See, similarly, regarding the generic term "vinegar", Case 193/80 *EC Commission* v. *Italy: vinegar* [1981] ECR 3019, 3036.

from their Member State of origin to another Member State solely to avoid the national rules of their Member State of origin and then only market their products in their Member State of origin.[61] In general, however, the Treaty seems to benefit traders who produce in one Member State and export their production to another Member State, irrespective of whether they comply with rules in the former. For example, *Schutzverband* concerned German legislation which prohibited the marketing of imported vermouth containing a lower level of alcohol than that prescribed in the state of manufacture for domestic marketing. The Court ruled that the marketing of vermouth lawfully made in another Member State might be prevented by such legislation contrary to Article 30.[62]

Therefore, while the equivalence doctrine and the proviso in *Rewe* with which it is associated may exemplify the operation of Article 30, they do not exhaustively define the requirements of this provision. These requirements mean that a Member State is not only prohibited from invoking national rules against imported products which satisfy equivalent rules in another Member State. A Member State may also be prohibited from invoking such rules against products which are simply allowed to be manufactured or marketed in another Member State.[63]

The formal rationale for the far-reaching trade liberalisation requirements which are entailed is that fundamental freedoms are at stake.[64] The classical concept of equality may, subject to certain modifications, be capable of capturing these requirements. This concept may prohibit differential treatment of what are alike and like treatment of what are different. Without more, such a concept would be inoperable, not least within the Union law context.[65] Products from the various Member States will usually be alike in some respects and different in other respects.[66] Hence, criteria are necessary to determine which similarities demand like treatment and which differences demand differential treatment.[67] These criteria are provided by market unification demands, which are taken to require that traders should be free to

[61] Cf. Case 229/83 *Association des Centres Distributeurs Edouard Leclerc v. Sárl "Au Blé Vert"* [1985] ECR 1, 35.

[62] Case 59/82 *Schutzverband gegen Unwesen ID Wirtschaft v. Weinvertriebs-GmbH* [1983] ECR 1217, 1226.

[63] The mutual recognition of national regulations which is impliedly demanded may go beyond a process conditioned by equivalence.

[64] Cf. Case 41/74 *Yvonne van Duyn v. Home Office* [1974] ECR 1337, 1350.

[65] According to Lagrange AG in Joined Cases 17 & 20/61 *Klöckner-Werke AG and Hoesch AG v. ECSC High Authority* [1962] ECR 325, 355, it was necessary to judge a "complaint of discrimination *in relation to a legislative system,* that is to say, within a general framework".

[66] As Lagrange AG put it in Case 13/63 *EEC Commission v. Italy: refrigerators* [1963] ECR 165, 190, the "concept of relativity . . . permeates" the equality principle.

[67] As the ECJ observed in Joined Cases 3–18, 25 & 26/58 *Barbara Erzergebau AG v. ECSC High Authority* [1960] ECR 173, 191, the opinion that any comparison between several undertakings must take into account all the circumstances in which they are placed would entail that an undertaking would only be comparable with itself, and thus the equality principle would become devoid of all meaning.

engage in trading activity beyond the confines of a single Member State. In effect, they should be as free to compete throughout the Union as they are in their own Member State. Thus differential treatment is prohibited where products are sufficiently similar that such treatment restricts exercise of this freedom,[68] and like treatment is prohibited where products are sufficiently different that such treatment has the same effect. What classical equality theory would describe as comparability problems[69] are reducible to problems of establishing the presence or absence of an effect restricting freedom of trade between Member States. Resolution of these problems depends, in turn, on whether there is a distortion of competition.

8.3.4 Distortion of Competition

Not all restrictions on imports or exports between Member States are prohibited by Articles 30 and 34. It is inherent in the idea of liberalising trading activity in an expanded market that prohibited restrictions are those which affect competition in such activity. Restrictions which do not affect the competitive position of products are not, therefore, prohibited. Were they prohibited, a competitive advantage would be created for traders to whom the restrictions were rendered inapplicable. In other words, distortions of competition incompatible with the requirement in Article 3(g) of the Treaty of undistorted competition in the common market would be created. Such creation would differ from the consequences of the Treaty failure to liberalise trading activity internal to a Member State.[70] It would differ, because a distortion[71] would not simply be replaced by another but would be created where none existed before.

Efforts to identify restrictions which are prohibited tend to rely on fine analytical distinctions. For example, according to the Commission, application of rules governing the characteristics or presentation of a product is prohibited even in the absence of discrimination. In contrast, application of rules governing the circumstances in which products may be marketed is

---

[68] Cf. Art. 2(3) of the GATT Agreement on the Application of Sanitary and Phytosanitary Measures, which prohibits measures which "arbitrarily or unjustifiably discriminate between Members where identical or similar conditions prevail" (Annex Ia to the WTO Agreement, OJ 1994 L336/1).

[69] However, as the ECJ observed in Joined Cases 7 & 9/54 *Groupement des Industries Sidérurgiques Luxembourgeoises* v. *ECSC High Authority* [1954–6] ECR 175, 195, the comparability test in itself only supplies a relative and transitory criterion for application of provisions prohibiting discrimination, because its effect depends on the scope of its field of application. Hence, recourse must be had to the objectives of the legal framework of such provisions, so as to ensure that the results of the use of that criterion are consistent with those intended by that framework.

[70] N. 3 above.

[71] Cf., regarding the anti-competitive effects of a failure to liberalise trade within a Member State, Dutheillet de Lamothe AG in Case 13/70 *Francesco Cinzano & Cia GmbH* v. *Hauptzollamt Saarbrücken* [1970] ECR 1089, 1103.

only prohibited where discrimination is entailed.[72] A further distinction may be made between "market circumstances" rules with a territorial element and those without such an element, the latter being said to be more objectionable from the perspective of trade liberalisation. The terms "static" and "dynamic" may be used to make the same distinction.[73]

Such distinctions are designed to assist national courts called upon to apply preliminary rulings delivered by the Court of Justice under Article 177 of the Treaty.[74] The need for such assistance may seem pressing. The questions to be tackled by the courts may often be comparable with those largely reserved for the economic appreciation of the Commission under Articles 85 and 92 of the Treaty.[75] However, efforts made to meet this need reflect formalistic conceptions[76] of the relationship between economy and law. According to these conceptions, questions involving economic appreciation should be resolved by the Commission, and courts should be left to determine, pursuant to the preliminary rulings procedure, questions of the interpretation of Union law.[77] As a result, the distinctions which are advanced with a view to assisting national courts may tend to obscure the underlying issues—those of "access to the market"[78]—involved. They may thus be ill adapted to the real needs of trade liberalisation. In practice, for example, "market circumstances" rules may be more onerous for traders than those regulating the labelling or characteristics of a product.[79] Yet application of the former kind of rules is said only to be prohibited where their application entails discrimination.

To rely on such distinctions may be less helpful than squarely to address questions of anti-competitive effects. Measures which differentiate between domestic and imported goods or which apply only to the latter have an inherent capacity to distort conditions of competition for trade between

[72] Management of the mutual recognition of national rules after 1992 (OJ 1993 C353/4), para. 22. See also K. Mortelmans, "Art. 30 EC and Legislation Relating to Market Circumstances: A Time to Consider a New Definition?" (1991) 28 *CMLRev.* 115–36.

[73] N. Reich, "The 'November Revolution' of the European Court of Justice: Keck, Meng and Audi Revisited" (1994) 31 *CMLRev.* 459–92, 471.

[74] Though the distinctions may not be readily reconcilable with the case law of the ECJ. Cf. D.T. Keeling, "The Free Movement of Goods in EEC Law: Basic Principles and Recent Developments in the Case Law of the Court of Justice of the European Communities" [1992] *International Lawyer* 467–83.

[75] See Chaps. 13 and 17. Hence, the Commission sought an expanded role in tackling questions of the former kind, pursuant to the mutual recognition requirements of Art. 100b EEC. See Management of the mutual recognition of national rules after 1992 (OJ 1993 C353/4).

[76] It is not the formalism of these distinctions in itself which is problematic – an element of formalism is inevitable in the process of constructing reality to permit application of legal rules – but the degree of formalism involved.

[77] Lenz AG in C–44/93 *Namur – Les Assurances du Crédit SA* v. *Office National du Ducroire and Belgium* [1994] ECR I–3829, I–3855.

[78] Joined Cases C–267 & 268/91 *Bernard Keck and Daniel Mithouard* [1993] ECR I–6097, I–6131; and Case C–292/92 *Ruth Hunermund* v. *Landesapothekerkamer* [1993] ECR I–6787, I–6823.

[79] A. Mattera, n. 37 above, 153–4.

Member States. Moreover, such a distortion may be inferred where products which may be freely marketed in their Member State of origin (or the Member State in which they are put into free circulation) have to be modified in order to satisfy the (different) legal requirements for their marketing in another Member State. In such cases a distortion of competition may be a necessary consequence of the restriction of trade. In other cases it may have to be positively established[80] that a trade restriction entails a distortion of competition. For example, a national measure which made access of imported products to the domestic market conditional on the presence of a representative in the importing Member State has been found to be contrary to Article 30. It has been found contrary to this provision, as being likely to involve additional costs for importers.[81] Similarly, national legislation which reserved the sale of contact lenses and ancillary products to holders of an optician's certificate has been found contrary to this provision, because it "restricted sales to certain channels".[82] Ultimately, the acceptability or otherwise of such measures may depend on "the conditions prevailing on the market of the Member State" concerned.[83] Recognition of such dependence is implied in the case law regarding measures of types such as the following.

Price Controls

It cannot be inferred from the fact that a product may be freely marketed in one Member State that its subjection to price controls in another Member State will affect its competitiveness in the latter. Hence, the Court has found it necessary to illustrate the circumstances in which price controls may distort competition. Such circumstances will be present where maximum price controls take no account of the additional costs associated with importation or prevent increased prices of raw materials or finished products being passed on, so that the products concerned may only be sold at a loss. They will also be present where minimum prices prevent imports from competing with domestic products through a lower sale price.[84] In other circumstances

---

[80] A. Evans, "Economic Policy and the Free Movement of Goods in EEC Law" [1983] *ICLQ* 577–99. Note, more particularly, the questions put by the ECJ in Joined Cases C–267 & 268/91 *Bernard Keck and Daniel Mithouard* [1993] ECR I–6097, I–6102, regarding the effects of the national legislation at issue.

[81] Case 247/81 *EC Commission* v. *Germany: pharmaceutical products* [1984] ECR 1111, 1119.

[82] Case C–271/92 *Laboratoire de Prothèses Oculaires (LPO)* v. *Union Nationale des Syndicats d'Opticiens de France (UNSOF)* [1993] ECR I–2899, I–2922. See also, regarding a requirement that an auctioneer must have been registered for 2 years in the place where the auction sale is to take place, Case 239/90 *SCP Boscher, Studer, and Fromentin* v. *SA British Motors Wright* [1991] ECR I–2023, I–2039; regarding a pharmacists' monopoly for the retail sale of certain drugs, Case C–369/88 *Jean-Marie Delattre* [1991] ECR I–1487, I–1539–40; and regarding the prohibition of canvassing in connection with the sale of educational materials, Case 382/87 *Regina Buet and Educational Business Services (EBS) SARL* v. *Ministère Public* [1989] ECR 1235, 1251.

[83] Case 181/82 *Roussel Laboratoria* v. *Netherlands* [1983] ECR 3849, 3869.

[84] Case 13/77 *NV GB-Inno-BM* v. *Vereniging van de Kleinhandelaars in Tabak (ATAB)* [1977] ECR 2115, 2148.

price controls may be permissible. Thus, for example, the imposition on imported bread sold below the minimum price applicable to domestic bread of a compulsory distribution margin applicable also to domestic products is not prohibited by Article 30.[85]

The conclusion drawn from the case law is that "discrimination of substance" must be present before price controls may be caught by Article 30.[86] Such a condition for application of the prohibition in Article 30 may not necessarily be, as is usually imagined, an anomaly in the case law concerning this provision. Rather, it may simply be a consequence of the fact that the likelihood of anti-competitive effects necessary for application of Article 30 cannot be inferred from the imposition of price controls. As the Court puts it, a prohibition which makes no distinction between domestic products and imports, on sales by a retailer at a price below his purchase price, may entail no detrimental effects on the marketing of imported products alone.[87]

Advertising Restrictions

Advertising restrictions in themselves entail a cost reduction for traders, and it cannot be assumed that such restrictions distort competition, in particular, by affecting their comparative advantages.[88] For example, *EC Commission* v. *France*[89] concerned French restrictions on the advertising of alcoholic drinks. The Court found it necessary to establish that the restrictions had anti-competitive effects before ruling that they were caught by Article 30.[90] It has been argued that in this case the Court was only concerned with establishing the presence of such effects in order to rule on the admissibility of an exception from the prohibition.[91] However, the Court began by noting the agreement between the parties to the effect that *a* restriction of advertising for certain products could affect marketing prospects for imported products and thus be prohibited. The question to be resolved, ruled the Court, was whether *the* restrictions to which the Commission objected placed a handicap on the importation of alcoholic products from other Member

---

[85] Case 80/85 *Nederlandse Bakkerij Stichting* v. *Edah BV* [1986] ECR 3359, 3381. Cf. Case 78/82 *EC Commission* v. *Italy: tobacco monopoly* [1983] ECR 1955, 1968–9.

[86] P. Oliver, n. 35 above, 229, n. 53.

[87] Case 82/77 *Openbaar Ministerie* v. *Jacobus Philippus van Tiggele* [1978] ECR 25, 39. Such thinking may underlie the controversial judgment in *Keck* (see 225 below).

[88] Cf. Case 286/81 *Oosthoek's Uitgeversmaatschappij BV* [1982] ECR 4575, 4587; and Case C–126/91 *Schutzverband gegen Unwesen in der Wirtschaft* v. *Yves Rocher GmbH* [1993] ECR I–2361, I–2388.

[89] Case 152/78 [1980] ECR 2299.

[90] Cf., regarding a prohibition on the advertising of alcoholic drinks of more than 23 degrees, Joined Cases C–1 & 176/90 *Aragonesa de Publicidad Exterior SA and Publivia SAE* [1991] ECR I–4151, I–4183; and, regarding restrictions on televised advertising, Case C–412/93 *Société d'Importation Edouard Leclerc-Siplec* v. *TF1 Publicité SA and M6 Publicité SA* [1995] ECR I–179, I–217.

[91] L. Gormley, *Prohibiting Restrictions on Trade Within the EEC* (North-Holland, Amsterdam, 1985), 263.

States.[92] The answer to this question was, therefore, essential for determination of whether the restrictions at issue were, in principle, prohibited by Article 30.

The presence of such a handicap may be more readily established in the case of some advertising restrictions than in the case of others. For example, where a trader seeks to attract consumers to travel from another Member State to purchase his products in his Member State of establishment, advertising may be an effective precondition for the trade sought. Therefore, at least if "strategic trade" thinking[93] is adopted and problems of market entry are recognised, restrictions on his advertising may be found to be prohibited.[94]

Measures Governing Consumption or Production

Blesgen[95] concerned Belgian legislation prohibiting the sale in pubs and restaurants of alcoholic drinks exceeding twenty-two degrees in strength. Since this legislation applied to particular forms of consumption rather than marketing generally, a distortion of competition could not be inferred from any need to adapt imported products simply for their marketing in Belgium. Consequently, it had to be established that the legislation put imported spirits at a competitive disadvantage on the Belgian market. Such an effect was not established. Hence, the Court ruled, noting that the legislation made no distinction based on the origin of the products concerned, that it was not caught by Article 30.[96] Likewise, a prohibition of the distillation of raw materials applying "without discrimination" to imports and domestic products is not contrary to Article 30.[97]

Export Restrictions

Article 34 of the Treaty prohibits quantitative restrictions and measures having equivalent effect on exports between Member States. *Groenveld* [98]

[92] [1980] ECR 2299, 2314.

[93] I.e. if emphasis is placed on strategies which traders need to pursue rather than on comparative advantages.

[94] Case C–362/88 *GB-Inno-BM* v. *Confédération du Commerce Luxembourgeois* [1990] ECR I–667, I–686. Cf., regarding a Dutch prohibition of "cold calling" by suppliers of financial services, Case C–384/93 *Alpine Investments BV* v. *Minister van Financiën* [1995] ECR I–1141, I–1176. See, however, regarding the possibility that restrictions "reflect cultural sensitivities to which firms would wish to adapt their marketing strategies to operate effectively in the relevant Member States", the Reply by Mr Vanni d'Archirafi to WQ E–2036/94 (OJ 1995 C81/5) by Bryan Cassidy.

[95] Case 75/81 *Joseph Henri Thomas Blesgen* v. *Belgium* [1982] ECR 1211, 1299.

[96] See, similarly, regarding restrictions on certain kinds of Sunday trading, Joined Cases C–69 & 258/93 *Punto Casa SpA* v. *Sindaco del Commune di Capon and Comune di Capon* [1994] ECR I–2355, I–2368.

[97] Case 86/78 *SA des Grandes Distilleries Peureux* v. *Directeur des Services Fiscaux de la Haute-Saône et du Territoire de Belfort* [1979] ECR 975, 985.

[98] Case 15/79 *Groenveld* v. *Produktschap voor Vee en Vlees* [1979] ECR 3409, 3415. See also Case C–47/90 *Etablissements Delhaize Frères et Compagnie de Lion SA* v. *Promalvin SA and AGE Bodegas Unidas SA* [1992] ECR I–3669, I–3708.

involved a Dutch ban on the processing or stocking of horsemeat by sausage manufacturers. Here the Court ruled that such a ban would only be caught by Article 34, where it had as its specific object or effect the restriction of patterns of exports and thereby the establishment of a difference in treatment between the domestic trade of a Member State and its export trade, in such a way as to provide a particular advantage for national production or for the domestic trade of the Member State in question. In other words, it is only measures distorting conditions of competition as between exporters and those marketing products domestically which are caught by this provision. Consequently, Article 34 allows a Member State to impose high quality standards on domestic producers. A Member State may do so, even if that policy exposes its producers to the risk of price competition from producers of other Member States who are not bound by the same standards.[99]

Fundamentally, this interpretation of Article 34, which highlights the significance of a distortion of competition, seems consistent with that of Article 30. Certainly, *Oebel*[100] concerned German legislation banning night-time delivery of bakery products to the retailer or ultimate consumer. The Court ruled that the legislation applied equally to domestic products and imports or exports and was not prohibited by either Treaty provision. The legislation was clearly capable of restricting imports and exports. However, it was not established that the legislation distorted competition as between importers or exporters and those marketing products domestically, because deliveries to wholesalers were unaffected.[101] In contrast, pricing rules which operate on the basis of transportation costs from a domestic wholesaler to domestic retailers and do not take account of importation costs, including costs of delivery to the wholesaler, distort competition and are prohibited.[102]

Against this background, the controversy[103] raised by rulings such as *Forest*[104] and *Keck*[105] seems less justified. The former case involved French legislation imposing quotas on the quantities of wheat which could be milled in France. The Court ruled that even though the legislation might limit the quantities of wheat purchased by millers, they were free to buy domestic or imported wheat within their quotas. In addition, the Court noted that there were no such quotas which could have restricted flour imports. Hence, the

[99] Case 237/82 *Jongeneel Kaas BV* v. *Netherlands and Stichting Centraal Orgaan Zuivelcontrole* [1984] ECR 483, 505.

[100] Case 155/80 *Sergius Oebel* [1981] ECR 1993.

[101] *Ibid.*, 2010. Likewise, the legislation at issue in Joined Cases C–267 & 268/91 *Bernard Keck and Daniel Mithouard* [1993] ECR I–6097 did not prevent a producer from another Member State selling to a wholesaler at a loss (Van Gerven AG, I–6123–4).

[102] Case 188/86 *Ministère Public* v. *Régis Lefèvre* [1987] ECR 2963, 2979.

[103] See, e.g., P. Oliver, *The Free Movement of Goods in the EEC* (European Law Centre, London, 1988), 89 and D. Chalmers, "Repackaging the Internal Market – The Ramifications of the *Keck* Judgment" [1994] ELR 385–403, 393.

[104] Case 148/85 *Direction Générale des Impôts et Procureur de la République* v. *Marie-Louise Forest, née Sangoy, and Forest SA* [1986] ECR 3449.

[105] Joined Cases C-267 & 268/91 *Bernard Keck and Daniel Mithouard* [1993] ECR I–6097.

competitive position of imports into the French market was taken to be unaffected,[106] and so there was found to be no restrictive effect of the kind prohibited by Article 30.[107]

The *Keck* ruling concerned French legislation which prohibited shops from selling products at a price below that for which they purchased these products.[108] The Court ruled that legislation prohibiting "certain selling arrangements" did not restrict trade between Member States, provided that it applied to all affected traders operating within the national territory and affected in the same manner in law and in fact the marketing of domestic products and those from other Member States. Where these provisos were met, the legislation did not prevent access of products from other Member States to the market or impede their access any more than it impeded the access of domestic products. In other words, there were no anti-competitive effects. Hence, such legislation was not prohibited by Article 30. The Court prefaced this part of the ruling with the words "contrary to what has previously been decided".[109] In reality, the Court seems to have refined previous formulations of what it seeks to reduce to a "rule" in Article 30 rather than to have redefined the underlying requirements of this provision.[110]

General Restrictions and Measures Having Remote Effects

Instead of seeking directly to establish whether a national measure has anti-competitive effects, the Court may prefer to draw inferences from the characteristics of the measure concerned. Thus measures characterised as part of "the general legislative framework of business activities"[111] or of "the general regulation of commerce"[112] may be treated as lacking the requisite anti-competitive effects to be prohibited by Article 30. For example, in *Duphar*[113] the Court ruled that a Dutch scheme excluding listed pharmaceutical products from reimbursement from a state social security fund was not prohibited by Article 30, provided that certain conditions were met. Specifically, the lists had to be drawn up according to objective criteria without reference to the origin of the products. Moreover, the lists had to be verifiable by any importer, and amendment of the lists had to be possible

---

[106] The view of Van Gerven AG in Case C–145/88 *Torfaen Borough Council* v. *B & Q plc* [1989] ECR I–3851, I–3868 that the ECJ found no actual or potential restriction of imports in *Forest* is not necessarily justified.

[107] [1986] ECR 3449, 3475.

[108] See, similarly, regarding the prohibition of sales yielding only a very low profit margin, Case C–63/94 *Groupement National des Négociants en Pommes de Terre de Belgique (Belgapom)* v. *ITM Belgium SA and Vocarex SA* [1995] ECR I–2467.

[109] [1993] ECR I–6097, I–6131.

[110] According to the ECJ itself, its aim was "to reexamine and clarify" its case law (*ibid.*).

[111] Darmon AG in Case C–69/88 *H Krantz & Co.* v. *Ontvanger der Directe Belastingen and Netherlands* [1990] ECR I–583, I–589.

[112] Case C–391/92 *EC Commission* v. *Greece: processed milk for infants* [1995] ECR I–1621, I–1647–8.

[113] Case 238/82 *Duphar* v. *Netherlands* [1984] ECR 523, 541–2.

where there was compliance with the requisite criteria. Similarly, national legislation may limit the number of processors of a product, with the consequence that domestic processors need only pay "minimal prices" for the product concerned. However, Article 30 is not infringed, "since [the legislation] merely concerns the way in which a business is conducted".[114]

The underlying idea is that the competition sought by the free movement of goods does not aim to remove fundamental differences between cost structures of the Member States which contribute to the wider economic and social framework for trading activity in each Member State. Pursuit of such an aim would undermine the basis for mutually beneficial trade.[115] Accordingly, a national measure designed to improve the quality of domestic production so as to make it more attractive to consumers may be compatible with Article 30. It may be compatible, because the measure "complies with the requirement of sound and fair competition laid down by the Treaty".[116]

Apparently, then, the generality of a state measure may be such that it is treated as unobjectionable. However, "between generality and specificity there is a continuous but blurred range of positions, and placement on this scale is difficult".[117] Consequently, generality constitutes an imprecise criterion for determining whether competition is distorted.

Little may apparently be gained by concentrating not on the generality of a measure, but on the closeness of the relationship[118] between the measure and any possible anti-competitive effects.[119] Concentration on this relationship may mean that a measure may be characterised as having "insufficiently perceptible, direct, or certain effects" to be prohibited.[120]

However, a measure will not necessarily escape prohibition merely because its anti-competitive effects are only indirect.[121] For example, a requirement

---

[114] Case 118/86 *Openbaar Ministerie* v. *Nertsvoederfabriek Nederland BV* [1987] ECR 3883, 3907. The Court also described the legislation at issue in Joined Cases C–267 & 268/91 *Bernard Keck and Daniel Mithouard* [1993] ECR I–6097, I–6132 as "imposing a general prohibition".

[115] Cf. *First Survey on State Aids in the European Community* (EC Commission, Brussels, 1985), 7.

[116] Case 237/82 *Jongeneel Kaas BV* v. *Netherlands and Stichting Centraal Orgaan Zuivelcontrole* [1984] ECR 483, 504. Cf. Case 58/80 *Dansk Supermarked A/S* v. *Imerco A/S* [1981] ECR 181.

[117] R.H. Snape, "International Regulation of Subsidies" (1991) 14 *The World Economy* 139–63, 143.

[118] Cf., regarding the insufficiently close link between means of subsistence and access to vocational training for denial of maintenance grants to constitute discrimination prohibited by Art. 7 EEC, Slynn AG in Case 197/86 *Steven Malcolm Brown* v. *Secretary of State for Scotland* [1988] ECR 3205, 3230.

[119] It is not the "quantity" of the effects (see D. Chalmers, n. 103 above, 388), but their reality which is examined. As the ECJ puts it, Art. 30 is not concerned with "a merely hypothetical effect" (Case C–126/91 *Schutzverband gegen Unwesen in der Wirtschaft* v. *Yves Rocher GmbH* [1993] ECR I–2361, I–2390).

[120] Case C–69/88 *H. Krantz GmbH & Co.* v. *Ontvanger der Directe Belastingen and Netherlands* [1990] ECR I–583, I–597. See also Joined Cases C–140–142/94 *DIP SpA* v. *Comune di Bassano del Grappa and Comune di Chioggia* [1995] ECR I–3257, I–3297.

[121] Cf., regarding the old "criterion of operation" theory in Australian law, according to which measures were only treated as unlawfully restricting interstate trade where the measure applied to a fact, event, or thing itself forming part of trade, C. Staker, "Free Movement of Goods in the EEC and Australia: a Comparative Study" [1990] *YBEL* 209–42, 223.

that a person placing a product on the market for the first time must verify its conformity with the rules in force on that market may be prohibited by Article 30. It may be prohibited, because it may induce traders distributing similar domestic and imported products to prefer the domestic products, in regard to which verification is the responsibility not of the distributor but of the manufacturer.[122] Thus the criterion of remoteness, like that of generality, suffers from imprecision.

Reliance on such imprecise criteria highlights the difficulties involved in the operation of Articles 30 and 34. Their operation depends on whether a state measure can be characterised as having anti-competitive effects. The essential concern may be said to be with the impact of such action on the relative prices[123] of those extending their trading activity beyond the confines of their Member State of origin.

Identification of anti-competitive effects may be difficult in theory,[124] let alone in judicial proceedings. Much may apparently depend on the theoretical approach adopted. For example, in *Keck*[125] the French Government argued in terms of comparative advantage theory that the legislation at issue did not have anti-competitive effects.[126] In contrast, Advocate General van Gerven[127] and the Commission[128] maintained that in terms of strategic trade theory the legislation did have such effects.[129] The difficulties involved cannot be eliminated simply by distinguishing between "assessing (as a matter of law and policy) the current state of integration, the regulatory objective of a national measure, and the Community value of this objective" and "finding out (as an economic matter) whether a measure raises thresholds between national markets or acts as a deterrent to intra-Community trade".[130] They cannot be eliminated by this distinction, because effective assessment of the former involves findings as to the latter.

It may be an oversimplification to conclude that the approach of the Court is purely "casuistic", since consistency of underlying principles is discernible. What is apparent is the extent to which formulations of the requirements of a legal provision may vary according to the context in which the provision is applied. This variation may be exaggerated by the nature of preliminary rulings under Article 177 of the Treaty. In such

---

[122] Case 25/88 *Esther Renée Bouchara née Wurmser and Norlaine SA* [1989] ECR 1105, 1127.

[123] It is said that the protective effects of non-tariff barriers can be measured in terms of tariff equivalents. See Y. Bourdet and G. Hansson, "The Economics of Trade-Policy Harmonization: with Special Reference to the Passenger Car Industry" [1987] *World Competition* 25–41, 26.

[124] Cf. K.W. Dam, "The Economics and Law of Price Discrimination: herein of three Regulatory Schemes" (1963) 30 *Univ. of Chicago LR* 1–62.

[125] Joined Cases C–267 & 268/91 *Bernard Keck and Daniel Mithouard* [1993] ECR I–6097.

[126] *Ibid.*, I–6105.   [127] *Ibid.*, I–6119.   [128] *Ibid.*, I–6107.

[129] See also, regarding a prohibition of "cold calling" by telephone across national boundaries, Case C–384/93 *Alpine Investments BV* v. *Minister van Financiën* [1995] ECR I–1141, I–1176.

[130] W.P.J. Wils, "The Search for the Rule in Article 30EEC Much Ado About Nothing?" [1993] *ELR* 475–92, 490.

rulings the Court of Justice is supposed merely to rule on "questions" of Union law raised before the national court[131] and not to decide the case before the national court.[132] Hence, adjudication by national courts may tend, in practice, to play a greater role in determining the effective requirements of a legal provision in some contexts than in others. However, this tendency does not in itself justify the conclusion that the provision concerned loses its quality as such and has been transformed into a mere "standard".[133]

On the other hand, the quality of the evidence put to the Court of Justice regarding possible anti-competitive effects may often be decisive.[134] Indeed, the decisiveness of such evidence may bring into doubt the proposition that there is a simple trade-off between "administrative costs" (that is, the costs of the proceedings) and "error costs" (that is, the costs resulting from adoption of a "wrong" decision).[135] Since administrative costs may be met more easily by the party to a dispute having the greater resources, error costs may increase in direct proportion to administrative costs.

The case law which has resulted may be formally consistent with "statist" conceptions of supranationalism. Such conceptions treat integration as tending towards the centralisation of supreme power and assume that the only constraints on the tendency result from resistance by Member States. In *Rewe*, for example, the Court treated the "first best" solution to the problems raised in this case to be the introduction of common, that is, centralised, rules by the Union legislature.[136] It was only because such a solution had not been provided through harmonisation by the Union legislature that the Court considered the compatibility of the national rules concerned with Article 30 of the Treaty.

In practice, supranationalism so conceived has performed inadequately. Instead, the Court has developed its case law in response to the demands of traders, spurred by technological developments and increasing competitive pressures to engage in ever more complex transnational relations.[137] As a result, the case law may have substantial consistency with network

---

[131] Compare, e.g., Case 8/74 *Procureur du Roi* v. *Benoît and Gustave Dassonville* [1974] ECR 837 with Case 2/78 *EC Commission* v. *Belgium: certificates of authenticity* [1979] ECR 1761.

[132] See, e.g., Lenz AG in Case C–44/93 *Namur – Les Assurances du Crédit SA* v. *Office National du Ducroire and Belgium* [1994] ECR I–3829, I–3840–1.

[133] Cf. W.P.J. Wils, n. 130 above.

[134] More fundamentally, "the law's traditional taste for concreteness" may impede analysis of underlying economic issues. See A. Winters, "Goals and Own Goals in European Trade Policy" (1992) 15 *The World Economy* 557–74, 573.

[135] W.P.J. Wils, n. 130 above.

[136] Case 120/78 *Rewe-Zentral AG* v. *Bundesmonopolverwaltung für Branntwein* [1979] ECR 649, 662.

[137] Cf., regarding the "paradigm change in the rationality of modern law from materialisation to proceduralisation", N. Reich, "Protection of Diffuse Interests in the EEC and the Perspective of 'Progressively Establishing' an Internal Market" [1988] *Journal of Consumer Policy* 395–417, 401.

demands[138] and may facilitate "market-integration-from-below".[139] Indeed, the Court may have developed a capacity for learning and self-observa-tion,[140] which self-perceptions, based on statist conceptions of supranation-alism, may render more difficult in the case of an institution like the Commission.

On the other hand, it is said that judicial activity is, by its nature, highly discretionary and does not "match the legal certainty of a truly unified product market".[141] Whether this feature of judicial activity within the Union is held to be desirable is bound up with questions as to the relationship between diversity and uniformity.[142] Ultimately, the question is bound up with assumptions as to the proper relationship between state and market. According to such assumptions, the state pursues its economic and social policy, while the undertaking pursues, in the framework defined by this policy, its private interests, notably the realisation of profit.[143] The limita-tions of such thinking are sometimes admitted. It is admitted, for example, that the relationship between the public and private sectors being so close, a private holding company cannot ignore social and regional considerations in the pursuit of its private interests.[144] The implications of the case law for this relationship may be fundamental.

"Regulatory Competition"

The case law means that a Member State may not exclude products simply because they have been produced or marketed in accordance with the differing legal requirements of another Member State. Insofar as mutual recognition of national regulations is implicitly demanded, the regulatory autonomy of national institutions may be formally reconciled with reduction of trade obstacles. In substance, however, insofar as a Member State is prohibited from imposing restrictions on trade between Member States, the

[138] Cf., regarding the emergence of production systems based on economies of scope and the resulting opportunities for networks involving SMEs, Europe 2000: outlook for the development of the Community's territory, COM(91)452, 53.

[139] T. Heller and J. Pelkmans, "The Federal Economy: Law and Economic Integration and the Positive State – The USA and Europe Compared in an Economic Perspective" in M. Cappelletti, M. Seccombe, R.M. Buxbaum, K.J. Hopt, T. Daintith, S.F. Williams, T. Bourgoignie, and D. Trubek (eds.), *Integration Through Law* (de Gruyter, Berlin, 1986), i, 245–412, 320.

[140] Cf. K.-H. Ladeur, "European Community Institutional Reforms: Extra-National Management as an Alternative Model to Federalism" (1990/2) *LIEI* 1–21, 20.

[141] T. Heller and J. Pelkmans, n. 139 above, 359.

[142] Approaches to such questions may be couched in practical terms. E.g., the Commission may oppose such diversity of national rules as to render "virtually impossible" determination of the equivalence of health protection provided. See the explanatory memorandum to the Commission proposal for a directive on *in vitro* diagnostic medical devices, COM(95)130, 7.

[143] Lenz AG in Case C–44/93 *Namur – Les Assurances du Crédit SA* v. *Office National du Ducroire and Belgium* [1994] ECR I–3829, I–3853; and Darmon AG in Case C–185/91 *Bundesanstalt für den Guterfernverkehr* v. *Gebr. Reiff GmbH & Co. KG* [1993] ECR I–5801, I–5827.

[144] Van Gerven AG in Case C–303/88 *Italy* v. *EC Commission: Lanerossi* [1991] ECR I–1433, I–1459.

case law entails that the Member State may not employ such restrictions to protect domestic traders against the economic consequences of their subjection to the same restrictions. In other words, the capacity of a Member State to protect domestic traders against the consequences of its inefficient regulatory activities may be limited. Hence, costs may be incurred by Member States which fail to take into account and respond to regulatory developments in other Member States. In other words, "institutional competition"[145] or "regulatory competition",[146] which means that states compete to provide an attractive regulatory framework for economic actors and which is implied by globalisation, may be intensified.

The opportunity and the need for Member States to compete in the treatment of traders are implied. The opportunity for Member States derives from the fact that the application of national regulation does not prejudice the possibility for their traders to exercise freedom of movement. The opportunity may, indeed, be enhanced by the very fact that regulatory competition may counter a well-known source of regulatory failure – lack of information. A "market-driven" source of information is made available. The need for Member States to compete arises from the mobility of factors of production and increased consumer choice, though traditional consumer preferences[147] and "friction" applicable to the movement of such factors mean that the need should not be exaggerated.[148] Member States which do not compete effectively may not only face "exit" responses by their own traders but also increased "entry" by traders from other Member States.

8.4 State Trading Monopolies

Article 37(1) of the EC Treaty provides that Member States shall adjust any state monopolies of a commercial character so as to ensure that no discrimination regarding the conditions under which goods are produced and marketed exists between nationals of Member States.[149] This provision concerns any body through which a Member State, in law or in fact, either directly or indirectly, supervises, determines, or appreciably influences imports or exports between Member States.[150] According to the Court of Justice, it applies to bodies which have as their object transactions regarding

---

[145] H. Siebert and M.J. Koop, "Institutional Competition. A Concept for Europe" [1990] *Aussenwirtschaft* 439–62.

[146] J.-M. Sun and J. Pelkmans, "Regulatory Competition in the Single Market" [1995] JCMS 67–89.

[147] Note also "the problem of the installed base" in V. Curzon Price, *1992: Europe's Last Chance? From Common Market to Single Market* (Institute of Economic Affairs, London, 1988), 18.

[148] *Ibid.*

[149] Art. 37(3) EC contains special rules for the agricultural sector. See Case 91/75 *Hauptzollamt Göttingen and Bundesfinanzminister v. Wolfgang Miritz GmbH & Co.* [1976] ECR 217, 230.

[150] Art. 37(1) EC, 2nd para. Such bodies are defined as including monopolies delegated by the state to others (*ibid.*).

a commercial product capable of being the subject of competition and trade between Member States and play an effective part in such trade.[151]

Member States must refrain from introducing any new measure concerning such bodies which is contrary to the principles laid down in Article 37(1) or which restricts the scope of the Articles dealing with the abolition of customs duties and quantitative restrictions between Member States.[152]

The purpose of Article 37, as the Court of Justice has put it, is to ensure that the sales policy of a public monopoly is subject to the requirements of the free movement of goods and of equality of treatment in the terms granted for the products concerned.[153] Thus this provision only covers activities "intrinsically connected with the specific business" of the relevant monopoly.[154] It has been held, for example, to require elimination of an exclusive right to import from other Member States.[155]

However, Article 37 does not necessarily require the abolition of state monopolies, and Article 90 of the Treaty assumes the legality in principle of the grant of exclusive rights.[156] For example, *Sacchi*[157] concerned the Italian State television monopoly. Here the Court ruled that nothing in the Treaty prevents Member States, for reasons of public interest, of a non-economic nature, from removing radio and television transmissions, including cable transmissions, from the field of competition by conferring on one or more establishments an exclusive right to conduct them.[158]

In essence, the case law means that the existence of state monopolies and the grant of certain exclusive rights to them may be permitted. However, the case law also means that the exercise of these rights may be limited by the Treaty.[159] Problems arise where the existence of such rights and their exercise are, in practice, inseparable. In particular, an exclusive right of sale has been said to be intrinsically likely to cause discrimination within the meaning of Article 37(1).[160]

However, *France* v. *EC Commission*[161] concerned a French challenge to the legality of Directive 88/301[162] on competition in the markets in

---

[151] Case 6/64 *Flaminio Costa* v. *ENEL* [1964] ECR 585, 598.   [152] Art. 37(2) EC.

[153] Case 91/78 *Hansen GmbH & Co.* v. *Hauptzollamt Flensburg* [1979] ECR 935, 954.

[154] Case 86/78 *SA des Grandes Distilleries Peureux* v. *Dirécteur des Services Fiscaux de la Haute Saône et du Territoire de Belfort* [1979] ECR 897, 913.

[155] Case 59/75 *Pubblico Ministero* v. *Flavio Manghera* [1976] ECR 91; and Case C–347/88 *EC Commission* v. *Greece: state petroleum monopoly* [1990] ECR I–4747. See, similarly, the EFTA Court in Case E1/94 *Ravintoloitsijain Liiton Kustannos OY Restamark* v. *Helsingin Piiritullikamari* [1995] 1 CMLR 161, 181.

[156] Sect. 16.1 below.   [157] Case 155/73 *Giuseppe Sacchi* [1974] ECR 409.

[158] *Ibid.*, 429. See, more recently, Case C–260/89 *Elleniki Radiphonia Tileorassi Anonimi Etairia (ERT AE)* v. *Dimotiki Etairia Pliroforissis (DEP)* [1991] ECR I–2951, I–2959.

[159] Case C–202/88 *France* v. *EC Commission: telecommunications terminals* [1991] ECR I–1223, I–1270.

[160] Case 82/71 *Pubblico Ministero della Repubblica Italiana* v. *Società Agricola Industria Latte (SAIL)* [1972] ECR 119, 144 (Roemer AG).

[161] Case C–202/88 [1991] ECR I–1223.   [162] OJ 1988 L131/73.

telecommunications terminal equipment. The Court ruled that an exclusive right to import and market, which deprived economic operators of the possibility of selling their products to consumers, to advise consumers, or to guarantee the quality of the products, might be prohibited. This prohibition applied particularly where there was a wide range of technically different products, such that the monopolist might not be able to offer the whole range of products existing on the market.[163] A strictly literal interpretation of this ruling suggests that the Court was simply exemplifying the scope of the prohibition of exclusive rights to import and market. However, the ruling may also be read as an attempt to justify the prohibition of such rights on competition policy grounds.

8.4.1 Policy Considerations

The competition policy pursued in Union practice is concerned with maintaining the competitive structure of the market. For example, in the *Ninth Report on Competition Policy*[164] the Commission referred to the need to maintain "the right amount of competition in order for the Treaty's requirements to be met and its aims attained".[165] A state monopoly which makes available a wide range of products and facilitates entry onto the market of new products from other countries may be regarded as improving the competitive structure of the market. The implication of such policy is that certain exclusive rights, perhaps even an exclusive right of sale, are unaffected by Article 37.

8.4.2 Procedures

The application of Article 37 was apparently expected by the Treaty authors to be potentially problematic, and so special procedural arrangements were made. In particular, Article 37(6) provided for the Commission to make recommendations to Member States regarding the subjection of bodies covered to the requirements of the free movement of goods. Possibly, the Treaty authors considered that the distinctive problems raised by the operation of such bodies were not so much substantive. Rather, particularly in view of the need to unravel and reform the complex relations often maintained between such bodies and government ministers, the problems may have been regarded as procedural.[166]

---

[163] [1991] ECR I–1223, I–1268.

[164] (EC Commission, Brussels, 1980), 10.

[165] In seeking to meet this need, the Commission may have regard to market participation by companies from third states. See, e.g., Dec. 91/305 (OJ 1991 L156/39) concerning investment aid which the Belgian Government planned to grant to Mactac SA, Soignies.

[166] Cf. Case 91/75 *Hauptzollamt Göttingen and Bundesfinanzminister* v. *Wolfgang Miritz GmbH & Co.* [1976] ECR 217, 230.

8.5 Exceptions

The EC Treaty may permit the imposition of various restrictions on trade between Member States. The tendency of writers is to look first to see whether a given restriction may be prohibited at all by Treaty provisions guaranteeing the free movement of goods and then to consider the possibility of an exception being permissible from the prohibition. Such an approach may reflect a preference for regarding Articles 30 and 34 simply as rules which can be divorced from the structural requirements of the legal system in which they operate. It is true that the two-stage test which is involved may sometimes be convenient. Particularly where it is clear that state measures do not fall within the scope of a particular prohibition, such an approach avoids the need for a pointless investigation of requirements competing with those with which the prohibition is concerned. Frequently, however, the position will not be so clear-cut, and a choice may have to be made between different requirements embodied in the Union legal system. Here analysis based on the idea of the two-stage test may tend to obscure the reality of the exercise which takes place in the Court of Justice.

8.5.1 "Public Interest"

Article 36 of the EC Treaty[167] permits prohibitions or restrictions on imports, exports, or goods in transit between Member States on various grounds. These grounds are public morality,[168] public policy,[169] or public security;[170] the protection of life and health of humans, animals, or plants;[171] the protection of national treasures possessing artistic, historic, or architectural value;[172] or the protection of industrial or commercial property.[173] The second sentence of Article 36 stipulates that such prohibitions or restrictions must not constitute a means of arbitrary discrimination[174] or a disguised restriction on trade between Member States. In other words, the possibility of a derogation from the free movement of goods must not be abused.

Strict Construction

In interpreting Article 36, the Court of Justice has emphasised the importance

---

[167] Cf. Art. XX of GATT.

[168] Case 34/79 *R.* v. *Maurice Donald Henn and Frederick Ernest Darby* [1979] ECR 3795.

[169] Case 229/83 *Association des Centres Distributeurs Edouard Leclerc* v. *Sàrl "Au Blé Vert"* [1985] ECR 1.

[170] Sect. 8.5.2 below.

[171] Case 40/82 *EC Commission* v. *UK: poultry ban* [1982] ECR 2793.

[172] Case 7/68 *EC Commission* v. *Italy: exports of artistic or historic interest* [1968] ECR 423. See also A. Bondi, "The Merchant, the Thief and the Citizen: the Circulation of Works of Art within the European Union" (1997) 34 *CMLRev.* 1173–95.

[173] Sect. 8.5.3 below.

[174] Thus restrictions on imports must be matched by effective measures against domestic products. See Case 4/75 *Rewe-Zentralfinanz GmbH* v. *Landwirtschaftskammer* [1975] ECR 843, 860; and Case 121/85 *Conegate* v. *HM Customs and Excise* [1986] ECR 1007, 1022.

of establishment of the common market[175] and has characterised this provision as an exception from the fundamental principle of free movement. Since it has this character, the Court considers that its scope must be strictly construed.[176] Hence, the list of exceptions contained therein is exhaustive.[177]

Proportionality Principle

The case law owes much to the proportionality principle, that is, the principle that a measure must be no more restrictive than is necessary to secure a lawful end. Thus restrictive measures must not simply be necessary to protect the interests with which Article 36 is concerned. They must also be necessary in the sense that such interests are not already protected and cannot be as effectively safeguarded by measures less restrictive of free movement.[178] The burden of proving such necessity is on the Member State seeking to rely on Article 36.[179] More particularly, a risk to public health must be measured, not according to the yardstick of general conjecture, but on the basis of relevant scientific research.[180] Account may be taken of national diversity in relation to requirements of public health[181] and public morality.[182] However, if Union legislation harmonises national law in, and comprehensively occupies, a particular field, a Member State may no longer invoke Article 36.[183]

Neutrality

Campus Oil v. *Minister for Industry and Energy*[184] concerned a requirement in Irish legislation that petroleum importers should purchase a certain proportion of their supplies from the Irish National Petroleum Company. This requirement was designed to protect the viability of the sole oil refinery in the Republic and thereby to secure a supply of petroleum products. The Court of Justice ruled that the resulting restrictions on the importation of petroleum products might be justified on public security grounds under Article 36.[185]

---

[175] Cf., regarding the establishment of the common market and the need strictly to interpret exceptions from the prohibition of customs duties in Art. 12 EC, Joined Cases 90 & 91/63 *EEC Commission* v. *Luxembourg and Belgium: duty on milk products* [1964] ECR 625, 633.

[176] See, e.g., Case 46/76 *W.J.G. Bauhuis* v. *Netherlands* [1977] ECR 5, 15.

[177] See, e.g., Case 95/81 *EC Commission* v. *Italy: advance payments for imports* [1982] ECR 2187, 2204.

[178] See, e.g., Case 104/75 *Adriaan De Peijper, Managing Director of Centrafarm BV* [1976] ECR 613, 636.

[179] See, e.g., Case 227/82 *Leendert van Bennekom* [1983] ECR 3883, 3905.

[180] Case C–17/93 *Openbaar Ministerie* v. *J.J.J. van der Veldt* [1994] ECR I–3537, I–3560.

[181] Case 94/83 *Albert Heijn BV* [1984] ECR 3263, 3280.

[182] Case 34/79 *R.* v. *Maurice Donald Henn and Frederick Ernest Darby* [1979] ECR 3795, 3813.

[183] See, e.g., Case 5/77 *Carlo Tedeschi* v. *Denkavit Commerciale Srl* [1977] ECR 1555, 1576–7.

[184] Case 72/83 [1984] ECR 2727.

[185] *Ibid.*, 2755. See also, regarding essential medical supplies, Case C–324/93 *R.* v. *Secretary of State for the Home Dept, ex p. Evans Medical Ltd and Macfarlan Smith Ltd* [1995] ECR I–563, I–608. Cf. VerLoren van Themaat in Case 231/83 *Henri Cullet and Chambre Syndicale des Réparateurs.*

This provision may thus be of particular relevance to neutral Member States.[186] Possibly, it would permit action by a neutral Member State designed to ensure that essential supplies would be maintained in the event of war.[187]

Support for this view may be sought in *Richardt*.[188] This case concerned restrictions on the transit of electronic equipment being exported from France to the then Soviet Union via Luxembourg. Here the Court ruled that the concept of public security in Article 36 covered both the internal and the external security of a Member State. More particularly, imports, exports, and the transit of goods capable of being used for strategic purposes might affect the public security of a Member State, which the latter had the right to protect under this provision.[189] Insofar as neutrality is maintained in the interests of external security, this ruling implies that trade restrictions based on neutrality requirements may be permissible under Article 36.

8.5.2 Security

Security exceptions are permitted under Articles 223 and 224 as well as Article 36 of the EC Treaty.[190] As exceptions from freedom of movement, they are to be strictly construed.[191]

According to Article 223(1)(a), no Member State shall be obliged to supply information the disclosure of which it considers contrary to the essential interests of its security.[192] Moreover, any Member State may take such measures under Article 223(1)(b) as it considers necessary for the protection of the essential interests of its security which are connected with the production of or trade in arms, munitions, and war material.[193] Such measures shall not, however, adversely affect the conditions of competition in the common market regarding products which are not intended for specifically military purposes. A list of products covered by Article 223(1)(b) has been drawn up pursuant to Article 223(2). The list has not been published, but the products covered are said to be normally products

---

Automobiles and *Détaillants de Produits Pétroliers* v. *Centre Leclerc Toulouse and Centre Leclerc Saint-Orens-de-Gameville* [1985] ECR 305, 313, who maintained that minimum price rules designed to maintain an optimum geographical spread of petroleum supplies for purely individual needs were not covered by Art. 36 EC.

[186] I.e., Austria, Finland, Ireland, and Sweden.

[187] Cf., regarding action needed to be taken by a neutral country, P. Cramér, "Funderingar kring permanent neutralitet och integration i västeuropa" in U. Nordlöf-Lagerkranz (ed.), *Svensk Neutralitet, Europa, och EG* (Foreign Policy Institute, Stockholm, 1990), 27–51, 38.

[188] Case C–367/89 *Aimé Richardt and Les Accessoires Scientifiques SNC* [1991] ECR I–4621.

[189] *Ibid.*, I–4652.

[190] Cf. Art. 73l EC and Art. K.5 TEU.

[191] Case 13/68 *SpA Salgoil* v. *Italian Ministry for Foreign Trade* [1968] ECR 453, 463.

[192] This provision follows Art. XXI(a) of GATT.

[193] Art. XXI(b)(ii) of GATT also refers to traffic in "implements of war and . . . in other goods and materials as is carried on directly or indirectly for the purposes of supplying a military establishment".

of industries which do not work exclusively on military equipment.[194] Some writers favour an interpretation of Article 223(1)(b) broad enough to cover goods, such as uniforms, required by the military even in peacetime.[195] In practice, a narrower interpretation has apparently been adopted,[196] though the provision is said to be applied to "sensitive" goods which it was not originally intended to cover.[197]

According to Article 224, Member States shall consult each other with a view to taking together the steps needed to prevent the functioning of the common market being affected by measures which a Member State may be called upon to take in the event of serious internal disturbances affecting the maintenance of law and order, in the event of war or serious international tension constituting a threat of war,[198] or in order to carry out obligations it has accepted for the purpose of maintaining peace and international security. It is said that the "primary focus of Article 224 is not to protect national jurisdiction but to protect Community interests".[199] However, this provision may permit Member States, in the case of a serious crisis, to take necessary measures without being bound by the Treaty.[200]

For example, *Johnston*[201] concerned a prohibition of the training of female members of the Royal Ulster Constabulary in the use of guns. The Court of Justice ruled that Articles 36, 223, and 224 could not be interpreted widely. Hence, it was not possible to infer from them that there was inherent in the Treaty a general proviso covering all measures taken for reasons of "public safety".[202] On the other hand, these provisions might justify denial of a right to judicial review before national courts conferred by a directive.[203] They might do so where such review was rendered impossible

[194] Commission Reply to WQ 877/89 (OJ 1990 C79/33) by Mr Donnea.

[195] H. von der Groeben, H. von Boeckh, J. Thiesing, and C.-D. Ehlermann (eds), *Kommentar zum EWG Vertrag* (Nomos, Baden-Baden, 1983), i, 664. But cf. *ibid.*, ii, 1038.

[196] *Ninth Report on Competition Policy* (EC Commission, Brussels, 1980), 72–3.

[197] Report of the Committee on Foreign Affairs and Security on the Community's role in the supervision of arms exports and the armaments industry, EP Doc. A3–0260/92, 22.

[198] See, regarding such a threat, Jacobs AG in Case C–120/94 *EC Commission* v. *Greece: FYROM* [1996] ECR I–1513, I–1530.

[199] D. Kennedy and L. Specht, "Austrian Membership in the European Communities" (1990) 31 *Harvard International Law Journal* 407–61, 429.

[200] Gand AG in Case 15/69 *Württembergische Milchverwertung-Südmilch* v. *Salvatore Ugliola* [1969] ECR 363, 373

[201] Case 222/84 *Marguerite Johnston* v. *Chief Constable of the Royal Ulster Constabulary* [1986] ECR 1651.

[202] *Ibid.*, 1684. Similarly, the fact that Member States may take public security measures against nationals of third states does not mean that the whole field of migration policy in relation to third states falls within the scope of public security. See Joined Cases 281, 283–285 & 287/85 *Germany, France, Netherlands, Denmark, and the UK* v. *EC Commission: migration policy* [1987] ECR 3203, 3253.

[203] Dir. 76/207 (OJ 1976 L39/40) on the implementation of the principle of equal treatment for men and women.

by serious internal disturbances or if measures needed to protect public safety could be deprived of their effectiveness because of such review.[204]

Neutrality

A narrow interpretation of Article 223 may be thought consistent with one of the original aims of the Union, which was so to integrate the coal and steel industries of the Member States that they would be unable to mount a major war against each other.[205] Article 224 seems more favourable to neutral countries.[206] It may be argued that neutral Member States have undertaken the obligations of neutrality for the purpose of maintaining international peace and security within the meaning of Article 224. It may be inferred that they may invoke this provision in the case of measures needed to give effect to these obligations.[207] Such reasoning may offer a justification for the view of the Austrian Government[208] that its neutrality is compatible with Union membership.[209]

True, the Commission considers that neutrality requirements are not covered by Article 224. According to the Commission, this provision is concerned only with United Nations operations under Chapter VII of the UN Charter. This Chapter is headed "Action with Respect to Threats to the Peace, Breaches of the Peace, and Acts of Aggression".[210] Such an interpretation of Article 224 may be incompatible with the obligations of neutral Member States concerning trade with belligerents.[211]

However, in *Richardt* Advocate General Jacobs adopted a broader interpreta-

---

[204] [1986] ECR 1651, 1692. In Case 68/76 *EC Commission* v. *France: potatoes* [1977] ECR 515, 542 Capotorti AG also left open the possibility that unilateral measures by a Member State might be permissible "as being of unavoidable necessity and urgency".

[205] 5th recital in the preamble to the ECSC Treaty.

[206] In 1962 the Swedish Minister of Commerce suggested to the Council that a provision like Art. 224 EEC might be included in an association agreement and might be drafted in such a way as to allow for Sweden to withdraw from certain obligations or the whole agreement where neutrality requirements so demanded. See *Utrikesfrågor* (Utrikesdepartementet, Stockholm, 1962), 153.

[207] T. Muoser, *Finnlands Neutralität und die Europäische Wirtschaftsintegration* (Nomos, Baden-Baden, 1986), 206, regards this provision as a broad "neutrality reservation".

[208] House of Lord Select Committee on the European Communities, Enlargement of the Community HL (1992–3) 5, 17. See also the text of the Austrian membership application of 17 July 1989 (G. Stadler, *Die EG und Österreich* (Manz, Vienna, 1989), 464). See, *contra*, D. Kennedy and L. Specht, n. 199 above.

[209] Sweden considers that "neutrality is no longer an adequate overall term for Sweden's foreign and security policy". See the House of Lord Select Committee on the European Communities, Enlargement of the Community, HL (1992–3) 5, 17. However, while the Swedish membership application of 1 July 1991 (published in SvD, 2 July 1991) made no reference to neutrality, the application was made in accordance with a Parliamentary vote approving a report from the Foreign Affairs Committee, which favoured Union membership "with neutrality policy being retained" (Sweden and Western European Integration, 1990/91:UU8).

[210] *Commission Opinion on Austria's Application for Membership*, Bull. EC, Supp. 4/92, 17, n.1. See also G. Lysén, "Some Views on Neutrality and Membership of the European Communities: the Case of Sweden" (1992) 29 *CMLRev.* 229–55, 249. Art. XXI(c) of GATT expressly adopts this position.

[211] Art. 9 of Convention (No. V) Concerning the Rights and Duties of Neutral Powers in War on Land, The Hague 1907 (SFS 1910:153), provides that a neutral country must not apply discriminatory

tion of Article 224 than the Commission. He did not exclude the possibility
that application of CoCom[212] rules, which controlled the export of goods of
strategic importance to Central and Eastern European countries, by
Luxembourg could be justified under Article 224.[213] Moreover, this provision
may be invoked in connection with the imposition of sanctions on third states,
even where the United Nations Security Council has passed no resolution
requiring such action.[214] Therefore, Union practice does not unambiguously
support the narrow interpretation of Article 224 adopted by the Commission.

In short, the meaning of Articles 223 and 224 is insufficiently clear to
resolve such a fundamental question as whether the free movement of goods
is compatible with neutrality.[215] Particular problems may arise from the fact
that use of Articles 223 and 224 can be challenged before the Court of Justice
under Article 225 of the Treaty. The last provision concerns measures taken
in the circumstances referred to Articles 223 and 224. If such measures have
the effect of distorting competition in the common market, the Commission
and the Member State concerned shall examine how they can be adjusted to
the rules laid down in the Treaty. If a Member State is considered to be
making improper use of these provisions, the Commission or any Member
State may bring the matter before the Court.[216] The suggestion has been
advanced that such proceedings should be excluded where neutrality is
invoked as a basis for use of these provisions.[217]

CFSP

The meaning of Articles 36, 223 and 224 does not depend simply on their
terms or even on their relationship with Articles 30 and 34.[218] Their
meaning may also be affected by the demands of "European unity".[219] More
particularly, the development of the common foreign and security policy[220]

restrictions to trade with a belligerent. Art. 6 of Convention (No. XIII) Concerning the Rights and
Duties of Neutral Powers in Naval War, The Hague 1907 (SFS 1910:153), provides that a neutral
country must not supply war material of any kind to a belligerent. See P. Cramér and S. Åström,
"Sverige, EG och neutraliteten" in U. Nordlöf-Lagerkranz (ed.), n. 187 above 52–75, 56.

[212] Coordinating Committee for Multilateral Export Controls.
[213] Case C–367/89 *Aimé Richardt and Les Accessoires Scientifiques SNC* [1991] ECR I–4621, I–4643.
[214] See, in the case of Iran, EC Bull. 5-1980, 26.
[215] T. Muoser, n. 207 above, 192–3. See also P. Guggenheim, "Organisations économiques supranationales, indépendance et neutralité de la Suisse" [1962] *Zeitschrift für Schweizerisches Recht*
221–343, 320–1.
[216] Case C–120/94R *EC Commission* v. *Greece: FYROM* [1994] ECR I–3037; and Case C–120/94 *EC
Commission* v. *Greece: FYROM* [1996] ECR I–1513.
[217] W. Hummer and M. Schweitzer, "Möglichkeiten und Grenzen der Dynamisierung der
Beziehungen Österreichs zu den Europäischen Gemeinschaften" [1987] *Europa-Archiv* 343–50, 349.
[218] It was once thought that specific provisions in a treaty might not be necessary to render performance of neutrality obligations compatible with the treaty concerned. See the dissenting opinion of
Judges Anzillotti and Huber in *The S.S. Wimbledon* (PCIJ Ser. A, No. 1), 36–7.
[219] Opinion 1/91 *Draft Agreement between the Community and the EFTA Countries relating to the
Creation of the EEA* [1991] ECR I–6079, I–6102. See, regarding the implications for neutrality, M.
Torrelli, "La Neutralité en question" [1992] *RGDIP* 5–43.
[220] Sect. 21.14 below.

may imply that their scope of application should be narrowed. Certainly, security interests cannot justify trade-restrictive measures by Member States, if Union measures inadequately meet these interests.[221]

8.5.3 Intellectual Property Rights

Intellectual property rights[222] in national law may lead to restriction of trade between Member States.[223] National law may, for example, entitle the holder of a trade mark[224] to prevent the marketing by others of any products, domestic or imported, which bear the same or a similar mark.[225] Such law does not entail discrimination against imports. However, its application to imports from other Member States is prohibited by Article 30 of the EC Treaty, unless its application can be justified on grounds of the protection of commercial or industrial property under Article 36.[226] According to the latter provision, the free movement of goods does not preclude trade restrictions on such grounds.[227]

It is also stipulated in Article 36, however, that the restrictions must not constitute a means of arbitrary discrimination[228] or a disguised restriction on trade between Member States. Where a producer uses different trade marks in different Member States, there may be a disguised restriction of trade within the meaning of this stipulation, if he does so to partition the common market artificially.[229] In this connection, particular problems may arise where trade-marked products are repackaged and relabelled.[230]

---

[221] Case C–124/95 *R.* v. *HM Treasury and the Bank of England, ex p. Centro-Com srl* [1997] ECR I–81, I–127.

[222] Such rights may be broadly interpreted. See, e.g., regarding plant breeders' rights, Case 258/78 *L.G. Nungesser KG and Kurt Eisele* v. *EC Commission* [1982] ECR 2015; and Case 27/87 *Louis Erauw-Jacqéry Sprl* v. *La Hesbignonne Société Coopérative* [1988] ECR 1919.

[223] Cf., regarding designations of origin, Case 12/74 *EC Commission* v. *Germany: designations of origin* [1975] ECR 181 and Case C–3/91 *Expotur SA* v. *LOR SA and Confisserie du Tech* [1992] ECR I–5529.

[224] See also, in the case of patentees, Case 24/67 *Parke Davis & Co.* v. *Probel, Reese, Beintema-Interpharm and Centrafarm* [1968] ECR 55.

[225] Cf. Prot. 12, on conformity assessment agreements, to the EEA Agreement (OJ 1994 L1/3), according to which the Union will negotiate mutual recognition agreements on the use of the EC mark with third states on the basis that these states will conclude parallel agreements with EFTA states. Moreover, according to Art. 4 of Prot. 28, on intellectual property, the Contracting Parties will use their best endeavours to obtain protection for their own producers and those of other Contracting Parties.

[226] See, e.g., Case 119/75 *Terrapin (Overseas) Ltd* v. *Terranova Industrie C.A. Kapferer & Co* [1976] ECR 1039.

[227] In a joint declaration *ad* Art. 66 of the Europe Agreement with Poland (OJ 1993 L348/2), such property is defined as "copyright and neighbouring rights, patents, industrial designs, trade marks and service marks, topographies of integrated circuits, software, geographical indications, as well as protection against unfair competition and protection of undisclosed information or know-how".

[228] Cf. Case 434/85 *Allen and Hanburys Ltd* v. *Generics (UK) Ltd* [1988] ECR 1245, 1275.

[229] Case 3/78 *Centrafarm BV* v. *American Home Products Corporation* [1978] ECR 1823, 1841–2.

[230] Case 102/77 *Hoffmann-La Roche & Co. AG* v. *Centrafarm Vertriebsgesellschaft Pharmazeutischer Erzeugnisse mbH* [1978] ECR 1139.

Exhaustion of Rights

The case law concerning the protection of intellectual property allowed under Article 36 embodies the exhaustion of rights doctrine.[231] According to this doctrine, for example, where products are put into free circulation anywhere in the Union by the trade mark holder or with his consent,[232] his rights are "exhausted". Hence, he may not invoke them to prevent the products being traded between Member States.[233]

"Specific Subject Matter"

Only the "specific subject matter" of patents,[234] trade marks,[235] copyright,[236] and design rights[237] may be protected under Article 36. The specific subject matter of, for example, a patent is the guarantee that the patentee has the exclusive right to use an invention with a view to manufacturing industrial products and putting them into circulation for the first time, either directly or by the grant of licences to third parties, as well as the right to oppose infringements.[238] Thus a patent right may be exercised to exclude products exported by a compulsory licensee in another Member State.[239]

However, a patentee in one Member State may not use his patent to restrict imports from another Member State where he has placed the patented product on the market. He may not do so, even when he cannot obtain patent protection in that Member State and maximum prices are controlled by the government, so that he has never been able to obtain a monopoly profit.[240]

"Function"

In determining whether an intellectual property right may be protected under Article 36, the Court of Justice may have regard to the "function" of that right. For example, it is the function of a patent to foster creative activity.[241] Again, it is the function of a trade mark as a guarantee for

---

[231] Cf., regarding performance rights and copyright, Case 158/86 *Warner Bros Inc. and Metronome Video ApS* v. *Erik Viuff Christiansen* [1988] ECR 2605.

[232] Cf. when consent is absent, Case 192/73 *Van Zuylen Frères* v. *Hag AG* [1974] ECR 731. But see, now, Case C–10/89 *SA CNL-SUCAL* v. *HAG GF AG* [1990] ECR I–3711.

[233] Whether or not provisions such as Article 30 EC are at issue, Member States are required by Art. 6 EC to treat "persons in a situation governed by Community law" equally with their own nationals. See Joined Cases C–92 & 326/92 *Phil Collins* v. *Imtrat Handelsgesellschaft mbH* [1993] ECR I–5145, I–5181.

[234] Case 15/74 *Centrafarm BV and Adriaan de Peijper* v. *Sterling Drug Inc.* [1974] ECR 1147, 1162.

[235] Case 16/74 *Centrafarm and Adriaan de Peijper* v. *Winthrop* [1974] ECR 1183, 1194.

[236] Case 78/70 *Deutsche Grammophon GmbH* v. *Metro-SB-Grossmärkte GmbH & C. KG* [1971] ECR 487; and Joined Cases 55 & 57/78 *Musik-Vertrieb Membran GmbH* v. *Gesellschaft für Musikalische Aufführungs-und Mechanische Verfielfältigungsrechte* [1981] ECR 147.

[237] Case 144/81 *Keurkoop BV* v. *Nancy Kean Gifts BV* [1982] ECR 2853.

[238] Case 15/74 *Centrafarm BV and Adriaan de Peijper* v. *Sterling Drug Inc.* [1974] ECR 1147, 1162.

[239] Case 19/84 *Pharmon BV* v. *Hoechst AG* [1985] ECR 2281.

[240] Joined Cases C–267 & 268/95 *Merck & Co. Inc.* v. *Primecrown Ltd* [1996] ECR I–6285.

[241] Case 35/87 *Thetford Corporation* v. *Fiamma SpA* [1988] ECR 3585, 3607.

consumers of the origin of a product rather than as a means of safeguarding the investment of the holder incurred in the promotion of his product which constitutes the specific subject matter of the trade mark.[242] Hence, trade mark rights may only be applied to exclude products from other Member States when the mark fulfils this function.[243]

8.5.4 "Mandatory Requirements"

In *Rewe*[244] the Court of Justice ruled that national measures necessary to satisfy mandatory requirements, such as those relating to the protection of public health, the defence of the consumer, the fairness of commercial transactions, and the effectiveness of fiscal supervision, escaped the prohibition in Article 30 of the Treaty.

It is clear from the language of the Court in this ruling that the requirements indicated were not to be regarded as constituting an exhaustive enumeration of the grounds on which national measures might be permitted. Thus measures protecting the interests of workers[245] or the well-being of animals,[246] environmental protection measures,[247] and measures to encourage the creation of cinematographic works[248] have also been recognised as permissible. Where such measures "apply without discrimination to both domestic and imported products",[249] their application will be unaffected by Articles 30 and 34 of the Treaty.

However, the measures must be necessary, in the sense that they promote such requirements,[250] no measures less restrictive of trade can achieve the same ends,[251] the relevant interests are worthy of protection,[252] and the measures do not unjustifiably discriminate in their application[253] or their

---

[242] See, e.g., Case 119/75 *Terrapin (Overseas) Ltd* v. *Terranova Industrie CA Kapferer & Co.* [1976] ECR 1039, 1061.

[243] Case 192/73 *Van Zuylen Frères* v. *Hag AG* [1974] ECR 731. But see now Case C–9/93 *IHT Internationale Heiztechnic GmbH and Uwe Danziger* v. *Ideal-Standard GmbH and Wabco Standard GmbH* [1994] ECR I–2789, I–2850–1.

[244] Case 120/78 *Rewe-Zentral AG* v. *Bundesmonopolverwaltung für Branntwein* [1979] ECR 649, 662. Cf. the idea of "reasonable" measures in 8/74 *Procureur du Roi* v. *Benoît and Gustave Dassonville* [1974] ECR 837, 852.

[245] Case 155/80 *Sergius Oebel* [1981] ECR 1993, 2008.

[246] Joined Cases 141–143/81 *Gerrit Holdijk* [1982] ECR 1299, 1314. Cf., now, the Protocol to the EC Treaty on protection and welfare of animals.

[247] Case 240/83 *Procureur de la République* v. *Association de Défense des Brûleurs d'Huiles Usagées* [1985] ECR 531, 549; and Case 302/86 *EC Commission* v. *Denmark: beer containers* [1988] ECR 4607, 4630. See also the Commission Communication concerning the Consequences of the Judgment given by the ECJ on 20 Feb. 1978 (OJ 1980 C256/2).

[248] Joined Cases 60 & 61/84 *Cinéthèque* v. *Fédération Nationale des Cinémas Français* [1985] ECR 2605, 2626.

[249] Case 788/79 *Herbert Gilli and Paul Andres* [1980] ECR 2071, 2078.

[250] Case 16/83 *Karl Prantl* [1984] ECR 1299, 1328–9.

[251] Case 261/81 *Walter Rau Lebensmittelwerke* v. *De Smedt PvbA* [1982] ECR 3961, 3973.

[252] See also, regarding restrictions on advertising, Case C–362/88 *GB-Inno-BM* v. *Confédération du Commerce Luxembourgeois Asbl* [1990] ECR I–667, I–687.

[253] Case 113/80 *EC Commission* v. *Ireland: souvenirs* [1981] ECR 1625, 1639; and Case 59/82 *Schutzverband gegen Unwesen in der Wirtschaft* v. *Weinvertriebs-GmbH* [1983] ECR 1217, 1227.

effect.[254] To determine whether the interests are worthy of protection, the Court may examine whether the relevant interests are protected by the law of other Member States[255] or by international agreements.[256] More particularly, the Court may investigate whether a product banned pursuant to such measures is consumed elsewhere in the Union[257] or whether a banned additive is used elsewhere in the Union.[258] The measures must also be necessary, in the sense that the relevant interests are not adequately protected by the law of the Member State of origin of the goods concerned. For example, *Robertson*[259] concerned Belgian law prescribing hallmarking requirements for silver-plated ware sold in Belgium. Here the Court considered whether hallmarks borne by imported silver-plated articles provided the consumer with equivalent protection to that required by Belgian law.[260]

Public Policy Analogy

It may be thought that recognition of mandatory requirements merely involves acceptance of exceptions from Articles 30 and 34 on the basis of public policy.

True, the Court of Justice stipulated in *EEC Commission* v. *Italy: pigmeat*,[261] where the Italian authorities had suspended imports of pigmeat because of a crisis on the pigmeat market, that Article 36 did not permit restrictive measures to be adopted on the basis of economic considerations.[262] Since some at least of the mandatory requirements recognised by the Court concern matters having an economic background, the inference may be drawn that such requirements are not covered by this provision.

However, the case law concerning intellectual property rights suggests that the mere existence of an economic background to a restrictive measure does not in itself preclude the possibility of the measure being permitted under Article 36. More particularly, there is nothing in the above ruling to indicate that the Court meant that measures adopted by Member States would fall

---

[254] Case 207/83 *EC Commission* v. *UK: indications of origin* [1985] ECR 1201, 1212.

[255] See, e.g., Case 6/81 *BV Industrie Diensten Groep* v. *J.A. Beele Handelsmaatschappij BV* [1982] ECR 707, 717.

[256] See, e.g., the reference to Art. 10*bis* of the Paris Convention for the Protection of Industrial Property (*ibid.*, 717).

[257] See, e.g., Case 193/80 *EC Commission* v. *Italy: vinegar* [1981] ECR 3019, 3035.

[258] See, e.g., Case 53/80 *Officier van Justitie* v. *Koninklijke Kaasfabriek Eyssen BV* [1981] ECR 409, 422.

[259] Case 220/81 *Timothy Frederick Robertson* [1982] ECR 2349, 2361.

[260] However, Member States may exempt from quality requirements or inspections products intended for export or may not carry out inspections. In practice, therefore, legislative equivalence may offer uncertain protection of the interests concerned. See the explanatory memorandum to the Commission proposal for a directive on the official inspection of foodstuffs, COM(86)747. See, generally, G. Brouwers, "Free Movement of Foodstuffs and Quality Requirements: Has the Commission Got it Wrong?" (1988) 25 *CMLRev.* 237–62, 251–2.

[261] Case 7/61 [1961] ECR 317, 329.

[262] See also Case 352/85 *Bond van Adverteerders* v. *Netherlands* [1988] ECR 2085, 2135.

outside provisions such as Article 36 simply because of their economic consequences. Indeed, Treaty liberalisation provisions only apply in principle to economic activity,[263] that is, activity restrictions on which inevitably have such consequences. Hence, attribution of such a meaning to the above ruling would deprive provisions such as Article 36 of effective significance. Therefore, as the Court recognises, the mere fact that national rules, justified by objective circumstances corresponding to the needs of the interests referred to in Article 36, also enable other, economic objectives to be achieved does not exclude the application of that provision.[264]

The real meaning of the case law is, presumably, that a measure based on Article 36 must not simply be justified on one of the grounds specified therein. If it were not so justified, it would in any case constitute what Article 36 expressly prohibits as being a "disguised restriction on trade between Member States". Rather, it must be so justified independently of its economic consequences.[265]

For example, *Thompson*[266] concerned a ban on the export of silver alloy coins from the United Kingdom to other Member States, which was designed to prevent the coins being melted down or destroyed there. The Court found the ban to be justified on public policy grounds within the meaning of Article 36. The ban was considered justified, because it stemmed from the need to protect the right to mint coinage, which was traditionally regarded as involving the fundamental interests of the Member State. Conversely, Article 36 cannot justify a measure whose primary objective is budgetary, in as much as it is intended to reduce the operating costs of a sickness insurance scheme.[267]

On the other hand, the Court has insisted that, as an exception from the fundamental principle of free movement, the concept of public policy has to be strictly construed.[268] Consequently, it would run counter to the established case law for the Court to treat Article 36 as permitting trade restrictions on grounds not expressly laid down therein. In fact, care seems to have been taken to avoid any clear implication being given to the effect that Article 36 might provide the basis for the mandatory requirements

---

[263] Case 36/74 *B.N.O. Walrave and L.J.N. Koch v. Union Cycliste Internationale, Koninklijke Nederlandsche Wielren Unie and Federacion Español Ciclismo* [1974] ECR 1405, 1417–18. Cf., Case C–275/92 *HM Customs and Excise v. Gerhart Schindler and Jörg Schindler* [1994] ECR I–1039, I–1091. See, generally, A. Evans, "Freedom of Trade under the Common Law and European Community Law: The Case of the Football Bans" (1986) 102 *LQR* 510–48.

[264] Case 72/83 *Campus Oil Ltd v. Minister for Industry and Energy* [1984] ECR 2727, 2752. See also Case 118/86 *Openbaar Ministerie v. Nertsvoederfabriek Nederland* [1987] ECR 3883, 3908.

[265] According to Mancini AG in Case 238/82 *Duphar BV v. Netherlands* [1984] ECR 523, 550, it is enough that the specified grounds have "a decisive influence" on the restrictive measures adopted by a Member State.

[266] Case 7/78 *R. v. Ernest George Thompson, Brian Albert Johnson, and Colin Alex Norman Woodiwiss* [1978] ECR 2247, 2275.

[267] Case 238/82 *Duphar BV v. Netherlands* [1984] ECR 523, 542.

[268] Sect. 8.5.1 above.

recognised by the Court.[269] Moreover, *EC Commission* v. *Ireland*[270] concerned Irish legislation requiring all souvenirs and articles of jewelry imported from other Member States to bear an indication of origin or the word "foreign". Here the Court expressly stated that Article 36 did not do so. Subsequently, the Court began to deal separately with questions whether a justification for a restrictive measure could be based on the protection of public health within the meaning of Article 36, on the need to protect consumers, or on the requirements of fair trading.[271] Apparently, therefore, the Court regards the mandatory requirements recognised in its case law as being distinct from the grounds, including that of public policy, on which Article 36 permits trade restrictions.

Despite such rulings, the view persists that Article 36 provides the basis for the mandatory requirements recognised by the Court. This view is supported by the argument that measures otherwise qualifying by reference to such requirements would be treated with undue harshness where they were not equally applicable.[272] Certainly, as the Court continues to rule, such requirements may only cover national measures which are "applicable without discrimination".[273] In apparent contrast, provisions such as Article 36 may cover discriminatory measures, provided that the discrimination is not "arbitrary". Thus in *Campus Oil*[274] the Court accepted that the public security ground in Article 36 might justify the imposition of restrictions on imported products alone, provided that such restrictions were necessary to preserve the viability of the only oil refinery in the Irish Republic.

However, in *EC Commission* v. *Ireland*[275] the Court was prepared to examine whether the obligation imposed only on imported souvenirs that they be stamped with the country of origin or the word "foreign" could be justified on grounds of mandatory requirements relating to consumer protection. It was only because imported and domestic souvenirs were found to be comparable that imposition of this obligation on the former alone was held to be discriminatory and, hence, impermissible. The converse was demonstrated in *EC Commission* v. *Belgium: prohibition of waste from other Member States*.[276] According to this judgment, differentiation between waste from within a particular region and waste from outside that region may be justified and permissible on the basis of mandatory requirements, having regard to the principle in Article 130r(2) of the Treaty that pollution should

[269] See, in particular, Case 8/74 *Procureur du Roi* v. *Benoît and Gustave Dassonville* [1974] ECR 837, 852; and Case 12/74 *EC Commission* v. *Germany: designations of origin* [1975] ECR 181, 199.
[270] Case 113/80 [1981] ECR 1625, 1640–1.
[271] See, e.g., Case 25/88 *Esther Renée Bouchara, née Wurmser, and Norlaine SA* [1989] ECR 1105.
[272] See, e.g., P. Oliver, n. 103 above, 92–3.
[273] See, e.g., Case C–353/89 *EC Commission* v. *Netherlands: radio and television programmes* [1991] ECR I–4069, I–4093.
[274] Case 72/83 *Campus Oil* v. *Minister for Industry and Energy* [1984] ECR 2727, 2753.
[275] Case 113/80 [1981] ECR 1625, 1640.
[276] Case C–2/90 [1992] ECR I–4431, I–4480.

be rectified at source. In other words, the acceptability of a measure on grounds of a mandatory requirement may depend on whether or not there is "arbitrary discrimination" of the kind referred to in Article 36. It seems, then, *EC Commission* v. *Belgium* is not "a difficult judgment to fit within the legal trends in this area".[277]

The failure of the Court, in recognising such requirements, to reproduce the language of the Article 36 proviso may be partly attributable to a desire to emphasise that, as regards the possibility of a measure being treated as justified by reference to a mandatory requirement, it is the application rather than the effects of such a measure which is decisive.[278] If it were enough for a measure to be precluded from such treatment that it had the effect of making importation more difficult than the disposal of domestic products, such treatment would be available in respect of few measures which did not anyway fall outside the scope of Article 30, as currently defined by the case law of the Court. As a result, consideration of the possibility of a mandatory requirement being recognised would be largely pre-empted by determination of whether a measure could be prohibited at all by Article 30. Thus the willingness of the Court to recognise such requirements would have little real significance.

On the other hand, the fact that the protection of public health is covered by Article 36 and has been recognised as a mandatory requirement may be thought to imply that the requirements recognised by the Court have their basis in this provision. If not, then the Court may be thought to be engaging in unnecessary duplication.[279] However, the purpose of Article 36 is simply to enable public interest requirements of Member States to be taken into account in the application of Articles 30 and 34.[280] It cannot be assumed that the nature and function of the mandatory requirements recognised by the Court are identical to those of the exceptions provided for in Article 36.

"Reserved Powers"

It has been argued that mandatory requirements reflect recognition by the Court of "reserved powers" which are provisionally retained by Member States for the implementation of national policies and which are unaffected by Article 30. Specifically, it has been deduced from the inclusion in the Treaty of various provisions envisaging harmonisation of national law and policy[281] that national measures implementing such policies which do not

---

[277] S. Weatherill and P. Beaumont, *EC Law* (2nd edn. Penguin, London, 1995), 517.

[278] Cf. Van Gerven AG in Case 25/88 *Esther Renée Bouchara née Wurmser and Norlaine SA* [1989] ECR 1105, 1118.

[279] Note the clarification in Joined Cases C–1 & 176/90 *Aragonesa de Publicidad Exterior SA and Publivia SAE* [1991] ECR I–4151, I–4186.

[280] Cf. Case 153/78 *EC Commission* v. *Germany: health controls on imported meat* [1979] ECR 2555, 2564.

[281] See, e.g., Arts. 99 and 100 EC.

formally discriminate are to be harmonised and, pending such harmonisation, cannot be affected by provisions such as Article 30.[282] Some support for
this argument may be sought by analogy in the finding of the Court that
education policy was a matter for Member States and that, therefore,
discrimination against nationals of other Member States as regards the award
of maintenance grants for university studies was not prohibited by Article 7
of the EEC Treaty.[283]

If such an argument really were to have been adopted by the Court, the
consequence would be that the scope of trade liberalisation requirements
would vary from Member State to Member State. It would vary, depending
on the extent to which each chose to exercise its reserved powers. The
reasonableness or otherwise of such choices would be beyond the control of
Union law. Such a situation would run counter to the principle of the
uniform application of Union law.[284]

In its refined version this argument may seem more plausible. According
to this version, there is a division of powers between Member States and the
Union. This division implies that the former may, pending harmonisation,
enact "reasonable measures" in the exercise of their powers without falling
foul of Article 30.[285] The Commission may, perhaps, be thought to have
followed such thinking in drawing up Directive 70/50.[286] Here it was
accepted that national trading rules which were equally applicable to imports
and domestic products were permitted unless their effects exceeded those
intrinsic to such rules.[287] The consequence of relying on such thinking,
however, would also render further reduction of trade restrictions dependent
on harmonisation. Such dependence would not be readily reconcilable with
the possibility of the requirements of Article 30 being inherently capable of
evolution or, in other words, with the autonomy of Union law.[288]

It may have been for such reasons that the Court has avoided adopting such
thinking and has expressly rejected the argument that Article 100 of the Treaty
implies that all national law which does not formally discriminate against
imports is unaffected by Article 30.[289] The former provision envisages the

[282] See, e.g., Roemer AG in Joined Cases 51–54/71 *International Fruit Co. NV* v. *Produktschap voor
Groenten en Fruit* [1971] ECR 1107, 1123–4. See also the argument of the German Government in
Case 120/78 *Rewe-Zentral AG* v. *Bundesmonopolverwaltung für Branntwein* [1979] ECR 649, 655.
[283] Case 197/86 *Steven Malcolm Brown* v. *Secretary of State for Scotland* [1988] ECR 3205, 3243.
[284] See, e.g., Case 14/68 *Walt Wilhelm* v. *Bundeskartellamt* [1969] ECR 1, 14.
[285] R. Barents, "New Developments in Measures Having an Equivalent Effect" (1981) 18 *CMLRev.*
271–308, 283.
[286] JO 1970 L13/29.
[287] *Ibid.*, Art. 3.
[288] Cf. the insistence of the ECJ that a Member State "may not plead a mandatory requirement . . .
in order to shield a product from the effects of price competition on the pretext of economic difficulties brought about by the elimination of barriers to intra-Community trade" (Case 216/84 *EC
Commission* v. *France: labelling of milk substitutes* [1988] ECR 793, 812–13)
[289] Case 193/80 *EC Commission* v. *Italy: vinegar* [1981] ECR 3019, 3033. See also Capotorti AG in
Case 120/78 *Rewe-Zentral AG* v. *Bundesmonopolverwaltung für Branntwein* [1979] ECR 649, 655.

harmonisation of national law directly affecting the establishment or functioning of the common market.

Even so, it may be imagined that the Court, though unwilling to accept the existence of any reserved powers entailing limits to the scope of provisions such as Article 30, has sought to preserve the availability of such powers by admitting exceptions from such provisions not explicitly envisaged in the Treaty[290] and has merely reversed the burden of proof envisaged by the Commission in Directive 70/50.[291] In fact, however, the only rationale offered by the Court for recognition of mandatory requirements is that the requirements concerned accord with the "general interest".[292] Some Advocates General have gone further and have maintained that the requirements may be an inherent feature of the Union legal system.[293]

The "General Interest"

The interests with which the mandatory requirements recognised by the Court are concerned appear to be encompassed by Treaty objectives, as outlined in Article 2 and the Preamble.[294] In the light of this outline, the Court seems to treat mandatory requirements as implicit in the Treaty framework.[295]

That these requirements have a basis in the Treaty framework explains why they must be taken into account not only in judicial application of provisions such as Article 30 but also in legislative harmonisation.[296] At the same time, distinctions made by the Court between measures to protect purely national interests and those concerned with the general interest may be explained. For example, monetary compensatory amounts were not treated as levies introduced by some Member States unilaterally but Union measures which might be permissible within the framework of the common agricultural policy.[297] Similarly, as regards charges for health inspections of pigs and bovine animals, which were required by Union legislation,[298] the inspections were not prescribed by each Member State unilaterally to protect some interest of its own. Rather, the inspections

---

[290] Cf. the view of K. Mortelmans (n. 72 above), 116 that the ECJ has recognised exceptions necessary to take account of "market circumstances" legislation.

[291] JO 1970 L13/29.

[292] See, e.g., Case 130/80 *Fabriek voor Hoogwaardige Voedingsprodukten Kelderman BV* [1981] ECR 527, 535.

[293] See, e.g., Capotorti AG in Case 155/80 *Sergius Oebel* [1981] ECR 1993, 2017.

[294] Cf., earlier, regarding fishery conservation measures and sustainable development, Joined Cases 3, 4 & 6/76 *Cornelis Kramer* [1976] ECR 1279, 1313.

[295] Union instruments lacking formal legal force, such as the Council Resolution of 19 May 1981 (OJ 1981 C133/1) on a second programme for a consumer protection and information policy, may even be invoked by the ECJ, at least to articulate such requirements. See Case C–362/88 *GB-Inno-BM v. Confédération du Commerce Luxembourgeois Asbl* [1990] ECR I–667, I–687–8.

[296] Sect. 19.2 below.

[297] Case 10/73 *Rewe-Zentral AG v. Hauptzollamt Kehl* [1973] ECR 1175, 1192.

[298] Dir. 64/4324 (JO 1964 1977) on animal health problems affecting intra-Community trade in bovine animals and swine.

were prescribed by the Council in the general interest of the Union.[299] Hence, the charges might also be permissible.

It is consistent with such distinctions that exceptions expressly provided for in Treaty provisions such as Article 36 and the mandatory requirements recognised by the Court may not operate in identical fashion. An illustration is provided by the manner in which the prohibition of discrimination applies, on the one hand, to Article 36 measures and, on the other hand, to mandatory requirements. Since measures of the former kind are concerned with national interests, criteria for determining the comparability necessary for differential treatment to be characterised as prohibited discrimination must be found in such interests. As the *Campus Oil*[300] judgment illustrates, such interests may mean that imports and domestic products are non-comparable by reason of the very fact that the imports originate from outside the Member State concerned. Since the mandatory requirements recognised by the Court are concerned with the general interest, other criteria must, as in *EC Commission* v. *Ireland: souvenirs*,[301] be found to establish non-comparability. In this sense, provisions such as Article 36 may justify differentiation which cannot be justified on the basis of mandatory requirements recognised by the Court.

The significance of the latter requirements is that their recognition enables the Court to seek to go beyond the limits of the exceptions specifically envisaged in the Treaty, with a view to reconciling[302] trade liberalisation requirements with respect for other Treaty requirements.[303] Such reconciliation is implicit in the condition, employed by the Commission in Directive 70/50[304] and, later, by the Court,[305] that trading rules may be prohibited where their effects go beyond those intrinsic to such rules. According to the Court, to verify that the restrictive effects on Union trade do not exceed those necessary for attainment of a legitimate aim, it must be considered whether the effects are direct, indirect, or purely speculative and whether the marketing

---

[299] Case 46/76 *W.J.G. Bauhuis* v. *Netherlands* [1977] ECR 5, 17.

[300] Case 72/83 *Campus Oil* v. *Minister for Industry and Energy* [1984] ECR 2727.

[301] Case 113/80 [1981] ECR 1625.

[302] Union legislation, such as Dir. 79/112 (OJ 1979 L33/1) on the approximation of the laws of the Member States relating to the labelling, presentation, and advertising of foodstuffs, may produce different results. E.g., the Commission accepts that the indication of fat content is very important as an item of information which enables the consumer to make a distinction between the various types of food products on the market. However, for the Netherlands to apply unilaterally measures requiring such an indication would, according to the Commission, be bound to hamper trade between Member States considerably. Consequently, the Commission acted under Dir. 79/112 (*ibid.*), to require the Netherlands to suspend adoption of the draft measure for 12 months. See Dec. 92/238 (OJ 1992 L121/48) calling upon the Netherlands to postpone the adoption of a draft regulation in respect of the labelling of emulsified fats.

[303] Cf., in the agricultural sector, Case 139/79 *Maizena GmbH* v. *EC Commission* [1980] ECR 3393, 3421.

[304] JO 1970 L13/29.

[305] Case C–145/88 *Torfaen Borough Council* v. *B & Q plc* [1989] ECR I–3851, I–3889.

of imported products is impeded more than the marketing of national products.[306]

The relationship between trade liberalisation requirements and mandatory requirements entailed by such practice may not necessarily be one of conflict.[307] Hence, their interaction may not always be reducible to the simple balancing process[308] identified by some writers.[309] The more a measure is justified by reference to mandatory requirements, the less likely it will be to distort competition contrary to trade liberalisation requirements. Conversely, the less protection a national measure offers to mandatory requirements, the more likely it is to be treated as contrary to liberalisation requirements.[310]

This relationship may be captured by analysis based on the equality principle more satisfactorily than by one based on the idea of exceptions from a general prohibition. Liberalisation requirements may mean that certain likenesses render differential treatment prohibited or that certain differences render like treatment prohibited. Mandatory requirements may mean that certain differences justify differential treatment in the former case or that certain likenesses justify like treatment in the latter case. Hence, recognition of mandatory requirements may play an organic role in the decision making on which trade liberalisation depends. In essence, there is an interplay of trade liberalisation requirements and mandatory requirements – a "matrix of variables" – embodied in the Treaty.

8.5.5 Economic Policy Requirements

The Treaty may expressly authorise restrictions on the free movement of goods by reference to various economic policy requirements. However, authorisation of restrictive measures is gradually to be replaced by common policies,[311] which may be supposed to offer a more developed solution to "relative gains"[312] problems in integration. Pending such replacement, their

---

[306] Case C–169/91 *Council of the City of Stoke-on-Trent, Norwich City Council* v. *B & Q plc* [1992] ECR I–6635, I–6658–9.

[307] Even if a static conception of competition may suggest conflict, resort to a more dynamic conception may produce different conclusions. E.g., imposition of high standards of environmental protection may result in industries in the Member State concerned becoming more efficient and competitive.

[308] Cf. the Commission emphasis on the need for a balance to be achieved between high environmental standards and the requirements of free movement in the negotiations for Swedish Accession to the Union. See *Commission Opinion on Sweden's Application for Membership*, Bull. EC, Supp. 5/92, 30–1.

[309] See, e.g., W.P.J. Wils, "The Search for the Rule in Article 30EEC Much Ado About Nothing?" [1993] *ELR* 475–92, 478.

[310] See, e.g., Case 7/68 *EC Commission* v. *Italy: exports of artistic or historic interest* [1968] ECR 423, 430.

[311] See, in particular, regarding Art. 46 EC, Joined Cases 80 & 81/77 *Société Les Commissionnaires Réunis Sàrl* v. *Receveur des Douanes* [1978] ECR 927, 946. See, regarding Art. 103 EEC, Case 154/77 *Procureur du Roi* v. *P. Dechmann* [1978] ECR 1573, 1584 and Joined Cases 88–90/75 *Società SADAM* v. *Comitato Interministeriale dei Prezzi* [1976] ECR 323, 338.

[312] J.M. Grieco, *Co-operation among Nations* (Cornell University Press, Ithaca, N.Y., 1990).

authorisation is designed to counter adverse consequences of integration for the interests of the Union[313] rather than for the interests of individual Member States.[314] As the Court of Justice puts it, a Member State cannot be allowed to avoid the effects of free movement by pleading the economic difficulties caused by the elimination of barriers to trade with other Member States.[315] For such reasons, the Treaty allocates a central role in the adoption of restrictive measures to the Commission and Council, and the measures adopted may be challenged before the Court. Moreover, the burden is on the Member State concerned to establish compliance with procedural requirements for resort to such measures. Equally, the burden is on the Member State to show the presence of the material conditions for, and the appropriateness of, the adoption of the measures.[316]

Conjunctural Policy

Restrictive measures might be authorised under Article 226 of the EEC Treaty because of difficulties arising during the transitional period. The difficulties concerned included those attributable to operation of the Treaty.[317] However, they had to be serious and liable to persist in a sector of the economy or to bring about serious deterioration in the economic situation of a given area.[318] Permissible measures were to be designed to rectify the situation and to adjust the sector concerned to the economy of the common market. Priority was also to be given to such measures as would least disturb the functioning of the common market.

Article 103 of the Treaty has remained applicable after the end of the transitional period. It provides that Member States shall regard their conjunctural policies as a matter of common concern. Moreover, Article 103a(1) provides for the Council to decide what measures should be taken, in particular if serious difficulties arise in the supply of certain products.[319] Where a Member State is in difficulties or is seriously threatened with severe

---

[313] Cf., regarding Art. 67 ECSC, Joined Cases 27–29/58 *Compagnie des Hauts Fourneaux et Fonderies de Givors* v. *ECSC High Authority* [1960] ECR 241, 254; and Case 30/59 *De Gezamenlijke Steenkolenmijnen in Limburg* v. *ECSC High Authority* [1961] ECR 1, 24. Cf. also, in relation Art. 46 EC, Case 337/82 *St. Nikolaus Brennerei und Likörfabrik, Gustav Kniepf-Melde GmbH* v. *Hauptzollamt Krefeld* [1984] ECR 1051, 1063.

[314] See, e.g., Joined Cases 80 & 81/77 *Société Les Commissionnaires Réunis Sàrl.* v. *Receveur des Douanes* [1978] ECR 927, 947.

[315] Case 72/83 *Campus Oil* v. *Minister for Industry and Energy* [1984] ECR 2727, 2752.

[316] Roemer AG in Joined Cases 6 & 11/69 *EC Commission* v. *France: preferential rediscount rate for exporters* [1969] ECR 523, 555–6.

[317] Joined Cases 73 & 74/63 *NV Internationale Crediet-en Handelsvereniging "Rotterdam" and De Coöperatieve Suikerfabriek en Raffinederij G.A. "Puttenhoek"* v. *Minister van Landbouw en Visserij* [1964] ECR 1, 25.

[318] Cf. Art. XIX(1)(a) of GATT. See now the Agreement on Safeguards in Annex 1A to the WTO Agreement (OJ 1994 L336/1).

[319] See, e.g., under Art. 103(4) EEC, Dec. 63/689 (JO 1963 3108) authorising Belgium to restrict exports of pork and live pigs until 31 Jan. 1964 because of the serious shortage of such products in that country.

difficulties caused by exceptional occurrences beyond its control,[320] the Council may also grant Union financial assistance to the Member State concerned under Article 103a(2).

In the case of shortages of products covered by the ECSC Treaty, the Commission shall, in the absence of a unanimous decision of the Council, allocate the resources among the Member States and impose quotas on exports to third states under Article 59 of this Treaty.[321]

It appears that a physical shortage is not necessary for resort to such provisions. According to the Court of Justice, if the price of a raw material is driven up by demand to a level such that a significant part of Union industry is no longer in a position to pay the price demanded, a *prima facie* case exists for a finding that there is a shortage for the purposes of Article 59 of the ECSC Treaty. Such a case may exist, even though the material may be available in sufficient quantities.[322] Apparently, then, such provisions have the potential to permit serious interference with trade.

However, the involvement of Union institutions may have fundamental implications for the function of such provisions. Given their involvement, these provisions may not so much allow for avoidance of Treaty violations that may otherwise be induced by overly rigid obligations.[323] Rather, they create the possibility that exercise of the powers conferred on these institutions may entail further integration.

The underlying idea is that of "Community solidarity".[324] According to this idea, the Union is to treat the conjunctural problems of a Member State as a matter of "common concern"[325] and is to adopt measures necessary in the "common interest"[326] to safeguard Treaty objectives[327] without impeding trade between Member States.[328] Where such measures have been adopted by the Union, the Member State concerned may not act unilaterally.[329]

Commercial Policy

Article 115 of the Treaty provides that in order to ensure that the execution of measures of commercial policy taken in accordance with this Treaty by any

---

[320] Cf. Arts. XX(j) and XIX(2)(a) of GATT.

[321] Particular measures have also been adopted in the case of oil shortages. See, e.g., Dec. 77/706 (OJ 1977 L292/9) on the setting of a Community target for a reduction in the consumption of primary sources of energy in the event of difficulties in the supply of crude oil and petroleum products.

[322] Case 25/85R *Nuovo Campsider* v. *EC Commission* [1985] ECR 751, 757.

[323] Cf. A. Manin, "A Propos des clauses de sauvegarde" [1970] RTDE 1–42.

[324] Case 77/77 *Benzine en Petroleum Handelsmaatschappij BV* v. *EC Commission* [1978] ECR 1513, 1525.

[325] Case 43/72 *Merkur-Aussenhandels-GmbH* v. *EC Commission* [1973] ECR 1055, 1073.

[326] Joined Cases 9–11/71 *Compagnie d'Approvisionnent, de Transport, et de Crédit SA and Grands Moulins de Paris SA* v. *EC Commission* [1972] ECR 391, 406.

[327] Case 5/73 *Balkan-Import Export* v. *Hauptzollamt Berlin Packhoff* [1973] ECR 1091, 1108; and Case 9/73 *Carl Schlüter* v. *Hauptzollamt Lorrach* [1973] ECR 1135, 1152.

[328] Reischl AG in Case 65/75 *Riccardo Tasca* [1976] ECR 291, 318.

[329] See also Joined Cases 88–90/75 *Società SADAM* v. *Comitato Interministeriale dei Prezzi* [1976] ECR 323, 338.

Member State is not obstructed by deflection of trade[330] or where differences between such measures lead to economic difficulties in one or more of the Member States,[331] the Commission shall recommend the methods for the requisite co-operation between Member States. Failing this, the Commission shall authorise Member States to take the necessary protective measures, the conditions and details of which it shall determine.[332] In the selection of such measures, priority shall be given to those which cause the least disturbance to the functioning of the common market. Even so, this provision has in the past led to authorisation of national measures of commercial policy restricting trade between Member States in goods originating from third states.

The Court of Justice treated Article 115 as an exception from the fundamental principle of the free movement of goods and from the common commercial policy.[333] Accordingly, the Court sought to interpret this provision as strictly as the Treaty framework was considered to allow.[334] According to the Court, the Commission might, solely for serious reasons[335] and for a limited period, after a full examination of the situation in the Member State seeking a decision under Article 115[336] and having regard to the general interests of the Union, authorise the protective measures which caused the least disruption of trade between Member States.[337]

Even so, "complete uniformity" in the treatment of goods from third states by the various Member States might be considered necessary to eliminate the need for such measures.[338] In other words, a "completed" common commercial policy, to be introduced by the Union,[339] was considered necessary. Insofar as uniformity was lacking, Article 115 measures might fulfil the same kind of function as rules of origin in a free trade area.[340] Indeed, this provi-

---

[330] Case 1/84R *Ilford* v. *EC Commission* [1984] ECR 423. It was only this, narrower, aim which was apparently regarded as legitimate under the ECSC Treaty. See Roemer AG in Joined Cases 9 & 12/60 *Société Commerciale Antoine Vloeberghs SA* v. *ECSC High Authority* [1961] ECR 197, 233.

[331] Case 59/84 *Tezi Textiel BV* v. *EC Commission* [1986] ECR 887, 924.

[332] Before its amendment by the TEU, this provision stated that during the transitional period a Member State could itself decide on urgent measures. See also Dec. 87/433 (OJ 1987 L238/26) on surveillance and protective measures which Member States may be authorised to take pursuant to Art. 115.

[333] Sect. 21.12.

[334] See, e.g., Case 41/76 *Suzanne Criel, née Donckerwolcke, and Henri Schou* v. *Procureur de la République* [1976] ECR 1921, 1937.

[335] The Commission breached the proportionality principle if it acted under Art. 115 EC to authorise restriction of the importation of an "insignificant" quantity of the products concerned. See, e.g., Case 62/70 *Werner A. Bock* v. *EC Commission* [1971] ECR 897, 909–10.

[336] The Commission might not rely simply on the compatibility of a measure with the Treaty without examining the reasons for the measure. See Case 29/75 *Kauphof AG* v. *EC Commission* [1976] ECR 431, 443.

[337] Case 41/76 *Suzanne Criel, née Donckerwolcke, and Henri Schou* v. *Procureur de la République* [1976] ECR 1921, 1928–9.

[338] Case 59/84 *Tezi Textiel BV* v. *EC Commission* [1986] ECR 887, 924.   [339] Sect. 21.12 below.

[340] Such rules are used to differentiate within such an area between goods from another member, which benefit from freedom of movement within the area, and goods from non-members, which do not benefit from this freedom.

sion is said to have contributed to fragmentation of the common market along national lines, which made itself felt in wide price differences for identical products.[341] It is not simply that the customs union envisaged in Article 9 of the Treaty may have degenerated into a free trade area but that it degenerated into an imperfect free trade area.

Completion of the internal market may be thought to rule out continued use of any commercial policy measures in respect of trade between Member States. Its completion logically implies that the only restrictive measures which may now be adopted in pursuit of commercial policy requirements should be applicable to trade between third states and the Union as a whole.[342] In other words, any such measures should be adopted in implementation of the common commercial policy rather than to compensate for its inadequacies. Accordingly, Article 115 measures are no longer authorised.[343]

However, "regional safeguard measures", authorising a Member State to restrict trade with other Member States in goods from third states, may still be permissible in exceptional circumstances. The Commission may authorise such measures, "if it considers that such measures applied at that level are more appropriate than measures applied throughout the Community". They must be temporary and must disrupt the operation of the internal market as little as possible.[344]

More particularly, "sectoral back-up measures" have been approved for cars,[345] footwear,[346] and bananas.[347] Such measures may allow for restrictions on trade between Member States in these products. Textiles are also made subject to special treatment, involving replacement of national quotas with Union quotas, though again regional safeguard measures may still be authorised.[348] Moreover, in some instances at least, distortions of competition in Union trade may merely take less visible forms[349] than Article 115

---

[341] G. Koopman and H.-E. Scharrer, *Scenarios of a Common External Trade Policy for the EC after 1992* (Institut für Wirtschaftsforschung, Hamburg, 1990), 12.

[342] Disparities caused by differing national quantitative restrictions set out in Annex I to Reg. 288/82 (OJ 1982 L35/1) were eliminated by Reg. 518/94 (OJ 1994 L67/77) on common rules for imports and repealing Reg. 288/82. The latter measure has itself been replaced by Reg. 3285/94 (OJ 1994 L349/53) on the common rules for imports and repealing Reg. 518/94.

[343] The Community internal market – 1993 report, COM(94)55, 56–7.

[344] Art. 18 of Reg. 3285/94 (OJ 1994 L349/53); and Art. 17 of Reg. 519/94 (OJ 1994 L67/89) on common rules for imports from certain third countries and repealing Regs. 1765/82, 1766/82, and 3420/83.

[345] See, regarding Japanese cars, the *Twenty-Fifth EC General Report* (EC Commission, Brussels, 1992), 331; and Commission Replies to OQ 141 by Ms Tongue (EP Debs. No. 3–423, 265, 28 Oct. 1992) and to WQ 1195/93 (OJ 1994 C32/18) by Mr Christian de la Malène.

[346] See, regarding shoes from South Korea and Taiwan, *Financial Times*, 5 Aug. 1991.

[347] Reg. 404/93 (OJ 1993 L47/1) on the common organisation of the market in bananas.

[348] Art. 11 of Reg. 3030/93 (OJ 1993 L275/1) on common rules for imports of certain textile products from third countries; and Art. 16 of Reg. 517/94 (OJ 1994 L67/1) on common rules for imports of textile products from certain third countries not covered by bilateral agreements, protocols or other arrangements, or by other specific Community import rules.

[349] E.g., Dec. 95/130 (OJ 1995 L85/44) concerning the import of certain steel products into the new *Länder* of Germany from Russia permits certain duty-free imports of steel into the former GDR

measures.[350] They may, for example, take the form of "voluntary export restraints" (VERs) negotiated with third states,[351] even perhaps involving restrictive practices by undertakings sponsored or at least tolerated[352] by Union institutions.[353] In short, therefore, the real effect of completion of the internal market on the use of commercial policy measures in trade between Member States is uncertain.

Monetary Policy

According to Article 107(2) of the EEC Treaty, if a Member State made an alteration in its rate of exchange[354] which was inconsistent with Article 104 objectives[355] and seriously distorted competition, the Commission might authorise other Member States to take measures to counter the consequences of such alteration. However, moves towards monetary union are seen as obviating the need for such measures, and so Article 107(2) was repealed by the Treaty on European Union.

On the other hand, Article 109h of the EC Treaty[356] concerns circumstances where a Member State is in difficulties or is seriously threatened with difficulties as regards its balance of payments. The difficulties must result from an overall disequilibrium in its balance of payments or from the type of currency at its disposal.[357] The difficulties must also be liable to jeopardize the functioning of the common market or the progressive implementation of the common commercial policy. In such circumstances, the Commission is

and Berlin, but Arts. 1 and 2 require Germany and the Commission to "take all the measures necessary to ensure that those products are actually used only" there.

[350] Cf. the reference in Completing the internal market, COM(85)310, 11–12 to "alternative means" of meeting commercial policy requirements.

[351] See, regarding Union use of VERs generally, M. Kelly, N. Kirmani, M. Xaja, C. Boonekamp, and P. Winglee, *Issues and Developments in International Trade Policy* (IMF, Washington, 1988). In principle, they are prohibited by Art. 11(1)(b) of the Agreement on Safeguards in Annex 1a to the WTO Agreement (OJ 1994 L336/1).

[352] Cf. the failure of the Commission to act against a state-sponsored cartel to restrict imports of Japanese cars into France, which the CFI found unlawful in Case T–7/92 *SA Asia Motor France* v. *EC Commission* [1993] ECR II–669. See also Case T–37/92 *Bureau Européen des Consumateurs* v. *National Consumer Council* [1994] ECR II–285.

[353] It is envisaged that exclusive distributorship agreements may play a role in preventing trade deflection (*Financial Times*, 5 Aug. 1991).

[354] Art. 107(1) EEC provided that each Member State was to treat its policy with regard to rates of exchange as a matter of common concern.

[355] I.e. maintenance of a balance-of-payments equilibrium and confidence in the currency, while taking care to ensure a high level of employment and stable prices.

[356] It replaced Arts. 108 and 109 EEC, which allowed for protective measures to be adopted by Member States with balance-of-payments problems. E.g. under Art. 108(3) EEC the Commission authorised France to restrict imports of cars and certain other products (Dec. 68/301 (JO 1968 L178/15) authorising France to take certain safeguard measures according to Art. 108(3) EEC) and Greece to require interest-free deposits to be lodged for the importation of certain goods (Dec. 85/594 (OJ 1985 L375/9) authorising Greece to take certain safeguard measures under Art. 108(3) EEC).

[357] Cf. Art. XII of GATT.

to recommend the action to be taken by the Member State. If the recommended action proves insufficient, the Council may provide for the grant of mutual assistance.[358] Only if such assistance is not granted or proves insufficient, may the Commission authorise protective measures.[359] Article 109i also permits a Member State unilaterally to adopt such measures in the case of a sudden crisis, though the Council may decide by majority that these measures should be amended, suspended, or abolished.

However, subject to Article 109k(6),[360] Articles 109h and 109i shall cease to apply from the beginning of the third stage of monetary union,[361] that is, when national currencies are replaced by the Euro. Again, therefore, establishment of such a union is seen as removing the rationale for preserving national policy-making powers in this field.

8.6 Harmonisation

Harmonisation has played a particularly notable role in relation to public procurement and intellectual property. Other harmonisation, which concerns the goods themselves, is discussed in Chapter 19.

8.6.1 Public Procurement

Liberalisation of public procurement is secured partly by Treaty provisions such as Article 30[362] and partly by harmonisation measures enacted by the Council.[363] These measures may be extended to cover public procurement in third states by agreement with such states.

Public Supply

Rules regarding public supply contracts are contained in Directive 93/36.[364] For this Directive to apply, two conditions must be met. First, the contract

---

[358] The idea of Union solidarity is thus emphasised. Cf. Joined Cases 6 & 11/69 *EC Commission* v. *France: preferential rediscount rate for exporters* [1969] ECR 523, 540.

[359] Such authorisation must be formally, not tacitly, granted. Cf. Reischl AG in Case 27/74 *Demag AG* v. *Finanzamt Duisburg-Süd* [1974] ECR 1037, 1057.

[360] I.e. safeguard measures may still be adopted by Member States not participating in the third stage of monetary union.

[361] Arts 109h(4) and 109i(4) EC, respectively.

[362] Case 43/87 *EC Commission* v. *Ireland: Dundalk water supply* [1988] ECR 4929, 4965; and Case C–21/88 *Du Pont de Nemours Italiana SpA* v. *Unità Sanitaria Locale No. 2 di Carrara* [1990] ECR I–889, I–921.

[363] Besides the legislation, the Commission published a Guide to the Community rules on open government procurement (OJ 1987 C358/1).

[364] Co-ordinating procedures for the award of public supply contracts (OJ 1993 L199/1). Cf. Dir92/50 (OJ 1993 L209/1) relating to the co-ordination of procedures for the award of public service contracts. Amendments to implement the WTO Agreement on Government Purchasing (OJ 1994 L336/1) have been made by Dir. 97/52 (OJ 1997 L328/1).

must be for the supply of goods with a value above specified thresholds.[365] Secondly, the purchaser must be the state, a regional or local authority, a body governed by public law, or an association formed by one or several such authorities or bodies.[366] In the award of such contracts discrimination between suppliers from the different Member States is prohibited.

Utilities

Directive 93/38[367] concerns water, energy, transport, and telecommunications. It applies where the purchaser is a utility in one of these sectors. Contracts may be awarded on the basis of either the lowest price or the most economically advantageous tender. The criteria must be specified in the contract notice, by which bids are invited.[368]

The Directive not only prohibits discrimination between suppliers from different Member States. It also establishes "a Community preference".[369] Thus if a "Community bid" is no greater than three per cent more expensive than a bid from a third state, the former bid must be preferred.[370] A bid originates from a third state, unless at least half the goods are of Union origin.[371]

At the same time, effective access for Union undertakings to public procurement in third states is to be sought.[372] For this purpose, agreements may be concluded with such states which extend equality of treatment to the nationals of each party.[373]

Review Procedures

Requirements as to review procedures are laid down in Directive 89/665.[374] According to this Directive, Member States must adopt the measures necessary to ensure that decisions taken by contracting authorities may be reviewed

---

[365] Art. 5(1) of Dir. 93/36 (OJ 1993 L199/1).

[366] *Ibid.*, Art. 1. See also Case 31/87 *Gebroeders Beentjes NV* v. *Netherlands* [1988] ECR 4635, 4655.

[367] Co-ordinating the procurement procedures of entities operating in the water, energy, transport, and telecommunications sectors (OJ 1993 L199/84). Amendment is proposed. See OJ 1997 C28/4.

[368] Case C–31/87 *Gebroeders Beentjes NV* v. *Netherlands* [1988] ECR 4635; and Case C–87/94 *EC Commission* v. *Belgium: excluded sectors* [1996] ECR I–2043.

[369] The preference is now limited as a result of the WTO Agreement on Government Purchasing (OJ 1994 L336/1). See the Commission Notice concerning this Agreement (OJ 1995 C332/5).

[370] Art. 36(3) of Dir. 93/38 (OJ 1993 L199/84).

[371] *Ibid.*, Art. 36(2).

[372] *Ibid.*, Art. 37.

[373] *Ibid.*, Art. 36(1).

[374] On the co-ordination of the laws, regs., and administrative provisions relating to the application of review procedures to the award of public supply and public works contracts (OJ 1989 L395/33). See also Dir. 92/13 (OJ 1992 L76/14) co-ordinating the laws, regs., and administrative provisions relating to the application of Community rules on the procurement procedures of entities operating in the water, energy, transport, and telecommunications sectors.

effectively and as rapidly as possible on the grounds of violation of Union rules on public procurement or national implementing rules.[375]

8.6.2 Intellectual Property

With a view to reducing conflict between the requirements of free movement and those of intellectual property law, harmonisation of national law governing such property may take place. Such harmonisation concerns trade marks,[376] copyright,[377] supplementary protection certificates for medicines,[378] and computer programmes.[379]

Regulation 40/94[380] goes further.[381] It introduces a right for companies to register a "Community Trade Mark", which will be valid and enforceable throughout the Union. The rationale for introduction of this right is that in the internal market it is not enough to remove barriers to the free movement of goods and services and to ensure that competition is not distorted. It is also necessary to enable companies to adapt their activities to the scale of the Union.[382]

The Community Trade Mark may consist of any signs capable of being represented graphically, provided that such signs are capable of distinguishing the goods or services of one company from those of other companies.[383] It has equal effect throughout the Union, when it is registered with the Community Trade Mark Office. Application for registration may be made directly to this Office or through the national trade mark office. The application must contain: a request for registration of a Community Trade Mark; information identifying the applicant; a list of the goods or services in respect of which the registration is requested; and a representation of the

---

[375] Art. 1(1) of Dir. 89/665 (OJ 1989 L395/33).

[376] Dir. 89/104 (OJ 1989 L40/1), First Dir. to approximate the laws of the Member States relating to trade marks. See also Case C–352/95 *Phytheron International SA* v. *Jean Bourden SA* [1997] ECR I–1729.

[377] Dir. 92/100 (OJ 1992 L346/61) on rental right and lending right and on certain rights related to copyright in the field of intellectual property; Dir. 93/83 (OJ 1993 L248/15) on the co-ordination of certain rules concerning copyright and rights related to copyright applicable to satellite broadcasting and cable retransmission; and Dir. 93/98 (OJ 1993 L290/9) harmonising the term of protection of copyright and certain related rights.

[378] Reg. 1768/92 (OJ 1992 L182/1) concerning the creation of a supplementary protection certificate for medicinal products.

[379] Dir. 91/250 (OJ 1991 L122/42) on the legal protection of computer programmes. See also the proposal for a dir. approximating the legal arrangements for the protection of inventions by utility model, COM(97)691; and the proposal for a dir. on the legal protection of designs (OJ 1994 C345/14).

[380] On the Community trade mark (OJ 1994 L11/1).

[381] Cf. the Agreement relating to Community Patents (OJ 1989 L401/1). Cf. also the proposal for a regulation on the Community design (OJ 1994 C29/11).

[382] 1st recital in the preamble to Reg. 40/94 (OJ 1994 L11/1).

[383] *Ibid.*, Art. 4.

trade mark.[384] Registration will be for ten years, renewable for further periods of ten years. It shall not be registered, transferred, or surrendered or be the subject of a decision revoking the rights of the proprietor or declaring it invalid, nor shall its use be prohibited, save in respect of the whole Union.[385]

8.7 Goods from Third States

Where goods are produced or wholly obtained in a third state, they originate from that state. Where goods are processed in more than one state, the state of origin is that where the last economically justifiable process occurred, provided that that process resulted in a new good or was an important or essential phase of its manufacture.[386] In other words, there must be a significant qualitative change.[387]

If the concern of the free movement of goods is with competition, the question whether goods are from another Member State or from a third state loses significance, except for the purposes of the common commercial policy.[388] In practice, the concern of this policy to secure reciprocity dominates Union practice regarding goods from third states.

8.7.1 Reciprocity

The nature of the free movement of goods may be such that the search for reciprocity on the basis of this freedom may be problematic. This freedom lies at the heart of the "new legal order" created by the EC Treaty,[389] which, in turn, has an independent capacity to create rights and obligations for economic actors.[390] It is this capacity which enables the free movement of goods to go beyond the simple prohibition of discrimination between imports and domestic products. In these circumstances, a "public good" analogy, according to which reciprocity depends on processes[391] designed to

[384]   *Ibid.*, Art. 26(d).

[385]   *Ibid.*, Art. 1(2).

[386]   Reg. 2913/92 (OJ 1992 L302/1) establishing the Community Customs Code, Art. 24.

[387]   Case 49/76 *Gesellschaft für Überseehandel mbH* v. *Handelskammer Hamburg* [1977] ECR 41, 53.

[388]   Sect. 21.12.

[389]   Case 26/62 *NV Algemeine Transport- en Expeditie Onderneming Van Gend en Loos* v. *Nederlandse Administratie der Belastingen* [1963] ECR 1, 23.

[390]   Chap. 7.

[391]   Cf. L. Tsoukalis, *The New European Economy: The Politics and Economics of Integration* (Oxford University Press, Oxford, 1991), 272. Emphasis on "process reciprocity" in the context of international trade is said to reflect the increasing significance of structural rather than regulatory barriers to trade. See, e.g., Y.S. Lanneaux, "International Trade: Joint Report of the United States–Japan Working Group on the Structural Impediments Initiative" (1991) 32 *Harvard International Law Journal* 245–54.

prevent "free riding",[392] may seem applicable to the requirements of this freedom.

However, these requirements are so demanding as to entail serious intrusion into policy making. The implication is that political constraints may set limits to what can be achieved by way of reciprocal liberalisation between the Union and third states. Moreover, their operational content is so variable that an essential characteristic lies in their judicial determination in individual cases.

Their resulting potential for dynamism[393] and, at the same time, their failure to secure full uniformity of treatment for traders within the Union mean that the requirements of free movement may provide "no definite yardstick" by reference to which the appropriate treatment for third state traders can be determined.[394] Indeed, legislation may be found necessary to protect Union traders against being disadvantaged in relation to third state traders.[395]

Hence, extension by analogy of the free movement of goods to trade between the Union as such and third states may be problematic.[396] For example, comparatively liberal regulation in a third state would mean that traders therefrom, being entitled to free competition in extending throughout the Union what they were free to do in their own state, might enjoy greater freedom of trade within the Union than traders from Member States. More particularly, they would enjoy greater freedom of trade within any given Member State than nationals of that Member State trading domestically.[397] The result would be distortions of competition radically incompatible with the undistorted competition sought by freedom of movement between Member States.

Logically, reciprocal extension of the free movement of goods to trade with third states can only be achieved if it is done in such a way as to cover trade between each state involved. Such an extension not only necessitates adoption of common rules applicable to such trade. It also necessitates establishment of a judicial system capable of maintaining the common quality of those rules and the essence of the trade liberalisation requirements embodied therein.

These necessities cannot easily be met in respect of trade between the

---

[392] I.e. where one party to an arrangement benefits from sacrifices made by another without itself making such sacrifices. Cf., regarding opposition of the GATT system to free riding, A. Ahnlid, "Free or Forced Riders? Small States in the International Political Economy: The Example of Sweden" [1992] *Co-operation and Conflict* 241–76.

[393] The concept of *reciprocité pondérée* (see R. Schwok in J. Jamar and H. Wallace (eds.), *EEC–EFTA: More Than Just Good Friends?* (De Tempel, Bruges, 1988), 353) may be an unworkable substitute and may, indeed, be more of a statement of the problem than a solution thereto.

[394] Cf. Warner AG in Case 30/79 *Land of Berlin* v. *Wigei, Wild-Geflügel-Eier-Import GmbH & Co. KG* [1980] ECR 151, 171.

[395] *Ibid.*, 164.

[396] The problems may have been less apparent when early association agreements, such as that which Greece (JO 1963 294) and the Yaoundé Convention (JO 1964 1431) were concluded.

[397] According to the case law, freedom of movement does not apply to such trade. See n. 4 above.

Union and a single third state. The operation of the free movement of goods depends on the work of institutions, particularly the case law of the European Courts, which are independent of the Member States. Either the extension of this freedom must apply to a group of third states, so that they can create equivalent bodies, or the jurisdiction of the European Courts must be accepted by third states individually with consequences for sovereignty comparable with some of the most important constitutional consequences of Union membership. As former Commission President Delors once put it,[398] there must either be an agreement establishing a "two-pillar" framework with a group of third states or an agreement extending Union rules[399] to interested third states.

Such considerations may explain why the EC Treaty itself is not interpreted as requiring extension of the provisions on the free movement of goods to trade with third states.[400] Thus Article 30 only applies to restrictions on imports affecting trade between Member States.[401] Accordingly, the authorities competent to settle the terms of licences of right may grant or refuse the licensee authorisation to import the patented product from a third state without infringing Article 30.[402]

In essence, reciprocity concerns may demand separation of the free movement of goods from the regulation of trade with third states.[403] The consequence is not only that national legislation has a greater role in the regulation of such trade than in the regulation of trade between Member States. The further consequence is a situation in which Union legislation may play a limited role in resolving the problems involved.

8.7.2 National Legislation

To be marketed within the Union, products from third states must not only satisfy Union law requirements to be put into free circulation under Article 10 of the Treaty.[404] In the absence of Union harmonisation acts, they must also satisfy whatever requirements are stipulated for the marketing of the kind of products concerned by the legislation of the Member State where they are put into free circulation. Thus, for example, the mere fact that a

---

[398] EP Debs. No. 2–373, 76, 17 Jan. 1989.

[399] As in the Agreement on Civil Aviation between Norway, Sweden, and the EC (OJ 1992 L200/21).

[400] The ECJ also ruled in Case 91/78 *Hansen GmbH & Co.* v. *Hauptzollamt Flensburg* [1979] ECR 935, 956 that Art. 37 EC, concerning state trading monopolies, did not apply to goods from third states. Cf., however, the view of Capotorti AG (*ibid.*, 971).

[401] Case 51/75 *EMI Records Ltd* v. *CBS United Kingdom Ltd* [1976] ECR 811, 845.

[402] Case C–191/90 *Generics (UK) Ltd, Harris Pharmaceuticals Ltd* v. *Smith Kline and French Laboratories Ltd* [1992] ECR I–5335, I–5374.

[403] According to the Resolution of the European Parliament of 13 June 1985 (OJ 1985 C175/229) on consolidating the internal market, para. 6, "if a Community-wide market is to be established, it must also be capable of defending itself".

[404] 209 above.

product from a third state complies with Union law requirements to be put into free circulation in a Member State does not entail that it can be marketed, even in principle, in that Member State under a trade mark registered there by another undertaking.[405] Distortion of competition and deflection of trade may result.

Distortion of Competition

Traders from third states, like domestic traders within a Member State, may be disadvantaged in relation to those involved in trade between Member States. The disadvantages may arise where legal requirements in their own state differ from those laid down in legislation enacted by the Member State in which the products are to be put into free circulation. In such circumstances, competition is distorted.

That the concomitant of such distortion is protection of Union traders receives little attention. According to the Commission, pressing the European market towards internal unity, thereby reaffirming its separate identity *vis-à-vis* the outside world, would help to restore confidence. The aim was to expand European industry in a way that would create productive employment in the Union. Hence, steps had to be taken to ensure that it would indeed be Union companies that would effectively and in the first place benefit from measures to develop industry within the Union.[406] Such was said to be the thrust of an early Commission document[407] on the internal market.[408] In other words, association of liberalisation of Union trade with limitations to liberalisation of trade with third states may sometimes be thought desirable.

The consequences of tolerating, let alone espousing, the protectionism entailed may become increasingly serious. Insofar as completion of the internal market implies scale economies for Union traders, the latter, in the absence of effective exposure to competition from outside the Union, may internalise these economies and dissipate them through inefficiencies.

More particularly, protection may have redistributive effects as between import-competing producers and other Union traders. As a result, adjustment costs necessitated by developments in international market conditions may be shifted to traders within the Union who have no rational need so to adjust. The costs are not simply static losses associated with misallocations but also efficiency losses in protected firms and the loss of dynamism in the incentive system for performance.[409]

---

[405] Case 51/75 *EMI Records Ltd* v. *CBS United Kingdom Ltd* [1976] ECR 811, 846. Warner AG tended to obscure this point by apparently merging questions under Art. 30 EC with those under Art. 36 EC (*ibid.*, 860).

[406] A Community strategy to develop Europe's industry, COM(81)639, 17.

[407] State of the internal market, COM(81)313.

[408] A Community strategy to develop Europe's industry, COM(81)639, 7.

[409] Cf. J. Pelkmans, "The European Community and the Newly Industrializing Countries" in W. Maihofer (ed.), *Noi si Mura* (EUI, Florence, 1986), 510–39.

Such distortions are the opposite of what is sought by liberalisation of trade between Member States. They reflect, however, the unease with which Union law recognises the interdependence of the Union market and the markets of third states.[410]

Traders from third states may respond by establishing subsidiaries or taking over companies in a Member State where they trade on a large scale.[411] However, to the extent that traders feel compelled so to transfer their production because of legal obstacles, a trade distortion may be involved. In any case, such a course of action may not be a realistic option for most traders from third states.

Deflection of Trade

Insofar as Member States remain free to adopt their own legislation regarding trade with third states, such legislation may vary from one Member State to another, and trade may be deflected. For example, a third state trader wishing to sell his products in a Member State with legislation imposing restrictive requirements may seek to import them into that Member State through a Member State with less restrictive requirements. Such trade deflection may be accompanied by that of a less direct kind. The imports from the third state into the Member State with less restrictive requirements may displace domestic products from the market of that Member State. The latter may then be exported to the Member State with more restrictive requirements. At the same time, deflection may result not only from legislation governing imports from third states but also from legislation governing exports to third states.[412]

8.7.3 Union Legislation

Problems of trade with third states may not readily be resolved through Union legislation. For example, in *Richardt*[413] Advocate General Jacobs

---

[410] Cf., regarding the provision of services, Opinion 1/94 *International Agreements on Services and the Protection of Intellectual Property* [1994] ECR I–5267, I–5412–4. Cf. also the view of the ESA that a tax from which exports were exempted could not affect the international competitiveness of a national producer in Notice 95–002 – Norway (OJ 1995 C212/6) concerning aid which Norway proposed to grant in the form of a tax exemption for glass packaging from a basic tax on non-reusable beverage packaging.

[411] F. Capelli, "Les Relations CE/Etats-Unis et la réalisation du marché intérieur" in J. Schwarze (ed.), *The External Relations of the European Community, in Particular EC–US Relations* (Nomos, Baden-Baden, 1989), 139–43, 142. The effects of tariffs may be mitigated by the internalising ability of transnational enterprises. See P. Robson and I. Wooton, "The Transnational Enterprise and Regional Economic Integration" [1993] *JCMS* 71–89.

[412] In Case 86/85 *Alexander Moksel Import-Export GmbH & Co. Handels-KG v. Hauptzollamt-Jonas* [1987] ECR 369, 386, the ECJ reminded the Commission that restrictions on exports to third states could affect trade between Member States.

[413] Case C–367/89 *Aimé Richardt and Les Accessoires Scientifiques SNC* [1991] ECR I–4621, I–4642.

considered whether it was compatible with Union law, particularly Regulation 2603/69,[414] for Luxembourg to restrict the transit of electronic equipment being exported from France to the then Soviet Union via Luxembourg. Article 1 of this Regulation prohibited quantitative restrictions on exports to third states, unless the restrictions were covered by Article 11 thereof. The latter provision had similar wording to Article 36 of the Treaty. However, the proportionality principle might be less demanding in relation to Article 11 of the Regulation than in relation to Article 36 of the Treaty.[415] Hence, in the view of the Advocate General, the former provision might permit restrictions going beyond the kinds of restrictions permitted by the latter.

The significance of the context within which the acceptability of restrictions falls to be assessed may be all the more pronounced where the Union has enacted legislation on, for example, public health. According to the Court of Justice, Member States are not required to show the same degree of confidence towards third states as that which, on the basis of Union legislation, should characterise relations between Member States and which entails the abolition of systematic inspections in trade between Member States.[416] As a result, restrictions which, in the case of trade between Member States, are prohibited by such legislation may be permitted in relation to trade with third states. Distortion of competition may be entailed, and completion of the internal market may be undermined.

Distortion of Competition

Underlying issues are sometimes touched upon in judicial proceedings. For example, in determining whether scientific equipment from third states can be exempted from the Common Customs Tariff,[417] the Court of Justice considers it "necessary to balance the needs of Community scientific research against the possibilities of development of the Community industry in the sector of scientific instruments and apparatus."[418]

However, recognition of underlying issues does not apparently preclude acceptance of distortions of competition. For example, according to the Court, different treatment of Union traders must be regarded as compatible with Union law, where it is merely an automatic consequence of the different treatment accorded to third states with which those traders have entered into commercial relations.[419] The distortions accepted may be compounded,

---

[414] Establishing common rules for exports (JO 1969 L324/25).

[415] See also Jacobs AG in Case C–312/91 *Metalsa Srl* [1993] ECR I–3751, I–3766. Cf. Case 52/77 *Leonce Cayrol* v. *Giovanni Rivoira & Figli* [1977] ECR 2261, 2281.

[416] Case 30/79 *Land of Berlin* v. *Wigei, Wild-Geflügel-Eier-Import GmbH & Co. KG* [1980] ECR 151, 166. See, similarly, Rozès AG in Case 2/81 *Albert Clément, Gérard Ces* [1981] ECR 3339, 3355.

[417] Sect. 21.12.2 below.

[418] Case 232/86 *Nicolet Instrument GmbH* v. *Hauptzollamt Berlin-Packhof* [1987] ECR 5025, 5038.

[419] Case 52/81 *Offene Handelsgesellschaft in Firma Werner Faust* v. *EC Commission* [1982] ECR 3745, 3762.

insofar as the integration with third states which does take place[420] results in narrower production and export specialisation and less import substitution and increases the structural dependence of Member States on states outside as well as within the Union.[421]

Completion of the Internal Market

Completion of the internal market logically implies that the only restrictive measures which may now be applied specifically to goods from third states should be applicable to trade between third states and the Union as a whole. However, distortions of competition within the Union may continue as a result of substitution of Article 115 measures by less visible measures.[422] In essence, failure to liberalise trade with third states may set limits to what can be achieved by the free movement of goods and may thus undermine the completion of the internal market.

In short, therefore, completion of the internal market not only highlights the artificiality of separating the free movement of goods from the treatment of trade with third states. It also increases the urgency of developing a legal regime tending towards assimilation of the two. Assimilation may be sought, though not necessarily achieved, through conclusion of free trade agreements or association agreements.[423]

8.8 Agreements with Third States

Agreements with third states may reproduce provisions contained in the EC Treaty.[424] The agreements may thus be designed to secure a greater degree of trade liberalisation between the parties thereto than is secured by Union law in the case of trade with third states generally.[425] They may not, however, be designed to substitute the pursuit of reciprocity with extension of the free

---

[420] See, in connection with the globalisation process, A. de la Torre and M.R. Kelly, *Regional Trade Arrangements* (IMF Occasional Paper No. 93, Washington, 1992), 46.

[421] United Nations Conference on Trade and Development, *Common European Economic Space* (UNCTAD, New York, 1991), 5. According to J. Fagerberg, "The Process of Economic Integration in Europe: Consequences for EFTA Countries and Firms" [1991] *Co-operation and Conflict* 197–215, 201, the changing composition of trade between Member States in recent decades reflects not only European integration but also increasing "world integration".

[422] Sect. 8.5.5 above.

[423] Such agreements may be seen as implementing the principle in Art. 110 EC. See, e.g., the Opinion of the Economic and Social Committee of 25 Jan. 1995 (OJ 1995 C102/40) on relations between the EU and Russia, Ukraine, and Belarus, para. 3.23.

[424] See the list of such agreements in the Council Reply to WQ E–182/95 (OJ 1995 C196/16) by Jean-Pierre Raffarin.

[425] The traditional response to "international externalities" has been the formulation of policies for international co-operation. See P. Nicolaides, "How Fair is Fair Trade?" [1986] *JWTL* 148–62, 149.

movement of goods to trade with third states. On the one hand, there may be "external" impediments to such substitution. Union law does not require that all third states must be treated equally.[426] However, GATT requirements as to most-favoured-nation status[427] may be influential,[428] and in any case commitment to achieving uniformity in the treatment of products from third states may not easily be abandoned.[429] On the other hand, impediments may result from the unsuitability of the free movement of goods for transposition to an agreement designed to liberalise trade relations between the Union and a third state.

At the same time, limits to the effective reproduction of Treaty provisions in agreements with third states may be implied by the reluctance of the Court of Justice to interpret Treaty provisions solely by reference to their terms.[430] Both the limitations of language and social demands may preclude such a simple approach to interpretation. Rather, account may be taken of other Treaty provisions, and conclusions drawn from the general legal framework constituted by the Treaty may be influential. In other words, interpretation may be affected by features of the Treaty structure. If reproduction of these features is lacking in agreements with third states, Treaty provisions and textually equivalent provisions in such agreements may be interpreted differently. To imagine otherwise would, it said, be "heretical",[431] though differential interpretation is not inevitable.[432]

While they do not seem to have been fully explored in Union practice regarding agreements with third states, judicial proceedings illustrate aspects of the problems. In such proceedings these agreements may be treated as forming part of the common commercial policy. They are not usually treated as creating a duty incumbent on Member States to extend to trade with the third states concerned the binding principles of the free movement of goods between Member States.[433] According to the Court of Justice, EC Treaty

---

[426] Case 55/75 *Balkan Import-Export* v. *Hauptzollamt Berlin-Packhof* [1976] ECR 19, 32; and Case 245/81 *Edeka Zentrale AG* v. *Germany* [1982] ECR 2745, 2756.

[427] According to Art. I(1) of GATT, any trade liberalisation introduced for one Party to the Agreement must be extended to all other Parties.

[428] See, e.g., the explanatory memorandum to the proposal for a dir. on the procurement procedures of entities providing water, energy, transport, and telecommunications services, COM(88)377, 31.

[429] Case 52/77 *Leonce Cayrol* v. *Giovanni Rivoira & Figli* [1977] ECR 2261, 2278–9.

[430] Indeed, in one case AG Mancini took the extreme position that the function of CCT headings might be so changed by the practice of national authorities that it would be "impossible" for the ECJ to interpret them. See Case 166/84 *Thomasdünger GmbH* v. *Oberfinanzdirektion Frankfurt am Main* [1985] ECR 3001, 3003.

[431] Warner AG in Case 51/75 *EMI Records Ltd* v. *CBS United Kingdom Ltd* [1976] ECR 811, 861.

[432] See, e.g., regarding the concept of social security, Case C–18/90 *Office National de l'Emploi (ONEM)* v. *Bahia Kziber* [1991] ECR I–199, I–227. See also Darmon AG in Case C–355/93 *Hayriye Eroglu* v. *Land Baden-Württemberg* [1994] ECR I–5113, I–5121.

[433] Case 51/75 *EMI Records Ltd* v. *CBS United Kingdom Ltd* [1976] ECR 811, 846–7.

provisions "cannot as such be transposed to relations with non-member countries".[434] Hence, individual trade liberalisation provisions of these agreements need to be interpreted in the light of the "structure" of the relevant agreement.

8.8.1 Free Trade Agreements

Free trade agreements regularly reproduce Article 30 of the EC Treaty. For example, Article 14 of the Portuguese Free Trade Agreement[435] prohibited the introduction of new quantitative restrictions or measures having effect on imports between the Parties. It also required the abolition of existing restrictions and equivalent measures.

The meaning of the latter provision was at issue in *Polydor*.[436] This judgment concerned the importation of gramophone records from Portugal, where they had been purchased from the exclusive licensee for that country, and their sale in the United Kingdom without the consent of the copyright holder or his exclusive licensee in the United Kingdom. In particular, the question was whether the exclusion of such products from the United Kingdom was contrary to Article 14 of the Agreement. The Court of Justice ruled that their exclusion was justified under Article 23 of the same Agreement,[437] which was substantially identical to Article 36 of the EC Treaty. In contrast, within the context of trade between Member States the "exhaustion of rights"[438] doctrine would apply. Its application would prevent the holder of an intellectual property right from employing his right to exclude from a Member State products marketed in another Member State with his consent. Hence, their exclusion would be prohibited by Article 30 of the EC Treaty and would not be justified under Article 36 of the same Treaty.

Such a contrast between the operation of Articles 30 and 36 of the EC Treaty and the operation of provisions in free trade agreements may be acceptable to national courts in third states. For example, *Gramola*[439] concerned the Austrian Free Trade Agreement.[440] Here the Austrian Supreme Court found that an Austrian record shop proprietor who imported records from Germany, where they were lawfully marketed, infringed the rights in Austria of the Austrian music society. In so finding,

---

[434] Case 225/78 *Procureur de la République, Besançon* v. *Bouhelier* [1979] ECR 3151, 3160.

[435] JO 1972 L301/165.

[436] Case 270/80 *Polydor Ltd and RSC Records Inc.* v. *Harlequin Record Shops Ltd and Simon Records Ltd* [1982] ECR 329.

[437] Cf. Case 51/75 *EMI Records Ltd* v. *CBS United Kingdom Ltd* [1976] ECR 811, 847, where the ECJ implied that liberalisation requirements of free trade agreements might be more demanding.

[438] Sect. 8.5.3 above. This doctrine is extended to include the EFTA states by Prot. 28, on intellectual property, to the EEA Agreement (OJ 1994 L1/3).

[439] *Austro-Mechana Gesellschaft zur Verwaltung und Auswertung Mechanisch-Musikalischer-Urheberrechte GmbH* v. *Gramola Winter & Co.* [1984] 2 CMLR 626.

[440] JO 1972 L309/2.

this Court ruled that "the creation and exercise of copyrights in the widest sense" were not covered by the Agreement, "at least in so far as the restrictions stipulated by the parties [did] not extend beyond the substance of the property right".[441]

"Structural" Considerations

The case law apparently reflects "structural" considerations. According to the Court of Justice in *Polydor*,[442] the scope of the case law regarding Article 30 of the EC Treaty was to be determined in the light of the objectives and activities defined in Articles 2 and 3 of the Treaty, which were concerned with the unification of national markets into a single market having the characteristics of a domestic market.[443] More particularly, the Court observed:

> "the instruments which the Community has at its disposal in order to achieve the uniform application of Community law and the progressive abolition of legislative disparities within the common market have no equivalent in the context of relations between the Community and Portugal."[444]

Institutional arrangements may also have been influential.[445] Advocate General Rozès noted in the same case:

> "whilst with regard to the free movement of goods the structure of the [Portuguese Free Trade] agreement may indeed be comparable to that of the [EC] Treaty, there are many aspects to the Treaty other than the free movement of goods. Apart from the joint committee, . . . no 'common institution' was established [by the Portuguese Agreement]."[446]

Apparently, the liberalisation required by a particular provision of a free trade agreement may depend on the generality of the liberalisation sought by the agreement. It may also depend on the arrangements made therein for harmonisation[447] and institutional involvement.[448] Such thinking may partly, though not necessarily simply, reflect a concern that "reciprocity is . . . not guaranteed" by free trade agreements.[449] Presumably, in the absence of provisions requiring sufficiently generalised liberalisation and making arrangements for harmonisation and institutional involvement, application

---

[441] [1984] 2 CMLR 626, 639. See, later, *Mute*, [1989] GRUR, Int. 699.

[442] Case 270/80 *Polydor Ltd and RSC Records Inc.* v. *Harlequin Record Shops Ltd and Simon Records Ltd* [1982] ECR 329.

[443] *Ibid.*, 348. Cf., in connection with interpretation of Art. 95 EC, Case 15/81 *Gaston Schul* [1982] ECR 1409, 1431–2.

[444] [1982] ECR 329, 349.   [445] Cf. the link made in Art. 234 EC.   [446] [1982] ECR 329, 354.

[447] According to the *Ninth Report on Competition Policy* (EC Commission, Brussels, 1980), 9, the "metamorphosis of a heterogeneous collection of isolated national markets into a single vast market could not succeed without the establishment of some basic rules".

[448] Cf. the consequences which the Swiss Supreme Court in *Bosshard Partners Intertrading AG* v. *Sunlight AG* [1980] 3 CMLR 664, 674, attached to the fact that the Free Trade Agreement with Switzerland (JO 1972 L300/189) did "not aim to create a uniform internal market with supranational regulations governing competition, but merely a free trade area".

[449] [1982] ECR 329, 354.

of the same prohibition of measures having equivalent effect to quantitative restrictions in trade between the Union and third states as applies to trade between third states may enable undertakings engaged in international trade to exploit differences in competitive conditions which such provisions are designed to preclude. Certainly, the "complete" free movement of goods sought by the EC Treaty is seen as presupposing, *inter alia*, that the freedom to provide services and freedom of establishment are achieved at the same time.[450]

On the other hand, in its case law the Court of Justice implicitly recognises the inadequacies of harmonisation and the work of the Union institutions.[451] The impression is that rulings such as that in *Polydor* reflect underlying assumptions as to the limited degree of integration sought by free trade agreements.

Such rulings may be viewed in terms of a "pairing" or "matching" of "substance" (that is, trade liberalisation requirements) and "structure" (that is, institutional involvement in integration processes), which was successful until integration within the Union "took a further leap"[452] with the adoption of the Single European Act.[453] Thinking of this kind, however, begs questions why the pairing lacked the dynamism to respond to the integration also taking place between the parties to the free trade agreements.

It may be argued that, in view of the broad terms of the preambles to the free trade agreements with the EFTA states and their objectives, as outlined in Article 1 of these agreements and as confirmed by the "Luxembourg process",[454] such restrictive interpretations of liberalisation provisions in these agreements were not justified.[455] On the other hand, according to Article 1(b) of these agreements, they merely aimed "to provide fair conditions of competition for trade between the Contracting Parties" rather than to create a common market.[456] The implication might be that their provisions had to be interpreted more restrictively than corresponding provisions of the EEC Treaty.

---

[450] *Ibid.*, 356. See also Joined Cases 55 & 57/80 *Musik-Vertrieb Membran GmbH and K-tel International* v. *GEMA* [1981] ECR 147, 165.

[451] Case 120/78 *Rewe-Zentral AG* v. *Bundesmonopolverwaltung für Branntwein* [1979] ECR 649, 662.

[452] T. Cottier, "Constitutional Trade Regulation in National and International Law: Structure-Substance Pairings in the EFTA Experience" in M. Hilf and E.-U. Petersmann (eds), *National Constitutions and International Economic Law* (Kluwer, Deventer, 1993), 409–42, 423.

[453] OJ 1987 L169/1.

[454] I.e. practice following the EC–EFTA Ministerial Declaration of 9 Apr. 1984 (Bull. EC 4–1984, 1.2.1).

[455] U. Bernitz, "Sveriges EG-anknyting i rättsligt perspektiv" [1989/90] *JT* 47–69, 60. Cf., earlier, N. March Hunnings, "Enforceability of the EEC–EFTA Free Trade Agreements" [1977] *ELR* 163–89.

[456] In Case C–312/91 *Metalsa Srl* [1993] ECR I–3751, I–3774–5 the ECJ contrasted the objective of the Austrian Free Trade Agreement (JO 1972 L309/2) (the creation of a free trade area), as indicated in its Preamble, with the objective of creating a common market in Arts. 2 and 3 EEC. See, similarly, Jacobs AG (*ibid.*, I–3760)

Moreover, it cannot be assumed that the practical achievements of the Luxembourg process were such as to remove the justification for restrictive interpretations. For example, in *Bosshard Partners Intertrading AG* v. *Sunlight AG* the Swiss Supreme Court found that a Swiss trade mark holder was entitled to prevent the importation into Switzerland of German-made detergents lawfully branded in Germany with the trade mark concerned. In finding that this entitlement was unaffected by the Swiss Free Trade Agreement[457] the Court observed that the Agreement omitted to establish any institution comparable with the Court of Justice.[458] This omission was not remedied by the Luxembourg process. The absence of any such institution may not simply have rendered "public good" conceptions of the regime created by the Agreement less appropriate than an approach to interpretation emphasising the need for reciprocity.[459] It may also have meant that, in practice, reciprocity requirements could not easily be reconciled with a broad interpretation of liberalising provisions contained therein.

Practical Consequences

Consequences of major practical importance follow from a narrow interpretation of provisions of free trade agreements. In particular, such agreements may allow parties to adopt policy measures which are prohibited within the Union by the EC Treaty.

In Sweden, for example, the alcohol policy entailed the prohibition of the sale of strong beers, such as those lawfully brewed and marketed in Belgium. This prohibition would have been contrary to Article 30 of the EC Treaty, unless it could have been justified on public health grounds under Article 36 of the Treaty or, possibly, on the basis of a mandatory requirement recognised by the Court of Justice. Given that the sale of spirits was permitted in Sweden, such a justification would not have been easy to establish. Hence, the prohibition of the sale of strong beers would apparently have been unlawful under this Treaty.[460]

In contrast, provisions of free trade agreements corresponding to Article 30 of the EC Treaty are apparently interpreted merely as prohibiting a party from discriminating between imports from the other party and domestic

---

[457] JO 1972 L300/189.

[458] [1980] 3 CMLR 664, 674. See also Rozès AG in Case 104/81 *Hauptzollamt Mainz* v. *C.A. Kupferberg & Cie KG* [1982] ECR 3641, 3674.

[459] According to G. Porro, *L'Integrazione giuridica nell'Associazione europea di libero scambio* (Giuffré, Milan, 1983), 202–10, free trade agreements are based on the principle *do ut des* and do not involve the adoption of EC Treaty objectives or the same degree of institutional participation as do association agreements.

[460] It may be argued that the prohibition of drinks of intermediate strength is necessary to discourage "graduation" to strong drinks. However, this argument is, in substance, the same as that which was rejected by the ECJ in Case 120/78 *Rewe-Zentral AG* v. *Bundesmonopolverwaltung für Branntwein* [1979] ECR 649, 663.

goods.[461] Certainly, this interpretation was favoured by the Swiss Supreme Court[462] and has been implicitly adopted by the Court of Justice itself.[463] Thus Article 13 of the Austrian Free Trade Agreement[464] prohibited a Member State from making the marketing authorisation for a pharmaceutical product originating in Austria, identical in all respects to a pharmaceutical product already authorised by the health authority of that Member State, subject to the condition that the parallel importer submit documents already made available to that authority by the manufacturer at the time of the first request for a marketing authorisation.[465] In other words, a Member State was prohibited from discriminating between products from other Member States and its own products. In the absence of such discrimination, parties to such agreements remain free to pursue domestic policies affecting trade. Apparently, therefore, the prohibition of the sale of strong beers, regardless of origin, is permitted by such agreements.

On the other hand, a further consequence of a restrictive interpretation of liberalisation provisions in the free trade agreements is that most technical barriers to trade between the parties[466] are unaffected by the prohibition of measures having equivalent effect to quantitative restrictions. Such barriers, which are potentially of significance in relation to any preferential trading arrangements,[467] have increased in importance,[468] as a result of GATT successes in reducing tariffs.[469] Insofar as the relative benefits of tariff preferences decline,[470] traders have to rely more and more on comparative advantage or economies of scale. Comparative advantage, whether natural or man-made, may be sufficient to outweigh the costs associated with technical barriers. However, the need to maintain multiple "product lines" implied by

---

[461] Cf. Art. III(4) of GATT. The Swiss Supreme Court ruled in *Bosshard Partners Intertrading AG* v. *Sunlight AG* [1980] 3 CMLR 664, 675 that the prohibition of quantitative restrictions and measures having equivalent effect on imports in Art. 13 of the Swiss Free Trade Agreement (JO 1972 L300/189) only covered measures "directly affecting the import of goods".

[462] *Maison Godard-Burnet & Fils Sprl* v. *Direction Générale des Douanes* A486/85, 2 Sept. 1986.

[463] Case 104/81 *Hauptzollamt Mainz* v. *C. A. Kupferberg & Cie KG* [1982] ECR 3641.

[464] JO 1972 L309/2.

[465] Case C–207/91 *Eurim-Pharm GmbH* v. *Bundesgesundheitsamt* [1993] ECR I–3723.

[466] I.e. national rules and standards regarding product qualities. See, generally, H. Ewander, *Avveckling av teckniska handelshinder* (Industriförbundet Arbetsrapport 12, Stockholm, 1989).

[467] In *A Community strategy to develop Europe's industry* (COM(81)639, 16) the Commission noted that the "Community preference" had declined as CCT duties had fallen. In any case, owing to the increasing relative importance of non-tariff barriers to trade maintained or introduced by the Member States, market unity was not all that it should be.

[468] See, e.g., K. Shigehara, "External Dimension of Europe 1992: Its Effects on the Relationship between Europe, the United States and Japan" [1991] *Bank of Japan Monetary and Economic Studies* 87–102, 92.

[469] However, low average levels of customs duties may hide significant tariff peaks. See J. Greenwald, "Negotiating Strategy" in G.C. Hufbauer (ed.), *Europe 1992: An American Perspective* (Brookings Institution, Washington, DC, 1990), 345–88, 361.

[470] Communication on the management of preferential trade agreements, COM(97)402.

such barriers may have a more serious effect in relation to economies of scale and may, indeed, preclude them altogether.

8.8.2 Association Agreements

The Europe Agreements provide for creation of a free trade area in industrial goods between the parties.[471] Accordingly, they provide for abolition of customs duties and charges having equivalent effect as well as quantitative restrictions and measures having equivalent effect in trade between the parties. More particularly, they apply the asymmetrical principle.[472] In accordance with this principle, the Union market is to be opened up to traders from the other parties more rapidly than the latter are required to open up their markets to Union traders. Such asymmetry may be considered necessary to ensure that the reciprocity required of association agreements under Article 238 of the EC Treaty is real.[473]

For example, Article 9(4) of the Europe Agreement with Poland[474] provides that quantitative restrictions on imports to the Union and measures having equivalent effect shall be abolished on entry into force of the Agreement with regard to products originating in Poland. At the same time, Article 10(4) of the Agreement provides that quantitative restrictions on imports into Poland of products originating in the Union and measures having equivalent effect shall be abolished on entry into force of the Agreement with the exception of those listed in Annex V, which shall be abolished in accordance with the timetable provided in that Annex.

The terms of these provisions do not go so far as Article 5(1) of the Yaoundé Convention.[475] It provided that as regards the elimination of quantitative restrictions, the Member States were to apply to imports from the associated states the corresponding provisions of the EEC Treaty. Accordingly, the Court of Justice found Article 33 of the EEC Treaty applicable to trade between the Union and such associated states.[476]

The possibility may still be left open that Articles 9(4) and 10(4) of the Polish Agreement[477] can operate in the same fashion as corresponding provisions of the EC Treaty, particularly Article 30 thereof. Certainly, association agreements generally may be treated as demanding more intensive integration

---

[471] Art. 7 of the Europe Agreement with Poland (OJ 1993 L348/2).

[472] It is authorised by Art. XXXVI(8) of GATT.

[473] In relation to agreements with the OCT, asymmetry is envisaged in Art. 131 EC. Note also the conclusions drawn by the ECJ from the "fundamentally favourable approach of the Community towards the OCT" in Case C–430/92 *Netherlands* v. *EC Commission: OCT* [1994] ECR I–5197, I–5225.

[474] OJ 1993 L348/2.   [475] JO 1964 1431.

[476] Case 48/74 *Mr Charmasson* v. *Minister for Economic Affairs and Finance (Paris)* [1974] ECR 1383.

[477] OJ 1993 L348/2.

than free trade agreements.[478] For example, the Association Agreement with Greece[479] was said to "constitute much more than a free trade agreement of the classical type".[480] Not only did it envisage the future accession of Greece to the Union, but also its structure and content were based on the EEC Treaty.[481] The Europe Agreements also refer to the possibility of future Union membership for the states concerned.[482] However, the liberalisation sought by these Agreements centres on the creation of a free trade area in a transitional period of a maximum of ten years.[483] The liberalisation sought may not necessarily be regarded as comparable with that sought by the Greek Association Agreement. It is possible, therefore, that the Europe Agreements will be treated as allowing parties the same kind of freedom to adopt policy measures for themselves as did the free trade agreements.[484] If so, trade liberalisation may be seriously jeopardized.

The only solution may be for countries such as Poland to adapt their legislation to Union rules, if they are to seek to maximise the benefits of these agreements.[485] In other words, the Europe Agreements, like free trade agreements, may fail to overcome problems of the separation of Union trade liberalisation from trade liberalisation with third states.[486]

8.8.3 EEA Agreement

The EEA Agreement[487] constitutes an exceptionally sophisticated attempt not merely to liberalise trade between the Union and the third states

---

[478] Even so, in connection with the Turkish Association Agreement (JO 1964 368), Darmon AG maintained in Case 12/86 *Meryem Demirel* v. *Stadt Schwäbisch Gmünd* [1987] ECR 3719, 3744 that the "consensual nature" of such an agreement might preclude "the application of provisions without a clearly circumscribed content".

[479] JO 1963 26.

[480] Rozès AG in Case 17/81 *Pabst & Richarz KG* v. *Hauptzollamt Oldenberg* [1982] ECR 1331, 1359.

[481] The ECJ itself was rather less expressive (*ibid.*, 1350). In Joined Cases 37 & 38/73 *Sociaal Fonds voor de Diamantarbeiders* v. *NV Indiamex and Association de Fait de Belder* [1973] ECR 1609, 1619 the Commission distinguished simply between association agreements based on a customs union and agreements not creating such a union.

[482] See, e.g., the final recital in the preamble to the Polish Agreement (OJ 1993 L348/2). "When such a convention looks towards a further accession, the Community must of necessity hold the most extensive powers to conclude agreements with non-member countries in order to cover all the fields of activity contemplated by the EC Treaty" (Darmon AG in Case 12/86 *Meryem Demirel* v. *Stadt Schwäbisch Gmünd* [1987] ECR 3719, 3741).

[483] Art. 7 of the Polish Agreement (OJ 1993 L348/2).

[484] Cf. S. Peers, "An Ever Closer Waiting Room? The Case for Eastern European Accession to the European Economic Area" (1995) 32 *CMLRev.* 187–213, 208.

[485] See the view of the British Foreign Office in House of Lords Select Committee on the European Communities, European Agreements with Poland, Hungary, and the Czech and Slovak Federal Republic, HL (1990–1) 35, Minutes of Evidence, 9. See sect. 19.5.1 below, regarding "voluntary harmonisation".

[486] Cf. D. Kennedy and D.E. Webb, "The Limits of Integration: Eastern Europe and the European Communities" (1993) 30 *CMLRev.* 1095–117, 1097.

[487] OJ 1994 L1/3.

concerned but also to assimilate such liberalisation to that within the Union. As far as the EFTA states were concerned, the Agreement represented the results of a policy designed to secure for their citizens, institutions, and companies participation in the internal market on the same conditions as Union actors.[488]

"Homogeneity"

Article 1 of the EEA Agreement provides that the aim of the Agreement is to promote a continuous and balanced strengthening of trade and economic relations between the Contracting Parties with equal conditions of competition and respect for the same rules, with a view to creating a homogeneous European Economic Area.

Moreover, the fourth recital in the Preamble to the Agreement refers to the objective of establishing a dynamic and homogeneous European Economic Area. This Area is to be based on common rules and equal conditions of competition, adequate means of enforcement, including arrangements at the judicial level, and equality, reciprocity, and an overall balance of benefits, rights, and obligations for the Contracting Parties.[489] To achieve this objective, the Agreement reproduces EC Treaty provisions governing the "four freedoms" and competition policy. These provisions are to be interpreted having regard to the case law of the Court of Justice before signature of the Agreement.[490] At the same time, Union implementing measures listed in annexes to the Agreement are embodied in EEA law.

Formal Limits to "Homogeneity"

The EEA Agreement does not require establishment of a customs union or an internal market, and it does not embody the common commercial policy or the common agricultural policy. Hence, certain provisions of the Agreement differ in substance from EC Treaty provisions. In particular, Article 8(2) of the Agreement stipulates that its provisions only apply to products originating in the Contracting Parties.[491] The rules needed to determine origin are contained in Protocol 4 to the Agreement.[492] Moreover,

---

[488] See, e.g., European Economic Co-operation Area, prop. 1991/92:170, pt 1, annex 1, 4.

[489] It thus envisages an apparently sophisticated version of what is described by L.A. Winters, "Reciprocity" in J.M. Finger and A. Olechowski, *The Uruguay Round* (World Bank, Washington, DC, 1987), 45–51, 49 as "rules reciprocity", though the "overall balance" envisaged may have more in common with reciprocity by outcome. See, regarding the agreements on agriculture concluded by each EFTA state with the Union at the time of conclusion of the EEA Agreement itself, the Declaration by the EC on bilateral agreements, attached to the EEA Agreement.

[490] Art. 6 EEA.

[491] Though Arts 9(2) and 21(3) EEA envisage co-operation in customs matters regarding goods generally. See also Prot. 10 on simplification of inspections and formalities in respect of carriage of goods and Prot. 11 on mutual assistance in customs matters.

[492] On rules of origin. Particular problems may arise from the operation of rules of origin in relation to textiles. Note, however, the "evolutionary clauses" in Art. 9(2) and (3) EEA.

coal and steel remain under free trade agreements with the ECSC.[493] In addition, unprocessed agricultural products are basically excluded from liberalisation,[494] and special arrangements apply to processed agricultural products listed in Protocol 2 to the Agreement.[495]

These provisions mean that the goods benefiting from freedom of movement under the EEA Agreement are more narrowly defined than those benefiting from this freedom under the EC Treaty. Moreover, the abolition of frontier controls envisaged in Article 7a of the Treaty is not required. Subject to these provisos, the provisions defining the freedom of movement from which goods covered by the EEA Agreement will benefit may be expected formally to secure the same freedom as the EC Treaty provisions which they reproduce.

"Structural" Limitations to "Homogeneity"

In Opinion 1/91[496] the Court of Justice was requested by the Commission pursuant to Article 228(6) of the EC Treaty to give its opinion on the compatibility of the draft EEA Agreement with this Treaty. According to the Court, the fact that provisions of the EEA Agreement and the corresponding Union provisions were identically worded did not mean that they necessarily had to be interpreted identically. An international treaty was to be interpreted not only on the basis of its wording but also in the light of its objectives.[497]

The EEA Agreement was concerned with the application of rules on free trade and competition in economic and commercial relations between the Contracting Parties.[498] In contrast, the EC Treaty rules on free trade and competition, which the Agreement sought to extend to the whole territory of

---

[493] See, in the case of Norway, OJ 1974 L348/1. However, Art. 27 EEA and Prot. 14, on trade in coal and steel products, and Prot. 25, on competition regarding coal and steel, require elimination of all remaining restrictions and adoption of the competition rules of Union law in relation to these industries.

[494] Art. 8(3) EEA and Prot. 3, on products excluded from the scope of the Agreement in accordance with Art. 8(3)(a). However, Prot. 9, on trade in fish and other marine products, requires the elimination or reduction of duties on many fish products, and Prot. 42, on bilateral arrangements concerning specific agricultural products, envisages bilateral arrangements regarding specific agricultural products. More particularly, Prot. 47, on the abolition of technical barriers to trade in wine, provides for the abolition of technical barriers to trade in wine, and according to Art. 18 EEA, arrangements to ease veterinary and phytosanitary checks in Annex I, on veterinary and phytosanitary matters, apply to all agricultural products.

[495] Art. 8(3)(b) EEA. Prot. 3 simplifies rules regarding processed agricultural products, particularly as regards compensation for differences between the agricultural policies of the Contracting Parties. The compensation is to be calculated on the basis of the real agricultural content of the products. For certain such products complete freedom of movement is envisaged.

[496] Opinion 1/91 *Draft Agreement between the Community and the EFTA Countries relating to the Creation of the EEA* [1991] ECR I–6079, I–6101.

[497] Art. 31 of the Vienna Convention on the Law of Treaties (1969).

[498] Part VI of the Agreement, dealing with co-operation beyond the four freedoms was not apparently considered significant. Cf. the argument that the Court underestimated the degree of integration sought by the EEA Agreement in A. Epiney, "La Cour de justice des Communautés européennes et l'Espace économique européen" [1992] *Revue Suisse de Droit International et de Droit Européen* 275–304.

the Contracting Parties, had developed and formed part of the Union legal order. The objectives of this order went beyond that of the EEA Agreement. It followed, *inter alia*, from Articles 2, 7a, and 102a of the Treaty[499] that this Treaty aimed to achieve economic integration leading to the establishment of an internal market[500] and economic and monetary union. Article 1 of the Single European Act[501] made clear, moreover, that the objective of the Treaty was to contribute together to making concrete progress towards European unity.[502] Hence, the provisions of the Treaty on free movement and competition, far from being an end in themselves, were only means for attaining those objectives.

As in *Polydor*,[503] the importance of the objectives of a legal instrument for interpretation of its provisions was stressed by the Court. These objectives were classified in terms of integration intensities ranging from a free trade area, through an internal market, to a union.[504] The objective of monetary union may be particularly relevant for the development of the free movement of goods. For example, devaluation by an EFTA state might be countered by unilateral Union resort to safeguard measures.[505] In contrast, within the Union problems which might otherwise lead to devaluation are to be tackled within the framework of monetary union rules.[506]

A solution might have been for the EEA Agreement to have made "it completely clear that within the scope of this Agreement the objectives are the same as those pursued by the equivalent chapters in the EC Treaty".[507]

---

[499] Art. 2 defined the task of the Community, Art. 7a required the completion of the internal market, and Art. 102a envisaged convergence of the economic and monetary policies of the Member States.

[500] I.e., not the common market of *Polydor* (Case 270/80 *Polydor Ltd and RSC Records Inc.* v. *Harlequin Record Shops Ltd and Simon Records Ltd* [1982] ECR 329).

[501] However, Art. 31 SEA (OJ 1987 L169/1) provided that the provisions of the Treaties regarding the powers of the ECJ and exercise of these powers did not apply to the part of the Act in which Art. 1 was contained.

[502] [1991] ECR I–6079, I–6102. Such language echoes that used earlier by Commission President Delors (EP Debs. No. 2–373, 76, 17 Jan. 1989). The French text referred simply to "*l'Union européenne*" without the implication of joint action in use of the word "together". Later in the ruling ([1991] ECR I–6079, I–6108) the ECJ referred in the English version simply to "a European Union".

[503] Case 270/80 *Polydor Ltd and RSC Records Inc.* v. *Harlequin Record Shops Ltd and Simon Records Ltd* [1982] ECR 329.

[504] In referring to such a union, the Court "moved the goalposts", and the EC Treaty was regarded as requiring more intensive integration in broader fields than before. According to B. Brandtner, "The Drama of the EEA: Comments on Opinions 1/91 and 1/92" in O. Jacot-Guillarmod (ed.), *Accord EEE: commentaires et réflexions* (Schulthess, Bern, 1992) 300–28, 307, a paradigm shift had taken place.

[505] Sect. 12.4.2 below. However, in 1982 the Commission raised the question in the Joint Committee whether Swedish devaluation in that year was compatible with the spirit of the Free Trade Agreement (*Sverige–EG 1982* (Utrikesdepartementets handelsavdelning, Stockholm, 1983), 13).

[506] See sect. 21.11.2.

[507] O. Due, "General Introduction to a Discussion on the Principles of Community Law Seen in the EEA Perspective" [1991] *JFT* 288–94, 290–1.

The problem is that the relationship between the objectives and the scope of an agreement may be circular. Objectives may determine scope, but objectives may only be discernible by reference to scope.[508] However, implicit in recognition of this problem is a possible solution. Dynamic interpretation of scope may facilitate expansive definition of objectives.[509] In other words, the EEA Agreement may have the potential for overcoming problems of the separation of trade liberalisation within the Union from trade liberalisation with third states.

---

[508] Cf., regarding the "revelation" of the objectives of a directive by its content, the UK submission in Case C–295/90 *European Parliament* v. *EC Council: right of residence for students* [1992] ECR I–4193, I–4209.

[509] Para. 1 of Prot. 1 to the EEA Agreement, on horizontal adaptations, provides that the preambles to Union acts in the annexes "are relevant to the extent necessary for the proper interpretation and application, within the framework of the Agreement, of the provisions contained in such acts".

9

Free Movement of Workers

Article 48(1) of the EC Treaty provides that freedom of movement for workers shall be secured within the Union. Details of what this freedom includes are given in paragraphs two and three of the same provision. Article 48(2) prohibits any discrimination based on nationality between workers of Member States as regards employment, remuneration, and other conditions of work and employment. Article 48(3) provides, in turn, for rights of entry and residence in Member States. It is directly applicable.[1]

This provision seems originally to have been concerned to limit the social impact of immigration.[2] In particular, Article 48(3)(a) refers only to a right of entry to take up offers of employment "actually made". Thus the movement of the unemployed in search of employment was not apparently to be encouraged. In practice, however, the emphasis of legislation implementing Article 48[3] and the case law interpreting this provision has been on promoting the social integration of workers exercising their freedom of movement. The establishment of Union Citizenship also implies concern with their political integration, but integration of this kind poses fundamental challenges for Union law.

9.1 Persons Covered

To benefit from freedom of movement, individuals must meet economic and nationality conditions. They must do so either personally or, in the case of spouses or dependants,[4] through others.

9.1.1 Economic Conditions

The expression "worker" is not defined in the Treaty or in Union legislation. However, the Court of Justice has ruled that it is a Union law concept with a

---

[1] Case 167/73 *EC Commission* v. *France: merchant seamen* [1974] ECR 359, 371–2.

[2] Note also the Joint declaration on the free movement of persons, annexed to the Final Act adopting the First Accession Agreement.

[3] It is enacted under Art. 49 EC.   [4] Sect. 9.2.4 below.

Union law meaning.[5] This meaning is broadly interpreted. Thus a person is a worker for the purposes of Article 48, even if his reimbursement is at a rate lower than a minimum guaranteed wage in the Member State concerned,[6] the reimbursement is non-existent,[7] or the work is of part-time character. However, the pursuit of a genuine and effective activity must be involved.[8] A person paid a "share" may also be a worker.[9]

On the other hand, an activity does not qualify an individual as a worker if it is merely a means of rehabilitation or reintegration to enable him to recover the capacity to take ordinary work.[10] Moreover, self-employed persons[11] and students are not covered by Article 48,[12] though the latter may benefit under Directive 93/96[13] on the right of residence for students. However, provided that a person is "economically active", he may benefit from free movement without having to be classified as employed for the purposes of Article 48 or self-employed for the purposes of Articles 52 and 59.[14]

More particularly, job-seekers are not mentioned in Article 48. However, Regulation 1612/68[15] prohibits discrimination regarding access to the facilities provided by national employment bureaux,[16] thus implying that job-seekers may benefit from freedom of movement. A similar implication may be drawn from the right under Regulation 1408/71[17] for such persons to draw unemployment benefit for up to three months.[18] Certainly, the Court of Justice has accepted that they may benefit from free movement.[19]

---

[5] Case 75/63 *Mrs M.K.H. Unger (née Hoekstra)* v. *Bestuur der Bedrijfsvereniging voor Detailhandel en Ambachten* [1964] ECR 177, 184–5.

[6] Case 139/85 *R.H. Kempf* v. *Staatssecretaris van Justitie* [1986] ECR 1741, 1750–1.

[7] Case 196/87 *Udo Steymann* v. *Staatssecretaris van Justitie* [1988] ECR 6159, 6173.

[8] Case 53/81 *D.M. Levin* v. *Staatssecretaris van Justitie* [1982] ECR 1035, 1050–1.

[9] Case C–3/87 *R.* v. *Ministry of Agriculture, Fisheries, and Food, ex p. Agegate Ltd* [1989] ECR I–4459, I–4505.

[10] Case 344/87 *I. Bettray* v. *Staatssecretaris van Justitie* [1989] ECR 1621, 1646.

[11] Case C–15/90 *David Maxwell Middleburgh* v. *Chief Adjudication Officer* [1991] ECR I–4655, I–4682.

[12] *Ibid.*   [13] OJ 1993 L317/59.

[14] Case C–363/89 *Danielle Roux* v. *Belgium* [1991] ECR I–273, I–293. Arts. 48, 52 (freedom of establishment), and 59 EC (freedom to provide services) are based on the same principles as regards rights of entry and residence and equality of treatment. See Case 48/75 *Jean Noël Royer* [1976] ECR 497, 509. But cf. Case 15/90 *David Maxwell Middleburgh* v. *Chief Adjudication Officer* [1991] ECR I–4655, I–4682.

[15] On freedom of movement for workers within the Community (JO 1968 L257/2).

[16] *Ibid.*, Art. 5.

[17] On the application of social security schemes to employed persons and their families moving within the Community (JO 1971 L149/2).

[18] *Ibid.*, Art. 69(1).

[19] Case 48/75 *Jean Noël Royer* [1976] ECR 497, 512.

9.1.2 Nationality Conditions

Article 48 of the Treaty does not expressly limit the benefits of free movement to nationals of Member States.[20] However, Directive 68/360,[21] which was enacted under Article 49 to implement the requirements of Article 48(3), only provides for such nationals, their spouses, and dependants to enjoy rights of entry and residence. Likewise, the second paragraph of Article 8a(1) of the Treaty states that every person having the nationality of a Member State shall be a Union Citizen.[22] The natural, though not inevitable, implication is that the rights of Union Citizenship are limited to nationals of Member States.

Moreover, a Declaration concerning nationality of a Member State[23] was adopted along with the Treaty on European Union. According to this Declaration, whenever the EC Treaty refers to nationals of Member States, the question whether an individual possesses the nationality of a Member State shall be settled solely by reference to the national law of the Member State concerned.[24] In the view of the Commission, this Declaration "spells out" Article 8a(1) of the EC Treaty. It implies that rules on the acquisition and possession of the nationality of a Member State fall within the scope not of this Treaty, but of the national law of the Member State concerned.[25]

Declarations on Nationality

Germany[26] and, on two occasions, the United Kingdom[27] have made declarations defining those persons who qualify as their nationals for Union law purposes. The implicit assumption in these declarations is that it is for each Member State to define those who are its nationals for Union law purposes.

---

[20] See, generally, A. Evans and H.–U.J. d'Oliveira, "Nationality and Citizenship" in A. Cassese, A. Clapham, and J.H.H. Weiler (eds.), *Fundamental Rights and the European Community: Methods of Protection* (Nomos, Baden-Baden, 1991), 299–350.

[21] On the abolition of restrictions on movement and residence within the Community for workers of Member States and their families (JO 1968 L257/13), Art. 1.

[22] Art. 25(3) of the Declaration of Fundamental Rights and Freedoms of the European Parliament (OJ 1989 C120/51) also provided that "a Community citizen within the meaning of this Declaration shall be any person possessing the nationality of one of the Member States". Art. 3 of the Draft Treaty establishing a European Union (OJ 1984 C77/33) went further and expressly stated that Union citizenship could not be acquired or lost independently of the citizenship of a Member State.

[23] The legal status of the declaration is unclear. See J. Verhoeven, "Les Citoyens de l'Europe" [1993] *Annales de Droit de Louvain* 165–91, 170.

[24] This view had earlier been expressed by Mayras AG in Case 33/72 *Monique Gunnella* v. *EC Commission* [1973] ECR 475, 486 and Roemer AG in Case 14/68 *Walt Wilhelm* v. *Bundeskartellamt* [1969] ECR 1, 28.

[25] Explanatory memorandum to the proposal regarding rights to participate in elections to the European Parliament, COM(93)534, 11.

[26] Declaration of the German Government on the definition of the expression "German National", which was "noted" by the Conference and annexed to the Final Act adopting the EEC Treaty.

[27] Declaration by the UK Government on the definition of the term "nationals", annexed to the Final Act adopting the First Accession Agreement. See now OJ 1983 C23/1.

The implication is further developed in the Declaration on nationality of a Member State, adopted with the Treaty on European Union. According to this Declaration, Member States may declare, for information, who are to be considered their "nationals for Community purposes" by way of a declaration lodged with the Presidency. They may also amend any such declaration when necessary.

The validity of such declarations may have judicial recognition. Thus the current definition of United Kingdom nationals for Union law purposes, which does not cover British Overseas Citizens generally, was applied by the Court of First Instance in *Farrugia*.[28] In the light of this declaration, the Court held that a British Overseas Citizen was not rendered ineligible for a Union-financed research fellowship in the United Kingdom by virtue of possessing the nationality of that Member State.[29] It may be noted, however, that such application of the definition was consistent with the functional requirements of the Union scheme. Hence, questions remain how such a declaration is to be treated, if it conflicts with functional requirements of Union law.

Such conflict is not precluded. In particular, insofar as a Member State may alter its definition of nationality for Union law purposes, the rights of free movement may be precarious.[30] Even in the absence of alterations of nationality definitions, the continuing terms of such definitions may still jeopardize the exercise of free movement. For example, under United Kingdom law descendants of persons born to British Citizens who have exercised this freedom may be denied British Citizenship.[31] In other words, persons who exercise this freedom may only be able to pass on a "second class" citizenship under the national law of their state.[32]

The ruling of the Court of Justice in *Micheletti*[33] may be thought to offer a solution to such problems. This case concerned an Italian national who also held Argentine nationality. He had been refused a residence card in Spain, because his "habitual residence" before arrival in Spain had been in

---

[28] Case T–230/94 *Frederick Farrugia* v. *EC Commission* [1996] ECR II–195.

[29] *Ibid.*, II–207–8.

[30] Cf. the objections of the ECJ to an "ambiguous state of affairs" in Case 167/73 *EC Commission* v. *France: merchant seamen* [1974] ECR 359, 372. However, while the need for a Union law definition of "workers" was recognised in Case 75/63 *Mrs M.K.H. Unger (née Hoekstra)* v. *Bestuur der Bedrijfsvereniging voor Detailhandel en Ambachten* [1964] ECR 177, 184–5, it is argued that "nationality" is a qualitatively different concept because of its link with statehood. See H.-U.J. d'Oliveira, "European Citizenship: Its Meaning, Its Potential" in R. Dehousse (ed.), *Europe After Maastricht An Ever Closer Union?* (Beck, Munich, 1994), 126–48, 129.

[31] S. 2 of the British Nationality Act 1981. Cf. D. Bonner, "British Citizenship: Implications for UK Nationals in the European Communities" [1981] *ELR* 69–75.

[32] Cf. recognition by the ECJ that rights of entry and residence "cannot be fully effective if a [Union Citizen] may be deterred from exercising them by obstacles raised in his or her country of origin to the entry and residence of his or her spouse" in Case C–370/90 *R.* v. *Immigration Appeal Tribunal and Surinder Singh, ex p. Secretary of State for the Home Dept.* [1992] ECR I–4265, I–4294.

[33] Case C–369/90 *Mario Vicente Micheletti* v. *Delegacion del Gobierno en Cantabria* [1992] ECR I–4239.

Argentina and so under Spanish law he could not be treated as a national of a Member State. For the Court the decisive question was whether he possessed Italian nationality according to Italian law.[34] According to the Court, each Member State was competent to define the conditions for acquisition and loss of its nationality. However, Member States did not apparently have a free hand in the matter, because this competence had to be exercised "having due regard to Community law" (*doit être exercée dans le respect du droit communautaire*).[35] This obligation was presumably regarded as the necessary corollary of the obligation of Member States to recognise the Treaty rights of nationals of other Member States.[36] It was thus a prerequisite for ensuring that the application of free movement did not vary from Member State to Member State.

The legal foundation of the former obligation may be the duty of loyalty in Article 5 of the Treaty, taken together with provisions such as Article 48. However, its real significance for determination of those who are entitled to free movement depends on the content which may be given to it by Union law rules. Such rules in this area are at best rudimentary[37] and may not necessarily lend themselves easily to significant development through the case law.[38] In other words, nationality of a Member State may in itself be an unsatisfactory basis for determining the personal scope of free movement.

Possible Use of Alternative Conditions

Little consideration has been given to the fundamental issue whether conditions other than nationality can suitably be employed as a basis for recognition of entitlement to free movement. Resort to conditions other than nationality would not, however, be entirely novel.

For example, the nationality condition applies for the purposes of Union rules governing the social security rights of migrants at the time of acquisition of such rights.[39] Subsequent loss of the nationality of a Member State may not mean that these rights are also lost. Rather, a continuing link with a social security system may be a substitute for continued fulfilment of the nationality condition. Again, the Commission has proposed that derived

[34] Cf., regarding recognition of identity documents issued by other Member States, Case C–376/89 *Pangiottis Giagounidis* v. *Stadt Reutlingen* [1991] ECR I–1069.

[35] [1992] ECR I–4239, I–4262. Cf., earlier, the ruling in Case 21/74 *Jeanne Airola* v. *EC Commission* [1975] ECR 221, 228 that "the concept of 'nationals' in Art. 4(a) [of Annex VII to the Staff Regs. (JO 1962 1385)] must be interpreted in such a way as to avoid any unwarranted difference of treatment as between male and female officials who are, in fact, placed in comparable situations".

[36] Even where the persons concerned are also their own nationals. See, e.g., Case 292/86 *Claude Gullung* v. *Conseils de l'Ordre des Avocats du Barreau de Colmar et de Saverne* [1988] ECR 111, 136.

[37] According to Tesauro AG in *Micheletti* [1992] ECR I–4239, I–4254, they are non-existent.

[38] Cf. the question-begging argument that such rules may be developed on the basis of "the objectives and effective operation of the free movement provisions and Union citizenship", which is advocated by S. O'Leary, "Nationality Law and Community Citizenship: A Tale of Two Uneasy Bedfellows" [1992] *YBEL* 353–84, 378.

[39] Case 10/78 *Belbouab* v. *Bundesknappschaft* [1978] ECR 1915, 1924.

rights of residence for the spouse and dependants of a Union Citizen exercising his freedom of movement should continue after his death or the dissolution of the marriage.[40] In both cases a right which is originally based, directly or indirectly, on the nationality condition may develop into one which is exercisable independently of this condition.

Article 2 of the Protocol to the First Accession Act on the Channel Islands and the Isle of Man goes further. It provides that Channel Islanders and Manxmen shall not benefit from Union provisions relating to the free movement of persons and services. However, according to Article 6 of the same Protocol, those who have "at any time been ordinarily resident in the United Kingdom for five years" are not considered to be Channel Islanders or Manxmen for the purposes of these provisions. Thus entitlement to free movement may be founded on ordinary residence in a Member State for a given period.[41]

9.2 Rights of Entry and Residence

Article 48(3) of the EC Treaty refers to rights of entry and residence for persons entering a Member State "to accept offers of employment actually made", persons residing in the Member State concerned for the purpose of employment, and persons remaining there after employment has finished. The Treaty does not distinguish between rights of entry and residence in other Member States and such rights in one's own Member State. However, this distinction is made in the case law.

9.2.1 Other Member States

Persons taking up the offer of a job in another Member State enjoy a right of entry under Article 48(3)(a) and a right to move freely within the territory of Member States for this purpose under Article 48(3)(b). An analogous right has been found to exist for job-seekers. In the case of the latter, the right of

---

[40] Proposal of 11 Jan. 1989 (OJ 1989 C100/6) for a reg. amending Reg. 1612/68. The explanatory memorandum described the right as conditional on "a tie to the employment market of a Member State" (COM(88)815, 22). The European Parliament considers that such rights should be unaffected by the death of the primary beneficiary or divorce or *de facto* separation. See OJ 1990 C175/90, in the case of pensioners. In the case of students, protection against the effects of "dissolution of the marriage" rather than separation was envisaged (OJ 1990 C175/96). In the case of those exercising their right of residence under the draft for what became Dir. 90/364 (OJ 1990 L180/26) on the right of residence, protection against the effects of "final separation" was envisaged (OJ 1990 C175/84).

[41] An analogy may be drawn with the Council of Europe Convention on the Legal Status of Migrant Workers (ETS(1977)93). This instrument applies to nationals of a Contracting Party who have been authorised by another Contracting Party to reside in its territory in order to take up employment there. Cf. the amended proposal of 21 Mar. 1997 (OJ 1997 C139/6) for a directive on the right of TSNs to travel in the Community.

residence must extend for a reasonable period. In particular, it must continue for as long as the person concerned provides evidence that he is still seeking work and has genuine chances of being engaged.[42] He has a right of equal access to employment but no right to "social advantages".[43]

Persons who enter another Member State to take up a job and job-seekers who find one are entitled to reside there for the purposes of their employment under Article 48(3)(c). It provides that they are entitled to do so, in accordance with the provisions governing the employment of nationals of that Member State laid down by law, regulation, or adminis-trative action.[44]

They are to be granted a residence permit on production of the document on the basis of which they entered the territory and either a confirmation of engagement from the employer or a certificate of employment.[45] The permit is valid for five years and automatically renewable.[46] It cannot be withdrawn, if the holder becomes incapable of work through illness or accident or is involuntarily unemployed.[47] However, temporary workers, who are working for between three and twelve months, are only entitled to a temporary residence permit.[48] Seasonal workers and those working for less than three months are entitled to reside during the period of their employment without a residence permit.[49]

On the other hand, after twelve consecutive months of involuntary unemployment a first residence permit may be renewed for a limited period.[50] The implication is that long-term unemployment may lead to loss of the right of residence.

On retirement workers are entitled to remain under Article 48(3)(d), which has been implemented by Regulation 1251/70.[51] Pensioners generally may now benefit from free movement under Directive 90/365[52] on the right of residence for employees and self-employed persons who have ceased their occupational activity.

Directive 90/364[53] is broader. It confers rights of entry and residence on persons not enjoying free movement under other provisions of Union law. However, beneficiaries and their dependants must be covered by sickness

[42] Case C–292/88 *R.* v. *Immigration Appeal Tribunal, ex p. Gustaff Desiderius Antonissen* [1991] ECR I–745, I–779; and Case C–344/95 *EC Commission* v. *Belgium: residence restrictions* [1997] ECR I–1035, I–1053. Cf., where obtaining employment is objectively impossible, Case C–171/91 *Dimitrios Tsiotras* v. *Landeshauptstadt Stuttgart* [1993] ECR I–2925, I–2957.

[43] Case 316/85 *Centre Public d'Aide Sociale, Courcelles* v. *Marie-Christine Lebon* [1987] ECR 2811, 2839.

[44] No quantitative restrictions may be imposed. See Art. 4 of Dir. 68/360 (JO 1968 L257/13). See also Case 167/73 *EC Commission* v. *France: merchant seamen* [1974] ECR 359.

[45] Art. 4(3) of Dir. 68/360 (JO 1968 L257/13).

[46] *Ibid.*, Art. 6(1).   [47] *Ibid.*, Art. 7(1).   [48] *Ibid.*, Art. 6(3).   [49] *Ibid.*, Art. 8.

[50] *Ibid.*, Art. 7(2).

[51] On the right of workers to remain in the territory of a Member State after having been employed in that state (JO 1970 L142/1).

[52] OJ 1990 L180/28.   [53] On the right of residence (OJ 1990 L180/26).

insurance and have sufficient resources to avoid becoming a burden on the social assistance system of the host Member State.[54]

9.2.2 Own Member State

The question whether an individual enjoys rights of entry and residence under Union law in the Member State of which he possesses the nationality is controversial.

"Internal Situations"

According to the case law, an individual does not usually have the right under Union law to enter his own Member State. He only has this right, where he has already exercised his freedom of movement in order to carry out economic activities in another Member State.[55] The rationale for recognition of this limited right may be that, in the absence of such a right, Union Citizens may be deterred from exercising their rights in relation to a Member State other than their own.[56]

In other circumstances the issues are treated as "wholly internal"[57] to the Member State concerned or as being without "any element going beyond a purely national setting".[58] As a result, a Member State may be permitted by the Treaty to impose restrictions on the entry and residence of its own nationals which would be prohibited in the case of nationals of other Member States. A national of a Member State cannot challenge restrictions in his own Member State on the ground that he may someday seek work elsewhere in the Union.[59]

On the other hand, receipt of a service in another Member State[60] or even simply shopping there[61] may apparently constitute exercise of rights implied by the free movement of services under Articles 59 to 66 of the Treaty.[62] If so, then a person who has exercised these rights in other Member States may acquire rights of entry and residence in relation to his own Member State.

[54] Under a Council agreement of 1968 (excerpts from the unpublished agreement may be found in *R.* v. *Secretary of State for the Home Dept., ex p. Muhammed Ayub* [1983] 3 CMLR 140) job seekers were already required to satisfy a condition of the latter kind.
[55] Joined Cases 35 & 36/82 *Elestina Esselina Christina Morson* v. *Netherlands and Head of the Plaatselijke Politie within the meaning of the Vreemdelingenwet* [1982] ECR 3723, 3736–7.
[56] Case C–370/90 *R.* v. *Immigration Appeal Tribunal and Surinder Singh, ex p. Secretary of State for the Home Dept* [1992] ECR I–4265, I–4293–4.
[57] Case 175/78 *R.* v. *Vera Ann Saunders* [1979] ECR 1129, 1135.
[58] Case 20/87 *Ministère Public* v. *André Gauchard* [1987] ECR 4879, 4896.
[59] Case 180/83 *Hans Moser* v. *Land Baden-Württemberg* [1984] ECR 2539, 2547.
[60] Tourists who go to another Member State as recipients of services benefit from freedom of movement. See Case 186/87 *Ian William Cowan* v. *Trésor Public* [1989] ECR 195, 221.
[61] The right to go to another Member State to shop is also implied by the free movement of goods (see Case C–362/88 *GB-Inno-BM* v. *Confédération du Commerce Luxembourgeois Asbl* [1990] ECR I–667, I–686–7). The right exists, even if the shopper is carrying no means of payment. See Tesauro AG in Case C–68/89 *EC Commission* v. *Netherlands: frontier controls* [1991] ECR I–2637, I–2647.
[62] Chap. 11.

True, there is concern in the Court of Justice that Union law rights in relation to one's own Member State should not be employed as a device to evade "secondary" immigration control.[63] In other words, the rights should not be employed to evade control of immigration by dependants of nationals of the Member State concerned.[64] Nevertheless, the practical effect of the limits imposed on free movement may be less than is suggested by the language of the relevant judgments.

Internal Market and Union Citizenship

For Union law rights to depend on the prior crossing of a frontier between Member States may be thought inconsistent with the definition of the internal market in Article 7a of the Treaty. According to this provision, such frontiers were to have been abolished by the end of 1992. More fundamentally, it may be thought incompatible with the concept of Union Citizenship, which was "established" by Article 8(1) of the Treaty, for a Union Citizen wishing to acquire a Union law right to reside in his own Member State to have first to move to another Member State. According to the Court of Justice, however, "internal situations" are still unaffected by Union law.[65]

True, Article 8a(1) of the Treaty does provide that every Union citizen shall have the right to move and reside freely within the territory of the Member States. No distinction is made between one's own Member State and other Member States. However, the right is expressly subject to the limitations and conditions laid down in this Treaty and in the measures adopted to give it effect. The main object of this reference to other Treaty provisions is, presumably, Articles 48 to 66.[66] The effect of the reference may not only be to perpetuate the tendency for free movement for economic purposes, as sought by these provisions, to operate as the "core and origin" of Union Citizenship.[67] Certainly, the establishment of Union Citizenship has been found not to prejudice the condition for enjoyment of this freedom that persons not economically active must have sickness insurance.[68] More particularly, the effect may be

---

[63] See, e.g., A. Evans, "Secondary Immigration Control and EEC Law" [1984] *NLJ* 965–7.

[64] Slynn AG in Joined Cases 35 & 36/82 *Elestina Esselina Christina Morson* v. *Netherlands and Head of the Plaatselijke Politie within the meaning of the Vreemdelingenwet* [1982] ECR 3723, 3742. See, regarding "sham marriages", Case C–351/95 *Selma Kadiman* v. *Bavaria* [1997] ECR I–2133. Cf., regarding evasion of national legislation regulating vocational training, Case C–61/89 *Marc Gaston Bouchoucha* [1990] ECR I–3551, I–3568. Cf. also, regarding the need for persons to be genuinely travelling between Member States for purposes of tax exemption for goods contained in their personal luggage, Case 278/82 *Rewe-Handelsgesellschaft Nord mbH and Rewe-Markt Herbert Kureit* v. *Hauptzollamter Flensburg, Itzehoe, and Lübeck-West* [1984] ECR 721, 763.

[65] Joined Cases C–64 & 65/96 *Land Nordrhein-Westfalen* v. *Kari Uecker* (15 June 1997). See, generally, regarding the practical problems of realizing Union Citizenship, Second report on Citizenship of the Union, COM(97)230.

[66] Arts. 48–51 EC govern the free movement of workers, Arts 52–58 EC freedom of establishment, and Arts. 59–66 EC free movement of services.

[67] See, e.g., H.-U.J. d'Oliveira, n.30 above, 132 and 147.

[68] See, in connection with Dirs. 90/364 (OJ 1990 L180/26) and 90/365 (OJ 1990 L180/28), Case T–66/95 *Hedwig Kuchlenz-Winter* v. *EC Commission* [1997] ECR II–637, II–656.

to perpetuate the distinction in Union law between rights of entry and residence in other Member States and such rights in one's own Member State.

9.2.3 Frontier Checks and Internal Controls

Beneficiaries of free movement may be subject to frontier checks on entry into a Member State and to internal controls on their residence there.

Frontier Checks

When travelling within the Union, beneficiaries of freedom of movement may, in practice, be subjected to systematic frontier checks.[69] However, these checks may not go beyond the requirement that a valid passport or identity card is produced.[70] Thus, for example, rights of entry cannot be made dependent on statements as to the purpose and duration of the stay and the financial means available for it.[71]

Abolition of such checks within the Union generally is envisaged in Article 73i(a) of the EC Treaty, as introduced by the Treaty of Amsterdam.[72] It provides for the Council to adopt measures aimed at ensuring the free movement of persons in accordance with Article 7a. These measures are to ensure the absence of any controls on persons, be they Union Citizens or third-state nationals, when crossing borders within the Union. They are to be adopted in conjunction with flanking measures regarding external border controls, asylum, and immigration, and measures to prevent and combat crime. In addition, the Council may adopt other measures regarding asylum,[73] immigration, and safeguarding the rights of third-state nationals;[74] measures regarding judicial co-operation in civil matters;[75] measures to encourage and strengthen administrative co-operation;[76] and police and judicial co-operation in criminal matters.[77]

---

[69] Note the checks which the ECJ found acceptable in Case 321/87 *EC Commission* v. *Belgium: frontier checks* [1989] ECR 997.

[70] Case 157/79 *R.* v. *Stanislaus Pieck* [1980] ECR 2171.

[71] Case C–68/89 *EC Commission* v. *Netherlands: frontier controls* [1991] ECR I–2637.

[72] OJ 1997 C340/1.

[73] Cf. the Convention determining the state responsible for examining applications for asylum lodged in one of the Member States of the EC (OJ 1997 C254/1); and Joint Position 96/196 (OJ 1996 L63/2) on the definition of the term "refugee" in the Geneva Convention relating to the status of refugees. The desire to adopt such formal measures is said to be a manifestation of resistance to refugees. See T. Hoogenboom, "The Position of Those who are not Nationals of a Community Member State" in A. Cassese, A. Clapham, and J.H.H. Weiler (eds), *Human Fundamental Rights and the European Community: Methods of Protection* (Nomos, Baden-Baden, 1991), 351–422, 377. Cf. the Resolution of 25 Sept. 1995 (OJ 1995 C262/1) on burden-sharing with regard to the admission and residence of displaced persons on a temporary basis.

[74] Art. 73i(b) EC.   [75] Art. 73i(c) EC.   [76] Art. 73i(d) EC.

[77] Art. 73i(e) EC. This co-operation is to be achieved in accordance with Arts. K.1–14 TEU. See, e.g., Joint Action 97/339 (OJ 1997 L147/1) with regard to co-operation on law and order andsecurity; Resolution on preventing and restraining football hooliganism through the exchange of experience, exclusion from stadiums, and media policy (OJ 1997 C193/1); and Convention on the fight against

However, the United Kingdom may maintain frontier controls, to verify the rights of the persons concerned under Union law and to determine whether other persons should be granted permission to enter this country. Corresponding controls may be applied to persons travelling from the United Kingdom to other Member States. Similar controls may apply in the case of Ireland.[78] These exceptional arrangements for the United Kingdom and Ireland are designed to preserve the common travel area between these two Member States.

Internal Controls

Beneficiaries of freedom of movement may be subject to internal controls within Member States. Thus they may be required to obtain the residence permit prescribed by Union legislation.[79] Charges for any such residence document must not exceed those payable when an identity card is issued to a national of the Member State concerned.[80] They may also be required to report their presence on a local population register[81] or to register with the police.[82]

However, a residence permit is simply declaratory of Union law rights. Hence, failure to comply with such requirements does not in itself justify denial of the rights entailed by freedom of movement.[83] Similarly, exercise of this freedom cannot be made dependent on registration with the social security authorities.[84] Moreover, the right of residence must be recognised, even on the basis of an identity card which does not allow the holder to leave the territory of the Member State which issued it.[85]

9.2.4 Family Members

Members of the family of a worker exercising his freedom of movement are entitled to enter and reside with him and have the right to take up employment.[86] Regulation 1612/68[87] defines members of the family of a worker as:

corruption involving EC officials of officials of Member States (OJ 1997 L195/1); Convention relating to extradition between Member States (OJ 1996 C313/11).

[78] Protocol on the application of certain aspects of Art. 14 EC to the UK and Ireland.
[79] Case 8/77 *Concetta Sagulo, Gennaro Brenca, and Addelmadjid Bakhouche* [1977] ECR 1495.
[80] Case 344/95 *EC Commission* v. *Belgium: residence restrictions* [1997] ECR I–1035.
[81] Case 48/75 *Jean Noël Royer* [1976] ECR 497.
[82] Case 118/75 *Lynn Watson and Alessandro Belmann* [1976] ECR 1185. Note also the controls which the ECJ found acceptable in Case C–265/88 *Lothar Messner* [1989] ECR 4209.
[83] See, e.g., Joined Cases 389 & 390/87 *G.B.C. Echternach and A. Moritz* v. *Netherlands Minister for Education and Science* [1989] ECR 723, 755.
[84] Case C–363/89 *Danielle Roux* v. *Belgium* [1991] ECR I–273.
[85] Case C–376/89 *Panagiotis Giagounidis* [1991] ECR I–1069.
[86] Art. 11 of Reg. 1612/68 (JO 1968 L257/2). See also Case 131/85 *Emir Gül* v. *Regierungspräsident Düsseldorf* [1986] ECR 1573.
[87] JO 1968 L257/2, Art. 10(1).

- his spouse[88] and descendants who are under the age of 21 years or are dependants; and
- dependent relatives in the ascending line of the worker and his spouse.[89]

If such persons lack the nationality of a Member State, they may be required to obtain a visa in order to accompany a primary beneficiary of freedom of movement. According to Directive 68/360,[90] "every facility" for obtaining the visa must be granted by the Member State concerned. This obligation, however, is uncertain in its terms and may not always have been taken seriously by Member States.[91]

They do not lose their derived right of residence merely because the person with primary rights separates from them[92] or because they have recourse to public funds.[93] Moreover, although a worker must provide housing for his dependants, this requirement must not lead to discrimination,[94] and the same housing assistance must be provided as in the case of nationals of the host Member State.[95] On the other hand, Union legislation does not preserve a right of residence for them where the primary beneficiary dies,[96] unless the latter has acquired the right to remain under Regulation 1251/70.[97]

9.3 Equality of Treatment

Article 48(2) of the EC Treaty provides that freedom of movement for workers shall entail the abolition of any discrimination based on nationality

---

[88] Cf., regarding unmarried "partners", Case 59/85 *Netherlands* v. *Ann Florence Reed* [1986] ECR 1283.

[89] The Commission proposed an amendment of this provision, so as to broaden its scope (proposal of 11 Jan. 1989 (OJ 1989 C100/6) for a reg. amending Reg. 1612/68).

[90] JO 1968 L257/13, Art. 3(2). See, similarly, regarding self-employed persons, Art. 3(2) of Dir. 73/148 (OJ 1973 L172/14) on the abolition of restrictions on movement and residence within the Community for nationals of Member States with regard to establishment and the provision of services.

[91] The Commission belatedly sought to secure respect for this obligation (Seventh annual report on Commission monitoring of the application of Community law, COM(90)288, 24). In practice, problems remain. See Action plan for the free movement of workers, COM(97)586.

[92] Case 267/83 *Aissatou Diatta* v. *Berlin Land* [1985] ECR 574, 590. The English High Court has also taken the view that divorce may not automatically lead to loss of such a right. See *R.* v. *Home Secretary, ex p. Sandhu* [1982] 2 CMLR 553.

[93] Case 316/85 *Centre Public d'Aide Sociale, Courcelles* v. *Marie-Christine Lebon* [1987] ECR 2811, 2838.

[94] Art. 10(3) of Reg. 1612/68 (JO 1968 L257/2). See also Case 249/86 *EC Commission* v. *Germany: housing requirements* [1989] ECR 1263.

[95] Art. 9 of Reg. 1612/68 (JO 1968 L257/2).

[96] The Commission proposed amendment of Art. 11 of Reg. 1612/68, to provide that their rights continue after the death of the primary beneficiary or dissolution of the marriage (OJ 1989 C100/6).

[97] JO 1970 L142/1.

between workers of the Member States as regards employment, remuneration, and other conditions of work and employment.

9.3.1 Working Conditions and Social Benefits

Equality of treatment regarding working conditions and social benefits is required by Article 48(2) of the Treaty and Regulation 1612/68.[98] The requirements have been broadly interpreted in practice.

Working Conditions

Article 48(2) of the Treaty and Regulation 1612/68[99] require equality of treatment as regards access to employment and pay and conditions of employment. This requirement extends beyond state measures and also concerns discriminatory clauses in collective or individual agreements on employment.[100] It applies, for example, to the length of employment contracts,[101] conditions of dismissal,[102] calculation of seniority,[103] separation allowances,[104] reimbursement of overpaid tax,[105] and tax deductions in respect of pension contributions.[106] It also applies to vocational training and retraining.[107]

Again, Article 8(1) of the Regulation prohibits discrimination regarding membership of trades unions and exercise of the rights attaching thereto.[108] This prohibition extends beyond the bounds of trade-union organisations in the strict sense. It concerns participation in other bodies which perform similar functions, as regards the defence and representation of workers' interests.[109]

Not only is formal discrimination based on nationality prohibited but also differential treatment based on other criteria which have discriminatory effect. In particular, Article 3(1) of the Regulation refers to national measures which are applicable irrespective of nationality. Where their exclusive or principal aim or effect is to keep nationals of other Member States away from the employment offered, they are prohibited. Discrimination may be found,

---

[98] JO 1968 L257/2.   [99] *Ibid.* Arts. 1–9.   [100] *Ibid.*, Art. 7(4).

[101] Joined Cases C–259, 331 & 332/91 *Pilar Allué* v. *Università degli Studi di Venezia* [1993] ECR I–4309; and Case C–272/92 *Maria Chiara Spotti* v. *Freistaat Bayern* [1993] ECR I–5185.

[102] Case 44/72 *Pieter Massman* v. *M. Rosskamp* [1972] ECR 1243.

[103] Case 15/69 *Württembergische Milchverwertung-Südmilch-AG* v. *Salvatore Ugliola* [1969] ECR 363.

[104] Case 152/73 *Giovanni Maria Sotgiu* v. *Deutsche Bundespost* [1974] ECR 153, 163–4.

[105] Case C–175/88 *Klaus Biehl* v. *Administration des Contributions du Grand-Duché de Luxembourg* [1990] ECR I–1779.

[106] Case C–204/90 *Hans-Martin Bachmann* v. *Belgium* [1992] ECR I–249, I–280.

[107] Art. 7(3) of Reg. 1612/68 (JO 1968 L257/2).

[108] A. Evans, "European Community Law and the Trade Union and Related Rights of Migrant Workers" [1979] *ICLQ* 354–66.

[109] Case C–213/90 *ASTI (Association de Soutien aux Travailleurs Immigrés)* v. *Chambre des Employés Privés* [1991] ECR I–3507, I–3530.

even where 25 per cent of the persons adversely affected are nationals of the host Member State.[110] However, conditions relating to linguistic knowledge required by reason of the nature of the work may be permissible.[111] Thus language conditions necessary for the performance of the duties of a post and conditions designed to promote the national language may be covered.[112]

Social Benefits

Article 7(2) of Regulation 1612/68[113] requires equality of treatment in relation to social benefits. Such benefits include, for example, birth and maternity allowances,[114] interest-free loans to families in respect of newly born children,[115] family benefits,[116] handicap allowances,[117] a minimum subsistence allowance,[118] unemployment benefit for young persons,[119] an old-age benefit for those lacking entitlement to a pension under the national social security system for old persons,[120] a guaranteed minimum income for old persons,[121] education of dependent children,[122] railway discounts,[123] a scholarship to study abroad,[124] use of one's own language in court proceedings,[125] and registration of pleasure boats.[126] Tax concessions are also covered.[127] In addition, special arrangements for tuition of the children of the worker are made.[128]

---

[110] Case 33/88 *Pilar Allué and Carmel Mary Coonan* v. *Università degli Studi di Venezia* [1989] ECR 1591.

[111] Art. 3(1) of Reg. 1612/68 (JO 1968 L257/2).

[112] Case 378/87 *Anita Groener* v. *Minister for Education and the City of Dublin Vocational Education Committee* [1989] ECR 3967, 3993.

[113] JO 1968 L257/2.

[114] Case C–111/91 *EC Commission* v. *Luxembourg: childbirth and maternity allowances* [1993] ECR I–817.

[115] Case 65/81 *Francesco Reina and Letizia Reina* v. *Landeskredietbank Baden-Württemberg* [1982] ECR 33.

[116] Case C–266/95 *Pascual Merino Garcia* v. *Bundesanstalt für Arbeit* (12 June 1997).

[117] Case 63/76 *Vito Inzirillo* v. *Caisse d'Allocations Familiales de l'Arrondissement de Lyon* [1976] ECR 2057.

[118] Case 249/83 *Vera Hoeckx* v. *Openbaar Centrum voor Maatschappelijk Welzijn Kalmthout* [1985] ECR 973.

[119] Case 94/84 *Office National de l'Emploi* v. *Joszej Deak* [1985] ECR 1873.

[120] Case 157/84 *Maria Frascogna* v. *Caisse des Dépôts et Consignations* [1985] ECR 1739.

[121] Case 261/83 *Carmela Castelli* v. *Office National des Pensions pour Travailleurs Salariés (ONPTS)* [1984] ECR 3199.

[122] Joined Cases 389 & 390/87 *GBC Echternach and A. Moritz* v. *Netherlands Minister for Education and Science* [1989] ECR 723.

[123] Case 32/75 *Anita Cristini* v. *Société Nationale des Chemins de Fer Français* [1975] ECR 1085.

[124] Case 235/87 *Annunziata Matteuci* v. *Communauté Française of Belgium and Commissariat Général aux Relations Internationales de la Communauté Française de Belgique* [1988] ECR 5589.

[125] Case 137/84 *Ministère Public* v. *Robert Heinrich Maria Mutsch* [1985] ECR 2681.

[126] Case C–151/96 *EC Commission* v. *Ireland: registration of vessels other than fishing vessels* (12 June 1997).

[127] See, regarding taxation of non-residents, Case C–279/93 *Finanzamt Köln-Alstadt* v. *Roland Schumacker* [1995] ECR I–225.

[128] Dir. 77/486 (OJ 1977 L199/32) on the education of the children of migrant workers.

There may be important implications for national policy making. For example, in *Casagrande*[129] an Italian national, who was a child of an Italian worker in Germany, had been refused an education grant there. The Court of Justice observed that competence in the field of education and training policy had not as such been transferred to the Union institutions. However, exercise of those competences which had been transferred could not be affected by national measures implementing national education or training policy. Hence, such measures could not interfere with the equality of treatment enjoyed by migrant workers and their dependants, and the latter could not be denied education grants available to nationals of the host Member State.[130]

In short, as the Court of Justice puts it, Article 48 requires equal treatment in relation to social advantages where two conditions are met. First, they must be advantages which are generally granted to national workers because of their objective status as workers or their residence on the national territory. Secondly, they must be advantages the extension of which to workers from other Member States seems likely to facilitate their movement within the Union. The equality requirement does not, however, apply to advantages "essentially linked to the performance of military service".[131]

Such practice originates principally[132] in efforts to liberalise the movement of persons as factors of production[133] and to prevent "social dumping". According to the Court, "the purpose of the [relevant] provisions is to assist in the abolition of all obstacles to the establishment of a common market in which the nationals of a Member State may move freely within the territory of those Member States in order to pursue their economic activities".[134] At the same time, also according to the Court, Article 48(2) "has the effect . . . in accordance with Article 117 of the Treaty,[135] of guaranteeing to the Member State's own nationals that they should not suffer the unfavourable consequences which could result from the offer or acceptance by nationals of other Member States of conditions of employment or remuneration less advantageous than those obtaining under national law".[136]

In the evolution of its case law, however, the Court is said to have shown a

---

[129] Case 9/74 *Casagrande* v. *Landeshauptstadt München* [1974] ECR 773.

[130] *Ibid.*, 779.

[131] Case 207/78 *Ministère Public* v. *Gilbert Even and Office National des Pensions pour Travailleurs Salariés* [1979] ECR 2019, 2034; and Case C–315/94 *Peter de Vos* v. *Stadt Bielefeld* [1996] ECR I–1417, I–1441.

[132] Though the evolution of free movement as an element of Union Citizenship may have been anticipated by some. See C.F. Ophuls, "La Rélance européenne" (1958) *European Yearbook* 3–15, 13; and Presidenza del Consiglio dei Ministri, *Comunità economica europea* (Servizi informazioni, Rome, 1958), 106.

[133] Comité intergouvernemental créé par la Conférence de Messine, *Rapport des chefs de délégation aux ministres des affaires étrangères* (Secretariat of the Committee, Brussels, 1956), 89–91.

[134] Case 298/84 *Iorio* v. *Azienda Autonoma delle Ferrovie dello Stato* [1986] ECR 247, 255.

[135] Sect. 21.4.1 below.

[136] Case 167/73 *EC Commission* v. *France: merchant seamen* [1974] ECR 359, 373.

"social" tendency marked by the choice, in case of doubt, of the most favorable interpretation for the worker.[137] Hence, Article 48 is interpreted not merely as seeking elimination of obstacles to the free movement of persons arising from inequalities which place migrants at a disadvantage in comparison with nationals of the host Member State.[138] It is also interpreted as requiring that individuals established in one Member State should have free access to employment in other Member States[139] and as opposing any national measures which may be unfavourable to individuals wishing to extend their activities beyond the territory of a single Member State.[140]

Therefore, prohibited measures are not only those which deny national treatment to persons moving between Member States but also those which disadvantage such movement in comparison with remaining at home.[141] For example, the obligation to cancel a policy taken out with an insurer in one Member State in order to take advantage of the tax deductions in respect of contributions available in another Member State, when the person concerned considers continuation of that policy to be in his best interests, is prohibited because of the procedures and expenditure involved.[142] The objection that migrant workers obtain more advantageous treatment than workers who have never left their own country is rejected by the Court, since the situations of the two categories of workers are not comparable.[143]

9.3.2 Direct Elections to the European Parliament

Member States were left free by Article 7(1) of the Act on Direct Elections[144] to prohibit resident nationals of other Member States from participating in elections to the European Parliament held on their territories. Member States were also left free by the Act to deny their own nationals resident abroad the opportunity to participate in these elections held on their territories. Consequently, Union Citizens resident in a Member State other than their

---

[137] Capotorti AG in Case 55/77 *Maris* v. *Rijksdienst voor Werknemerspensioenen* [1977] ECR 2327, 2338.

[138] Trabucchi AG in Case 66/74 *Alfonso Farrauto* v. *Bau-Berufsgenossenschaft* [1975] ECR 157, 168.

[139] Case 298/84 *Iorio* v. *Azienda Autonoma delle Ferrovie dello Stato* [1986] ECR 247, 255; and Case C–415/93 *Union Royale Belge des Sociétés de Football Association* v. *Jean-Marc Bosman* [1995] ECR I–5040, I–5068.

[140] Case 143/87 *Christopher Stanton and SA Belge d'Assurances l'Etoile 1905* v. *Inasti (Institute National d'Assurances Sociales pour Travailleurs Indépendents)* [1988] ECR 3877, 3894; and Joined Cases 154 & 155/87 *Rijksinstituut voor de Sociale Verzekeringen der Zelfstendingen* v. *Heinrich Wolf and Microtherm Europe NV* [1988] ECR 3897, 3912.

[141] See, e.g., Case C–19/92 *Dieter Kraus* v. *Land Baden-Württemberg* [1993] ECR I–1663.

[142] Case C–204/90 *Hans-Martin Bachmann* v. *Belgium* [1992] ECR I–249, I–280. Cf. the Proposal for a dir. on safeguarding the supplementary pension rights of employed and self-employed persons moving within the EU, COM(97)486.

[143] Case 22/77 *Fonds National de Retraite des Ouvriers Mineurs* v. *Giovanni Mura* [1977] ECR 1699, 1707.

[144] OJ 1976 L278/5.

own might be denied the opportunity to participate in these elections at all.

Article 8b(2) of the Treaty now provides that every Union Citizen residing in a Member State of which he is not a national has the right to vote and stand as a candidate in elections to the European Parliament, subject to detailed arrangements to be adopted by the Council. However, the Treaty also attaches significance to the "bond of nationality"[145] lying at the heart of the nation state,[146] and the implication is that major differences between Union Citizens may remain.[147] In particular, the implication is that nationals of different Member States are not comparable[148] for the purposes of enjoyment of political rights and may thus be treated differently in respect of enjoyment of such rights.[149] Certainly, Article 8b(2) of the Treaty allows for some differentiation regarding participation in direct elections "where warranted by problems specific to a Member State".

In implementation of this provision Directive 93/109[150] has been enacted.[151] In the preamble to this measure, the right to vote and stand as a candidate in elections to the European Parliament in the Member State of residence is described as an instance of the application of the equality principle and a corollary of the right to move and reside freely.[152] Hence, nationals of other Member States must be subject to the same conditions as nationals of the host Member State for participation in such elections.[153] To preclude effective discrimination, Article 5 of the Directive provides that where a national of a Member State must have completed a minimum period of residence in his own Member State to be eligible to vote there, an equivalent period of residence for "Community voters" in another Member State will suffice. On the other hand, requirements of a minimum period of residence in order to vote in a particular locality are unaffected by this

---

[145] Case 149/79 *EC Commission v. Belgium: employment in the public service* [1980] ECR 3883, 3900; [1982] ECR 1845, 1851.

[146] Cf. the idea of "l'obligation mutuelle du souverain au subject" in Jean Bodin, *Les Six livres de la République* (ed. J.M. Franklin, Cambridge University Press, Cambridge, 1972), Bk 1, chap. 6.

[147] Cf. Case 207/78 *Ministère Public v. Gilbert Even and Office National des Pensions pour Travailleurs Salariés* [1979] ECR 2019, 2034.

[148] Cf. the early view that equality of treatment was only required under the ECSC Treaty in respect of economic actors in a comparable position (Case 9/57 *Chambre Syndicale de la Sidérurgie Française v. ECSC High Authority* [1957–8] ECR 319, 330).

[149] Cf. the view that it was necessary, where doubts existed, to reinforce the criterion of comparability by comparing the result to which it led with that intended by the ECSC Treaty in Joined Cases 7 & 9/54 *Groupement des Industries Sidérurgiques Luxembourgeoises v. ECSC High Authority* [1954–6] ECR 175, 195.

[150] Laying down detailed arrangements for the exercise of the right to vote and stand as a candidate in elections to the European Parliament for Union Citizens residing in a Member State of which they are not nationals (OJ 1993 L329/34).

[151] The participation rate by Union Citizens resident in another Member State may be very low. See Voting rights of EU Citizens living in a Member State of which they are not nationals, COM(97)731.

[152] Dir., 3rd recital in the preamble.

[153] *Ibid.*, 6th recital. See also the explanatory memorandum to the proposal, COM(93)534, 8.

provision. Nationals of the Member State concerned are more likely to be able to meet such requirements than nationals of other Member States. As a result, the latter may not be as free to participate in such elections if they move to another Member State as if they stay in their own.

9.3.3 Local Elections

Article 8b(1) of the Treaty provides that every Union Citizen residing in a Member State of which he is not a national has the right to vote and stand as a candidate in local government elections in that Member State under the same conditions as nationals of that Member State. These rights are to be exercised subject to detailed arrangements to be made by the Council. The arrangements may provide for derogations "where warranted by problems specific to a Member State". This provision has been implemented by Directive 94/80.[154]

9.4 Exceptions

Exceptions from the requirements of free movement may be permissible on public interest grounds and in relation to employment in the public service.

9.4.1 Public Interest Exceptions

Article 48(3) of the Treaty provides that rights of entry and residence are subject to limitations justified on grounds of public policy, public security, or public health.

Public policy is the expression adopted in the English language version of the Treaty to denote the civil law concept of *ordre public*. In the context of Union law, however, it has a more restricted meaning than in national law.[155] In particular, Directive 64/221[156] introduced restrictions on its scope. Thus public policy measures may not be employed for economic purposes.[157] They must be based on the personal conduct of the individual concerned,[158] and they may not be based solely on a previous criminal conviction[159] or on expiry of the passport or identity card on the basis of which entry was gained.[160]

---

[154] Laying down detailed arrangements for the exercise of the right to vote and stand as a candidate in municipal elections by Union Citizens residing in a Member State of which they are not nationals (OJ 1994 L368/38).

[155] Cf. A. Evans, "*Ordre Public* in French Immigration Law" [1980] *Public Law* 132–49.

[156] On the co-ordination of special measures concerning the movement and residence of foreign nationals which are justified on grounds of public policy, public security, or public health (JO 1964 850). It was extended by Dir. 72/194 (JO 1972 L121/32) to persons staying on after having been employed in another Member State.

[157] Art. 2(2) of Dir. 64/221 (JO 1964 850).   [158] *Ibid.*, Art. 3(1).   [159] *Ibid.*, Art. 3(2).
[160] *Ibid.*, Art. 3(3).

The Court of Justice in a series of rulings has further restricted the scope of public policy. As a result, a person benefiting from free movement may only be excluded or expelled from a Member State other than his own where his own conduct[161] constitutes a genuine and sufficiently serious threat to public policy[162] affecting a fundamental interest of society.[163] Moreover, his exclusion or expulsion must be "necessary in a democratic society",[164] and effective measures must be adopted against nationals of the Member State concerned who engage in the same conduct.[165]

The Directive also limits the diseases or disabilities which may justify exclusion on public health grounds and lists them in an annex.[166] Moreover, it is stipulated that the contracting of a disease or development of a disability in another Member State does not justify expulsion.[167]

At the same time, procedural safeguards for persons affected by restrictions on their entry or residence are laid down by the Directive.[168] In particular, reasons must be given for their exclusion from a Member State, unless security would be threatened.[169] Fifteen days notice must also be given of a refusal to issue or renew a residence permit or of an expulsion, unless the matter is urgent.[170] Moreover, the same legal remedies must be available as are available to nationals of the Member State concerned when challenging administrative acts.[171] Finally, an opinion must be obtained from a body independent of the one which decides to impose the restrictions on entry or residence.[172]

9.4.2 Public Service Exception

Article 48(4) of the Treaty states that the provisions of this Article shall not apply to employment in the public service. The Court of Justice has insisted that the scope of Article 48(4) must be strictly construed and, more particularly, cannot be dependent simply on domestic law distinctions between public and private bodies. Accordingly, it only covers posts which are typical

[161] Case 67/74 *Carmelo Angelo Bonsignore* v. *Oberstadtdirektor der Stadt Köln* [1975] ECR 297, 307.

[162] Case 56/75 *Roland Rutili* v. *Minister of the Interior* [1975] ECR 1219, 1231.

[163] Case 30/77 *R.* v. *Pierre Bouchereau* [1977] ECR 1999, 2014.

[164] Case 36/75 *Roland Rutili* v. *Minister of the Interior* [1975] ECR 1219, 1232.

[165] Joined Cases 115 & 116/81 *Rezguia Adoui* v. *Belgium and City of Liège; Dominique Cornouaille* v. *Belgium* [1982] ECR 1665, 1708.

[166] Art. 4(1) of Dir. 64/221 (JO 1964 850).

[167] *Ibid.*, Art. 4(2).

[168] *Ibid.*, Arts. 5–9. See also Case 98/79 *Josette Pecastaing* v. *Belgium* [1980] ECR 691; and Joined Cases C–65 & 111/95 *R.* v. *Secretary of State for the Home Dept, ex p. Mann Singh Shingara* (17 June 1997).

[169] Art. 6 of Dir. 64/221 (JO 1964 850).   [170] *Ibid.*, Art. 7.

[171] *Ibid.*, Art. 8. See also Joined Cases C–65 & 111/95 *R.* v. *Secretary of State for the Home Dept., ex p. Marin Singh Shingaru* (17 June 1997).

[172] Art. 9 of Dir. 64/221 (JO 1964 850). See also Joined Cases C–65 & 111/95 *R.* v. *Secretary of State for the Home Dept., ex p. Marin Singh Shingaru* (17 June 1997).

of the specific activities of the public service. These are posts whose holders exercise powers conferred by public law and have responsibility for safeguarding the general interests of the state.[173] The posts of a nurse in a public hospital,[174] a trainee teacher,[175] or a foreign language assistant at a university[176] are not covered.

More particularly, Article 8(1) of Regulation 1612/68[177] limits the equality of treatment guaranteed as regards access to trades union posts and membership of other bodies representing workers within the undertaking. It provides that this equality does not apply to the holding of offices "governed by public law" or to participation in the management of bodies "governed by public law". In including this clause in the Regulation, the Council apparently assumed that Article 48(4) of the Treaty had a scope broader than that subsequently defined by the Court of Justice. The clause was not part of the original Commission draft, and the French Government is thought to have been particularly insistent on its inclusion, because in France such politically important bodies as the Economic and Social Council contain trades union representatives.[178] Since, however, the clause extends beyond such bodies, it has been criticised as permitting undue restriction of migrant participation in trade union and related activity.[179]

In fact, it is far from clear that all public law offices and bodies covered by the terms of Article 8(1) of the Regulation fall under Article 48(4) of the Treaty. According to the established case law of the Court of Justice, ambiguous provisions of Union legislation are, wherever possible, to be given a construction consistent with Treaty provisions.[180] The implication is that Article 8(1) of the Regulation has to be strictly construed. In practice, the Court[181] and the Commission[182] seek to ensure that the limits of Article 48(4) of the Treaty are not exceeded in the operation of Article 8(1) of the Regulation.

---

[173] Case 149/79 *EC Commission* v. *Belgium: employment in the public service* [1980] ECR 3881, 3901 and [1982] ECR 1845, 1851.

[174] Case 307/84 *EC Commission* v. *France: nurses* [1986] ECR 1725.

[175] Case 66/85 *Deborah Lawrie-Blum* v. *Land Baden-Württemberg* [1986] ECR 2121.

[176] Case 33/88 *Pilar Allué and Carmel Mary Coonan* v. *Università degli Studi di Venezia* [1989] ECR 1591.

[177] JO 1968 L257/2.

[178] The Economic and Social Committee considers that a distinction should be made between such bodies and those concerned with work and vocational activity (Opinion of 30 Oct. 1976 (OJ 1976 C12/4) on the action programme in favour of migrant workers and their families, para. 7.6).

[179] Cf., regarding the need for a narrow interpretation, the European Parliament Resolution of 17 Jan. 1972 (JO 1972 C10/4) on the definition of the concepts of public service and public power in Member States and their consequences for the application of Arts. 48(4) and 55 EEC, para. 11.

[180] See, e.g., Case 220/83 *EC Commission* v. *France: coinsurance* [1986] ECR 3663, 3707.

[181] Case C–213/90 *ASTI (Association de Soutien aux Travailleurs Immigrés)* v. *Chambre des Employés Privés* [1991] ECR I–3507, I–3531.

[182] Free movement of persons and access to posts in the public administration of Member States: action of the Commission relating to the application of Art. 48(4) EEC (OJ 1988 C72/2).

9. 5 Mandatory Requirements

Measures restricting free movement may be justified on grounds of mandatory requirements. For example, national legislation may impose restrictions on a worker from another Member State who seeks to make misleading use of academic titles awarded outside the territory of the Member State concerned. According to the Court of Justice, it is a legitimate interest of the Member State to counter such abuse of freedom of movement. However, the restrictive measures must be proportionate to the needs of protecting this interest.[183]

9.6 Social Security

Article 51 of the EC Treaty states that the Council shall adopt such measures in the field of social security as are necessary to provide freedom of movement for workers. To this end, it shall make arrangements to secure for migrant workers and their dependants the aggregation of qualifying periods for benefits and the payment of benefits to persons resident in the territories of Member States. Harmonisation of the social security systems of Member States is not envisaged.[184] This provision has been implemented by Regulation 1408/71.[185]

9.6.1 Persons Covered

Regulation 1408/71[186] applies to employed[187] or self-employed persons[188] who are or have been subject to the legislation of one or more Member States and who are nationals of a Member State.[189] It also applies to the members of their families and their survivors, irrespective of their nationality.[190] Family members are defined by reference to national law.[191] However,

---

[183] Case C–19/92 *Dieter Kraus* v. *Land Baden-Württemberg* [1993] ECR I–1663, I–1697. Cf., regarding the interests of sport, Case C–415/93 *Union Royale Belge des Sociétés de Football Association ASBL* v. *Jean-Marc Bosmanm* [1995] ECR I–4921, I–5071.

[184] But cf. Rec. 92/441 (OJ 1992 L245/46) on common criteria concerning sufficient resources and social assistance in the national social protection systems.

[185] JO 1971 L149/2. It has been consolidated by Reg. 118/97 (OJ 1997 L28/1).

[186] *Ibid.*   [187] *Ibid.*, Art. 2(1).

[188] Reg. 1390/81 (OJ 1981 L143/1) extending Reg. 1408/71 to self-employed persons and members of their families.

[189] But see the benefits envisaged for TSNs in the proposal for a reg. amending Reg. 1408/71, COM(97)294. Cf. H. Verschueren, "EC Social Security Coordination Excluding Third Country Nationals: Still in Line with Fundamental Rights after the Gaygusuz Judgment?" (1997) 34 CMLRev. 991–1017.

[190] See also Rec. 21 of the Administrative Commission for Social Security for Migrant Workers (OJ 1997 C67/3) concerning the application of Reg. 1408/71 to unemployed persons accompanying their spouses employed in a Member State other than the competent state.

[191] Art. 1(f) of Reg. 1408/71 (JO 1971 L149/2).

freedom of movement must not be jeopardized by the definition.[192] In addition, stateless persons and refugees resident in the territory of a Member State as well as civil servants are covered.[193]

Such persons may benefit under the Regulation, if they are insured, compulsorily or on an optional basis, for one or more of the contingencies covered by the branches of a social security scheme for employed or self-employed persons.[194] Those who have been but are not now insured may also benefit.[195] They may even benefit in respect of work outside the Union.[196]

In principle, they are entitled to benefits under the social security legislation of the Member State where they are employed.[197] However, special rules apply to temporary workers, workers employed in two or more Member States, and frontier workers.[198] Moreover, unemployment benefits[199] and family benefits[200] may be payable to persons resident outside the competent Member State.

9.6.2 Benefits Covered

Regulation 1408/71[201] covers sickness and maternity benefits; invalidity benefits; old-age benefits; survivors' benefits; benefits in respect of accidents at work and occupational diseases; death grants; unemployment benefits;[202] and orphans' benefits.[203]

"Social and medical assistance" is excluded from the scope of the Regulation.[204] However, this exclusion is narrowly construed.[205] Moreover, in the case of Union Citizens employed in a Member State other than their own, such assistance may be covered by Article 7(2) of Regulation 1612/68.[206]

9.6.3 Equal Treatment

According to the Court of Justice, Regulation 1408/71[207] seeks to ensure that, as a consequence of exercising free movement, workers do not lose the advantages in the field of social security which are guaranteed to them by the

---

[192] Case 7/75 *Mr and Mrs F.* v. *Belgium* [1975] ECR 679, 690–1.

[193] Art. 2(1) and (3) of Reg. 1408/71 (JO 1971 L149/2).

[194] *Ibid.*, Art. 1(a)(i).   [195] *Ibid.*, Art. 2(1).

[196] Joined Cases 82 & 103/86 *Giancarlo Laborero and Francesca Sabato* v. *Office de Sécurité Sociale d'Outre-Mer* [1987] ECR 3401, 3428.

[197] Art. 13(2)(a) of Reg. 1408/71 (JO 1971 L149/2).   [198] *Ibid.*, Art. 14.   [199] *Ibid.*, Art. 69.

[200] *Ibid.*, Art. 73(1).   [201] *Ibid.*   [202] *Ibid.*, Art. 4(1).

[203] *Ibid.*, Art. 3(1). See also Case C–131/96 *Carlos Mora Romero* v. *Landesversicherungsanstalt Rheinproving* [25 June 1997].

[204] JO 1971 L149/2, Art. 4(4).

[205] Case 7/75 *Mr and Mrs F.* v. *Belgium* [1975] ECR 679, regarding a special grant for the handicapped.

[206] JO 1968 L257/2. See sect. 9.3.1 above.   [207] JO 1971 L149/2.

laws of a single Member State.[208] To this end, discrimination, including "reverse discrimination" against nationals of the Member State concerned,[209] is prohibited.[210] For example, where a benefit, or a higher rate of benefit, is payable to such workers in respect of family members, the national authorities must take account of such members, even if they are resident in another Member State.[211] If the national authorities disregard family members resident in another Member State, they effectively discriminate against workers from other Member States. Effective discrimination is present, because such workers are more likely than nationals of the Member State concerned to have family members elsewhere in the Union.

9.6.4 Aggregation

Article 51 of the Treaty provides for the aggregation, for the purpose of acquiring and retaining the right to benefit and of calculating the amount of benefit, of all periods taken into account under the laws of the several countries in which an individual may have worked. This provision thus envisages aggregation of social security benefits in the case of migrant workers, even though it is not clear that non-aggregation would entail discrimination between migrants and nationals of the host Member State. In particular, aggregation is to take place in the case of sickness and maternity benefits,[212] invalidity,[213] old-age and death pensions,[214] death grants,[215] unemployment benefits,[216] and family benefits and allowances.[217]

While no overlapping of benefits is to result,[218] benefits accruing under the Regulation must not be less than those which would result from national law alone.[219] More generally, the Court has tended to interpret Regulation 1408/71[220] in such a way as to maximise the benefits to which claimants are entitled.[221] The premise for such practice is said to be that the Treaty looks at people as human beings, with the ordinary concerns of human beings, rather than simply as economic factors of production.[222]

---

[208] Case 254/84 *G.J.J. De Jong* v. *Bestuur van de Sociale Verzekeringsbank* [1986] ECR 671, 682.

[209] Case 1/78 *Patrick Christopher Kenny* v. *Insurance Officer* [1978] ECR 1489.

[210] Art. 3(1) of Reg. 1408/71 (JO 1971 L149/2).

[211] *Ibid.*, Art. 23, regarding sickness and maternity benefit; Art. 68 (*ibid.*), regarding unemployment benefit; and Art. 73 (*ibid.*), regarding family benefits. See, similarly, in the case of the self-employed, Joined Cases C–4 & 5/95 *Fritz Stöber and José Manuel Piosa Pereira* v. *Bundesanstalt für Arbeit* [1997] ECR I–511, I–546.

[212] Art. 18(1) of Reg. 1408/71 (JO 1971 L149/2).   [213] *Ibid.*, Art. 38.   [214] *Ibid.*, Art. 45.

[215] *Ibid.*, Art. 64.   [216] *Ibid.*, Art. 67.   [217] *Ibid.*, Art. 72.   [218] *Ibid.*, Art. 12(1).

[219] Case 112/76 *Renato Manzioni* v. *Fonds National de Retraite des Ouvriers Mineurs* [1977] ECR 1647.

[220] JO 1971 L149/2.

[221] See, e.g., Case 7/75 *Mr and Mrs F.* v. *Belgium* [1975] ECR 679; and Case 24/75 *Teresa and Silvana Petroni* v. *Office National des Pensions pour Travailleurs Salariés (ONPTS)* [1975] ECR 1149.

[222] AG Trabucchi in Case 7/75 *Mr and Mrs F.* v. *Belgium* [1975] ECR 679, 696.

9.7 Harmonisation

Reliance has been placed on the prohibition of discrimination rather than harmonisation of working conditions, such harmonisation being treated as a matter of social policy.[223] However, harmonisation necessary for the elimination of frontier controls on movement within the Union is envisaged.[224]

Special legislation has also been adopted regarding "posted" workers,[225] to ensure for such persons equality of treatment in the Member State to which they are posted.[226] Such a worker is one who, for a limited period, carries out his work in the territory of a Member State other than the one in which he normally works.[227] The legislation covers both Union Citizens and third-state nationals. Undertakings established in a third state are covered as well as those established in a Member State.[228] It is stipulated that the former must not be given more favourable treatment than the latter.[229]

9.8 Workers from Third States

Article 48(1) of the EC Treaty refers to freedom of movement for "workers of Member States". While this expression requires some link between a beneficiary of this freedom and a Member State, it does not appear necessarily to exclude third-state nationals. Hence, the Treaty may provide a basis for the development of rules determining those third-state nationals who have a sufficient link with a Member State to enjoy freedom of movement within the Union.[230] Certainly, Article 48(3), which confers no rights on job-seekers, may constitute a possible basis for liberalisation of movement by such persons.

However, Union practice seeks to treat third-state nationals separately from Union Citizens. Such separation may be problematic, particularly because of the derived rights which third-state nationals may enjoy under Union law.

9.8.1 Separate Treatment

Nationality law was chosen by the Union legislature as a substitute for common rules regarding immigration from third states.[231] Presumably, it

---

[223] Sect. 21.4.1 below.   [224] Sect. 9.2.3 above

[225] Dir. 96/71 (OJ 1997 L18/1) concerning the posting of workers in the framework of the provision of services.

[226] *Ibid.*, Art. 3.   [227] *Ibid.*, Art. 2(1).   [228] *Ibid.*, Art. 1(1).

[229] *Ibid.*, Art. 1(4). See, generally, P. Davies, "Posted Workers: Single Market or Protection of National Labour Law Systems" (1997) 34 *CMLRev.* 571–602.

[230] Academic research is said to have shown that extending free movement within the Union to cover TSNs would be unlikely to cause significant immigration flows having an economically disruptive effect. See T. Hoogenboom, "The Position of Those who are not Nationals of a Community Member State" in A. Cassese, A. Clapham, and J.H.H. Weiler (eds), n.20 above, 351–422, 359.

[231] See, e.g., A. Evans, "Nationals of Third Countries and the Treaty on European Union" [1994] EJIL 199–219.

was supposed to operate analogously to rules of origin within a free trade area for goods.[232] The separate treatment of Union Citizens and third-state nationals which is entailed may be claimed to have support in the Treaty. According to the Commission, the wording of Article 49 of the Treaty "militates against" extension of Regulation 1612/68[233] to cover nationals of third states.[234] However, Article 49 does not mention nationality as a condition for enjoyment of free movement.

At the same time, if a Member State may unilaterally alter its nationality law, such law may not perform the role envisaged for it. Steps are now being taken towards adoption in Union law of common rules regarding movement between third states and the Union. Indeed, effective rules of this kind are seen as a precondition for removal of border controls within the Union.[235] However, the effectiveness of the rules may be undermined by reliance on the nationality criterion for determining their applicability. In particular, insofar as Member States may alter their nationality law, they may thereby vary the persons to whom such rules are to apply. Equally, insofar as a Member State may employ a different definition of its nationality for Union law purposes from that employed for other purposes, persons having a right of entry and residence in the Member State concerned may be subject to control of their entry and residence elsewhere in the Union.[236]

9.8.2 "Community Priority"

Separate treatment of Union citizens and third-state nationals is accompanied by provision for "Community priority" for the former. Thus nationals of other Member States enjoy the priority over third-state nationals which is granted to nationals of the Member State of employment.[237]

In particular, in Article 43 of Regulation 15/61[238] Member States were requested to draw up their policies in the light of the conditions on the markets of the other Member States. They were to endeavour to have only limited recourse to third-state nationals. In Regulation 38/64[239] the Member

[232] Compare the Declaration by the German Government on the definition of the expression "German National" with the Protocol on German Internal Trade and Connected Problems.
[233] JO 1968 L257/2.
[234] Joined Cases 281, 283–285 & 287/85 *Germany, France, Netherlands, Denmark, and the UK v. EC Commission: migration policy* [1987] ECR 3203, 3216.
[235] A. Evans, 'Nationals of Third Countries and the Treaty on European Union' (1994) EJIL 199–219.
[236] Conversely, British Dependent Territories Citizens from Gibraltar are formally subject to immigration control under UK law but as UK Nationals for Union law purposes benefit from free movement under Union law.
[237] Mancini AG in Joined Cases 281, 283–285 & 287/85 *Germany, France, Netherlands, Denmark, and the UK v. EC Commission: migration policy* [1987] ECR 3203, 3238.
[238] Concerning the first measures for introduction of the free movement of workers within the Community (JO 1961 1073).
[239] Concerning the free movement of workers within the Community (JO 1964 965).

States were to take account of "Community priority" in their practice. Article 1(2) of Regulation 1612/68[240] now defines this priority as a right. It is implemented by the clearing system for vacancies established by Articles 15 and 16. According to this system, applications from nationals of other Member States are to be submitted to employers with the same priority as that granted to national workers over third-state nationals. The Member State in question may only offer vacancies to third-state nationals, if it considers that there are insufficient workers available who are Union Citizens.[241]

9.8.3 "External Controls"

The EC Treaty recognises the difficulty of removing frontier checks solely for Union Citizens. Hence, harmonisation of national law governing the entry and residence of persons lacking the nationality of a Member State is envisaged.[242]

Article 73j(2) of the Treaty provides for the adoption of measures on the crossing of the external borders of the Member States. The measures shall establish standards and procedures to be followed by Member States in carrying out checks on persons at such borders[243] and rules on visas for intended stays of no more than three months. These rules shall include: a list of third countries whose nationals must be in possession of visas when crossing the external borders[244] and those whose nationals are exempt from that requirement;[245] the procedures and conditions for issuing visas by Member States; a uniform format for visas;[246] and rules on a uniform visa. At the same time, there are to be measures setting out the conditions under which third-state nationals shall have the freedom to travel within the territory of the Member States during a period of no more than three months.[247]

---

[240] JO 1968 L257/2.

[241] See now Reg. 2434/92 (OJ 1992 L245/1) amending Part II of Reg. 1612/68.

[242] The White Paper on Completing the internal market (COM(85)310, para. 48) advocated adoption of a dir. on the status of TSNs. See, generally, T. Hoogenboom, "Integration into Society and Free Movement of Non-EC Nationals" [1992] *EJIL* 36–52. The Dutch draft for the TEU would have made provision in Art. 100a*bis* EEC for enactment of measures generally concerning entry into, and movement on the territory of, Member States by TSNs. See *Europe Doc.* 1733/1734 (3 Oct. 1991).

[243] But see the Protocol on external relations of the Member States with regard to the crossing of external borders.

[244] Reg. 2317/95 (OJ 1995 L234/1) determining the third countries whose nationals must be in possession of visas when crossing the external borders of the Member States.

[245] This provision may entail formal recognition of a competence already acquired in practice. E.g. the Council, acting on a Commission proposal, abolished the visa requirement from 7 May 1990 for nationals of the then GDR. See the statement of Commissioner Papandreou to the European Parliament (EP Debs. No 3–391, 181, 13 June 1990).

[246] Reg. 1683/95 (OJ 1995 L164/1) laying down a uniform format for visas.

[247] Joint Action 97/1 (OJ 1997 L7/1) concerning a uniform format for residence permits; and Joint Action 96/749 (OJ 1996 L342/5) on monitoring the implementation of instruments adopted by the Council concerning illegal immigration, readmission, the unlawful employment of TSNs, and co-operation in the implementation of expulsion orders.

State Powers

Care is taken by the Treaty to limit encroachment on state powers. Thus, according to Article 73l(1), the exercise of responsibilities incumbent upon Member States with regard to the maintenance of law and order and the safeguarding of internal security is not affected.[248]

It seems unlikely that this provision will be interpreted as narrowly as provisions permitting exceptions from the freedom of movement of Union Citizens. According to the Court of Justice, Member States may take measures with regard to nationals of third states which are based on considerations of public policy, public security, and public health. Such measures are their sole responsibility. They may take the form of national rules or international instruments. The only proviso is that the whole field of migration policy in relation to third states does not necessarily fall within the scope of public security.[249] Whereas in the case of Union Citizens, restrictions on their freedom of movement must be justified under Union law,[250] in the case of nationals of third countries, restrictions on state powers must be so justified.

More particularly, if one or more Member States are confronted by an emergency characterised by a sudden inflow of third-state nationals, the Council may under Article 73l(2) adopt provisional measures of a duration not exceeding six months for the benefit of the Member States concerned.

Schengen Agreement

According to the Schengen arrangements, most Member States have agreed to lift frontier controls between themselves. Iceland and Norway are associated.[251] These arrangements are now to be integrated into Union law, in so far as they are compatible with such law.[252] In fact, the extent of their compatibility with Union law is uncertain.

For example, Article 3(1) of the Schengen Agreement[253] provides that, in principle, "external frontiers" may only be crossed at official crossing-points and during fixed hours.[254] Such frontiers include those between Schengen Parties and the rest of the Union.[255] Moreover, Article 5(1) lays down the

---

[248] See also Art. 2 of the Protocol integrating the Schengen *acquis* into the framework of the EU.

[249] Joined Cases 281, 283–285 & 287/85 *Germany, France, Netherlands, Denmark, and the UK* v. *EC Commission: migration policy* [1987] ECR 3203, 3253. The evolution of the CFSP under Arts. J.1–18 TEU may also have an impact on the freedom of Member States to adopt unilateral measures of security policy. Indeed, at one stage in the drafting of the TEU it was envisaged that visa policy, asylum, and immigration matters would be covered by the CFSP. See the draft of 20 June 1990 in *Europe Doc.* 1722/1723 (5 July 1991).

[250] Sect. 9.4.1 above.

[251] Art. 6 of the Schengen Agreement, (1991) ILM 68.

[252] 3rd recital in the preamble to the Protocol integrating the Schengen *acquis* into the framework of the EU.

[253] [1991] ILM 68. See also the Convention applying the Schengen Agreement [1991] ILM 84.

[254] In Art. 4(1) (*ibid.*) Contracting Parties guarantee that all passengers on flights from non-Contracting Parties who board a flight to another Contracting Party will be subject to a check.

[255] See the definitions in Art. 1 (*ibid.*).

conditions on the basis of which a third-state national may be admitted for up to three months. Article 5(2) requires that admission should, in principle, be refused to those who do not meet these conditions. Application of these provisions assumes the need to maintain frontiers which are supposed to be abolished within the Union under Article 7a of the EC Treaty.

More particularly, Article 6(1) of the Schengen Agreement provides for controls at "external frontiers" to be based on uniform principles. According to Article 6(2)(a), controls involve not only the checking of travel documents and other conditions of entry, residence, work, and exit. The controls also involve investigation of threats to the public policy and national security of the Parties. Moreover, Article 6(2)(b) requires that all persons must at least be required to establish their identity through the production or presentation of travel documents. Non-Union Citizens must, according to Article 6(2)(c), be subjected to more rigorous controls within the meaning of Article 6(2)(a). The controls implicitly envisaged for Union Citizens moving within the Union between a party and a non-party to the Schengen Agreement also seem incompatible with Article 7a of the EC Treaty.

9.8.4 Derived Rights

Separate treatment of third-state nationals may be undermined by the availability of certain derived rights to such persons. In particular, they may enjoy derived rights of entry and residence as employees of firms exercising their freedom to provide services in another Member State.[256] Similarly, third-state nationals who are spouses or dependants of Union Citizens enjoy derived rights to accompany Union Citizens exercising their freedom of movement.[257]

Problems in the relationship between such derived rights and primary rights have not been squarely addressed in Union practice. For example, in *Diatta*[258] the position of a third-state dependant of a Union Citizen was at issue. Here Advocate General Darmon demonstrated his "concern to provide a strict interpretation"[259] of Article 11 of Regulation 1612/68,[260] which requires equal treatment for the dependants of a worker exercising his

---

[256] Joined Cases 62 & 63/81 *Seco SA and Desquenne & Giral SA* v. *Etablissement d'Assurances contre la Vieillesse et l'Invalidité* [1984] ECR 236; and Case C–119/89 *Rush Portuguesa Lda* v. *Office National d'Immigration* [1990] ECR I–1417, I–1443.

[257] Art. 11 of Reg. 1612/68 (JO 1968 L257/2) covers spouses and dependants of Union Citizens, "irrespective of their nationality".

[258] Case 267/83 *Aissatou Diatta* v. *Land Berlin* [1985] ECR 567.

[259] *Ibid.*, 572.

[260] JO 1968 L257/2. This provision entails the right for dependants to take up work, but if they do so they cease to be dependants and lose the right to work. They also only have the right to reside in the Member State where the worker resides. The Commission proposed amendments to Reg. 1612/68 (OJ 1989 C100/6).

freedom of movement. The Court of Justice itself ruled that this provision could not entail independent rights of residence. This strict interpretation may be contrasted with the expansive interpretation adopted of Articles 6 and 48(2) of the Treaty. According to the interpretation of these provisions, discrimination against an unmarried couple with Union Citizenship, where the Member State concerned grants certain advantages to unmarried couples having its nationality, may be prohibited.[261] These contrasting interpretations may have consequences of practical significance, even for Union Citizens. In particular, the safeguarding of derived rights alone may not necessarily effectively secure freedom of movement for the holder of primary rights.[262] For example, a Union Citizen may be deterred from moving between Member States by the thought that the derived rights of a third-state spouse or dependant may be extinguished on his death.

9.9 Agreements with Third States

Separate treatment of Union Citizens and third-state nationals may be accompanied by demands for the conclusion of reciprocal agreements with third states. For example, according to the Commission, the passport union envisaged in the 1970s went beyond a mere area of free movement and implied that third-state nationals would receive equal treatment from all Member States.[263] Accordingly, negotiations with third states to secure identical[264] and reciprocal treatment[265] for all Union Citizens and the replacement of bilateral agreements between Member States and third states by agreements with the Union[266] were considered necessary.

However, Union practice "varies widely" depending on whether rights derive from the freedom of movement of Union Citizens or from agreements concluded by the Union. It varies because the former is treated as concerning the common market and the latter as concerning the external relations of the Union.[267] As a practical consequence, the emphasis in the case law of the

---

[261] Case 59/85 *Netherlands* v. *Ann Florence Reed* [1986] ECR 1283, 1300 and 1303.

[262] J.H.H. Weiler, "Thou Shalt Not Oppress a Stranger: on the Judicial Protection of the Human Rights of Non-EC Nationals – A Critique" [1992] *EJIL* 65–91.

[263] *Towards a Citizens' Europe*, Bull. EC 7/75, 11.

[264] *Ibid.*, 10.

[265] Consultation on migration policies *vis-à-vis* third countries, COM(79)115; and the Legal Affairs Committee of the European Parliament, The problem of migrant workers, EP Doc. 1–811/83, 43.

[266] *Towards a Citizens' Europe*, Bull. EC 7/75, 15. In practice, however, agreements are likely to depend on negotiations between "*couples*" of states of origin and host states and to lead to demands for similar privileges from other third states. See H. de Lary, "Libre circulation et immigrés à l'horizon 1993" [1989] *Revue Française des Affaires Sociales* 93–117, 110.

[267] W. Alexander, "Free Movement of Non-EC Nationals: A Review of the Case-Law of the Court of Justice" [1992] *EJIL* 53–64, 63.

Court of Justice, like that of the agreements themselves, is on the need for securing reciprocity in relations with third states rather than equality between third-state nationals and Union Citizens.

9.9.1 Association Agreements

The Europe Agreements seek to secure equal treatment for nationals of the parties, but without conferring rights of entry and residence. For example, Article 37(1) of the Europe Agreement with Poland[268] covers Polish workers legally employed in the territory of a Member State. Each Member State must treat such workers equally with its own nationals, as regards working conditions, remuneration, or dismissal.[269]

The Turkish Association Agreement[270] goes further. Article 12 provides that the Parties agree "to be guided by Articles 48, 49, and 50 of the [EEC] Treaty for the purpose of progressively securing freedom of movement for workers between them". The Court of Justice considers that "to ensure compliance with that objective, it would seem to be essential to transpose, so far as is possible, the principles contained in those Articles to Turkish workers", who enjoy rights conferred by implementing measures adopted by the Association Council.[271]

The implementing measures include Decision 1/80.[272] Article 6 of this Decision provides that a Turkish worker duly registered as belonging to the labour force of a Member State shall enjoy free access to any paid employment of his choice after four years of legal employment. From this provision rights to employment, and residence rights may be implied.[273] In particular, there are implied rights to remain for work-seeking purposes after employment which are analogous to the rights of Union Citizens.[274]

9.9.2 EEA Agreement

The EEA Agreement[275] provides for extension of freedom of movement[276] and the prohibition of discrimination[277] to benefit nationals of EFTA States.

---

[268] OJ 1993 L348/2.

[269] According to the Joint Declaration *ad* Chap. II of Title IV of the Agreement, treatment by one Party of the nationals or companies of another Party which is either formally or *de facto* less favourable than that accorded to its own nationals or companies is prohibited.

[270] JO 1964, 3687.

[271] Case C–434/93 *Ahmet Bozkurt* v. *Staatssecretaris van Justitie* [1995] ECR I–1475, I–1501.

[272] EC-Turkish Association Council, 20 Dec. 1976.

[273] Case C–285/95 *Suat Kol* v. *Land Berlin* (5 June 1997).

[274] Case C–171/95 *Recep Tetik* v. *Land Berlin* [1997] ECR I–329.   [275] OJ 1993 L1/3.

[276] Art. 28 EEA is substantially identical to Art. 48 EC, and Art. 29 EEA is substantially identical to Art. 51 EC. Union implementing measures are referred to in Annex V, on free movement of workers, and Annex VI, on social security, to the Agreement. A Declaration by the Governments of the Member States of the EC and the EFTA states on the facilitation of border controls, attached to the EEA Agreement, also provides for co-operation to facilitate border controls for each others' citizens.

[277] See, generally, Art. 4 EEA.

Thus persons lacking the nationality of a Member State will enjoy the protection of the very principles which lie at the heart of Union Citizenship. It, therefore, becomes increasingly implausible to treat as rights dependent on the nationality of a Member State what could be treated as fundamental rights and protected as such by Union law.

9.10 Fundamental Rights

The approach to fundamental rights in the case law of the Court of Justice regarding the free movement of workers is exemplified by a comparison of rulings such as those in *Rutili* and *Demirel*. The compatibility of the approach with the European Convention on Human Rights may be questioned.

9.10.1 Fundamental Rights and Free Movement

Rutili[278] concerned restrictions on the movement of an Italian trade unionist in France. Here the Court of Justice considered the powers of Member States under Article 48(3) of the Treaty and Directive 64/221[279] to restrict the movement of nationals of other Member States on public policy grounds. The Court ruled that, in restricting such movement, Member States had to respect principles enshrined in the European Convention on Human Rights.[280]

Demirel[281] concerned the expulsion from Germany of a Turkish woman who had gone to Germany to join her husband who was working there. In this ruling provisions of the Turkish Association Agreement[282] requiring the progressive introduction of the free movement of workers between the Parties[283] were at issue. The Court of Justice noted that the free movement of workers was, by virtue of Article 48 of the EC Treaty, one of the fields covered by this Treaty. Accordingly, the Court did not accept that the Member States entered into commitments to Turkey concerning this freedom in the exercise of their own powers. Rather, these commitments fell within the powers conferred on the European Community by Article 238 of the Treaty.[284] However, the commitments merely set out programmes and were "not sufficiently precise and unconditional to be capable of governing directly the movement of workers."[285] The Court did not address the

---

[278] Case 36/75 *Roland Rutili* v. *Minister of the Interior* [1976] ECR 1219.
[279] JO 1964 850.
[280] [1976] ECR 1219, 1232. See also, regarding the need for Reg. 1612/68 (JO 1968 L257/2) to be interpreted in the light of the requirement of respect for family life in Art. 8 ECHR, Case 249/86 *EC Commission* v. *Germany: housing requirements* [1989] ECR 1263, 1290.
[281] Case 12/86 *Meryem Demirel* v. *Stadt Schwäbisch Gmünd* [1987] ECR 3719.
[282] JO 1964, 3687. [283] *Ibid.*, Art. 12. [284] [1987] ECR 3719, 3751. [285] *Ibid.*, 3753.

question whether in implementing the commitments the Member States had to respect the Treaty[286] and, more particularly, fundamental rights[287] embodied in Union law.

9.10.2 European Convention on Human Rights

The implicit failure of the case law to utilise the potential of Union law for promoting fundamental rights in the case of third-state nationals may ultimately lead to clashes with the requirements of the European Convention on Human Rights. The Convention does not guarantee rights of entry and residence as such, and the Fourth Protocol to the Convention[288] only guarantees these rights in the case of nationals of the state concerned. However, exclusion or expulsion may involve action contrary to other rights which are guaranteed by the Convention.

For example, expulsion of a third-state national related to someone resident in a Member State may constitute a violation of the right to respect for family life in Article 8 of the Convention.[289] The possibility of there being a breach of the Convention in such circumstances is apparently heightened where discrimination of the kind prohibited by Article 14 of the Convention is involved.[290] Thus expulsion of such a person on grounds, for example of political activity, which would not lead to the expulsion of a Union Citizen may be contrary to the Convention.

Differential treatment of different categories of aliens, that is, nationals of other Member States and nationals of third states, may not necessarily be easy to justify for the purposes of the Convention.[291] Parties to the Convention and its Protocols cannot lawfully derogate from the rights embodied therein simply by concluding agreements, even one as important as the EC Treaty, amongst themselves.[292] Certainly, there is no equivalent in

[286] Cf. the finding that Art. 7 EEC applied to the tax treatment of teachers employed at the European Schools, i.e. such treatment fell within the scope of application of the Treaty for the purposes of this provision, in Case 44/84 *Derrick Guy Hurd* v. *Kenneth Jones (HM Inspector of Taxes)* [1986] ECR 29, 85. Where the Union had not acted, Art. 7 EEC might still apply. See Case 61/77 *EC Commission* v. *Ireland: sea fisheries* [1978] ECR 417, 450–1; and Case 88/77 *Minister for Fisheries* v. *Schonenberg* [1978] ECR 473, 491.

[287] Cf. J.H.H. Weiler, "Thou Shalt Not Oppress a Stranger: on the Judicial Protection of the Human Rights of Non-EC Nationals – A Critique" (1992) *EJIL* 65–91. Cf. also the argument regarding the need for Member States to respect fundamental rights in implementation of their obligation to hold direct elections in A. Evans, "Nationality Law and European Integration" [1991] *ELR* 190–215, 208. Cf. also Case 5/88 *Hubert Wachauf* v. *Germany* [1989] ECR 2609, 2639–40.

[288] ETS(1963)46.

[289] See, e.g., App. 8244/78 *Uppal Singh* (17 D. & R. 149).

[290] Home Affairs Sub-Committee on Race Relations and Immigration, Proposed new immigration rules and the European Convention on Human Rights, HC (1979–80) 434, memorandum by F. Jacobs, para. 4.

[291] Art. 1(3) of the International Convention on the Elimination of all Forms of Racial Discrimination (G.A. Res. 2106A(XX)) prohibits discrimination against a particular nationality.

[292] The ECJ has ruled that it was not contrary to the prohibition of discrimination as between

the Convention of Article XXIV of GATT.[293] Moreover, Union Citizenship lacks the historical foundation of, for example, Commonwealth Citizenship or the special treatment accorded Irish nationals in the United Kingdom. Hence, it is unclear whether Union Citizenship can always provide an adequate justification for such differentiation.[294]

Such questions appear to have received little attention from the European Court of Human Rights in *Moustaquin* v. *Belgium*.[295] This case concerned a Moroccan national who had arrived in Belgium in 1965, when he was one year old. He had lived there with his family, until he was deported in 1984 because of his criminal record in Belgium. Among the arguments against the compatibility of the deportation with the Convention was that his right to family life in Article 8 of the Convention was less well protected than it was in the case of nationals of other Member States. The Court stated that there was an "objective and reasonable justification" for "preferential treatment" of nationals of Member States in comparison with nationals of third states,[296] because Member States "belong . . . to a special legal order".

Certainly, if the right to family life within the meaning of Article 8(1) of the Convention is not at stake, the fact that family life may have a higher level of protection in the case of nationals of other Member States than in the case of nationals of third states need not in itself entail that interference with the family life of the latter constitutes a violation of this provision by the Member State concerned. However, where such a right is at stake, as in *Moustaquin*, and the question is whether the right may be restricted under Article 8(2) of the Convention, differential treatment between nationals of Member States and nationals of third states may be of greater significance. It is not apparent why expulsion of the latter alone could be justified on grounds such as public order or could be accepted as being "necessary in a democratic society" for the purposes of Article 8(2). This point, however,

nationals of different ACP countries in the Lomé Convention for a Member State to reserve more favourable treatment to nationals of one ACP country, provided that such treatment resulted from the provisions of an international agreement comprising reciprocal rights and obligations. See Case 65/77 *Jean Razanatsimba* [1977] ECR 2229, 2238–9. However, fundamental rights issues were not put to the Court.

[293] According to this provision, GATT parties which establish a customs union or a free trade agreement between themselves may derogate from fundamental requirements of most-favoured-nation treatment in relation to other GATT parties.

[294] Though there may be attractions for national authorities. E.g. the status of British Dependent Territories Citizens from Gibraltar as UK nationals for Union law purposes was used in s. 5 of the British Nationality Act 1981 to indicate the beneficiaries of the right of registration as British Citizens under this provision.

[295] Ser. A, No. 193, 1, 120; (1985) 13 EHRR 802, 816.

[296] The question did not arise whether preferential treatment of the latter in comparison with nationals of the Member State concerned, i.e. "reverse discrimination", which may be allowed by the EC Treaty, might similarly be justified. However, the ECJ accepts that national constitutional rules may be applied against such discrimination (Case C–132/93 *Volker Steen* v. *Deutsche Post* [1994] ECR I–2715, I–2724) and may also consider principles of the Convention to be applicable.

was not addressed by the Court, possibly because Article 8 had already been found to have been violated in this case.

In short, availability of fundamental rights remains dependent on integration requirements rather than *vice versa*.[297] Family reunification, for example, is treated by Union law as "a necessary element in giving effect to the freedom of movement of workers [and] does not become a right until the freedom which it presupposes has taken effect".[298] Such practice does not fit easily with the concern for fundamental rights professed in the Treaty on European Union.[299]

---

[297] Cf. Case C–159/90 *Society for the Protection of Unborn Children Ireland Ltd* v. *Stephen Grogan* [1991] ECR I–4685, I–4740–1.

[298] Darmon AG in Case 12/86, *Meryem Demirel* v. *Stadt Schwäbisch Gmünd* [1987] ECR 3719, 3745. According to the ECJ itself, such a right is dependent on a Union provision defining the conditions in which family reunification must be permitted (*ibid.*, 3754). See also Case C–295/90 *European Parliament* v. *EC Council: right of residence for students* [1992] ECR I–4193, I–4236.

[299] 3rd recital in the Preamble and Art. F.(2) TEU.

10

Establishment

Article 52(1) of the EC Treaty provides for restrictions on the freedom of establishment of nationals of a Member State in the territory of another Member State to be prohibited.[1] This provision benefits Union Citizens who are self-employed and their families.[2] It also benefits legal persons. It is to be observed by "all the competent public authorities, including legally recognised professional bodies".[3]

Establishment is defined by the Court of Justice as becoming "involved on a stable and continuous basis in the economic life" of a Member State.[4] Implicit in this definition is an indication of the difficulties of determining the presence of a prohibited restriction. On the one hand, restrictions which impede such involvement by a national of a Member State in another Member State may be expected to be prohibited. On the other hand, subjection to the same restrictions as nationals of the host Member State may be regarded as an integral element of such involvement.[5]

10.1 Natural Persons

Article 52(2) of the EC Treaty provides that freedom of establishment includes the right for natural persons to take up and pursue self-employed activities in a Member State other than their own under the conditions laid down for its own nationals by the law of the Member State where such establishment is effected. For these purposes, natural persons enjoy rights of entry and residence, which are defined in Directive 73/148.[6] The persons covered

---

[1] See, regarding Art. 52 EC and public procurement, Case 197/84 *P. Steinhauser* v. *City of Biarritz* [1985] ECR 1819, 1827; and Case C–272/91 *Commission* v. *Italy: lotteries* [1994] ECR I–1409, I–1435–6.

[2] Case 48/75 *Jean Noël Royer* [1976] ECR 497, 512.   [3] [1985] ECR 1819, 1826–7.

[4] Case C–70/95 *Sodemare SA* v. *Regione Lombardia* (17 June 1997).

[5] Cf. L. Daniele, "Non-Discriminatory Restrictions to the Free Movement of Persons" [1997] *ELR* 191–200.

[6] On the abolition of restrictions on movement and residence within the Community for nationals of Member States with regard to establishment and the provision of services (OJ 1973 L172/14), Arts. 3 and 4.

are also entitled to retire in the Member State concerned.[7] However, the rights do not operate in relation to "purely internal" situations.[8] In other words, they do not usually benefit individuals wishing to establish themselves in the Member State of which they are nationals. They do, in contrast, benefit a national of a Member State who returns to that Member State after having been resident in another Member State.[9]

Where this freedom does operate, national law may not formally discriminate against nationals of other Member States. For example, a Member State may not limit access to the legal profession to its own nationals[10] or prohibit nationals of other Member States from registering a fishing vessel.[11]

A Member State may also not apply national rules having discriminatory effects to the person concerned.[12] Such effects are unlikely to be found to derive simply from differences between national regulation in an individual's Member State of origin and the Member State where he establishes himself. His establishment in the latter means that he is no longer subject to the national regulation of the former. In other words, a distortion of competition cannot be inferred from the cumulative burden of complying with two different sets of regulations. Consequently, attention focuses on the question whether a distortion arises from discrimination in the Member State of establishment.

Discrimination against a person exercising his freedom of establishment is prohibited in the application of specific rules governing his activities. This prohibition is broadly defined. For example, beneficiaries have the right to set up and maintain, subject to observance of the professional rules of conduct, more than one place of work within the Union. Thus the right of a doctor or dentist[13] or a lawyer[14] to practise in a Member State cannot be made dependent on his termination of a practice in another Member State. Moreover, a formally non-discriminatory rule is prohibited, where its effect is to disadvantage someone having places of business in more than one Member State.[15] Thus a requirement that separate accounts be kept by each place of business may be prohibited.[16]

---

[7] Dir. 75/34 (OJ 1975 L14/10) concerning the right of nationals of a Member State to remain in the territory of another Member State after having pursued therein an activity in a self-employed capacity.
[8] Case 204/87 *Guy Bekaert* [1988] ECR 2029, 2039.
[9] Case 115/78 *J. Knoors* v. *Secretary of State for Economic Affairs* [1979] ECR 399, 410.
[10] Case 2/74 *Jean Reyners* v. *Belgium* [1974] ECR 631.
[11] Case C–246/89 *EC Commission* v. *UK: fishing vessels* [1991] ECR I–4585.
[12] Cf. Case 221/85 *EC Commission* v. *Belgium: clinical biology laboratories* [1987] ECR 719, 737.
[13] Case 96/85 *EC Commission* v. *France: medical professions* [1986] ECR 1475.
[14] Case 107/83 *Ordre des Avocats au Barreau de Paris* v. *Onno Klopp* [1984] ECR 2971.
[15] Case 143/87 *Christopher Stanton and SA Belge d'Assurances "L'Etat 1905"* v. *Inasti (Institut National d'Assurances Sociales pour Travailleurs Indépendants)* [1988] ECR 3877, 3895. Cf. Case 79/85 *D.H.M. Segers* v. *Bestuur van de Bedrijfsvereniging voor Bank-en Verzekeringswesen, Groothandel en Vrije Beroepen* [1986] ECR 2375, 2387–8.
[16] Case C–250/95 *Futura Participations SA, Singer* v. *Administration des Contributions* (15 May 1997).

The equality of treatment required by Article 52 also relates to general facilities relevant to pursuit of such activities.[17] Thus, for example, equal treatment is required as regards access to housing.[18]

Moreover, agreements and rules other than those of state authorities may be prohibited where they relate to such activities and are disadvantageous to those exercising their freedom of establishment.[19]

10.2 Companies

Article 52(2) of the EC Treaty provides that freedom of establishment includes the right to set up and manage undertakings, in particular companies or firms within the meaning of Article 58 of the Treaty, under the conditions laid down for its own nationals by the law of the Member State where such establishment is effected. According to Article 58, such "companies or firms" are those constituted under civil or commercial law, including co-operative societies and other legal persons governed by public or private law, save for those which are non-profit making. Thus non-profit-making persons are denied the benefit of this freedom, though the economic activities of a religious organisation may bring it within the scope of Article 52.[20]

As in the case of natural persons, "internal situations" are unaffected. For example, a company cannot evade planning rules in its own Member State on the ground that these rules violate its freedom of establishment.[21]

Even in relation to Member States other than that of which the person exercising freedom of establishment posses the nationality, this freedom may have limited practical significance for existing companies. For example, the Court of Justice ruled in *Regina* v. *HM Treasury and Commissioners of Inland Revenue, ex parte Daily Mail and General Trust PLC*[22] that a Member State might not hinder the establishment in another Member State of a company which was incorporated under its legislation and came within the definition in Article 58. However, Article 52 conferred no right on a company incorporated under the legislation of a Member State and having its registered office there to transfer its central management and control to another Member

---

[17] Cf. Case C–168/91 *Christos Konstantinidis* v. *Stadt Altensteig* [1993] ECR I–1191, I–1219, regarding a German requirement that a Greek national register his name according to the Latin alphabet.

[18] Case 63/86 *EC Commission* v. *Italy: social housing* [1988] ECR 29.

[19] Case 36/74 *B.N.O. Walrave and L.J.N. Koch* v. *Union Cycliste Internationale, Koninklijke Nederlandsche Wielren Unie, and Federacion Española Ciclismo* [1974] ECR 1405, 1419.

[20] Case 196/87 *Udo Steymann* v. *Staatssecretaris van Justitie* [1988] ECR 6159. Cf. the Declaration on the status of churches and non-confessional organisations, adopted with the Amsterdam Treaty (OJ 1997 C340/1).

[21] Case 20/87 *Ministère Public* v. *André Gauchard* [1987] ECR 4879; and Case 204/87 *Guy Bekaert* [1988] ECR 2029.

[22] Case 81/87 [1988] ECR 5483.

State.[23] Therefore, if a company wishes to move to another Member State, it must liquidate and incorporate itself according to the law of that Member State.

10.3 Agencies, Branches, and Subsidiaries

Under Article 52(1) of the EC Treaty freedom of establishment covers the setting up of agencies, branches, or subsidiaries[24] by nationals of any Member State established in the territory of any Member State.

This provision is interpreted broadly. Thus, for example, it covers the setting up of "an office managed by the undertaking's own staff or by a person who is independent, but authorised to act on a permanent basis for the undertaking, as would be the case with an agency".[25] It is also interpreted as entitling a company to establish a subsidiary in another Member State and to conduct its business solely through that subsidiary.[26]

A Member State in which a company carries on its business may not treat that company differently from other companies solely because its registered office is in another Member State.[27] For example, discriminatory tax treatment as between companies of the host Member State and branches of a company registered in another Member States is prohibited.[28]

10.4 Exceptions

The EC Treaty permits certain restrictions on freedom of establishment under Articles 55 and 56(1).

10.4.1 Public Interest

Article 56(1) of the Treaty permits the exclusion or expulsion of persons seeking to exercise their freedom of establishment on grounds of public policy, public health, or public security. However, Directive 64/221[29] restricts the scope of public policy and lays down procedural safeguards for persons affected.[30] Further restrictions on its scope result from the case law of the Court of Justice.[31]

---

[23] *Ibid.*, 5510.   [24] *Ibid.*, 5511.

[25] Case 205/84 *EC Commission* v. *Germany: insurance services* [1986] ECR 3755, 3801.

[26] Case 79/85 *D.H.M. Segers* v. *Bestuur van de Bedrijfsvereninging voor Bank-en Verzekeringswesen, Groothandel en Vrije Beroepen* [1986] ECR 2375, 2388.

[27] Case C–330/91 *R.* v. *Inland Revenue Commissioners, ex p. Commerzbank AG* [1993] ECR I–4017.

[28] Case 270/83 *EC Commission* v. *France: taxation of insurance companies* [1986] ECR 273.

[29] On the co-ordination of special measures concerning the movement and residence of foreign nationals which are justified on grounds of public policy, public security, or public health (JO 1964 850).

[30] It was extended to persons remaining in a Member State after having pursued a self-employed activity there by Dir. 75/35 (OJ 1975 L14/14).

[31] Sect. 9.2.5 above.

10.4.2 Official Authority

Article 55 of the Treaty permits a Member State to exclude beneficiaries of freedom of establishment from "activities which in that State are connected, even occasionally, with the exercise of official authority". However, this provision only covers activities which have a direct and specific connection with the exercise of official authority.[32] Activities entailing only "auxiliary and preparatory functions" in relation to such authority are not covered.[33]

10.5 "Mandatory Requirements"

The Court of Justice has ruled that freedom of establishment is subject to the application of national professional rules justified by the general good, provided that such application is effected without discrimination.[34] Thus non-discriminatory rules regulating a profession, such as the requirement that lawyers be registered at the bar of the host Member State are permissible, since they pursue "an objective worthy of protection".[35] State measures necessary for the effectiveness of fiscal supervision may also be permitted.[36]

The relationship between such "mandatory requirements" and freedom of establishment may not be solely conflictual. The more a measure is justified by reference to such requirements, the less likely it will be to distort competition contrary to freedom of establishment.[37]

10.6 Harmonisation

To make it easier for persons to take up and pursue self-employed activities, Article 57(2) of the EC Treaty provides for harmonisation of national law governing such activities. Such harmonisation may seek the co-ordination of the provisions laid down by law, regulation, or administrative action in Member States concerning the taking up and pursuit of activities as self-employed persons.[38]

---

[32] Case 2/74 *Jean Reyners* v. *Belgium* [1974] ECR 631, 654.

[33] Case C–42/92 *Adrianus Thijssen* v. *Controledienst voor de Verzekeringen* [1993] ECR I–4047, I–4073. See also Case C–3/88 *EC Commission* v. *Italy: data processors* [1989] ECR 4035, 4060.

[34] Case 71/76 *Jean Thieffry* v. *Conseil de l'Ordre des Avocats à la Cour de Paris* [1977] ECR 765, 776.

[35] Case 292/86 *Claude Gullung* v. *Conseils de l'Ordre des Avocats du Barreau de Colmar et de Saverne* [1988] ECR 111, 139; and Case C–55/94 *Reinhard Gebhard* v. *Consiglio dell'Ordine degli Avvocati e Procuratori di Milano* [1995] ECR I–4165, I–4197–8.

[36] Case C–250/95 *Futura Participations SA, Singer* v. *Administration des Contributions* (15 May 1997).

[37] Case 96/85 *EC Commission* v. *France: medical professions* [1986] ECR 1475, 1485–6.

[38] See, e.g., Dir. 89/299 (OJ 1989 L 124/16) on the own funds of credit institutions; and Dir. 97/9 (OJ 1997 L84/22) on investor-compensation schemes. Cf., under Art. 100a EC, Dir. 89/592 (OJ 1989 L334/30) co-ordinating regulations on insider dealings

Accordingly, directives have been adopted for manufacturers and processors,[39] wholesale traders,[40] retail traders,[41] commercial agents,[42] pharmacists,[43] traders in toxic products,[44] wholesale coal traders,[45] food and beverage producers,[46] transporters,[47] insurance agents,[48] reinsurers,[49] banks and other financial institutions,[50] direct insurers other than life assurers,[51] credit institutions,[52] coinsurers,[53] film distributors,[54] hairdressers,[55] and

---

[39] Dir. 64/427 (JO 1964 1863) laying down detailed provisions concerning transitional measures in respect of activities of self-employed persons in manufacturing and processing industries.

[40] Dir. 64/222 (JO 1964 857) laying down detailed provisions concerning transitional measures in respect of activities in wholesale trade and activities of intermediaries in commerce, industry, and small craft industry; and Dir. 64/223 (JO 1964 863) concerning the attainment of freedom of establishment and freedom to provide services in respect of activities in the wholesale trade.

[41] Dir. 68/363 (JO 1968 L260/1) concerning the attainment of freedom of establishment and freedom to provide services in respect of activities of self-employed persons in the retail trade; and Dir. 68/364 (JO 1968 L260/6) laying down detailed provisions concerning transitional measures in respect of activities of self-employed persons in retail trade.

[42] Dir. 64/224 (JO 1964 869) concerning the attainment of freedom of establishment and freedom to provide services in respect of activities of intermediaries in commerce, industry, and small craft industries.

[43] Dir. 88/432 (OJ 1988 L253/34) concerning the co-ordination of provisions laid down by law, reg., or administrative action in respect of certain activities in the field of pharmacy.

[44] Dir. 74/556 (OJ 1974 L307/1) laying down detailed provisions concerning transitional measures relating to activities, trade in, and distribution of toxic products and activities entailing the professional use of such products, including activities of intermediaries; and Dir. 74/557 (OJ 1974 L307/5) on the attainment of freedom of establishment and freedom to provide services in respect of activities of self-employed persons and of intermediaries engaging in the trade and distribution of toxic products.

[45] Dir. 70/523 (JO 1970 L267/18) laying down detailed provisions concerning transitional measures relating to activities in the wholesale coal trade and in respect of activities of intermediaries in the whole trade.

[46] Dir. 68/365 (JO 1968 L260/9) concerning attainment of freedom of establishment and freedom to provide services in respect of activities of self-employed persons in the food manufacturing and beverage industries; and Dir. 68/366 (JO 1968 L260/12) laying down detailed provisions concerning transitional measures relating to activities in the food manufacturing and beverage industries.

[47] Dir. 82/470 (OJ 1982 L213/1) on measures to facilitate the effective exercise of freedom of establishment and freedom to provide services in respect of activities of self-employed persons in certain activities incidental to transport and travel agencies and in storage and ware-housing.

[48] Dir. 77/92 (OJ 1977 L26/14) on measures to facilitate the effective exercise of freedom of establishment and freedom to provide services in respect of the activities of insurance agents and brokers and, in particular, transitional measures in respect of these activities.

[49] Dir. 64/225 (JO 1964 878) on the abolition of restrictions on freedom of establishment and freedom to provide services in respect of reinsurance and retrocession.

[50] Dir. 73/183 (OJ 1973 L194/1) on the abolition of restrictions on freedom of establishment and freedom to provide services in respect of self-employed activities of banks and other financial institutions.

[51] Dir. 73/239 (OJ 1973 L228/3) on the co-ordination of laws, regs., and administrative provisions relating to the taking up and pursuit of the business of direct insurance other than life assurance.

[52] Dir. 77/780 (OJ 1977 L322/30) on the co-ordination of laws, regs., and administrative provisions relating to the taking up and pursuit of the business of credit institutions.

[53] Dir. 78/473 (OJ 1978 L151/25) on the co-ordination of laws, regs., and administrative provisions relating to Community coinsurance.

[54] Dir. 65/264 (OJ 1965 1437) implementing in respect of the film industry the provisions of the general programme for the abolition of restrictions on freedom of establishment and freedom to

providers of personal services.[56]

More particularly, a series of directives has been enacted under Article 54(2)(g) of the Treaty. These directives seek to co-ordinate the safeguards which, for the protection of the interests of members and others, are required by Member States of companies or firms. As a result, much harmonisation of the company law of the Member States has taken place. The directives cover safeguards for members and others;[57] safeguards in respect of the formation of public limited companies;[58] annual accounts;[59] mergers;[60] division of public limited companies;[61] consolidated accounts;[62] approval of auditors;[63] branch disclosure requirements;[64] and single-member limited-liability companies.[65] On the other hand, a proposal from the Commission, originally drawn up in the 1960s, providing for incorporation of "Euro-companies" has not been adopted by the Council.[66]

Such harmonisation may extend to persons from third states. For example, branches of undertakings from third states are covered by the Eleventh Directive on Company Law,[67] which concerns branch disclosure requirements.

provide services; and Dir. 68/369 (JO 1968 L260/12) concerning the attainment of freedom of establishment in respect of activities of self-employed persons in film distribution.

[55] Dir. 82/489 (OJ 1982 L218/24) laying down measures to facilitate the effective exercise of the right of establishment and freedom to provide services in hairdressing.

[56] Dir. 68/368 (JO 1968 L260/19) laying down detailed provisions concerning transitional measures relating to activities in the personal services sector.

[57] Dir. 68/151 (JO 1968 L65/8) on co-ordination of safeguards which, for the protection of the interests of member and others, are required by Member States of companies within the meaning of Art. 58 EEC, with a view to making such safeguards equivalent throughout the Community.

[58] Dir. 77/91 (OJ 1977 L26/1) on co-ordination of safeguards in respect of the formation of public limited liability companies and the maintenance and alteration of their capital, with a view to making such safeguards equivalent throughout the Community.

[59] Dir. 78/660 (OJ 1978 L222/11) on the annual accounts of certain types of companies. See, more particularly, Dir. 91/674 (OJ 1991 L374/7) on the annual accounts of insurance undertakings.

[60] Dir. 78/855 (OJ 1978 L295/36) concerning mergers of public limited companies.

[61] Dir. 82/891 (OJ 1982 L378/47) concerning the division of public limited liability companies.

[62] Dir. 83/349 (OJ 1983 L193/1) on consolidated accounts.

[63] Dir. 84/253 (OJ 1984 L126/20) on the approval of persons responsible for carrying out the statutory audits of accounting documents.

[64] Dir. 89/666 (OJ 1989 L395/36) concerning disclosure requirements in respect of branches opened in a Member State by certain types of company governed by the law of another Member State.

[65] Dir. 89/667 (OJ 1989 L395/40) on single-member limited-liability companies.

[66] See, currently, OJ 1989 C334/30. Cf., however, Reg. 2137/85 (OJ 1985 L199/1) on European economic interest groupings.

[67] Dir. 89/666 (OJ 1989 L395/36), Arts. 7–10.

10.7 Mutual Recognition

To make it easier for persons to take up and pursue activities as self-employed persons, Article 57(1) of the EC Treaty provides for the issue of Council directives for the mutual recognition of diplomas, certificates, and other evidence of formal qualifications. Accordingly, directives have been adopted for doctors,[68] dentists,[69] veterinary surgeons,[70] nurses,[71] midwives,[72] pharmacists,[73] architects,[74] carriers of goods by waterway,[75] and for civil aviation.[76] In the case of medical professions, such action has had considerable success, because medical techniques vary little between Member States.

Directive 89/48[77] established a general system for the recognition of higher-education diplomas awarded on completion of professional education and training of at least three years' duration. There is, however, provision for safeguards and adaptation periods or aptitude tests in the host Member State.

The enactment of such legislation is not a precondition for the operation

---

[68] Dir. 93/16 (OJ 1993 L165/1) to facilitate the free movement of doctors and the mutual recognition of their diplomas, certificates, and other evidence of formal qualifications.

[69] Dir. 78/686 (OJ 1978 L233/1) concerning the mutual recognition of diplomas, certificates, and other evidence of formal qualifications in dentistry, including measures to facilitate the effective exercise of the right of establishment and freedom to provide services.

[70] Dir. 78/1026 (OJ 1978 L362/1) concerning the mutual recognition of diplomas, certificates, and other evidence of formal qualifications in veterinary medicine, including measures to facilitate the effective exercise of the right of establishment and freedom to provide services.

[71] Dir. 77/452 (OJ 1977 L176/1) concerning the mutual recognition of diplomas, certificates, and other evidence of formal qualifications of nurses responsible for general care, including measures to facilitate the effective exercise of the right of establishment and freedom to provide services.

[72] Dir. 80/154 (OJ 1980 L33/1) concerning the mutual recognition of diplomas, certificates, and other evidence of formal qualifications in midwifery, including measures to facilitate the effective exercise of the right of establishment and freedom to provide services.

[73] Dir. 85/433 (OJ 1985 L253/37) concerning the mutual recognition of diplomas, certificates, and other evidence of formal qualifications in pharmacy, including measures to facilitate the effective exercise of the right of establishment relating to certain activities in the field of pharmacy.

[74] Dir. 85/384 (OJ 1985 L223/15) on the mutual recognition of diplomas, certificates, and other evidence of formal qualifications in architecture, including measures to facilitate the effective exercise of the right of establishment and freedom to provide services.

[75] Dir. 87/540 (OJ 1987 L322/20) on access to the occupation of carrier of goods by waterway in national and international transport and on the mutual recognition of diplomas, certificates, and other evidence of formal qualifications for this occupation.

[76] Dir. 91/670 (OJ 1991 L373/21) on mutual acceptance of personnel licences for the exercise of functions in civil aviation.

[77] OJ 1989 L19/16. According to Rec. 89/49 (OJ 1989 L19/24) concerning nationals of Member States who hold a diploma conferred on a third state, Member States should apply the provisions of Dir. 89/48 to persons who hold diplomas or other formal qualifications awarded in a third state and are in a position comparable to one of those described in the Dir. See also Dir. 92/51 (OJ 1992 L209/25) on a second general system for the recognition of professional education and training and to supplement Dir. 89/48. See, regarding diplomas or certificates issued by a third state, a Resolution (OJ 1992 C187/1) concerning nationals of Member States who hold a diploma or certificate awarded in a third country.

of freedom of establishment.[78] According to the Court of Justice, Member States must recognise the professional qualifications of a national of another Member State, if those qualifications would be recognised when held by their own nationals.[79] The refusal by a national authority to recognise a qualification gained elsewhere must be reasoned and subject to judicial review.[80] More particularly, in *Vlassopoulu*[81] the Court of Justice dealt with the question of a national of a Member State with a law diploma obtained in that Member State who wished to work in another Member State. According to the Court, the latter Member State had to determine whether the knowledge and qualifications attested by that diploma corresponded to its own requirements. If not, the national authorities had to determine whether the person concerned had acquired the knowledge and qualifications lacking.[82]

10.8 Persons from Third States

By virtue of Article 58 of the EC Treaty, freedom of establishment applies to any company or firm formed according to the law of a Member State and having its registered office, central administration, or principal place of business within the Union. However, companies whose registered office is in the Union but whose central management or principal place of business is in a third state must have "an effective and continuous link with the economy of a Member State".[83]

The basic implication in Article 58 is that subsidiaries of companies from third states having registered offices within a Member State are to be treated in the same way as natural persons who are nationals of that Member State. This implication may be confronted by controversies concerning local content requirements[84] and application of anti-dumping rules[85] to the products of "screwdriver" plants. Local content requirements are those which must be met for a product to be regarded as originating within the Union and thus not having to be put into free circulation.[86] According to

---

[78] Case 11/77 *Richard Hugh Patrick* v. *Ministre des Affaires Culturelles* [1977] ECR 1199, 1205.

[79] Case 71/76 *Jean Thieffry* v. *Conseil de l'Ordre des Avocats à la Cour de Paris* [1977] ECR 765, 778.

[80] Case 222/86 *Union Nationale des Entrâineurs et Cadres Techniques Professionnels de Football* v. *Georges Heylens* [1987] ECR 4097, 4117.

[81] Case C–340/89 *Irene Vlassopoulou* v. *Ministerium für Justiz, Bundes- und Europaangelegenheiten Baden-Württemberg* [1991] ECR I–2357, I–2384–5.

[82] See also Case C–104/91 *Collegio Oficial de Agentes de la Propiedad Inmobiliaria* v. *José Luis Aguirre Borrell* [1992] ECR I–3003, I–3028–9.

[83] General programme on the abolition of restrictions on freedom of establishment (JO 1962 36), Title I.

[84] The confrontation may be even more pronounced, when agreements between the Union and third states embody particularly strict rules of origin. See, e.g., the arguments in the GATT Working Party on the Swedish Free Trade Agreement (BISD, Twentieth Supp., 183–96).

[85] Sect. 21.12.4 below. [86] Sect. 8.7 above.

these requirements, "simple" assembly work does not confer Union origin,[87] though more substantial assembly work may do so.[88] "Screwdriver plants" are plants established within the Union to avoid anti-dumping measures imposed on the finished product entering from a third state.[89]

Such controversies may be treated by "fundamental external bargains" with countries such as the United States.[90] However, bargains of this kind depend on exceptions being made from the normal decision-making processes of the Union. Moreover, if they are only made with certain third states, they may as well increase as decrease distortions of competition in overall terms.

10.9 Agreements with Third States

While free trade agreements may be limited to trade in goods, association agreements may contain provisions regarding establishment.

10.9.1 Free Trade Agreements

The failure of free trade agreements to secure freedom of establishment may jeopardize liberalisation of trade in goods. It means, for example, that there is no right to establish an office to facilitate such trade in the territory of the other party.

10.9.2 Association Agreements

Limited requirements regarding freedom of establishment may be made in association agreements. For example, Article 113 of the Europe Agreement with Poland[91] provides that, in the fields covered by this Agreement and without prejudice to any special provisions contained therein, Poland must not discriminate between Member States, their companies, or firms. Conversely, the arrangements applied by the Union in respect of Poland shall not give rise to discrimination between Polish nationals or companies or firms.[92]

[87] Case C–26/88 *Brother International GmbH* v. *Hauptzollamt Giessen* [1989] ECR I–4253, I–4281.

[88] Case 34/78 *Yoshida Nederland BV* v. *Kamer van Koophandel en Fabrieken voor Friesland* [1979] ECR 115, 136.

[89] See, in particular, the finding of the GATT Panel in *Re Screwdriver Assembly: Japan* v. *European Economic Community* [1990] 2 CMLR 639. The GATT Director General suggested less demanding requirements than the Union in the context of Uruguay Round negotiations. See the Tenth annual report on the anti-dumping and anti-subsidy activities of the Community, COM(92)716, 23. No agreement was reached. See the Decision on Anti-circumvention, in the Final Act Embodying the Results of the Uruguay Round of Multilateral Trade Negotiations (OJ 1994 L336/1).

[90] Cf. W. Sandholtz and J. Zysman, "1992: Recasting the European Bargain" (1989/90) 42 *World Politics* 94–128.

[91] OJ 1993 L348/2.

[92] Note the problems raised by a Polish plan to divide between Fiat, General Motors, and Volkswagen the quota of duty-free car imports from the Union (*Financial Times*, 26 Feb. 1992).

10.9.3 EEA Agreement

The EEA Agreement[93] goes further than other association agreements. Article 31 of this Agreement reproduces Article 52 of the EC Treaty. More particularly, harmonisation measures, such as those adopted under Article 54(2)(g) of the EC Treaty, are listed in Annex XXII[94] to the EEA Agreement.

---

[93] OJ 1994 L1/3.   [94] Company law.

11

Services

Articles 59 to 66 of the EC Treaty deal with the freedom to provide services.[1] Article 60(1) defines the services concerned as those "normally provided for remuneration",[2] in so far as they are not governed by the Treaty provisions relating to freedom of movement for goods, capital, and persons. According to Article 60(2), they include activities of an industrial character, of a commercial character, of craftsmen, and of the professions. More particularly, according to the case law, they include education,[3] health care,[4] and tourism.[5]

However, freedom to provide services in the field of transport is governed by the provisions of the Title of the Treaty relating to transport.[6] Moreover, as regards banking and insurance services connected with movement of capital, their liberalisation has had to be effected in step with the progressive liberalisation of the movement of capital.[7]

The original emphasis in Articles 59 to 66 was on securing freedom of movement for the provider of services.[8] This freedom, like freedom of establishment, benefits self-employed persons and legal persons moving between Member States. The two freedoms may be distinguished, however, in that the freedom to provide services only envisages temporary residence by the provider of services in the Member State where the service is provided.[9] Thus the burden of complying with national rules in his Member State of establishment and of complying with national rules in the Member State where the services are provided may cumulate. In the case of this freedom, therefore, national rules in the latter Member State are more likely to be found to

---

[1] See, regarding Art. 59 EC and public procurement, Case 76/81 *SA Transporoute et Travaux* v. *Minister of Public Works* [1982] ECR 417, 427–8; and Case 272/91 *EC Commission* v. *Italy: lotteries* [1994] ECR I–1409, I–1436.

[2] It is not necessary that the remuneration is paid by the recipient of the service. See Case 352/85 *Bond van Averteerders* v. *The Netherlands* [1988] ECR 2085, 2131.

[3] Slynn AG in Case 293/83 *Françoise Gravier* v. *City of Liège* [1985] ECR 593, 602–4.

[4] Joined Cases 186/82 & 26/83 *Graziana Luisi and Giuseppe Carbone* v. *Ministero del Tesoro* [1984] ECR 377, 403.

[5] Case 186/87 *Ian William Cowan* v. *Trésor Public* [1989] ECR 195, 221.

[6] Art. 61(1) EC.   [7] Art. 61(2) EC.   [8] See, in particular, Art. 60(3) EEC.

[9] Art. 60(3) EC.

distort competition and to entail prohibited restrictions because of differences from rules in the former Member State than they are in the case of freedom of establishment.

More fundamental differences between Articles 59 to 66 and the provisions on freedom of establishment reflect the evolution of Union practice. Such practice presumably reflects the tendency for technological developments to blur the distinction between goods and services.[10] It has come to treat Articles 59 to 66 as liberalising the movement of services generally rather than merely the movement of their provider.

11.1 Persons Covered

Both providers and recipients of services may be covered by Articles 59 to 66 of the EC Treaty. These provisions only make express reference to nationals of Member States as beneficiaries of the freedom entailed.[11]

11.1.1 Providers

Article 59 of the Treaty provides that restrictions on the freedom to provide services are prohibited in respect of nationals of Member States who are established in a Member State other than that of the person for whom the services are intended.[12] According to the case law, restrictions must also be abolished in respect of providers who are resident in a Member State other than that where the service is to be provided.[13]

11.1.2 Recipients

Recipients as well as providers of services are covered by Directive 73/148,[14] which was enacted to implement the freedom to provide services. However, express reference is only made in Articles 59 to 66 of the Treaty to the provider,[15] and recipients are not mentioned in these provisions. Hence, in

---

[10] Cf. Case 155/73 *Giuseppe Sacchi* [1974] ECR 409; and Case 52/79 *Procureur du Roi* v. *Marc J.V.C. Debauve* [1980] ECR 833. Cf. also the finding that "goods" include goods supplied in the context of the provision of a service in Case 45/87 *EC Commission* v. *Ireland: Dundalk water supply* [1988] ECR 4929, 4963.

[11] But see sect. 11.9 below.

[12] It seems that movement between Member States and provision of the service need not be contemporaneous. See Case 15/78 *Société Générale Alsacienne de Banque SA* v. *Walter Koestler* [1978] ECR 1971, 1980.

[13] Case 39/75 *Robert Gerardus Coenen* v. *Sociaal-Economische Raad* [1975] ECR 1547, 1555.

[14] On the abolition of restrictions on movement and residence within the Community for nationals of Member States with regard to establishment and the provision of services (OJ 1973 L172/14), Art. 1(1)(b).

[15] Art. 60(3) EC.

Watson and Belmann,[16] which concerned a British *au pair* in Italy, Advocate General Trabucchi expressed the opinion that recipients would only benefit from freedom of movement in strictly limited circumstances. The Court of Justice itself avoided ruling on this issue.

On the other hand, Articles 59 to 66 fall within the chapter of the Treaty headed "services".[17] These provisions may, therefore, be said to envisage the free movement of services rather than merely the free movement of providers of services. If so, this freedom will also apply where it is the recipients rather than the providers who move from one Member State to another.

For example, in *Luisi and Carbone*[18] two Italian residents had purchased various foreign currencies for use abroad to an amount exceeding that permitted by Italian law. Here the Court of Justice accepted that recipients of services generally, including tourists, benefited from free movement. Again, *Cowan*[19] concerned a British Citizen on holiday in France, who suffered injuries during an assault at the exit of a metro station but was refused an award under a publicly financed compensation scheme for victims of violent assaults. The Court ruled that Member States were prohibited from excluding tourists from other Member States, in their capacity as recipients of services, from the benefits of the scheme.[20]

11.2 Rights of Entry and Residence

Persons covered by Articles 59 to 66 of the EC Treaty may enjoy rights of entry and residence under these provisions.

11.2.1 Entry

Article 60(3) of the Treaty provides that without prejudice to provisions regarding freedom of establishment, the person providing a service may, in order to do so, temporarily pursue his activity in the Member State where the service is provided.[21] A right of entry is implied for such providers of services. Moreover, interpretation of Articles 59 to 66 as covering recipients implies that recipients and, hence, virtually all nationals of Member States also benefit from a right of entry. The abolition of systematic border controls

---

[16] Case 118/75 *Lynn Watson and Alessandro Belmann* [1976] ECR 1185, 1204.

[17] Part Three, Title III, Chap. 3 of the EC Treaty.

[18] Joined Cases 186/82 & 26/83 *Graziana Luisi and Giuseppe Carbone* v. *Ministero del Tesoro* [1984] ECR 377, 403.

[19] Case 186/87 *Ian William Cowan* v. *Trésor Public* [1989] ECR 195, 221.

[20] Cf. the early ruling regarding social security rules and tourists in Case 44/65 *Hessische Knappschaft* v. *Maison Singer et Fils* [1965] ECR 965, 971.

[21] Cf., regarding nationals of the Member State concerned, Case 52/79 *Procureur du Roi* v. *Debauve* [1980] ECR 833, 857.

within the Union required by Article 7a of the Treaty may give further reality to these rights of entry.

11.2.2 Residence

A right of residence is entailed by Articles 59 to 66, though Article 60 implies that such a right may only be available for a "temporary period".[22] According to the Court of Justice, this means that no right either for providers[23] or recipients[24] is available on a permanent basis or without a foreseeable limit to duration. However, there is no definition of just how temporary the period should be. For example, *EC Commission* v. *Italy: social housing*[25] concerned Italian law permitting only Italians to purchase or lease housing built or renovated with the aid of public funds or to obtain reduced-rate mortgage loans. The Court of Justice ruled that the freedom to provide services might entail for the provider of the services concerned the right to equal treatment as regards the purchase or renting of residential accommodation. Assuming, as Directive 73/148[26] appears to do, that the rights of providers and recipients of services are co-extensive, the apparent implication is that both enjoy the right of residence under Articles 59 to 66 for a substantial period.

11.3 Equality of Treatment

Article 60(3) of the EC Treaty states that the person providing a service may, in order to do so, temporarily pursue his activity in the Member State where the service is provided under the same conditions as are imposed by that Member State on its own nationals. The implied prohibition of discrimination applies whenever the provider or recipient moves between Member States. Hence, it applies to the Member State where the provider is established, the Member State of the recipient of the service, and to any third Member State, if the service is provided there.[27]

---

[22] Provision of the services themselves need not be temporary, and the provider need not provide any such services in his own Member State. See Case C–56/96 *VT4 Ltd and Vlaamse Gemeenschap* (5 June 1997).

[23] Case 196/87 *Udo Steymann* v. *Staatssecretaris van Justitie* [1988] ECR 6159, 6173.

[24] Case C–70/95 *Sodemare SA* v. *Regione Lombardia* (17 June 1997).

[25] Case 63/86 [1988] ECR 29, 53. See also Case 305/87 *EC Commission* v. *Greece: property rights* [1989] ECR 1461, 1479.

[26] OJ 1973 L172/14, Art. 1(1).

[27] Case C–381/93 *EC Commission* v. *France: maritime transport* [1994] ECR I–5145, I–5168; and Jacobs AG in Case C–384/93 *Alpine Investments BV* v. *Minister van Financiën* [1995] ECR I–1141, I–1155.

11.3.1 Regulation of Services

Equality requirements as regards the regulation of services may be far-reaching.

Formal Discrimination

The principal aim of Article 60(3) is to enable the provider of the service to pursue his activities in the Member State where the service is provided without suffering discrimination in favour of nationals of that Member State. Hence, restrictions may not be imposed on the person providing the service by reason in particular of his nationality or of his residence outside the Member State where the service is provided, if the restrictions do not apply to persons established within the national territory or they may prevent or otherwise obstruct the activities of the person providing the service.[28]

Material Discrimination

It does not follow from Article 60(3) that all national regulation applicable to nationals of that Member State and usually applied to undertakings established there may be applied in its entirety to the temporary activities of undertakings established in other Member States.[29] Rather, application of such regulation to the latter undertakings may be prohibited. It may be prohibited, because Articles 59 to 66 are designed to create a common market in the provision of services, and not merely to abolish formal discrimination between providers of services.[30]

Accordingly, the prohibition of discrimination in Article 60(3) extends to material discrimination. If, for example, an undertaking is established in another Member State and is liable to pay the employer's share of social security contributions there, the undertaking cannot be required to make such contributions under the law of the Member State where it provides a service. The requirement is prohibited, because it cumulates with the liability of the undertaking in its Member State of establishment. Such cumulation means that the requirement is more onerous in economic terms for undertakings established in another Member State than for those undertakings established in the Member State where the service is provided.[31]

Again, if an insurer is established in another Member State, authorised by the supervisory authority of that Member State, and subject to the supervision of that authority, he cannot be required to have a permanent establishment within the territory of the Member State where the service is provided.

[28] Case 33/74 *Johannes Henricus Maria van Binsbergen* v. *Bestuur van de Bedrijfsvereniging voor de Metaalnijverheid* [1974] ECR 1299, 1309.

[29] Case 205/84 *EC Commission* v. *Germany: insurance services* [1986] ECR 3755, 3802. See, earlier, Case 279/80 *Alfred John Webb* [1981] ECR 3305, 3324.

[30] Warner AG in Case 52/79 *Procureur du Roi* v. *Debauve* [1980] ECR 833, 871–2.

[31] Joined Cases 62 & 63/81 *Seco SA and Desquenne and Giral SA* v. *Etablissement d'Assurance contre la Veillesse et l'Invalidité* [1982] ECR 223, 235.

Nor can he be required to obtain a separate authorisation from the supervisory authority of the latter Member State. The requirements are prohibited, because they increase the cost of such services in the Member State in which they are provided, particularly where the insurer conducts business in that Member State only occasionally.[32]

Distortion of Competition

It is not only the cumulation of regulatory requirements in the Member State where the provider is established with regulatory requirements in the Member State where the service is provided and the implied "dual burden" which render the latter requirements inapplicable. For example, where patent-monitoring services in a Member State are reserved to persons holding a special professional qualification, an undertaking established in another Member State cannot be prohibited from providing such services in the former Member State.[33] Even the prescription of a mandatory form of employment relationship for employees of the provider of a service may be prohibited.[34]

In short, therefore, the application of any national regulation which is found to have the effect of distorting competition in the provision of services between Member States is precluded.[35] On the other hand, the freedom to provide services must not be "abused". For example, if an undertaking established in one Member State directs its activity entirely or principally towards another Member State, the latter Member State may apply to the undertaking the professional rules of conduct applicable to providers of similar services established on its territory.[36]

Similarly, national regulation may be rendered inapplicable because of its impact on recipients of services. For example, discrimination in a Member State as regards charges for access to museums is prohibited.[37] The imposition on tourists from other Member States of museum charges from which nationals are exempt may be seen as likely to influence decisions of such persons to visit the Member State concerned.[38] In other words, it is conceivable that conditions of competition in the tourist industry are distorted.

---

[32] Case 205/84 *EC Commission* v. *Germany: insurance services* [1986] ECR 3755, 3803.

[33] Case C–76/90 *Manfred Säger* v. *Dennemeyer & Co. Ltd* [1991] ECR I–4221, I–4224–5. Cf. Case C–275/92 *HM Customs & Excise* v. *Gerhart Schindler and Jörg Schindler* [1994] ECR I–1039, I–1093, regarding restrictions on the holding of lotteries.

[34] Case C–398/95 *Syndesmos ton en Elladi Touristikos kai Taxidiotikon* v. *Ypourgas Ergasias* (5 June 1997).

[35] Case C–381/93 *EC Commission* v. *France: maritime transport* [1994] ECR I–5145, I–5169; and Jacobs AG in Case C–384/93 *Alpine Investments BV* v. *Minister van Financiën* [1995] ECR I–1143, I–1155.

[36] Case 33/74 *Johannes Henricus Maria van Binsbergen* v. *Bestuur van de Bedrijfsvereniging voor de Metaalnijverheid* [1974] ECR 1299, 1309; and Case 205/84 *EC Commission* v. *Germany: insurance services* [1986] ECR 3755, 3801.

[37] Case C–45/93 *EC Commission* v. *Spain: museum charges* [1994] ECR I–911.

[38] This argument was expressly approved by Gulmann AG (*ibid.*, I–914–15) and tacitly accepted by the Court itself (*ibid.*, I–919)

11.3.2 Facilities

The prohibition of discrimination covers not only specific rules governing the provision of a service. The prohibition also covers rules relating to the various general facilities which are of assistance for the provision of that service. The prohibition applies, for example, to rules governing the purchase of property;[39] rules governing access to social housing;[40] and rules requiring that nationals of other Member States, but not nationals of the Member State concerned, pay a security for the costs of court proceedings.[41]

The prohibition of discrimination against recipients is similarly broad. For example, in *Cowan*[42] the Court of Justice ruled that Member States were prohibited from excluding tourists from other Member States, in their capacity as recipients of services under Articles 59 to 66, from the benefits of a state scheme to compensate victims of violent crimes. The rationale was that protection from harm was a corollary of free movement.[43] Hence, equality of treatment had to apply both to state protection against the risk of assault and to compensation provided for by national law when that risk materialised.[44] In other words, discrimination was prohibited in state performance of a public duty which constituted a precondition for competition in the tourist industry.[45]

Hence, the freedom to provide services precludes the application of any national legislation which has the effect of making the provision of services between Member States more difficult than the provision of services purely within one Member State.[46]

Such case law entails an expansive approach to definition of the equality of treatment necessary for implementation of the freedom to provide services as an element in the establishment of the common market. However, it does not meet the implication in establishment of Union Citizenship that discrimination between Union Citizens should in itself be prohibited.

---

[39] Case 305/87 *EC Commission* v. *Greece: property rights* [1989] ECR 1461, 1478.

[40] Case 63/86 *EC Commission* v. *Italy: social housing* [1988] ECR 29, 53.

[41] Case C–20/92 *Anthony Hubbard* v. *Peter Hamburger* [1993] ECR I–3777, I–3794.

[42] Case 186/87 *Ian William Cowan* v. *Trésor Public* [1989] ECR 195. See, generally, F. Schockweiler, "La Portée du principe de non-discrimination de l'art. 7 du traité CEE" [1991] *RTDE* 3–24.

[43] Cf., regarding the right to pursue leisure activities and freedom of establishment, Case C–334/94 *EC Commission* v. *France: registration of vessels* [1996] ECR I–1307, I–1341.

[44] [1989] ECR 195, 221.

[45] Cf., regarding attacks by French farmers on lorries carrying strawberries from Spain, the Reply by Mr Fischler to WQ P–1344/95 (OJ 1995 C222/67) by Maria Izquiredo Rojo.

[46] Case C–381/93 *EC Commission* v. *France: maritime transport* [1994] ECR I–5145, I–5169. Cf. Jacobs AG in Case C–384/93 *Alpine Investments BV* v. *Minister van Financiën* [1995] ECR I–1141, I–1155.

11.4 Exceptions

The rights entailed by the freedom to provide services are rendered subject by Article 66 of the EC Treaty to the exceptions provided for in Articles 55 and 56 of the Treaty. These exceptions were examined in Chapter 10.

11.5 Intellectual Property

Intellectual property rights are protected by an analogy with Article 36 of the EC Treaty. However, the nature of such rights in relation to the provision of services may mean that the exhaustion of rights doctrine may be less restrictive of such rights than it is in connection with the free movement of goods. For example, broadcast diffusion rights are not exhausted by a performance in another Member State.[47]

11.6 "Mandatory Requirements"

The freedom to provide services may be restricted on the basis of mandatory requirements recognised by the Court of Justice. The restrictions entailed must be objectively justified by the need to ensure that professional rules of conduct are complied with and that the interests which such rules seek to safeguard are protected; they must not have economic aims;[48] they must be applied to all persons or undertakings operating in the Member State where the service is provided; and the interest concerned must not already be safeguarded by the provisions to which the provider of a service is subject in the Member State of his establishment.[49] Where these conditions are met, such restrictions may be justified on grounds such as consumer protection;[50] cultural policy;[51] encouragement of media pluralism;[52] conservation of historical, artistic, and archaeological treasures;[53] the maintenance of order in society;[54] and the maintenance of the good reputation of the national financial sector.[55]

---

[47] Case 62/79 *SA Compagnie Générale pour la Diffusion de la Télévision, Coditel* v. *SA Ciné Vog Films* [1980] ECR 881, 903–4.

[48] Case C–398/95 *Syndesmos ton en Elladi Touristikos kai Taxidiotikon* v. *Ypourgas Ergasias* (5 June 1997).

[49] Joined Cases 110 & 111/78 *Ministère Public and Chambre Syndicale des Agents Artistiques et Impresarii de Belgique ASBL* v. *Willy van Wesemael* [1979] ECR 35, 52; and Case 279/80 *Alfred John Webb* [1981] ECR 3305, 3325.

[50] Case 205/84 *EC Commission* v. *Germany: insurance services* [1986] ECR 3755, 3803–4.

[51] Case C–353/89 *EC Commission* v. *Netherlands: radio and television programmes* [1991] ECR I–4069, I–4094.

[52] Case C–23/93 *TV10 SA* v. *Commissariaat voor de Media* [1994] ECR I–4795.

[53] Case C–154/89 *EC Commission* v. *France: tourist guides* [1991] ECR I–659, I–687.

[54] Case C–275/92 *HM Customs & Excise Commissioners* v. *Gerhart Schindler and Jörg Schindler* [1994] ECR I–1039, I–1096.

[55] Case C–384/93 *Alpine Investments BV* v. *Minister van Financiën* [1995] ECR I–1141, I–1179.

For example, *EC Commission* v. *Germany: insurance services*[56] concerned restrictions on the provision of insurance services in Germany. Here the Court of Justice ruled that, regard being had to the particular nature of certain services, specific requirements imposed on suppliers established in other Member States were not incompatible with the Treaty where they had as their purpose the application of rules governing such services. However, the freedom to provide services was one of the fundamental principles of the Treaty. Hence, requirements restricting this freedom might only be applied if they met the above conditions. Only insofar as these conditions were met could requirements relating to the public interest in consumer protection justify the imposition of restrictions on the freedom to provide insurance services.[57]

11.7 Harmonisation

Article 63 of the EC Treaty provides for the adoption of directives to abolish restrictions on freedom to provide services within the Union. Moreover, by virtue of Article 66 of the Treaty, Article 57(2) harmonisation procedures apply to services. Hence, legislation may cover both freedom to establishment and freedom to provide services.[58]

Harmonisation also relates to public procurement. Rules regarding public works contracts are contained in Directive 93/37[59] and rules regarding public service contracts in Directive 92/50.[60] The rules apply to contracts with a value above specified thresholds, concluded by the state, regional and local authorities, associations formed by one or several such authorities, and bodies governed by public law.[61] Special rules apply to the "excluded sectors".[62] Besides the legislation, a Guide to the Community rules on open government procurement has been published by the Commission.[63] Requirements as to review procedures are laid down in Directive 89/665.[64]

---

[56] Case 205/84 [1986] ECR 3755.   [57] *Ibid.*, 3803.

[58] See the measures cited in sect. 10.6 above.

[59] Concerning the co-ordination of procedures for the award of public works contracts (OJ 1993 L199/54).

[60] Relating to the co-ordination of procedures for the award of public service contracts (OJ 1992 L209/1). Amendments have been made by Dir. 97/52 (OJ 1997 L328/1).

[61] Art. 1 of Dir. 93/37 (OJ 1993 L199/54). See also Case 31/87 *Gebroeders Beentjes NV* v. *Netherlands* [1988] ECR 4635, 4655.

[62] Sect. 8.6.1 above.   [63] OJ 1987 C358/1.

[64] On the co-ordination of the laws, regs., and administrative provisions relating to the application of review procedures to the award of public supply and public works contracts (OJ 1989 L395/33).

11.8 Mutual Recognition

Rather than engaging in detailed harmonisation the Union legislature may seek to establish minimum standards, on the basis of which there is to be mutual recognition of "home country control". For example, according to Article 16 of Directive 75/362,[65] medical practitioners established outside the Member State where they provide services do not have to register with professional organisations or bodies in that Member State. They are, however, subject to the applicable national rules of professional conduct. Similar rules apply to lawyers under Directive 77/249.[66] They may also be required to "work in conjunction with" a local lawyer,[67] but this requirement must not be applied disproportionately.[68]

11.9 Services from Third States

Article 66 of the EC Treaty renders Article 58 of the Treaty applicable to services. By virtue of the latter provision, freedom to provide services applies to any company or firm formed according to the law of a Member State and having its registered office, central administration or principal place of business within the Union. However, companies whose registered office is in the Union but whose central management or principal place of business is in a third state must have "an effective and continuous link with the economy of a Member State".[69] Moreover, according to Article 59(2) of the Treaty, the Council may extend the benefits of free movement of services to nationals of third states established in the Union.[70]

However, there may be reluctance unilaterally to extend the benefits of this freedom. For example, in the case of subsidiaries within the Union of third-state financial institutions, the Commission sought to render their enjoyment of liberalisation within the Union dependent on reciprocal treatment of Union institutions in the third state concerned.[71] This approach was only

[65] Concerning the mutual recognition of diplomas, certificates, and other evidence of formal qualifications in medicine, including measures to facilitate the effective exercise of the right of establishment and freedom to provide services (OJ 1975 L167/1).

[66] To facilitate the effective exercise by lawyers of freedom to provide services (OJ 1977 L78/17), Art. 4.

[67] *Ibid.*, Art. 5. See also Case C–427/85 *EC Commission* v. *Germany: lawyers* [1988] ECR I–1123, I–1161–3.

[68] See also Case C–294/89 *EC Commission* v. *France: lawyers* [1991] ECR I–3591, I–3610–11.

[69] General programme on the abolition of restrictions on freedom of establishment (JO 1962 36), Title I.

[70] See, e.g., Arts. 27–32 of Dir. 79/267 (OJ 1979 L63/1) on the co-ordination of laws, regs., and administrative provisions relating to the taking up and pursuit of the business of direct life insurance.

[71] Art. 7 of the proposal of 23 Feb. 1988 (OJ 1988 C84/1) on the co-ordination of laws, regs., and administrative provisions relating to the taking up and pursuit of the business of credit institutions and amending Dir. 77/780.

acceptable to the Council, possibly influenced by GATT negotiations,[72] in a limited form.[73] In the case of such subsidiaries,[74] as in the case of public procurement,[75] the aim now is to secure "comparable and effective" access. Most recently, the Council has resolved that "the use of non-Community resources [by Union air carriers] affords a possibility for access by third countries to the internal market which needs to be looked at in the framework of relations with those countries".[76]

11.10 Agreements with Third States

Free trade agreements have been limited to trade in goods. However, association agreements may contain provisions regarding the supply of services between the parties. Thus, for example, Articles 55 to 57 of the Europe Agreement with Poland[77] provide for the liberalisation of such services.

Moreover, Articles 36 and 37 of the EEA Agreement[78] reproduce, respectively, Articles 59 and 60 of the EC Treaty. More particularly, Article 65(1) of the EEA Agreement refers to the specific provisions and arrangements in Union law concerning public procurement. The relevant acts are listed in Annex XVI[79] to the EEA Agreement.[80]

---

[72] *Europe,* No. 5375 (22 Nov.).

[73] Art. 9 of Dir. 89/646 (OJ 1989 L124/16) on the co-ordination of laws, regs., and administrative provisions relating to the taking up and pursuit of the business of credit institutions. See also Art. 4 of Dir. 90/618 (OJ 1990 L330/44) amending, particularly as regards motor vehicle insurance, Dir. 73/239 and Dir. 88/357 which concern the co-ordination of the laws, regs., and administrative provisions relating to direct insurance other than life insurance; Art. 8 of Dir. 90/619 (OJ 1990 L330/50) on the co-ordination of laws, regs., and administrative provisions relating to life assurance, laying down provisions to facilitate the effective exercise of freedom to provide services and amending Dir. 79/267; and Art. 7(5) of Dir. 93/22 (OJ 1993 L141/27) on investment services in the securities field.

[74] Art. 9(4) of Dir. 89/646 (OJ 1989 L124/16)

[75] Art. 29 of Dir. 90/531 (OJ 1990 L297/1) on procurement procedures of entities operating in the water, transport, and telecommunications sectors.

[76] Council Resolution of 19 June 1995 (OJ 1995 C169/3) on relocation in air transport.

[77] OJ 1993 L348/2.   [78] OJ 1994 L1/3.   [79] Procurement.

[80] EEA arrangements may be regarded as securing "effective and comparable access" for Union undertakings. See the explanatory memorandum to Commission proposal for a decision concerning the extension of the benefit of the provisions of Dir. 90/531 in respect of Austria, Finland, Iceland, Liechtenstein, Norway, and Sweden, COM(93)667.

12

Free Movement of Capital and Payments

The distinction between the free movement of capital and the free movement of current payments was controversial under the EEC Treaty, which made only limited progress in limiting the movement of capital. The distinction may retain importance under agreements with third states which do not provide at all for liberalisation of the movement of capital.

12.1 Capital

Articles 67 to 73 of the EEC Treaty concerned the free movement of capital. In particular, Article 67 of the Treaty required the abolition between Member States of all restrictions on the movement of capital belonging to persons resident in Member States. It also required the abolition of any discrimination based on the nationality or the place of residence of the parties or on the place where such capital was invested. However, abolition of the restrictions was only required to the extent necessary to ensure the proper functioning of the common market.

Article 67 led to little case law, principally because the Court of Justice did not recognise its direct applicability.[1] However, implementing directives were enacted under Article 69 of the Treaty. In particular, Directive 88/361[2] required elimination of all restrictions on monetary transactions, including financial loans and credits, current and deposit account operations, transactions in securities, and other instruments normally dealt in on the money market.

At the same time, measures were adopted under Articles 54(3)(g) and 100 of the EEC Treaty,[3] to "establish a European capital market".[4] The measures

---

[1] Cf., regarding Art. 71 EEC, Case 203/80 *Guerrino Casati* [1981] ECR 2595, 2616.

[2] For the implementation of Art. 67 EEC (OJ 1988 L178/5). It replaced the Dir. of 11 May 1960 (JO 1960 921) First Dir. for the implementation of Art. 67 EEC; Dir. 63/21 (JO 1963 62) Second Dir. for the implementation of Art. 67 EEC; and Dir. 86/566 (OJ 1986 L332/22) amending the First Dir. for the implementation of Art. 67 EEC

[3] Sect. 19.3 below.

[4] 5th recital in the preamble to Dir. 79/279 (OJ 1979 L66/21) co-ordinating the conditions for the admission of securities to official stock exchange listing.

concerned such matters as conditions for admission to stock exchange listing[5] and publication requirements for listed securities.[6]

Articles 67 to 73h of the EC Treaty now deal with the free movement of capital. In particular, Article 73b of the Treaty prohibits all restrictions on the movement of capital between Member States.

Moreover, Article 221 of the EC Treaty is relevant to capital movements. It prohibits discrimination regarding participation in the formation of companies.

12.2 Current Payments

Article 106(1) of the EEC Treaty liberalised current payments. Each Member State undertook to authorise, in the currency of the Member State in which the creditor or beneficiary resided, any payments connected with the movement of goods, services, or capital, and any transfers of capital and earnings. However, such liberalisation was only required to the extent that the movement of goods, services, capital, and persons between Member States had been liberalised pursuant to the Treaty.[7] Article 67(2), in turn, required that current payments connected with the movement of capital between Member States were to be freed from all restrictions. The payments covered were those made by way of consideration for benefits obtained.[8]

The case law made clear that freedom of movement for current payments under the EEC Treaty could not be used as a substitute for systematic liberalisation of capital movements. Some coinage might be treated as covered by the free movement of goods. However, coinage which constituted a means of legal payment or could be regarded as "equivalent to currency" on money markets was not so covered.[9]

True, in *Luisi and Carbone*[10] the Court of Justice ruled that the physical export of bank notes which the exporter concerned said would be used to pay for services to be received in another Member State was covered by Article 106. It might be difficult, in practice, to deny the benefit of this provision where money was moved ostensibly for the purpose of purchasing

    [5] *Ibid.*

    [6] Dir. 80/390 (OJ 1980 L100/1) co-ordinating the requirements for the drawing up, scrutiny, and distribution of the listing particulars to be published for the admission of securities to official stock exchange listing.

    [7] See also Dir. 97/5 (OJ 1997 L43/25) on cross-border credit transfers. Cf. Reg. 3604/93 (OJ 1993 L332/4) specifying definitions for the application of the prohibition of privileged access referred to in Art. 104a EC.

    [8] Joined Cases 286/82 & 26/83 *Graziana Luisi and Giuseppe Carbone* v. *Ministero del Tesoro* [1984] ECR 377, 404.

    [9] Case 7/78 *R.* v. *Ernest George Thompson, Brian Albert Johnson, and Colin Alex Norman Woodiwiss* [1978] ECR 2247, 2274.

    [10] Joined Cases 286/82 & 26/83 *Graziana Luisi and Giuseppe Carbone* v. *Ministero del Tesoro* [1984] ECR 377, 404.

goods or services but, in reality, for investment purposes. However, where goods were imported into a Member State at a price which suggested that a capital transfer was taking place, the importing Member State might act against the transaction.[11] Moreover, according to the Court, Article 106 did not apply to re-exportation of money previously imported with a view to purchasing goods, if the purchase had not materialised.[12] Therefore, an investor who sought to abuse Article 106 for the purpose of effecting capital movements might find himself in a precarious position.

Article 73b(2) of the EC Treaty now provides for the prohibition of restrictions on all payments between Member States.

12.3 Exceptions

Article 73d of the EC Treaty preserves the freedom of Member States to apply tax law provisions which distinguish between tax-payers who are not in the same situation with regard to their place of residence or with regard to the place where the capital is invested.[13] Moreover, Member States may take all requisite measures to prevent infringements of national law and regulations, particularly in the field of taxation and the prudential supervision of financial institutions. They may also lay down procedures for the declaration of capital movements for purposes of administrative or statistical information, and take measures justified on grounds of public policy or public security.[14]

At the same time, restrictions on the right of establishment which are compatible with the Treaty are unaffected by the liberalisation requirements of Article 73b.[15] However, no such measures or procedures may constitute a means of arbitrary discrimination or a disguised restriction on the free movement of capital and payments.[16]

Finally, protective measures to deal with balance-of-payments problems may be adopted under Article 109h.[17] However, subject to Article 109k(6),[18] Article 109h shall cease to apply from the beginning of the third stage of monetary union,[19] that is, when national currencies are replaced by the Euro.[20]

---

[11] Case 65/79 *Procureur de la République* v. *René Chatain* [1980] ECR 1345, 1384, concerning the Swiss Free Trade Agreement (JO 1972 L300/189).

[12] Case 203/80 *Guerrino Casati* [1981] ECR 2595, 2617.

[13] Art. 73d(1)(a) EC. According to a declaration on Art. 73d EC, adopted with the TEU, Member States would only exercise this freedom in respect of capital movements and payments between Member States only on the basis of provisions existing at the end of 1993.

[14] Art. 73d(1)(b) EC.

[15] Art. 73d(2) EC. Conversely, according to Art. 52(2) EC, freedom of establishment is subject to the Treaty provisions concerning capital.

[16] Art. 73d(3) EC.   [17] Sect. 8.5.5 above.

[18] I.e. safeguard measures may still be adopted by Member States not participating in the 3rd stage of monetary union.

[19] Arts 109h(4) and 109i(4) EC respectively.   [20] Art. 109l(4) EC.

12.4 Capital, Payments, and Third States

In relation to the movement of capital and current payments between the Union and third states, the EEC Treaty envisaged co-ordination of national practice. The EC Treaty, instead, focuses on liberalisation.

12.4.1 Co-ordination

Article 70(1) of the EEC Treaty provided for Council adoption of measures for the progressive co-ordination of the exchange policies of Member States in respect of the movement of capital between Member States and third states. However, Article 70(2) dealt with situations where such measures did not permit the elimination of differences between the exchange rules of Member States and where such differences could lead persons resident in one Member State to use the freer transfer facilities within the Union in order to evade the rules of a Member State regarding movement of capital to or from third states. In such situations the Member State might take appropriate measures to overcome the difficulties.

Moreover, according to Article 72 of the same Treaty, Member States were to keep the Commission informed of any movements of capital to and from third states which came to their knowledge. The Commission might deliver to Member States any opinions which it considered appropriate on this subject.

12.4.2 Liberalisation

Article 73b of the EC Treaty now requires, in principle, the same liberalisation of movements of capital and payments between Member States and third states as that applying between Member States.[21] Thus Article 73b(1) prohibits all restrictions on the movement of capital between Member States and third states, and Article 73b(2) prohibits all restrictions on payments between Member States and third states. Restrictions on such payments may, more particularly, be prohibited as quantitative restrictions on exports contrary to Article 11 of Regulation 2603/69.[22]

12.4.3 Exceptions

Various restrictions, additional to those which are also permitted in respect of capital movements between Member States,[23] are permitted specifically in relation to capital movements between the Union and third states.[24]

---

[21] Cf. Art. 7 of Dir. 88/361 (OJ 1988 L178/5) for the implementation of Art. 67 EC.
[22] Case C–124/95 *R.* v. *HM Treasury and the Bank of England, ex p. Centro-Com srl* [1997] ECR I–81, I–126.
[23] Sect. 12.3 above.   [24] Arts. 73c, 73f, and 73g EC.

Residuary National Restrictions

Article 73c(1) of the Treaty allows Member States to continue to apply restrictions on capital movements with third states[25] existing on 31 December 1993.[26]

Article 73c(2) provides for the Council to enact measures by a qualified majority to further the objective of liberalisation of such movements "to the greatest extent possible". However, the Council may, provided it reaches unanimous agreement, also enact measures which "constitute a step back in Community law" as regards such liberalisation.

Economic and Monetary Union

Safeguard measures may be adopted by the Council under Article 73d of the Treaty, where movements of capital to or from third states cause or threaten to cause serious difficulties for the operation of economic and monetary union. Such measures must be strictly necessary and may not be taken for a period exceeding six months.

CFSP

The common foreign and security policy may affect liberalisation of the movement of capital and payments. In particular, Article 73g(1) of the Treaty concerns boycotts adopted against trade with a third state pursuant to this policy and implemented under Article 228a of the Treaty.[27] According to the former provision, the Council may "take the necessary urgent measures on the movement of capital and on payments as regards the third countries concerned".

In addition, Article 73g(2) permits, without prejudice to Article 224,[28] measures to be taken for serious political reasons and on grounds of urgency unilaterally by a Member State against a third state with regard to capital movements and payments. However, the Council may require such measures to be amended or abolished.

12.5 Agreements with Third States

Agreements with third states may contain provisions relating to current payments and capital movements between the parties.

---

[25] cf. Art. 72 EEC.

[26] Where they enjoyed a derogation on the basis of existing Union law, they might continue to apply restrictions covered by that derogation until 31 Dec. 1995.

[27] Sect. 21.14.3 below.

[28] Sect. 8.5.2 above.

12.5.1 Free Trade Agreements

Free trade agreements seek to liberalise current payments. For example, Article 19 of the Swiss Free Trade Agreement[29] provides that payments relating to trade in goods and the transfer of such payments to the Member State in which the creditor is resident or Switzerland shall be free from any restrictions. Moreover, the Contracting Parties to this Agreement must refrain from any exchange or administrative restrictions on the grant, repayment, or acceptance of short and medium-term credits covering commercial transactions in which a resident participates. These obligations, however, only relate to current payments for imported goods "within the limit of their true value".[30]

12.5.2 Association Agreements

Association agreements may seek to secure liberalisation of current payments and some liberalisation of capital movements. For example, according to Article 59 of the Europe Agreement with Poland,[31] the Contracting Parties undertake to authorise, in freely convertible currency, any payments on the current account of balance of payments to the extent that the transaction underlying the payment concerns movements of goods, persons, or services between Parties which have been liberalised pursuant to this Agreement.

Moreover, Article 60(1) of the Agreement concerns transactions on the capital account. As regards such transactions, the Member States and Poland shall ensure the free movement of capital in companies formed in accordance with the laws of the host country and investments made in accordance with provisions on establishment. They shall also ensure the liquidation or repatriation of these investments and of any profit stemming from them. Further liberalisation is envisaged in Article 61 of the Agreement.

12.5.3 EEA Agreement

Articles 40 and 41 of the EEA Agreement[32] are substantially identical to Article 67 of the EEC Treaty, Article 42 of the Agreement reproduces Article 68(2) and (3) of the EEC Treaty,[33] and relevant Union acts are listed in Annex XII to the Agreement.[34] Moreover, Article 41 of the Agreement is

---

[29] JO 1972 L300/189.

[30] Capotorti AG in Case 65/79 *Procureur de la République* v. *René Chatain* [1980] ECR 1345, 1407–8.

[31] OJ 1993 L348/2.   [32] OJ 1994 L1/3.

[33] Art. 124 EEA is also substantially identical to Art. 221 EC.

[34] Annex XII, free movement of capital, introduced transitional periods for EFTA states for implementation of Dir. 88/361 (OJ 1988 L178/5) for the implementation of Art. 67 EC. In addition, Iceland and Norway may continue to restrict foreign ownership of fishing vessels.

substantially identical to Article 106 of the EEC Treaty.[35] Article 46 of the Agreement, which provides for exchange of information and views on a non-binding basis, envisages limited co-operation to deal with problems that arise from the liberalisation entailed.

---

[35] Cf. the Declaration by the Government of Liechtenstein, on the Specific Situation of the Country, regarding Art. 112 EEA and capital inflows liable to endanger access of the resident population to real estate or extraordinary increase in number of nationals from other Contracting Parties or in the number of jobs in the economy, both in comparison with the number of the resident population.

13

Cartels

Article 85 of the EC Treaty concerns cartels. In other words, it concerns restrictive practices arising from collusion between two or more undertakings. In particular, Article 85(1) provides that all agreements between undertakings, decisions by associations of undertakings, and concerted practices which may affect trade between Member States and which have as their object or effect the prevention, restriction, or distortion of competition within the common market are prohibited.

According to Article 85(2), agreements or decisions prohibited pursuant to this Article[1] shall be automatically void.[2] In practice, only those clauses of an agreement that interfere with competition are void and, therefore, unenforceable before national courts. The consequences for other parts of the agreement are not a matter for Union law, but must be determined by the national court concerned according to its national law.[3]

Since Article 85(1) has been held to be directly applicable,[4] there may be further consequences for national court proceedings. For example, an injunction may be granted to restrain practices in breach of this provision, and damages may be awarded in respect of harm occasioned by such practices.[5]

In addition, parties to a restrictive practice prohibited by Article 85(1) may be fined by the Commission pursuant to Regulation 17.[6] Interim measures may also be adopted by the Commission.[7]

---

[1] A distinction is made between "old" and "new" agreements. See Arts 4 and 5 of Reg. 17 (JO 1962 204), First Reg. implementing Arts. 85 and 86 EEC.

[2] Cf., regarding the provisional validity of pre-Reg. 17 agreements, Case C–39/96 *Koninklijke Vereeniging ter Bevordering van de Belangen des Boekhandels* v. *Free Record Shop BV and Free Record Shop Holding NV* [1997] ECR I–2303.

[3] Case 319/82 *Société de Vente de Ciments et Bétons de l'Est* v. *Kerpen and Kerpen GmbH & Co. KG* [1983] ECR 4173, 4184.

[4] Case 127/73 *Belgische Radio en Televisie (BRT) and Société Belge des Auteurs, Compositeurs, et Editeurs* v. *SV SABAM and NV Fonior* [1974] ECR 51, 62.

[5] V. Korah, *An Introductory Guide to EC Competition Law and Practice* (Hart Publishing, Oxford, 1997).

[6] First Reg. implementing Arts. 85 and 86 EEC (JO 1962 204), Art. 15. See also Reg. 2988/74 (OJ 1974 L319/1) concerning limitation periods in proceedings and the enforcement of sanctions under the rules of the EEC Treaty relating to transport and competition.

[7] Case 792/79R *Camera Care Ltd* v. *EC Commission* [1980] ECR 119, 131; and Case T–44/90 *La Cinq Srl* v. *EC Commission* [1992] ECR II–1, II–13.

However, Article 85(3) provides that certain agreements or decisions may be exempted from the prohibition in Article 85(1). Exemption may be granted on an individual or group basis.

These provisions are all to be interpreted in the light of Articles 2 and 3(g) of the Treaty.[8] Their original concern may have been with ensuring that the state barriers to trade abolished by provisions such as Articles 30 and 34 were not replaced by cartels.[9] In particular, the concern may have been to prevent traders in different Member States from agreeing reciprocally to keep out of each other's home market.[10] Increasingly, however, Article 85 has been seen as having the further function of promoting efficiency.[11] Its application may perform this function through encouraging the expansion of efficient firms and sectors of the economy at the expense of those less good at supplying what people want to buy.[12]

13.1 Undertakings

"Undertakings" are not defined in the EC Treaty "common rules on competition".[13] However, they are defined by the Court of Justice for the purposes of Article 85[14] as entities pursuing economic or commercial activity.[15] Non-profit making bodies,[16] co-operatives of workers,[17] and individuals,[18] such as opera singers,[19] may be covered by the term.

On the other hand, a subsidiary may lack the independence from its mother company to be covered.[20] Moreover, bodies entrusted with responsibilities

---

[8] Joined Cases 6 & 7/73 *Istituto Chemioterapico Italiano SpA and Commercial Solvents Corporation* v. *EC Commission* [1974] ECR 223, 252.

[9] Cf. Case 26/76 *Metro-SB-Großmärkte GmbH & Co. KG* v. *EC Commission and Binon AMP* [1977] ECR 1875, 1904.

[10] Cf., regarding the limiting or controlling of markets, Art. 85(1)(b) EC.

[11] Though reconcilation of concern for market integration with concern for efficiency may be problematic. Cf. B. Hawk, "The American (Anti-trust) Revolution: Lessons for the EEC?" [1988] *ECLR* 53–87.

[12] V. Korah, n. 5 above.

[13] Chap. 1 of Title V of Part Three of the EC Treaty is so headed. It contains Arts. 81–89 EC.

[14] Cf. the definitions in Art. 58 EC, concerning freedom of establishment, Art. 80 ECSC, and Art. 196 Euratom.

[15] Roemer AG in Case 32/65 *Italy* v. *EEC Council and EEC Commission: block exemptions* [1966] ECR 389, 418. See also Art. 1 of Prot. 22, concerning the definition of "undertaking" and "turnover", to the EEA Agreement (OJ 1994 L1/3).

[16] Joined Cases 209–215 & 218/78 *Heintz von Landewyck Sàrl* v. *EC Commission* [1980] ECR 3125.

[17] Case C–179/90 *Merci Convenzionali Porto di Genova SpA* v. *Siderurgica Gabrielli SpA* [1991] ECR I–5889.

[18] Dec. 76/743 (OJ 1976 L254/40) relating to a proceeding under Art. 85 EEC (IV/28.996 – Reuter/BASF).

[19] Dec. 78/516 (OJ 1978 L157/39) relating to a proceeding under Art. 85 EEC (IV/29.559 – RAI/UNITEL).

[20] Case 170/83 *Hydrotherm Gerätebau GmbH* v. *Compact del Dott. Ing. Mario Andreoli & C. sas* [1984] ECR 2999, 3016. Cf. Case 15/74 *Centrafarm BV and de Pijper* v. *Sterling Drug Inc.* [1974] ECR 1147, 1183.

such as the management of a public social security system fulfil exclusively social functions. Their activity is based on the principle of national solidarity and is not profit-making. The benefits that are paid out are statutory benefits, bearing no relation to the amount of the contributions. Hence, it is not an economic activity, and bodies entrusted with it are not undertakings for the purposes of Article 85.[21]

13.2 Practices

Article 85(1) of the EC Treaty is concerned with agreements, decisions of associations of undertakings, and concerted practices. These concepts have been broadly interpreted, and in practice their application may tend to overlap.[22]

13.2.1 Agreements

Not only binding agreements but also "gentlemen's agreements", at least when combined with a binding agreement,[23] are covered.[24] It is not necessary that the agreement has been signed[25] or that consent to its terms has been formally expressed.[26] Thus implied terms of an agreement may be covered.[27] Equally, it is not necessary that steps are taken to secure compliance with an agreement.[28] However, "concessions" granted by public authorities do not constitute agreements.[29]

---

[21] Joined Cases C–159 & 160/91 *Christian Poucet* v. *Assurances Générales de France (AGF) and Caisse Mutuelle Régionale du Languedoc-Rousillon (Camulrac)* [1993] ECR I–637, I–670. See also Case C–364/92 *SAT Fluggesellschaft mbH* v. *Eurocontrol* [1994] ECR I–43. On the other hand, the German state labour exchange constituted an undertaking, even though it did not charge for its services and could not make a profit. See Case C–41/90 *Klaus Höfner and Fritz Elser* v. *Macrotron GmbH* [1991] ECR I–1979, I–2016–17.

[22] See, e.g., M. Antunes, "Agreements and Concerted Practices under EEC Competition Law: Is the Distinction Relevant?" [1991] *YBEL* 57–81.

[23] Case 41/69 *ACF Chemiefarma NV* v. *EC Commission* [1970] ECR 661, 693.

[24] Dec. 86/39 (OJ 1986 L230/1, [1988] CMLR 347) relating to a proceeding under Art. 5 EEC (IV/31.149 – Polypropylene); and Case T–7/89 *SA Hercules Chemicals* v. *EC Commission* [1991] ECR II–1711. See regarding "target prices", Case 8/72 *Vereeniging van Cementhandelaren* v. *EC Commission* [1972] ECR 977.

[25] *BP Kemi* [1979] 3 CMLR 684.

[26] Case T–41/96R *Bayer AG* v. *EC Commission* [1996] ECR II–381, II–397.

[27] Case 107/82 *Allgemeine Elektricitäts-Gesellschaft AEG-Telefunken AG* v. *EC Commission* [1983] ECR 3151, 3195; and Case C–277/87 *Sandoz Prodotti Farmaceutici SpA* v. *EC Commission* [1990] ECR I–45.

[28] *Ibid.*

[29] Case 30/87 *Corine Bodson* v. *Pompes Funèbres des Régions Liberées SA* [1988] ECR 2479, 2512.

13.2.2 Decisions of Associations

Decisions of associations[30] need not be binding to be covered by Article 85(1). They may include recommendations lacking legal force,[31] and the framework within which decisions are taken is irrelevant.[32] As a result, an association may be liable for the conduct of its members.[33] Moreover, the constitution of an association may be a decision rather than an agreement,[34] as may its regulations.[35]

13.2.3 Concerted Practices

The concept of concerted practices is broad.[36] In essence, it concerns replacement of the risks of competition[37] or replacement of the independent determination of conduct to be followed[38] by practical co-operation. Such a practice may, for example, be present where information is exchanged.[39] The underlying idea is that intention to concert is sufficient to constitute such a practice, even if there are no actual effects.[40] For example, acquisition of an equity interest in a competitor may be covered by this concept because of the likely effects on the market where the undertakings concerned carry on business.[41]

However, distinguishing between legitimate parallelism and unlawful

[30] See, also regarding decisions of an association of associations of undertakings, Case 123/83 *Bureau National Interprofessionnel du Cognac* v. *Guy Clair* [1985] ECR 391, 423. Cf. Case 71/74 *Nederlandse Vereniging voor Fruit en Groentenimporthandel, Nederlandse Bond van Grossiers in Zuidruchten en ander Geimporteerd Fruit "Frubo"* v. *EC Commission and Vereniging de Fruiturie* [1975] ECR 563, 583.

[31] Case 8/72 *Vereeniging van Cementhandelaren* v. *EC Commission* [1972] ECR 977, 989–90. Cf. Case 246/86 *SC Belasco* v. *EC Commission* [1989] ECR 2117.

[32] Case 123/83 *Bureau National Interprofessionnel du Cognac* v. *Guy Clair* [1985] ECR 391, 423; and Joined Cases 96–102, 104, 105, 108 & 110/82 *IAZ International* v. *EC Commission* [1983] ECR 3369.

[33] Dec. 82/896 (OJ 1982 L379/1; [1983] 2 CMLR 240) relating to a proceeding under Art. 85 EEC (IV/29.883 – AROW/BNIC).

[34] Dec. 80/917 (OJ 1980 L260/24; [1980] 3 CMLR 429) relating to a proceeding under Art. 85 EEC (IV/27.958 – National Sulphuric Acid Association).

[35] Case T–66/89 *Publishers' Association* v. *EC Commission* [1992] ECR II–2016.

[36] See e.g. Joined Cases 100–103/80 *SA Musique Diffusion Française* v. *EC Commission* [1983] ECR 1825, 1898.

[37] Joined Cases 48/69 *Imperial Chemical Industries Ltd* v. *EC Commission* [1972] ECR 619, 655.

[38] Joined Cases 40–48, 50, 54–56 111, 113 & 114/73 *Coöperatieve Vereniging "Suiker Unie" UA* v. *EC Commission* [1975] ECR 1663,

[39] Dec. 77/592 (OJ 1977 L242/10, [1977] 2 CMLR D28) relating to a proceeding under Art. 85 EEC (IV/312-366 – COBELPA/VNP).

[40] Case T–11/89 *Shell International Company Ltd* v. *EC Commission* [1992] ECR II–757, II–881; and Case T–1/89 *Rhône Poulenc SA* v. *EC Commission* [1991] ECR II–867, II–1073. Cf., regarding an option, Joined Cases 19 & 20/74 *Kali und Salz AG and Kali-Chemie* v. *EC Commission* [1975] ECR 499.

[41] Joined Cases 142 & 156/84 *British-American Tobacco Co. Ltd and R.J. Reynolds Industries Inc.* v. *EC Commission* [1987] ECR 4487, 4577. Certain powers for the Commission to control mergers were implied.

concertation may be problematic, and it may be found necessary to rely on circumstantial evidence.[42] There may, for example, be "parallel courses of conduct that are peculiar to oligopolies", in that the courses of conduct of oligopolists interact.[43]

According to the Court of Justice, parallel conduct provides proof of concertation where concertation constitutes the only plausible explanation for such conduct.[44] Article 85 does not, on the other hand, prevent undertakings from adapting themselves "rationally" to the existing and anticipated conduct of their competitors.[45] More particularly, a refusal to supply may be contrary to Article 85(1), but freedom of contract must remain the general rule.[46]

13.3 Distortion of Competition

Article 85(1) of the Treaty contains five sub-paragraphs that exemplify rather than enumerate practices which have as their object or effect the prevention, restriction, or distortion of competition within the common market. The examples cover practices which:

(a) directly or indirectly fix purchase or selling prices or any other trading conditions;

(b) limit or control production, markets, technical development, or investment;

(c) share markets or sources of supply;

(d) apply dissimilar conditions to equivalent transactions with other trading parties, thereby placing them at a competitive disadvantage;

(e) make the conclusion of contracts subject to acceptance by the other parties of supplementary obligations which, by their nature or according to commercial usage, have no connection with the subject of such contracts.

Such practices need not actually have an effect on competition, and intention is irrelevant.[47] It is sufficient that their "object" is to distort

---

[42] See e.g. Case 48/69 *Imperial Chemical Industries Ltd* v. *EC Commission* [1972] ECR 619, 653. But cf. Joined Cases 29 & 30/83 *Compagnie Royale Asturienne des Mines SA and Rheinzink GmbH* v. *EC Commission* [1984] ECR 1679, 1702.

[43] Case 85/76 *Hoffmann-La Roche & Co. AG* v. *EC Commission* [1979] ECR 461, 520. Cf., regarding the possibility of controlling oligopolies through the concept of "collective dominance" for the purposes of Art. 86 EC, sect. 14.1 below.

[44] Joined Cases 29 & 30/83 *Compagnie Royale Asturienne des Mines SA and Rheinzink GmbH* v. *EC Commission* [1984] ECR 1679.

[45] Joined Cases C–89, 104, 114, 116, 117 & 125–129/85 *A. Åhlström Osakeyhtiö* v. *EC Commission* [1993] ECR I–1307, I–1613. Cf. Case 395/87 *Ministère Public* v. *Jean-Louis Tournier* [1989] ECR 2521, 2574.

[46] Case T–41/96R *Bayer AG* v. *EC Commission* [1996] ECR II–381, II–401.

[47] Joined Cases 29 & 30/83 *Compagnie Royale Asturienne des Mines SA and Rheinzink GmbH* v. *EC Commission* [1984] ECR 1679, 1703–4.

competition.[48] Otherwise, the consequences of implementing the agreement must be considered, and factors must be found which show that competition has, in fact, been appreciably distorted.[49]

The concept of distortion of competition is broader than that of prevention or restriction of competition. Apparently, all that is required for a distortion to be present is that competition within the common market should be different from what it would have been without the practices concerned. For example, while state regulation may mean that there is little competition to distort, if some scope for competition remains, it must not be distorted by the practices of undertakings.[50]

A distortion may arise not only from practices by undertakings which differentiate between nationals of Member States or between domestic products and imports or exports. It may also arise from conduct that does not differentiate in this way.[51] Thus agreements to raise prices or to share markets[52] or to tie the sale of one item to another[53] may be prohibited. For example, an agreement among tobacco manufacturers relating to maximum margins to be granted to certain defined categories of wholesalers was covered. The agreement was regarded as distorting competition, because manufacturers no longer had the opportunity of competing against each other as regards mark-ups. At the same time, wholesalers no longer had the opportunity of competing in the services they rendered to the manufacturer.[54]

Where the practices which distort competition are encouraged by the state, the applicability of Article 85 to the undertakings concerned is unaffected.[55] However, where state measures reinforce the effects of such practices, these measures may themselves violate Articles 3(g), 5, and 85 of the Treaty.[56]

---

[48] Joined Cases 56–58/64 *Etablissements Consten SARL and Grundig-Verkaufs GmbH* v. *EEC Commission* [1966] ECR 299, 342.

[49] Case 56/65 *Société Technique Minière* v. *Maschinenbau Ulm* [1966] ECR 235, 249.

[50] Joined Cases 209–215 & 218/78 *Heintz van Landewyck Sàrl* v. *EC Commission* [1980] ECR 3125, 3263–5; and Case T–7/92 *Asia Motor France SA* v. *EC Commission* [1993] ECR II–669, II–696–7.

[51] The market may have to be defined. See e.g., Joined Cases T–68, 77 & 78/89 *Società Italiana Vetro SpA* v. *EC Commission* [1992] ECR II–1403, II–1463.

[52] Case 41/69 *ACF Chemiefarma NV* v. *EC Commission* [1970] ECR 661.

[53] Case T–83/91 *Tetra Pak International SA* v. *EC Commission* [1994] ECR II–755.

[54] Joined Cases 209–215 & 218/78 *Heintz van Landewyck Sàrl* v. *EC Commission* [1980] ECR 3125, 3265. Cf. Joined Cases 240-242, 261, 262, 268 & 269/82 *Stichting Sigarettenindustrie* v. *EC Commission* [1985] ECR 3831.

[55] Case 123/83 *Bureau National Interprofessionnel du Cognac* v. *Guy Clair* [1985] ECR 391, 423–4.

[56] Case 136/86 *Bureau National Interprofessionel du Cognac* v. *Yves Aubert* [1987] ECR 4789, 4815; and Case 311/85 *Vereniging van Vlaamse Reisbureaus* v. *Sociale Dienst van de Plaatselijke en Gewestelijke Overheidsdiensten* [1987] ECR 3801, 3829. But cf. Case C–2/91 *Meng* [1993] ECR I–5751.

13.4 Effect on Trade Between Member States

Practices of undertakings that distort competition within the meaning of Article 85(1) of the EC Treaty are prohibited where trade between Member States may be affected. For example, in *Consten and Grundig*[57] it had been agreed that Consten would be the sole representative of Grundig in France. It had also been agreed that Grundig would only supply in France to Consten and that Consten would not sell outside France. The Court of Justice stated that Article 85(1) applied to agreements which were capable of constituting a threat, either direct or indirect, actual or potential, to freedom of trade between Member States in a manner which might harm the attainment of a single market between Member States.[58] In other words, this provision applies to agreements which may influence the pattern of trade between Member States in such a way as to prejudice the attainment of this objective.[59]

While trade between Member States must be affected, it is not necessary that the goods or services which are the subject of an agreement are themselves traded between Member States.[60] Moreover, such trade may cover the movement of suppliers as well as of goods and services.[61]

13.4.1 *De Minimis* Issues

Determination whether trade between Member States is affected may involve the application of a *de minimis* rule.[62] Insofar as such a rule is applicable, a restrictive practice may fall outside Article 85(1) because of its limited impact on competition and trade between Member States. It appears that the applicability of this rule depends on qualitative rather than quantitative criteria.[63] In other words, its application depends on whether there is a real rather than purely theoretical possibility that competition in such trade may be distorted.

[57] Joined Cases 56–58/64 *Etablissements Consten SARL and Grundig-Verkaufs GmbH* v. *EEC Commission* [1966] ECR 299.

[58] *Ibid.*, 341. The importance attached to market unification may explain why the ECJ does not, like US courts, as in *Continental T.V. Inc.* v. *G.T.E. Sylvania Inc.* (1977) 433 US 36, treat restrictive practices affecting intrabrand competition more leniently than those affecting interbrand competition.

[59] Case 42/84 *Remia BV and Verenigde Bedrijven Nutricia* v. *EC Commission* [1985] ECR 2545, 2572.

[60] Case 123/83 *Bureau National Interprofessionnel du Cognac* v. *Guy Clair* [1985] ECR 391, 425. See also Case 8/72 *Vereeniging van Cementhandelaren* v. *EC Commission* [1972] ECR 977, 991.

[61] Case 161/84 *Pronuptia de Paris GmbH* v. *Pronuptia de Paris Irmgard Schillgalis* [1986] ECR 353, 384; and Case 45/85 *Verband der Sachversicherer eV* v. *EC Commission* [1987] ECR 405.

[62] Notice on agreements of minor importance which do not fall under Art. 85(1) EEC (OJ 1994 C368/20). Amendment and concentration on questions of market share are envisaged by the Commission (OJ 1997 C29/3). See, generally, F. Barr, "The New Commission Notice on Agreements of Minor Importance: Is Appreciability a Useful Measure" [1997] *ECLR* 202–13.

[63] Note the rejection of a quantitative analysis by the ECJ in Case 30/78 *Distillers Co. Ltd* v. *EC Commission* [1980] ECR 2229, 2265.

For example, an exclusive dealing agreement, even with absolute territorial protection, may escape the prohibition in Article 85(1) because of the weak position of the persons concerned in the relevant market.[64] Such an agreement may do so, because it is not considered to affect trade between Member States.[65] It is, therefore, necessary to take into account the nature and quantity, limited or otherwise, of the products concerned; the isolated nature of the agreement or, alternatively, its position in a series of agreements; and the severity of the clauses intended to limit trade or, alternatively, the opportunities allowed for competitors in the same products by way of parallel re-exportation or importation.[66]

13.4.2 "Domestic Agreements"

De minimis questions may be bound up with the question whether restrictive practices between undertakings within the same Member State relating exclusively to products sold domestically are covered by Article 85(1). Practices of this kind are only covered where they have the effect of making the domestic market more difficult to penetrate by undertakings from other Member States.[67] Such an effect depends on various factors, including the market position of the parties to the agreements[68] and the actual impact of the agreements on imports.[69] The effect may be present where the agreement is part of a network or networks of agreements "sewing up" the market in the Member State concerned and thereby impeding trade with other Member States.[70]

The judgment of the Court of Justice in *Delimitis*[71] has elaborated on the circumstances in which the effect may be present. This judgment concerned a beer supply agreement between a brewery and a publican in Germany. The Court ruled that an agreement which both formally and as a matter of practical reality permitted purchases from other Member States was not prohibited. An agreement only had the requisite effect on trade between Member States to be prohibited by Article 85(1) where access to the national market was, in the economic and legal context of the agreement at issue, made more difficult for competitors. The fact that the agreement might be

---

[64] Case 5/69 *Franz Völk* v. *Etablissements J. Vervaecke* [1969] ECR 295, 303.

[65] See e.g. Case 28/77 *Tepea BV* v. *EC Commission* [1978] ECR 1391, 1461. But cf. Case 319/82 *Société de Vente de Ciments et Bétons de l'Est* v. *Kerpen and Kerpen GmbH & Co. KG* [1983] ECR 4173, 4183.

[66] Case 56/65 *Société Technique Minière* v. *Maschinenbau Ulm* [1966] ECR 235, 250.

[67] See e.g. Case C–234/89 *Stergios Delimitis* v. *Henninger Bräu AG* [1991] ECR I–935, I–984–7. See earlier, Case 23/67 *SA Brasserie de Haecht* v. *Wilkin* [1967] ECR 407, 415–16.

[68] Case 5/69 *Franz Völk* v. *Etablissements J. Vervaecke* [1969] ECR 295, 302.

[69] Case 247/86 *Société Alsacienne et Lorraine de Télécommunications et d'Electronique (Alsatel)* v. *SA Novasam* [1988] ECR 5987, 6008.

[70] Case 23/67 *SA Brasserie de Haecht* v. *Wilkin* [1967] ECR 407, 415; and Case C–393/92 *Municipality of Almelo* v. *Energiebedrijf Ijsselmij NV* [1994] ECR I–1477.

[71] Case C–234/89 *Stergios Delimitis* v. *Henninger Brau AG* [1991] ECR I–935.

one of a number of agreements having a cumulative effect on competition within that market was only one of several factors relevant to a determination whether access was obstructed. The agreement also had to contribute significantly to the obstructive effect of the network of agreements viewed as a whole in their economic and legal context. The scale of the contributory effect depended on the position of the parties in the market and on the duration of the agreement.[72]

13.5 Exemptions, "Comfort Letters", and Negative Clearance

Article 85(3) of the EC Treaty provides that the Commission may, on an individual or group basis, grant exemptions from the Article 85(1) prohibition. As the Court of Justice recognises, this provision concerns practices compatible with the promotion of Treaty objectives.[73] In addition, "comfort letters" may be issued by the Commission, or negative clearance may be granted.

13.5.1 Individual Exemptions

Where an individual exemption is granted, the Commission declares Article 85(1) inapplicable to the conduct concerned. The grant of such an exemption is subject to both substantive and procedural conditions.

Substantive Conditions

To qualify for an individual exemption, an agreement, decision, or concerted practice must satisfy four substantive conditions set out in Article 85(3). The first condition is that it must contribute to improving the production or distribution of goods or to promoting technical or economic progress. According to Commission practice, such a benefit must exceed that which would result from undistorted competition.[74] The second condition is that consumers[75] should be allowed a fair share of the resulting benefit.[76] In practice, where the first condition is met, the Commission tends to assume the second also to be met, provided that a sufficient degree of competition remains in the relevant market.[77] However, in view of the requirements of the

---

[72] *Ibid.*, I–987.

[73] Case 14/68 *Walt Wilhelm* v. *Bundeskartellamt* [1969] ECR 1, 14.

[74] Dec. 76/172 (OJ 1976 L30/13) relating to a proceeding under Art. 85 EEC (IV/27.073 – Bayer/Gist-Brocades).

[75] I.e. ultimate purchasers. See Dec. 68/319 (JO 1968 L201/7; [1968] CMLR D35).

[76] In Joined Cases 43 & 63/82 *Vereniging ter Bevordering van het Vlaamse Boekwezen and Vereeniging ter Bevordering van de Belangen des Boekhandels* v. *EC Commission* [1984] ECR 19, 67–70 this condition was not met because of lack of consumer choice.

[77] Dec. 75/76 (OJ 1975 L29/20) relating to a proceeding under Art. 85 EEC (IV/26.603 – Rank/Sopelem).

two further conditions for exemption, it is questionable whether any independent significance is really given to the condition concerning consumer benefit.[78] According to the third condition, restrictions must not be imposed on the undertakings concerned which are not indispensable to attainment of the objectives outlined in the first condition.[79] Finally, the fourth condition stipulates that the undertakings must not be afforded the possibility of eliminating competition in respect of a substantial part of the common market.[80]

Notification Requirements

To obtain an individual exemption, the parties must notify their conduct to the Commission.[81] Proper notifications provide immunity from the Commission's power to impose fines in respect of any act occurring after notification. This immunity is operative from the date of notification until the Commission adopts a formal decision refusing to grant exemption or issues a preliminary notice to that effect.[82] However, a notification that does not comply with all the procedural requirements laid down by Regulation 17[83] will be deemed not to have taken place.[84]

13.5.2 Group Exemptions

Group exemptions have been provided for in regulations concerning exclusive distributorship agreements,[85] exclusive purchasing agreements,[86] motor vehicle distribution and servicing agreements,[87] patent licensing agreements,[88] specialisation agreements,[89] research and development agreements,[90] franchise

---

[78] A. Evans, "Article 85(3) Exemption: 'Allowing Consumers a Fair Share of the Resulting Benefit'" in M. Goyens (ed.), *European Competition Policy and the Consumer Interest* (Bruylant, Brussels, 1985), 99–120.

[79] See also Case T–66/89 *Publishers' Association* v. *EC Commission* [1992] ECR II–1995.

[80] See also Joined Cases 209–215 & 218/78 *Heintz van Landewyck Sàrl* v. *EC Commission* [1980] ECR 3125. The exemption of an agreement may be annulled by the CFI because the agreement entails discrimination. See Case T–88/92 *Groupement d'Achat Edouard Leclerc* v. *EC Commission* [1996] ECR II–1961, II–2020.

[81] Art. 4 of Reg. 17 (JO 1962 204); Reg. 27 (JO 1962 1118) First Regulation implementing Reg. 17; and Notice on procedure concerning notification (OJ 1983 C295/6).

[82] Art. 15(5) and (6) of Reg. 17 (JO 1962 204).

[83] As to what constitutes notification, see Case 106/79 *Vereniging ter Bevordering van de Belangen des Boekhandels* v. *Eldi Records BV* [1980] ECR 1137, 1148. See also Reg. 3385/94 (OJ 1994 L377/28) on the form, detail, content, and other details of applications and notifications provided for in Reg. 17.

[84] Case 30/78 *Distillers Co. Ltd* v. *EC Commission* [1980] ECR 2229, 2264.

[85] Reg. 1983/83 (OJ 1983 L173/1) on certain categories of exclusive distribution agreements.

[86] Reg. 1984/83 (OJ 1983 L173/5) on certain categories of exclusive purchasing agreements. A Commission Notice (OJ 1984 C101/2) deals with both categories of agreements.

[87] Reg. 1475/95 (OJ 1995 L145/25) on certain categories of motor vehicle distribution and servicing arrangements.

[88] Reg. 2349/84 (OJ 1984 L219/15) on certain categories of patent licensing agreements.

[89] Reg. 417/85 (OJ 1985 L53/1) on certain categories of specialisation agreements.

[90] Reg. 418/85 (OJ 1985 L53/5) on certain categories of R & D agreements.

agreements,[91] know-how licensing agreements,[92] technology transfer agreements,[93] insurance,[94] maritime transport,[95] and air transport arrangements[96] and cooperation.[97] Where agreements meet the conditions laid down in the relevant regulation, they are exempt from the prohibition in Article 85(1) without the need for notification.[98] Even though they do not meet the conditions, an individual exemption may still be available.[99]

13.5.3 "Comfort Letters"

The Commission may send a "comfort letter" to undertakings. Such a letter states the view of the Commission that their conduct does not breach Article 85(1) or that an exemption under Article 85(3) is available. As far as the Commission is concerned, such a letter closes the file, unless material legal or factual circumstances change.[100]

13.5.4 Negative Clearance

Undertakings may apply to the Commission for a negative clearance.[101] A negative clearance may be granted in the case of minor agreements and agreements unlikely to have any significant effect on trade between Member States. In granting such a clearance, the Commission states that there is no reason, in the light of the information available, to intervene under the Treaty.

More generally, the Commission has issued notices indicating categories of

---

[91] Reg. 4087/88 (OJ 1988 L359/46) on certain categories of franchise agreements.

[92] Reg. 556/89 (OJ 1989 L61/1) on certain categories of know-how licensing agreements.

[93] Reg. 240/96 (OJ 1996 L31/2) on certain categories of technology transfer agreements.

[94] Reg. 1534/91 (OJ 1991 L143/1) on certain categories of agreements, decisions, and concerted practices in the insurance sector.

[95] Reg. 479/92 (OJ 1992 L55/3) on certain categories of agreements, decisions, and concerted practices between liner shipping companies (consortia); and Reg. 870/95 (OJ 1995 L89/7) on certain categories of agreements, decisions, and concerted practices between liner shipping companies (consortia) pursuant to Reg. 479/92.

[96] Reg. 3976/87 (OJ 1987 L374/9) on certain categories of agreements and concerted practices in the air transport system; Reg. 83/91 (OJ 1991 L10/9); and Reg. 3652/93 (OJ 1993 L333/37) on certain categories of agreements between undertakings relating to computerised reservation systems for air transport services.

[97] Reg. 1617/93 (OJ 1993 L155/18) on certain categories of agreements and concerted practices concerning joint planning and coordination of schedules, joint operations, consultations on passenger and cargo tariffs on scheduled air services, and slot allocation at airports.

[98] The position of third parties is not affected. See Case C–41/96 *VAG – Handlerbeirat eV* v. *SYD – Consult* (5 June 1997). See, generally, regarding group exemptions and third parties, Case C–128/95 *Fontaine SA* v. *Aqueducs Automobiles SARL* [1997] ECR I–967, I–980.

[99] Dec. 90/46 (OJ 1990 L32/19; [1991] 4 CMLR 208) relating to a proceeding under Art. 85 EEC (IV/32.006 – Alcatel Espace/ANT Nachrichtentechnik).

[100] Notice on procedures concerning notifications pursuant to Art. 4 of Reg. 17 (OJ 1983 C295/6).

[101] Art. 2 of Reg. 17 (JO 1962 204).

agreements that it does not consider to be prohibited by Article 85(1).[102] In other words, "group negative clearances" are granted. The categories concern exclusive dealing contracts with commercial agents;[103] cooperation agreements between small and medium-sized enterprises;[104] subcontracting agreements, particularly those involving small and medium-sized enterprises;[105] and agreements of minor importance.[106] A "Green Paper" setting out proposals for reform has been published.[107]

13.6 "Rule of Reason"

The Court of Justice, consistently with its recognition of mandatory requirements in relation to the "four freedoms",[108] applies a "rule of reason" to Article 85(1) of the EC Treaty.[109] According to the case law, certain restrictive agreements may not be caught by Article 85(1), where they are consistent with what the Court regards as fair competition. Such competition is seen in structural terms[110] and should be such as to enable new entrants to participate in a unified market.[111]

For example, the Court has ruled that franchising agreements may escape the Article 85(1) prohibition.[112] Similarly, a selective distribution agreement may be "an aspect of competition which accords with Article 85(1)", provided that the criteria for selection of distributors are applied uniformly and objectively.[113] Qualitative criteria for selection, such as those related to

---

[102] Cf. the guidelines on the application of EEC competition rules in the telecommunications sector (OJ 1991 C233/2).

[103] Communication concerning exclusive representation contracts with commercial representatives (JO 1962 2921).

[104] Communication concerning agreements, decisions, and concerted practices related to co-operation between undertakings (JO 1968 C75/3).

[105] Communication concerning assessment of certain subcontracting agreements in relation to Art. 85(1) EEC (OJ 1979 C1/2).

[106] Notice on agreements of minor importance which do not fall under Art. 85(1) EC (OJ 1994 C368/20).

[107] Green paper on vertical restraints in EC competition policy, COM(96)721.

[108] Cf. VerLoren van Themaat AG in Case 286/81 *Oosthoek's Uitgeversmaatschappij BV* [1982] ECR 4575, 4592.

[109] Cf. Case C–234/89 *Stergios Delimitis* v. *Henninger Bräu AG* [1991] ECR I–935, I–984, where the ECJ examined a beer supply agreement by reference to its effect rather than its object, apparently because the restrictions of competition entailed by such agreements were necessary to achieve pro-competitive ends.

[110] Cf. the consideration given to employment effects for the purposes of application of Art. 85(3) EC in Case 28/76 *Metro-SB-Großmärkte GmbH & Co. KG* v. *EC Commission* [1977] ECR 1875, 1916.

[111] Case 56/65 *Société Technique Minière* v. *Maschinenbau Ulm* [1966] ECR 235, 250.

[112] Case 161/84 *Pronuptia de Paris GmbH* v. *Pronuptia de Paris Irmgard Schillgalis* [1986] ECR 353.

[113] Case 26/76 *Metro-SB-Großmärkte GmbH & Co. KG* v. *EC Commission and Binon AMP* [1977] ECR 1875, 1904; and Case T–19/92 *Groupement d'Achat Edouard Leclerc* v. *EC Commission* [1996] ECR II–1851, II–1896. Cf., regarding an "open exclusive licence", Case 258/78 *L.C. Nungesser KG and Kurt Eisele* v. *EC Commission* [1982] ECR 2015, 2069.

professional qualifications, technical knowledge of staff, and equipment in establishments,[114] are acceptable in the case of consumer durables of high quality and technical sophistication. However, such criteria must not be more restrictive than necessary,[115] and parallel importation must not be prohibited.[116]

Such case law has particular importance for national courts, which may apply Article 85(1) but not Article 85(3).[117] It means that such courts may find a practice to be lawful independently of an individual exemption by the Commission or the availability of a group exemption.

13.7 Intellectual Property

The exercise of intellectual property rights must not distort competition. On the other hand, the "specific subject matter" of such rights is respected by Union law, provided that there is no abuse.

13.7.1 Distortions of Competition

Undertakings that employ intellectual property rights as part of an agreement to partition the common market[118] or otherwise to distort competition[119] violate Article 85(1) of the Treaty. On the other hand, the grant of exclusive rights to different broadcasters in different Member States entails no such violation.[120] In fact, determination of the presence of a violation may be a complicated process.

Before assignment of an intellectual property right can be treated as giving effect to an agreement prohibited by Article 85(1), it is necessary to analyse the context, the commitment underlying the assignment, the intention of the parties, and the consideration for the assignment.[121] For example, in *Consten and Grundig*[122] Grundig had assigned its trade mark in France to Consten.

---

[114] Dec. 92/33 (OJ 1992 L12/24) relating to a proceeding under Art. 85 EEC (IV/33.242 – Yves Saint Laurent Parfums).

[115] But cf., regarding guarantees, Case C–367/92 *Metro SB-Großmärkte GmbH & Co. KG* v. *Cartier SA* [1994] ECR I–15.

[116] Dec. 91/532 (OJ 1991 L287/37) relating to a proceeding under Art. 85 EEC (IV/32.879 – Viho/Toshiba). Cf., regarding covenants on the sale of a business, Case 42/84 *Remia BV* v. *EC Commission* [1985] ECR 2545.

[117] Case 48/72 *SA Brasserie de Haecht* v. *Wilkin-Janssen* [1973] ECR 77, 87.

[118] Joined Cases 56 & 58/64 *Etablissements Consten SARL and Grundig-Verkaufs GmbH* v. *EEC Commission* [1966] ECR 299, 345.

[119] Case 193/83 *Windsurfing International Inc.* v. *EC Commission* [1986] ECR 611.

[120] Case 262/81 *Coditel SA* v. *Ciné Vog Films* [1982] ECR 3361.

[121] Case C–9/93 *IHT Internationale Heiztechnik GmbH and Uwe Danziger* v. *Ideal-Standard GmbH and Wabco Standard GmbH* [1994] ECR I–2789, I–2855.

[122] Joined Cases 56 & 58/64 *Etablissements Consten SARL and Grundig-Verkaufs GmbH* v. *EEC Commission* [1966] ECR 299.

This assignment was treated as giving effect to the restrictive agreement discussed above.[123]

In *Sirena*[124] the Court of Justice went further. In this case an American corporation had assigned its trade mark rights to an Italian undertaking and to a German undertaking. These two undertakings duly registered the mark in their respective countries. These arrangements were made before entry into force of the Treaty, and so there was no agreement to which Article 85(1) could apply. However, the Court found it sufficient that an agreement concluded earlier continued to have restrictive effects after entry into force of the Treaty.[125] Accordingly, the Court ruled that one party to the agreement violated Article 85 by seeking to employ its rights to exclude imports from the other party.[126] On the other hand, trade mark delimitation agreements that serve a legitimate function and do not attempt to partition the common market fall outside Article 85(1).[127]

13.7.2 "Specific Subject Matter"

In *Consten* the Court of Justice accepted that the "grant" of trade mark rights was protected by Article 222 of the EC Treaty. However, the Court maintained that the exercise of such rights might be restricted by Article 85(1).[128] In *Sirena* the Court relied on the principle underlying Article 36 of the Treaty[129] and ruled that this principle protected the "existence" of trade mark rights. Again, however, the Court maintained that their exercise could be restricted by Article 85(1).[130] As the case law has evolved, it has become clear that the "specific subject matter" of intellectual property rights generally, as discussed in Chapter 8,[131] is in principle unaffected by Article 85(1).

13.7.3 "Abuse of Right"

Rights that constitute the specific subject matter of an intellectual property right must not be abused. A formal basis for this proposition may be found in Article 36(2) of the Treaty. It states that derogations on the grounds specified in the first paragraph this provision may not constitute a disguised restriction on trade between Member States. For example, in *Terrapin*[132] the Court of Justice ruled that a restrictive agreement would render the proviso in Article 36(2) operative. In the presence of such an agreement exercise of

---

[123] Sect. 13.4.   [124] Case 40/70 *Sirena Srl* v. *Eda Srl* [1971] ECR 69.   [125] *Ibid.*, 83.
[126] *Ibid.*, 83.
[127] Case 35/83 *BAT Cigaretten-Fabriken GmbH* v. *EC Commission* [1985] ECR 363, 385.
[128] [1966] ECR 299, 345.   [129] Sect. 8.5.1 above.
[130] Case 40/70 *Sirena Srl* v. *Eda Srl* [1971] ECR 69, 83.   [131] Sect. 8.5.3.
[132] Case 119/75 *Terrapin (Overseas) Ltd* v. *Terranova Industrie C.A. Kapferer & Co.* [1976] ECR 1039.

the trade mark rights concerned to exclude imports bearing a similar would be prohibited by Article 85(1).[133]

Moreover, a trade mark owner who employs different marks[134] or different packaging[135] in different Member States with a view to partitioning the common market is not entitled to prevent the importation of the products concerned. He is not entitled to do so, even if the products have been repackaged by a third party. Again, the Commission has decided that agreements between undertakings with the same or confusingly similar trade marks to divide the common market are prohibited by Article 85(1). According to the Commission, they are prohibited, even if the ostensible purpose of such agreements is to protect consumers from confusion.[136]

13.8 Procedures

The Commission plays a central role in competition law procedures. According to the Commission, its role is to act in the public interest, whereas national courts have the task of safeguarding the subjective rights of private individuals.[137] A distinction may also be made between the role of courts and Commission concern with "the substance" of competition issues.[138] Even so, as the Commission itself maintains, "if the competition process is to work well in the internal market", co-operation is necessary between the Commission, national competition authorities, and national and European Courts.[139]

13.8.1 Commission

The procedural role of the Commission is outlined in Regulation 17.[140]

Initiation of Proceedings

The Commission may initiate proceedings on its own initiative,[141] following a notification for exemption or an application for negative clearance, or in response to a complaint. Complaints may be made by a Member State or a natural or legal person claiming a legitimate interest.[142]

---

[133]   *Ibid.*, 1062.

[134]   Case 3/78 *Centrafarm BV* v. *American Home Products Corporation* [1978] ECR 1823, 1842.

[135]   Case 102/77 *Hoffmann-La Roche & Co. AG* v. *Centrafarm Vertriebsgesellschaft Pharmazeutischer Erzeugnisse mbH* [1978] ECR 1139, 1164.

[136]   *Re the Persil Trade Mark* [1978] 1 CMLR 395.

[137]   Notice on co-operation between national courts and the Commission in applying Arts. 85 and 86 EC (OJ 1993 C39/6), para. 4. Cf. Case T–24/90 *Automec Srl* v. *EC Commission* [1992] ECR II–2223, II–2277, and Case C–354/90 *Fédération Nationale Extérieur des Produits Alimentaires and Syndicat National des Négociants et Transformateurs de Saumon* v. *France* [1991] ECR I–5505, I–5528.

[138]   Jacobs AG (*ibid.*, I–5519).

[139]   Notice on co-operation between national courts and the Commission in applying Arts. 85 and 86 EC (OJ 1993 C39/6), para. 3.

[140]   JO 1962 204.   [141]   *Ibid.*, Art. 3(1).   [142]   *Ibid.*, Art. 3(2).

The Commission cannot be compelled to initiate proceedings. However, it must examine carefully the factual and legal particulars brought to its notice by a complainant. On the basis of such an examination, it is to decide whether these particulars disclose conduct of such a kind as to distort competition in trade between Member States.[143] Where the Commission rejects a complaint, the Court of First Instance will review the legality of the decision.[144]

Investigative Powers

The Commission may request information from national authorities, undertakings, and associations of undertakings under Article 11 of Regulation 17.[145] However, there must be a link between the information requested and the breach of competition law being investigated. Moreover, the burden implied for the undertaking concerned in providing the information must not be disproportionate to the requirements of the investigation.[146]

The information provided must not be misleading. On the other hand, the undertaking concerned is not compelled to admit having violated competition law. In other words, there is some protection against self-incrimination.[147]

If the request is not met, the Commission may adopt a decision requiring the information to be provided. The Commission also has "search and seizure" powers[148] under Article 14 of the Regulation. However, written communications between a lawyer and client are protected by professional privilege, which means that the communications need not be revealed.[149] Moreover, according to Article 20 of the Regulation, the information obtained by the Commission may only be used for the purpose of the relevant investigation.

Hearings

The undertakings or associations of undertakings being investigated must, according to Article 19 of Regulation 17,[150] be given an opportunity to present their views before the Commission takes a decision on the merits.[151]

---

[143] Case T–24/90 *Automec Srl* v. *EC Commission* [1992] ECR II–2223, II–2276.
[144] Case T–114/92 *BEMIM* v. *EC Commission* [1995] ECR II–147, II–176.
[145] JO 1962 204.
[146] Case C–36/92 *P. Samenwerkende Elektriciteits-produktiebedrijven NV* v. *EC Commission* [1994] ECR I–1911.
[147] Case 374/87 *Orkem* v. *EC Commission* [1989] ECR 3283.
[148] Case 136/79 *National Panasonic (UK) Ltd* v. *EC Commission* [1980] ECR 2033; Joined Cases 46/87 & 227/88 *Hoechst* v. *EC Commission* [1989] ECR 2859.
[149] Case 155/79 *AM & S (Europe) Ltd* v. *EC Commission* [1982] ECR 1575.
[150] JO 1962 204.
[151] See also the Notice (OJ 1997 C23/3) on the internal rules of procedure for processing requests for access to the file in cases pursuant to Arts. 85 & 86 EC, Arts. 65 & 66 ECSC, and Reg. 4064/89. It was issued following the ruling in Joined Cases T–30/91 *Solvay SA* v. *EC Commission* [1995] ECR II–1775.

Such a decision is one which clears, prohibits, or exempts an agreement, or imposes fines or periodic penalty payments.[152] If the Commission considers it necessary, other natural or legal persons may be heard. Applications by such persons to be heard shall, where they show a sufficient interest, be granted.

More particularly, where the Commission intends to give a negative clearance or to take a decision in application of Article 85(3) of the Treaty, it shall publish a summary notice. In the notice it shall invite interested third parties to submit their observances within a time limit of not less than one month. Publication shall have regard to the legitimate interest of undertakings in the protection of their business secrets.[153]

Decisions

If the Commission finds that there is an infringement of Article 85, it may by decision require the undertakings or associations of undertakings concerned to end such infringement.[154] Otherwise, the Commission may decide to grant a negative clearance[155] or an exemption.[156]

Publication

Decisions to clear, prohibit, exempt, or impose conditions on an exemption must, according to Article 21 of Regulation 17,[157] be published in the Official Journal. The publication shall state the names of the parties and the main content of the decision. However, it shall have regard to the legitimate interest of undertakings in the protection of their business secrets.

Fines

Fines may be imposed for the supply of incorrect, incomplete or misleading information under Article 15(1) of Regulation 17.[158] Fines of up to one million Euro or 10 per cent of turnover for the previous year[159] may also be imposed under Article 15(2) of the Regulation for intentional or negligent infringement of Article 85 of the Treaty. In the case of associations of undertakings, the turnover of all the members may be aggregated for the purpose of calculating the amount of the fine.[160] Alternatively, periodic penalty payments may be imposed under Article 16 of the Regulation.

13.8.2 National Authorities

The Treaty makes no provision for national administrative enforcement of competition law requirements, but such enforcement may be permitted. In

---

[152] See also Reg. 99/63 (JO 1963 2268) on hearings provided for in Art. 19(1) and (2) of Reg. 17.
[153] JO 1962 204, Art. 19(3).   [154] *Ibid.*, Art. 3.   [155] *Ibid.*, Art. 2.   [156] *Ibid.*, Art. 6.
[157] *Ibid.*   [158] *Ibid.*
[159] Joined Cases 100–103/80 *Musique Diffusion Française SA* v. *EC Commission* [1983] ECR 1823.
[160] Joined Cases T–39 & 49/92 *Groupement des Cartes Bancaires "CB" and Europay International SA* v. *EC Commission* [1994] ECR II–49.

particular, as long as the Commission has not initiated a procedure to grant a negative clearance, to grant an exemption, or to require the termination of an infringement, the national authorities remain competent to apply Article 85(1).[161] Indeed, for the purposes of Swedish accession to the Union, the Commission considered that the Swedish Government "need[ed] to adopt implementing measures that [would] give it the effective tools it ha[d] hitherto lacked" to enforce competition policy.[162]

However, the ruling of the Court of Justice in *Walt Wilhelm*[163] concerned the legality of action by the German Cartel Office against restrictive practices that were also the subject of Commission proceedings. The Court ruled that national authorities were not to act in such a way as to interfere with the uniform application of Union competition law. Rather, they had to co-operate with the Commission.[164]

The practical operation of the basic principle embodied in this ruling may be problematic.[165] In particular, it is disputed whether national authorities may apply their national competition law to agreements favoured by the Commission. On the one hand, Commission decisions rejecting a complaint of violation of Union competition law[166] and "comfort letters" do not affect application of national competition law.[167] On the other hand, block exemptions do affect its application.[168]

13.8.3 National Courts

Article 85(1) of the Treaty has been held to be directly applicable.[169] Hence, national courts may find an agreement prohibited by this provision to be void under Article 85(2). They may also grant injunctions to restrain a violation of the former provision and award damages for a violation.[170]

On the other hand, since Article 85(3) necessitates the exercise of Commission discretion, it has been held not to be directly applicable. Hence,

---

[161] Art. 9(3) of Reg. 17 (JO 1962 204).

[162] *Commission Opinion on Sweden's Application for Membership*, Bull. EC, Supp. 5/92, 25.

[163] Case 14/68 *Walt Wilhelm* v. *Bundeskartellamt* [1969] ECR 1.

[164] *Ibid.*, 14–15.

[165] See, now, Notice on co-operation between national competition authorities and the Commission in handling cases falling within the scope of Art. 85 or 86 EC (OJ 1997 C313/3). See, generally, P.B. Marsden, "Inducing Member State Enforcement of European Competition Law: a Competition Policy Approach to 'Antitrust Federalism'" [1997] *ECLR* 234–41.

[166] Case T–575/93 *Caspar Koelman* v. *EC Commission* [1996] ECR II–1, II–19–20.

[167] Joined Cases 253/78 & 1–37/79 *Procureur de la République* v. *Bruno Giry and Guerlain SA* [1980] ECR 2327, 2375; and Case 31/80 *NV L'Oréal and SA L'Oréal* v. *PVBA De Nieuwe AMCK* [1980] ECR 3775, 3793. Cf. *Iberian UK Ltd* v. *BPB Industries PLC*, English High Court, Chancery Division [1996] 2 CMLR 601.

[168] Case C–234/89 *Stergios Delimitis* v. *Henninger Bräu AG* [1991] ECR I–935, I–992; and Case T–51/89 *Tetra Pak Rausing SA* v. *EC Commission* [1990] ECR II–309, II–362–3.

[169] Case 127/73 *Belgische Radio en Televisie (BRT) and Société Belge des Auteurs, Compositeurs, et Editeurs* v. *SV SABAM and NV Fonior* [1974] ECR 51, 62.

[170] Sect. 7.3.1 above.

national courts cannot grant exemptions. Therefore, if a national court considers that an unnotified agreement is contrary to Article 85(1) but may qualify for exemption under Article 85(3), it should stay proceedings pending the outcome of consideration of the matter by the Commission.[171]

13.9 Undertakings from Third States

Recognition that restrictive practices by undertakings from third states may affect competition within the Union is well established in Commission decision-making.[172] However, the question of the legal basis on which the Commission may exercise jurisdiction over such undertakings is not without controversy.

13.9.1 Enterprise Unity

In the case of third-state undertakings with subsidiaries within the Union, the doctrine of enterprise unity may be employed as a basis of jurisdiction over the parent company. At least, it may be employed as a ground for rejecting the argument that the actions of the subsidiaries are not imputable to the parent company.[173]

13.9.2 Effects Doctrine

In general, the Commission prefers to base its claim to jurisdiction on the effects within the Union of the conduct of third-state undertakings. A broad application of the "effects doctrine" is favoured. According to the Commission, the individual participation in restrictive practices by a particular undertaking from a third state may in itself have no appreciable effect within the Union. However, it is enough to establish jurisdiction that the overall practices in which the undertaking participates have such an effect.[174]

---

[171] Case 48/72 *SA Brasserie de Haecht* v. *Wilkin-Janssen* [1973] ECR 77, 87. See now the Notice on co-operation between national courts and the Commission in applying Arts. 85 and 86 EEC (OJ 1993 C39/6). See, regarding information from the Commission to assist national courts, Case C–91/95P *Roger Tremblay* v. *EC Commission* [1996] ECR I–5547, I–5579.

[172] Though exemptions may be available in respect of restrictive practices involving such undertakings. See, e.g., Dec. 88/541 (OJ 1988 L301/68, [1989] 4 CMLR 610) relating to a proceeding under Art. 85 EEC (IV/32.368 – BBC Brown Boveri).

[173] Case 48/69 *Imperial Chemical Industries Ltd.* v. *EC Commission* [1972] ECR 619, 662. See also Case 52/69 *J.R. Geigy* v. *EC Commission* [1972] ECR 787, 835–6; Dec. 74/634 (OJ 1974 L343/19) relating to proceedings under Art. 85 EEC (IV/27.095 – Franco-Japanese ball-bearings agreement); and Dec. 75/497 (OJ 1975 L228/3) relating to a proceeding under Art. 85 EEC (IV/27.000 – IFTRA rules for producers of virgin aluminium).

[174] Dec. 85/206 (OJ 1985 L92/1) relating to a proceeding under Art. 85 EEC (IV/26.870 – aluminium imports from Eastern Europe).

13.9.3 Implementation

The Court of Justice accepts that Article 85 applies to conduct of third-state undertakings which is "implemented"[175] within the Union.[176] However, it is not clear that the Court has in mind the effects doctrine. In particular, it may not be enough for the Court that an agreement has effects within the Union for Article 85 to apply.[177] According to the express terms of this provision, trade between Member States must also be affected. This condition may be reflected in the requirement in the case law that conduct must be implemented within the Union.

For example, in *EMI Records*[178] the question was whether the owner of a trade mark in a Member State could prevent the sale in that Member State of products bearing the same mark and coming from a third state or manufactured in the Union by a subsidiary of the owner of that mark in that third state. The Court of Justice observed that an agreement between traders within the Union and competitors in third states could bring about an isolation of the common market as a whole. Such an agreement could reduce the supply in the Union of products originating in third states and similar to those protected by a trade mark within the Union. Hence, conditions of competition within the common market might be distorted. Moreover, if the proprietor of the mark in the third state had subsidiaries established in different Member States that could sell the products at issue within the common market, trade between Member States might also be affected.[179]

The implication is that the conduct of a third-state undertaking must not only have the effect of distorting competition within the Union. If the conduct is to be prohibited, it must also affect trade between Member States.[180]

---

[175] The potentially broader term "materialise" is preferred by P. Pescatore, "The Dynamics and Homogeneity of the European Economic System" [1991] *JFT* 295–320, 314.

[176] Joined Cases 89, 104, 114, 116–117 & 125–129/85 *A. Åhlström Osakeyhtiö* v. *EC Commission* [1988] ECR 5193, 5243. Cf., earlier, the ambiguity of the approach of the ECJ in Case 22/71 *Béguelin Import Co.* v. *SAGL Import Export* [1971] ECR 949, 959, concerning a restrictive practice which was "operative" within the Union. Cf. also Case 28/77 *Tepea BV* v. *EC Commission* [1978] ECR 1391.

[177] Cf. the view that the Commission "can now address almost any alleged global pricing scheme under the claim that the scheme affects competition among the Member States of the European Community" (E. Breibart, "The Wood Pulp Case: the Application of EEC Competition Law to Foreign-Based Undertakings" (1989) 19 *Georgia Journal of International and Comparative Law* 149–73, 168).

[178] Case 51/75 *EMI Records Ltd* v. *CBS United Kingdom Ltd* [1976] ECR 811.

[179] *Ibid.*, 848. See also Warner AG (*ibid.*, 863–4) and Case 71/74 *Nederlandse Vereniging voor Fruit en Groentenimporthandel, Nederlandse Bond van Grossiers in Zuidruchten en ander Geimporteerd Fruit "Frubo"* v. *EC Commission and Vereniging de Fruiturie* [1975] ECR 563, 584.

[180] See e.g. Dec. 69/202 (JO 1969 L168/22) relating to a proceeding under Art. 85 EEC (IV/597 – VVVF) and Dec. 71/22 (JO 1971 L10/12) relating to a proceeding under Art. 85 EEC (IV/337 – Supexie).

13.9.4 Practical Considerations

Practical considerations may have influenced the reasoning of the Court of Justice in its approach to anti-competitive behaviour by third-state undertakings. If such behaviour is implemented within the Union by means of agreements, the latter will be void under Article 85(2) of the Treaty. If it is implemented through subsidiaries, fines may be imposed on the latter. If neither condition is met, there may be practical problems in enforcing Union law.

13.9.5 Policy Considerations

The concentration of the Court of Justice on the "internal" Union effects of the conduct of third-state undertakings has its counterpart in the policy of states. States tend to exempt from their competition law national cartels or monopolies that seek to extract rents from foreign markets.[181] However, the more integrated the economies of different states become, the less rational may be the implicit distinction between "internal" and "external" competition.[182]

13.9.6 Procedural Constraints

The realities of globalisation may not be reflected in the procedural framework within which the Commission operates. The Commission, like other Union institutions, may only "act within the limits of the powers conferred upon it" by the EC Treaty.[183] More particularly, Article 89 of the Treaty requires the Commission to ensure the application of the principles laid down in Articles 85 and 86. However, no reference is made to conduct of undertakings distorting competition in trade with third states. Indeed, Article 3(2) of Regulation 17[184] does not even provide for third states to complain to the Commission concerning anti-competitive conduct.[185] The implication is that the Commission is only to proceed against practices having internal effects within the Union. The question is begged, however, why the Council has not legislated under Article 87,[186] to provide the

---

[181] See e.g. R.E. Caves, "Industrial Policy and Trade Policy: the Connections" in H. Kierzkowski (ed.), *Protection and Competition in International Trade* (Blackwell, Oxford, 1987), 68–85, 81.

[182] Cf. an early decision, where the Commission granted a negative clearance to an exclusive distributorship agreement between a French company and a Swiss company. This agreement prohibited the latter company from selling within the Union. However, there was considered to be no distortion of competition within the Union, because, among other reasons, the products had to cross a customs frontier to be sold within the Union. See Dec. 64/233 (JO 1964 915) concerning a request for negative clearance under Art. 2 of Reg. 17 (IV/A – 00061).

[183] Art. 4(1) EC.   [184] JO 1962 204.

[185] Cf. Tesauro AG in Case C–327/91 *France* v. *EC Commission: EC–US competition law agreement* [1994] ECR I–3641, I–3662–4.

[186] According to Art. 87 EC, the Council is to adopt any appropriate measures to give effect to the principles set out in Arts. 85 and 86 EC.

Commission with greater powers to investigate cartels operating in trade with third states.[187]

13.10 Agreements with Third States

The Union may conclude "international anti-trust agreements"[188] with third states,[189] such as that with the United States.[190] Moreover, free trade and association agreements with third states may reproduce competition law provisions of the EC Treaty.

13.10.1 Free Trade Agreements

Article 23 of the Swiss Free Trade Agreement[191] apparently incorporates much of Union competition law into the Agreement. It specifies anti-competitive conduct that is incompatible with the proper functioning of the Agreement, in so far as trade between the Parties may be affected. A broad prohibition of anti-competitive practices in trade between the Parties may be thought to be entailed.[192]

In particular, Article 23(1)(i) of the Swiss Agreement provides that all agreements between undertakings, decisions of associations of undertakings, and concerted practices between undertakings which have as their object or effect the prevention, restriction, or distortion of competition as regards the production of, or trade in, goods are incompatible with the Agreement, insofar as trade between the Parties may be affected. This provision thus adopts much of the terminology of Article 85 of the EC Treaty. However, in

---

[187] Cf. Art. 213 EC.

[188] See, e.g., regarding the development of GATT, A consistent and global approach: a review of the Community's relations with Japan, COM(92)219, 6. More generally, it is considered "desirable that a genuine body of competition rules should be developed at international level". See the *Twenty-Fourth Report on Competition Policy* (EC Commission, Brussels, 1995), 27.

[189] Conclusion of such agreements is favoured by the European Parliament. See, e.g., the Resolution of 13 Dec. 1991 (OJ 1992 C13/472) on the Twentieth Report on Competition Policy, para. 27. See also J.H.J. Bourgeois, "EEC Control over International Mergers" [1990] *YBEL* 103–32, 132.

[190] Agreement with the Government of the USA regarding the application of their competition laws (OJ 1995 L95/47). The ECJ had found the Commission alone not to be competent to conclude the Agreement in Case C–327/91 *France* v. *EC Commission: EC–US competition law agreement* [1994] ECR I–3641. See also the Draft Agreement with the Government of the USA regarding the application of positive comity principles in the enforcement of competition laws (COM(97)233) and the Draft Agreement with Canada regarding the application of their competition laws (Bull. EU 1/2–1995, 1.3.59).

[191] JO 1972 L300/191.

[192] See e.g. N. March Hunnings, "Enforceability of the EEC-EFTA Agreements" [1977] *ELR* 163–9. See also J. Dunlop and R.N. King, "Regional Economic Integration and GATT: the Effects of the EEC–EFTA Agreements on International Trade" [1974] *Law and Policy in International Business* 207–35, 216.

view of the more limited objectives of free trade agreements, use of equivalent terms does not necessarily mean that Article 23(1)(i) of the Swiss Agreement has the same function as does Article 85 of the EC Treaty.[193]

In this connection, account may be taken of a declaration attached to the Swiss Agreement.[194] According to the declaration, Article 23 of this Agreement is to be applied on the basis of the same principles as those in Article 85 of the EC Treaty. This application is to take place in "the autonomous implementation of Article 23(1) of the Agreement which is incumbent on the Contracting Parties".[195] The legal status of this declaration is uncertain,[196] though there may be agreement as to its practical consequences. The Commission considers it to mean that Article 23(1) "must be applied by each Party on the basis of its own law".[197] Switzerland may, in turn, consider that the declaration does not prevent it from interpreting Article 23(1) independently.[198] The implication is that this provision is intended to apply to restrictive practices affecting trade between the Parties. However, there is little apparent interest in securing the harmonisation of competition policy necessary for application of this provision to be mutually acceptable.[199]

Even so, the Court of Justice recognised that anti-competitive conduct of undertakings might be "contrary both to the objective and the terms of the [Austrian Free Trade] Agreement",[200] Article 23 of which was equivalent to Article 23 of the Swiss Agreement.[201]

Moreover, procedures under free trade agreements may be seen as having some role to play in efforts to curb restrictive practices.[202] For example, in 1975 the Commission instituted concurrent procedures against a Swiss

[193] Cf. M.V. LLavero, "The Possible Direct Effect of the Provisions on Competition in the EEC–EFTA Free Trade Agreements in the Light of the Kupferberg Decision" (1984/2) LIEI 83–101, 96.

[194] JO 1972 L300/191.

[195] At the same time, the *Second Report on Competition Policy* (EC Commission, Brussels, 1973), 17, stressed the need for "joint discipline" of competition in trade relations with third states.

[196] Art. 1 of Reg. 2839/72 (JO 1972 L300/186) concluding an Agreement with Switzerland and adopting provisions for its implementation provided for the texts of the Agreement and the Final Act to be annexed to the Regulation. According to the Final Act, the Declaration, which was "noted" by the representatives of Switzerland and the EEC, was annexed to this Act. Hence, the Declaration might be said to have been part of the Reg. See generally, Th. Öhlinger, "Rechtsfragen des Freihandelsabkommen zwischen Österreich und der EWG" [1974] *ZaöRV* 656–87, 677.

[197] Reply to WQ 152/75 (OJ 1975 C209/14) by Mr Cousté.

[198] Cf. the Bill concerning an agreement with the EEC, prop. 1972:135, 50.

[199] In contrast, the Swedish Free Trade Agreement with the ECSC (OJ 1973 L350/76) provided in Art. 20(1) that Sweden would apply the pricing rules in Art. 60 ECSC even to domestic sales by the Swedish iron and steel industry.

[200] JO 1972 L300/2.

[201] Case C–334/93 *Bonapharma Arzneimittel GmbH* v. *Hauptzollamt Krefeld* [1995] ECR I–319, I–339.

[202] Cf. Case 174/84 *Bulk Oil (Zug) AG* v. *Sun International Ltd and Sun Oil Trading Co.* [1986] ECR 559, 583, where the ECJ left open the question whether Art. 12 of the Agreement with Israel (OJ 1975 L136/3) prohibited anything.

company, Hoffmann-La Roche. One procedure was for presumed breaches
of Articles 85 and 86 of the EC Treaty. The other procedure took the form of
a reference to the Joint Committee under Article 27 of the Swiss Free Trade
Agreement[203] in respect of effects on trade between the Union and
Switzerland.[204] On the other hand, discussion of the possibility that the Joint
Committee established by the Swedish Free Trade Agreement[205] should
establish a sub-committee on restrictive practices came to nothing.[206]

Safeguard Measures

According to Article 23(2) of the Swiss Agreement,[207] safeguard measures
may be adopted where a Party considers that a given practice is incompatible
with Article 23(1). It may be thought that Article 23 of the Agreement merely
authorises the Parties to adopt measures of this kind rather than prohibiting
any restrictive practices.[208]

Indeed, the Commission considers that third states are not prohibited by
such agreements from employing their criminal law to penalise persons
assisting its investigations of restrictive practices.[209] If Article 23 prohibited
restrictive practices, then, taken together with Article 22, which prohibits the
Parties from taking measures jeopardizing achievement of the objectives of
the Agreement, such use of the criminal law would also apparently be
prohibited.[210]

Commission thinking seems to have been shared by the Swiss Supreme
Court in *Adams* v. *Public Prosecutor, Canton Basle*.[211] This case concerned an
ex-employee of Hoffman-La Roche who had informed the Commission of
the involvement by this company in restrictive practices. When he was
convicted of infringing Swiss law concerning business secrets, he appealed to
the Supreme Court. This Court dismissed the appeal. In dismissing the
appeal, the Court ruled that Article 23 of the Swiss Agreement did not
prohibit the prosecution or, indeed, anything else. It merely authorised the
Parties to take suitable measures against conduct specified therein.[212]

---

[203] JO 1972 L300/191.
[204] Commission Reply to WQ 152/75 (OJ 1975 C209/14) by Mr Cousté.
[205] JO 1972 L300/96.
[206] H. Lidgard, "Tre års frihandelssamarbete med EEC" [1976] *SvJT* 689–714, 702.
[207] JO 1972 L300/191.
[208] Cf., regarding the equivalent provision in the Swedish Free Trade Agreement (JO 1972 L300/96), Report of the Foreign Affairs Committee on the bill concerning the agreement with the EEC (UU 1977:20), 17–18.
[209] Commission Reply to WQ 152/75 (OJ 1975 C209/14) by Mr Cousté.
[210] Cf. the view that Member States may be obliged by Art. 5 EC to employ their criminal law to give effect to the trade liberalisation required by this Treaty in the Reply by Mr Steichen to WQ E–1818/94 (OJ 1995 C24/30) by Juan Colino Salamanca.
[211] [1978] 3 CMLR 480.
[212] *Ibid.*, 485–6. See also *Bosshard Partners Intertrading AG* v. *Sunlight AG* [1980] 3 CMLR 664, 675. The ECJ may have impliedly adopted a similar approach in Case 53/84 *Stanley George Adams* v. *EC Commission* [1985] ECR 3595, 3601.

Application of Article 85 EC

In practice, the Commission has applied Article 85 of the EC Treaty rather than provisions of free trade agreements in the face of anti-competitive conduct by undertakings from the third states which are party to such agreements.[213] Reliance on the former provision may only partly reflect the failure of the agreements to seek to delimit the respective jurisdictions of the Joint Committees established pursuant thereto,[214] national authorities, and the Commission;[215] the lack of direct effectiveness of the relevant provisions in such agreements;[216] or a Commission desire to demonstrate the importance of the Union as an international economic actor.[217] It may also reflect concern to maintain the uniform application of Union competition law within the Union where competition therein is distorted by the conduct of undertakings from third states.

Thus, for example, in May 1979 the Commission took proceedings against three Swedish companies for breach of Article 85 of the EC Treaty. The matter was not referred to the Joint Committee, the Free Trade Agreement with Sweden[218] was not invoked, and it was not shown that trade between the Union and Sweden was affected. Instead, informal consultations took place.[219]

In the *Wood Pulp* case,[220] where wood pulp producers established in Canada, Finland, and the United States had engaged in price-fixing arrangements which affected the prices paid by purchasers in the Union, the Court of Justice did not object to Commission reliance on such practice. However, the point does not seem to have been put squarely to the Court that the Commission might have been interfering with the trade which the Free Trade Agreement with Finland[221] sought to liberalise without satisfying the procedural conditions laid down in the Agreement for resort to safeguard measures.[222]

---

[213] See e.g. *Sverige – EG 1981* (Utrikes- och handelsdepartementen, Stockholm, 1981), 22. See, generally, M. Haymann, "Joint Ventures and Mergers as a Test-Mark for a European Competition Law Between EEC and EFTA: Switzerland as an Example" [1990] *World Competition* 5–29.

[214] See sect. 4.5.1.

[215] According to N.G. van der Pas, "The European Economic Area: Aspects concerning Free Movement of Goods" in O. Jacot-Guillarmod (ed.), *Accord EEE: commentaires et réflexions* (Schulthess, Bern, 1992), 101–14, 106, "although allowing Contracting Parties to defend themselves if a dispute cannot be solved in the Free Trade Agreement Joint Committee, the Agreements do not provide the means to act efficiently against illicit behaviour".

[216] Cf. the argument of the Commission in Joined Cases 89, 104, 114, 116–117 & 125–129/85 *A. Åhlström Osakeyhtiö* v. *EC Commission* [1988] ECR 5193, 5211 that a breach of Art. 23 of the Finnish Free Trade Agreement (OJ 1973 L328/2) could only be invoked by a Contracting Party.

[217] D.P. Fidler, "Competition Law and International Relations" [1992] *ICLQ* 563–89, 569.

[218] JO 1972 L300/96.

[219] *Sverige –EG 1981* (Utrikes-och handelsdepartementen, Stockholm, 1981), 22.

[220] Joined Cases 89, 104, 114, 116, 117, 125–129/85 *A. Åhlström Osakeyhtiö* v. *EC Commission* [1988] ECR 5193.

[221] OJ 1973 L328/2.

[222] *Ibid.*, Arts. 23(2) and 27. Cf. the provision for Commission negotiations under Council authorisation with third states where application of Reg. 4056/86 (OJ 1986 L378/4) laying down detailed

It is true that confidentiality requirements imposed by Article 20 of Regulation 17[223] may constrain the Commission in using procedures established by free trade agreements.[224] However, the Commission seems generally willing to hold consultations with officials from third states,[225] according to an OECD Recommendation of 1979.[226] Moreover, the question is begged why the Council has not acted under provisions such as Articles 87 and 113 of the EC Treaty to confer the necessary powers on the Commission to act against conduct incompatible with the free trade agreements.

Practical Considerations

If free trade agreements do not affect the application of Article 85 of the EC Treaty, the Commission may feel little practical need to resort to procedures contained in such agreements. Most of the larger companies from third states which are parties to such agreements have subsidiaries within the Union. Hence, the Commission may, in practice, often have the same opportunities for investigation of anti-competitive practices and imposition of sanctions on offenders as if their country were a Member State. Moreover, although Regulation 17[227] does not refer to Commission investigations outside the Union,[228] such investigations may be permitted by international law with the consent of the state concerned. Consent may be forthcoming from the governments of third states, which may favour co-operation with the Commission.[229] As for the companies themselves, they may also tend to be compliant so as to maintain "good relations" with the Commission.[230]

Economic Considerations

The presence of an "extra-Union" element in a restrictive practice may be relevant to its effect on competitive conditions within the Union, which should be taken into account in order to secure real uniformity in the application of Union competition law. Moreover, collaboration between parties to

rules for the application of Arts. 85 and 86 EEC to maritime transport is liable to conflict with the laws of such states (Art. 9).

[223] JO 1962 204.
[224] Cf. Co-operation with the US regarding the application of their competition rules, COM(94)430, 2 and Annex I, 6; and the Report on the application of the Agreement with the Government of the USA regarding the application of competition laws, COM(97)346.
[225] *Sverige – EG 1984* (Utrikesdepartementets handelsavdelning, Stockholm, 1985), 23–4.
[226] *Competition Policy and International Trade: OECD Instruments of Co-operation* (OECD, Paris, 1987); and the *Ninth Report on Competition Policy* (EC Commission, Brussels, 1980), 35.
[227] JO 1962 204.
[228] Art. 14(2) (*ibid.*) requires the Commission to exercise its powers to investigate undertakings suspected of anti-competitive conduct after notifying the authorities of the Member State concerned. The implication is that only investigations within the Union are envisaged.
[229] *Redovisning av det Svenska Integrationsarbetet Våren 1988 – Mars 1989* (Utrikesdepartementets handelsavdelning, Stockholm, 1989), 150–1.
[230] *Industri och EG* (Industriförbundet Arbetsrapport 11, Stockholm, 1988), 8. In particular, exchange of confidential information may apparently be "authorised" by the undertaking concerned. See the *Twenty-Fourth Report on Competition Policy* (EC Commission, Brussels, 1995), 27.

free trade agreements may be of practical necessity in such circumstances. However, such considerations may not be impressive to the Commission.[231] Even less so may be the possibility that treatment of the restrictive practice according to the provisions of such an agreement can make a positive contribution to improving the competitive structure of the Union market.[232]

The consequence may be that the role of competition provisions in free trade agreements becomes dependent on prior harmonisation of competition policy as between the parties. Unless both the content and the application of their competition law are harmonised—in other words, unless common competition law applies to trade between parties to such agreements—uniform application of competition law within the Union may be jeopardised by a Commission failure to apply Article 85 of the EC Treaty to restrictive practices affecting trade between the parties as well as trade between Member States.[233]

13.10.2 Association Agreements

Article 63(1)(i) of the Europe Agreement with Poland[234] follows Article 23(1)(i) of the Swiss Free Trade Agreement.[235] However, Article 63(2) of the Polish Agreement provides that any practices contrary to this provision shall be assessed on the basis of "criteria" arising from the application of Article 85 of the EC Treaty.[236] More particularly, it is required that "the principles contained in the block exemption regulations in force in the EC are applied in full" by Poland.[237] This Agreement may thus be thought to seek closer harmonisation of competition policy than do free trade agreements. Such

---

[231] The attitude of the Commission seems to be changing, now that the "phenomenon of globalisation . . . is becoming more marked". See the *Twenty-Fourth Report on Competition Policy* (EC Commission, Brussels, 1995), 27.

[232] "Rather than contributing to a harmonious exchange of trade, these [provisions] have added an element of confusion and uncertainty to the implementation" of the free trade agreements. See D. Horovitz, "The Impending 'Second Generation' Agreements between the European Community and Eastern Europe – Some Practical Considerations" [1991] *JWT* 55–80, 70. However, the logic of Union practice means that the alternative to application of Union competition law may be resort to anti-dumping measures. See R. Kulms, "Competition, Trade Policy and Competition Policy in the EEC: the Example of Antidumping" (1990) 27 *CMLRev.* 285–313. This alternative may be even more damaging to trade.

[233] Cf., regarding the related risk of "forum shopping", the Recommendations by the EEA Joint Parliamentary Committee of 26 and 27 Apr. 1994 (OJ 1994 L247/36), para. II.D.

[234] OJ 1993 L348/2.   [235] JO 1972 L300/191.

[236] A Joint Declaration is also attached to the Polish Agreement (OJ 1993 L348/2) to the effect that when applying the criteria arising from the application of the rules of Art. 85 EC, the notion of affectation of trade between Member States defined in this Article shall be replaced by the notion of affectation of trade between the Union and Poland.

[237] Art. 6 of the implementing rules for the application of the competition provisions applicable to undertakings provided for in Art. 63(1)(i) and (ii) and 63(2) of the Polish Agreement (OJ 1996 L208/25).

harmonisation may be expected to be important for the future development of trading relations between the Parties.[238]

The search for such harmonisation may be seen as a manifestation of a desire to lessen the artificial separation of competition policy from the common commercial policy[239] of the Union. More fundamentally, it may be seen as manifesting a desire to lessen the artificial separation of liberalisation of trade between Member States from liberalisation of trade with third states. At the same time, such harmonisation may have a central role to play in developing an efficient system of competition in Central and Eastern Europe.[240] However, very close co-operation between the Parties will apparently be necessary for Article 63(1) of the Polish Agreement to play such a role. This co-operation may depend on such consistency in the application of competition law as to impose considerable demands on the emerging private sector in Poland.

In this connection, particular importance may attach to the use made of Article 63(3) of the Agreement. This provision requires the Association Council to adopt, within three years of the entry into force of the Agreement, the necessary rules for the implementation of Article 63(1).[241] Such rules may presumably provide for imposition of penalties for conduct incompatible with Article 63(1) and stipulate that agreements incompatible therewith are void. If such rules do not do so, Article 63(1) may be treated simply as preserving Commission powers to apply Article 85 of the EC Treaty.[242]

Certainly, safeguard measures may be adopted under Article 63(6) of the Agreement, where the Union or Poland considers that a particular practice is incompatible with the terms of Article 63(1) and is not adequately dealt with under the implementing rules.[243] To this extent, therefore, the Commission apparently remains competent to apply Article 85 of EC Treaty, where trade between Member States is affected, instead of invoking Article 63(1)(i) of the Polish Agreement.

---

[238] Though it is the "actual implementation" of competition law which, according to the Commission, "is a prerequisite for the smooth development of trade relations between the two". Cf. the explanatory memorandum to the proposal concerning implementation arrangements under the Europe Agreement with the Czech Republic, COM(95)57, 2.

[239] Sect. 21.12 below.

[240] Resolution of the European Parliament of 13 Dec. 1991 (OJ 1992 C13/472) on the Twentieth Report on Competition Policy, para. 29.

[241] See, similarly, Art. 8(3) of Prot. 2, on ECSC products, to the Polish Agreement (OJ 1993 L348/2).

[242] In fact, no provision for imposition of penalties seems currently to be envisaged, and Commission competence to apply Arts. 85 and 86 EC is carefully preserved. See Arts. 1, 2.2 and 9.3 of the implementing rules for the application of the competition provisions applicable to undertakings provided for in Art. 63(1)(i) and (ii) and 63(2) of the Polish Agreement (OJ 1996 L208/25).

[243] *Ibid.*

13.10.3 EEA Agreement

Article 53 of the EEA Agreement[244] reproduces the terms of Article 85 of the EC Treaty, though "the territory covered by this Agreement" substitutes "the common market", and "trade between Contracting Parties" substitutes "trade between Member States".

This provision is unlikely to have a major impact on larger EFTA companies. Such companies, because of their trading activity in the Union, have long been subject to Union competition law in much the same way as Union companies.[245] Only insofar as Article 53 of the Agreement results in more account of competitive conditions on the EU–EFTA market being taken in the application of competition law, is this provision likely to affect such companies.

On the other hand, Article 53 of the Agreement may apply to practices only affecting trade between EFTA states. There may be important implications for the trading activity of smaller companies in EFTA states. This provision may, therefore, be expected to be at least as significant in liberalising trade within the EFTA area and, more particularly, within individual EFTA states as in liberalising EU–EFTA trade.

Application of this provision is primarily the responsibility of the Commission and the EFTA Surveillance Authority.[246]

Commission

Article 56(1)(c) of the EEA Agreement provides that the Commission decides cases under Article 53 where trade between Member States is affected. However, Article 56(3) denies such jurisdiction to the Commission where effects on trade between Member States or on competition within the Union are not appreciable.[247] Thus existing Commission practice is put on a more secure legal basis.

The Commission also decides cases where EU-EFTA trade, though not trade between Member States, is affected and the turnover of the undertakings concerned in the EFTA states is less than 33 per cent[248] of their total

---

[244] OJ 1994 L1/3.

[245] See e.g. Case 238/87 *AB Volvo* v. *Erik Veng (UK) Ltd* [1988] ECR 624.

[246] Cf. ESA Notice on co-operation between national courts and the ESA in applying Arts 53 and 56 EEA (OJ 1995 C112/7). Cf. also, regarding national authorities, Art. 10 of Prot. 21, on the implementation of competition rules applicable to undertakings, to the EEA Agreement.

[247] According to an Agreed Minute, the word "appreciable" in Art. 56(3) EEA is understood to have the meaning it has in the Commission Notice on agreements of minor importance which do not fall under Art. 85(1) EEC (OJ 1994 C368/20). Within the Union the notice has uncertain effect (cf. Warner AG in Case 19/77 *Miller International Schallplatten GmbH* v. *EC Commission* [1978] ECR 131, 158), and the effect of the Agreed Minute is also uncertain. See Case C–292/89 *R.* v. *Immigration Appeal Tribunal, ex p. Gustaff Desiderius Antonissen* [1991] ECR I–745, I–778.

[248] This figure was apparently chosen with a view to allowing the ESA sufficient work to justify its establishment. However, it is reminiscent of Art. 1(2) of Reg. 4064/89 (OJ 1989 L395/1, as corrected by OJ 1990 L257/13) on the control of concentrations between undertakings. See sect. 15.2.1 below.

turnover.[249] The Commission thus acquires a new competence in relation to restrictive practices that only affect trade between one Member State and one or more EFTA states. It may also be a new competence for the Commission to be entitled to act where only trade between the Union as a whole and one or more EFTA states is affected.

The precise significance of these provisions may be unclear, because the failure of the Court of Justice unambiguously to adopt the effects doctrine renders the limits to the pre-existing competences of the Commission uncertain. The Joint Declaration Concerning Rules on Competition, attached to the Agreement, offers little clarification. In the Declaration the Contracting Parties merely declare that the implementation of the EEA competition rules, in cases falling within the competence of the Commission, is "based on the existing Community competences", supplemented by the provisions contained in the Agreement. In practice, the Commission apparently intends to apply jointly the rules in the EC Treaty and the EEA Agreement, particularly to take account of the effects of cartels on trade between the Union and EFTA.[250]

ESA

Where only trade between EFTA states is affected, cases falling under Article 53 are decided by the EFTA Surveillance Authority under Article 56(1)(a) of the EEA Agreement. Moreover, where EU–EFTA trade is affected and where the turnover of the undertakings concerned in the territory of the EFTA states is 33 per cent or more of their turnover in the territory covered by this Agreement, cases are decided by this Authority under Article 56(1)(b). However, this latter competence is without prejudice to Article 56(1)(c). Article 56(1)(c), taken together with Article 56(3), entails that when trade between Member States is appreciably affected, the Authority lacks jurisdiction.

Co-operation

Article 109(2) of the EEA Agreement seeks to ensure a uniform surveillance throughout the European Economic Area. It provides that the EFTA Surveillance Authority and the Commission shall co-operate, exchange information, and consult each other on surveillance policy issues and individual cases. They are to inform each other of complaints received concerning application and implementation of the Agreement.[251] Moreover, each is to examine all complaints falling within its competence and pass to the other any complaints which fall outside.[252]

More particularly, Article 59 of the Agreement provides for developing

[249] The terms "turnover" and "undertaking" are defined in Prot. 22, concerning the definition of "undertaking" and "turnover", to the EEA Agreement.
[250] *Twenty-First Report on Competition Policy* (EC Commission, Brussels, 1992), 51.
[251] Art. 109(3) EEA.   [252] Art. 109(4) EEA.

and maintaining a uniform surveillance throughout the European Economic Area in the field of competition. It also provides for promoting a homogeneous implementation, application, and interpretation of the provisions of this Agreement. To these ends, the competent authorities shall co-operate according to the provisions set out in Protocol 23, concerning co-operation between the surveillance authorities.[253] Disagreements between the Commission and the EFTA Surveillance Authority about the action to be taken on a complaint or about the result of the examination may be referred by either body to the EEA Joint Committee.[254] These arrangements create the possibility of developing competition policy adapted to conditions on EU–EFTA markets.

[253] See also Prot. 25 to the EEA Agreement, concerning co-operation in relation to competition in the coal and steel sectors.

[254] Art. 109(5) EEA. The latter is to deal with the matter under Art. 111 EEA.

14

Monopolies

Article 86 of the EC Treaty concerns monopolies. It provides that any abuse by one or more undertakings[1] of a dominant position within the common market or a substantial part of it shall be prohibited as incompatible with the common market, in so far as it may affect trade between Member States. There are basically three conditions that must be met before the conduct of undertakings will be prohibited by this provision: dominance, abuse of a dominant position, and the likelihood of an effect on trade between Member States. There is no provision for exemption,[2] though a negative clearance may be granted under Regulation 17.[3]

As with cartels, there may be controversy about the relationship between market integration and efficiency. In particular, it may be disputed whether application of Article 86 with a view to securing market integration is compatible with maximisation of competition. The relationship is complicated by controversy, in turn, about the relationship between market structure and efficiency. In other words, it may be disputed whether application of Article 86 in accordance with the needs of maintaining the competitive structure of an integrated market is consistent with securing the greatest possible efficiency.[4]

14.1 Dominance

To be prohibited, conduct must be attributable to an undertaking in a dominant position.[5] Both geographical and economic considerations may be relevant to determination whether such a position exists.

---

[1] For the purposes of Art. 86 EC, undertakings are defined in the same way as under Art. 85 EC.

[2] Indeed, a practice covered by a block exemption under Art. 85(3) EC may be prohibited by Art. 86 EC. See Case T–51/89 *Tetra Pak Rausing SA* v. *EC Commission* [1990] ECR II–309.

[3] First Reg. implementing Arts. 85 and 86 EEC (JO 1962 204), Art. 2.

[4] V. Korah, *An Introductory Guide to EC Competition Law and Practice* (Hart Publishing, Oxford, 1997).

[5] See also, regarding "collective dominance", Joined Cases T–68, 77 & 78/89 *Società Italiana Vetro SpA* v. *EC Commission* [1992] ECR II–1403, II–1548; Case C–393/92 *Municipality of Almelo* v. *Energiebedrijf Ijsselmij NV* [1994] ECR I–1477, I–1520; and Case C–70/95 *Sodemare SA* v. *Regione Lombardia* (17 June 1997).

14.1.1 Geographical Considerations

The geographical market may be defined as the territory in which all the traders concerned are exposed to objective conditions of competition that are similar or sufficiently homogenous.[6] An important position on the market of one of the "big four" Member States is more likely to be regarded as dominance than the same position in, say, Luxembourg.[7] However, if most undertakings active in a particular market were established in Luxembourg, the dominance of one of them might relate to a substantial part of the common market.[8] Certainly, the port of Genoa has been treated as a substantial part of the common market because of its importance to trade into and out of Italy.[9]

14.1.2 Economic Considerations

Dominance was defined by the Commission in *Continental Can*,[10] where a United States producer of food containers took over a Dutch manufacturer of the same product. According to this definition, dominance denotes the ability of the undertaking concerned to act, to a substantial degree, without taking account of its competitors, suppliers, or customers. The definition was accepted by the Court of Justice in *United Brands*,[11] which concerned the trading activities of the largest group on the world banana market.

Commission thinking has undergone some evolution. Thus, according to the Commission, dominance may also be defined as the ability to prevent potential competitors from entering the market.[12]

Dominance may be indicated by various factors,[13] such as price

---

[6] Case T–504/93 *Tiercé Ladbroke SA* v. *EC Commission* (12 June 1997).

[7] Warner AG in Case 77/77 *Benzine en Petroleum Handelsmaatschappij BV* v. *EC Commission* [1978] ECR 1513, 1537.

[8] Cf. Joined Cases 40–48, 50, 54–56 111, 113 & 114/73 *Co-operatiëve Vereniging "Suiker Unie" UA* v. *EC Commission* [1975] ECR 1663, 1993–4. Cf. also Case 247/86 *Société Alsacienne et Lorraine de Télécommunications et d'Electronique* v. *Novasam SA* [1988] ECR 5987, 6010. See, in the case of the Netherlands, Case 322/81 *NV Nederlandsche Banden-Industrie Michelin* v. *EC Commission* [1983] ECR 3461, 3510–12.

[9] Case C–179/90 *Merci Convenzionali Porto di Genova SpA* v. *Siderurgica Gabrielli SpA* [1991] ECR I–5889, I–5928. But cf. the reluctance to accept a geographical market smaller than that of the Union as a whole in Case T–83/91 *Tetra Pak International SA* v. *EC Commission* [1994] ECR II–755.

[10] Dec. 72/21 (JO 1972 L7/25) relating to a proceeding under Art. 86 EEC (IV/26811 – Continental Can Company).

[11] Case 27/76 *United Brands Company and United Brands Continental BV* v. *EC Commission* [1978] ECR 207, 277. See, more recently, Case C–250/96 *Gøttrup-Klim Grovvareforening* v. *Dansk Landsbrugs Grovvareselskab AmbA* [1984] ECR I–5641, I–5680.

[12] Dec. 85/609 (OJ 1985 L374/1) relating to a proceeding under Art. 86 EEC (IV/30.698 – ECS/AKZO). See also Dec. 91/299 (OJ 1991 L152/21) relating to a proceeding under Art. 86 EEC (IV/33.133 – Soda-ash – Solvay). Cf. Case 27/76 *United Brands Company and United Brands Continental BV* v. *EC Commission* [1978] ECR 207, 284. See, regarding barriers to entry generally, R. P. Whish, *Competition Law* (3rd edn., Butterworths, London, 1993), 263.

[13] Case 85/76 *Hoffmann-La Roche & Co. AG* v. *EC Commission* [1979] ECR 461, 524.

discrimination.[14] Very large market shares are in themselves, save in exceptional circumstances, also indicators of the existence of a dominant position.[15] At the same time, a dominant position may result from law.[16] Moreover, an undertaking that finds itself in a dominant position because of changes in market conditions rather than its own conduct may be "supposed" to be dominant for the purposes of Article 86.[17]

More fundamentally, determination whether an undertaking is in a dominant position necessarily presupposes a definition of the relevant market. In economic terms, the relevant market includes products or services that are substitutable with the product or service of the undertaking in question.[18] Their substitutability depends not only on their objective characteristics, by virtue of which they are particularly suitable for satisfying the constant needs of consumers. It also depends on the conditions of competition and the structure of supply and demand in the market in question.[19]

Definition of the relevant market may not always be an easy matter. For example, in *Continental Can*[20] the question was whether there was a market for meat tins, fish tins, and metal closures for glass jars distinct from the market for tins. The Court of Justice concentrated on the substitutability of production. The Court held that no distinct market for the manufacture of products of the former kinds had been shown to exist. Consequently, the position of the undertaking concerned as a major manufacturer of such products could not as such be regarded as entailing dominance.

On the other hand, in *United Brands*[21] the question was whether there was a market for bananas distinct from the market for fresh fruit generally. Here the emphasis was on the substitutability of demand. According to the Commission, this question depended on cross-elasticity of demand. In its view, there was little such cross-elasticity, because only a banana tasted like a banana.[22] The Court itself observed that bananas were a particularly valuable

---

[14] Case 322/81 *Nederlandsche Banden-Industrie Michelin NV* v. *EC Commission* [1993] ECR I–3461, I–3503.

[15] Case 85/76 *Hoffmann-La Roche & Co. AG* v. *EC Commission* [1979] ECR 461, 520; and Case C–62/86 *AKZO Chemie BV* v. *EC Commission* [1991] ECR I–3359, I–3453.

[16] Case 26/75 *General Motors Continental NV* v. *EC Commission* [1975] ECR 1367, 1378; and Case C–179/90 *Merci Convenzionali Porto di Genova SpA* v. *Siderurgica Gabrielli SpA* [1991] ECR I–5889, I–5928.

[17] Case 77/77 *Benzine en Petroleum Handelsmaatschappij BV* v. *EC Commission* [1978] ECR 1513, 1526.

[18] Cf., regarding effects on potential competition, Dec. 96/435 (OJ 1996 L183/1) declaring a concentration to be compatible with the common market and the functioning of the EEA Agreement (Case IV/M.623 – Kimberly-Clark/Scott). See, generally, the *Twenty-First Report on Competition Policy* (EC Commission, Brussels, 1992), 138.

[19] Case T–504/93 *Tiercé Ladbroke SA* v. *EC Commission* (12 June 1997).

[20] Case 6/72 *Europemballage Corporation and Continental Can Company Inc.* v. *EC Commission* [1973] ECR 215, 247–9.

[21] Case 27/76 *United Brands Company and United Brands Continental BV* v. *EC Commission* [1978] ECR 207.

[22] *Ibid.*, 226–7.

source of nutrition for babies, old people, and the sick.[23] In these circumstances, the Court concluded that there was a distinct market for bananas.[24]

14.2 Abuse

The condition for operation of the Article 86 prohibition which has proved most controversial is that of abuse. Four illustrative examples[25] of abuse are given in Article 86. These are:

  (a) directly or indirectly imposing unfair purchase or selling prices or any other unfair trading conditions;
  (b) limiting production, markets, or technical development to the prejudice of the consumer;
  (c) applying dissimilar conditions to equivalent transactions with other trading parties, thereby placing them at a competitive disadvantage; and
  (d) making the conclusion of contracts subject to acceptance by the other parties of supplementary obligations which, by their nature or according to commercial usage, have no connection with the subject of such contracts.

The examples of abuse given in this provision imply that the conduct must be objectionable in itself.

14.2.1 Unfair Pricing

As Article 86(a) provides, unfair pricing may constitute an abuse of a dominant position. For example, it may be abusive to charge prices that are excessively high.[26] It may also be abusive to charge prices that are above those in other markets.[27]

14.2.2 Discrimination

As Article 86(c) implies, discrimination may constitute abuse. For example, *Gessellschaft zur Verwertung von Leistungsschutzrechten mbH v. EC*

---

[23] *Ibid.*, 273.

[24] However, competition between bananas and other table fruit has been found to be such that national taxation favouring the former may be prohibited by Art. 95 EC. See Case 184/85 *EC Commission* v. *Italy: consumption tax on bananas* [1987] ECR 2013, 2026.

[25] Case 6/72 *Europemballage Corporation and Continental Can* v. *EC Commission* [1973] ECR 215, 245.

[26] Case 26/75 *General Motors Continental NV* v. *EC Commission* [1975] ECR 1367, 1379. Cf. Case 27/76 *United Brands Company and United Brands Continental BV* v. *EC Commission* [1978] ECR 207, 301.

[27] Case 395/87 *Ministère Public* v. *Jean-Louis Tournier* [1989] ECR 2521, 2579. See also Case 30/87 *Corine Bodson* v. *Pompes Funèbres des Régions Liberées SA* [1988] ECR 2479, 2516–17.

Commission[28] concerned a German company established to exploit and manage "performers' rights". According to this ruling, a refusal by a monopoly to provide services to persons falling outside a certain category defined by nationality or residence constituted an abuse. Similarly, *Sacchi*[29] concerned the legality of the exclusive right of the Italian State to operate television. Here the Court of Justice ruled that discrimination between undertakings or products of a given Member State and those of other Member States as regards access to television advertising would be abusive, if practised by a dominant firm. More particularly, discriminatory pricing may be abusive.[30]

14.2.3 Consolidation of a Dominant Position

An undertaking in a dominant position has a "special responsibility not to allow its conduct to impair genuine undistorted competition on the market".[31] Hence, such an undertaking commits an abuse, where it acts in such a way as to consolidate its position by means of a form of competition that is not based on transactions effected.[32]

For example, as Article 86(c) indicates, a refusal to supply is abusive. It may be abusive where the refusal to supply concerns a product essential for the exercise of a given activity, in that there is no real or potential substitute. A refusal to supply a new product whose introduction may be prevented, despite specific, constant, and regular demand from consumers may also be abusive.[33] Similarly, it may be abusive to grant discounts to large customers, which makes it difficult for smaller suppliers to compete;[34] to require that musicians assign rights in all present and future works;[35] or to charge prices below average variable costs[36] or, if elimination of competition is the aim, to charge prices below average total costs but above average variable costs.[37]

Improved trading opportunities may be implied for smaller companies. Such opportunities are exemplified by the *Hilti* case.[38] Hilti was the largest

---

[28] Case 7/82 [1983] ECR 483, 509.   [29] Case 155/73 *Giuseppe Sacchi* [1974] ECR 409, 430.

[30] Case 27/76 *United Brands Company and United Brands Continental BV v. EC Commission* [1978] ECR 207, 299.

[31] Case 322/81 *NV Nederlandsche Banden-Industrie Michelin* v. *EC Commission* [1983] ECR 3461, 3511.

[32] Case 85/76 *Hoffmann-La Roche & Co. AG* v. *EC Commission* [1979] ECR 461, 540.

[33] Case T–504/93 *Tiercé Ladbroke SA* v. *EC Commission* (12 June 1997). See, earlier, Joined Cases 6 & 7/73 *Istituto Chemioterapico Italiano SpA and Commercial Solvents Corporation* v. *EC Commission* [1974] ECR 223, 251.

[34] Case 85/76 *Hoffmann-La Roche & Co. AG* v. *EC Commission* [1979] ECR 461; Case T–65/89 *BPB Industries and British Gypsum* v. *EC Commission* [1993] ECR II–389.

[35] Dec. 71/224 (JO 1971 L134/151, [1971] CMLR D35) relating to a proceeding under Art. 86 EEC (IV/26760 – GEMA).

[36] I.e. costs which vary depending on the quantities produced.

[37] Case C–62/86 *AKZO Chemie BV* v. *EC Commission* [1991] ECR I–3359, I–3455. Cf. Dec. 92/163 (OJ 1992 L72/1) relating to a proceeding pursuant to Art. 86 EEC (IV.31043 – Tetra Pak II).

[38] Case T–30/89 *Hilti AG* v. *EC Commission* [1991] ECR II–1439.

European producer of "power-actuated fastening" nail guns, nails, and cartridge strips. Profix Distribution Ltd and Bauco (UK) Ltd produced, *inter alia*, nails intended for use in Hilti nail guns. They complained to the Commission that Hilti was trying to exclude them from the market in such nails through refusing to supply cartridges independently of a corresponding quantity of nails. Hilti also refused to supply cartridges directly to the complainants and induced its independent dealer in the Netherlands to cut off supplies to them. Without these cartridges the complainants could not sell nails manufactured by them for use in Hilti guns. The Commission decided that such conduct by Hilti constituted an abuse of a dominant position contrary to Article 86,[39] and this decision was upheld by the Court of First Instance.[40]

However, in *Continental Can*[41] the Court of Justice, relying partly on the general principle in Article 3(f) of the EEC Treaty,[42] seemed to take the view that conduct which was objectionable only because of its impact on the structure of the market might be abusive. In particular, an undertaking that acquired a dominant position through a takeover might commit such an abuse.[43] In effect, certain powers for the Commission to control mergers were apparently inferred from Article 86 of the Treaty.[44] Controversy arose, because the language used by the Court in *Continental Can* raised questions whether an undertaking in a dominant position might fall foul of this provision merely because of growth attributable to efficient trading.

14.2.4 Commercial Legitimacy

Article 86(d) implies that certain conduct may be permissible, because it accords with commercial usage. For example, in *BP*[45] the Court of Justice ruled that in an international oil shortage it was not abusive for an oil company to reduce supplies to occasional customers more than in the case of its contractual or regular customers.[46] The fact that the effect of such conduct might have been to drive some smaller oil companies out of business did not render the conduct abusive.

Thus an undertaking that differentiates between trading partners according

---

[39] Dec. 88/138 (OJ 1988 L65/19) relating to a proceeding under Art. 86 EEC (IV/30.787 and 31.488 – Eurofix-Bauco v. Hilti).

[40] [1991] ECR II–1439.

[41] Case 6/72 *Europemballage Corporation and Continental Can* v. *EC Commission* [1973] ECR 215, 245.

[42] Now Art. 3(g) EC.

[43] The acquisition by a dominant firm of a potential competitor which has an exclusive licence to the main alternative technology may also be abusive. See Case T–51/89 *Tetra Pak Rausing SA* v. *EC Commission* [1990] ECR II–309, II–357-8.

[44] Now Art. 86 EC.

[45] Case 77/77 *Benzine en Petroleum Handelsmaatschappij BV* v. *EC Commission* [1978] ECR 1513.

[46] *Ibid.*, 1528.

to legitimate commercial reasons does not commit an abuse of a dominant position contrary to Article 86.[47] In particular, price differentiation is permitted, provided it is justified by objectively established distinctions[48] and is not designed to eliminate a competitor.[49] Only in cases where these provisos are not met, will differential pricing be prohibited by Article 86.[50]

Apparently, therefore, abuse constitutes conduct other than that which would take place in conditions of effective competition. It relates to conduct which, through recourse to methods different from those conditioning normal competition, has the effect of distorting competition.[51]

14.3 Effect on Trade Between Member States

Abuse of a dominant position is only prohibited where it may affect trade between Member States, though it is not necessary that the abuse must relate to the exports or the trade between Member States of the dominant undertaking.[52]

For example, *Alsatel*[53] concerned telephone-system rental and maintenance contracts between Alsatel and its customers. Here the Court of Justice observed that trade between Member States was only affected where the clauses of the contracts had the effect of restricting imports of telephone equipment from other Member States, thus partitioning the market. There was no evidence before the Court suggesting that such effects arose. Therefore, the conduct of Alsatel could not be held to be prohibited by Article 86 of the Treaty.[54]

Again, *Hugin*[55] concerned a Commission decision[56] that the refusal of Hugin to supply Lipton with spare parts constituted a violation of Article 86. The Court annulled the decision, on the ground that the refusal to supply did not have any effects outside the London region in which Lipton was

---

[47] Case 322/81 *NV Nederlandsche Banden-Industrie Michelin* v. *EC Commission* [1983] ECR 3461, 3520.

[48] Cf. Case 8/57 *Groupement des Hauts Fourneaux et Aciéries Belges* v. *ECSC High Authority* [1957–8] ECR 245, 256.

[49] Case C–62/86 *AKZO Chemie BV* v. *EC Commission* [1991] ECR I–3359, I–3473. See, generally, U. Springer, "Meeting Competition: Justification of Price Discrimination under EC and US Antitrust Law" [1997] *ECLR* 251–8.

[50] Case 27/76 *United Brands Company and United Brands Continental BV* v. *EC Commission* [1978] ECR 207, 301.

[51] Case 85/76 *Hoffmann-La Roche & Co. AG* v. *EC Commission* [1979] ECR 461, 541.

[52] Joined Cases 6 & 7/73 *Istituto Chemioterapico Italiano SpA and Commercial Solvents Corporation* v. *EC Commission* [1974] ECR 223, 252–3.

[53] Case 247/86 *Société Alsacienne et Lorraine de Télécommunications et d'Electronique* v. *Novasam SA* [1988] ECR 5987.   [54] *Ibid.*, 6008.

[55] Case 22/78 *Hugin Kassaregister AB and Hugin Cash Registers Ltd* v. *EC Commission* [1979] ECR 1869, 1899.

[56] Dec. 78/68 (OJ 1978 L22/23) relating to a proceeding under Art. 86 EEC (IV/29.132 – Hugin/Liptons).

active. The absence of such effects was due to the nature of the activities performed by Lipton. The maintenance, repair, and renting out of cash registers, as well as the sale of used machines, were found not to be profitable beyond a certain area around the commercial base of an undertaking. Such services were apparently performed by a large number of small, local undertakings. For that reason, the refusal of Hugin to supply spare parts to independent companies which specialised in the provision of maintenance services could not be deemed to affect trade between Member States.

In short, abuse of a dominant position is only prohibited by Article 86 where it may have such repercussions on the structure of competition within the common market as to affect trade between Member States.[57]

14.4 Intellectual Property

The exercise or, in certain circumstances, the acquisition of intellectual property rights[58] may be prohibited by Article 86 of the Treaty. For example, a refusal to supply under copyright may constitute an abuse of a dominant position contrary to this provision.[59] It may also be abusive to refuse to license the production of goods covered by a design right, to refuse to sell them, or to overcharge for them.[60] Similarly, a copyright holder may commit an abuse by imposing unfairly high and arbitrarily fixed royalties.[61]

14.5 Procedures

Article 86 of the EC Treaty is directly applicable before national courts.[62] The roles of the Commission and the national authorities correspond to their roles in connection with Article 85 of the Treaty, except that there is no provision for exemption of conduct covered by this provision.

---

[57] Joined Cases 6 & 7/73 *Istituto Chemioterapico Italiano SpA and Commercial Solvents Corporation* v. *EC Commission* [1974] ECR 223, 252–3.

[58] T–51/89 *Tetra Pak Rausing SA* v. *EC Commission* [1990] ECR II–309, II–357–8.

[59] Case T–69/89 *Radio Telefis Eireann* v. *EC Commission* [1991] ECR II–485, II–519; Case T–70/89 *BBC and BBC Enterprises Ltd* v. *EC Commission* [1991] ECR II–535, II–563; and Case T–76/89 *Independent Television Publications Ltd* v. *EC Commission* [1991] ECR II–575, II–601.

[60] Dec. 71/224 (JO 1971 L134/15, [1971] CMLR D35); Case 238/87 *AB Volvo* v. *Erik Veng (UK) Ltd* [1988] ECR 6211, 6235; Case 53/87 *Consorzio Italiano della Componentistica di Ricambio per Autoveicoli and Maxicar* v. *Régie Nationale des Usines Renault* [1988] ECR 6039, 6073.

[61] Case 395/87 *Ministère Public* v. *Jean-Louis Tournier* [1989] ECR 2521.

[62] Case 127/73 *Belgische Radio en Televisie (BRT) and Société Belge des Auteurs, Compositeurs, et Editeurs* v. *SV SABAM and NV Fonior* [1974] ECR 51, 62.

14.6 Undertakings from Third States

In the application of Article 86 of the EC Treaty the activities of third-state undertakings may be relevant to definition of the market in which there may be dominance. At the same time, Article 86 of the Treaty may apply to third-state undertakings themselves. According to *Continental Can*,[63] Article 86 is applicable to conduct of such undertakings which "influences market conditions within the Community".[64] Control of their conduct may be expected to be facilitated by agreements with third states.

14.7 Agreements with Third States

Free trade agreements and association agreements may reproduce Article 86 of the EC Treaty.

14.7.1 Free Trade Agreements

Article 23(1)(ii) of the Swiss Free Trade Agreement[65] follows Article 86 of the EC Treaty. It concerns abuse by one or more undertakings of a dominant position in the territories of the Parties as a whole or in a substantial part thereof. It provides that such abuse is incompatible with the Agreement, insofar as trade between the Parties may be affected. This provision thus adopts much of the terminology of Article 86 of the EC Treaty. However, free trade agreements have more limited objectives than the EC Treaty. Hence, use of equivalent terms does not necessarily mean that Article 23(1)(ii) of the Swiss Agreement has the same function as Article 86 of the EC Treaty.[66]

According to the declaration attached to the Swiss Agreement, which has already been discussed,[67] Article 23 of this Agreement is to be applied on the basis of the same principles as those in Article 86 of the EC Treaty. This is to be done in "the autonomous implementation of Article 23(1) of the Agreement which is incumbent on the Contracting Parties".[68] The implication is that this provision is intended to apply to any abuse of a dominant position affecting trade between the Parties.

---

[63] Case 6/72 *Europemballage Corporation and Continental Can Company Inc.* v. *EC Commission* [1973] ECR 215.

[64] *Ibid.*, 242. See also Case T–83/91 *Tetra Pak International SA* v. *EC Commission* [1994] ECR II–755.

[65] JO 1972 L300/191.

[66] Cf. M.V. LLavero, "The Possible Direct Effect of the Provisions on Competition in the EEC–EFTA Free Trade Agreements in the Light of the Kupferberg Decision" (1984/2) *LIEI* 83–101, 96.

[67] Sect. 13.10.1 above.

[68] At the same time, the *Second Report on Competition Policy* (EC Commission, Brussels, 1973), 17, stressed the need for "joint discipline" of competition in trade relations with third states.

In practice, however, provisions of such agreements have been regarded merely as authorising application of Article 86 of the EC Treaty to undertakings from third states abusing a dominant position within the Union.[69] In other words, application of the former provisions has been more concerned with competition within the Union than with competition in trade between the parties.

14.7.2 Association Agreements

Article 63(1)(ii) of the Europe Agreement with Poland[70] follows Article 23(1)(ii) of the Swiss Free Trade Agreement.[71] However, Article 63(2) of the Polish Agreement provides that any practices contrary to this provision shall be assessed on the basis of "criteria" arising from the application of Article 86 of the EC Treaty.[72] This Agreement may thus be thought to seek closer harmonisation of competition policy than do free trade agreements. Such harmonisation may be expected to be of potential importance for the future development of trading relations between the Parties. For the same reasons as those discussed in the previous chapter,[73] it is uncertain whether this potential will be realised.

14.7.3 EEA Agreement

Article 54 of the EEA Agreement[74] reproduces the terms of Article 86 of the EC Treaty. However, the dominant position must be within the territory covered by this Agreement or a substantial part of it. Moreover, it is trade between the Contracting Parties which must be likely to be affected.

Commission

Article 56(2) of the EEA Agreement provides for the Commission to decide cases under Article 54 where dominance is found to exist within the Union. If dominance exists both within the Union and the EFTA States, the Commission has equivalent jurisdiction to that provided by Article 56(1)(c) of the Agreement.[75]

ESA

Article 56(2) of the EEA Agreement provides for the EFTA Surveillance Authority to decide cases under Article 54 where dominance exists only within EFTA. If dominance also exists within the Union, this Authority may

---

[69] cf. Sect. 13.10.1 above.   [70] OJ 1993 L348/2.   [71] JO 1972 L300/191.

[72] A Joint Declaration is also attached to the Polish Agreement to the effect that when applying the criteria arising from the application of the rules of Art. 86 EC, the notion of affectation of trade between Member States defined in this Art. shall be replaced by the notion of affectation of trade between the Union and Poland.

[73] Sect. 13.10.2 above.   [74] OJ 1994 L1/3.   [75] Sect. 13.10.3 above.

still decide the case, provided that the turnover of the undertaking concerned within the territory of EFTA states is 33 per cent or more of its total turnover within the territory covered by the Agreement. However, this competence is without prejudice to the competence of the Commission to decide the case where trade between Member States is appreciably affected.

Co-operation

Article 59 of the EEA Agreement provides for developing and maintaining a uniform surveillance throughout the European Economic Area in the field of competition. It also provides for promoting a homogeneous implementation, application, and interpretation of the provisions of this Agreement. To these ends, the competent authorities shall co-operate according to the provisions set out in Protocol 23 to the Agreement, concerning co-operation between the surveillance authorities. These co-operation arrangements are the same as those discussed in the previous Chapter.[76]

---

[76] *Ibid.*

15

Mergers

Unlike the ECSC Treaty,[1] the EC Treaty makes no express provision for control of mergers having anti-competitive effects. Hence, Regulation 4064/89[2] had to be enacted by the Council under Article 87, which provides for the enactment of appropriate regulations or directives to give effect to the principles set out in Articles 85 and 86, and Article 235 of the EC Treaty.[3]

It was noted in the preamble to the Regulation that a system ensuring undistorted competition, as required by Article 3(g) of the EC Treaty, was essential for the achievement of the internal market and its development. However, the dismantling of internal frontiers was resulting in major corporate reorganisations in the Union, particularly in the form of concentrations. Such a development was in line with the requirements of dynamic competition. It was also capable of increasing the competitiveness of European industry, improving the conditions of growth, and raising the standard of living in the Union. On the other hand, it had to be ensured that the process of reorganisation did not result in lasting damage to competition. Union law, therefore, had to include provisions governing those concentrations that might significantly impede effective competition in the common market or in a substantial part of it.

Articles 85 and 86 of the Treaty, though applicable to certain concentrations, were considered insufficient to control all concentrations that might prove to be incompatible with the system of undistorted competition envisaged in the Treaty. A new legal instrument, therefore, had to be created in the form of a regulation to permit effective control of all concentrations from the point of view of their effect on the structure of competition in the Union.[4]

---

[1] Art. 66 ECSC.
[2] On the control of concentrations between undertakings (OJ 1989 L395/1, as corrected by OJ 1990 L257/13).
[3] Sect. 19.1.1 below.
[4] 6th and 7th recitals in the preamble to Reg. 4064/89 (OJ 1989 L395/1).

15.1 Definition of a Concentration

According to Regulation 4064/89,[5] there is a concentration where:

- two or more previously independent undertakings merge, or
- one or more persons already controlling at least one undertaking, or one or more undertakings acquire, whether by purchase of securities or assets, by contract, or by any other means, direct or indirect control of the whole or parts of one or more other undertakings.[6]

15.1.1 Control

Control is constituted by rights, contracts, or any other means that, either separately or in combination, confer the possibility of exercising decisive influence on an undertaking. In particular, it is constituted by:

- ownership or the right to use all or part of the assets of an undertaking;
- rights or contracts that confer decisive influence on the composition, voting, or decisions of the organs of an undertaking.[7]

Control is acquired by persons or undertakings which:

- are holders of the rights or entitled to rights under the contracts concerned; or
- while not being holders of such rights or entitled to rights under such contracts, have the power to exercise the rights deriving therefrom.[8]

Credit Institutions

Allowance is made for the special position of credit institutions, other financial institutions, or insurance companies, the normal activities of which include transactions and dealing in securities for their own account or for the account of others. A concentration is deemed not to arise where such institutions hold on a temporary basis securities which they have acquired in an undertaking with a view to reselling them.

However, the institutions must not exercise voting rights in respect of those securities to determine the competitive behaviour of the undertaking concerned.[9] They must exercise such rights only to prepare the disposal of all or part of that undertaking or of its assets or the disposal of those securities.

---

[5] *Ibid.*

[6] *Ibid.*, Art. 3(1). See also Communication regarding the notion of concentration within the meaning of Reg. 4064/89 (OJ 1994 C385/5); and Communication concerning supplementary restrictions to concentrations (OJ 1990 C203/5).

[7] Art. 3(3) of Reg. 4064/89 (OJ 1989 L395/1). See, e.g., regarding a minority shareholding combined with contractual guarantees of control over management decisions, Lyonnaise des Eaux Dumez/Brochier (IV/M.76) (OJ 1991 C188/20).

[8] Art. 3(4) of Reg. 4064/89 (OJ 1989 L395/1).

[9] Communic. on the notion of undertakings concerned in the meaning of Reg. 4064/89 (OJ 1994 C385/12).

The disposal must take place within one year of the date of acquisition. This period may be extended by the Commission on request where such institutions or companies can show that the disposal was not reasonably possible within the period set.[10]

Liquidators

A concentration is deemed not to arise where control of an undertaking is acquired by an office-holder according to the law of a Member State relating to liquidation, winding up, insolvency, cessation of payments, compositions, or analogous proceedings.[11]

15.1.2 Joint Ventures

The creation of a joint venture performing on a lasting basis all the functions of an autonomous economic entity constitutes a concentration.[12] If a joint venture has as its object or effect the co-ordination of the competitive behaviour of undertakings that remain independent, such coordination is appraised in accordance with the criteria of Article 85(1) and (3) of the EC Treaty.[13]

15.2 "Community Dimension"

The concern of the Regulation is with significant structural changes the market impact of which goes beyond the national borders of any one Member State.[14] Therefore, the scope of application of the Regulation is limited by quantitative thresholds to concentrations having a "Community dimension".[15]

15.2.1 Turnover Thresholds

A concentration has a Community dimension where two turnover thresholds are met. First, the combined aggregate worldwide turnover of all the undertakings concerned in the concentration must be more than 5, 000 million Euro. Secondly, the aggregate Union-wide turnover of each of at least two of the undertakings concerned must be more than 250 million Euro. This condition is not met where each of the undertakings concerned achieves more than two-thirds of its aggregate Union-wide turnover within the same

[10] Art. 3(5)(a) of Reg. 4064/89 (OJ 1989 L395/1).
[11] *Ibid.*, Art. 3(5)(b).
[12] Art. 3(2) of Reg. 4064/89 (OJ 1989 L395/1), as amended by Reg. 1310/97 (OJ 1977 L180/1).
[13] *Ibid.*, Art. 2(4).
[14] But see sect. 15.4.15 below, regarding "national mergers".
[15] Art. 1(1) of Reg. 4064/89 (OJ 1989 L395/1).

Member State.[16] Lower thresholds apply in the case of concentrations having a significant interest in three of more Member States.[17]

15.2.2 Calculation of Turnover

Aggregate turnover comprises the amounts derived by the undertakings concerned in the concentration during the preceding financial year from the sale of products and the provision of services falling within their ordinary activities after deduction of sales rebates, value-added tax, and other taxes directly related to turnover. It does not include the sale of products or the provision of services between any of the undertakings concerned. More particularly, turnover in the Union or in a Member State comprises products sold and services provided to undertakings or consumers in the Union or in that Member State, as the case may be.[18]

Credit Institutions

In the case of credit and financial institutions, "banking income" is used to calculate their turnover.[19]

Insurance Companies

In the case of insurance companies, worldwide turnover is replaced by the value of gross premiums written. This value comprises all amounts received and receivable in respect of insurance contracts issued by or on behalf of the insurance undertakings. Outgoing reinsurance premiums are included, but taxes, parafiscal contributions, and levies charged by reference to the amounts of individual premiums or the total volume of premiums are deducted. As regards Union-wide turnover and turnover within one Member State, gross premiums received from Union residents and from residents of that Member State, respectively, are taken into account.[20]

Public Undertakings

The arrangements for the control of concentrations are without prejudice to Article 90(2) of the EC Treaty[21] and respect the principle of non-discrimination between the public and the private sectors. In the public sector, therefore, calculation of the turnover of an undertaking concerned in a concentration takes account of undertakings making up an economic unit with an independent power of decision. The way in which their capital is held and the rules of administrative supervision applicable to them are disregarded.[22]

---

[16] *Ibid.*, Art. 1(2).   [17] *Ibid.*, Art. 1(3), as amended by Reg. 1310/97 (OJ 1997 L180/1).
[18] Art. 5(1) of Reg. 4064/89 (OJ 1989 L395/1).   [19] *Ibid.*, Art. 5(3)(a).
[20] *Ibid.*, Art. 5(3)(b).   [21] Sect. 16.3 below.
[22] 12th recital in the Preamble to Reg. 4064/89 (OJ 1989 L395/1).

15.3 Distortion of Competition

The Commission appraises concentrations within the scope of the Regulation to establish whether they are compatible with the common market. In making this appraisal, the Commission takes into account the need to maintain and develop effective competition within the Union.[23] In particular, the Commission takes into account the market position of the undertakings concerned and their economic and financial power; the alternatives available to suppliers and users and their access to supplies or markets; any legal or other barriers to entry; supply and demand trends for the relevant goods and services; the interests of the intermediate and ultimate consumers; and technical and economic progress, provided that it benefits consumers and does not form an obstacle to competition.[24]

A concentration that is found to create or to strengthen a dominant position[25] as a result of which effective competition may be significantly impeded in the common market or in a substantial part of it shall be declared incompatible with the common market.[26] Otherwise, the concentration shall be declared compatible with the common market.[27] In particular, concentrations that, by reason of the limited market share of the undertakings concerned, are not liable to impede effective competition may be presumed to be compatible. Without prejudice to Articles 85 and 86 of the EC Treaty, an indication that a concentration is not so liable exists where the market share of the undertakings concerned does not exceed 25 per cent, either in the common market or in a substantial part of it.[28]

The concern of the appraisal is with maintaining and developing effective competition in the common market. At the same time, the Commission must place its appraisal within the general framework of the achievement of the objectives in Article 2 of the EC Treaty, including that of strengthening economic and social cohesion.[29]

---

[23] See, e.g., Dec. 91/251 (OJ 1991 L122/48; [1991] 4 CMLR 778) declaring the compatibility with the common market of a concentration (Case No. IV/M042 – Alcatel/Telettra).

[24] Art. 2(1) of Reg. 4064/89 (OJ 1989 L395/1).

[25] Dominance is defined similarly to dominance under Art. 86 EC. See, e.g., Dec. 96/435 (OJ 1996 L183/1) declaring a concentration to be compatible with the common market and the functioning of the EEA Agreement (Case IV/M.623 – Kimberly-Clark/Scott). See, regarding barriers to market entry, Dec. 95/354 (OJ 1995 L211/1) relating to a proceeding pursuant to Reg. 4064/89 (Case IV/M.477 – Mercedes-Benz/Kässbohrer).

[26] Art. 2(3) of Reg. 4064/89 (OJ 1989 L395/1).

[27] *Ibid.*, Art. 2(2).

[28] 15th recital in the preamble (*ibid.*). See, generally, regarding the significance of market shares, the *Twenty-Second Report on Competition Policy* (EC Commission, Brussels, 1993), 138.

[29] 13th recital in the preamble to Reg. 4064/89 (OJ 1989 L395/1).

15.4 Procedures

Procedural rules are contained in Regulation 4064/89[30] and Regulation 3384/94.[31]

15.4.1 Prior Notification of Concentrations

To ensure effective control, undertakings are obliged to notify concentrations with a Community dimension.[32] Such concentrations must be notified to the Commission not more than one week after the conclusion of the agreement, the announcement of the public bid, or the acquisition of a controlling interest. The week begins when the first of those events occurs.[33]

A concentration that consists of a merger or the acquisition of joint control must be notified jointly by the parties. In other cases, the notification must be made by the person or undertaking acquiring control of the whole or parts of one or more undertakings.[34]

Where the Commission finds that a notified concentration falls within the scope of Regulation 4064/89,[35] it shall publish the fact of the notification. The names of the parties, the nature of the concentration, and the economic sectors involved are to be indicated. However, the Commission must take account of the legitimate interest of undertakings in the protection of their business secrets.[36]

15.4.2 Preliminary Examination and Initiation of Proceedings

The Commission examines the notification as soon as it is received. Where the Commission finds that a notified concentration does not raise serious doubts about its compatibility with the common market, it must declare the concentration to be compatible with the common market. If, on the other hand, the Commission finds that the concentration falls within the scope of the Regulation and raises serious doubts about its compatibility with the common market, proceedings must be initiated. The Commission must notify its decision to the undertakings concerned and the competent authorities of the Member States without delay.[37]

The decisions must be taken within one month. That period normally begins on the day following that of the receipt of a notification. However, if the information to be supplied with the notification is incomplete, it begins on the day following that of the receipt of the complete information.

The period is extended to six weeks, if the Commission receives a request from a Member State for referral.[38]

[30] *Ibid.*
[31] On the notifications, time limits, and hearings provided for in Reg. 4064/89 (OJ 1994 L377/1).
[32] Detailed notification requirements are laid down by Reg. 2367/90 (OJ 1990 L219/5).
[33] Art. 4(1) of Reg. 4064/89 (OJ 1989 L395/1).   [34] *Ibid.*, Art. 4(2).   [35] *Ibid.*
[36] *Ibid.*, Art. 4(3).   [37] *Ibid.*, Art. 6.   [38] *Ibid.*, Art. 10. See sect. 15.4.5 below, regarding referrals.

15.4.3 Suspension of Concentrations

In principle, a concentration covered by the Regulation shall not be put into effect either before its notification or before a final decision has been reached on its compatibility with the common market.[39]

A public bid that has been properly notified to the Commission may still be implemented. However, the acquirer must not exercise the voting rights attached to the securities in question or must do so only to maintain the full value of those investments and on the basis of a derogation granted by the Commission.[40]

Derogations

The Commission may, on request, grant a derogation from suspension requirements, to prevent serious damage to one or more undertakings concerned by a concentration or to a third party. The derogation may be made subject to conditions and obligations to ensure conditions of effective competition. It may be applied for and granted at any time, even before notification or after the transaction.[41]

Legal Certainty

The validity of any transaction carried out in contravention of a suspension depends on a Commission decision concerning the concentration. In the absence of a decision, its validity depends on a presumption established by Regulation 4064/89.[42] According to the presumption, where the Commission has not decided on the compatibility of a concentration with the common market within the deadline set by the Regulation, it is compatible.

However, in the interests of legal certainty, the validity of transactions must be protected as much as necessary. Thus the Regulation does not normally affect the validity of transactions in securities, including those convertible into other securities admitted to trading on a market which is regulated and supervised by authorities recognised by public bodies, operates regularly, and is accessible directly or indirectly to the public. It may only affect their validity, if the buyer and seller knew or ought to have known that the transaction was carried out in contravention of suspension requirements.[43]

15.4.4 Decisions on Compatibility

All proceedings initiated pursuant to a finding that a concentration falls within the scope of the Regulation and that there are serious doubts about its compatibility with the common market must be closed by means of a decision.

---

[39] Art. 7(1) of Reg. 4064/89 (OJ 1989 L395/1), as amended by Reg. 1310/97 (OJ 1997 L180/1).
[40] *Ibid.*, Art. 7(3).   [41] *Ibid.*, Art. 7(4).   [42] *Ibid.*   [43] *Ibid.*, Art. 7(5).

Compatibility

Where serious doubts about the compatibility of a concentration with the common market appear to have been removed, a decision to this effect must be taken by the Commission.

Conditional Compatibility

Where the Commission finds that, following any necessary modification by the undertakings concerned, a notified concentration is compatible with the common market, a decision to this effect is to be issued. It may attach to its decision conditions and obligations intended to ensure that the undertakings concerned comply with the commitments they have entered into *vis-à-vis* the Commission concerning modification of the original concentration plan. The decision also covers restrictions directly related and necessary to the implementation of the concentration.

Incompatibility

Where the Commission finds that a concentration is incompatible with the common market, a decision to this effect is to be issued. Where a concentration has already been implemented, the Commission may require the separation of the undertakings or assets brought together, the cessation of joint control, or any other action that may be appropriate to restore conditions of effective competition.[44]

Time Limits

Decisions that a concentration is compatible with the common market must be taken as soon as serious doubts about its compatibility appear to have been removed, particularly as a result of modifications made by the undertakings concerned. At the latest such decisions must be taken within four months of the initiation of proceedings.

Similarly, decisions declaring a notified concentration to be incompatible with the common market must be taken within four months of the initiation of proceedings. This period may exceptionally be suspended where, owing to circumstances for which one of the undertakings involved in the concentration is responsible, the Commission has had to request information by decision or to order an investigation. Moreover, the deadline does not apply where a decision declaring the compatibility of the concentration has been based on incorrect information supplied by one of the undertakings concerned; where the decision has been obtained by deceit; or where the undertakings have violated an obligation attached to the decision.

If the Commission does not take a decision declaring a concentration compatible or incompatible within the deadlines set, the concentration shall

---

[44] *Ibid.*, Art. 8.

be deemed to have been declared compatible with the common market, without prejudice the rights of Member States.[45]

Publication

The Commission publishes the decisions that it takes regarding the compatibility or incompatibility of concentrations in the Official Journal. The publication states the names of the parties and the main content of the decision. It shall, however, have regard to the legitimate interest of undertakings in the protection of their business secrets.[46]

Revocation

The Commission may revoke a decision finding a concentration to be compatible where the decision has been based on incorrect information supplied by one of the undertakings or has been obtained by deceit. The Commission may also revoke such a decision where the undertakings concerned commit a breach of an obligation attached to the decision.[47]

15.4.5 Referral to the Competent Authorities of the Member States

A Member State may inform the Commission that a concentration threatens to create or to strengthen a dominant position, as a result of which effective competition will be significantly impeded on a distinct market within that Member State.[48] If the Commission considers that, having regard to the market for the products or services in question and the geographical reference market, there is such a distinct market and that such a threat exists, the Commission may itself deal with the case. It may do so to maintain or restore effective competition on the market concerned. Alternatively, the Commission may refer the case to the competent authorities of the Member State concerned to apply the national competition law of that Member State.[49]

Geographical Reference Market

The geographical reference market is the area in which the undertakings concerned are involved in the supply and demand of products or services and in which the conditions of competition are sufficiently homogeneous. It must be distinguishable from neighbouring areas because, in particular, conditions of competition are appreciably different in those areas. Particular account is to be taken of the nature and characteristics of the products or services concerned. Particular account is also to be taken of the existence of entry barriers, consumer preferences, appreciable differences of the undertakings' market shares between the area concerned and neighbouring areas, and substantial price differences.[50]

---

[45] *Ibid.*, Art. 10.   [46] *Ibid.*, Art. 20.   [47] *Ibid.*, Art. 8.   [48] *Ibid.*, Art. 9(2).
[49] *Ibid.*, Art. 9(3).   [50] *Ibid.*, Art. 9(7).

Time Limits

A decision to refer or not to refer must be taken, as a general rule, within six weeks of the notification of the concentration concerned where the Commission has not initiated proceedings. It must be taken within three months of the notification where the Commission has initiated proceedings, without taking the preparatory steps to require modification of the original concentration plan. It must also be taken within three months in the case of a concentration already implemented where the Commission has initiated proceedings, without taking the preparatory steps to restore effective competition on the market concerned.[51] If within the three months the Commission, despite a reminder from the Member State concerned, has not taken a decision on referral or the preparatory steps provided for, it shall be deemed to have decided to refer the case to the Member State concerned.[52]

If a concentration is referred, or deemed to be referred, by the Commission, the Member State concerned may take the measures strictly necessary to safeguard or restore effective competition on the market concerned.[53]

A report or announcement of the findings of the examination of the concentration by the competent authority of the Member State concerned shall be published not more than four months after the referral.[54]

15.4.6 Information Gathering

The Commission may obtain all necessary information from the governments and competent authorities of the Member States, from the parties, and from undertakings and associations of undertakings.[55]

Requests

The Commission may send a request for information to a person, an undertaking, or an association of undertakings. The Commission shall send a copy of the request to the competent authority of the Member State where the person is resident or the seat of the undertaking or association of undertakings is situated. In its request the Commission shall state the legal basis and the purpose of the request and the penalties provided for in Regulation 4064/89[56] for supplying incorrect information.

In the case of undertakings, the requested information must be provided by their owners or their representatives. In the case of legal persons, companies or firms, or associations having no legal personality, it must be provided by the persons authorised to represent them by law or by their statutes.[57]

---

[51] *Ibid.*, Art. 9(4).   [52] *Ibid.*, Art. 9(5).   [53] *Ibid.*, Art. 9(8).   [54] *Ibid.*, Art. 9(6).
[55] *Ibid.*, Art. 11(1).   [56] *Ibid.*   [57] *Ibid.*, Art. 11(2)–(4).

Orders

Where the requested information is not provided within the period fixed by the Commission or is incomplete, the Commission may by decision require the information to be provided. The decision shall specify what information is required, fix an appropriate period within which it is to be supplied, indicate the penalties provided for in Regulation 4064/89,[58] and refer to the right to have the decision reviewed by the Court of Justice. The Commission shall at the same time send a copy of its decision to the competent authority of the Member State where the person is resident or the seat of the under-taking or association of undertakings is situated.[59]

15.4.7 Assistance from the National Authorities of the Member States

The Commission must be afforded assistance by the Member States. It must also be empowered to require information to be given and to carry out the necessary investigations in order to appraise concentrations.[60]

In particular, at the request of the Commission, the competent authorities of the Member States shall undertake the investigations which the Commission considers to be necessary or which it has ordered by decision. The officials of the competent authorities of the Member States responsible for conducting those investigations shall exercise their powers upon produc-tion of an authorisation in writing issued by the competent authority of the Member State where the investigation is take place. The authorisation shall specify the subject matter and purpose of the investigation. If so requested by the Commission or by the competent authority of the Member State where the investigation is to take place, Commission officials may assist the officials of that authority in carrying out their duties.[61]

15.4.8 Investigations by the Commission

The Commission may undertake all necessary investigations into undertak-ings and associations of undertakings. To that end, officials authorised by the Commission are empowered: to examine books and other business records; to take or demand copies of or extracts from books and business records; to ask for oral explanations on the spot; and to enter any premises, land, and means of transport of undertakings.

The officials exercise their powers on production of an authorisation in writing. The authorisation must specify the subject matter and purpose of the investigation and the penalties provided for in cases where production of the required books or other business records is incomplete. In good time before the investigation, the Commission shall inform, in writing, the competent authority of the Member State where the investigation is to

---

[58] *Ibid.*   [59] *Ibid.*, Art. 11(5) and (6).   [60] *Ibid.*, Art. 19(2).   [61] *Ibid.*, Art. 12.

be made of the investigation and of the identities of the authorised officials.

Undertakings and associations of undertakings must submit to such an investigation, provided that it has been ordered by a decision of the Commission. The decision must specify the subject matter and purpose of the investigation, appoint the date on which it shall begin, state the penalties provided for, and refer to the right to have the decision reviewed by the Court of Justice.

The Commission shall in good time and in writing inform the competent authority of the Member State where the investigation is to be made of its intention to take a decision. It shall hear the competent authority before taking its decision.

Officials of the competent authority of the Member State where the investigation is to be made may, at the request of that authority or of the Commission, assist Commission officials in carrying out their duties. In particular, where an undertaking or association of undertakings opposes an investigation, the Member State concerned shall afford the necessary assistance to the officials authorised by the Commission, to enable them to carry out their investigation.[62]

15.4.9 Fines

The Commission may by decision impose on the parties to a merger fines of from 1,000 to 50,000 Euro where, intentionally or negligently: they fail to notify a concentration in accordance with the Regulation; they supply incorrect or misleading information in a notification; they supply incorrect information in response to a Commission request or fail to supply information within the period fixed by a Commission decision; or they produce the required books or other business records in incomplete form during investigations or refuse to submit to an investigation ordered by a Commission decision.[63]

Moreover, the Commission may impose fines not exceeding 10 per cent of the aggregate turnover of the undertakings concerned on the persons or undertakings concerned where, either intentionally or negligently, they fail to comply with an obligation imposed by decision; they put into effect a concentration without prior notification within the first three weeks following notification or in breach of a suspension order or other interim measures adopted by the Commission; or they put into effect a concentration declared incompatible with the common market by decision or do not take the measures ordered to restore effective competition after a merger has been implemented.[64]

In setting the amount of a fine, the Commission shall have regard to the

---

[62] *Ibid.*, Art. 13.   [63] *Ibid.*, Art. 14(1).   [64] *Ibid.*, Art. 14(2).

nature and gravity of the infringement.[65] Decisions taken shall not be of criminal law nature.[66]

15.4.10 Periodic Penalty Payments

The Commission may by decision impose on the parties to a concentration, undertakings, or associations of undertakings concerned periodic penalty payments of up to 25,000 Euro for each day of delay calculated from the date set in the decision. These penalty payments are designed to compel them to supply complete and correct information which has been requested by decision or to submit to an investigation which has been ordered by decision.[67]

In some cases periodic penalty payments of up to 100,000 Euro per day may be imposed. These penalty payments are designed to compel those concerned to comply with an obligation imposed by a decision granting a derogation from suspension obligations; to comply with a decision declaring a modified concentration to be compatible; or to apply the measures ordered to restore conditions of effective competition following implementation of an unnotified concentration.[68]

15.4.11 Professional Secrecy

Information acquired as a result of the application of the Regulation may be used only for the purposes of the relevant request, investigation, or hearing. Moreover, the Commission and the competent authorities of the Member States, their officials, and other servants must not disclose such information where it is of the kind covered by the obligation of professional secrecy. However, disclosure of information necessary to allow for the parties to be heard and publication of decisions finding compatibility or incompatibility after the initiation of proceedings or requiring action to restore conditions of effective competition or the revocation of such decisions in the Official Journal are authorised. General information and surveys that do not contain information relating to particular undertakings or associations of undertakings may also be published.[69]

15.4.12 Hearings

Before taking any decision provided for in Regulation 4064/89,[70] the Commission shall give the persons, undertakings, and associations of undertakings concerned the opportunity, at every stage of the procedure up to the consultation of the Advisory Committee,[71] of making known their views on the objections against them.[72]

[65] *Ibid.*, Art. 14(3).   [66] *Ibid.*, Art. 14(4).   [67] *Ibid.*, Art. 15(1).   [68] *Ibid.*, Art. 15(2).
[69] *Ibid.*, Art. 17.   [70] *Ibid.*   [71] See sect. 15.4.13 below.
[72] Art. 18 of Reg. 4064/89 (OJ 1989 L395/1).

Moreover, the Commission shall base its decision only on objections on which the parties have been able to submit their observations. The rights of the defence shall be fully respected in the proceedings. Access to the file shall be open at least to the parties directly involved, subject to the legitimate interest of undertakings in the protection of their business secrets.[73]

In so far as the Commission or the competent authorities of the Member States deem it necessary, other natural or legal persons may also be heard. Persons showing a sufficient interest, especially members of the administrative or management bodies of the undertakings concerned or the recognised representatives of their employees, are entitled, upon application, to be heard.[74]

However, a decision to continue the suspension of a concentration or to grant a derogation from suspension as referred may be taken provisionally. Such a decision may be taken without the persons, undertakings, or associations of undertakings concerned being given the opportunity to make known their views beforehand. The Commission must give them that opportunity as soon as possible after having taken its decision.[75]

15.4.13 Liaison with the Authorities of the Member States

The Commission shall carry out the procedures set out in the Regulation in close and constant liaison with the competent authorities of the Member States, which may express their views on them.[76] More particularly, the Commission shall transmit to such authorities copies of notifications within three working days. As soon as possible, copies of the most important documents lodged with or issued by the Commission pursuant to this Regulation must also be transmitted to them.[77]

Moreover, the Advisory Committee on concentrations may have to be consulted.[78] The Committee consists of representatives of the authorities of the Member States. Each Member State appoints one or two representatives. At least one of the representatives of a Member State must be competent in matters of restrictive practices and dominant positions.

The Committee meets at the invitation of, and is chaired by, the Commission. A summary of the case, together with an indication of the most important documents and a preliminary draft of the decision to be taken for each case considered, shall be sent with the invitation. The meeting shall be held not less than fourteen days after the invitation has been sent. The Commission may in exceptional cases shorten that period, as appropriate, to avoid serious harm to one or more of the undertakings concerned by a concentration.

---

[73] *Ibid.*, Art. 18(3).   [74] *Ibid.*, Art. 18(4).   [75] *Ibid.*, Art. 18(2).   [76] *Ibid.*, Art. 19(1).
[77] *Ibid.*, Art. 19(2).
[78] *Ibid.*, Art. 19(3). It is to be consulted before any decision is taken pursuant to Art. 8(2) to (5), 14, or 15 or any provisions are adopted pursuant to Art. 23 (*ibid.*).

The Committee shall deliver an opinion on the Commission's draft decision, if necessary by taking a vote. The Committee may do so, even if some members are absent and unrepresented. The opinion shall be delivered in writing and appended to the draft decision. The Commission shall take the utmost account of the opinion delivered by the Committee and shall inform the Committee of the manner in which its opinion has been taken into account. The Committee may recommend publication of the opinion by the Commission. The decision to publish shall take due account of the legitimate interest of undertakings in the protection of their business secrets and of the interest of the undertakings concerned in such publication.[79]

15.4.14 Legitimate Interests of Member States

The national authorities of a Member State may take appropriate measures to protect legitimate interests other than those taken into account by Regulation 4064/89.[80] The interests must, however, be compatible with the general principles and other provisions of Union law. Public security, plurality of the media, and prudential rules shall be regarded as being compatible. Any other public interest must be communicated to, and assessed by, the Commission.[81]

15.4.15 "Requests" from Member States

A Member State may request Commission assistance where its own national legislation does not permit it to act against a concentration.[82] Following such a request, the Commission examines whether a concentration without a Community dimension creates or strengthens a dominant position as a result of which competition would be significantly impeded within the territory of the Member State concerned. If the concentration is found to do so, the Commission may, insofar as the concentration affects trade between Member States, declare it incompatible with the common market; declare it compatible only after changes have been made; or, if already implemented, require action necessary to restore conditions of effective competition.[83] However, the Commission may only take the measures strictly necessary to maintain or restore effective competition within the Member State at the request of which it intervenes.[84]

---

[79] *Ibid.*, Art. 19(4)–(7).   [80] *Ibid.*   [81] *Ibid.*, Art. 21(3).
[82] See e.g. Request of examination of a concentration (Case IV/M.890 – Blokker/Toys "R" Us) (OJ 1997 C32/6).
[83] Art. 22(3) of Reg. 4064/89 (OJ 1989 L395/1).   [84] *Ibid.*, Art. 22(5).

15.5 Undertakings from Third States

Regulation 4064/89[85] assumes that concentrations involving undertakings from third states may be controlled. According to the Preamble, the thresholds for a concentration to have a Community dimension may be met where the concentrations are effected by undertakings which do not have their principal fields of activities in the Union but which have substantial operations there.[86] For example, in 1995 the Commission required the United States tissue maker, Kimberly-Clark,[87] to sell interests in the United Kingdom as a condition for authorisation of its merger with another United States company, Scott Paper.[88]

15.6 Merger Control in Third States

Consistency is sought between merger control under Regulation 4064/89[89] and merger control in third states. Thus Member States are to inform the Commission of any general difficulties encountered by their undertakings with concentrations in third states. The Commission is to report on treatment accorded to Union undertakings as regards such concentrations. If it appears to the Commission that a third state does not grant Union undertakings treatment comparable to that granted by the Union to undertakings from that state, the Commission may request from the Council a negotiating mandate with a view to obtaining comparable treatment for Union undertakings.[90]

15.7 Agreements with Third States

Agreements with third states do not usually refer to merger control. The EEA Agreement[91] is exceptional. Article 57(1) of this Agreement provides that concentrations which create or strengthen a dominant position as a result of which competition may be significantly impeded within the territory covered by this Agreement or a substantial part of it may be declared incompatible with the Agreement. The responsibility for their control is basically that of the Commission, which is alone competent to apply to Regulation 4064/89.[92]

---

[85] *Ibid.*   [86] *Ibid.*, 11th recital in the preamble.

[87] Dec. 96/435 (OJ 1996 L183/1) declaring a concentration to be compatible with the common market and the functioning of the EEA Agreement (Case IV/M.623 – Kimberly-Clark/Scott).

[88] See also the conditions imposed in Dec. 97/816 (OJ 1997 L336/16) declaring a concentration compatible with the common market and the functioning of the EEA Agreement (Case IV/M.877 – Boeing/ McDonnell Douglas).

[89] OJ 1989 L395/1.   [90] *Ibid.*, Art. 24. Art. 234 EC requirements are not prejudiced.

[91] OJ 1994 L1/3.   [92] OJ 1989 L395/1.

15.7.1 Commission

Article 57(2)(a) of the EEA Agreement provides for the control of concentrations covered by Article 57(1) of the Agreement to be carried out by the Commission in cases falling under Regulation 4064/89.[93] The Commission shall, subject to review by the Court of Justice, have sole competence to take decisions on those cases.

These arrangements apparently reflect Union concern to retain the competence to control concentrations involving EFTA undertakings which is implied by the Regulation. However, it may also be observed that this Regulation does not rely on a criterion related to the effect on trade between Member States. Hence, there might have been no other readily available means of ensuring that the uniform application of merger control within the Union was not jeopardized. In return, the EFTA States secured special co-operation arrangements in Protocol 24 to the Agreement, on co-operation in the field of concentrations.

15.7.2 ESA

Article 57(2)(b) of the EEA Agreement provides for the control of concentrations falling under Article 57(1) to be carried out by the EFTA Surveillance Authority in cases not falling under subparagraph (a) where the relevant thresholds are fulfilled in the territory of the EFTA states. Thus the EFTA Surveillance Authority is only competent to act in limited circumstances.[94]

15.7.3 Co-operation

Article 59 of the EEA Agreement provides for developing and maintaining a uniform surveillance throughout the European Economic Area in the field of competition. It also provides for promoting a homogeneous implementation, application, and interpretation of the provisions of this Agreement. To these ends, the competent authorities shall cooperate according to the provisions set out in Protocol 23, concerning co-operation between the surveillance authorities, and 24, on co-operation in the field of concentrations. Other co-operation arrangements are the same as those concerning cartels and monopolies.

---

[93] *Ibid.*

[94] This competence is without prejudice to the competence of Member States.

16

Public Undertakings

EC Treaty provisions on competition apply not only to the private sector but also to the public sector. Their applicability to the latter sector is confirmed by Article 90 of the Treaty, which covers public undertakings.[1] This provision originated in concern that Member States should not be able through their operation of public undertakings to adopt measures restricting trade between Member States which would in regulatory form be prohibited by provisions such as Article 36 of the Treaty. In more policy-oriented terms, its rationale is that the benefit of the economic rent created for such undertakings should be used for delivering public services or should accrue to the state as revenue. However, limiting the distortions of competition often associated with the operation of public undertakings to those strictly necessary for such ends is "a delicate task".[2]

16.1 State Measures Relating to Public Undertakings

Article 90(1) of the EC Treaty refers to public undertakings and undertakings to which Member States grant special or exclusive rights. It provides that in the case of such undertakings, Member States must neither enact nor maintain in force any measure contrary to the rules contained in the Treaty, in particular to those rules provided for in Article 7 and Articles 77 to 85.[3] Infringements of other provisions, such as those concerning freedom of establishment,[4] must also be avoided

Article 90(1) constitutes a specific statement, in relation to the operation of public undertakings, of the general proposition that the Member States

---

[1] L.M. Pais Antunes, "L'Art. 90 du traité CEE: obligations des états membres et pouvoirs de la Commission" [1991] *RTDE* 187–209.

[2] Preparation of the associated countries of Central and Eastern Europe for integration into the internal market of the Union, COM(95)163, Annex, 150.

[3] See, regarding Arts. 90(1) and 86 EC, Dec. 97/744 (OJ 1997 L301/17) on the provisions of Italian ports legislation relating to employment; and Dec. 97/745 (OJ 1997 L301/27) regarding the tariffs for piloting in the port of Genoa.

[4] See, regarding Arts. 90(1) and 52 EC, Dec. 97/606 (OJ 1997 L244/18) on the exclusive right to broadcast television advertising in Flanders.

must respect the Treaty. It may thus be regarded as *lex specialis* in relation to Article 5.[5] The latter provision requires Member States to collaborate in the achievement of the Treaty objectives and to abstain from any measure which could jeopardize their achievement.

16.1.1 Undertakings Covered

The undertakings concerned by Article 90 are not defined in the Treaty. However, according to Directive 80/723,[6] on the transparency of financial relations between Member States and public undertakings, public undertakings are those over which a Member State may exercise dominant influence.[7]

16.1.2 Meaning of "Measures"

The expression "measures" in Article 90(1) of the Treaty is broadly interpreted.[8] It not only covers binding measures adopted by public authorities.[9] It may also cover non-binding "requests" from governments to undertakings covered by this provision. A generalised obligation is implied for Member States not to operate such undertakings in a manner contrary to the requirements of provisions such as Articles 85 and 86 of the Treaty.[10] For example, discriminatory charges may be prohibited by Articles 85(1) and 86.[11]

However, it seems from *Macrotron*[12] that a Member State does not violate Article 90(1) simply by permitting conduct contrary to such requirements. This ruling concerned the activities of German recruitment firms which were tolerated by the Federal Office for Employment in derogation from its own exclusive right of employment procurement. Advocate General Jacobs considered that Article 90(1) would be violated where a Member State had "brought about" conduct contrary to the requirements of Article 85 or 86.[13] The Court of Justice itself, however, ruled that Article 90(1) was only violated where a Member State created a situation in which an undertaking covered by this provision could not avoid acting contrary to such requirements.[14]

---

[5] Case 13/77 *GB-Inno BM BV* v. *Vereniging van de Kleinhandelaars in Tabak* [1977] ECR 2115, 2144–5.

[6] OJ 1980 L195/35.

[7] *Ibid.*, Art. 2. The definition was approved by the ECJ in Joined Cases 188–90/80 *France, Italy, and the UK* v. *EC Commission: transparency directive* [1982] ECR 2545. See, generally, A. Evans, "Public Undertakings in EEC Law: Commission Directive on the Transparency of Financial Relations" [1983] *JWTL* 445–57.

[8] A. Evans, "Public Corporations" in *Stair Memorial Encyclopaedia of the Laws of Scotland*, (Butterworths, London, 1989) vol. xix, 59–114.

[9] Case 30/87 *Corine Bodson* v. *Pompes Funèbres des Régions Libérées SA* [1988] ECR 2479.

[10] Case C–41/90 *Klaus Höfner and Fritz Elser* v. *Macrotron GmbH* [1991] ECR I–1979, I–2017–18; and C–18/88 *Régie des Télégraphes et des Téléphones* v. *GB–Inno–BM SA* [1991] ECR I–5941, I–5981.

[11] See, regarding discounts from airport landing charges in Belgium, Dec. 95/364 (OJ 1995 L216/8) relating to a proceeding pursuant to Art. 90(3) EC.

[12] Case C–41/90 *Klaus Höfner and Fritz Elser* v. *Macrotron GmbH* [1991] ECR I–1979.

[13] *Ibid.*, I–2007.   [14] *Ibid.*, I–2017.

16.2 Conduct of Public Undertakings

Provided that they have "economic objects", public undertakings constitute undertakings for the purposes of Articles 85 and 86 of the EC Treaty. Such undertakings must themselves, therefore, respect these provisions.[15]

It appears that the term "economic" is defined by reference to Article 2 of the Treaty,[16] which speaks of the establishment of the common market and the implementation of common policies, and to the activities mentioned in Articles 3 and 3a.[17] Thus the term is not given any narrow technical meaning. Accordingly, a public undertaking, even one exercising powers conferred by legislation to fix charges and conditions of service for customers, is treated as being engaged in "business activity" for the purposes of Article 86.[18] Hence, it must respect this provision. Even if it is "integrated into the state administration", it may still be treated as an undertaking.[19] Only a public body exercising "powers . . . which are typically those of a public authority" falls outside the concept of an undertaking for the purposes of Articles 85 and 86.[20]

However, since these provisions are concerned with the unification of markets, that is, economic systems, economic activity is apparently defined by reference to such systems. Accordingly, Union law only applies to activity pursued within the framework of an economic system. Thus, for example, insofar as relationships are based on purely cultural or educational criteria, Union law is inapplicable, and the conduct of the relevant bodies is unaffected by Articles 85 and 86. Moreover, the activities of a public body, even if it is autonomous, insofar as they are adopted in the public interest and lack a commercial character, fall outside the scope of Articles 85 and 86.[21] Rather, Article 90(1) may be applicable to measures adopted by the Member State concerned.

Subject to these provisos, the conduct of public undertakings must respect Articles 85 and 86. Thus, for example, British Telecom has been found to have violated Article 86 through imposing restrictions on the use of telephone and telex services by third parties.[22] Similarly, British Leyland has been found to have violated this provision through imposing restrictions on the grant of type-approval certificates for its products.[23]

---

[15] This requirement is implicitly confirmed by Art. 90(2) EC.

[16] Case 36/74 *B.N.O. Walrave and L.J.N. Koch* v. *Union Cycliste Internationale Koninklijke Nederlandsche Wielren Unie, and Federacion Española Ciclismo* [1974] ECR 1405, 1418.

[17] Chap. 1.

[18] Case 41/83 *Italy* v. *EC Commission: British Telecom* [1985] ECR 873, 885.

[19] Case 118/85 *EC Commission* v. *Italy: AAMS* [1987] ECR 2599, 2622.

[20] Case C–364/92 *SAT Fluggesellschaft mbH* v. *Eurocontrol* [1994] ECR I–43, I–63–4.

[21] Case 94/74 *Industria Gomma Articoli Vari, IGAV* v. *Ente Nazionale per la Cellulosa e per la Carta, ENCC* [1975] ECR 699, 713 (Rec. 714). Note that the English version of the judgment is misleading.

[22] Dec. 82/861 (OJ 1982 L360/36) relating to a proceeding under Art. 86 EC (IV/29.877 – British Telecommunications).

[23] Dec. 84/379 (OJ 1984 L207/11) relating to a proceeding under Art. 86 (IV/30.615–BL).

16.3 Exceptions

Article 222 of the EC Treaty provides that the rules of the Member States governing the system of property ownership shall in no way be prejudiced by the Treaty. In principle, therefore, the creation and operation of public undertakings are not prohibited by the Treaty.[24] More particularly, Article 90(2) of the Treaty[25] concerns undertakings entrusted with the operation of services of general economic interest or having the character of a revenue-producing monopoly. It states that these undertakings are only subject to the rules of the Treaty, including those governing competition, insofar as the application of such rules does not obstruct the performance, in law or in fact, of the particular tasks assigned to them.[26] It is stipulated, however, that the development of trade must not be affected to such an extent as would be contrary to "the interests of the Community". Subject to this proviso, the requirements of the Treaty may be relaxed as regards the conduct of public undertakings. The natural implication is that such relaxation under Article 90(2) is also available as regards state measures relating to such undertakings.

This provision covers, for example, an exclusive purchasing requirement[27] and the grant of exclusive rights as regards the collection, carriage, and distribution of mail.[28] It may also cover state aid. The sole purpose of the aid must be to offset the additional costs incurred in performing the particular task assigned to the undertaking entrusted with the operation of a service of general economic interest. Moreover, the aid must be necessary to enable the undertaking to perform its public service obligations under conditions of economic equilibrium.[29]

The Court of Justice, however, favours a strict interpretation of Article 90(2), since it constitutes an exception to fundamental Treaty requirements. The Court has strictly interpreted the stipulation that the task must be entrusted to the undertaking concerned[30] and that the application of Treaty rules would obstruct its performance.[31] Thus the task must be entrusted to a specific undertaking and must not arise from the application of general

---

[24] See also the Protocol on the system of public broadcasting in the Member States, annexed to the EC Treaty, and the Declaration on public credit institutions in Germany, adopted with the Treaty of Amsterdam (OJ 1997 C340/1).

[25] See also Art. 7d EC.

[26] Case T–106/95 *Fédération Française des Sociétés d'Assurances (FFSA)* v. *EC Commission* [1997] ECR II–229, II–281–7.

[27] Case C–393/92 *Municipality of Almelo* v. *Energiebedrijf Ijsselmij NV* [1994] ECR I–1477, I–1521.

[28] Case C–320/91 *Paul Corbeau* [1993] ECR I–2533, I–2568.

[29] Case T–106/95 *Fédération Française des Sociétés d'Assurances (FFSA)* v. *EC Commission* [1997] ECR II–229, II–283.

[30] Case 10/71 *Ministère Public Luxembourg* v. *Madeleine Hein (née Muller)* [1971] ECR 723, 730, and Case 66/86 *Ahmed Saeed Flugreisen and Silver Line Reisebüro GmbH* v. *Zentrale zur Bekämpfung Unlauteren Wettbewerbs eV* [1989] ECR 803.

[31] Case 30/87 *Corinne Bodson* v. *Pompes Funèbres des Régions Libérées SA* [1988] ECR 2479, 2499–500.

rules.[32] Moreover, its performance must be "put in jeopardy from the economic point of view", not simply made more difficult.[33] Hence, there must be no appropriate alternative system.[34]

At the same time, the activity of a public undertaking which constitutes performance of its task is strictly interpreted.[35] For example, in the case of a body established to promote research activity, Article 90(2) does not apply to its marketing arrangements.[36] Again, while a public monopoly may be justified by reason of the need for cross-subsidies, Article 90(2) does not apply to specific services separable from the service of general interest.[37]

16.4 Procedures

Article 90(3) of the EC Treaty provides for the Commission to ensure the application of this Article through addressing appropriate directives[38] or decisions[39] to Member States. Thus Directive 80/723,[40] which requires the transparency of financial relations between Member States and their public undertakings, could be adopted under Article 90(3). It could be adopted under this provision, because particular difficulties in the application of the Treaty rules regarding state aid arose from the complex financial relations maintained between public undertakings and public authorities.[41]

---

[32] Case 7/82 *Gesellschaft zur Verwertung von Leistungsschutzrechten mbH (GVL)* v. *EC Commission* [1983] ECR 483, 504.

[33] Case 41/83 *Italy* v. *EC Commission: British Telecom* [1985] ECR 873, 888.

[34] Case T–260/94 *Air Inter SA* v. *EC Commission* (19 June 1997).

[35] This provision does not cover measures regulating the relations of private bodies with a public undertaking. See Case 72/83 *Campus Oil Limited* v. *Minister for Industry and Energy* [1984] ECR 2727, 2747.

[36] Case 258/78 *L.C. Nungesser KG and Kurt Eisele* v. *EC Commission* [1982] ECR 2015, 2056–7.

[37] Case C–320/91 *Paul Corbeau* [1993] ECR I–2533, I–2569.

[38] See, e.g., Dir. 88/301 (OJ 1988 L131/73) on competition in the markets in telecommunications terminal equipment; and Case C–202/88 *France* v. *EC Commission* [1991] ECR I–1223. See also Dir. 90/388 (OJ 1990 L192/10) on competition in the markets for telecommunications services; and Joined Cases C–271, 281 & 289/90 *Spain, Belgium, and Italy* v. *EC Commission* [1992] ECR I–5833.

[39] See, e.g., Dec. 87/359 (OJ 1987 L194/28) concerning reductions in air and sea transport fares available only to Spanish nationals resident in the Canary Islands and the Balearic Islands, regarding reduced airfares in Spain. See also Case 226/87 *EC Commission* v. *Greece: public sector insurance companies* [1988] ECR 3611. See, regarding hearing requirements, Joined Cases C–48 & 66/90 *Netherlands* v. *EC Commission: messenger services* [1992] ECR I–565, I–640.

[40] OJ 1980 L195/35, as amended by Dirs. 85/413 (OJ 1985 L229/20) and 93/84 (OJ 1993 L254/16).

[41] Joined Cases 188–190/80 *France, Italy, and the UK* v. *EC Commission: transparency directive* [1982] ECR 2545, 2577–8.

16.5 Public Undertakings from Third States

Public undertakings from third states may be subject to Articles 85 and 86, like other undertakings from third states. However, in practice the tendency may have been to rely on application of anti-dumping rules[42] to trade-distorting activities of public undertakings from third states. Such practice has been particularly controversial in the case of public undertakings from countries classified as non-market economies for the purposes of anti-dumping rules.[43]

16.6 Agreements with Third States

Agreements with third states may recognise the potential impact of public undertakings on economic activity between the parties.

16.6.1 Free Trade Agreements

Reference may be made to Article 90 of the EC Treaty in declarations attached to free trade agreements, such as the declaration attached to the Swiss Agreement.[44] The declaration relates to Article 23 of this Agreement, which concerns restrictive practices of undertakings and state aid. According to the declaration, this provision is to be applied on the basis of the same principles as those in Article 90 of the EC Treaty. This application is to take place in "the autonomous implementation of Article 23(1) of the Agreement which is incumbent on the Contracting Parties".[45] The implication is that Article 23 of the Agreement is intended to apply to restrictive practices involving public undertakings, where trade between the Parties is affected. In practice, however, its significance may be no greater for public undertakings than for private undertakings.[46]

16.6.2 Association Agreements

The Europe Agreements refer to public undertakings. For example, Article 65 of the Europe Agreement with Poland[47] requires that the principles of Article 90 of the EC Treaty are upheld. The problems posed by the major role retained by the public sector in countries such as Poland have no apparent recognition.

---

[42] Sect. 21.12.14 below.

[43] See, e.g., R. Denton, "The Non-Market Economy Rules of the European Community's Anti-Dumping and Countervailing Duties Legislation" [1987] *ICLQ* 198–239.

[44] JO 1972 L300/191.

[45] At the same time, the *Second Report on Competition Policy* (EC Commission, Brussels, 1973), 17, stressed the need for "joint discipline" of competition in trade with third states.

[46] Sects. 13.10.1 and 14.7.1 above.   [47] OJ 1993 L348/2.

16.6.3 EEA Agreement

Article 59 of the EEA Agreement[48] is substantially identical to Article 90 of the EC Treaty. More particularly, Article 59(3) of the Agreement provides for the Commission and the EFTA Surveillance Authority to ensure within their respective competence the application of the provisions of this Article. Where necessary, they are to address appropriate measures to the states falling within their respective territory.

[48] OJ 1994 L1/3.

17

State Aid

Article 92 of the EC Treaty relates to distortions of competition arising from state use of financial resources. In particular, Article 92(1) provides that, save as otherwise provided in this Treaty,[1] any aid granted by a Member State or through state resources in any form whatsoever which distorts or threatens to distort competition by favouring certain undertakings or the production of certain goods shall, in so far as it affects trade between Member States, be incompatible with the common market.

Strictly speaking, Article 92(1) merely indicates that aid which is incompatible with the common market. Unlike Article 5(c) of the ECSC Treaty, it does not expressly state that aid is prohibited. However, the Court of Justice, possibly having regard to the general duty imposed on Member States by Article 5 of the EC Treaty to refrain from any measures jeopardizing attainment of Treaty objectives, treats Article 92(1) as entailing a prohibition of the aid indicated therein.[2]

The prohibition is apparently regarded as implementing the principle in Article 3(g) of the Treaty that undistorted competition should prevail throughout the Union. Hence, there are said to be a "basic principle stated in the Treaty that state aids are incompatible with the common market"[3] and, indeed, a "rebuttable presumption" that aid covered by Article 92(1) is prohibited.[4] As the Court of First Instance puts it, Article 92 "seeks in principle, as a rule of competition, to prevent aid granted by Member States from distorting competition or affecting intra-Community trade".[5]

However, the prohibition of state aid is tempered by the power of the Union institutions to take economic, social, and political considerations into

---

[1] Arts 42, 77, 90 (2), 92(2) and (3), and 93(2) EC.

[2] See the references to "aid which is prohibited" in Joined Cases 6 & 11/69 *EC Commission* v. *France: preferential rediscount rate for exporters* [1969] ECR 523, 540 and to "the prohibition in Article 92(1)" in Case 78/76 *Firma Steinike und Weinlig* v. *Germany* [1977] ECR 595, 608 and in Case C–354/90 *Fédération Nationale du Commerce Extérieur des Produits Alimentaires and Syndicat Nationale des Négociants et Transformateurs de Saumon* v. *France* [1991] ECR I–5505, I–5528.

[3] *Tenth Report on Competition Policy* (EC Commission, Brussels, 1981), 111.

[4] Darmon AG in Case 248/84 *Germany* v. *EC Commission: regional aid* [1987] ECR 4013, 4028.

[5] Joined Cases T–447–449/93 *Associazione Italiana Tecnico Economica del Cemento* v. *EC Commission* [1995] ECR II–1971, II–2017.

account under Article 92(2) and (3) and Article 93(2) of the Treaty.[6] They provide for authorisation by the Commission or Council of certain aid or categories of aid covered by Article 92(1).

These provisions originate in concern that Member States may seek to protect their industries through the grant of aid. In their application, however, the original macroeconomic approach of the Treaty authors is being supplanted progressively by a microeconomic perspective, similar to that favoured in anti-trust law.[7] Nevertheless, it is questionable whether this evolution in Union practice has gone far enough to recognise that state aid control should not simply be an instrument of competition policy. Such control should also promote such Union objectives as cohesion[8] and environmental protection.[9]

17.1 Definition of State Aid

The EC Treaty does not define state aid, though the concept "falls exclusively within the ambit of Community law".[10] In Union practice aid has been variously defined. Most definitions treat aid as simultaneously entailing benefits for undertakings and burdens for the state.[11] Some definitions concentrate on the benefits for aid recipients.[12] The underlying idea is that a grant from the state for no consideration[13] or for inadequate consideration[14] constitutes aid. Other definitions concentrate on the burden undertaken by the state.[15] Still other definitions concentrate on state purposes.[16]

[6] Warner AG in Case 74/76 *Iannelli & Volpi SpA* v. *Ditta Paolo Meroni* [1977] ECR 557, 582. See similarly, regarding the legislative power of the Council under Art. 92(3)(e) EC, Case C–400/92 *Germany* v. *EC Commission: shipbuilding aid* [1994] ECR I–4701, I–4730 and Joined Cases C–356/90 & 180/91 *Belgium* v. *EC Commission: shipbuilding aid* [1993] ECR I-2323, I-2358.

[7] C.-D. Ehlermann, "State Aid Control in the European Union: Success or Failure?" (1995) 18 *Fordham Int. Law J* 1212–29, 1219.

[8] According to Art. 130b EC, the formulation and implementation of Union actions, presumably including application of competition law, shall take into account cohesion objectives and contribute to their achievement.

[9] Art. 3c EC provides that environmental protection requirements must be integrated into the definition and implementation of other Union policies and activities, implicitly including application of competition law.

[10] See the submission of the Commission in Case T–459/93 *Siemens SA* v. *EC Commission* [1995] ECR II–1675, II–1698.

[11] Fourth survey on state aids in the EC in the manufacturing and certain other sectors, COM(95)365, 51.

[12] Lenz AG in Case C–44/93 *Namur – Les Assurances du Crédit* v. *Office National du Ducroire and Belgium* [1994] ECR I–3829, I–3847.

[13] Reischl AG in Case 61/79 *Amministrazione delle Finanze dello Stato* v. *Denkavit Italiana Srl* [1980] ECR 1205, 1235.

[14] Fenelly AG in Case C–56/93 *Belgium* v. *EC Commission: natural gas tariff* [1996] ECR I–723, I–733.

[15] Dec. 82/73 (OJ 1982 L37/29) on the preferential tariff charged to glasshouse growers for natural gas in the Netherlands.

[16] Case 61/79 *Amministrazione delle Finanze dello Stato* v. *Denkavit Italiana Srl* [1980] ECR 1205, 1228. See, similarly, H. Desterbecq-Fobelets, "Le Contrôle externe de l'octroi des aides étatiques aux entreprises privées en Belgique" [1979] *Administration Publique* 277–301, 278.

Paragraph 1.1 of the Guidelines for the examination of state aid to fisheries and aquaculture[17] apparently attempts a comprehensive definition of aid for the purposes of Article 92. It treats as aid:

"all measures entailing a financial advantage in any form whatsoever funded directly or indirectly from the budgets of public authorities (national, regional or provincial, departmental or local) . . . capital transfers, reduced-interest loans, interest subsidies, certain state holdings in the capital of undertakings, aid financed by special levies and aid granted in the form of state securities against bank loans or the reduction of or exemption from charges or taxes, including accelerated depreciation and the reduction of social contributions."

In reality, even this definition tends not so much exhaustively to define aid for the purposes of Article 92(1) as to provide examples of such aid. In more detailed Union practice the following examples figure prominently.

17.1.1 Financial Measures

Besides the outright grant of funds, various financial measures may be treated as aid.

Credit

The provision of credit,[18] including export credit,[19] assistance with the costs of obtaining credit,[20] and interest rebates thereon,[21] as well as the grant of a loan with inadequate security[22] or with a premium too low to reflect the risk actually involved,[23] may constitute aid. Decisions under Article 113 of the Treaty, which provides for establishment of the common commercial policy, may accept the legality of aid in the form of credits for exporters to third states.[24] However, these decisions do not imply the acceptability of such aid in trade between Member States.[25]

---

[17] OJ 1997 C100/12.

[18] Joined Cases 6 & 11/69 *EC Commission* v. *France: preferential rediscount rate for exporters* [1969] ECR 523, 540.

[19] Case 57/86 *Greece* v. *EC Commission: interest rebates on export credits* [1988] ECR 2855, 2871. See, now, Communication pursuant to Art. 93(1) EC applying Arts. 92 and 93 EC to short-term export-credit insurance (OJ 1997 C281/4).

[20] Communication C30/93 (ex N348/93) (OJ 1993 C336/9) concerning financing measures for the fisheries bank.

[21] See, e.g., Dec. 82/364 (OJ 1982 L159/44) concerning the subsidising of interest rates on credits for exports from France to Greece after the accession of that country to the EEC.

[22] Communication C26/93 (ex NN23/93) (OJ 1993 C235/6) concerning aid decided by the German Government in favour of Märkische Faser AG in Premnitz, Brandenburg.

[23] Notice C17/93 (NN77/93) (OJ 1994 C71/3) concerning aid granted by Belgium to SA Forges de Clabecq in the form of a cash loan of 5 million Bfrs.

[24] Dec. 97/173 (OJ 1997 L69/19) amending the Dec. of 4 April 1978 on the application of certain guidelines in the field of officially supported export credits.

[25] Note the Commission statement in the Council when the Dec. of 4 Apr. 1978 (*ibid*) was adopted, which was quoted in Dec. 82/364 (OJ 1982 L159/44).

Guarantees

The provision of a state guarantee,[26] including a "comfort letter . . . assuring the lenders that the Government is behind" an undertaking,[27] constitutes aid.[28] It does so, whether or not the Member State concerned later has to make good a loss.[29] Such characterisation of a guarantee as aid is not affected by alleged imperfections in the capital market.[30] Equally, such characterisation is not affected by the fact that the benefit represented by the guarantee is of a qualitative nature and cannot be quantified, save where a "mishap" entails actual disbursement of state funds under the guarantee.[31] Indeed, the mere publication of a decision to award a guarantee may constitute aid, because it gives the undertaking concerned an advantage in its relations with banks and suppliers.[32]

Tax Concessions

Aid may be entailed where the state reduces the public charges generally imposed on undertakings through tax concessions.[33] For example, such concessions may mean that a bank is able to finance investments which others are unable or unwilling to finance. In such circumstances, aid may be found to be present. Imperfections in the capital market do not affect such a finding.[34] On the other hand, tax concessions compensating the French Post Office for the costs involved in performance of public service obligations relating to the provision of a rural postal service do not constitute aid, because the costs are greater than the tax concessions.[35]

More particularly, special depreciation rules,[36] deferment of tax payments, failure by the public authorities to take proceedings to enforce tax debts, and

---

[26] Commission Letter to Member States SG(89)D/4328, 5 Apr. 1989 (*Competition Law in the European Communities*, ii: *Rules Applicable to State Aids* (EC Commission, Brussels, 1990), 37).

[27] Dec. 94/698 (OJ 1994 L279/29) concerning increase in capital, credit guarantees, and tax exemption in favour of TAP (Transportes Aéreos Portugueses).

[28] See, regarding a guarantee where the commission charged did not reflect the degree of risk involved, Bull. EC 12–1992, 1.3.80.

[29] Dec. 79/519 (OJ 1979 L138/30) concerning the special financing scheme for investments to increase exporting firms' production capacity in France.

[30] Notice C49/91 (E15/90) (OJ 1992 C22/6) regarding a general aid scheme in the Netherlands entitled "Regeling Bijzondere Financiering".

[31] *Third Report on Competition Policy* (EC Commission, Brussels, 1973), 98.

[32] Communication C29/92 (NN12/92) (OJ 1992 C234/8) concerning aid decided by the Basque country in favour of La Papelera Española.

[33] Dec. 73/263 (OJ 1973 L253/10) on the tax concessions granted, pursuant to Art. 34 of French Law 65–66 of 12 July 1965 and to the Circular of 24 Mar. 1967, to French undertakings setting up business abroad; and Case C–387/92 *Banco de Crédito Industrial SA* v. *Ayuntamiento de Valencia* [1994] ECR I–877, I–908.

[34] Notice C49/91 (E15/90) (OJ 1992 C22/6) regarding a general aid scheme in the Netherlands entitled 'Regeling Bijzondere Financiering'.

[35] Bull. EU 1/2–1995, 1.3.39.

[36] Commission Letter E/93 (OJ 1993 C289/2) proposing action to be taken in respect of fiscal aid given to German airlines in the form of a depreciation allowance.

any divergence from the ordinary procedure for recovering tax debts may entail the grant of aid,[37] as may exemption from rules requiring a delay in making value-added tax deductions.[38] Moreover, while inadvertent adoption of a wrong valuation for tax assessment purposes may not constitute aid, aid may be present where a state agency knowingly persists in a misapplication of a legislative provision having such a consequence.[39]

Social Security Concessions

Assistance with,[40] or reduction of,[41] social security payments may entail the grant of aid. This may be so where the state assists the undertaking in meeting its obligations under employment legislation or collective agreements with trades unions to provide redundancy benefits and/or early retirement pensions.[42] It may also be the case where in particular industries the state covers the cost of benefits provided by undertakings to redundant workers going beyond the statutory or contractual obligations of the undertaking.[43]

Reduced Returns

Failure by the state to maximise the return on its capital may constitute aid. In particular, the behaviour of a public authority in disposing of an asset to a commercial interest, trading in the Union, should correspond to the rationale of a private vendor operating under normal market economy conditions. In the absence of such correspondence, aid may be involved. A "break-even approach" by the public authority does not exclude the possibility of aid being involved.[44]

A preferential tariff fixed by a public undertaking for a particular customer

---

[37] Notice C20/92 (ex NN18/92) (OJ 1992 C198/9) concerning aid which Spain planned to grant to the undertaking Fundix SA.

[38] Dec. 92/35 (OJ 1992 L14/35) requiring France to suspend the implementation of aid in favour of the Pari Mutuel Urbain, introduced in breach of Art. 93(3) EC.

[39] Lord Oliver of Aylmerton in *R. v. Attorney-General, ex p. Imperial Chemical Industries PLC* [1987] 1 CMLR 72, 105–6.

[40] Dec. 80/932 (OJ 1980 L264/28) concerning the partial taking-over by the state of employers' contributions to sickness insurance schemes in Italy.

[41] Notice concerning the Greek Currency Committee Dec. 1574/80 and its amendments, in particular Dec. 350/82 and the reduction of the employer's share of social security charges attributable to exports which was unavailable to a small number of undertakings as an alternative aid measure (OJ 1984 C149/3).

[42] Guidelines on state aid for rescuing and restructuring firms in difficulty (OJ 1994 C368/12), para. 3.2.5.

[43] Though such aid is usually authorised "because the workers are then the primary beneficiaries of the aid". See, e.g., Notice C7/95 (N412/94) (OJ 1995 C262/16) concerning the aid the German Government intended to grant to Maschinenfabrik Sangerhausen i. K., Sachsen-Anhalt. The ECJ avoided ruling on the matter in Case C–241/94 *France v. EC Commission: Kimberly Clark* [1996] ECR I–4551.

[44] Dec. 92/11 (OJ 1992 L6/36) concerning aid provided by the Derbyshire County Council to Toyota Motor Corporation.

or class of customer can also constitute aid, if it results in reduced revenue for the state.[45] Only if such a tariff is objectively justified on commercial grounds, does it fall outside Article 92(1). Such grounds may include cost savings, the need to resist competition on the same market from other sources of supply,[46] or economies of scale. However, in the case of economies of scale, the magnitude of the tariff reduction must be reasonably related to production costs.[47]

In such practice the aid definition applied sometimes takes as its starting-point the effects for the state. Sometimes the starting-point may be the effects for the recipient. Often the result may be unaffected by the choice of starting-point. For example, *Amministrazione delle Finanze dello Stato* v. *Denkavit Italiana Srl*[48] concerned the repayment of sums unlawfully levied by the Italian authorities as charges having equivalent effect to customs duties on products from other Member States. According to Advocate General Reischl, the repayment of charges wrongly levied was not aid, because there was "no distribution of state resources".[49] On the other hand, the Court of Justice in the same case ruled that such a repayment was not aid, because undertakings received no advantages to "encourage the attainment of the economic or social objectives sought".[50]

17.1.2 Coercive Measures

Whatever starting-point for definition of state aid is adopted, financial resources must be found to be involved. Apparently Article 92 is interpreted as being exclusively concerned with state "use"[51] of financial resources rather than with state regulation of the use of such resources by others.

This interpretation does not, according to the Court of Justice, mean that aid must necessarily be financed from state resources.[52] Certainly, Article 92(1) implies that aid granted by a state need not necessarily derive from state resources. More particularly, according to Article 1(2) of Decision 3632/93,[53] aid to the coal industry may be present, even if there is no

---

[45] Dec. 85/215 (OJ 1985 L97/49) on the preferential tariff charged to glasshouse growers for natural gas in the Netherlands. This decision was upheld by the ECJ in Case 213/85 *EC Commission* v. *Netherlands: natural gas tariffs* [1988] ECR 281 and Joined Cases 67, 68 & 70/85 *Kwekerij Gebroeders van der Kooy BV, Johannes van Vliet, Landbouwschap, and Belgium* v. *EC Commission* [1988] ECR 219.

[46] *Ibid.*, 270.

[47] Notice C38/92 (NN128/92) (OJ 1993 C75/2) regarding aid which Italy had decided to grant to EFIM.

[48] Case 61/79 [1980] ECR 1205. [49] *Ibid.*, 1235.

[50] *Ibid.*, 1228. See also Case T–471/93 *Tiercé Ladbroke SA* v. *EC Commission* [1995] ECR II–2537, II–2561.

[51] The expression "use" is found in Case 259/85 *France* v. *EC Commission: aid to textiles and clothing* [1987] ECR 4393, 4418.

[52] Case 290/83 *EC Commission* v. *France: aid to poor farmers* [1985] ECR 439, 449.

[53] Establishing Community rules for state aid to the coal industry (OJ 1993 L329/12).

"burden on public budgets". In fact, a measure adopted by the public authority and favouring certain undertakings or products does not lose the character of an aid because it is wholly or partly financed by contributions imposed by the public authority and levied on the undertakings concerned.[54] Hence, the use by the state of a levy imposed on private undertakings may constitute aid.

In *Sloman Neptun*[55] the Commission sought to go further.[56] It argued that the exemption of non-residents employed on German-registered ships from German labour law, including minimum pay requirements, constituted aid.[57] The Court of Justice, however, ruled that no aid was present. According to the Court, the exemption conferred no advantage constituting a charge on the state, but only altered the framework for labour relations in the shipping industry.[58] Again, in *Kirsammer-Hack*[59] the Commission argued that the exemption of small companies from unfair dismissal legislation in Germany constituted aid.[60] However, the Court of Justice ruled that no aid was present, because the exemption only concerned the legislative framework for labour relations in small companies.[61] In both cases state regulation of the use of resources by others, which does not constitute the grant of aid under Article 92(1), was apparently assumed by the Court to be present.

The position may be more complicated where the state imposes price controls.

Minimum Price Controls

"Regulatory subsidies" may be said to be present where the state lays down minimum prices in a particular sector which are above market prices.[62] Thus a legislative power to align the prices of newsprint purchased from several manufacturers in favour of the least competitive has been found by the Commission to involve aid.[63] However, such findings may not necessarily have the support of the European Courts. The Court of Justice has ruled that the fixing of minimum prices by the state does not involve the grant of aid. According to the Court, no aid is involved, because advantages accruing to

[54] Case 78/76 *Firma Steinike und Weinlig* v. *Germany* [1977] ECR 595, 611.

[55] Joined Cases C–72-73/91 *Sloman Neptun Schiffahrts AG* v. *Seebetriebsrat Bodo Ziesemer der Sloman Neptun Schiffahrts AG* [1993] ECR I–887.

[56] See, generally, M.M. Slotboom, "State Aid in Community Law: Broad or Narrow Definition?" [1995] ELR. 289–301.

[57] [1993] ECR I–887, I–900–1.

[58] *Ibid.*, I–934.

[59] Case C–189/91 *Petra Kirsammer-Hack* v. *Nurhan Sidal* [1993] ECR I–6185.

[60] *Ibid.*, I–6192–3.

[61] *Ibid.*, I–6220.

[62] S. Lehner and R. Meiklejohn, "Fair Competition in the Internal Market" (*European Economy* No. 48, EC Commission, Brussels, 1991), 7–114, 17.

[63] Bull. EC 7/8–1987, 2.1.115.

certain producers "are not granted directly or indirectly through state resources in the meaning of Article 92(1)".[64]

Maximum Price Controls

Maximum price controls may involve loss of indirect tax revenue[65] and the grant of aid, at least where the state makes up the losses of undertakings whose prices are controlled. In *BALM*[66] the question at issue was whether allocation of a share in a Union tariff quota constituted state aid. The Court of Justice found no such aid to be present in this particular case. However, according to Advocate General VerLoren van Themaat, the independent grant by the state of pecuniary advantages which were not paid for by the state might constitute aid. Examples given by the Advocate General included reduced rates which a Member State might require private electricity companies or haulage contractors to apply, with reimbursement, to certain undertakings or in respect of certain products.[67]

Overlapping Treaty Provisions

The fact that the grant of aid is accompanied by regulation does not prevent application of Article 92(1) to state use of financial resources.[68] Furthermore, the compatibility of regulation with a Treaty provision other than Article 92 does not preclude application of the latter provision to associated aid. For example, the compatibility of a system of tax imposition with Article 95 of the Treaty does not affect the Commission's appraisal of the aid funded by it having regard to Article 92.[69] Moreover, Article 54(2)(h) of the Treaty expressly provides that the Council and Commission, in securing the elimination of restrictions on freedom of establishment, must satisfy themselves "that the conditions of establishment are not distorted by aids granted by Member States".

Conversely, the mere fact that state use of financial resources may be

---

[64] Case 82/77 *Openbar Ministerie* v. *Jacobus Philippus van Tiggele* [1978] ECR 25, 41.

[65] Cf. Slynn AG in Joined Cases 67, 68, & 70/85 *Kwekerij Gebroeders Van der Kooy BV* v. *EC Commission* [1988] ECR 219, 250. Cf. also Darmon AG in Joined Cases C–72 & 73/91 *Sloman Neptune Schiffahrts AG* v. *Seebetriebsrat Bodo Ziesemer der Sloman Neptune Schiffahrts SA* [1993] ECR I–887, I–905, I–934.

[66] Joined Cases 213–215/81 *Norddeutsches Vieh-und Fleischkontor Herbert Will Trawako, Transit-Warenhandels-Kontor GmbH & Co., and Gedelfi Grosseinkauf GmbH & Co.* v. *Bundesanstalt für Landwirtschaftliche Marktordnung* [1982] ECR 3583.

[67] *Ibid.*, 3617. Cf. Dec. 92/327 (OJ 1992 L182/89) concerning aid granted by the Belgian Government to undertakings in the pharmaceutical industry in the form of programme contracts. Cf. also Case T–95/94 *Chambre Syndicale Nationale des Entreprises de Transport de Fonds et Valeurs (Sytraval) and Brinks France SARL* v. *EC Commission* [1995] ECR II–2651, II–2674.

[68] Art. 1(3) of Dec. 3632/93 (OJ 1993 L329/12) establishing Community rules for state aid to the coal industry.

[69] Case 47/69 *France* v. *EC Commission: textiles aid* [1970] ECR 487, 495. See also Dec. 95/486 (OJ 1995 L227/10) concerning aid and compulsory contributions to promote market outlets for poultry and rabbit farming products in Belgium.

involved does not prevent application to regulatory measures of the Article 30 prohibition of quantitative restrictions and measures having equivalent effect on imports between Member States;[70] the Article 12 prohibition of charges having equivalent effect to a customs duty on such imports[71]; or the Article 95 prohibition of discriminatory taxation.[72] Nor is the application of Article 85 or 86 to aid recipients precluded.[73]

Such provisions seek the same ends – freedom of movement under "normal" conditions of competition – as Article 92.[74] However, they do not make the same provision for aid authorisation as Article 92(2) and (3), and the Commission cannot act under these last two provisions to authorise exceptions from Treaty provisions other than Article 92(1).[75] As the Commission puts it, if a Member State proposes a measure incorporating aid which infringes Union rules (including those of secondary legislation) other than Article 92, the application of Article 92 may not produce a result which would be contrary to those rules.[76] Hence, the technique employed by a Member State to provide aid may affect the permissibility of the aid. The role of national courts may also be affected, given that provisions such as Articles 12, 30, and 95 of the Treaty, but not Article 92,[77] are directly effective before such courts.

17.1.3 General State Interventions

Problems may arise in distinguishing the grant of aid from state interventions through the operation of general fiscal rules, social security measures, conjunctural policy measures,[78] and so on. The established position of the

---

[70] Case 74/76 *Iannelli and Volpi SpA v. Ditta Paolo Meroni* [1977] ECR 557, 576; and Case C–21/88 *Du Pont de Namours Italiana SpA v. Unità Sanitaria Locale No. 2 di Carrara* [1990] ECR I–889, I–922. Cf. the idea of "non-cumulation" in R. Barents, "Recente ontwikkelingen in de rechtspraak over steunmaatregelen" [1988] *SEW* 352–64, 354.

[71] Case 77/72 *Carmine Capolongo* v. *Azienda Agricola Maya* [1973] ECR 611, 623; and Case 103/84 *EC Commission* v. *Italy: aid for the purchase of domestically produced cars* [1986] ECR 1759, 1774.

[72] Case 277/83 *EC Commission* v. *Italy: Marsala* [1985] ECR 2049, 2058. See, similarly, regarding Art. 37 EC and state trading monopolies, Case 91/78 *Hansen GmbH* v. *Hauptzollamt Flensburg* [1979] ECR 935, 953 and Case 253/83 *Sektkellerei CA Kupferberg & Cie KG* v. *Hauptzollamt Mainz* [1985] ECR 157, 185.

[73] Case 225/91 *Matra SA* v. *EC Commission* [1993] ECR I–3203, I–3260.

[74] See also, regarding freedom of establishment, Dec. 73/263 (OJ 1973 L253/10) on the tax concessions granted, pursuant to Art. 34 of French Law 65–566 of 12 July 1965 and to the Circular of 24 Mar. 1967, to French undertakings setting up abroad; and, regarding the free movement of workers and freedom to supply services, Dec. 89/441 (OJ 1989 L208/38) on aid granted by the Greek Government to the film industry for the production of Greek films.

[75] Joined Cases C–134 & 135/91 *Kerafina-Keramische und Finanz-Holding AG and Vioktimatiki AEVE* v. *Elliniko Dimisio and Organismos Oikonomikis Anasygkratissis Epicheirisseon AE* [1992] ECR I–5699, I–5720.

[76] Dec. 88/167 (OJ 1988 L76/18) concerning Law 1386/1983 by which the Greek Government granted aid to Greek industry.

[77] Sect. 7.1.1 above.

[78] Darmon AG in Case 310/85 *Deufil GmbH & Co. KG* v. *EC Commission* [1987] ECR 901, 915.

Court of Justice is that Article 92 does not distinguish between measures of state intervention by reference to their causes or aims but defines them in relation to their effects. Thus, for example, according to the Court, aid may be present where a particular industrial sector is exempted from the normal application of a general social security system, without there being any justification for the exemption in the nature or general scheme of the system.[79]

In practice, the approach of the Court may be more problematic in its application than such language suggests. In particular, questions of discretion may be decisive. Thus, for example, the suspension of debt repayments in favour of a Spanish steel company did not in itself constitute aid, but a general measure taken within the framework of Spanish insolvency legislation applicable to all companies.[80] On the other hand, a Finnish employment aid scheme available to all undertakings in every sector of industry and every region of the country did fall within Article 92(1). It did so, because the authorities could decide on a discretionary basis the level of aid and the length of the subsidised period for each unemployed person taken on by a company.[81]

The underlying problems may be particularly prominent in the case of taxation and training.

As the Commission puts it, a tax measure falls under Article 92(1), where it constitutes a departure from the generally accepted or benchmark tax structure and produces favourable tax treatment for particular types of activities or groups of taxpayers. Thus, for example, tax reliefs granted to certain development areas (reduction in corporation taxes or favourable depreciation terms) are regarded as aid, whereas the rate structure is regarded as an integral part of the benchmark tax system.[82] However, in some cases such departures from the benchmark system are on the borderline between aid within the meaning of Article 92(1) and general measures. The Commission considers that further work is needed to elucidate this "grey area".[83]

Again, assistance provided by the public authorities for education, including vocational training, does not usually constitute aid within the meaning of Article 92(1).[84] Certainly, according to the Court of Justice, training which is not provided for the sole benefit of a particular undertaking does not do so.[85] However, where specific training goes beyond the general system of education and vocational training and corresponds to the

---

[79] Case 173/73 *Italy* v. *EC Commission: social charges* [1974] ECR 709, 719; and Case 310/85 *Deufil GmbH & Co KG* v. *EC Commission* [1987] ECR 901, 923–4.

[80] H. Morch, "Summary of the Most Important Recent Developments" (1995) 4 *Competition Policy Newsletter* 47–51, 49.

[81] *Ibid.*

[82] *Second Survey on State Aids in the European Community in the Manufacturing and Certain Other Sectors* (EC Commission, Brussels, 1990), 7.

[83] *Ibid.*, Technical Annex, 10.

[84] Dec. 91/390 (OJ 1991 L215/11) on aid granted by the French Government to the undertaking Saint-Gobain (Eurofleet) at Salaisse-sur-Sanne (glass sector).

[85] Case C–225/91 *Matra SA* v. *EC Commission* [1993] ECR I–3203, I–3257.

particular needs of a given undertaking, sector, or region, a contribution by the public authorities to training costs may constitute aid.[86]

17.1.4 Infrastructure Provision

The provision by public authorities of infrastructures which are traditionally covered by the state budget is not aid in the sense of Article 92(1).[87] Thus finance for hospitals,[88] the building of schools, prisons, and public offices,[89] port administration,[90] a logistic supply base for oil exploration rigs,[91] or for fundamental research, designed generally to increase scientific and technical knowledge,[92] is not treated by the Commission as aid falling under Article 92(1). The Commission position may apparently be supported by the Court of Justice. Certainly, according to the Court, provision of infrastructure not for the exclusive benefit of a given undertaking falls outside Article 92(1).[93]

However, aid may be present, where infrastructure is provided for the benefit of one or more particular undertakings or productive activities[94] rather than being open to all potential users who pay the charges prescribed by legislation.[95] It may also be present, where assistance is provided to specific companies using the infrastructure.[96] Moreover, where infrastructures, such as the connection of an industrial site to the public railway system, renewal of a sewage system, and site preparation before the start of construction work,[97] usually have to be built by the private sector,[98] their provision by public authorities may constitute aid.[99]

---

[86] Notice C20/94 (NN27/94) (OJ 1994 C170/8) concerning aid for the development of the site occupied by Kimberly Clark Industries at Toul/Villey-St-Etienne (Meurthe-et-Moselle).

[87] *Seventeenth Report on Competition Policy* (EC Commission, Brussels, 1988), 143.

[88] Commission Reply to WQ 564/91 (OJ 1991 C227/29) by Mr Antony.

[89] Notice C27 & 28/90 (ex NN71 & 73/89) (OJ 1992 C181/5) concerning interest subsidies on loans to small and medium-sized industrial and commercial enterprises and works projects and miscellaneous assistance schemes.

[90] Dec. 94/374 (OJ 1994 L170/36) on Sicilian Law No 23/1991 concerning extraordinary assistance for industry and Art. 5 of Sicilian Regional Law 8/1991 concerning, in particular, financing for Sitas.

[91] *Ibid.*

[92] Dec. 91/500 (OJ 1991 L262/29) concerning aid granted to enterprises in the Friuli-Venezia Giulia region.

[93] Case C–225/91 *Matra SA* v. *EC Commission* [1993] ECR I–3203, I–3257. Van Gerven AG (*ibid.*, I–3235) also relied on the fact that the undertaking would, like other undertakings, pay for the infrastructure services in the future.

[94] Notice C20/94 (NN27/94) (OJ 1994 C170/8) concerning aid for the development of the site occupied by Kimberly Clark Industries at Toul/Villey-St-Etienne (Meurthe-et-Moselle).

[95] Notice C35/91 (ex N658/90) (OJ 1993 C59/4) concerning aid which Italy had decided to grant to the alkaline salts industry.

[96] See, regarding assistance for the second Munich airport, the Reply by Mr Kinnock to WQ E–1347/95 (OJ 1995 C222/68) by Wolfgang Kreissl-Dorfer.

[97] Communic. C60/91 (ex NN73 & 76/91) (OJ 1993 C43/14) regarding the proposal by the German Government to award state aid to the Opel group in support of its investment plans in the new *Länder*.

[98] Summary of the Commission decision not to raise objections to the aid which the Portuguese Government planned to grant to the joint-venture of Ford and Volkswagen to establish a multipurpose vehicle plant in the Setubal peninsula (OJ 1991 C257/5).

[99] C. Quigley, "The Notion of State Aid in the EEC" [1988] *ECLR* 242–56, 253.

17.1.5 Nationalisation

Serious definitional problems may arise from exercise by a Member State of its freedom under the Treaty to nationalise. State participation in the ownership of undertakings is normally dictated by exigencies going beyond the profit motive. However, this factor is inherent in public ownership, the "existence and special nature of which are confirmed" by Article 222 of the Treaty.[100] Hence, as the Court of Justice notes, such participation is not automatically contrary to Article 92.[101]

In examining such participation, the Commission seeks to distinguish between state investment, which may be made without being subject to Union supervision, and the granting of aid by public authorities to promote the public good, which is supervised under Article 92.[102] However, although the Union has special rules designed to facilitate detection of the grant of aid to public undertakings,[103] problems of distinguishing state investment from state aid may remain.

Private Investor Test

The Commission considers whether the private sector would have provided the finance associated with state participation. In the view of the Commission, this test – the private investor test – is necessary to uphold the principle of neutrality with regard to the system of property ownership and the principle of equal treatment[104] between public and private undertakings.[105]

Efforts to apply the test may proceed on the basis of simplified conceptions of the aims of private investors. Such conceptions underlie the view that "private undertakings determine their industrial and commercial strategy by taking into account in particular requirements of profitability. Decisions of public undertakings, on the other hand, may be affected by factors of a different kind within the framework of the pursuit of objectives of public interest."[106]

Ultimately, simplified conceptions of the relationship between state and market may be revealed. For example, *Belgium* v. *EC Commission: Meura*[107] concerned capital subscriptions by public authorities in a Belgian producer of equipment for the food industry. Here the Court of Justice accepted

[100] *Second Report on Competition Policy* (EC Commission, Brussels, 1973), 127.
[101] Case 323/82 *Intermills SA* v. *EC Commission* [1984] ECR 3809, 3830.
[102] Lenz AG in Case 234/84 *Belgium* v. *EC Commission: Meura* [1986] ECR 2263, 2270 and Case 40/85 *Belgium* v. *EC Commission: Boch* [1986] ECR 2321, 2328.
[103] Dir. 80/723 (OJ 1980 L195/35, as amended by Dir. 85/413, OJ 1985 L229/20 and Dir. 93/84, OJ 1993 L254/16) on the transparency of financial relations between Member States and public undertakings.
[104] *Ninth Report on Competition Policy* (EC Commission, Brussels, 1980), 103.
[105] Application of Arts. 92 and 93 EC and of Art. 5 of Dir. 80/723 to public undertakings in the manufacturing sector (OJ 1991 C273/2), para. 11.
[106] Joined Cases 188–190/80 *France, Italy, and the UK* v. *EC Commission: transparency directive* [1982] ECR 2545, 2577.
[107] Case 234/84 [1986] ECR 2263, 2286.

Commission characterisation of the subscriptions as aid. The Court ruled that such subscriptions would constitute aid, unless a private shareholder having regard to the foreseeability of obtaining a return and leaving aside all social, regional policy, and sectoral considerations would have made the investment. Consistently with this ruling, the Commission has found aid to be involved where the state subscribes capital to support restructuring.[108] The Commission has also found aid to be present where the state acquires holdings in firms to help them until they overcome temporary difficulties or to achieve regional policy goals.[109] In such practice a test based on the conduct of a "model" investor acting competitively, given what was foreseeable at the time, seems to have been envisaged.

Commission thinking was summarised in a Communication of 17 September 1984.[110] According to this Communication,[111] aid is present where:

- the financial structure and, in particular, the debt structure of the undertaking concerned mean that a normal return cannot be expected within a reasonable time;
- the undertaking would be unable, because of the lack of its own financing capacity, to raise on the market the capital needed for investment;
- the participation involves the taking over or the continuation of non-viable activity of an undertaking in difficulty through the creation of a new legal entity;
- the holding is a short-term one, with the duration and selling price fixed in advance, so that the return to the provider of capital is considerably less than he could have expected from a capital market investment for a similar period;
- there is an obvious imbalance between public and private participation,[112] and the relative disengagement of private shareholders is largely due to the company's poor profit outlook; or
- the participation exceeds the real value of the undertaking concerned.

Reasonableness

Italy v. *EC Commission: Lanerossi*[113] concerned capital injections by the Italian authorities in a nationalised producer of clothing. Here it was argued

---

[108] Dec. 90/224 (OJ 1990 L118/42) on aid granted by the Italian Government to Aluminia and Comsal, 2 state-owned undertakings in the aluminium industry.

[109] *Second Report on Competition Policy* (EC Commission, Brussels, 1973), 108.

[110] *Public Authorities' Holding in Company Capital: the Commission's Position* (Bull. EC 9–1984, 3.5.1).

[111] *Ibid.*, para. 3.3.

[112] Negligible private investment does not affect the aid character of state participation. See Case T–358/94 *Compagnie Nationale Air France* v. *EC Commission* [1996] ECR II–2109, II–2160–2.

[113] Case C–303/88 [1991] ECR I–1433, I–1475. Cf. Case C–305/89 *Italy* v. *EC Commission: Alfa Romeo* [1991] ECR I–1603, I–1640.

that the test whether aid was involved should relate to the actions of the private entrepreneur rather than the private investor. This argument seems to have been influential.[114] Certainly, Advocate General van Gerven accepted that, the relationship between the public and private sectors being so close, a private holding company could not ignore social and regional considerations.[115] The state could also reasonably take account of such considerations in its participation decisions, though it could not continue to support a loss-making subsidiary in a sector suffering from overcapacity without adopting a restructuring plan.[116] According to the Court of Justice itself, state participation in pursuit of a structural policy, general or sectoral, guided by long-term profitability perspectives would not constitute aid. However, aid would be present where the participation took no account of the question of returns, even in the long term.[117]

The need for a "more concrete" evaluation of state participation is implicit in this ruling[118] and is reflected in the evolution of Commission practice. In other words, the case law of the Court has "enriched" Commission practice.[119]

According to a Communication of 1991,[120] the Commission recognises that investors, public or private, must engage in risk analysis. Such analysis requires the exercise of managerial skills, which necessarily implies a wide margin of judgment by the investor. Within that wide margin the exercise of judgement cannot be regarded as involving the grant of aid, though the Commission excludes the possibility that a public authority may happen to be better at foreseeing future market developments than anyone else.[121] Only where there are no objective grounds reasonably to expect that participation will give an adequate rate of return that would be acceptable to a private investor in a comparable undertaking operating under normal market conditions is aid involved.[122] No distinction is now made between projects which have short or long-term pay back periods, as long as the risks are adequately and objectively assessed and discounted at the time the decision to invest is made.[123]

---

[114] F. Minneci, "Le Partecipazioni pubbliche al capitale di imprese" [1991] *Diritto Comunitario e degli Scambi Internazionali* 365–72.

[115] This point also seems to have been recognized by Reischl AG in Joined Cases 188–190/80 *France, Italy, and the UK* v. *EC Commission: transparency directive* [1982] ECR 2545, 2591.

[116] [1991] ECR I–1433, I–1459.

[117] *Ibid.*, I–1476; and [1991] ECR I–1603, I–1640. See also Van Gerven AG (*ibid.*, I–1626) and in Case C–261/89 *Italy* v. *EC Commission: Aluminia* [1991] ECR I–4437, I–4449.

[118] F. Minneci, n. 114 above, 371.

[119] R. Kovar, "Les Prises de participation publiques et le régime communautaire des aides d'état" [1992] *RTDE* 109–57, 122.

[120] Application of Arts. 92 and 93 EC and of Art. 5 of Dir. 80/723 to public undertakings in the manufacturing sector (OJ 1991 C273/2).

[121] Communication C18/89 (ex N121/87–63/89) (OJ 1991 C45/3) regarding aid which Germany had decided to grant to Bremen and Niedersachsen.

[122] OJ 1991 C273/2, para. 27.   [123] *Ibid.*, para. 28.

Equally, it is recognised that a private undertaking may engage in cross-subsidisation, when it has a strategic plan with good hopes of long-term gain or where the cross-subsidy has a net benefit to the group as a whole. The Commission takes account of similar strategic goals where there is cross-subsidisation in public holding companies. Such cross-subsidisation is only treated as aid where the Commission considers that there is no reasonable explanation for the flow of funds other than that aid is involved.[124]

Finally, the Commission recognises the differences in approach a private investor may have between his minority holding in a company and full control of a large group. The former relationship may often be characterised as more of a speculative or short-term interest, whereas the latter usually involves a longer-term interest. Similarly, where a public authority controls an individual undertaking, it will normally be less motivated by purely short-term profit considerations than if it had merely a minority or non-controlling holding. Its time horizon will correspondingly be longer. Nevertheless, there must be a possibility of a return on its capital within "the foreseeable future". Accordingly, the Commission takes account of the nature of the public authority's holding in comparing its behaviour with the benchmark of the equivalent private investor. More particularly, where a decision is made to abandon a line of activity because of its lack of medium or long-term commercial viability, the Commission accepts that a public group, like a private group, can be expected to decide the timing and scale of its run down in the light of the impact on the overall credibility and structure of the group.[125]

In short, the test employed by the Commission has evolved. It is not so much that of a "model" private investor,[126] which would entail discrimination against the public sector, as that of a "reasonable" investor or entrepreneur.[127] As a result, state financing of conversion operations, including redeployment of workers and mitigation of the regional effects of a cutback, may not be treated as aid for the purposes of Article 92(1). Such operations involve a number of benefits, such as "indirect material profit", "image maintenance",[128] and "redirection of activities".[129] However, there must be a coherent restructuring plan,[130] and the financing of regional development operations may still be treated as aid. More particularly, where capital injections coincide

---

[124] *Ibid.*, para. 29.   [125] *Ibid.*, para. 30.

[126] Though the model has not been entirely eliminated from Commission practice. See, e.g., Dec. 93/133 (OJ 1993 L55/54) concerning aid granted by the Spanish Government to Merco (an agricultural processing company).

[127] Van Gerven AG in Case C–305/89 *Italy* v. *EC Commission: Alfa Romeo* [1991] ECR I–1603, I–1640.

[128] See also Joined Cases C–278–280/92 *Spain* v. *EC Commission: Hytasa* [1994] ECR I–4103, I–4154.

[129] Dec. 92/266 (OJ 1992 L138/24) on the conversion activities of French industrial groups outside the steel and coal industries and excluding the Compagnie Générale Maritime.

[130] Communication C39/93 (NN87/93) (OJ 1993 C334/7) concerning the subscription by CDC-participations to 2 bond issues of Air France.

with the sale of publicly owned shares in the company concerned, the prospect of profit from the injections is removed, and so they constitute aid.[131]

17.1.6 Privatisation

Privatisation may be favoured in Commission practice.[132] A reduction in the size of the public sector may not only render the use of state aid more transparent but, more fundamentally, may also be expected to lead to increased competition.

Commission practice is elaborated in guidelines regarding privatisation.[133] According to these guidelines, privatisation by means of a stock market flotation is generally assumed to take place on market conditions. Moreover, disposals made by unconditional invitation to tender involve no aid, if:

- the company is sold to the highest bidder;
- the terms and conditions of the invitation to tender are non-discriminatory and transparent; and
- interested parties are given ample time to prepare their offer and are given all the information needed to carry out a correct evaluation.

However, the following may involve aid:

- disposals made through restricted procedures or direct sales;
- disposals preceded by a debt write-off by the state, public enterprise, or any other public body;
- disposals preceded by conversion of debts into capital or by a capital increase; and
- disposals subject to conditions which would not be acceptable for a transaction between market-economy investors.

17.2 Anti-competitive Effects

Where aid of the kind covered by the above definitions is granted on a scale other than the purely negligible, competition within the common market will inevitably be different from what it would be if left to market forces.[134]

---

[131] H. Morch, "Summary of the Most Important Recent Developments" (1995) 5 *Competition Policy Newsletter* 43–9, 45.

[132] See, regarding privatisation as a solution to "recidivism", the *Twenty-Fourth Report on Competition Policy* (EC Commission, Brussels, 1995), 173. See, generally, A. Evans, "Privatization and State Aid Control in EC Law" [1997] *ECLR* 259–64 and W. Devroe, "Privatizations and Community Law: Neutrality versus Policy" (1997) 34 CMLRev. 267–306.

[133] *Twenty-Third Report on Competition Policy* (EC Commission, Brussels, 1994), 255–6.

[134] Cf., exceptionally, Dec. 93/625 (OJ 1993 L300/15) concerning aid granted by the French Government to the Pari Mutuel Urbain and to the racecourse undertakings; and Dec. 87/506 (OJ 1987 L290/21) concerning aid granted by the French Government to 2 steel groups.

According to the Commission, any aid granted to an undertaking gives it an advantage over others and by its nature tends to affect competition.[135] Hence, there may be a presumption that aid distorts or threatens to distort competition, unless exceptional circumstances exist,[136] and that trade between Member States may be affected.[137] Even if an aid recipient has ceased trading, a distortion may still arise. For example, it may arise, because the economic advantage is transferred to investors in the recipient and the entrepreneurial risk for such investors may be reduced or removed.[138]

Nevertheless, Article 92(1) of the Treaty stipulates that aid is only contrary to this provision where three conditions are met. First, certain undertakings or the production of certain goods must be favoured. Secondly, there must be a distortion of competition or threat thereof. Thirdly, trade between Member States must be affected.[139]

17.2.1 Favouritism

In Commission practice the requirement of favouritism in Article 92(1) is treated as meaning that there must be an element of selection or discrimination in the grant of aid.[140]

Such practice does not imply that only aid to individual sectors or regions is covered by Article 92(1). For example, the grant of export aid to undertakings generally in a Member State is also covered thereby.[141] Similarly, tax concessions limited to firms in difficulty are treated as aid covered by Article 92(1).[142] Such treatment may be supported by the wording of Article 92. In particular, Article 92(2) and (3) allow for aids other than those limited to particular sectors or regions to be authorised. They thus imply that aids other than those so limited may be covered by Article 92(1).

Moreover, Commission practice does not rely on purely formal consideration of the aid concerned. Hence, aid which is formally available to undertakings generally may be treated as effectively favouring a particular sector[143]

---

[135] Case 304/85 *Acciairie e Ferriere Lombarde Falck* v. *EC Commission* [1987] ECR 871, 895.

[136] Capotorti AG in Case 730/79 *Philip Morris Holland BV* v. *EC Commission* [1980] ECR 2671, 2698.

[137] Slynn AG in Case 57/86 *Greece* v. *EC Commission: interest rebates on export credits* [1987] ECR 2855, 2867; and Lenz AG in Case 234/84 *Belgium* v. *EC Commission: Meura* [1986] ECR 2263, 2274–5. But cf. Reischl AG in Case 52/76 *Luigi Benedetti* v. *Munari Flli s.a.s.* [1977] ECR 163, 191.

[138] Dec. 95/366 (OJ 1995 L218/20) on aid granted by Italy (Sardinia) in the agricultural sector. But cf. Dec. 95/524 (OJ 1995 L300/23) concerning aid granted by the Italian State to Iritecna SpA.

[139] Provision for control of planned aid in Art. 93(3) EC implies that a potential effect on trade is sufficient. See R. Kovar, n. 119 above, 131.

[140] *Twenty-Third Report on Competition Policy* (EC Commission, Brussels, 1994), 246–7.

[141] Roemer AG in Joined Cases 6 & 11/69 *EC Commission* v. *France: preferential rediscount rate for exporters* [1969] ECR 523, 552.

[142] Dec. 95/547 (OJ 1995 L308/92) giving conditional approval to the aid granted by France to Crédit Lyonnais.

[143] Case C–169/84 *Société CdF Chimie et Fertilisants SA* v. *EC Commission* [1990] ECR I–3083, I–3116.

or a particular undertaking[144] contrary to Article 92(1). For example, a greater reduction of social charges in respect of female than male employees may be found to favour undertakings relying heavily on female labour.[145] Likewise, tax measures which are "structured in such a way as to apply to only a very small number of operations, if not just to a single operation", are limited in time, only apply to large companies, and depend on the exercise of discretion may be treated as aid favouring the companies concerned.[146]

Such practice entails a sufficiently broad conception of favouritism to raise serious doubts about what this condition adds to the condition implicit in aid definitions that exclude general state interventions from the scope of Article 92(1).

17.2.2 Distortion of Competition

In determining whether there is a distortion of competition or threat thereof for the purposes of Article 92(1), the Commission may have regard not only to the direct and immediate effects of aid on the market position of the recipient. The Commission may also consider the effects for potential competitors.[147] The Commission may even consider the "downstream" effects[148] on competition in industries which purchase goods from the aided undertaking[149] or the effects of aid to the production of raw materials on the costing of the final product and profit margins.[150] Similarly, "upstream" effects may be considered where aid to the purchaser affects competition between producers.[151]

Theory of the "Second Best"

The economics theory of the "second best" may be thought relevant to the

---

[144] Dec. 80/932 (OJ 1980 L264/29) concerning the partial taking-over by the state of employers' contributions to sickness insurance schemes in Italy. Cf. ESA Notice 95–002 (OJ 1995 C212/6) concerning aid which Norway proposed to grant in the form of a tax exemption for glass packaging from a basic tax on non-reusable beverage packaging.

[145] Case 173/73 *Italy* v. *EC Commission: social charges* [1974] ECR 709.

[146] Dec. 92/389 (OJ 1992 L207/47) concerning the state aid provided for in Decree–Laws 174 of 15 May 1989 and 254 of 13 July 1989 and in draft Law 4230 regularising the effects produced by these Decree–Laws.

[147] Dec. 67/217 (OJ 1967 1275) concerning the amendment of certain aids granted by the Netherlands to the processing of cereals for human consumption.

[148] See, generally, regarding "upstream" and "downstream" subsidies and "cross-subsides", G.M. Roberti, "Le Contrôle de la Commission des Communautés européennes sur les aides nationales" [1993] *AJDA* 397–411, 404–5.

[149] See, e.g., Dec. 72/253 (JO 1972 L164/22) concerning the grant of aid to encourage the rationalisation of the production and processing of forage and the co-operation of agricultural producers in the Netherlands.

[150] Dec. 84/508 (OJ 1984 L283/42) on the aid granted by the Belgian Government to a producer of polypropylene fibre and yarn.

[151] Dec. 66/556 (JO 1966 3141) concerning an aid system established by the French Government for the acquisition of gliders.

determinations made by the Commission. According to this theory, a distortion of competition reduces welfare because it results in a shift of resources to the production of goods that are, from a social point of view, less desirable. If there is only one distortion of competition, such theory holds that removing the distortion will improve welfare. If, on the other hand, there is more than one distortion, removing only one of them need not necessarily improve welfare. Its removal may mean that the misallocation of resources resulting from remaining distortions is increased. In other words, the effect of partial elimination of distortions may be to reduce overall welfare.[152] In such circumstances, as well as in the face of other market imperfections, such as externalities[153] or economies of scale, aid can in theory restore efficiency and increase welfare.

In other words, since competition requires efficient allocation of resources, aid which merely corrects inefficient allocation associated with market imperfections may not be regarded as distorting competition. For example, since an undertaking may be unable fully to appropriate the benefit of infrastructure and training, they may only be imperfectly provided by the market. Aid to remedy this market imperfection may not distort competition. Hence, as the Court of Justice has ruled, financial assistance for infrastructure and training, which do not exclusively benefit one undertaking, may not constitute aid for the purposes of Article 92(1).[154]

Political Economy Perspective

From a political economy perspective, a critical role may be implied for supranational control.[155] Specifically, such control may prevent special interest groups securing aid detrimental to the economy as a whole. In other words, it may distinguish between aid designed to correct market failure and aid which merely increases distortion of competition.[156]

However, the importance attached by the Union institutions to market integration jeopardizes realisation of the potential of supranational control. Indeed, it is said that the economic foundations of the criteria employed to control aid are unclear. Commission practice is not consistently based on the above distinction, and there is no evidence that it is primarily concerned with ensuring that aid does not increase the welfare of a Member State at the expense of other Member States by altering the terms of trade.[157]

---

[152] R.G. Lipsey and K. Lancaster, "The General Theory of the Second Best" [1956] *Review of Economic Studies* 11–32.

[153] Externalities are costs or benefits not recognised by the market. They may be negative, as in the case of pollution, or positive, as in the case of R & D or vocational training ("State Aid Control in the Context of Other Community Policies" [1994] *European Economy*, Supp. A, No. 4, 3).

[154] Case C–225/91 *Matra SA* v. *EC Commission* [1993] ECR I–3203, I–3257.

[155] R.E. Baldwin, "Assessing the Fair Trade and Safeguards Laws in Terms of Modern Trade and Political Economy Analysis" [1992] *The World Economy* 185–202, 195.

[156] J. S. Chard and M.J. Macmillan, "Sectoral Aids and Community Competition Rules: The Case of Textiles" [1979] *JWTL* 132–57.   [157] *Ibid.*, 155.

Market Unification

Judicial perspectives on the function of the condition for application of Article 92(1) that there be a distortion of competition were developed in *Italy* v. *EC Commission*.[158] This case concerned a reduction of social charges on Italian textile firms. Here the Court of Justice ruled that in the application of Article 92(1) the appropriate reference point for deciding whether there was a distortion had to be the competitive position existing within the common market before the grant of the aid in question.[159] In so ruling, the Court implicitly followed Advocate General Warner. The latter approved an early characterisation[160] of the relationship between the prohibition of state aid and the establishment of the common market. He observed that there would be no real common market in an industry straddling several countries if one of those countries subsidised its own industry.[161]

Such thinking may lead to a broad interpretation of the concept of a distortion of competition. Accordingly, aid may be regarded as distorting competition, simply because it calculably improves the recipient's return on his investment, thereby strengthening his financial position compared with competitors who do not receive such assistance.[162]

It was argued in *Philip Morris Holland BV* v. *EC Commission*[163] that a more developed economic analysis was necessary under Article 92(1) than is entailed by such practice. In this case a Dutch investment aid scheme had been approved by the Commission, subject to the condition of prior notification of individual grants. One such grant involved a project of Philip Morris International to close a cigarette factory at one location in the Netherlands, while expanding capacity at another. There was substantial Union trade in cigarettes, and the Netherlands was one of the largest importers and exporters of cigarettes. Philip Morris, the second largest group of tobacco manufacturers in the world, expected the project to give it half of Dutch manufacturing of cigarettes and anticipated that more than 80 per cent of its Dutch production would be exported to other Member States. On the basis of this information, the Commission decided that the proposed aid was likely to distort competition by favouring the recipient within the meaning of Article 92(1) and was prohibited.

Philip Morris challenged this decision before the Court of Justice on several grounds. One was that the economic analysis performed by the Commission was not sufficient to justify a finding of distortion to competition. According to the challenger, to decide whether aid was incompatible with the common market, it was appropriate to apply the criteria for deciding whether there was

---

[158] Case 173/73 [1974] ECR 709.   [159] *Ibid.*, 720.
[160] Case 30/59 *De Gezamenlijke Steenkolenmijnen in Limburg* v. *ECSC High Authority* [1961] ECR 1, 41 (Lagrange AG).
[161] [1974] ECR 709, 722.
[162] Dec. 87/15 (OJ 1987 L12/17) on the compatibility with the common market of aid under the German Federal/*Land* Government Joint Regional Aid Programme in 6 labour market regions.
[163] Case 730/79 [1980] ECR 2671.

a distortion of competition under Articles 85 and 86 of the Treaty, which concern restrictive practices by undertakings.[164] Thus the Commission had, first, to determine the relevant market and, for this purpose, had to take account of the product, the territory, and the period of time in question. It had then to consider the "pattern" of this market in order to be able to assess how far the aid affected relations between competitors.[165]

However, the Court simply noted that the aid strengthened the position of an undertaking compared with other undertakings competing in trade between Member States.[166] In particular, it reduced the cost of converting the production facilities. It thereby gave the recipient a competitive advantage over manufacturers who had completed or intended to complete at their own expense a similar increase in the production capacity of their plant. The Court considered these effects sufficient to justify the Commission decision that the aid threatened to distort competition.

17.2.3 Effect on Trade between Member States

Aid may be found to affect trade between Member States, simply because the sector concerned has "cross-border characteristics",[167] the sector is one where producers from different Member States are in effective competition, or the recipient is engaged in trade between Member States.[168] According to the Commission, when aid strengthens the position of all national undertakings in a particular sector involved in such trade, the latter must be considered as affected by that aid.[169]

Domestic Activity

It is not only export activity which is taken into account in a determination whether trade between Member States is affected by aid. In *France* v. *EC Commission: a brewery loan*[170] the Court of Justice ruled that aid may be such as to affect trade between Member States where the recipient competes with products coming from other Member States, even if the recipient does not export its products. In particular, the aid may enable the recipient to maintain or increase domestic production, with the result that undertakings established in other Member States have less chance of exporting their products to that Member State. Such aid is, therefore, likely to affect trade between Member States.

---

[164] Chaps. 13 and 14.   [165] [1980] ECR 2671, 2688.   [166] *Ibid.*, 2688–9.

[167] See, regarding aid to airlines, Communication C34/93 (N557/93) (OJ 1993 C291/4) on equity injections by the Irish Government in favour of Aer Lingus.

[168] Dec. 88/565 (OJ 1988 L310/28) on planned aid by the French Government for certain areas of Haute-Normande, Franche-Comté, and Sarthe, in the conversion centres of Dunkirk, Le Creusot, Fos, Caen, and the area of Roubaix-Tourcoing.

[169] Communication C32/92 (ex NN67/92) (OJ 1992 C316/7) on aids granted by Italy to professional road hauliers.

[170] Case 102/87 [1988] ECR 4067, 4087–8.

Absence of International Trade

Aid may be found not to affect trade between Member States because of the lack of integration of the markets. For example, according to Advocate General van Gerven in *Italy* v. *EC Commission: Lanerossi*,[171] there may exist no international trade in certain products, by reason of high transport costs or other particular circumstances. In the present state of integration of the markets, aid to such products may be found not to affect trade between Member States.

Lack of a "Trading Infrastructure"

Aid may be found not to affect trade between Member States, because the lack of a "trading infrastructure" obliges aid recipients to operate almost exclusively on the local market.[172] For example, in the case of the foundry industry, customers need to be in close contact with foundries, and the transport costs of castings are relatively high. For these reasons, international trade in castings is relatively limited.[173] Hence, aid to the production of castings may be found not to affect trade between Member States.

Evolution of Trading Conditions

While at a given time aid may be found not to affect trade between Member States, the evolution of trading conditions may be significant. For example, Irish aid to bakeries to enable them to lower the price of bread was accepted in 1975, because there did not seem to be trade in bread between Member States. Later, trade between Ireland and Northern Ireland developed, and so the Commission considered that trade between Member States could be affected by the aid.[174]

Again, although it may not be "possible to say exactly where the recipients' markets are, since the prospective recipients are not known, past experience [may] indicate that some of the aided firms will be active in intra-Community trade" and, hence, that such trade may be affected.[175] According to the Commission, if the investigation of the effect on trade is not to be restricted to a purely static or retrospective approach, the analysis must take into account the potential competition which can reasonably be expected to affect trade flows.[176]

---

[171] Case C–303/88 [1991] ECR I–1433, I–1464.

[172] *Sixteenth Report on Competition Policy* (EC Commission, Brussels, 1987), 173.

[173] *Seventh Report on Competition Policy* (EC Commission, Brussels, 1978), 155.

[174] Bull. EC 4–1979, 2.1.28.

[175] Dec. 87/15 (OJ 1987 L12/17) on the compatibility with the common market of aid under the German Federal/*Land* Government Joint Regional Aid Programme in 6 labour market regions.

[176] *Fourteenth Report on Competition Policy* (EC Commission, Brussels, 1985), 129.

17.2.4 *De Minimis* Issues

Controversy surrounds the question whether the application of Article 92(1) is subject to a *de minimis* rule. In other words, controversy surrounds the question whether aid falls outside this provision because of its limited impact on competition and trade between Member States.

Objections to a De Minimis *Rule*

It may be argued that the formal structure of Article 92 excludes application of a *de minimis* rule. In particular, account may be taken of the availability of "exceptions" from the Article 92(1) prohibition in Article 92(2) and (3). In view of the availability of such exceptions, it may be argued that minor hindrances to competition and trade between Member States which do not qualify for such an exception cannot be permitted.[177]

Objections to application of a *de minimis* rule may also emphasise qualitative considerations. It is said, for example, that "the very idea of states ignoring their Treaty obligations is intrinsically more destructive to political harmony and market unity than occasional restrictive practices between firms".[178]

At the same time, stress may be placed on practical considerations. According to Advocate General Warner in *Italy* v. *EC Commission: social charges,*[179] this was a field where the difficulties of positive proof were often insurmountable. Accordingly, once it was clear that the natural consequence of aid to an industry in a Member State was to increase the competitiveness of that industry *vis-à-vis* its competitors in other Member States,[180] the inference could properly be drawn that the aid would distort competition and affect trade between Member States.[181]

There may, however, be a rationale for rejection of a *de minimis* rule which goes beyond legal form, "intrinsic" considerations, or practical considerations. Whereas it is in the nature of a market with a competitive structure that conduct of undertakings with a limited effect on this structure is tolerable,[182] the same may be less true of state action.

This rationale may have support in *France* v. *EC Commission: textiles aid.*[183] This case concerned an aid scheme, financed by a tax on all textiles sold in France and used to assist reorganisation of that industry. The goals of

---

[177] Case 234/84 *Belgium* v. *EC Commission: Meura* [1986] ECR 2263, 2274; and Case 102/87 *France* v. *EC Commission: brewery loan* [1988] ECR 4067, 4078.

[178] M. Ross, "A Review of Developments in State Aids 1987–8" (1989) 26 *CMLRev.* 167–92, 170. In particular, respect for the duty to notify planned aid under Art. 93(3) EC might become more difficult to secure.

[179] Case 173/73 [1974] ECR 709.

[180] To require that the real effects of aid already granted be demonstrated would favour Member States which granted unnotified aid. See Darmon AG in Joined Cases C–324 & 342/90 *Germany and Pleuger Worthington GmbH* v. *EC Commission* [1994] ECR I–1173, I–1184.

[181] Case 173/73 [1974] ECR 709, 728.   [182] Sect. 13.4.1 above.

[183] Case 47/69 [1970] ECR 487.

the scheme may have been acceptable to the Commission. However, the Commission found the scheme objectionable, because the tax extended to imports from other Member States, whereas the benefits went mainly to French firms.[184] In challenging this finding before the Court of Justice, the French Government stressed the relatively small size of the tax. The rate had been initially fixed at 0.20 per cent. and had been raised to 0.44 per cent.

Advocate General Roemer accepted the assertion of the French government that such low rates could have only a small effect on prices. However, he also doubted whether the situation should really be assessed in such quantitative terms. If the matter was considered from a qualitative point of view, the Advocate General had no doubt that imposing handicaps on foreign producers to the detriment of their competitive position, especially as a result of tax measures taken within the framework of a system of aid, distorted competition.[185]

The Court itself ruled that the rate of tax was not the essential element in finding a distortion of competition. According to the Court, the Commission rightly decided that this aid, whatever might be the rate of tax, had the effect, because of its method of financing, of distorting competition in trade between Member States.[186]

Guidelines

Although the various objections to a *de minimis* rule may seem convincing, the Commission has drawn up guidelines on aids of "minor importance".[187] These guidelines entail that outside sectors covered by specific "policy statements" (steel, shipbuilding, synthetic fibres and motor vehicles) and the agricultural (as defined in Annex II to the Treaty), fishery, transport, and coal sectors the Commission will not, in principle, object to the grant of minor aids.[188]

Such aids are present where

– the recipient does not employ more than 250 people, has an annual turnover of not more than 20 million Euro or a balance sheet total not exceeding 10 million Euro, and is not more than 25 per cent owned by one or more companies not falling within this definition, except public investment corporations, venture capital companies or, provided no control is exercised, institutional investors, and
– the aid intensity does not exceed 7.5 per cent.,

---

[184] Dec. 69/266 (JO 1969 L220/1) concerning the French aid system to encourage research and the modernisation of industrial and commercial structures in the textiles sector.

[185] Case 47/69 [1970] ECR 487, 501–2.

[186] *Ibid.*, 495.

[187] Communication on the accelerated clearance of aid schemes for SMEs and of amendments of existing schemes (OJ 1992 C213/10).

[188] *Ibid.*, para. 5.

- the aid is designed to lead to job creation and amounts to no more than 3,000 Euro per job created, or
- in the absence of specific investment or job creation objectives, the total volume of aid a recipient may receive is not more than 200,000 Euro.

These guidelines may reflect considerations of substance[189] as well as administrative convenience. According to the Commission, all financial assistance to enterprises alters competitive conditions to some extent. However, not all aid has a perceptible or appreciable impact[190] on competition in trade between Member States. Certainly, the Court of Justice has accepted the possibility that "aid properly so-called, although not in conformity with Community law, does not substantially affect trade between Member States and may thus be acknowledged as permissible"[191]. Such aid may have effects "of such small dimension as to be of interest to only a very limited section of the market"[192] or effects which are so minimal that they can be disregarded for the purposes of Article 92(1).[193]

Apparently, therefore, aid must be such as to be capable of having a real rather than purely theoretical effect on the market, if it is to be prohibited by this provision.

17.3 Aid Authorisations

Article 92(2) of the EC Treaty provides for mandatory authorisations of aid, while Article 92(3) provides for authorisations at the discretion of the Commission. Further authorisations may be granted by the Council.

17.3.1 Mandatory Authorisations

Article 92(2) provides that three categories of aid are compatible with the common market.[194] Aid falling within one of these categories must be authorised by the Commission, though it has to be established that the aid does so fall.[195] Moreover, it is implicit in Article 92(2) that aid under this provision must not be "misused".[196]

---

[189] Cf., regarding the express requirement in Art. 67(1) ECSC of appreciable repercussions on conditions of competition, Lagrange AG in Case 30/59 *De Gezamenlijke Steenkolenmijnen in Limburg* v. *ECSC High Authority* [1961] ECR 1, 41.

[190] Case 248/84 *Germany* v. *EC Commission: regional aid* [1987] ECR 4013, 4041; and Dec. 87/99 (OJ 1987 L40/22) on aid proposed by Rheinland-Pfalz for a fibre processing firm in Scheuerfeld.

[191] Case 47/69 *France* v. *EC Commission: textiles aid* [1970] ECR 487, 495.

[192] Reischl AG in Case 40/75 *Société des Produits Bertrand SA* v. *EC Commission* [1976] ECR 1, 17.

[193] Capotorti AG in Case 730/79 *Philip Morris Holland BV* v. *EC Commission* [1980] ECR 2671, 2697.

[194] Cf. also regarding aid covered by Art. 223(1)(b) EC, Dec. 89/633 (OJ 1989 L367/62) concerning aid provided or to be provided by the Spanish Government to Enasa, an undertaking producing commercial vehicles.

[195] Notice on co-operation between national courts and the Commission in the state aid field (OJ 1995 C312/8), para. 14.

[196] According to Art. 93(2) EC, the Commission may act against aid which is incompatible with the common market or which is being misused.

Social Aid

Aid which has a social character and is granted to individual consumers,[197] provided that it is granted without discrimination related to the origin of the products concerned, is compatible with the common market under Article 92(2)(a).[198]

The acquisition of wheat by the state and its subsequent resale at a discount, which has the effect of reducing bread prices, may be an example of aid covered by this provision.[199] Tax relief for individual consumers purchasing cars fitted with pollution reduction devices may be a further example.[200]

"Disaster Aid"

Aid to make good the damage caused by natural disasters or exceptional occurrences is compatible with the common market under Article 92(2)(b).

Earthquakes, volcanic eruptions,[201] floods,[202] and weather of an exceptional and short-term character[203] may be treated as such a disaster, where the damage suffered "attains a certain severity at individual level".[204] Apparently, temporary aid to re-establish the equilibrium disturbed is envisaged. Thus aid to irrigation, granted even during "normal" weather conditions, is not covered by Article 92(2)(b).[205]

Exceptional occurrences for the purposes of this provision may cover "man-made" damage,[206] such as that associated with a strike, war, serious internal political disturbances, explosions or catastrophic mine accidents,[207] or social or religious persecution.[208]

---

[197] In the French, Italian, and Dutch versions respectively the terms "*consommateurs*", "*consumatori*", and "*verbruikers*" are found. These terms relate to the final consumer and are thus narrower than "*utilisateurs*", "*utilizzatori*", and "*gebruikers*", which are found in Art. 85(3) EC.

[198] Cf., regarding Art. 56 ECSC, which provides for "readaptation aid" in favour of workers in the coal and steel industries, sect. 20.6.2 below.

[199] Reischl AG in Case 52/76 *Luigi Benedetti* v. *Munari F.lli s.a.s.* [1977] ECR 163, 190.

[200] *Europe* 5234 (31 Mar. 1990).

[201] Notice C11/92 (ex NN134/91) (OJ 1993 C59/7) concerning aid which Italy had decided to introduce by Law 34/1991 of the Sicilian region concerning the marketing and sale of Sicilian products.

[202] See, in the case of North Rhine Westphalia, Bull. 7/8–1995, 1.3.154.

[203] Dec. 82/743 (OJ 1982 L315/21) on the aids provided for in Campania to help producers of plums.

[204] Communication C16/91 (OJ 1994 C58/8) concerning aids which Italy had decided to grant to agricultural holdings following drought.

[205] Communication C6/90 (ex NN91/89) (OJ 1994 C19/4) concerning aid granted by Sardinia (reduction of irrigation tariffs).

[206] Cf. M. Schütte and J.-P. Hix, "The Application of the EC State Aid Rules to Privatizations: The East German Example" (1995) 32 *CMLRev.* 215–48, 226.

[207] Bull. EC 12-1968, 32.

[208] H. von der Groeben, H. von Boeckh, J. Thiesing, and C.-D. Ehlermann (eds.), *Kommentar zum EWG-Vertrag* (Nomos, Baden-Baden, 1983), 1604. Cf. E. Wohlfarth, U. Everling, H.J. Glaesner, and R. Sprung, *Die Europäische Wirtschaftsgemeinschaft* (Vahlen, Berlin, 1960), 276.

Aid to a Divided Germany

Article 92(2)(c) provides that aid to the economy of certain areas of the Federal Republic of Germany affected by the division of Germany is compatible with the common market, in so far as such aid is required to compensate for the economic disadvantages caused by that division.[209]

Deletion of this provision was envisaged in drafts for the Treaty on European Union,[210] apparently because "the economic justification for continuous subsidisation of these regions has ceased to exist".[211] However, the Commission is reluctant to take a position on the question whether it has been rendered inapplicable by German reunification. The Commission is apparently content to secure its strict interpretation and the gradual phasing-out of the aid concerned.[212]

17.3.2 Discretionary Authorisations

Article 92(3) provides that various categories of aid may be considered to be compatible with the common market. The Commission may exercise discretion, subject to possible review by the European Courts, in deciding whether to authorise such aid. In exercising its discretion, the Commission considers whether: the aid promotes a project that is in the Union interest as a whole; the aid is necessary for the achievement of the result envisaged; and the duration, intensity, and scope of the aid are proportional to the importance of the result.[213]

Aid to Peripheral Regions

Article 92(3)(a) provides that aid to promote the economic development of areas where the standard of living is abnormally low or where there is serious underemployment may be considered compatible with the common market. This paragraph is treated as covering certain aid to the "peripheral regions" of the Union.[214]

Aid to Projects of Common European Interest

Article 92(3)(b) provides that two kinds of aid may be considered compatible with the common market. The first kind of aid concerned is that to promote the execution of an important project of common European

---

[209] The categories of permissible aids were indicated in Bull. EC 2–1965, 33.

[210] *Europe Doc.* 1709/1710 (3 May 1991) and *Europe Doc.* 1722/1723 (5 July 1991). It was excluded from Art. 6(2) of the Agreement on Civil Aviation between Norway, Sweden, and the EEC (OJ 1992 L200/21), which otherwise reproduced Art. 92(2) EC.

[211] *The European Community and German Unification*, Bull. EC., Supp. 4/90, 75.

[212] Dec. 94/266 (OJ 1994 L114/21) on the proposal to award aid to SST-Garngesellschaft mbH, Thüringen.

[213] *Twelfth Report on Competition Policy* (EC Commission, Brussels, 1983), 160.

[214] Communication on the method for the application of Art. 92(3)(a) and (c) to regional aid (OJ 1988 C212/2), para. I; and Changes to the method for the application of Art. 92(3)(a) to regional aid (OJ 1994 C364/8).

interest. Such a project must form part of a transnational European programme supported jointly by a number of Member States or arise from concerted action by a number of Member States to combat a common threat such as environmental pollution.[215] The project must be promoted by the aid, in the sense that without the aid the project would not go ahead or would only do so in such a manner that it would no longer be considered an important project of common European interest.[216]

Aid to Remedy a Serious Disturbance

Article 92(3)(b) also provides that aid to remedy a serious disturbance in the economy of a Member State may be considered compatible with the common market. The disturbance must, it seems, be cyclical rather than structural,[217] and there must be an abnormal situation by reference to the cyclical fluctuations which may be expected in the sector concerned.[218] The disturbance must also be serious by Union standards.[219] Apparently, a disturbance is not considered serious if it lacks national significance.[220] At the same time, the aid must be of such a scope and scale as to be capable of remedying the disturbance. Hence, aid to a particular sub-sector is not covered by Article 92(3)(b).[221]

Aid for Regional or Sectoral Development

Article 92(3)(c) provides that aid to facilitate the development of certain economic activities or of certain economic areas may be compatible with the common market. However, the aid must not adversely affect trading conditions[222] to an extent contrary to the common interest. This subparagraph concerns sectoral aid[223] and aid to the "central regions".[224]

---

[215] Joined Cases 62 & 72/87 *Exécutif Régional Wallon and SA Glaverbel* v. *EC Commission* [1988] ECR 1573, 1595.

[216] Notice C32/94 (N48/94) (OJ 1994 C293/6) with regard to the aid for the construction of a rape seed oil methylester pilot plan operated by the Raiffeisen Hauptgenossenschaft Nord AG, Kiel.

[217] Hence, aid cannot be granted for as long as 3 years. See Dec. 73/274 (OJ 1973 L254/14) on Art. 20 of Italian Law 1101 of 1 Dec. 1971 on the restructuring, reorganisation, and conversion of the textile industry.

[218] Dec. 77/172 (OJ 1977 L54/39) concerning an aid for the pigmeat sector in the UK.

[219] Dec. 84/94 (OJ 1984 L51/17) on the aid that the UK Government proposed to grant for an investment to expand production capacity for polypropylene film.

[220] Case 730/79 *Philip Morris Holland BV* v. *EC Commission* [1980] ECR 2671, 2692. See also Dec. 94/725 (OJ 1994 L289/26) on measures adopted by the French Government concerning pigmeat.

[221] Dec. 94/813 (OJ 1994 L335/82) concerning aid to French pig farmers – Stabiporc adjustment fund. But see, regarding the possibility that sectoral problems may justify aid under this provision, Mayras AG in Joined Cases 31 & 53/77R *EC Commission* v. *UK and UK* v. *EC Commission: aid to pig producers* [1977] ECR 921, 934.

[222] This condition seems broader than that relating to "the development of trade" in Art. 86(2) EC. Cf. Rozès AG in Case 78/82 *EC Commission* v. *Italy: state monopoly for tobacco* [1983] ECR 1955, 1989.

[223] See, generally, Guidelines on state aid for rescuing and restructuring firms in difficulty (OJ 1997 C283/2).

[224] Para. II.2 of the Communication on the method for the application of Art. 92(3)(a) and (c) to regional aid (OJ 1988 C212/2; OJ 1997 C198/9); and Guidelines for state aid for undertakings in deprived urban areas (OJ 1997 C146/6).

In considering whether to authorise such aid, the Commission may have regard to considerations of international competitiveness and to any special rules for aid to the relevant sector.[225] Special rules apply to aid to various sectors, including: agriculture,[226] fishing,[227] transport,[228] shipbuilding,[229] textiles,[230] synthetic fibres,[231] and motor vehicles.[232] Special rules also apply to aid to the coal[233] and steel industries[234] under the ECSC Treaty.

Cultural Aid

Article 92(3)(d) provides that aid to promote culture and heritage conservation may be compatible with the common market. However, the aid must not affect trading conditions and competition in the Union to an extent that is contrary to the common interest. This provision was introduced into the EC Treaty by the Treaty on European Union. It follows Commission practice under Article 92(3)(b) and (c) of the EEC Treaty, regarding aid to the film industry.[235]

On the basis of these various provisions, the Commission has adopted guidelines concerning aid granted in pursuit of "horizontal policies", that is policies not limited by region or industrial sector. In particular, they have been adopted for employment aid,[236] aid to research and development,[237] aid to small and medium-sized enterprises,[238] and environmental aid.[239]

Council Authorisations

Further categories of aid may be authorised by Council enactments under Article 92(3)(e).[240] So far, this power has only been used in the case of

[225] Bull. EC 1–1979, 2.1.36.
[226] See, in particular, the Communication regarding state aid for investments in the processing and marketing of agricultural products (OJ 1996 C29/4).
[227] Guidelines for the examination of state aid to fisheries and aquaculture (OJ 1997 C100/12).
[228] A. Evans, *EC Law of State Aid* (Oxford Series in EC Law, Clarendon Press, Oxford, 1997), 263–74.
[229] Reg. 1013/97 (OJ 1997 L148/1) on aid to certain shipyards under restructuring.
[230] Framework for aid to textiles (*Competition Law in the European Communities*, ii: *Rules Applicable to State Aids* (EC Commission, Brussels, 1990), 44–7).
[231] Code on aid to the synthetic fibres industry (OJ 1992 C346/2).
[232] Framework on state aid to the motor vehicle industry (OJ 1997 C279/1).
[233] Dec. 3632/93 (OJ 1993 L329/12) establishing Community rules for state aid to the coal industry.
[234] Dec. 2496/96 (OJ 1996 L338/42) establishing Community rules for state aid to the steel industry.
[235] See, e.g., Dec. 89/441 (OJ 1989 L208/3) on aid granted by the Greek Government to the film industry for the production of Greek films.
[236] Guidelines on aid to employment (OJ 1995 C334/4).
[237] H. Morch, "Summary of the Most Important Recent Developments" (1995) 6 *Competition Policy Newsletter* 41–7, 41–3.
[238] Guidelines on state aid for SMEs (OJ 1992 C213/2).
[239] Community guidelines on state aid for environmental purposes (OJ 1994 C72/3).
[240] I.e., "an abstract and general framework" may be established. See Darmon AG in Case C–400/92 *Germany* v. *EC Commission: Cosco* [1994] ECR I–4701, I–4708.

shipbuilding, notably to permit the grant of operating aid.[241] The Council may also authorise particular aid measures on application by the Member State concerned under Article 93(2).[242]

Formally, therefore, the Treaty framework for state aid control comprises a prohibition of aid in Article 92(1) and the possibility of its authorisation under Article 92(2) or (3) or Article 93(2). In substance, these provisions embody various legal requirements – that competition should not be distorted, that regional development should be promoted or facilitated, that sectoral development should be facilitated, and so on – to be given effect in the application of these provisions.[243]

17.3.3 "Compensatory Justification"

In pursuing the various requirements embodied in Articles 92 and 93 of the Treaty, the Commission applies the principle of "compensatory justification".[244] According to this principle, aid falling within Article 92(1) may only be authorised where it is necessary to accomplish one of the goals of Article 92(2) or (3). The national interests of a Member State or the benefits obtained by the aid recipient do not in themselves justify an authorisation. Rather, the aid must contribute to the attainment of objectives which, under normal market conditions, the recipient firms would not attain by their own actions.[245] To authorise aid where there was no such compensatory justification would be tantamount to allowing trade between Member States to be affected and competition to be distorted without any benefit in terms of the Union interest, while at the same time accepting that undue advantages accrued to some Member States.[246]

The formal rationale for this practice may be that Article 92(2) and (3) permit exceptions to the fundamental principle of free competition enshrined in Article 3(g) of the Treaty. For this reason, the former provisions have to be strictly construed. In substance, however, the rationale may be that aid which distorts competition will be authorised only to accomplish a Union objectives and only in the presence of market failure. If market forces will accomplish the objective without aid, and the aid will distort competition, then it will be prohibited. In other words, microeconomic inefficiency

---

[241] That is, aid merely to keep the recipient in business. See Dir. 90/684 (OJ 1990 L380/27) on aid to shipbuilding.

[242] See, e.g., Case C–122/94 *EC Commission* v. *EU Council aid to wine producers* [1996] ECR I–881.

[243] Case C–169/95 *Spain* v. *EC Commission: aid to Teruel* [1997] ECR I–135, I–155–6.

[244] See, generally, K. Mortelmans, "The Compensatory Justification Criterion in the Practice of the Commission in Decisions on State Aids" (1984) 21 *CMLRev.* 405–34.

[245] *Tenth Report on Competition Policy* (EC Commission, Brussels, 1981), 149–51.

[246] Dec. 81/626 (OJ 1981 L229/12) on a scheme of aid by the Belgian Government in respect of certain investments carried out by a Belgian undertaking to modernise its butyl rubber production plant.

will only be accepted to the extent that it is necessary to alleviate macroeconomic problems.

In *Philip Morris*[247] the applicants argued that the role of the Commission should be much more limited than was implied by the principle of compensatory justification. In particular, the applicants objected to the Commission position that aid should only be approved if the market, unaided, would not produce the desired objective. Rather, it was argued, the Treaty should be interpreted as requiring approval of all aid that fell within the categories laid down in Article 92(3). This argument was rejected both by Advocate General Capotorti and the Court of Justice itself. The Commission therefore, has the support of the Court in applying the principle of compensatory justification to determine whether aid covered by Article 92(1) may be authorised.

17.4 Procedures

Procedural rules are contained in Article 93 of the EC Treaty and have been elaborated in the case law of the Court of Justice.

17.4.1 Review of Existing Aid

Article 93(1) provides that the Commission shall, in co-operation with Member States, keep under constant review all[248] systems of aid existing in those Member States. More particularly, the Commission is to propose to the Member States any appropriate measures required by the progressive development or the functioning of the common market.[249] The proposals are "simple recommendations" within the meaning of Article 189,[250] though they must be reasoned.[251]

This procedure "assumes constant co-operation between states and the Commission",[252] and is said by the Commission to allow account to be taken of changed conditions.[253]

If the Member State concerned does not follow a Commission proposal, the aid may be examined under Article 93(2).[254]

---

[247] Case 730/79 *Philip Morris Holland BV* v. *EC Commission* [1980] ECR 2671.

[248] There is no express requirement that the aid be incompatible with the common market.

[249] E.g. by letter of 19 May 1993 (OJ 1993 C163/5) the Commission proposed that the Portuguese Government abolish the taxation exemption enjoyed by the national airline, TAP.

[250] Darmon AG in Joined Cases 166 & 220/86 *Irish Cement Limited* v. *EC Commission* [1988] ECR 6473, 6492.

[251] Case 78/76 *Firma Steinike und Weinlig* v. *Germany* [1977] ECR 595, 609.

[252] Case 173/73 *Italy* v. *EC Commission: aids to the textile industry* [1974] ECR 709, 716 and Lenz AG in Case 40/85 *Belgium* v. *EC Commission: Boch* [1986] ECR 2321, 2332.

[253] Joint Reply by Mr Van Miert to WQs E–2197–2199/93 (OJ 1994 C306/9) by Nel van Dijk.

[254] Sects. 17.4.3 and 4 below.

17.4.2 Notification of New Aid

Article 93(3) provides that the Commission shall be informed, in sufficient time to enable it to submit its comments,[255] of any plans to grant or alter aid. The role of the Commission is principally to react to the initiatives thus notified by Member States.[256]

Scope of Notification Obligations

The notification obligations imposed on Member States are broad. Thus as well as planned aid schemes, "non-negligible",[257] "substantial",[258] or "material"[259] alterations of existing aid are to be notified.

Moreover, not only do measures which "unquestionably constitute aid" have to be notified. "Measures whose very character as aid may appear to be in doubt"[260] also have to be notified. According to the Commission, notification is obligatory "whenever there is sufficient likelihood", in the light of the case law of the Court of Justice and Commission practice, that aid is involved.[261]

Again, notification obligations apply at an early stage and not only in relation to "effective payment" of aid.[262] Aid is deemed to have been put into effect as soon as the legislative machinery enabling it to be granted has been introduced.[263] Thus legislative provision for aid and any draft laws granting aid[264] must be notified, even if the authorities say that the legislation will only become operative after Commission approval.[265]

Requests for Information

The Commission may issue an interim order requiring the Member State to supply information about new aid. If the Member State does not comply, the

[255] See, regarding "the distinction between the observations of the Commission provided for in Art. 93(3) and the opinions in Art. 93(1)", Capotorti AG in Joined Cases 142–143/80 *Amministrazione delle Finanze dello Stato* v. *Essevi SpA and Carlo Salengo* [1981] ECR 1413, 1443.

[256] Commission policy on sectoral aid schemes, COM(78)221, 5.

[257] Case 177/78 *Pigs and Bacon Commission* v. *McCarren & Co. Ltd* [1979] ECR 2161, 2204; and Joined Cases 91 & 127/83 *Heineken Brouwereijen BV* v. *Inspecteur der Vennootschapsbelasting* [1984] ECR 3435, 3453–4.

[258] Trabucchi AG in Case 51/74 *Hulst/Produktschap voor Siergewassen* [1975] ECR 79, 104–5.

[259] Lenz AG in Case C–44/93 *Namur – Les Assurances du Crédit SA* v. *Office National du Ducroire and Belgium* [1994] ECR I–3829, I–3850.

[260] Lenz AG in Case 40/85 *Belgium* v. *EC Commission: Boch* [1986] ECR 2321, 2332.

[261] *Competition Law in the European Communities,* iia: *Rules Applicable to State Aid* (EC Commission, Brussels, 1995), 31.

[262] Notice C37/93 (NN 63/93) (OJ 1994 C170/5) concerning Art. 29*ter* of the Walloon decree of 25 June 1992 on support for Walloon firms participating in Community industrial programmes which are the subject of specific international agreements.

[263] Dec. 93/627 (OJ 1993 L309/21) concerning aid granted by the Spanish authorities on the occasion of the sale by Cenemesa/Cadmesa/Conelec of certain selected assets to Asea-Brown Boveri.

[264] Case 169/82 *EC Commission* v. *Italy: agricultural aid for Sicily* [1984] ECR 1603, 1615.

[265] Dec. 93/508 (OJ 1993 L238/38) concerning aid granted by the Italian Government in favour of the ceramics industry of Lazio.

Commission may conclude its examination of the aid and issue a decision on the basis of the information received.[266]

Implementation of Notified Aid

If the Commission does not act within two months of a notification, the Member State concerned may implement the notified aid, provided the Member State has informed the Commission that it intends to do so.[267] The aid then becomes existing aid for the purposes of Article 93(1).[268] What is involved is not aid "authorisations *en bloc*" but the logical consequence of the fact that aid systems "crystallise" under Article 93(1).[269]

Suspension of Unnotified Aid

The Commission may require the suspension of aid which is unnotified[270] or which is implemented before the Commission has had the opportunity to comment.[271] If the Member State does not suspend the aid, the Commission may bring the violation of Article 93(3) or a decision requiring suspension before the Court of Justice.[272] However, the Commission may not require suspension simply because it has doubts whether the aid falls within a previous approval.[273]

Provisional Recovery of Unnotified Aid

Advocate General Jacobs in *Spain* v. *EC Commission: Merco*,[274] which concerned Spanish aid to an agricultural processor, expressed the view that the Commission was entitled to require immediate repayment of unnotified aid.[275] Consistently with this view, the Commission "intends in appropriate cases to adopt, by decision, interim measures designed to neutralise the aid and charge interest, so as to cancel out any advantage illegally conferred on

---

[266] Case C–301/87 *France* v. *EC Commission: Boussac* [1990] ECR I–307, I–356; and Case 142/87 *Belgium* v. *EC Commission: Tubemeuse* [1990] ECR I–959, I–1009.

[267] According to *Competition Law in the European Communities*, iia: *Rules Applicable to State Aid* (EC Commission, Brussels, 1995), 41, n. 3, this proviso means that it still has a reasonable period (2 weeks) within which to initiate the Art. 93(2) EC procedure.

[268] Case 120/73 *Gebr. Lorenz GmbH* v. *Germany* [1973] ECR 1471, 1481–2; and Case 84/82 *Germany* v. *EC Commission: aid to textiles and clothing* [1984] ECR 1451, 1488.

[269] Darmon AG in Joined Cases 166 & 220/86 *Irish Cement Limited* v. *EC Commission* [1988] ECR 6473, 6492–3.

[270] SG(91)D/4577 (*Competition Law in the European Communities*, iia: *Rules Applicable to State Aid* (EC Commission, Brussels, 1995), 63–4).

[271] Case 301/87 *France* v. *EC Commission: Boussac* [1990] ECR I–307, I–356; and Case 173/73 *Italy* v. *EC Commission: aids to the textile industry* [1974] ECR 709, 717.

[272] Case C–301/87 *France* v. *EC Commission: Boussac* [1990] ECR I–307, I–357.

[273] Case 47/91 *Italy* v. *EC Commission: Italgrani* [1994] ECR I–4635, I–4658.

[274] Case C–42/93 [1994] ECR I–4175.

[275] *Ibid.*, I–4186. Jacobs AG in Case C–301/87 *France* v. *EC Commission: Boussac* [1990] ECR I–307, I–341 considered that the Commission had power to order recovery for breach of Art. 93(3) EC alone. In support of this view he cited Tesauro AG in Case 142/87 *Belgium* v. *EC Commission: Tubemeuse* [1990] ECR I–959, I–997. The latter, however, only had in mind provisional orders.

the recipient, regardless of whatever final decision it takes on the compatibility of the aid with the common market".[276] In particular, provisional decisions requiring recovery of unnotified aid are envisaged in a 1995 Communication to the Member States.[277] Such action is considered necessary, because a decision requiring recovery after a finding of incompatibility with the common market, even with interest, may not eliminate the advantages to the recipient of having had the use of the aid. The advantages may include factors such as the positive tax implications, the increase in available cash funds, the "substantive advantages" deriving from the aid, the intermediate investments, and the possibilities of obtaining supplementary loans.[278]

17.4.3 Examination of Aid

If the Commission has any reason to think that aid may be incompatible with the common market,[279] has serious difficulties in determining whether aid is compatible with the common market,[280] is unable to satisfy itself after a preliminary examination that aid is compatible, or is not convinced that the aid is compatible,[281] it must examine the aid under Article 93(2).[282] The Commission must also examine the aid under this provision, where the terms of an earlier authorisation have not been respected or aid additional to that authorised has been granted.[283] In the former case the Commission may also refer the matter directly to the Court of Justice.[284]

The Commission must open the procedure under Article 93(2) by giving notice to the parties concerned to submit their comments. If the Commission finds that aid is not compatible with the common market having regard to Article 92 or that aid is being misused, it must require the Member State concerned to abolish or alter the aid within a specified period.[285]

When this procedure is opened, Member States are invited to comment by a letter addressed to them. Other interested parties are invited to comment

---

[276] *Twenty-Fourth Report on Competition Policy* (EC Commission, Brussels, 1995), 32.

[277] OJ 1995 C156/5.

[278] Joined Cases T–244 & 486/93 *TWD Textilwerke Deggendorf GmbH* v. *EC Commission* [1995] ECR II–2265, II–2299–300.

[279] Case C–198/91 *William Cook PLC* v. *EC Commission* [1993] ECR I–2487, I–2529.

[280] Case 84/82 *Germany* v. *EC Commission: aid to textiles and clothing* [1984] ECR 1451, 1488.

[281] Case T–49/93 *Société Internationale de Diffusion et de l'Edition* v. *EC Commission* [1995] ECR II–2501, II–2523.

[282] A corresponding procedure is contained in Art. 6(4) of Dec. 2496/96 (OJ 1996 L338/42) establishing Community rules for state aid to the steel industry and Art. 8 of Dec. 3632/93 (OJ 1993 L329/12) establishing Community rules for state aid to the coal industry

[283] Case C–294/90 *British Aerospace and Rover Group Holdings* v. *EC Commission* [1992] ECR I–493.

[284] *Ibid.*, I–522.

[285] Where the Commission considers an aid system to be contrary to Union law rules other than Art. 92 EC, it may bring proceedings under Art. 169 EC. See Case C–35/88 *EC Commission* v. *Greece: Kydep I* [1990] ECR I–3125, I–3154.

by a notice published in the C section of the Official Journal.[286] Interested parties include customers, employees, and trade associations.[287] According to the Court of Justice, such parties constitute "an indeterminate group", including "the persons, undertakings, or associations whose interests might be affected by the grant of the aid"[288]

Once the procedure is opened, aid may not be granted, until the Commission has reached a positive decision. Aid granted before the Commission has reached a final decision under Article 93(2) may be subject to a recovery procedure.[289] However, aid may be permitted where the investments to be aided are "compellingly urgent".[290]

If the Member State does not reply to the initiation of the procedure, the Commission may adopt a decision on the basis of the information it has.[291] If the Commission does not have sufficient information, it must order the Member State concerned to supply the missing information.[292]

17.4.4 Closure of Proceedings

Decisions to close the Article 93(2) procedure may be negative or positive.

Positive Decisions

A positive decision may be unconditional. Alternatively, it may be conditional, as to the type of aid, its amount, the recipients, its duration, and so on. The Commission may also approve an aid scheme subject to notification requirements in the case of "significant" individual grants of aid above certain thresholds. It must then assess the compatibility of any such grants with the common market and not merely with the conditions stipulated in the earlier decision.[293]

Negative Decisions

If the Commission adopts a negative decision, finding that the aid is incompatible with the common market, it may decide that the Member State concerned shall abolish or alter the aid. A decision prohibiting existing aid is constitutive, and so the aid need only be eliminated by the future date speci-

---

[286] VerLoren van Themaat AG in Case 323/82 *Intermills SA* v. *EC Commission* [1984] ECR 3809, 3837.

[287] *Ibid.*, 3837.   [288] *Ibid.*, 3827.

[289] Communication of 24 Nov. 1983 (OJ 1983 C318/3).

[290] Notice C4, 61 & 62/94, NN2, 3 & 467/95 (OJ 1995 C203/6) concerning aid the German Government intended to grant to Sächsische Olefinwerke GmbH, Leuna-Werke GmbH, and Buna GmbH.

[291] Letter to Member States, 30 Apr. 1987 (*Competition Law in the European Communities,* iia: *Rules Applicable to State Aids* (EC Commission, Brussels, 1995), 91).

[292] Joined Cases C–324 & 342/90 *Germany and Pleuger Worthington GmbH* v. *EC Commission* [1994] ECR I–1173, I–1206.

[293] Joined Cases T–447–449/93 *Associazione Italiana Tecnico Economica del Cemento* v. *EC Commission* [1995] ECR II–1971, II–2020.

fied in the decision.[294] A reasonable period for elimination must be allowed.[295] A decision prohibiting unnotified aid is declaratory, and the aid is *ab initio*[296] incompatible with the common market.

The Commission must indicate those aspects of the aid which it finds incompatible with the common market and which require elimination or modification.[297] The Commission fixes the date by which the aid has to be discontinued. Where the Member State is obliged to inform the Commission of action to comply with the decision by a given date, that date constitutes the deadline for discontinuation of the aid.[298]

If the Member State concerned does not comply with the decision by the date prescribed, the Commission or any other interested Member State may, in derogation from Articles 169 and 170, refer the matter to the Court of Justice direct.[299] States which are not "interested" may only proceed under Article 170.

17.4.5 Recovery

Unnotified aid or aid granted prior to closure of the Article 93(2) procedure which is found to be incompatible with the common market may have to be recovered by the Member State concerned,[300] so as to "restore the *status quo*".[301]

Although Article 93(2) refers only to the abolition or alteration of aid,[302] recovery may be considered necessary to give practical effect to either.[303] The withdrawal by recovery of illegal aid is a logical consequence of the finding that the aid is illegal. In principle, recovery cannot be held to be disproportionate with regard to the aims of the Treaty provisions concerning state aid.[304] Rather, it is considered necessary to deprive the aid recipient of any advantages on the market relative to its competitors.[305]

---

[294] Case 70/72 *EC Commission* v. *Germany: investment grants for mining* [1973] ECR 813, 831.

[295] Case 173/73 *Italy* v. *EC Commission: aids to the textile industry* [1974] ECR 709, 716–7.

[296] Dec. 94/725 (OJ 1994 L289/26) on measures adopted by the French Government concerning pigmeat.

[297] Case 70/72 *EC Commission* v. *Germany: investment grants for mining* [1973] ECR 813, 831.

[298] Case 213/85 *EC Commission* v. *Netherlands: preferential gas tariff for horticulturalists* [1988] ECR 281, 299–300.

[299] I.e. there is no need for a reasoned opinion.

[300] Cf. Case 70/72 *EC Commission* v. *Germany: investment grants for mining* [1973] ECR 813, 829; and Case 310/85 *Deufil GmbH & Co. KG* v. *EC Commission* [1987] ECR 901, 927.

[301] Notice C33/B/93 (NN12/94) (OJ 1994 C80/4) regarding aid which France had decided to grant to Groupe Bull. The deterrent effect of recovery has been doubted. See H-J. Priess, "Recovery of Illegal State Aid: An Overview of Recent Developments in the Case Law" (1996) 33 *CMLRev.* 69–91, 71.

[302] Darmon AG in Joined Cases C–324 & 342/90 *Germany and Pleuger Worthington GmbH* v. *EC Commission* [1994] ECR I–1173, I–1194.

[303] Case T–459/93 *Siemens SA* v. *EC Commission* [1995] ECR II–1675, II–1712.

[304] Case C–142/87 *Belgium* v. *EC Commission: Tubemeuse* [1990] ECR I–959, I–1020.

[305] See e.g. Case C–350/93 *EC Commission* v. *Italy: Lanerossi II* [1995] ECR I–699, I–716; and Case C–348/93 *EC Commission* v. *Italy: Alfa Romeo II* [1995] ECR I–673, I–696.

The aid is to be repaid with interest from the date it was granted.[306] Payment of interest is necessary to prevent the recipient from retaining financial advantages resulting from the grant of the illegal aid, in the form of an interest-free loan.[307]

Impossibility

Where recovery is required and the Member State concerned fails to respect the requirement, the Commission may bring proceedings before the Court of Justice. The only defence to such proceedings is absolute impossibility[308] or, presumably, imprecision in the recovery requirements.[309] The former defence is not constituted by bankruptcy rules,[310] intangibility of capital,[311] or the likelihood that recovery will entail liquidation of the recipient.[312] However, recovery is only required "within the limits of the possibilities afforded by the firm's liquidation".[313]

Legitimate Expectations

The legitimate expectations of aid recipients are recognised by Union law,[314] though undertakings are responsible for verifying that aid to be received is lawful.[315] Such expectations may be relied on in proceedings before a national court[316] in "exceptional circumstances".[317] The Court of Justice has not explained what such circumstances might be, but Advocate General Darmon has referred to doubts which some undertakings might have whether "atypical" forms of aid are subject to notification requirements.[318] A delay of twenty-six months by the Commission in reaching a final decision may also establish such an expectation.[319] Moreover, the recipient's good faith and the difficulties caused by the sharing of powers between the local

---

[306] Communication to the Member States supplementing Letter SG(91)D/4577 concerning the procedures for the notification of aid plans and procedures applicable when aid is provided in breach of the rules of Art. 93(3) EC (OJ 1995 C156/5).

[307] Case T–459/93 *Siemens SA* v. *EC Commission* [1995] ECR II–1675, II–1712. See also Case C–350/93 *EC Commission* v. *Italy: Lanerossi II* [1995] ECR I–699, I–716.

[308] Case 52/84 *EC Commission* v. *Belgium: Boch* [1986] ECR 89, 104.

[309] Case 70/72 *EC Commission* v. *Germany: investment grants for mining* [1973] ECR 813, 832.

[310] Case 142/87 *Belgium* v. *EC Commission: Tubemeuse* [1990] ECR I–959, 1019–20.

[311] Case 52/84 *EC Commission* v. *Belgium: Boch* [1986] ECR 89, 104; and Case 5/86 *EC Commission* v. *Belgium: aid to synthetic fibres* [1987] ECR 1773, 1779.

[312] Case 52/84 *EC Commission* v. *Belgium: Boch* [1986] ECR 89, 104.

[313] Dec. 86/366 (JO 1986 L223/30) concerning aid which the Belgian Government had granted to a ceramic sanitary ware and crockery manufacturer.

[314] Case 223/85 *Rijn-Schelde-Verolme (RSV) Maschinenfabrieken en Scheepswerven NV* v. *EC Commission* [1987] ECR 4617, 4659.

[315] Slynn AG (*ibid.*, 4652); and Case C–5/89 *EC Commission* v. *Germany: Alutechnik* [1990] ECR I–3437, I–3457.

[316] Case T–459/93 *Siemens SA* v. *EC Commission* [1995] ECR II–1675, II–1675.

[317] Case C–5/89 *EC Commission* v. *Germany: Alutechnik* [1990] ECR I–3437, I–3456–7.

[318] *Ibid.*, I–3449.

[319] Case 223/85 *Rijn-Schelde-Verolme (RSV) Maschinenfabrieken en Scheepswerven NV* v. *EC Commission* [1987] ECR 4617, 4659.

and central authorities may dissuade the Commission from requiring recovery of the aid.[320]

17.5 Aid and Third States

Article 112(1) of the EC Treaty provides for harmonisation of aid to exports to third states, to the extent necessary to ensure that competition between "undertakings of the Community" is not distorted. The position of this provision within Title IX, which is headed "Common Commercial Policy", of Part Three of the Treaty may seem significant. The implication is that the Treaty seeks to separate commercial policy issues from aid issues under Article 92. In practice, however, it may be problematic to seek to insulate pursuit of the common commercial policy from issues arising under Article 92.[321]

17.5.1 Aid to Extra-Union Activities

The Commission has tended to regard aid to the extra-Union activities of recipients as unobjectionable.[322] However, in *Belgium* v. *EC Commission: Tubemeuse*,[323] which concerned Belgian aid to a producer of steel pipes, the Court of Justice ruled that the fact that aid for exports to third states was dealt with in Article 112 of the Treaty did not preclude the application of Article 92 to such aid. The Court considered that, given the interdependence of markets, the possibility of trade between Member States being affected by the aid could not be ruled out *a priori*.[324]

Such thinking increasingly affects Commission practice. For example, according to the Commission, even if a recipient of aid has previously exported almost all its output outside the Union, the existence of world overcapacity may mean that the aid is likely to affect trade between Member States.[325] More generally, the Commission has come to the view that the aided operations of a Union undertaking in a third state may be relevant to the application of Article 92(1). According to the Commission, they may be

---

[320] Notice C39/95 (ex NN47/95) (OJ 1995 C344/8) concerning aid granted by Italy to Acciaierie di Bolzano.

[321] Cf. Darmon AG in Joined Cases 72 & 73/91 *Sloman Neptun Schiffahrts AG* v. *Seebetriebsrat Bodo Ziesemer der Sloman Neptun Schiffahrts AG* [1993] ECR I–887, I–913; and Case C–142/87 *Belgium* v. *EC Commission: Tubemeuse* [1990] ECR I–959, I–1000.

[322] See e.g. regarding acceptance of aid to the export of witloof chicory to Japan and the US, N323/93 (OJ 1994 C42/16). See also Van Gerven AG in Case C–294/90 *British Aerospace plc and Rover Group Holdings plc* v. *EC Commission* [1992] ECR I–493, I–516.

[323] Case 142/87 [1990] ECR I–959.

[324] *Ibid.*, I–1013–14. See also Darmon AG in Case 310/85 *Deufil GmbH & Co. KG* v. *EC Commission* [1987] ECR 901, 916.

[325] Dec. 87/418 (OJ 1987 L227/45) concerning aid to a Belgian steel pipe and tube manufacturer.

relevant, because these operations can strengthen the position of the recipient in intra-Union markets and trade.[326]

17.5.2 Competition from Third States

The impact of non-Union producers may be found to increase the likelihood of trade between Member States being affected by aid.[327] The fact that the production of an aided undertaking may serve mainly to replace goods imported from a third state does not preclude the possibility of trade between Member States being affected.[328]

On the other hand, aid which may result in replacement of imports predominantly from third states with domestic production is less likely than other aid to be treated as distorting competition to an extent contrary to the common interest for the purposes of Article 92(3)(c).[329] More particularly, the Court of Justice does not exclude the possibility that aid specifically designed to strengthen the competitiveness of Union undertakings in the face of imports from third states with low labour costs may be authorised.[330]

17.5.3 Compensatory Aid

The exposure of Union undertakings to competition from third states may be increased by international trade liberalisation associated with the General Agreement on Tariffs and Trade and the World Trade Organisation. The Commission is generally opposed to "compensatory aid" for Union industries exposed to such increased competition. In fact, the Commission maintains that the reduction of aid levels will lead to increased trade within the Union and with third states and thus to a general increase in prosperity for all Member States.[331] Thus, for example, the Commission refuses to accept that every time changes are made to the common customs tariff, aid to adversely affected industries must be sympathetically considered.[332] However, the Commission may face pressures from other Union institutions to modify its position.[333]

---

[326] Dec. 92/35 (OJ 1992 L14/35) requiring France to suspend the implementation of the aid in favour of the Pari Mutuel Urbain, introduced in breach of Art. 93(3) EC.

[327] Dec. 91/305 (OJ 1991 L156/39) concerning investment aid which the Belgian Government planned to grant to Mactac SA, Soignies.

[328] Dec. 81/626 (OJ 1981 L229/12) on a scheme of aid by the Belgian Government in respect of certain investments carried out by a Belgian undertaking to modernise its butyl rubber production plant.

[329] Notice C27/92 (N295/92) (OJ 1993 C46/5) on aid to SCA Aylesford, a manufacturer of newsprint.

[330] Case 259/85 *France* v. *EC Commission: aid to textiles and clothing* [1987] ECR 4393, 4419.

[331] Fourth survey on state aids in the European Community in the manufacturing and certain other sectors, COM(95)365, 46–7.

[332] Dec. 82/670 (OJ 1982 L280/30) on aid granted by the Belgian Government to a paper-manufacturing undertaking.

[333] See e.g. the Opinion of the Economic and Social Committee of 26 May 1992 (OJ 1992 C223/36) on the communication on new challenges for maritime industries, para. 2.5.

Such pressures may not be without their impact. For example, the Commission examines aid requests in the light of problems which the industrial situation and the abolition of intra-Union border controls under Article 115 of the Treaty pose for certain products and sectors.[334] Recognition of such problems may lead to the authorisation of restructuring[335] or even operating aid.[336]

17.5.4 Regulatory Protection

Where problems allegedly arise for Union undertakings from the grant of aid by third states, regulatory protection may sometimes be regarded as a more appropriate response than the grant of aid by a Member State.[337]

In particular, "voluntary export restraints" (VERs) may be seen as means of tackling the consequences of the grant of aid by third states.[338] Moreover, the common commercial policy may allow for certain "autonomous" measures to be taken by the Union against the grant of aid by third states.[339] In the past, Article 115 authorisations might also permit restriction of intra-Union trade in aided products from third states.[340]

Such measures may sometimes be presented as being compatible with the restructuring of Union industry and, more particularly, with the use of restructuring aid.[341] In other words, regulatory protection and the controlled use of aid may be seen as mutually supportive.

17.5.5 Retaliatory Aid

At least where measures of regulatory protection are unavailable or ineffective, the Commission may authorise aid to Union undertakings competing with third-state undertakings in receipt of aid from their own authorities. The Commission seems to be particularly willing to do so in the case of aid to the aerospace and shipbuilding industries.

In relation to the former industry, aid, including production aid and

---

[334] Implementation of the reform of the Structural Funds 1989, COM(90)516, 11.

[335] See e.g. the *Twelfth Report on Competition Policy* (EC Commission, Brussels, 1983), 128-9. See, more particularly, Dec. 82/670 (OJ 1982 L280/30) on aid granted by the Belgian Government to a paper-manufacturing undertaking.

[336] See e.g. Dec. of 19 Dec. 1960 (JO 1960 1972) concerning the French aid system for certain types of paper pulp. See also Reg. 3687/91 (OJ 1991 L354/1) on the common organisation of the market in fishery products, Art. 20 and recital 39 in the preamble.

[337] Dec. 88/282 (OJ 1988 L119/38) on aid from the French Government to the wood-processing sector (Isoroy and Pinault).

[338] See, regarding Austrian beef and veal, the Reply by Mr MacSharry to WQ 581/91 (OJ 1992 C2/6) by Mr Bocklet. Cf., regarding hazel nuts, the Reply by Mr Steichen to WQ E–2255/93 (OJ 1994 C240/15) by Mr Giuseppe Mottola *et al.*

[339] Sect. 21.12.5 below.

[340] See e.g. Reg. 1087/84 (OJ 1984 L112/31) introducing protective measures in respect of certain electronic piezo-electric quartz watches with digital display.

[341] *Twelfth Report on Competition Policy* (EC Commission, Brussels, 1983), 126.

export aid in trade between Member States, may be authorised under Article 92(3)(b), as promoting the execution of projects of common European interest.[342] In relation to shipbuilding, the Commission considers that aid may be needed because of the reluctance of major shipbuilding countries outside the Union to "undertake wholeheartedly the structural adjustments necessary to restore normal market conditions to this industry".[343]

17.5.6 Strategic Aid

Aid to enable Union undertakings to capture or recapture markets from third-state competitors may be authorised.[344] Authorisation of such aid is all the more likely where technological development[345] or exploitation of natural resources[346] is involved.

However, a strategic interest in authorising aid to Union industry is not always recognised. For example, *Glaverbel*[347] concerned Belgian aid to a flat-glass producer in Namur. Here it was argued that the aid at issue served to strengthen the position of the Union on export markets and to ensure its independence with regard to imports. In other words, it served an important project of common European interest within the meaning of Article 92(3)(b) and could thus be authorised thereunder. Such thinking was said to have influenced the Union approach to the grant of aid to the coal industry. Advocate General Lenz responded by observing that, according to Article 3(b) of the Treaty, the principles of the Union included the establishment of a common commercial policy towards third states. Moreover, according to Article 110, the same policy served to contribute to the harmonious development of world trade. Hence, the attempt to achieve self-sufficiency and to conquer world markets could not be regarded as a project covered by Article 92(3)(b).[348] Indeed, the inadequate information possessed by public authorities leads some economists to doubt whether "strategic trade policies" can ever be economically justified.[349]

---

[342] *Memorandum on Industrial and Technological Policy Measures to be Adopted in the Aircraft Industry* (EC Commission, Brussels, 1973), 89–93.

[343] *Seventeenth Report on Competition Policy* (EC Commission, Brussels, 1988), 152.

[344] See, e.g., Dec. 94/996 (OJ 1994 L379/13) concerning the transfer by the Netherlands of a pilot school to the Royal Dutch Airline.

[345] *Sixteenth Report on Competition Policy* (EC Commission, Brussels, 1987), 158.

[346] See e.g. Notice C27/92 (N295/92) (OJ 1993 C46/5) on aid to SCA Aylsford, a manufacturer of newsprint.

[347] Joined Cases 62 & 72/87 *Exécutif Régional Wallon and Glaverbel* v. *EC Commission* [1988] ECR 1573.

[348] *Ibid.*, 1588.

[349] A. Winters, "Goals and Own Goals in European Trade Policy" (1992) 15 *The World Economy* 557–74, 570.

17.6 Agreements with Third States

Agreements with third states may be reflected in Union legislation governing aid.[350] Thus, for example, the Preamble to Decision 3855/91,[351] which dealt with aid to the steel industry,[352] referred to the "consensus" reached with the United States concerning trade in certain steel products.[353] Application of the Decision is to be consistent with this consensus. Its application is also to be consistent with current or future international obligations of the Union concerning aid to this sector.[354] Similarly, legislation concerning aid to shipbuilding has been enacted "without prejudice to any amendments that may be necessary in order to comply with international obligations entered into by the Community".[355]

Various agreements may be relevant to Commission control of aid granted by Member States.

17.6.1 Multilateral Agreements

In pursuit of the common commercial policy the Union may undertake obligations regarding aid in trade with third states.

World Trade Organisation

Obligations such as those in the Agreement on Subsidies and Countervailing Measures,[356] annexed to the Agreement establishing the World Trade Organisation, may have implications for aid control within the Union.[357]

Such control is seen by the Commission as a means of demonstrating Union commitment to free trade.[358] At the same time, there may be concern that third states may "benefit gratuitously from the EU's internal control

---

[350] Enforcement of bilateral agreements to control aid may be problematic. See the Resolution of the European Parliament of 14 July 1995 (OJ 1995 C249/230) on the bilateral negotiations between the EU and the US on civil aircraft, paras. 4–7.

[351] Establishing Community rules for aid to the steel industry (OJ 1991 L362/57).

[352] The 11th recital in the preamble to Dec. 2496/96 (OJ 1996 L338/42) establishing Community rules for state aid to the steel industry now refers, more generally, to "international commitments of the Community concerning state aid to the steel industry".

[353] OJ 1989 L368/185. Cf. the Agreement between the EC and the US Government concerning the application of the GATT Agreement on Trade in Civil Aircraft (OJ 1992 L301/32).

[354] In 1991 the Commission examined R & D aid for a Luxembourg steel producer for compatibility with Dec. 322/89 (OJ 1989 L38/8) establishing Community rules for aid to the steel industry and with the "consensus". See the *Twenty-First Report on Competition Policy* (EC Commission, Brussels, 1992), 144.

[355] See e.g. 7th recital in the preamble to Dir. 93/115 (OJ 1993 L326/62) amending Dir. 90/684.

[356] OJ 1994 L336/156.

[357] Though Reg. 3284/94 (OJ 1994 L349/22) on protection against subsidised imports from countries not members of the EC, which was introduced to implement the results of the Uruguay Round, may be less permissive of aid than practice under Arts. 92–93 EC.

[358] *Second Survey on State Aids in the European Community in the Manufacturing and Certain Other Sectors* (EC Commission, Brussels, 1990), 51.

mechanism" for state aid.[359] Hence, limitations to disclosure of information regarding authorised aid may be considered justified, because the Union should not "give possible ammunition to its trading partners in international trading disputes".[360] However, the preferred solution of the Commission is to seek reciprocity in aid control. If reciprocity is achieved, it is hoped that aid will become less a cause of dispute than at present and that "all the main actors on the world trade scene" will benefit.[361]

In practice, achievement of reciprocity may be problematic. On the one hand, pursuant to sectoral policy considerations, the Commission is willing to permit aid to increase the international competitiveness of Union industry. As a result, attempts within the context of the commercial policy to negotiate elimination of international distortions of competition in this industry may be impeded.[362] On the other hand, unilateral elimination of aid within the Union would leave the latter with little to offer in a multilateral framework in exchange for agreed aid reductions by others. Hence, insofar as international agreements can be reached, the practical effect may be to set limits to aid control within the Union. For example, conclusion of the Agreement on Subsidies and Countervailing Measures[363] was taken by the Commission to necessitate some relaxation in control of research and development aid within the Union.[364]

Organisation for Economic Cooperation and Development

An OECD agreement requires, in principle, the elimination of operating aid to shipbuilding from 1 January 1996.[365] In implementation of the agreement, Regulation 3094/95 has been adopted.[366] Even so, the European Parliament considers that such aid should still be authorised by the Commission, if the agreement is not respected by other parties.[367]

Underlying problems of negotiating and enforcing international agreements may be problems of reconciling sectoral policy with commercial

[359] C.-D. Ehlermann, "State Aid Control in the European Union: Success or Failure?" (1995) 18 *Fordham Int. Law J* 1212–29, 1219–20.

[360] C.-D. Ehlermann, "State Aids under European Community Law" (1994) 18 *Fordham Int. Law J* 410–36, 431.

[361] *Second Survey on State Aids in the European Community in the Manufacturing and Certain Other Sectors* (EC Commission, Brussels, 1990), 51.

[362] The Commission proposed that the criteria for setting the aid ceiling under Dir. 90/684 should be expressly stated to be without prejudice to future international agreements requiring a lower level (OJ 1990 C223/4). However, this part of the proposal was not apparently acceptable to the Council.

[363] OJ 1994 L336/156.

[364] H. Morch, "Summary of the Most Important Recent Developments" (1995) 6 *Competition Policy Newsletter* 41–7, 41.

[365] Agreement respecting normal competitive conditions in the commercial shipbuilding and repair industry (OJ 1994 C375/3).

[366] On aid to shipbuilding (OJ 1995 L332/1).

[367] Resolution of 7 Apr. 1995 (OJ 1995 C109/302) on prospects for the future development of the shipbuilding industry, para. 11. See also the explanatory memorandum to the proposal for a reg. amending Reg. 3094/95, COM(97)469.

policy. For example, the Commission considers that "duty exemptions which are common in all Member States and therefore . . . constitute a part of the economic environment in the Community" are an acceptable form of shipbuilding aid.[368] Moreover, efforts to compensate for international distortions of competition through aid for Union shipbuilders are well established.[369] Even more fundamental problems arise in reconciling a defensive response to international overcapacity, exaggerated by distortions of competition by third states, with achievement of "a level playing field so far as intra-Community competition in shipbuilding is concerned".[370]

The general tendency seems to be to seek "management" of international trade. Thus although Article XVI of GATT prohibits export aid, OECD agreements harmonising export credits[371] have been concluded. Such harmonisation may be regarded as "an effective instrument of international discipline, assisting in lowering subsidies and reducing counterproductive competition" in this field.[372] Its effect has been to allow the grant of aid in the form of credit at rates comparable to those enjoyed by competing industries in third states.[373]

17.6.2 Free Trade Agreements

Free trade agreements may contain rules regarding aid which affects trade between the parties.

Anti-subsidy Measures

Article 23(1)(iii) of the Free Trade Agreement with Austria[374] provided that any public aid which distorted or threatened to distort competition by favouring certain undertakings or the production of certain goods was, in so far as trade between the Parties might be affected, incompatible with the Agreement. According to a declaration attached to the Agreement,[375] this provision was to be applied on the basis of the same principles as those in Article 92 of the EC Treaty. This application was to take place in "the autonomous implementation of Article 23(1) of the Agreement which [was] incumbent on the Contracting Parties".[376]

---

[368] Notice C10, 11 & 12/91 (ex NN54, 56 & 58/90) (OJ 1991 C123/16) regarding aid which Greece had granted to shipbuilding in the period 1987–90.

[369] See e.g. the *Medium-Term Economic Policy Programme* (EC Commission, Brussels, 1969), App. I, 21.

[370] Explanatory memorandum to the proposal for a reg. on aid to shipbuilding, COM(95)410, 1.

[371] Dec. 93/112 (OJ 1993 L44/1) extending the Dec. of 4 Apr. 1978 on the application of certain guidelines in the field of officially supported export credits.

[372] *Ibid.*, 8th recital in the preamble.

[373] *First Report on Competition Policy* (EC Commission, Brussels, 1972), 138.

[374] JO 1972 L300/2.   [375] Sect. 13.10.1.

[376] At the same time, the *Second Report on Competition Policy* (EC Commission, Brussels, 1973), 17, stressed the need for "joint discipline" of competition in trade with third states.

Before Austrian accession to the Union this provision was invoked against Austrian aid to General Motors. The grounds were that the aid breached Union "principles" regarding regional aid[377] and regarding aid to the car industry sector.[378] In the absence of Austrian acceptance of the Union position, safeguard measures were adopted, which took the form of reintroduction of the Common Customs Tariff in respect of the products concerned.[379] Following Austrian accession to the Union, the Commission authorised Austrian aid to General Motors for research and development, environmental protection, and training.[380]

Anti-dumping Measures

Under free trade agreements anti-dumping procedures may be employed against recipients of aid granted by the third state concerned.[381] In 1977, for example, the Commission expressed concern about Swedish aid to the chipboard industry.[382] In the following year the Commission secured price undertakings from Swedish exporters of chipboard in the course of an anti-dumping procedure.[383]

Such practice means that the effects of aid may be assessed in isolation from consideration of the broader economic policy context in which the aid is granted. Consequently, not only may the grant of aid in third states lead to the imposition of trade restrictions which cannot result within the Union from the grant of aid by a Member State. These restrictions may also be imposed on an undertaking in receipt of aid which might be permissible within the Union. Certainly, aid may be authorised within the Union specifically because it enables a producer to sell at a price which is below his real costs.[384]

17.6.3 Association Agreements

Association agreements may require the third states concerned to adapt their aids to "the rules laid down in the relevant Community frameworks and guidelines".[385]

---

[377] Communication on the method for the application of Art. 92(3)(a) and (c) to regional aid (OJ 1988 C212/2).

[378] Framework on state aid to the motor vehicle industry (OJ 1997 C279/1).

[379] Reg. 3697/93 (OJ 1993 L343/1) withdrawing tariff concessions in accordance with Arts. 23(2) and 27(3)(a) of the Free Trade Agreement with Austria (General Motors Austria).

[380] H. Morch, "Summary of the Most Important Recent Developments" (1995) 6 *Competition Policy Newsletter* 41–7, 45.

[381] See, e.g., Art. 25 of the Swedish Free Trade Agreement (JO 1972 L300/96).

[382] *Sverige – EG 1977* (Utrikes-och handelsdepartementen, Stockholm, 1978), 20.

[383] Notice of termination of the anti-dumping/anti-subsidies procedure concerning imports of reconstituted wood (wood chipboard) from Spain and Sweden (OJ 1978 C75/3).

[384] See, e.g., Dec. 88/437 (OJ 1988 L211/24) concerning aids planned by the French Government in favour of a shipbuilding contract for which there was competition between yards in several Member States.

[385] See, e.g., Art. 39(2)(c) and (d) of Dec. 1/95 of the EC–Turkey Association Council (OJ 1996 L35/1) on implementing the final phase of the customs union.

For example, Article 63(1)(iii) of the Europe Agreement with Poland[386] provides that any public aid which distorts or threatens to distort competition by favouring certain undertakings or the production of certain goods is, in so far as trade between the Parties may be affected, incompatible with the proper functioning of the Agreement. Article 63(2) of the Agreement requires that any practices contrary to this Article shall be assessed on the basis of criteria arising from the application of the rules of Article 92 of the EC Treaty.

Regional Aid

The Polish Agreement envisages that practice regarding aid to regions covered by Article 92(3)(a) of the EC Treaty will be extended by analogy to Poland. According to Article 63(4)(a) of the Agreement, for the purposes of applying Article 63(1)(iii), the Parties recognise that during the first five years after the entry into force of the Agreement, any public aid granted by Poland shall be assessed taking into account the fact that Poland shall be regarded as an area identical to those areas of the Union described in Article 92(3)(a) of the EC Treaty. The Association Council shall, taking into account the economic situation of Poland, decide whether to extend that period for further periods of five years.

Procedures

The Polish Agreement implicitly seeks to rely on Commission control of aid within the Union and control by the Polish authorities of aid within Poland. Thus Article 63(4)(b) of the Agreement requires each Party to ensure transparency in the area of state aid. Each Party is to do so, *inter alia*, by reporting annually to the other Party on the total amount and the distribution of the aid given and by providing, upon request, information on aid schemes. Upon request by one Party, the other Party shall also provide information on individual cases of aid. More generally, Article 63(7) provides that the Parties shall exchange information taking into account the limitations imposed by the requirements of professional and business secrecy.[387] Presumably, such reports and information are designed to enable each Party to determine whether the other Party is satisfactorily controlling aid within its jurisdiction.

Safeguard Measures

Article 63(6) of the Polish Agreement provides for situations where a Party considers that a particular practice is incompatible with the terms of Article 63(1)(iii) and is not adequately dealt with under the implementing rules

---

[386] OJ 1993 L348/2.

[387] According to a Joint Declaration annexed to the Agreement, the Parties shall not make improper use of provisions on professional secrecy to prevent the disclosure of information in the field of competition.

referred to in Article 63(3).[388] In such situations appropriate measures may be taken by that Party after consultation within the Association Council established by this Agreement[389] or after thirty working days following referral for such consultation.

17.6.4 EEA Agreement

Article 61(1) of the EEA Agreement[390] is substantially identical to Article 92(1) of the EC Treaty. According to the former provision, any aid granted by Member States or EFTA States or through state resources in any form whatsoever which distorts or threatens to distort competition by favouring certain undertakings or the production of certain goods shall, in so far as it affects trade between Contracting Parties, be incompatible with the functioning of the Agreement. It thus extends the prohibition of state aid to three EFTA states (Iceland, Liechtenstein, and Norway) as well as to aid granted by Member States[391] affecting trade with or between these EFTA states.

At the same time, Article 61(2) of the Agreement follows Article 92(2) of the EC Treaty, and Article 61(3) of the Agreement, follows Article 92(3) of the EC Treaty.[392] More particularly, according to a Joint Declaration annexed to the Agreement, the Contracting Parties declare that in deciding whether to authorise aid under Article 61(3)(b) of the Agreement, the Commission shall take the interest of the EFTA states into account and the EFTA Surveillance Authority shall take the interest of the Union into account.[393] Finally, Article 61(3)(d) allows for other categories of aid to be authorised by the EEA Joint Committee.

In addition, various Union enactments relating to state aid and other "instruments" adopted by the Commission, such as those concerning aid to textiles, environmental aid, and aid to research and development, are included in Annex XV[394] to the Agreement. The latter kind of instruments has an uncertain status within the Union,[395] and they are listed in the Annex as "acts which the EC Commission and the ESA shall take due account of".

---

[388] This provision requires the Association Council to adopt, within 3 years of the entry into force of the Agreement, the necessary rules for the implementation of Art. 63(1). See the implementing rules for the application of the competition provisions applicable to undertakings provided for in Art. 63(1)(i) and (ii) and 63(2) of the Agreement (OJ 1996 L208/25).

[389] Art. 103 of the Polish Agreement (OJ 1993 L348/2).

[390] OJ 1994 L1/3.

[391] The Commission assesses aid granted by Member States for compatibility with the EEA Agreement as well as the EC Treaty. See e.g. Communication C15/94 (N122/94, NN22/94, & E3/93) (OJ 1994 C93/12) concerning the existing tax exemption and planned recapitalisation of TAP.

[392] In its version before amendment by the TEU.

[393] Joint Declaration on Art. 61(3)(b) EEA.

[394] On state aid.   [395] Sect. 2.3.1 above.

Regional Aid

In a Joint Declaration annexed to the EEA Agreement[396] the Contracting Parties take note that even if eligibility of a region for aid has to be denied in the context of Article 61(3)(a) of the Agreement and according to the first stage of analysis under subparagraph (c), examination according to other criterion, such as very low population density, is possible.

This Declaration relates to a 1988 Commission Communication concerning regional aid within the Union.[397] The EFTA Surveillance Authority draws the conclusion from the Declaration that "a very low population density" may qualify a region for aid under Article 61(3)(a).[398] It cannot be assumed that this conclusion will be acceptable to the Commission.[399] For example, rural areas in Scotland may have much in common with those in Norway (though not necessarily in terms of *per capita* gross domestic product). However, they have traditionally been treated as being covered by Article 92(3)(c) rather than Article 92(3)(a) of the EC Treaty.[400] In the case of rural Norwegian areas having a higher *per capita* gross domestic product[401] than rural areas of Scotland, it is doubtful whether the Commission would agree that they should be treated as eligible for aid under Article 61(3)(a) of the Agreement.[402]

On the other hand, the EFTA Surveillance Authority has also relied on the Joint Declaration to adapt previous Commission practice to the perceived requirements of Article 61(3)(c) of the Agreement. According to the Authority,[403] a region where the population density is less than 12.5 per square kilometre may, on this ground alone, be found eligible for aid under Article 61(3)(c) of the Agreement. The Commission has similarly adapted its

---

[396] Joint Declaration on Art. 61(3)(c) EEA.

[397] Communication on the method for the application of Art. 92(3)(a) and (c) to regional aid (OJ 1988 C212/2).

[398] Para. 28.1.3 of Dec. 4/94/COL (OJ 1994 C231/1) on the adoption and issuing of the procedural and substantive rules in the field of state aid (Guidelines on the application and interpretation of Arts. 61 and 62 EEA and Art. 1 of Prot. 3 to the Surveillance and Court Agreement).

[399] Cf. Changes to the method for the application of Art. 92(3)(a) EC to regional aid (OJ 1994 C364/8), para. 1.1.

[400] Only as their *per capita* GDP has fallen towards the 75% level, has the possibility arisen that they may be treated as Art. 92(3)(a) regions. Reg. 2081/93 (OJ 1993 L193/5) amends Annex I to Reg. 2052/88, so as to classify them as Objective 1 regions for the purposes of allocations from the Structural Funds. The possible implication is that they will now also be treated as regions covered by Art. 92(3)(a) EC. However, Hainaut in Belgium, which has also become an Objective 1 region, is still treated as being covered by Art. 92(3)(c) EC. See the *Twenty-Fourth Report on Competition Policy*, COM(95)142, 524.

[401] Cf. the Swedish figures published in *Norbotten inför EG-förhandlingen* (Länstyrelsen Norbottens län, Luleå, 1992).

[402] Finnmark and the 4 most northerly municipalities of Troms have been found by the ESA to be covered by Art. 61(3)(a) of the EEA Agreement. See the ESA decision not to raise objections (OJ 1995 C14/4).

[403] Dec. 88/94/COL (OJ 1994 L240/33) on the second amendment of the procedural and substantive rules in the field of state aid, para. 28.2.3.1.

practice under Article 92(3)(c) of the EC Treaty.[404] These adaptations are justified by both the EFTA Surveillance Authority and the Commission on the ground that the other indicators used do not properly reflect regional problems specific to certain Contracting Parties, particularly the Nordic countries. These problems result from the remote northern location of some areas, harsh weather, very long distances inside the borders of the country concerned, and the very low population density in some parts.

More particularly, it is recognised by both surveillance authorities that such problems may induce firms to relocate to less remote areas or dissuade them from locating in remote areas. Hence, partial compensation for the additional transport costs of undertakings in such areas, provided their population density is less than 12.5 per square kilometre, may be authorised.[405] To this extent, objections to operating aid in regions outside the scope of Article 92(3)(a) of the EC treaty or Article 61(3)(a) of the EEA Agreement have been lifted.

Procedures

Article 62(2) of the EEA Agreement provides in relation to state aid for co-operation between the Commission and the EFTA Surveillance Authority according to Protocol 27 to the Agreement.[406] Such co-operation is apparently leading to some harmonisation of aid control policies as between the parties, though it seems from the above discussion that such harmonisation is not without problems.

---

[404] Changes to the method for the application of Art. 92(3)(c) EC to regional aid (OJ 1994 C364/8), paras. 2.5–6.

[405] *Ibid.*

[406] See also the Joint Declaration on Para. (c) of Prot. 27, on co-operation in the field of state aid.

18

Taxation

Articles 95 to 99 of the EC Treaty recognise that taxation of goods may have anti-competitive effects. In particular, discriminatory taxation is prohibited by Article 95 of the Treaty. This provision is interpreted in the light of Union objectives and activities as defined in Articles 2 and 3 of the Treaty,[1] notably the unification of national markets into a single market having the characteristics of a domestic market.[2]

Ultimately, however, questions may arise about whether a tax rate or even a tax system distorts competition.[3] It is assumed in the Treaty that legislative action may be necessary to address such questions.[4] Hence, Article 99 of the Treaty makes specific provision for harmonisation in this area.[5]

18.1 Formal Discrimination

Article 95(1) of the EC Treaty provides that no Member State shall impose, directly or indirectly, on the products of other Member States any internal taxation of any kind in excess of that imposed directly or indirectly on similar domestic products. For the purposes of this paragraph, products are similar when they come within the same customs, fiscal, or statistical classification[6] or when they have similar characteristics and meet the same needs from the point of view of the consumer.[7] Only taxation which formally discriminates against imports in favour of domestic products which are similar in this sense is prohibited by this paragraph. The mere possibility of such discrimination may be sufficient to bring the prohibition into play,[8] as

---

[1] Chap. 1.

[2] Case 15/81 *Gaston Schul Douane Expediteur BV* v. *Inspecteur der Invoerrechten en Accijnzen, Rosendaal* [1982] ECR 1409, 1431–2.

[3] See e.g. a package to tackle harmful tax competition in the EU, COM(97)564.

[4] Cf. the judgment of the *Bundesfinanzhof* in *Bobie Getränkevertrieb* [1988] 1 CMLR 482.

[5] The relationship with Art. 12 EC may be complicated. See e.g. Case 105/76 *Interzuccheri SpA* v. *Ditta Rezzano e Cavassa* [1977] ECR 1029. See also sect. 8.2 above.

[6] Case 27/67 *Firma Fink-Frucht GmbH* v. *Hauptzollamt München-Landsbergerstrasse* [1968] ECR 223, 232.

[7] Case 168/78 *EC Commission* v. *France: taxation of spirits* [1980] ECR 347, 359–60.

[8] Case 127/75 *Bobie Getränkevertrieb* v. *Hauptzollamt Aachen-Nord* [1976] ECR 1079.

may discrimination in the conditions of application of a tax.[9] However, taxation which differentiates between products by criteria other than their origin and applies equally to domestic and imported products is unaffected by this paragraph.

18.2 Material Discrimination

Article 95(2) of the EC Treaty provides that no Member State shall impose on the products of other Member States any internal taxation of such a nature as to afford indirect protection to other products. This paragraph applies where there are no domestic products similar to imported products for the purposes of Article 95(1).[10]

Article 95(2) covers all forms of indirect tax protection in the case of products which, without being similar, are nevertheless in competition, even partial, indirect, or potential,[11] with certain products of the importing Member State. Thus it prohibits taxation which does not formally discriminate between domestic products and imports but has the effect of putting the latter at a competitive disadvantage. For example, if a Member State has a system of taxation imposed on the sale of cars which is graduated so that the highest rate is paid by the largest cars and no such cars are produced in that Member State, there may be a violation of this paragraph.[12] Measures having protective effect are envisaged, and it may be deduced that material discrimination is prohibited by this paragraph.[13]

According to the Court of Justice, it is the competitive effect of a tax difference which determines whether the difference amounts to such discrimination.[14] Therefore, to be prohibited, taxation must have the effect of reducing potential consumption of imports to the advantage of domestic products.[15] The mere fact that imports may be restricted by tax measures does not mean that the measures are prohibited.

The reasoning is that Article 95 aims, in line with the Treaty objectives outlined in Articles 2 and 3,[16] is to ensure the free movement of goods

---

[9] Case 55/79 *EC Commission* v. *Ireland: periods of grace* [1980] ECR 481.

[10] Case 170/78 *EC Commission* v. *UK: taxation of wine* [1980] ECR 417, 432.

[11] Case 27/67 *Firma Fink-Frucht GmbH* v. *Hauptzollamt München-Landsbergerstrasse* [1968] ECR 223, 232–3; and Case 170/78 *EC Commission* v. *United Kingdom: taxation of wine* [1980] ECR 417, 432.

[12] Case 112/84 *Michel Humblot* v. *Directeur des Services Fiscaux* [1985] ECR 1367, 1379. See also Case 433/85 *Feldain* v. *Directeur des Services Fiscaux* [1987] ECR 3536.

[13] Cf. regarding taxation of goods graduated according to the size of the production units where the goods are made, Warner AG in Case 127/75 *Bobie Getränkevertrieb GmbH* v. *Hauptzollamt Aachen-Nord* [1976] ECR 1079, 1094.

[14] Case 169/78 *EC Commission* v. *Italy: taxation of spirits* [1980] ECR 385, 399.

[15] See e.g. Case 356/85 *EC Commission* v. *Belgium: taxation of beer and wine* [1987] ECR 3299, 3325.

[16] Case 15/81 *Gaston Schul Douane Expediteur BV* v. *Inspecteur der Invoerrechten en Accijnzen, Rosendaal* [1982] ECR 1409, 1431–2. See also Jacobs AG in Case C–312/91 *Metalsa Srl* [1993] ECR I–3751, I–3763.

between Member States in undistorted conditions of competition. It seeks to achieve this end through the elimination of all forms of protection resulting from the application of internal taxation which discriminates against products from other Member States or is protectionist in its scope.[17] In other words, Article 95 seeks to guarantee generally the neutrality of the systems of internal taxation with regard to trade between Member States whenever an economic transaction going beyond the frontiers of a Member State at the same time constitutes the chargeable event giving rise to a fiscal charge within the context of such a system.[18]

If a distortion of competition contrary to this guarantee is not established, national taxation arrangements are unaffected by Article 95. For example, *Schul*[19] concerned the imposition of Dutch value-added tax on the importation into the Netherlands of a second-hand pleasure boat purchased by a private person resident in the Netherlands from a private person in France. Here the Court ruled that adoption of the country of destination principle for taxation purposes was a political choice for the Union legislature.[20] The importing Member States merely had to reduce the value-added tax charged on imported goods by the amount levied in the exporting Member State. Provided they did so, there would be no breach of Article 95.

Moreover, this provision does not aim to place imports in a privileged position in relation to domestic products.[21] Hence, a Member State is not required to exempt imports from its tax system simply because there are no domestic products burdened by a given tax.[22]

18.3 "Reverse Discrimination"

Article 95 of the EC Treaty has been held not to prohibit the imposition on national products of internal taxation in excess of that on imported products. In the view of the Court of Justice, such disparities result from the special features of national laws which have not been harmonised in spheres for which Member States are responsible.[23] In other words, "reverse discrimination" is not prohibited by this provision. The implication is that the Court seeks to limit the disruption of national policy making by judicial decisions.

In other contexts the Court has been guided more by the function than the

---

[17] Case 142/77 *Statens Kontrol med Aedle Metaller* v. *Preben Larsen* [1978] ECR 1543, 1558.

[18] *Ibid.*, 1558. See also Case 169/78 *EC Commission* v. *Italy: taxation of spirits* [1980] ECR 385, 399.

[19] Case 15/81 *Gaston Schul Douane Expediteur BV* v. *Inspecteur der Invoerrechten en Accijnzen, Rosendaal* [1982] ECR 1409, 1432–3.

[20] Cf. Ruiz-Jarabo AG in Case C–296/95 *R.* v. *Commissioners of Customs and Excise, ex p. EMU Tabac* (17 April 1997).

[21] Case 78/76 *Firma Steinike and Weinlig* v. *Germany* [1977] ECR 595, 613.

[22] Case 20/67 *Firma Kunstmülhle Tivoli* v. *Hauptzollamt Würtzburg* [1968] ECR 199. Cf. Case 193/85 *Cooperativa Cofrutta* v. *Amministrazione delle Finanze dello Stato* [1987] ECR 2085.

[23] Case 86/78 *SA des Grands Distilleries Peureux* v. *Directeur des Services Fiscaux de la Haute-Sâone et du Territoire de Belfort* [1979] ECR 897, 913.

wording provisions governing taxation. For example, Article 96 expressly prohibits the refund of internal taxes on exports at a level higher than that at which taxes have been paid in the Member State of exportation. Trade within Member States is thus liberalised, insofar as Member States are prohibited from employing fiscal measures to disadvantage such trade in comparison with export trade. Moreover, although Article 96 only refers to discrimination in favour of exports, the Court finds implicit in the Treaty system a prohibition of discrimination against exports.[24] It may be argued that the function of Articles 95 and 96 within the Treaty system also requires that protection of certain imports against competition from domestic products should similarly be prohibited. However, such an argument does not seem to be favoured by the Court.

18.4 Objective Differentiation

Article 95 of the EC Treaty does not prohibit a Member State from differentiating between products according to objective criteria, if it pursues aims which are themselves compatible with the requirements of the Treaty and secondary legislation and if detailed rules of implementation avoid discrimination or protection.[25] Thus, for example, economic policy goals[26] and social policy goals[27] may be pursued.

In principle, the identification of social policy goals is a matter of political choice for the Member States. The choice can only be subject to supervision at the Union level if, by distorting the concept of social policy, it leads to measures which because of their effects and their true objectives lie outside the scope of this concept.[28]

The case law concerning such differentiation has much in common with the recognition of "mandatory requirements" in connection with provisions such as Article 30 of the EC Treaty.[29]

18.5 Harmonisation

Even when no discrimination or protectionist effects contrary to Article 95 or 96 of the EC Treaty can be established, differences in national tax law may interfere with economically efficient utilisation of resources within the Union. For this reason, Article 99 of the Treaty envisages harmonisation of indirect taxation which directly affects the establishment or functioning of the internal market.

---

[24] Case 142/77 *Statens Kontrol med Aedle Metaller* v. *Preben Larsen* [1978] ECR 1543, 1558.
[25] Case 140/79 *Chemical Farmaceutici SpA* v. *DAF SpA* [1981] ECR 1, 15. Cf. Warner AG in Case 46/80 *SpA Vinal* v. *SpA Orbat* [1981] ECR 77, 103.
[26] See e.g. regarding regional policy, Case 196/85 *EC Commission* v. *France: taxation of natural sweet wines and liqueur wines* [1987] ECR 1597, 1615. See, regarding industrial policy, Case 140/79 *Chemical Farmaceutici SpA* v. *DAF SpA* [1981] ECR 1.
[27] Case C–132/88 *EC Commission* v. *Greece: taxation of motor cars* [1990] ECR I–1567, I–1592.
[28] Case 415/85 *EC Commission* v. *Ireland: VAT zero rating* [1988] ECR 3097, 3120.
[29] Sect. 8.5.4 above.

The inclusion of this provision in the Treaty may have affected interpretation of Article 95. In particular, its inclusion has allowed interpretation of Article 95 to proceed on the assumption that restriction of the fiscal sovereignty of the Member States is compatible with the Treaty.[30] Its inclusion also implicitly recognises that fiscal harmonisation is necessary for the realisation of a common market.[31] True, only limited harmonisation may have taken place under Article 99 of the Treaty. However, the accomplishment of harmonisation may be less decisive[32] than the implications which may be drawn from its very contemplation in the Treaty.

In fact, some harmonisation of national law regarding value-added tax has taken place. Basic principles and rules for implementing them were established by the First[33] and Second Directives[34] on value-added tax, and the Sixth Directive[35] laid down a uniform base of assessment. Other directives concern duty-free allowances in international travel,[36] exemption for fuel held in commercial motor vehicle tanks,[37] common rates of capital duty,[38] and administrative co-operation.[39] Minimum levels of value-added tax[40] and excise duties[41] have also been agreed.[42]

[30] Lenz AG in Case 193/85 *Cooperativa Co-Frutta* v. *Amministrazione delle Finanze dello Stato* [1987] ECR 2085, 2101 and 2111–13.

[31] Gand AG in Case 28/67 *Firma Mölkerei-Zentrale Westfalens/Lippe GmbH* v. *Hauptzollamt Paderborn* [1968] ECR 143, 165.

[32] Cf. P. Demaret, "Le Régime des échanges internes et externes de la Communauté à la lumière des notions d'union douanière et de zone de libre-échange" in F. Capotorti, C.-D. Ehlermann, J.A. Fröwein, F. Jacobs, R. Joliet, T. Koopmans, and R. Kovar (eds.), *Du Droit International au Droit de l'Intégration, Liber Amicorum Pierre Pescatore* (Nomos, Baden-Baden, 1987), 139–65, 164–5.

[33] Dir. 67/227 (JO 1967 1301) on the harmonisation of legislation of Member States concerning turnover taxes.

[34] Dir. 67/228 (JO 1967 1303) on the harmonisation of legislation of Member States concerning turnover taxes; and Dir. 68/221 (JO 1968 L115/14) on a common method for calculating the average rates provided for in Art. 97 EEC.

[35] Dir. 77/388 (OJ 1977 L145/1) on the harmonisation of the laws of the Member States relating to turnover taxes – common system of VAT: uniform basis of assessment.

[36] Dir. 69/169 (JO 1969 L133/6) on the harmonisation of provisions laid down by law, regulation, or administrative action relating to exemption from turnover tax and excise duty on imports in international travel. But see, now, Dir. 91/680 (OJ 1991 L376/1) supplementing the common system of VAT and amending Dir. 77/388 with a view to the abolition of fiscal frontiers.

[37] Dir. 68/297 (JO 1968 L175/15) on the standardisation of provisions regarding the duty-free admission of fuel contained in the fuel tanks of commercial motor vehicles.

[38] Dir. 73/80 (OJ 1973 L103/15) fixing common rates of capital duty.

[39] Dir. 76/308 (OJ 1976 L73/18) on mutual assistance for recovery of claims resulting from operations governing part of the system of financing the EAGGF and of the agricultural levies and customs duties; Dir. 77/799 (OJ 1977 L336/15) concerning mutual assistance by the competent authorities of the Member States in the field of direct taxation; and Reg. 218/92 (OJ 1992 L24/1) on administrative co-operation in the field of indirect taxation (VAT).

[40] Dir. 92/77 (OJ 1992 L316/1) supplementing the common system of VAT and amending Dir. 77/38.

[41] See e.g. Dir. 92/84 (OJ 1992 L316/29) on the approximation of the rates of excise duty on alcohol and alcoholic beverages and Dir. 92/82 (OJ 1992 L365/46) on the approximation of rates of excise duties on mineral oils. See, generally, the Report on excise duties, COM(95)285.

[42] See also the proposal for a dir. restructuring the Community framework for the taxation of energy products (OJ 1997 C139/14).

18.6 Goods from Third States

Article 95 of the EC Treaty only expressly benefits "products of other Member States", and Article 9(2) of the Treaty[43] does not mention tax provisions.[44] However, the Court of Justice has assimilated products from third states in free circulation to products originating within the Union in connection with the prohibition of fiscal discrimination in Article 95.[45] According to the Court, Article 95 prohibits fiscal discrimination or protectionism against products from third states in free circulation within the Union.[46]

18.7 Agreements with Third States

Free trade agreements and association agreements usually contain provisions prohibiting discriminatory taxation.

18.7.1 Free Trade Agreements

In *Kupferberg*,[47] which concerned German taxation of port from Portugal, the Court of Justice had to interpret Article 21(1) of the Portuguese Free Trade Agreement.[48] According to this provision, the Parties were to refrain from any measure or practice of an internal fiscal nature establishing, whether directly or indirectly, discrimination between the products of one Party and like products originating in the territory of another Party. It was interpreted by the Court as only prohibiting differential treatment of products which had similar characteristics and were manufactured in a similar way.[49] According to the Commission, only "effective discrimination rather than the mere fact of a difference in taxation" was prohibited.[50]

Hence, the taxation of port from Portugal was not affected by the Free

---

[43] Art. 9(2) EC states that Arts. 12 and 30–37 EC apply to goods from third states in free circulation.

[44] In Case 7/67 *Milchwerke H. Wöhrmann und Sohn KG v. Hauptzollamt Bad Reichenhall* [1968] ECR 177, 183, the ECJ ruled that Art. 95 EC applied exclusively to products originating in the Member States. See also Case 20/67 *Firma Kunstmühle Tivoli* v. *Hauptzollamt Würtzburg* [1968] ECR 199, 204 and Case 148/77 *H. Hansen Jun. and O.C. Balle GmbH & Co.* v. *Hauptzollamt Flensburg* [1978] ECR 1787, 1808.

[45] Case 193/85 *Cooperativa Co-Frutta* v. *Amministrazione delle Finanze dello Stato* [1987] ECR 2085. In contrast, Lenz AG maintained that the intention of Art. 95 EC was to secure undistorted competition in the common market, whereas protection against competition from third states was ensured by the CCT and specific agreements (*ibid.*, 2101–2).

[46] [1987] ECR 2085, 2112.

[47] Case 104/81 *Hauptzollamt Mainz* v. *C.A. Kupferberg & Cie KG* [1982] ECR 3641.

[48] JO 1972 L301/2.

[49] [1982] ECR 3641, 3669. See also Case 253/83 *Sektkellerei C.A. Kupferberg & Cie KG* v. *Hauptzollamt Mainz* [1985] ECR 166, 186.

[50] [1982] ECR 3641, 3652.

Trade Agreement, because no similar products were made in Germany. In contrast, Germany would not be permitted by Article 95 of the EC Treaty to impose any tax on port from a Member State which put this product at a disadvantage in relation to competing national products. Such a tax would only be permissible where there was no national product capable of being protected by a tax on products imported from another Member State.[51]

Again, Article 18(1) of the Austrian Free Trade Agreement[52] was the equivalent of Article 21(1) of the Portuguese Agreement. Unlike Article 95 of the EC Treaty,[53] Article 18(1) of the Austrian Agreement was interpreted as not prohibiting national rules punishing offences concerning value-added tax on importation more severely than those concerning value-added tax on domestic sales.[54]

"Structural" Considerations

The reasoning of Advocate General Rozès in *Kupferberg*[55] was that, unlike the EC Treaty, the Portuguese Free Trade Agreement[56] was not intended to create an area of "complete neutrality with regard to competition" in an enlarged market.[57] She continued:

> "In view of the more restricted purpose of that Agreement, where there is such a non-discrimination clause, the only important question is whether the taxation measures actually have a protectionist effect as regards the importation of goods and thus jeopardize the abolition of obstacles to trade".[58]

In other words, taxation measures were only prohibited where they entailed "the actual economic effect of discrimination".[59]

The underlying idea is that while the EC Treaty seeks to remove obstacles to participation in an enlarged market, the Portuguese Agreement had a more limited objective.[60] The former entails that taxation should not distort competition within the common market, whereas the latter only entailed the prohibition of discrimination against imports.[61] While a simple prohibition of discrimination as between domestic goods and imports may not be considered adequate for the purposes of establishing the common market or the "total equality with regard to competition"[62] required by the EC Treaty, it may satisfy the requirements of a free trade agreement. It may, indeed, be regarded as the most practical approach to securing reciprocity.

---

[51] Case 27/67 *Firma Finkt-Frucht* v. *Hauptzollamt München-Landsbergerstrasse* [1968] ECR 223, 232–3.

[52] JO 1972 L300/2.   [53] Case 299/86 *Rainer Drexl* [1988] ECR 1213, 1235.

[54] Case C–312/91 *Metalsa Srl* [1993] ECR I–3751, I–3775.   [55] [1982] ECR 3641.

[56] JO 1972 L301/2.   [57] [1982] ECR 3641, 3676.   [58] *Ibid.*, 3676.   [59] *Ibid.*, 3677.

[60] See, similarly, regarding the Austrian Free Trade Agreement (JO 1972 L300/2), Case C–312/91 *Metalsa Srl* [1993] ECR I–3751, I–3774.

[61] Though the prohibition of such discrimination may be imperfect. See, regarding the Austrian Free Trade Agreement (JO 1972 L300/2), *ibid.*

[62] See the submission of the Commission in Case 253/83 *Sektkellerei C.A. Kupferberg & Cie KG* v. *Hauptzollamt Mainz* [1985] ECR 157, 180.

However, the concepts of discrimination and protectionism may have been invoked too loosely[63] by the Advocate General to express adequately the difference between requirements of the EC Treaty and those of free trade agreements. More fundamentally, these concepts may have been invoked too loosely to expose the need for justification of the limited approach adopted to interpretation of liberalisation provisions in such agreements.

The Court of Justice itself apparently sought a slightly more concrete basis for its approach. The Court stated that Article 21 of the Portuguese Agreement merely aimed to ensure that the liberalisation of trade in goods sought by abolition of customs duties and charges having equivalent effect and quantitative restrictions and measures having equivalent effect (which was required by Articles 3 to 14 of the same Agreement) was not rendered nugatory by fiscal practices of the Parties.[64] Apparently, a conservative approach to abolition of fiscal barriers to trade was felt to be justified by what was assumed to be a conservative approach in the Agreement to abolition of other trade barriers.[65] However, the basis for this assumption was not indicated.

Sovereignty

The implicit concern of the Court of Justice may be to avoid excessive encroachment on the fiscal autonomy of parties which have not demonstrated in free trade agreements the same willingness to contemplate fiscal policy harmonisation[66] as has been demonstrated in the EC Treaty. In particular, the Portuguese Agreement contained no equivalent of Article 99 of the EC Treaty. In other words, the issues involved may be pictured in terms of acceptance of sovereignty limitations.

18.7.2 Association Agreements

In relation to internal taxation, association agreements may follow free trade agreements. For example, Article 26 of the Europe Agreement with Poland[67]

---

[63] Case 104/81 *Hauptzollamt Mainz* v. *C.A. Kupferberg & Cie KG* [1982] ECR 3641, 3669.

[64] *Ibid.*, 3665.

[65] However, Art. 6 of the Swedish Free Trade Agreement (JO 1972 L300/96) prohibited a Member State from levying a charge proportional to the customs value of goods on goods imported from Sweden by reason of their entry into a region of that Member State, notwithstanding the fact that the charge was also imposed on goods entering that region from another part of the territory of the Member State concerned. See Case C–163/90 *Administration des Douanes et Droits Indirects* v. *Léopold Legros, Louise Alidor, Epouse Brun, Armand-Joseph Payet, Henri-Michel Techer* [1992] ECR I–5335.

[66] Cf. Case 218/83 *Les Rapides Savoyards* v. *Directeur Général des Douanes et Droits Indirects* [1984] ECR 3105, 3124, where the ECJ felt obliged to point out that rules in free trade agreements regarding determination of the origin of products did not encroach on fiscal autonomy, because the rules were established on the basis of reciprocal obligations placing the parties on an equal footing in their relations with each other.

[67] OJ 1993 L348/2.

states that the Parties shall refrain from any measure or practice of an internal fiscal nature establishing, whether directly or indirectly, discrimination between the products of one Party and like products originating in the territory of the other Party.

18.7.3 EEA Agreement

Articles 14 and 15 of the EEA Agreement[68] are substantially identical to Articles 95 and 96 of the EC Treaty. No similar provision to Article 99 of the EC Treaty is contained in the EEA Agreement. Hence, questions arise whether Articles 14 and 15 of the Agreement really will be interpreted as being substantially identical to Article 95 of the Treaty.

Part Three

LAW OF HARMONISATION
AND
COMMON POLICIES

19

Legislative Harmonisation

Legislative harmonisation[1] is envisaged in various EC Treaty provisions. Such harmonisation seeks to reduce obstacles to economic activity through eliminating differences in state measures which distort the costs of such activity. According to Article 3(h) of the Treaty, it is to take place to the extent required for the functioning of the common market. At the same time, attainment of Union objectives other than market unification may be sought by legislative harmonisation.[2]

Such harmonisation proceeds on the basis of acts, usually directives, adopted by the Union institutions. According to Article 189(3) of the Treaty, a directive shall be binding, as to the result to be achieved, upon each Member State to which it is addressed. However, it shall leave to the national authorities the choice of form and methods.

19.1 Treaty Provisions

Various EC Treaty provisions formally empower the Union institutions to engage in legislative harmonisation. Other Treaty provisions imply "guidelines" for the content of the harmonisation measures enacted.

19.1.1 Empowering Provisions

Treaty provisions empowering the Union to engage in harmonisation concern market unification and policy implementation.

Market Unification

The scope of certain Treaty provisions empowering the Union to engage in harmonisation may, as in the case, for example, of Articles 100 and 100a, be defined simply by reference to the need to harmonise national law which

---

[1] Various terms – "approximation", "co-ordination", and "harmonisation" – are to be found in the EC Treaty. They appear, however, to be used interchangeably.

[2] Cf. Case 43/75 *Defrenne* v. *SA Belge de Navigation Aérienne (Sabena)* [1976] ECR 455, 472.

impedes economic activity between Member States. In particular, the latter provision envisages the enactment of directives for the approximation of national law, regulation, or administrative action in Member States which have as their object the establishment or functioning of the internal market.[3]

Policy Implementation

The scope of some Treaty provisions empowering the Union to engage in harmonisation is defined by reference to particular sectors, such as agriculture[4] and transport,[5] in which the implementation of Union policies is sought. Other provisions may have their scope of application defined by reference to "horizontal" policies, such as environmental protection.[6] If the necessary powers cannot be found elsewhere, Article 235 provides for the adoption of acts necessary in the operation of the common market for the attainment of Treaty objectives.[7] Acts adopted pursuant to such provisions may be complemented, particularly in the case of the agricultural and regional policies, by the grant of Union aid, designed to assist implementation of the relevant Union policy.[8]

Such Treaty provisions may be seen as enabling the Union to move from "negative" integration towards "positive" integration.[9] The former kind of integration is said merely to involve elimination of obstacles to economic activity between Member States. The latter kind of integration is said to involve co-operation in efforts to secure other economic policy goals. This distinction between the two kinds of integration relies essentially on a reformulation of the traditional distinction between liberalism and interventionism.[10] It may thus be inadequate for the purposes of analysis of Union harmonisation.[11] In particular, the relationship between liberalisation and harmonisation in the Union context is more complicated than is suggested

---

[3] Harmonisation may not necessarily have to be based on Art. 100a EC, even though trade liberalisation is involved. See Case C–70/88 *European Parliament* v. *EC Council: radioactive contamination of foodstuffs* [1991] ECR I–4529, I–4566, where a reg. based on Art. 31 Euratom was found to have only "the incidental effect of harmonising the conditions for the free movement of goods within the Community". See also Case C–155/91 *EC Commission* v. *EC Council: waste* [1993] ECR I–939, I–968.

[4] Art. 43 EC.   [5] Art. 75 EC.   [6] Art. 130s EC.

[7] Resort to this provision may be justified in the interests of legal certainty. See Case 8/73 *Hauptzollamt Bremerhaven* v. *Massey-Ferguson* [1973] ECR 897, 908.

[8] Chap. 20.

[9] In 1987 G. Sjöstedt, "Nordic and World Economic-Political Co-operation: Competition, Adaptation or Participation?" [1987] *Co-operation and Conflict* 209–26, 223 wrote that EU–EFTA relations were in a process of transition from "negative" to "positive" integration.

[10] L. Pålsson, *EG-rätt* (Studentlitteratur, Lund, 1976), 16, treats this distinction as being central to Union law. The underlying assumptions remain dominant in Union law studies. See, e.g., W.P.J. Wils, "The Search for the Rule in Article 30EEC: Much Ado About Nothing" [1993] *ELR* 475–92.

[11] L. Tsoukalis, *The New European Economy: The Politics and Economics of Integration* (Oxford University Press, Oxford, 1991), 251.

by the distinction.[12] The complications are implicit in various Treaty provisions which "guide" harmonisation.

19.1.2 "Guideline Provisions"

The Union legislature may be bound by Treaty provisions, such as Article 30[13] and Article 95.[14] Hence, the harmonisation process must take account of liberalisation requirements entailed by such provisions.

Moreover, Member States retain considerable policy-making powers. Even if the Treaty required nothing more than the reduction of obstacles to economic activity, the drive towards their reduction might still be compromised by the need to make some allowance for the exercise of such powers by Member States.[15] In fact, the Treaty embodies various requirements other than those of liberalisation, which must also be respected by the Union legislature.[16] Consequently, harmonisation, like the operation of liberalisation provisions, may reflect the interplay of the underlying Treaty requirements.[17]

For example, Article 57 of the Treaty seeks to facilitate exercise of freedom of establishment through providing for the enactment of directives on the mutual recognition of diplomas, certificates, and other evidence of formal qualifications[18] and on the harmonisation of training requirements and conditions of access.[19] Special arrangements are made in the case of medical and allied and pharmaceutical professions. In their case, the progressive abolition of restrictions is to depend on co-ordination of the conditions for their exercise in the various Member States.[20] This provision thus seeks to reconcile freedom of establishment with the application of national professional rules justified by the general good.[21]

---

[12] It is said, e.g., that in a mixed economy positive-market-integration-from-above may be a prerequisite of negative-market-integration-from-above. See J. Pelkmans and T. Heller, "The Federal Economy: Law and Economic Integration and the Positive State – The USA and Europe Compared in an Economic Perspective" in M. Cappelletti, M. Seccombe, R.M. Buxbaum, K.J. Hopt, T. Daintith, S.F. Williams, T. Bourgoignie, and D. Trubek (eds.), *Integration Through Law* (De Gruyter, Berlin, 1986), i, 245–412, 325.

[13] Case C–39/90 *Denkavit Futtermittel* v. *Land Baden-Württemberg* [1991] ECR I–3099, I–3108.

[14] Case 15/81 *Gaston Schul Douane Expediteur BV* v. *Inspecteur der Invoerrechten en Accijnen, Roosendaal* [1982] ECR 1409, 1432. Cf. under the ECSC Treaty, Joined Cases 32 & 33/58 *Société Nouvelle des Usines de Pontlieue Aciéries du Temple (SNUPAT)* v. *ECSC High Authority* [1959] ECR 127, 143.

[15] Harmonisation measures may specifically preserve the power of Member States to adopt restrictive measures on "general good" grounds. See e.g. Art. 19(6) of Dir. 93/22 (OJ 1993 L141/27) on investment services in the securities field.

[16] Union measures requiring a high standard of protection for such requirements may be envisaged, as by Art. 100a(3) EC.

[17] See e.g. Case C–114/96 *Rene Kieffer and Romain Thill* (25 June 1997). Cf., regarding the significance which harmonisation measures may attach to the case law concerning such requirements, Dec. 97/42 (OJ 1997 L17/38) on a request from France for a derogation under Art. 14 of Dir. 92/51.

[18] Art. 57(1) EC.   [19] Art. 57(2) EC.   [20] Art. 57(3) EC.

[21] Case 33/74 *Johannes Henricus Maria van Binsbergen* v. *Bedrijfsvereniging* [1974] ECR 1299, 1309; and Case 71/76 *Jean Thieffry* v. *Conseil de l'Ordre des Avocats à la Cour de Paris* [1977] ECR 765, 776.

The need for such reconciliation in Union harmonisation practice generally is recognised in the case law of the Court of Justice. According to the case law, harmonisation must, for example, take account of requirements relating to protection of consumers and the health and life of persons[22] and requirements of "fair trading".[23] Again, since the protection of the environment is "one of the Community's essential objectives", harmonisation must, according to the Court, take account of environmental protection requirements.[24]

Pluralism

The implications for the Union legislature and, more fundamentally, for the relationship between Union law and national law are underlined by Article 100a(4) of the Treaty.[25] According to this provision, when a harmonisation measure has been adopted, a Member State may be authorised by the Commission to maintain national provisions on grounds of major needs referred to in Article 36 or related to protection of the environment or the working environment.[26] Article 100a(5) goes further. According to this provision, a Member State may, on the same grounds, introduce national provisions going beyond the requirements of a directive. Two conditions must be met. First, the new legislation must be based on new scientific evidence. Secondly, there must be problems specific to that Member State arising after the adoption of the directive. More particularly, Article 130t of the Treaty provides that environmental protection measures adopted under Article 130s shall not prevent any Member State from maintaining or introducing more stringent measures.[27] Hence, even if legislation taking inadequate account of such "needs" may lawfully be enacted, such legislation risks being ineffective in reducing obstacles to trade between Member States.

The implication is that the Union legislature lacks a legal monopoly to determine the requirements with which harmonisation is concerned. Consequently, the concept of the supremacy of Union law may be inadequate to capture and express the pluralism of the legal framework for harmonisation.[28]

---

[22] C–146/91 *Koinopraxia Enoséon Georgikon Diacheiriséos Enchorion Proionton Syn. PE (KYDEP)* v. *EU Council and EC Commission* [1994] ECR I–4199, I–4239–40 and I–4242–3.

[23] Case 249/85 *Albako Margarinefabrik Maria von der Linde GmbH & Co. KG* v. *Bundesanstalt für Landwirtschaftliche Marktordnung* [1987] ECR 2345, 2360.

[24] Case 240/83 *Procureur de la République* v. *Association de Défense des Brûleurs d'Huiles Usagées* [1985] ECR 531, 549. Art. 3c EC now provides that environmental protection requirements must be integrated into the definition and implementation of other Union policies and activities.

[25] See, more particularly, the exhortation to the Union legislature in the Declarations on the protection of animals and on assessment of the environmental impact of Community measures and, in connection with nature conservation, the Declaration on Part Three, Title XVI of the EC Treaty, which were adopted along with the TEU.

[26] Case C–41/93 *France* v. *EC Commission: PCP* [1994] ECR I–1829.

[27] See also, regarding positive discrimination in favour of women, Art. 119(4) EC.

[28] Cf. the preference for viewing the relationship as one of parallelism (N. Reich, "Protection of Diffuse Interests in the EEC and the Perspective of 'Progressively Establishing' an Internal Market"[1988] *Journal of Consumer Policy* 395–417) or co-operation (S. Weatherill and P. Beaumont, *EC Law* (2nd edn., Penguin, London, 1995), 517).

Dynamism

Harmonisation may be viewed as reintroducing dynamism into a situation rendered static at any given time by exhaustion of liberalisation provisions.[29] However, this view may be an oversimplification of the role of harmonisation within the Union legal system. The requirements underlying the harmonisation process are essentially the same as those which determine liberalisation and may be invoked by Member States and others in the context of either process. Hence, the two processes may be capable of dynamic interaction.[30] Such interaction may occur in the sense that the approach of one process to underlying Treaty requirements may affect the operation of the other process.[31] In other words, "the mere threat of regulatory competition as a realistic alternative to . . . harmonisation disciplines the harmonisation process itself".[32]

Recognition of these underlying requirements may establish guidelines[33] for the Council and Commission "for defining the economic order to be respected by their policies".[34] At the same time, their recognition may narrow down the area in which Member States can continue to apply national policies.[35] As policy options become narrower, the policy autonomy of each Member State becomes increasingly illusory,[36] and the time needed for completion of Union legislative procedures can be expected to decrease.[37]

Limitations

Harmonisation seeks the kind of equality which depends on traders becoming and remaining more alike. To this extent, harmonisation risks

---

[29] A. McGee and S. Weatherill, "The Evolution of the Single Market–Harmonization or Liberalization" (1990) 30 *MLR* 578–96, 578, begin by "examining the distinction between lawful and unlawful trade barriers, before considering the ways in which lawful barriers are being treated in the run up to 1992". In reality, the "lawfulness" of trade barriers under EC Treaty provisions may be affected by harmonisation. See e.g. Case 382/87 *Regina Buet and Educational Business Services (EBS) SARL* v. *Ministère Public* [1989] ECR 1235, 1252.

[30] I.e. their relationship may be more than what J.-M. Sun and J. Pelkmans, "Regulatory Competition in the Single Market" [1995] *JCMS* 67–89, 67, describe as "complementary".

[31] *Ibid.*   [32] *Ibid.*, 87.

[33] But cf., regarding the limited amenability to judicial review of choices of policy priorities by the Union legislature under Art. 39 EC, Tesauro AG in Case C–204/88 *Ministère Public* v. *Jean-Jacques Paris* [1989] ECR I–4361, I–4372–3.

[34] P. VerLoren van Themaat, "Some Preliminary Observations on the Intergovernmental Conferences: The Relations between the Concepts of a Common Market, a Monetary Union, an Economic Union, a Political Union, and Sovereignty" (1991) 28 *CMLRev.* 291–318, 316.

[35] See e.g. G. Schricker, "European Harmonization of Unfair Competition Law – a Futile Venture?" [1991] *International Review of Industrial Property and Copyright Law* 788–801.

[36] It may, however, have been an exaggeration to regard the free movement of capital and the common market as "a first legal argument against a rejection of monetary union for political reasons" (P. VerLoren van Themaat, n.34 above, 295–6).

[37] T. Sloot and P. Verschuren, "Decision-Making Speed in the European Community" [1990] *JCMS* 75–85, 77.

confronting the dynamism of liberalisation and other requirements in the Treaty with a static element.[38] Indeed, harmonisation may be sought precisely to "control" judicial decision-making.[39]

Even if threats to dynamism are disregarded, harmonisation may remain problematic. The capacity of harmonisation to reconcile reduction of obstacles to economic activity with promotion of other Treaty requirements is not unlimited. Harmonisation cannot by its nature be infinitely variegated,[40] and so it necessarily has an impact on the relative costs of economic actors, depending on their particular circumstances. Limitations to the utility of the process may be implied.

For example, Article 101 of the Treaty provides for harmonisation where a difference between the provisions laid down by law, regulation, or administrative action in Member States distorts competition in the common market and the resultant distortion needs to be eliminated. According to the Commission, this provision could not apply to the competitive distortions in horticulture which resulted from the fixing of prices for petroleum products at different levels in the various Member States. It would, in particular, be arbitrary to take in isolation one of the general conditions in which the undertakings of a Member State operated (such as the price of fuels) which handicapped production in that Member State by comparison with other Member States. To do so would be to ignore the fact that other general conditions affecting production (for example, social security payments, direct taxation, and credit conditions) resulted in that production enjoying a more favourable position than its competitors.[41] Indeed, the ultimate consequence would be treatment of the Member State where undertakings were most handicapped as the norm.[42] Such considerations may explain why Article 101 has been little used.[43]

19.2 Practice

While harmonisation and the operation of liberalisation provisions are not independent processes, there are important differences between the two processes. In practice, the substantial difference lies in their capacity to reach

[38] Solutions may be seen in terms of selecting "the appropriate intensity" of harmonisation to be sought by each Union act (Report of the group of independent experts on legislative and administrative simplification, COM(95)288, 53).

[39] S. Weatherill and P. Beaumont, n. 28 above, 527.

[40] Cf. Case C–233/94 *Germany* v. *European Parliament and EU Council: directive on deposit-guarantee schemes* (13 May 1997).

[41] Distortions of competition in hothouse agriculture, COM(80)306, 33.

[42] Cf. R.H. Snape, "International Regulation of Subsidies" [1991] *The World Economy* 139–63, 143.

[43] Cf. P. Collins and M. Hutchings, "Articles 101 and 102 of the EEC Treaty: Completing the Internal Market" [1986] *ELR* 191–9.

different conclusions about the need for reduction of obstacles to economic activity. More fundamentally, they may reach different conclusions about the appropriate relationship between meeting this need and respecting other requirements embodied in the EC Treaty.[44] Harmonisation may not only promote respect for such requirements through incorporating them into harmonised national policies. By simultaneously lessening divergences between such policies it may also tend towards equalising competitive conditions. Hence, it may tend towards reducing obstacles to economic activity. In other words, reduction of "market failures"[45] and reduction of obstacles to economic activity may be simultaneously achieved through harmonisation.[46]

More particularly, sensitivity for national sovereignty may limit the capacity of the Court of Justice to secure liberalisation of domestic activity through interpretation of liberalisation provisions in the Treaty as applying to such activity.[47] However, the same consideration need not inhibit the Union legislature from securing reduction of obstacles to such activity through a harmonisation process in which representatives of each Member State participate. As a result, harmonisation may go beyond simply prohibiting public or private conduct which distorts competition in economic activity between Member States. It may tend towards securing the same freedom of economic activity for everyone[48] within the Union.[49] In doing so, it may also compensate for the failure of Treaty provisions themselves to liberalise economic activity with third states. In these senses, harmonisation may offer a more developed kind of equality than operation of liberalisation provisions. Indeed, Article 40(2) of the Treaty expressly states that common organisations of agricultural markets are to exclude any discrimination between producers or consumers within the Union.[50]

However, the results of harmonisation may have depended on whether the "old" or the "new" approach to harmonisation has been favoured.

---

[44] Cf. Joined Cases 80 & 81/77 *Société Les Commissionnaires Réunis Srl* v. *Receveur des Douanes* [1978] ECR 927, 944.

[45] I.e. failures by the market to meet certain public interest requirements.

[46] E.g. there may be "added value", both for health protection and for industry. See the explanatory memorandum to the proposal for a directive on *in vitro* diagnostic medical devices, COM(95)130, 9.

[47] A. Evans, *The Integration of the European Community and Third States in Europe: A Legal Analysis* (Clarendon Press, Oxford, 1996), 12–19.

[48] Including, e.g., Union branches of undertakings from third states, as in Dir. 89/666 (OJ 1989 L395/36) concerning disclosure requirements in respect of branches opened in a Member State by certain types of company governed by the law of another state, Arts. 7–10.

[49] Though the emphasis on minimum harmonisation within the context of the "new approach" (see sect. 19.4 below) may do little to realise such potential. See e.g. Case C–11/92 *R.* v. *Secretary of State for Health, ex p. Gallaher Ltd* [1993] ECR I–3545, I–3566.

[50] Cf., in connection with the iron and steel sectors, Art. 4 ECSC. The affirmative equality sought by financial instruments such as the ERDF may be thought to be even more developed. See Chap. 20.

19.3 "Old Approach"

Harmonisation by way of adoption of identical rules for application throughout the Union – the "old approach" – may, at first sight, seem to be demanded by the EC Treaty. Insofar as such rules are adopted, disparities in competitive conditions attributable to differences in national laws will be eliminated. At the same time, Treaty requirements other than those of liberalisation may be promoted.

In some respects, adoption of such an approach to harmonisation also seems consistent with the case law of the Court of Justice. The Court has stressed the need for uniform application of Union law,[51] as an aspect of the general prohibition of discrimination in Article 6 of the Treaty. More particularly, provisions of Union measures, even directives, which are sufficiently precise may have direct effects within national legal systems. To this extent, failure by a Member State to implement a directive by the specified deadline means that the Member State concerned may lose the discretion in implementing the directive implied by Article 189(3). Even where the directive is implemented by the deadline, the meaning of the national implementing legislation may be determined by the interpretation of the directive favoured by the Court of Justice.[52]

Moreover, the Court has ruled that Member States may be unable to rely on Treaty provisions such as Article 36, to justify derogations from directives designed exhaustively to protect the interests invoked.[53] Therefore, the case law seems to provide the Commission with incentives to propose detailed harmonisation.

Accordingly, the removal of obstacles to economic activity used to be sought through the adoption of detailed harmonisation measures. In every area where national legislation served an accepted interest and thereby restricted trade between Member States, it was thought necessary for this interest to be protected in the same way in every Member State. In most cases this thinking meant that directives were designed to specify the requirements which national law was to satisfy. They usually had to be agreed upon unanimously by the Council under provisions such as Article 100 of the Treaty. According to this provision, the Council, acting unanimously, may enact directives for the approximation of such provisions laid down by law, regulation, or administrative action in Member States as directly affect the establishment or functioning of the common market.

As a result of such thinking, a directive might become so technically detailed that it completely determined the requisite characteristics of the product concerned. Similarly, in the case of services, the Commission envisaged

---

[51] Case 6/64 *Flaminio Costa* v. *ENEL* [1964] ECR 583, 594; and Case 14/68 *Walt Wilhelm* v. *Bundeskartellamt* [1969] ECR 1, 14.

[52] Sect. 7.1.2 above.

[53] Case 5/77 *Carlo Tedeschi* v. *Denkavit Commerciale srl* [1977] ECR 1555, 1576–7.

detailed harmonisation of national law, particularly that concerning insurance and the professions. However, because of the detail required such measures were often agreed, if at all, only after years of negotiation. Even where agreement was reached, the resulting measures might not be geared to potential technological developments and might even be capable of obstructing them.

19.4 "New Approach"

The need to enable Union industry to have a chance of competing with the United States, Japan, and the newly industrialised countries led to a review of harmonisation practice.[54] The principle which emerged was that no more harmonisation should take place than was strictly necessary for removing obstacles to economic activity.

This "new approach" to harmonisation was envisaged in the Commission report on *Completing the Internal Market*[55] and in the Single European Act.[56] The latter inserted into the EEC Treaty what is now Article 100a of the EC Treaty. It allows for Council adoption of measures necessary for the establishment and functioning of the internal market by qualified majority. This approach is characterised by a willingness to allow certain derogations from harmonisation measures and a reliance on outline legislation and mutual recognition.

19.4.1 Derogations

Article 100a(4) and (5) of the EC Treaty allow for derogations from Article 100a measures to be authorised by the Commission.[57] Moreover, Article 100a(10) provides that a safeguard clause may be included in the measures themselves.[58] Such clauses may authorise Member States to take, for one or more of the non-economic reasons referred to in Article 36, provisional measures subject to a Union control procedure.[59]

Arrangements of this kind are not entirely novel. In fact, they were sometimes employed in measures enacted under Article 100 of the EEC Treaty. An example may be found in Article 9 of Directive 73/23[60] on the harmonisation of the laws of Member States relating to electrical equipment designed for use within certain voltage limits. This Directive allowed for

---

[54] Technical barriers to trade are said often to be greatest in high-technology sectors, where market fragmentation in Europe is a major disadvantage in competition with producers in the US and Japan.

[55] COM(85)310.   [56] OJ 1987 L169/1.   [57] Sect. 19.1.2 above.

[58] See, more particularly, in the environmental field, Art. 130r(2) EC.

[59] See e.g. Dec. 97/140 (OJ 1997 L56/12) concerning a request for exemption submitted by the UK pursuant to Art. 8(2)(c) of Dir. 70/156 on the approximation of the laws of the Member States relating to the type-approval of motor vehicles and their trailers.

[60] OJ 1973 L77/29.

derogations from harmonised standards. Moreover, even before the introduction of Article 100a, a Member State could rely on Article 36, to justify
the application of higher standards than those contained in harmonisation
measures, where harmonisation was shown to be incomplete.[61] Therefore, it
is not simply the introduction of Article 100a(4), (5), and (10) which is
significant. These provisions have also apparently legitimated a change in the
philosophy underlying general harmonisation practice.

19.4.2 Outline Legislation

Directives may be couched in general terms, and detailed implementation
may be left to others. This aspect of the "new approach" may be regarded as
consistent with the conception of directives in Article 189(3) of the EC
Treaty. According to this provision, directives lay down objectives to be
achieved by the Member States, while leaving the latter free, in principle, to
choose the means of implementation.[62]

In practice, a single directive may be drawn up for a group of products
which may involve similar risks regarding, for example, health and safety.
Such directives prescribe the safeguards necessary, but the technical requirements for specific products may be formulated by European standards
bodies,[63] so as to achieve the aims of the directive.[64] Compliance with the
technical requirements thus formulated is not compulsory. Rather, a
manufacturer benefiting from the free movement of goods may ensure in his
own way that his product meets the safeguards required by the directive. If
he chooses to do so, the only disadvantage is that stricter forms of control
may take place in order to determine whether the product really does meet
the safeguards.

19.4.3 Mutual Recognition

A major role for mutual recognition is envisaged by the "new approach".
Thus products which in one Member State are found to satisfy the safeguards
required by the relevant directives are free to circulate throughout the Union.
Their technical specifications may be entirely different from those used in
other Member States. However, the former specifications must be accepted,
as must approval of the product, providing that both satisfy the requisite
safeguards.

---

[61] See e.g. Case 227/82 *Leendert van Bennekom* [1983] ECR 3883, 3904.
[62] Case 48/75 *Jean Noël Royer* [1976] ECR 497, 518.
[63] Particularly CEN and CENELEC. See sect. 6.4.1 above.
[64] An aim may be to depoliticise the exercise, though the approach may be criticised on the
grounds that privatisation of public functions and their performance by laboratories of large companies are involved. See e.g. Sweden and West European integration, 1988/89:UU19, 28.

Goods

The role of mutual recognition reflects the significance attached by Union practice to the doctrine of equivalence, which is said to be embodied in the case law of the Court of Justice.[65] According to this doctrine, Member States may not rely on Article 36 of the Treaty or mandatory requirements to justify exclusion of imports from other Member States which have complied with standards equivalent to their own. The implication that the standards need not be identical was confirmed by Article 100b of the EEC Treaty, which was added by the Single European Act.[66] It provided for the Council to decide that provisions in force in a Member State had to be recognised as being equivalent to those applied by another Member State.

Services

Union legislation accepts that differences exist between Member States in professional training courses. However, the final qualifications giving access to similar fields of activity are in practice broadly comparable.[67] Accordingly, directives on the mutual recognition of professional qualifications and on the co-ordination of access to the professions under Article 57 of the Treaty resort as little as possible to the prescription of detailed training requirements.

19.4.4 "Regulatory Failure"

Not only is harmonisation simplified by the new approach. The possibility of Union measures being enacted which entail impediments to economic activity not clearly demanded by the Treaty itself may also be reduced. True, the "new approach" has been criticised for failure to have sufficient regard to requirements other than those of trade liberalisation.[68] However, Article 100a(3) of the Treaty refers to proposals under Article 100a(1) for directives concerning health, safety, environmental protection, and consumer protection. It provides for the Commission, in its proposals, to take as a base a high level of protection. Within their respective powers, the European Parliament and the Council must also seek to achieve this objective. Moreover, derogations from the resulting directives may be possible in the case of national measures providing a higher level of protection than the directives themselves.[69]

---

[65] Case 120/78 *Rewe-Zentral AG v. Bundesmonopolverwaltung für Branntwein* [1979] ECR 649.

[66] OJ 1987 L169/1. See also Operational conclusions reached in the light of the inventory drawn up pursuant to Art. 100b EC (OJ 1993 C353/4).

[67] See, in particular, Dir. 89/48 (OJ 1989 L19/16) on a general system for the recognition of higher-education diplomas awarded on completion of professional education and training of at least 3 years' duration.

[68] The European Parliament has also expressed concern that creation of the EEA should not lead to a lowering of standards regarding environmental protection, social rights, and employee rights (Resolution of 12 June 1990 (OJ 1990 C175/51) on economic and trade relations between the EC and the EFTA States, para. 7).

[69] Sect. 19.4.1 above.

Even so, any regulation, whether at Union or national level, risks "regulatory failure". The risk may be exaggerated, insofar as the Union legislature feels itself free of the need to engage in regulatory competition.[70] It may also be exaggerated, because the political and administrative costs of enforcing Union enactments are borne by the Member States rather than the Union institutions.

On the one hand, opportunities for "capture" and "rent-seeking",[71] lost at the national level, may be recreated at the Union level. The consequence may be that the Union institutions are persuaded to introduce unjustified trade restrictions in their directives. For example, powerful traders may lobby the Union institutions to adopt directives which are favourable to their products but which restrict opportunities for new market entrants to compete with products having different characteristics.

On the other hand, directives may be perceived as inadequately meeting requirements other than those of trade liberalisation. Unless formulated and implemented with regard both to liberalisation and to other requirements recognised by Union law, the directives may also prove ineffective. Unless they take full account of liberalisation requirements, they may be ineffective in reducing obstacles to economic activity between Member States. Unless they take full account of other requirements recognised by Union law, they may be ineffective in promoting such requirements. At the same time, insofar as Member States are free to maintain or introduce national rules more effectively promoting these requirements, directives may again prove ineffective in removing obstacles to economic activity between Member States. For such reasons, harmonisation may remain problematic, despite adoption of the new approach.

19.4.5 "Proper" Role of Harmonisation

The new approach may expose rather than resolve fundamental questions about the conceptual basis for determining the "proper" role of harmonisation. The close inter-relationship between state and market means that the concept of market failure, according to which the legislature should only intervene to secure goals which cannot be secured by the market unaided, may not necessarily provide an adequate basis for the determination.[72]

For example, harmonisation affects the relative costs of traders, and the legislature is uncertain of such costs.[73] The response of the latter to a condition

---

[70] This kind of competition takes place where public authorities compete to provide a regulatory environment attractive to market actors.

[71] Where undertakings seek to compete through obtaining a regulatory framework more favourable to them than their competitors.

[72] See e.g. J.A. Hart, "The Effects of State-Societal Arrangements on International Competitiveness: Steel, Motor Vehicles, and Semiconductors in the United States, Japan, and Western Europe" [1992] *British Journal of Political Science* 255–300.

[73] E.g. the practical problems of determining a socially optimal pollution charge are "staggering". See G. Majone, *Evidence, Argument and Persuasion in the Policy Process* (Yale University Press, New Haven, Conn., 1989), 122.

of "bounded rationality"[74] may be to collude with the traders.[75] As a result of such collusion, market demands may come to play an organic role,[76] of which pressure groups may be no more than an institutionalised manifestation,[77] in affecting the content of directives.[78]

19.5 Harmonisation and Third States

Harmonisation problems may not only be of interest to the Member States and Union institutions. They may also be of interest to third states. Harmonisation of Union law and that of third states may take place in various forms, notably the multilateral and the "voluntary". Insofar as such harmonisation does take place, its separation from harmonisation within the Union may be problematic.

19.5.1 Multilateral Harmonisation

Multilateral harmonisation with third states may have an informal basis, such as the EC–EFTA Declaration in Luxembourg of April 1984[79] and the EC–EFTA Declaration in Brussels of December 1989.[80] Techniques may include information exchanges, consultation, and even judicial decision making.

Information Exchanges

Information exchanges may take place as a precondition for multilateral harmonisation between the Union and third states. For example, EFTA states and the Union co-operated to combat trade in counterfeit goods. In particular, they exchanged information concerning legislation, including information on implementing measures following the entry into force of Regulation 3842/86,[81] which prohibited the release for free circulation in the Union of

---

[74] H.A. Simon, *Models of Man* (John Wiley, New York, 1957); and H.A. Simon, "Rational Decision Making in Business Organizations" [1979] *American Economic Review* 493–513.

[75] Though the phenomenon of "regulatory capture" (see G.J. Stigler, *The Citizen and the State* (University of Chicago Press, Chicago, Ill., 1975)) is said not to be widespread. See G. Majone, "Regulating Europe" [1989] *Jahrbuch zur Staats-und Verwaltungswissenschaft* 159–77, 164.

[76] "Reverse causality", according to which interest intermediation may rely on state sponsorship (see F. Traxler, "Interests, Politics and European Integration" [1992] *European Journal of Political Research* 193–217, 210), adds to the complexity of the relationships.

[77] It is said that "no modern government can govern without the assistance of organised interests" (J. Greenwood, "Introduction: Organized Interests and the Transnational Dimension" in J. Greenwood (ed.), *Organized Interests and the European Community* (Pinter, London, 1992), 1–41, 7).

[78] Firms face "fiercer forms of competition generated by a curious mixture of market forces and industrial policies, of natural selection and strategic manipulation". See S. Urban and S. Vendemini, *European Strategic Alliances* (Blackwell, Oxford, 1992), 9.

[79] Bull. EC 4–1984, 1.2.1.

[80] EFTA Bull. 4/1989–1/1990, 5–7.

[81] Laying down measures to prohibit the release for free circulation of counterfeit goods (OJ 1987 L134/1). It has been replaced by Reg. 3295/94 (OJ 1994 L341/8).

counterfeit goods.[82] More generally, information was exchanged[83] within the framework of the GATT Agreement on Technical Barriers to Trade.[84]

Consultation

Arrangements for exchange of information may be reinforced by procedures for consultation before the adoption of legislation. For example, an agreement between the Union and EFTA states was concluded concerning mutual notification of proposed changes in technical rules and providing for a delay in implementation of such rules to allow adequate consultation.[85] This procedure followed that established within the Union by Directive 83/189.[86]

Judicial Decision Making

Judicial decision making may play a role in multilateral harmonisation between the Union and third states. Comparatively demanding arrangements resulted from the Lugano Convention.[87] The Convention laid down rules of international jurisdiction and simplified procedures for recognition and enforcement of judgments and embodied the substance of the 1968 Brussels Convention.[88] Protocol 2 to the Lugano Convention required that the courts of each Contracting Party, when applying and interpreting the Convention, pay "due account" to the principles laid down by any decision of the courts of other Contracting Parties concerning the Convention.[89] More particularly, the Member States would take all measures in their power to ensure respect for the principles of the Convention when Union acts governing jurisdiction and recognition and enforcement of judgments were drafted. They also considered it appropriate that the Court of Justice when interpreting the Brussels Convention should pay due account to the rulings contained in the case law of the Lugano Convention. Likewise, EFTA states considered it appropriate that their courts when interpreting the Lugano Convention should pay due account to the rulings contained in the case law

---

[82] The EFTA states also agreed to adoption of their own national legislation having equivalent effect to Union legislation *(Sverige – EFTA – EG 1988* (Utrikesdepartementets handelsavdelning, Stockholm, 1989), 123; and *Sverige – EFTA – EG 1989* (Utrikesdepartementets handelsavdelning, Stockholm, 1990), 140).

[83] *Sverige – EG 1980* (Utrikes-och handelsdepartementen, Stockholm, 1981), 24.

[84] BISD, Twenty-Sixth Supp., 8. A new agreement is contained in Annex 1A to the WTO Agreement (OJ 1994 C336/3).

[85] Agreement laying down a procedure for the exchange of information in the field of technical regulations (OJ 1990 L291/2).

[86] Laying down a procedure for the provision of information in the field of technical standards and regulations (OJ 1983 L109/8). According to Case C–194/94 *CIA Security International SA and Securitel SPRL* [1996] ECR I–2201, Arts. 8 and 9 of the Dir. are directly effective, and so national courts must not apply a national technical reg. which has not been notified to the Commission.

[87] OJ 1988 L319/9.   [88] OJ 1978 L304/36. See now OJ 1990 C189/2.

[89] The practical effectiveness of such a requirement is uncertain. See e.g. J.H.J. Bourgeois, "The EFTA States and EC Legal Systems: Is Integration Possible? Comment" in J.J. Jamar and H. Wallace (eds.), *EEC–EFTA: More Than Just Good Friends?* (De Tempel, Bruges, 1988), 299–304, 301.

of the Court of Justice and of courts of Member States concerning provisions of the Brussels Convention which were substantially reproduced in the Lugano Convention.

19.5.2 Voluntary Harmonisation by Third States

Third states may engage in "voluntary harmonisation"[90] with Union law. Harmonisation of this kind takes place where a third state adapts its internal legal provisions to Union law provisions which have no binding force in relation to that state.[91] Such harmonisation means that third states adopt the substance of Union rules in the framing of which they may have had no real participation.[92] Hence, it is said that, by resorting to such harmonisation, third states have "reacted against marginalisation, but at the inevitable price of satellisation".[93]

From the Union point of view, voluntary harmonisation by third states has the advantage of entailing no legal constraints on its future freedom of action.[94] The Union may also have more positive reasons to be sympathetic to such harmonisation. For example, in *A Community Strategy to Develop Europe's Industry*[95] the Commission maintained that the promotion of norms and standards for a larger market and even the world market might be advantageous for European industry in sectors where it was in a relatively strong position. At the same time, there may be concern that harmonisation within the Union alone will unduly assist traders from third states.[96]

"Shadow Membership"

Voluntary harmonisation may be claimed by third states to entail no loss of sovereignty, the necessary decisions being taken internally.[97] However, the extent to which the inherent contradictions between such harmonisation and formal retention of sovereignty really can be reconciled is questionable.

---

[90] A. Evans, "Voluntary Harmonization in Integration between the European Community and Eastern Europe" [1997] *ELR* 201–20.

[91] The "force exerted by a foreign model on domestic policy can be of two types: push and pull". See G. Majone, "Cross-National Sources of Regulatory Policy-Making in Europe and the United States", EUI Working Paper SPS No. 90/6 (EUI, Florence, 1990), 47.

[92] Even the old Soviet Union apparently engaged in such harmonisation. See the Opinion of the Economic and Social Committee of 25 Jan. 1995 (OJ 1995 C102/40) on relations between the EU and Russia, Ukraine, and Belarus, para. 2.1.5.

[93] P. G. Nell, "EFTA in the 1990s: The Search for a New Identity" [1990] *JCMS* 327–58, 352.

[94] It was, presumably, for this reason that the Commission felt able to suggest adoption of the practice as a possibility for Sweden during the negotiation of the Free Trade Agreement (*Commission Opinion to the Council on the Relations of the Enlarged Community with the Members and Associated States of EFTA not Applying for Admission*, Bull. EC, Supp. 3/71, 12–13).

[95] COM(81)639, 18.

[96] See e.g. Commission activities and Community requirements for the automobile industry in 1981–3, COM(83)633, 21.

[97] *Redovisning av det svenska integrationsarbetet våren 1988–mars 1989* (Utrikesdepartementets handelsavdelning, Stockholm, 1989), 215.

In practice, the contradictions may lead to the undermining of "open government" within the third state concerned.[98]

On the other hand, insofar as voluntary harmonisation takes place, undertakings from third states will be subject to the same legal conditions as competitors within the Union. In essence, what is involved for the states concerned is "shadow membership" of the Union without formal acceptance of obligations which may be seen as threatening important national policy interests. Moreover, the markets of these states may be unified with the Union market. In these circumstances, the Union institutions may be inhibited from introducing future divergent rules without consideration of the position of the third states concerned and even consultation at least of an informal kind.

"Bridging Agreements"

In practice, voluntary harmonisation is said to be subject to delay and uncertainty, which impede business planning.[99] More particularly, agreements may still have to be concluded between the Union and the third states concerned to secure mutual recognition of voluntarily harmonised law. While harmonisation may mean that mutual recognition is "automatic" within the Union, an agreement may be necessary with a third state.[100] The prospects of concluding such agreements may be adversely affected by the concern of the Commission that they must not endanger the autonomy of Union decision making.[101] Indeed, proposals for such agreements may be perceived as attempts by particular third states to secure a *de facto* right of co-decision in the event of any changes in the relevant Union law.[102]

Where such agreements are not concluded, the position of third states and their undertakings may be precarious. It may be precarious, in that mutual recognition may be based on a Commission assessment of the equivalence of Union legislation and the national legislation of the third state concerned. Such recognition may be subject to the possibility of revocation, should subsequent legislative amendments lead to incompatibility.[103]

---

[98] See e.g. the criticism by the Constitutional Committee of the Swedish Parliament, Inquiry into the work of the Cabinet and its handling of governmental affairs (1989/90:KU30).

[99] L. Ohlsson, *Consequences of the EC for Swedish Manufacturing Industry* (Industriförbundet Working Paper 7, Stockholm, 1988), 14.

[100] Case C–154/93 *Abdullah Tawil-Albertini* v. *Ministre des Affaires Sociales* [1994] ECR I–451, I–462–3.

[101] H.G. Krenzler, "Zwischen Protektionismus und Liberalismus: Europäischer Binnenmarkt und Drittlandsbeziehungen" [1988] *Europa-Archiv* 241–48, 248.

[102] T. Pedersen, "EC–EFTA Relations: Neighbours in Search of a New Partnership" in G. Edwards and E. Regelsberger (eds.), *Europe's Global Links* (Pinter, London, 1990), 97–111, 104.

[103] P. Baragiola, *EC/EFTA: the Future European Economic Area* (Club de Bruxelles, Brussels, 1991), 17–18.

19.6 Agreements with Third States

Agreements with third states may formally provide for harmonisation between the parties.

19.6.1 Free Trade Agreements

Free trade agreements may contain "evolutionary" clauses envisaging bilateral harmonisation by the parties. Such a clause was included, for example, in Article 32 of the Swedish Free Trade Agreement.[104] Article 32(1) envisaged the possibility that a Party might consider it useful in the common interest of both Parties to develop the relations established by the Agreement by extending them to fields not covered thereby. If so, that Party had to submit a reasoned request to the other Party. The Parties might instruct the Joint Committee to examine this request and, where appropriate, to make recommendations to them, particularly with a view to opening negotiations.

Scope of Harmonisation

The Swedish Government considered that Article 32(1) of the Free Trade Agreement could usefully operate in relation to technical or non-tariff barriers to trade. However, the Commission was apparently concerned to preserve Union autonomy of decision-making. Thus the Commission preferred reliance on voluntary harmonisation[105] and the mutual recognition of test results.[106] In other words, the permissible scope of harmonisation under Article 32 of the Agreement was problematic.

Nature of Harmonisation

The second paragraph of Article 32(1) of the Swedish Agreement provided that recommendations emanating from the Joint Committee might, where appropriate, aim at the attainment of "concerted harmonisation".[107] The implication was that Sweden was not expected unilaterally to harmonise its rules with Union law.[108]

On the other hand, the extent of the concertation envisaged in Article 32(1) seems to have been limited.[109] It was stipulated in this provision that

---

[104] JO 1972 L300/96.

[105] See, later, the Commission suggestion of Apr. 1984 in *A new regulatory regime for electrical materials*, prop. 1987/88:82, 3.

[106] AiH 4/1972, 18.

[107] The same terminology was employed in the Free Trade Agreement (OJ 1973 L171/2) with Norway.

[108] H. Danelius, "Sveriges avtal med de europeiska gemenskaperna – juridiska aspekter" [1973] *SvJT* 97–114, 110.

[109] The Commissioner responsible for the negotiation of the Free Trade Agreements with the EFTA states merely described these clauses as "*à la base de progrès futurs*". See also *Agreements with the EFTA States not Applying for Membership*, Bull. EC 9–1972, 11–21, 19. See, generally, R. Milas, "Les Relations entre la Communauté européenne et les pays nordiques" [1984] *RMC* 534–43, 538.

the autonomy of decision of each Party was not to be impaired. Thus during negotiation of the Agreement the Commission made clear that there could be no question of including a special procedure, as sought by Sweden, for information and consultation relating to Union harmonisation efforts.[110]

Moreover, any recommendations that might be made by the Joint Committee would not be binding on the Parties. The recommendations would also be subject to ratification or approval by the Parties according to their own procedures.[111] It appears, then, that parallel rules, rather than rules deriving direct legal force from a common source,[112] were envisaged in Article 32.

Hence, while the Agreement clearly laid down a framework for the Parties to engage in harmonisation, it might better be described as a framework of an intergovernmental kind rather than one involving supranationalism. In other words, the harmonisation envisaged did not require participation by institutions independent of the Parties in adoption of measures having internal legal effects within the Parties.

In fact, it has been argued that since no prior commitment to bilateral harmonisation is expressed in such clauses, anything done pursuant to them can also be done without them.[113] Such arguments may be favoured by national courts in third states. For example, in the case of the Free Trade Agreement with Switzerland,[114] the Swiss Supreme Court has taken the view not simply that an obligation to harmonise is "deliberately excluded" from the Agreement. The Supreme Court also considers that existing legal rules within Switzerland and the Union are mutually recognised and "approval is given to the unrestricted, independent implementation of these rules".[115]

Practice

In practice, little use was made of the procedure laid down in Article 32(1) of the Swedish Agreement, though the corresponding clause in the Portuguese Free Trade Agreement[116] was invoked to some effect.[117] At a meeting of

---

[110] Report of the Foreign Affairs Committee on the agreement with the EEC (UU1972:20), 20 and 28.

[111] Art. 32(2) of the Swedish Agreement (JO 1972 L300/96).

[112] As in the case of Union regs. (Art. 189(2) EC).

[113] E.P. Wellenstein, "The Free Trade Agreements Between the Enlarged European Communities and the EFTA-States" (1973) 10 *CMLRev.* 137–49, 145–6. See also M. Jäger, "Die sogenannte Entwicklungsklauseln in den Abkommen der EWG mit den Rest-EFTA-Staaten, insbesondere der Schweiz" [1972] *Aussenwirtschaft* 323–39.

[114] JO 1972 L300/189.

[115] *Adams* v. *Public Prosecutor, Canton Basle* [1978] 3 CMLR 480, 485. Such thinking, if followed literally, might have led to the non-application of much of the Agreement. Cf., regarding the Competition Agreement with the US, Tesauro AG in Case C–327/91 *France* v. *EC Commission* [1994] ECR I–3641, I–3664.

[116] JO 1972 L301/66.

[117] *EG under första halvåret 1975: Rapport från svenska delegationen i Bryssel* (Utrikes-och handels-departementen, Stockholm, 1975), 15.

officials from EFTA states in 1982 it was noted that co-operation outside their free trade agreements was taking place on an *ad hoc* basis. Evolutionary clauses were rarely invoked as the legal basis for such co-operation, though such clauses are said to have served as expressions of the willingness of the Parties to co-operate in new fields.[118] Certainly, the Preamble to the Protocol to the Swedish Agreement concerning export restrictions[119] referred both to Article 32 of this Agreement and to what was then described as the European Economic Space.[120] On the other hand, the absence of such a clause in the Free Trade Agreement with Finland[121] did not prevent adoption of a corresponding protocol to this Agreement.[122]

At most, therefore, provisions for bilateral harmonisation may merely offer a formal basis for giving effect to harmonisation agreed through contacts outside the framework of the procedures laid down by the free trade agreements concerned. The limited effect of such provisions may be an inevitable consequence of the fact that, according to Union law, free trade agreements are commercial policy instruments adopted under Article 113 of the Treaty.[123] Hence, harmonisation under the agreements must fall within the scope of commercial policy. The result is that the approach to economic problems between parties to such an agreement may differ from that applied to corresponding problems within the Union.[124] Such differences of approach may leave little scope for use of formal procedures for bilateral harmonisation by the parties.

19.6.2 Association Agreements

Association agreements may make formal provision for voluntary harmonisation by third states[125] and for collaboration between third states in such harmonisation.

Voluntary Harmonisation by Third States

Article 68 of the Europe Agreement with Poland[126] expressly refers to

---

[118] *Sverige – EG 1982* (Utrikesdepartementets handelsavdelning, Stockholm, 1983), 33. See also H. Lidgard, "Sverige–EEG och konkurrensen" [1974] *SvJT* 18–33, 32.

[119] OJ 1989 L295/22.

[120] See also, regarding bilateral agreements between Switzerland and the Union, R. Senti, *EG EFTA Binnenmarkt* (2nd edn., Schulthess, Zurich, 1992), 144.

[121] OJ 1973 L328/2.   [122] OJ 1989 L295/2.

[123] Procedures such as that in Art. 32 of the Swedish Agreement (JO 1972 L300/96) may not affect the competence of the Union under Art. 113 EC. See Opinion 1/94 *International Agreements on Services and the Protection of Industrial Property* [1994] ECR I–5267, I–5408.

[124] Capotorti AG in Case 225/78 *Procureur de la République, Besançon* v. *Bouhelier* [1979] ECR 3151, 3165.

[125] See, more particularly, the mutual recognition agreements envisaged in Preparation of the associated countries of Central and Eastern Europe for integration into the internal market of the Union, COM(95)163, 5.

[126] OJ 1993 L348/2.

voluntary harmonisation. According to this provision, the Parties recognise that the major precondition for Poland's economic integration into the Union is the approximation of its existing and future legislation to that of the Union. Accordingly, Poland shall use its best endeavours to ensure that its future legislation is compatible with Union legislation in various fields. The fields covered include: customs law, company law, banking law, company accounts and taxes, intellectual property, protection of workers at the workplace, financial services, rules on competition, protection of health and life of humans, animals and plants, consumer protection, indirect taxation, technical rules and standards, transport, and the environment.[127] Arrangements are also envisaged for participation by Poland in Union framework programmes, specific programmes, projects, or other actions in fields relevant to "economic and cultural co-operation".[128]

It is apparently envisaged that Poland will shape the legal foundations for its new economic system on the Union model.[129] While the imposition of considerable demands on Poland may be implied, any obligations on the Union to provide support are expressed only in generalised terms. Article 70 of the Agreement merely envisages that the Union will provide Poland with technical assistance.[130] Such assistance is to include the exchange of experts,[131] the provision of information, organisation of seminars, training activities, and aid for the translation of Union legislation in the relevant fields. In practice, informal contacts also take place with the Commission, which notifies Polish officials of the progress of Union harmonisation work.[132] Moreover, specialised sub-committees of the Association Council, established by the Polish Agreement,[133] have been given responsibility for "co-ordination and monitoring" of voluntary harmonisation.[134]

However, the Union aims to provide similar assistance to most Central and East European countries, and it is doubtful whether its human and financial resources are sufficient to enable the aim effectively to be met.[135]

---

[127] Art. 69 (*ibid.*). "Guidelines for the content and organisation of an intensive and coherent programme" are provided in Preparation of the associated countries of Central and Eastern Europe for integration into the internal market of the Union, COM(95)163, 5.

[128] 3rd recital in the preamble to the Additional Protocol to the Europe Agreement with Poland (OJ 1995 L317/35).

[129] H. Kramer, "The EC and the Stabilisation of Eastern Europe" [1992] *Aussenpolitik* 12–21, 15.

[130] Such assistance may be provided through the Phare Programme (Follow up to Commission communication on "The Europe Agreements and beyond: a strategy to prepare the countries of Central and Eastern Europe for accession", COM(94)361, 5).

[131] See also, regarding participation in standards bodies, such as CENELEC, Preparation of the associated countries of Central and Eastern Europe for integration to the internal market of the Union, COM(95)163, annex, 13.

[132] S.S. Nello, "Some Recent Developments in EC–East European Economic Relations" [1990] *JWT* 5–24, 12.

[133] OJ 1993 L348/2, Art. 103.

[134] Follow up to the communication on "The Europe Agreements and beyond: a strategy to prepare the countries of Central and Eastern Europe for accession", COM(94)361, 5.

[135] Cf. the Opinion of the Economic and Social Committee of 25 Jan. 1995 (OJ 1995 C102/40) on relations between the EU and Russia, Ukraine, and Belarus, para. 3.38.

More fundamentally, no arrangements are made to secure for Poland any real say in the development of the rules with which it is supposed to harmonise its law. The failure to make such arrangements may be rendered all the more "disturbing" by challenges, even within the Union, to the legitimacy of the institutions responsible for the development of such rules.[136]

While arrangements in association agreements to facilitate voluntary harmonisation may thus be limited, third states may make their own institutional arrangements to facilitate such harmonisation. For example, an Integration Office has been established within the Polish Government. This Office is to ensure the consistency of new legislation with Union law. It is also to facilitate adaptations of existing legislation to bring it into line with such law.[137] Such arrangements have apparently been the source of some tensions within the Polish Government.[138]

Collaboration between Third States

Collaboration between third states in voluntary harmonisation may be encouraged by the Union. In September 1992, for example, the Heads of the then Czechoslovak, Hungarian, and Polish Delegations to the Union submitted a joint memorandum to the Commission concerning closer co-operation with the Union and prospects for Union membership.[139] The Union response included a call for these countries to collaborate in voluntary harmonisation with Union law.[140]

Collaboration may be difficult to achieve between these states.[141] However, encouragement is provided by the Europe Agreements. For example, Article 71(3) of the Polish Agreement[142] deals with economic co-operation. It requires that special attention must be devoted to measures capable of fostering co-operation between Central and Eastern European countries with a view to the integrated development of the region.

Accordingly, the Union encourages the development of a free trade area and co-operation between these countries in fields such as agricultural, environmental, and transport policy.[143] More particularly, Protocol 4 to the Polish Agreement concerns the definition of the concept of "originating

---

[136] D. Kennedy and D.E. Webb, "The Limits of Integration: Eastern Europe and the European Communities" (1993) 30 *CMLRev.* 1095–117, 1102, n. 9.

[137] *Europe Report* 1650 (6 Feb. 1991).

[138] C. Brzezinski, "The EC-Poland Association Agreement: Harmonization of an Aspiring Member State's Company Law" (1993) 34 *Harvard International Law Journal* 105–48, 132–4.

[139] *Europe* 5813 (12 Sept. 1992).

[140] Joint Statement by the Foreign Ministers of the EC and the Visegrad countries of 5 Oct. 1992, Bull. EC 10–1992, 2.3.1. "Moves to create a Central European Free Trade Area point in the right direction." See the Report from the Council to the Essen European Council on a strategy to prepare for accession of the associated CCEE, Bull. EU 12–1994, I.39.

[141] A. Deen and D.A. Westbrook, "Return to Europe: Integrating Eastern European Economies into the European Market through Alliance with the European Community" (1990) 31 *Harvard International Law Journal* 660–70.

[142] OJ 1993 L348/2.

[143] Council Reply to WQ E–191/95 (OJ 1995 C202/4) by Jean-Pierre Raffarin.

products" and methods of administrative co-operation. Article 37 of this Protocol provides that the Parties shall take any measures necessary for the conclusion of arrangements with Hungary, the Czech Republic, and Slovakia enabling this Protocol to be applied. The Parties are to notify each other of measures taken to this effect.

19.6.3 EEA Agreement

The EEA Agreement[144] provides for EU–EFTA harmonisation in relation to the free movement of goods, persons, services, establishment, capital, and payments. Union acts embodied in EEA law at the time of conclusion of the Agreement are listed in annexes, which form an integral part of the Agreement.[145] Future Union legislation in relation to these freedoms will be subject to procedures for harmonisation at the EEA level. If such legislation is acceptable to the EFTA states, it will be incorporated into EEA law through amendment of the relevant annex to the Agreement.

Similarly, the Agreement provides for harmonisation in relation to certain areas treated as "relevant to the four freedoms". These areas comprise social policy,[146] consumer protection,[147] environmental protection,[148] statistics,[149] and company law.[150]

In addition, Articles 78 to 88 of the Agreement provide for "co-operation outside the four freedoms". In particular, Article 78 provides that the Contracting Parties shall strengthen and broaden co-operation in the framework of Union activities in various fields. The fields include: research and technological development, information services, the environment, education, training and youth, social policy, consumer protection, small and medium-sised enterprises, tourism, the audiovisual sector, and civil protection. Exchanges of information and consultation are envisaged as well as EFTA participation in Union programmes. Article 79(3) provides that legislative harmonisation may also be involved.

Harmonisation procedures are set out in Chapter 2 of Part VII of the Agreement. These procedures distinguish between decision shaping and decision taking. Provision is also made for suspension of annexes to the Agreement, where harmonisation does not take place satisfactorily.

Decision "Shaping"

In addition to the requirement in Article 99(1) of the EEA Agreement

---

[144] OJ 1994 L1/3.   [145] Art. 119 EEA.

[146] Arts. 66–71 EEA and Annex XVIII, health and safety at work, labour law, and equal treatment for men and women.

[147] Art. 72 EEA and Annex XIX, consumer protection.

[148] Arts 73–75 EEA and Annex XX, environment.

[149] Art. 76 EEA and Annex XXI, statistics.

[150] Art. 77 EEA and Annex XXII, company law. More limited harmonisation of economic and social policy is envisaged in Art. 46 EEA.

regarding early consultation of EFTA experts,[151] opportunities for EFTA participation in decision "shaping" are entailed by Article 99(2). It provides that when transmitting a proposal for legislation in a field covered by this Agreement to the Council of the Union, the Commission shall transmit copies thereof to the EFTA states.

At the request of one of the Contracting Parties, a preliminary exchange of views on the proposal takes place in the EEA Joint Committee.[152] Moreover, during the phase preceding the decision of the Council of the Union, a continuous information and consultation process takes place. In particular, the Contracting Parties consult each other again in the Joint Committee at significant moments at the request of one of them.[153] The Contracting Parties shall co-operate in good faith during this phase with a view to facilitating decision "taking" in the Joint Committee.[154]

Decision "Taking"

To guarantee the legal security and the homogeneity of the European Economic Area, the EEA Joint Committee shall take a decision concerning the amendment of an annex to the EEA Agreement as closely as possible to the adoption by the Union of the corresponding new Union legislation. Simultaneous application of such legislation and amendments of the annexes to the Agreement is sought thereby.[155] To this end, whenever adopting a legislative act on an issue which is governed by this Agreement, the Union shall as soon as possible inform the other Contracting Parties in the Joint Committee. The part of an annex to this Agreement which will be directly affected by the new legislation is assessed in the Joint Committee under Article 102(2) of the Agreement.

The Agreement contains no equivalent of Article 100a(4) or (5) of the EC Treaty.[156] However, the Contracting Parties are required to make all efforts to arrive at an agreement on matters relevant to the Agreement. The Joint Committee shall, in particular, make every effort to find a mutually acceptable solution where a serious problem arises in any area which, in the EFTA states, falls within the competence of the legislator.[157]

If an agreement on an amendment of an annex to the Agreement cannot be reached, the Joint Committee shall examine all further possibilities to maintain the good functioning of this Agreement. It shall also take any decision necessary to this effect, including the possibility of taking notice of the equivalence of legislation. According to Article 102(4) of the Agreement, such a decision

---

[151] Sect. 6.5.3 above.   [152] Art. 99(2) EEA.   [153] Art. 99(3) EEA.   [154] Art. 99(4) EEA.

[155] Art. 102(1) EEA. More particularly, Prot. 17, concerning Art. 34 EEA, provides that any legislation concerning third country access to their markets in a field governed by the Agreement shall be dealt with according to the procedures laid down in this Agreement, and the Contracting Parties shall endeavour to elaborate corresponding EEA rules.

[156] Cf., regarding environmental policy measures referred to in Annex XX, environment, Art. 75 EEA.

[157] Art. 102(3) EEA.

shall be taken within six months of the referral to the Joint Committee or, if later, on the date of entry into force of the corresponding Union legislation.

Such arrangements are designed to secure a European Economic Area which is homogeneous and dynamic without the internal autonomy of either of its constituent EEA "pillars" – the Union and the EFTA states – being jeopardized.[158] However, the possibility is not apparently excluded that the Joint Committee may agree that not all EFTA states should be bound by the act concerned. In other words, opting out by an individual EFTA state may be possible through negotiation.

Suspension

If EU–EFTA harmonisation does not take place and a solution cannot be reached within the Joint Committee, EFTA states will not be bound by the Union act concerned. In this sense, such states together may be in a more advantageous position than individual Member States of the Union. The latter may be bound by a Union act adopted in the Council of the Union by majority. The more advantageous position of the EFTA states reflects the fact that they are not fully involved in the negotiations for adoption of a Union act. However, the EEA Agreement seeks to ensure that there are effective disincentives to irresponsible exploitation of their position.[159]

Accordingly, Article 102(5) of the Agreement provides that if, at the end of the period indicated in paragraph 4, the Joint Committee has not taken a decision on an amendment of an annex to the Agreement, the affected part thereof, as determined in accordance with paragraph 2, is regarded as provisionally suspended, subject to a decision to the contrary by the Joint Committee. Such a suspension shall take effect six months after the end of the period referred to in paragraph 4. In no event may it take effect earlier than the date on which the corresponding Union act is implemented in the Union.[160] The Joint Committee shall pursue its efforts to agree on a mutually acceptable solution in order for the suspension to be terminated as soon as possible.

The practical consequences of such suspension are to be discussed in the Joint Committee.[161] The rights and obligations which individuals and economic operators have already acquired under the Agreement shall remain.[162] The Contracting Parties shall, as appropriate, decide on the adjustments necessary due to the suspension.

[158] See, generally, *EFTA–EF Forhandlingene: Kartlegging og forberedelser* (Regjerings-utvalget for EF-Saker, Oslo, 1990).

[159] House of Lords Select Committee on the European Communities, Relations between the Community and EFTA, HL (1989–90) 55–I, 26.

[160] Art. 111(3) EEA also permits such action to be taken, in the event of a dispute, which cannot be resolved by the Joint Committee, concerning case law under the EEA Agreement and corresponding provisions of Union law. Alternatively, safeguard measures under Art. 112(2) EEA may be taken.

[161] Art. 102(6) EEA.

[162] Mere expectations are not covered. Examples of the rights protected are given in an Agreed Minute *ad* Art. 102(6) EEA.

20

Harmonisation Through Financial Instruments

The implementation of common policies and activities, as envisaged in Article 2 of the EC Treaty, may be sought not only through the enactment of legislative measures. Their implementation may also be sought through the operations of the Structural Funds and other financial instruments of the Union. These "Union funds", in contrast to most of the work of the Guarantee Section of the European Agricultural Guidance and Guarantee Fund (EAGGF)[1] and the financing of the "administrative" costs of the Union institutions,[2] are concerned with the structural development of the Union.

20.1 Classification of the Union Funds

The Structural Funds comprise: the European Regional Development Fund (ERDF), the Guidance Section of the European Agricultural Guidance and Guarantee Fund, and the European Social Fund (ESF).[3] The "other financial instruments" of the Union are, according to Union legislation:[4] European Coal and Steel Community (ECSC) assistance in the form of readaptation aid, loans, interest subsidies, and guarantees; European Investment Bank (EIB) loans and guarantees; New Community Instrument (NCI) loans and guarantees; Euratom loans and guarantees; the Cohesion Fund; and Budgetary resources (particularly "other actions for structural purposes").[5] The Budgetary resources treated by the legislation as financial instruments include those associated with: measures accompanying reform of the common agricultural policy; Framework Programmes for Research

---

[1] Subsect. B1 of the Budget for 1997 (OJ 1997 L44/3).

[2] Part A of the Budget for 1997 (*ibid.*).

[3] Art. 2(1) of Reg. 2081/93 (OJ 1993 L193/5) amending Reg. 2052/88 on the tasks of the Structural Funds and their effectiveness and on the co-ordination of their activities between themselves and with the operations of the EIB and the other existing financial instruments.

[4] Art. 3(1) of Reg. 2082/93 (OJ 1993 L193/20) amending Reg. 4253/88 laying down provisions for implementing Reg. 2052/88 as regards co-ordination of the activities of the different Structural Funds between themselves and with the operations of the EIB and the other existing financial instruments.

[5] Chap. B2–2 of the 1997 Budget (OJ 1997 L44/3) is headed "Other Structural Operations" and includes Pedip, IMPs, and the Community Programme in the coal and steel sector.

and Technological Development; trans-European networks; and Phare.[6]

In addition, there are the Financial Instrument for Fisheries Guidance (FIFG),[7] the Financial Instrument for the Environment (LIFE),[8] and the EFTA Financial Mechanism.[9] These seem classifiable as "other financial instruments", since they are concerned with the structural development of the Union. In other words, they are designed to modify its existing economic structure, in order to direct market forces towards an improved configuration.[10]

These instruments may be sectoral or "horizontal". Sectoral instruments include, for example, ECSC assistance and the Financial Instrument for Fisheries Guidance. Horizontal instruments, in turn, may seek to assist in the attainment of horizontal policies of the Union, as for example do the Financial Instrument for the Environment and the Framework Programmes for Research and Technological Development. They may, as in the case of the European Investment Bank, have more general objectives. This Bank is to contribute "to the balanced and steady development of the common market"[11] and to economic and social cohesion.[12]

20.2 Policy Implications of the Work of the Union Funds

The work of the Union funds may be subject to the principles of "complementarity" and "additionality". According to the former principle, the provision of Union assistance presupposes complementary national assistance.[13] This principle may thus be considered necessary to avoid "fiscal illusion" and to ensure that spending reflects needs within Member States.[14] Moreover, according to the additionality principle, assistance from the funds should not lead Member States to reduce their overall level of support for cohesion.[15] As the current legislation puts it, Union assistance may not be used simply to

---

[6] 3rd recital in the preamble to Reg. 2082/93 (OJ 1993 L193/20).

[7] Reg. 2080/93 (OJ 1993 L193/1) laying down provisions for implementing Reg. 2052/88 as regards the FIFG. The FIFG is included in Chap. B2–1, headed "Structural Funds", of the 1997 Budget (OJ 1997 L44/3), though inclusion within this heading is inconsistent with legislative terminology.

[8] Reg. 1973/92 (OJ 1992 L206/1) establishing a financial instrument for the environment, as amended by Reg. 1404/96 (OJ 1996 L181/1).

[9] Art. 116 EEA.

[10] Cf. P. Bianchi, 'La Réorientation des politiques structurelles de la CEE' [1991] *RMC* 599–603, 599.

[11] Art. 188e EC.   [12] Art. 130b EC.   [13] Art. 4(1) of Reg. 2081/93 (OJ 1993 L193/5).

[14] D. Costello, "The Redistributive Effects of Interregional Transfers: A Comparison of the European Community and Germany" in *The Economics of Community Public Finance, European Economy* 5/1993 (EC Commission, Brussels, 1993), 269–94.

[15] 15th recital in the preamble to Reg. 724/75 (OJ 1975 L73/1) establishing an ERDF. See also J.A. Winter, "The ERDF and the Principle of Additionality" in *In Orde, Liber Amicorum Pieter VerLoren van Themaat* (Kluwer, Deventer, 1982), 365–80.

replace public (or comparable) expenditure for structural purposes[16] under-taken by the Member State in the whole of the territory eligible for such assistance.[17]

20.2.1 Competition Policy

In granting assistance the Union not only encourages what may be charac-terised, from the perspective of competition policy, as financial interventions by Member States distorting competition contrary to Article 92(1) of the EC Treaty.[18] It also opposes any reductions in the overall levels of interventions which might conceivably offset distortions arising from Union-assisted inter-ventions. The operation of the Union funds may thus have wide-ranging implications for Union policies.

20.2.2 Convergence

The principles of complementarity and additionality highlight problems in the relationship between cohesion and the convergence criteria for participa-tion in the third stage of economic and monetary union.[19] Assistance from the Union funds may be designed to promote cohesion. However, such assis-tance necessitates public expenditure which these criteria require to be limited. The problems are alleviated rather than resolved by the Cohesion Fund.[20] It seeks to assist certain Member States with a programme for meeting the convergence criteria to tackle their cohesion problems. In partic-ular, it provides assistance at a higher rate than is usual in the practice of the Union funds.[21]

20.2.3 National Policies

National authorities are likely to favour interventions of a kind which qualify for Union assistance, because the burden of financing such interventions will not fall exclusively on domestic resources. Insofar as they do so, national policies may be significantly affected by the availability of such assistance. For example, according to the Committee on Regional Policy and Regional Planning of the European Parliament, the conditions which the Union attaches to the grant of aid from the European Regional Development Fund

---

[16] "Le spese pubbliche o assimilabili a finalità strutturale". Note that the English version of this provision does not make sense.

[17] Art. 9(1) of Reg. 2082/93 (OJ 1993 L193/20).

[18] See, generally, A. Evans, *EC Law of State Aid* (Oxford Series in EC Law, Clarendon Press, Oxford, 1997).

[19] Art.109j(1) EC and the Protocol on the convergence criteria.

[20] Reg. 1164/94 (OJ 1994 L130/1) establishing a Cohesion Fund.

[21] Art. 13(3) of Reg. 2081/93 (OJ 1993/5) and Art. 7(1) of Reg. 1164/94 (OJ 1994 L130/1).

have a significant influence on the shape of the regional policy of the Member States. However, as the Committee observes, the influence would be even greater if the additionality principle were fully implemented.[22] In other words, harmonisation of national policies, and even of the conduct of undertakings which benefit from Union assistance,[23] is implied.

20.3 European Regional Development Fund

The European Regional Development Fund was the last of the three Structural Funds to be established. It only acquired an express legal basis in the EEC Treaty as a result of the Single European Act.[24] However, in terms of the amount of resources used,[25] it has now become the most important of the three.

According to Article 130c of the EC Treaty, the Fund is to help to redress the main regional imbalances[26] in the Union. It is to do so through participation in the development and structural adjustment of regions whose development is lagging behind and in the conversion of declining industrial regions. Accordingly, the "essential task" of the Fund is to support Objectives 1 and 2. It shall also participate in Objective 5b operations[27] and contribute to Objective 6 operations.[28]

To avoid previous administrative difficulties,[29] Article 14(3) of Regulation 2081/93[30] now provides that a region can be eligible under only one of these Objectives. To promote full coherence between Objectives 2 and 5b, the Commission also considers that the lists of eligible areas under each Objective should as far as possible be decided at the same time.[31]

20.3.1 Objective 1

Objective 1 is promoting the development and structural adjustment of regions whose development is lagging behind.[32] It is Objective 1 regions to

[22] Report on the tenth annual report on the activities of the ERDF, EP Doc. A2–76/86, 6.

[23] The Commission implicitly admits that, by providing financial assistance, it influences the investment decisions of companies. See the Reply by Mr Millan to WQ 251/91 (OJ 1991 C227/15) by Mrs Cristiana Muacandini.

[24] OJ 1987 L169/1. See, in particular, Art. 130c EEC.

[25] See the conclusions of the European Council meeting in Dec. 1992 (Bull. EC 12–1992, I.55).

[26] Art. 130c EEC referred to the "principal" regional imbalances.

[27] Art. 3(1) of Reg. 2081/93 (OJ 1993 L193/5).

[28] Prot. 6 to the Accession Agreement with Austria, Finland, and Sweden, as amended by Dec. 95/1 (OJ 1995 L1/1) adjusting the instruments concerning the accession of new Member States to the EU, Art. 1.

[29] Community Structural Fund operations 1994–9, COM(93)67, 14.

[30] Amending Reg. 2052/88 on the tasks of the Structural Funds and their effectiveness and on the co-ordination of their activities between themselves and with the operations of the EIB and the other existing financial instruments (OJ 1993 L193/5).

[31] Community Structural Fund operations 1994–9, COM(93)67, 14.

[32] Art. 1.1 of Reg. 2081/93 (OJ 1993 L193/5).

which the bulk of Union assistance is directed.[33] For the four Member States eligible for assistance under the Cohesion Fund,[34] resources available under this Fund and Objective 1 are to be doubled in real terms between 1992 and 1999.[35]

Regional Eligibility

The Commission originally envisaged that account would be taken of the situation of each Member State in determining whether any of its regions qualified for assistance under Objective 1. Hence, a Commission Statement was contained in Annex 2 to the March 1988 version of the proposal for what became Regulation 2052/88.[36] According to this statement, *per capita* gross domestic product of the Member State would be a criterion to be taken into account together with that of the *per capita* gross domestic product of the region in determining the least prosperous regions for which a special effort was to be undertaken.

Regulation 2052/88,[37] as adopted by the Council and subsequently amended by Regulation 2081/93,[38] makes no reference to the *per capita* gross domestic product of Member States. Article 8(1) provides that the regions concerned by Objective 1 shall be regions at NUTS[39] Level II whose *per capita* gross domestic product, according to figures for the last three years,[40] is less than 75 per cent of the Union average.[41] Northern Ireland, the five new German *Länder*, East Berlin,[42] the French overseas departments, the Azores, the Canary Islands, and Madeira shall be covered. Other regions whose *per capita* gross domestic product is close to that of the regions mentioned may have to be covered by Objective 1 for special reasons. In view of their unique adjacent position to Hainaut in Belgium and their regional gross domestic product, at NUTS Level III, the *arrondissements* of Avesnes, Douai, and Valenciennes are covered. Argyll and Bute, Arran, the Cambrae, and western Moray are also covered.

Article 8(2) of Regulation 2081/93[43] provides that the list of regions

---

[33] *Ibid.*, Art. 12(2).   [34] See sect. 20.7.4 below.

[35] Art. 12(3) of Reg. 2081/93 (OJ 1993 L193/5).   [36] COM(88)144.

[37] On the tasks of the Structural Funds and their effectiveness and on the co-ordination of their activities between themselves and with the operations of the EIB and the other existing financial instruments (OJ 1988 L185/9).

[38] OJ 1993 L193/5.

[39] Nomenclature of Territorial Units for Statistical Purposes.

[40] The European Parliament has complained about the lack of a transitional period for regions whose *per capita* GDP rises slightly above this figure. See the Resolution of 22 Jan. 1993 (OJ 1993 C42/211) on Community structural policies: assessment and outlook ("mid-term review"), para. 53. The Council decided in Art. 8(1) of Reg. 2081/93 (OJ 1993 L193/5) that Abruzzi, where the GDP figure had risen to 90%, would be eligible from 1 Jan. 1994 to 31 Dec. 1995.

[41] The figures for the 5 new *Länder* and East Berlin are not included in the calculation of this average.

[42] Its inclusion accords with the conclusions of the European Council in Dec. 1992 (Bull. EC 12–1992, I.55).

[43] OJ 1993 L193/5.

concerned by Objective 1 is given in Annex I. This list includes regions which are not specifically mentioned in Article 8(1) and have a gross domestic product above 75 per cent of the Union average. In particular, it includes Hainaut in Belgium and Merseyside in the United Kingdom. They have a *per capita* gross domestic product of 78 per cent and 77 per cent respectively of the Union average. The list also covers the Highlands and Islands of Scotland, with a figure of 75 per cent.[44]

Inclusion of Flevoland in the Netherlands, which had a *per capita* gross domestic product of 62 per cent of the Union average, was not proposed by the Commission. According to the Commission, there were "a lot of anomalies" in the position of this region.[45] Its low gross domestic product figure was largely a consequence of a dissociation between the place of work and the place of residence of the active population. Moreover, except for one city, this region was not eligible under the Dutch regional aid scheme.[46] Nevertheless, its inclusion in the list was agreed by the Council.[47]

Therefore, eligible regions are those which are underdeveloped by reference to the average gross domestic product *per capita* for the Union as a whole. Use of this indicator is defended on the grounds that it reflects the economic performance of the regions, in other words productivity. In contrast, an unemployment indicator can only reflect the manifest disequilibria on the labour market. The factor represented by underemployment cannot be taken into account by the latter indicator.[48] Besides, differences between the social policies of governments lead to different definitions of unemployment.

However, it is not universally accepted that gross domestic product figures alone are adequate to identify Union regions with the most serious problems. It may be objected, for example, that gross domestic product is only one of a number of relevant indicators, such as employment, emigration, and poverty,[49] and is too restrictive to permit proper assessment of the level of development of the regions.[50] More particularly, it may be objected that the principal indicators of regional problems are not the disparities in *per capita* gross domestic product but the disequilibria in the utilisation of regional

---

[44] The idea that Molise in Italy and the French island of Corsica, where the figure was 79%, should be removed from the list (*European Report* 1831 (30 Jan. 1993) was not pursued. These regions were peripheral and rural and were originally included in the list because of specific reasons of a technical and political nature. See Structural Funds: amendment of Regs. 2052/88 and 4253/88, SEC(93)651, 3.

[45] *European Report* 1831 (30 Jan. 1993).

[46] Structural Funds: amendment of Regs. 2052/88 and 4253/88, SEC(93)651, 3.

[47] The inclusion of Cantabria was also agreed by the Council. In the Fourth periodic report on the social and economic situation and the development of the regions of the Community, COM(90)609, Table A24 Cantabria was recorded as a having a *per capita* GDP of 72.3% of the Union average.

[48] Second periodic report on the social and economic situation and development of the regions of the Community, COM(84)40, ii.

[49] Opinion of the Economic and Social Committee of 25 May 1992 (OJ 1992 C106/20) on the annual report on the implementation of the reform of the Structural Funds, para. 2.2.5.

[50] Opinion of the Committee on Economic and Monetary Affairs and Industrial Policy in the Report of the Committee on Regional Policy, Regional Planning, and Relations with Regional and Local Authorities on the proposal for a regulation amending Reg. 4254/88 (EP Doc. A3–0191/93), 13).

resources. The latter are indicated by differences in unemployment rates and differences in the productivity levels of regional resources.[51] The only response to such objections seems to be an increasing willingness to apply the 75 per cent threshold with flexibility and to accept the eligibility of regions at NUTS III Level.[52]

Aid Allocation

Article 12(6) of Regulation 2052/88[53] sought to facilitate the planning of assistance in the regions concerned. It provided that the Commission should, for a period of five years and as a guide, establish the allocation for Member States of 80 per cent of the commitment appropriations of the Fund.[54] This allocation was to be based on the socio-economic criteria determining the eligibility of regions for Fund assistance under Objectives 1, 2, and 5b.[55]

Article 12(4) of Regulation 2081/93[56] now provides that the Commission shall, using transparent procedures, make indicative allocations by Member State for each of Objectives 1 to 4 and 5b of the Structural Fund commitment appropriations. Full account is to be taken of national prosperity; regional prosperity; population of the regions and the relative severity of structural problems, including the level of unemployment; and, for the appropriate Objective, the needs of rural development. These criteria are to be "appropriately" weighted in the allocation of aid. In practice, however, Council definition of each Objective and, more particularly its determination of regions covered by Objective 1 may limit the scope of effective Commission discretion in application of the criteria.

According to Decision 89/250,[57] no Objective 1 aid was originally allocated to Belgium, Denmark, Luxembourg, or the Netherlands, though Belgium and the Netherlands now receive allocations.[58] Most of such aid has been allocated to Spain and then Italy.[59]

---

[51] R. Camagni and R. Cappellin, "Policies for Full Employment and More Efficient Utilization of Resources and New Trends in European Regional Development" [1981] *Lo Spettatore Internazionale* 99–135, 120.

[52] The Commission considered that the stronger concentration of Structural Fund operations on Objective 1 (around 70% of total allocations in 1997) should be accompanied by increased flexibility in terms of both the rate of assistance and the eligibility criteria. See Community finances between now and 1997, COM(92)2001, 24. According to Commissioner Millan, "political considerations" ought to come into play in the application of the criterion (*Europe* 5927, 25 Feb. 1993).

[53] OJ 1988 L185/9.

[54] Member States apparently remain determined to secure firm guarantees regarding their allocations before adopting any Commission proposals in the Council. See e.g. *European Report* 1872 (3 July 1993).

[55] Art. 12(6) of Reg. 2052/88 (OJ 1988 L185/9) also required the Commission to ensure that the objective of doubling appropriations for the regions covered by Objective 1 involved a substantial increase in assistance in those regions, particularly in the least prosperous regions.

[56] OJ 1993 L193/5.

[57] Fixing an indicative allocation between Member States of 85% of the commitment appropriations of the ERDF under Objective 1 (OJ 1989 L101/41).

[58] Dec. 93/589 (OJ 1993 L280/30) fixing an indicative allocation between Member States of the commitment appropriations of the Structural Funds and the FIFG under Objective 1.

[59] *EU General Report 1994* (EC Commission, Brussels, 1995), 152.

20.3.2 Objective 2

Objective 2 is converting the regions, frontier regions, or parts of regions (including employment areas and urban communities) seriously affected by industrial decline.[60] According to the Preamble to the original version of Regulation 2052/88,[61] action in favour of Objective 2 regions could cover up to 15 per cent of the Community population living outside the regions whose development was lagging behind.[62] As amended by Regulation 2081/93,[63] the Preamble now refers simply to 15 per cent of the Union population.[64]

Regional Eligibility

Article 9(2), first paragraph, of Regulation 2081/93[65] provides that eligible regions must represent or belong to a NUTS Level III territorial unit and satisfy three criteria. First, the average rate of unemployment recorded over the last three years must have been above the Union average. Secondly, the percentage share of industrial employment in total employment must have equalled or exceeded the Union average in any reference year from 1975 onwards. Thirdly, there must have been an observable fall in industrial employment compared with that reference year.

The second paragraph of Article 9(2) of Regulation 2052/88[66] originally provided that assistance might also be granted to:

– adjacent areas meeting the same criteria;
– urban communities with an unemployment rate at least 50 per cent above the Union average which had recorded a substantial fall in industrial employment; and
– other areas which had recorded substantial job losses over the last three years or were experiencing or threatened with such losses in industrial sectors which were vital to their economic development, with a consequent serious worsening of unemployment in those areas.[67]

At the same time, Article 9(4) provided that the Commission should seek to ensure that assistance was genuinely concentrated on the areas most seriously affected, at the most appropriate geographical level. In doing so, it was to take into account the particular situation of the areas concerned.

According to the March 1988 version of the Commission proposal for what became Regulation 2052/88,[68] the sectors concerned would have been coal, steel, textiles and clothing, and shipbuilding. Other sectors might be

---

[60] Art. 1.2 of Reg. 20981/93 (OJ 1993 L193/5).
[61] OJ 1988 L185/9.   [62] *Ibid.*, 22nd recital in the preamble.   [63] OJ 1993 L193/5.
[64] *Ibid.*, 22nd recital in the preamble.   [65] *Ibid.*   [66] OJ 1988 L185/9.
[67] These criteria are less "objective" than those employed for determination of eligibility for state aid under Art. 92(3)(c) EC. See A. Evans, *EC Law of State Aid* (Oxford Series in EC Law, Clarendon Press, Oxford, 1997), chap. 4.
[68] Art. 9(3), 2nd para. (OJ 1988 C151/4).

considered where the Commission so decided, having regard to the general developments in those industries in the Union. The Council, however, was opposed to listing relevant sectors, and so this part of the proposal was not approved by the Council.

While the Council was apparently unwilling to limit Objective 2 activities to regions with problems in given sectors, it was willing to limit such activities to regions having industrial problems of some kind. Consequently, areas having a share of industrial employment in total employment below the Union average were denied Objective 2 aid, even if unemployment there was far above the Union average.[69] For example, coastal resorts, even though they might be suffering economically, were outside the scope of this Objective, because tourism was not considered industrial.[70] Industry was taken to refer to mining and quarrying and utilities, manufacturing, and building and civil engineering. Service industries are not taken into account.[71] Moreover, certain urban zones were excluded, because their economic and social problems could not be attributed to industrial decline.

The original list of beneficiary regions was contained in Decision 89/288.[72] The draft list covered 25 cent of the Union population and had to be revised, in line with the "15 per cent principle", and limited to the parts of regions considered to be most seriously affected by industrial decline.[73] As a result, of the 900 areas originally proposed by the Member States for treatment as Objective 2 regions, only sixty were selected.[74] In 1990 the average unemployment rate in the selected regions was $1^1/4$ percentage points higher than the Union average (9.5 per cent. against 8.3 per cent.).[75]

For the future, the Commission envisaged that the list of eligible regions would continue to be compiled according to unemployment and industrial employment statistics.[76] However, it was not possible to identify, according to Union statistics, all the areas currently affected by industrial decline[77] or to allow for the anticipation of the consequences of new industrial change. The Commission sought, therefore, a measure of discretion, to be used in consultation with the Member States concerned, but with no easing of the

---

[69] Reply by Mr Millan to WQ 1445/92 (OJ 1992 C345/19) by Mr Max Simeoni.

[70] EEC regional development policy, House of Lords Select Committee on the European Communities, HL (1991–2) 20, 16.

[71] Commission Reply to WQ 2955/90 (OJ 1991 C195/21) by Lord Inglewood.

[72] Establishing an initial list of declining industrial areas concerned by Objective 2 (OJ 1989 L112/19). See, for 1997–9, Dec. 96/472 (OJ 1996 L193/54).

[73] Fourth periodic report on the social and economic situation and the development of the regions of the Community, COM(90)609, 56.

[74] Annual report on the implementation of the reform of the Structural Funds, COM(90)516, 31.

[75] Fourth periodic report on the social and economic situation and the development of the regions of the Community, COM(90)609, 54.

[76] Increased transparency is now required by Art. 9(3) of Reg. 2081/93 (OJ 1993 L193/5).

[77] See, regarding some parts of Western Germany, the Resolution of the European Parliament of 22 Jan. 1993 (OJ 1993 C42/228) on the regional and social redevelopment plan and the CSF for the areas of Germany included in Objective 2, para. 10.

geographical concentration. Otherwise, strict interpretation of the statistics would make it impossible to assist the regions most in need of help.[78]

Accordingly, the third indent of the second paragraph of Article 9(2) has been amended by Regulation 2081/93.[79] It now includes a reference to job losses brought about by industrial changes and changes in production systems, with a consequent serious worsening of unemployment in the areas concerned. The aim is to introduce greater flexibility, so that a Member State may submit for consideration areas vulnerable to industrial decline.[80]

Moreover, two new indents have been added to the second paragraph of Article 9(2). The first new indent refers to areas, especially urban areas,[81] with severe problems linked to the rehabilitation of large numbers of derelict industrial sites. The second new indent refers to other industrial or urban areas where the socio-economic impact of restructuring of the fisheries sector, assessed according to objective criteria, justifies assistance. In applying these criteria, the Commission will take account of how the national situations with respect to unemployment, industrialisation, and industrial decline compare with the Union average.

Aid Allocation

According to Decision 89/289,[82] no Objective 2 aid was allocated to Greece, Ireland, or Portugal. Most was allocated to the United Kingdom, Spain, and France, though all the more developed Member States received some assistance. This allocation resulted from a share-out between the Member States.[83] There was no direct proportionality between the allocation of aid per head in the regions concerned and the seriousness of unemployment.[84] In the case of the Luxembourg allocation, it was admitted that the national unemployment rate had been only around 1.6 per cent since 1983. Nevertheless, the employment situation in the two cantons concerned by Objective 2 could not be measured directly and was "masked" by the national figure. In the period from 1986 to 1989, over 2,700 jobs would have been lost, and new reductions (of about 2,000 jobs) had been announced by

---

[78] From the Single Act to Maastricht and beyond: the means to match our ambitions, COM(92)2000; and Community structural policies: assessment and outlook, COM(92)84, 38.

[79] OJ 1993 L193/5.

[80] Community Structural Fund operations 1994–9, COM(93)67, 10. Art. 9(5) of Reg. 2081/93 (OJ 1993 L193/5) provided for West Berlin to continue to be eligible for 3 years. This provision reflected the inclusion of the new *Länder* and East Berlin in Objective 1 and the concern of the Commission to secure coherence in the development efforts for Berlin and Brandenburg as a whole, COM(93)67, 13.

[81] E.g. an area of Madrid with a population of 5,000 persons is now covered by Objective 2. See Dec. 96/472 (OJ 1996 L193/54) establishing the list of declining industrial areas concerned by Objective 2 for the programming period 1997–9.

[82] Fixing an indicative allocation between Member States of 85% of the commitment operations of the ERDF under Objective 2 (OJ 1989 L113/29).

[83] Bull. EC 10–1989, 2.1.101.

[84] Annual report of the Court of Auditors for 1991 (OJ 1992 C330/1), para. 5.36.

the steel industry for the years 1990 to 1992. Moreover, the economic situation in the south of the country had implications for the industrial areas just across the border with France, especially in view of the close links with the Longwy area.[85] Apparently, then, existing unemployment rates did not have to be shown to be high relative to the Union average as a condition for the allocation of aid under Objective 2.

The Commission based its current allocation of Objective 2 aid[86] on the population in each Member State's eligible areas compared with the total Union population eligible for such aid. It then combined these figures with the unemployment rate of each area as a proportion of the average unemployment rate across all the Objective 2 areas.[87]

20.3.3 Objective 5b

According to Article 1 of the original version of Regulation 2052/88,[88] Objective 5b was concerned with promoting rural development by facilitating the structural adjustment of rural areas. As amended by Regulation 2081/93,[89] this provision now states that Objective 5b is concerned with promoting rural development by facilitating the development and structural adjustment of rural areas.

Regional Eligibility

Article 11(2) of Regulation 2052/88[90] provided that Objective 5b regions were to be selected taking into account in particular the degree to which they were rural in character; the number of persons occupied in agriculture; their level of economic and agricultural development; the extent to which they were peripheral; and their sensitivity to changes in the agricultural sector, especially in the context of reform of the common agricultural policy.

More details were provided in Regulation 4253/88.[91] According to Article 4(1), the regions that might receive assistance under Objective 5b had to satisfy each of three criteria. First, there had to be a high share of agricultural employment in total employment. Secondly, there had to be a low level of agricultural income, notably as expressed in terms of value added by agricultural work unit. Thirdly, there had to be a low level of socio-economic development assessed by reference to gross domestic product per inhabitant. Moreover, account was to

---

[85] *CSF 1989–91 for Converting the Regions Affected by Industrial Decline, Luxembourg* (EC Commission, Brussels, 1990), 11.

[86] Dec. 94/176 (OJ 1994 L82/35) fixing an indicative allocation by Member State of Structural Fund commitment appropriations under Objective 2. See for 1997–9, Dec. 96/468 (OJ 1996 L192/29).

[87] *European Report* 1921 (29 Jan. 1994).

[88] OJ 1988 L185/9.   [89] OJ 1993 L193/5.   [90] OJ 1988 L185/9.

[91] Laying down provisions for implementing Reg. 2052/88 as regards co-ordination of the activities of the different Structural Funds between themselves and with the operations of the EIB and the other existing financial instruments (OJ 1988 L374/1).

be taken of socio-economic parameters which indicated the seriousness of the general situation in the regions concerned and how it was developing.

It was also provided in Article 4(2) of the same Regulation that, on receipt of a reasoned request from a Member State, assistance might be extended to other rural areas with a low level of socio-economic development on the basis of one or more of the following criteria:

- low population density and/or significant depopulation trend in the regions concerned;
- peripheral nature in relation to major centres of economic and commercial activity in the Union;
- sensitivity to developments in agriculture, especially in the context of reform of the common agricultural policy, assessed on the basis of the trend in agricultural incomes and the size of the agricultural labour force;
- pressures exerted on the environment and on the countryside; and
- status within mountain or less-favoured areas classified pursuant to Directive 75/268.[92]

In selecting regions to benefit, the Commission was required by Article 4(4) of the Regulation to ensure that assistance was effectively concentrated on regions suffering from the most serious problems of rural development.[93] Subject to this general requirement, it seems that rural problems other than that of the low *per capita* gross domestic product traditionally associated with the "peripheral regions", such as the Mezzogiorno, could be tackled.

Certainly, the Commission considered that *per capita* gross domestic product was "neither a sufficient measure of the gravity of the situation of the areas concerned nor a suitable instrument for determining the allocation of aid among the various areas".[94] "Very qualitative" assessments, which left the authorities broad discretion and favoured political compromises, might be preferred.[95]

In the event, the regions originally selected and listed in Decision 89/426,[96] were in Belgium, Denmark, France, Germany, Italy, Luxembourg, the Netherlands, Spain, and the United Kingdom. Thus the regions selected were not confined to the traditional periphery of the Union.[97]

[92] On mountain and hill farming and farming in less favoured areas (OJ 1975 L128/1).

[93] Concentration was to take place within the context of reform of the CAP, but this requirement has been removed in Art. 11a(4) of Reg. 2081/93 (OJ 1993 L193/5).

[94] Annual report of the Court of Auditors for 1991, OJ 1992 C330/1, para. 7.18 (Commission Reply).

[95] D. Gadbin, 'Le Droit communautaire des structures agricoles: organisation ou dilution?' [1991] *RMC* 218–30, 224.

[96] Selecting rural areas eligible to receive Community assistance under Objective 5b (OJ 1989 L198/1). See, for 1994–9, Dec. 94/197 (OJ 1994 L96/1). See also Dec. 95/37 (OJ 1995 L49/65) establishing, for 1995–9 in Austria and Finland, the list of rural areas under Objective 5b; and Dec. 95/43 (OJ 1995 L92/29) establishing, for 1995–9 in Sweden, the list of rural areas under Objective 5b.

[97] Increased transparency in the selection process is now required by Art. 11a(3) of Reg. 2081/93 (OJ 1993 L193/5).

The Commission considered that intervention in such regions should be "boosted". Aid should be directed towards all rural regions of the Union but should be concentrated where the needs were greatest and the capacity to contribute at the national level was weakest.[98] The criteria for what constituted an eligible region should be applied more flexibly and the range of measures broadened.[99] Particular attention should be paid to problems of rural exodus.[100] Accordingly, studies were carried out regarding definition of Objective 5b regions.[101]

However, only limited changes have been made by Regulation 2081/93.[102] The regions that may now receive aid under Objective 5b are those which have a low level of socio-economic development assessed on the basis of gross domestic product per inhabitant. They must also satisfy at least two of the following criteria:

– high share of agricultural employment in total employment;
– low level of agricultural income, notably as expressed in terms of agricultural value added by agricultural work unit; and
– low population density and/or a significant depopulation trend.[103]

Other rural regions with a low level of socio-economic development may receive Objective 5b assistance,[104] if they are affected by one or more of six listed criteria. These criteria are the same as those in the Article 4(2) of Regulation 4253/88,[105] except that the depopulation criterion has now been moved to the first paragraph. Two new criteria have also been added to the second paragraph. The new criteria are the structure of agricultural holdings and the age structure of the gainfully employed agricultural labour force; and the socio-economic impact on the area, as measured by objective criteria, of the restructuring of the fisheries sector.[106]

Aid Allocation

Most aid under Objective 5b is allocated to France and Germany.[107] It is designed to support development of the non-agricultural sectors of the economy, particularly small and medium-sized enterprises; tourism and recreation; environmental protection; and human resources.[108]

---

[98] Reply by Mr MacSharry to WQ 2860/91 (OJ 1992 C168/24) by Mr John Cushnahan.
[99] Community finances between now and 1997, COM(92)2001, 24.
[100] *Europe* 5927 (25 Feb. 1993).
[101] Reply by Mr MacSharry to WQ 1039/91 (OJ 1991 C315/26) by Mr Verbeek. See also Community Structural Fund operations 1994–9, COM(93)67, 13.
[102] OJ 1993 L193/5.　　[103] *Ibid.*, Art. 11a(1).
[104] A reasoned request from a Member State is no longer required.
[105] OJ 1988 L374/1.　　[106] Art. 11a(2) of Reg. 2081/93 (OJ 1993 L193/5).
[107] Dec. 89/379 (OJ 1989 L180/54) fixing an indicative allocation between Member States of 85% of the commitment appropriations of the ERDF under Objective 5b. See, for 1994–9, Dec. 94/203 (OJ 1994 L97/43).
[108] Decs 90/557 to 90/600 (OJ 1990 L322/1) on the establishment of CSFs for Objective 5b regions.

However, Union practice has been criticised on the ground that the amount of support provided is calculated on a *per capita* basis.[109] Indicative allocations are based on the criterion of the total population of each region covered, adjusted to take account of the impact of reform of the common agricultural policy on employment in the respective agricultural sectors. Hence, the more underpopulated is the rural area, the smaller will be the amount of support provided.[110]

A more particular problem for rural regions in more developed Member States may derive from Article 13 of Regulation 2081/93.[111] According to this provision, aid is to be differentiated taking into account, *inter alia*, the financial capacity of the Member State concerned. Such capacity is to be assessed in the light of, in particular, the relative prosperity of that Member State.

20.3.4 Objective 6

The northern parts of Finland and Sweden comprise what the Commission, in its *Opinion on Sweden's Application for Membership*,[112] described as "Arctic and sub-Arctic regions".[113] They exhibit problems of low population density, unfavourable climate, and peripherality comparable with, though more severe than, those of the Highlands and Islands of Scotland. On the other hand, the Northern counties of Sweden may fail to qualify as Objective 1 or even Objective 5b regions by reference to *per capita* gross domestic product.[114] They may also benefit little from Objective 2 assistance, because there is limited industry to decline and unemployment problems may not be serious by Union standards.

To cater for their problems, Objective 6 was created. This Objective covers regions of Finland and Sweden with a population density limited to eight people per square kilometre.[115] Objective 1 rules apply to regions covered by Objective 6.[116]

20.3.5 Scope of Assistance

The scope of the assistance which the European Regional Development Fund may provide is outlined in Article 1 of Regulation 2083/93.[117]

---

[109] Future of rural society, House of Lords Select Committee on the European Communities, HL (1989–90) 80–I, 33.

[110] This criterion meant that the Highlands and Islands was effectively penalised by its sparsity of population. See EEC regional development policy, House of Lords Select Committee on the European Communities, HL (1991–2) 20, 17.

[111] OJ 1993 L193/5.   [112] Bull. EC, Supp. 5/92, 14.

[113] See, similarly, the *Opinion on Finland's Application for Membership*, Bull. EC, Supp. 6/92, 12.

[114] Note the GDP figures for Swedish regions published in *Norbotten inför EG–förhandlingen* (Lanstyrelsen Norbottens län, Luleå, 1992).

[115] Prot. 6 to the Accession Agreement, as amended by Dec. 95/1 (OJ 1995 L1/1).

[116] *Ibid.*, Art. 4.

[117] Amending Reg. 4254/88 laying down provisions for implementing Reg. 2052/88 as regards the ERDF (OJ 1993 L193/34).

Productive Investment

The Fund may participate in the financing of productive investment to enable the creation or maintenance of permanent jobs.[118] However, the regional development impact of such investment may be limited, because the proportion of supplies bought within the relevant region may not be significant. Even where purchases within the region are reasonably important in quantitative terms, the products bought may be mainly raw materials or products which have only been slightly processed. Little exploitation of existing industrial capabilities may be entailed. Far from securing the self-sustained growth of these areas, aid to the investments concerned may even have a negative effect on local labour markets, jeopardizing the small, local industries already in existence.[119]

Infrastructure Investment

The Fund may participate in the funding of the creation or modernisation of infrastructure which contributes to the development or conversion of the regions concerned.[120] A broader range of investments may be supported in Objective 1 regions than in Objective 2 or 5b regions.

In Objective 1 regions infrastructure investments contributing to increasing the economic potential, development, and structural adjustment of these regions may be supported. Where appropriate, investments contributing to the establishment and development of trans-European networks in the areas of transport, telecommunications, and energy infrastructures, may be included. Where the need is demonstrated, financing may also be provided for investments in the field of education and health which contribute to structural adjustment.[121]

In Objective 2 regions eligible infrastructure investments are not only those relating to the regeneration of areas suffering from industrial decline, including inner cities. They are also those which provide the basis for the creation or development of economic activity. In Objective 5b regions eligible infrastructure investments are those directly linked to economic activity which creates jobs other than in agriculture. Investments in communications infrastructure, on which the development of economic activity depends, may also be eligible in Objective 5b regions.[122]

"Endogenous Development"

The Fund may assist measures to exploit the potential for internally generated development of the regions concerned.[123] In particular, the Fund may

---

[118] *Ibid.*, Art. 1(a).
[119] R.P. Camagni, "Development Scenarios and Policy Guidelines for the Lagging Regions in the 1990s" [1992] *Regional Studies* 361–74.
[120] Art. 1(b) of Reg. 2083/93 (OJ 1993 L193/34).
[121] *Ibid.*, Art. 1(d). See also Art. 3(1)(d) of Reg. 2081/93 (OJ 1993 L193/5).
[122] Art. 1(b) of Reg. 2083/93 (OJ 1993 L193/34).
[123] Art. 3(1)(c) of Reg. 2081/93 (OJ 1993 L193/5).

support local development initiatives and the activities of small and medium-sized enterprises.[124] Such support may involve: assistance towards services for firms, particularly in the fields of management, study and research of markets, and services common to several firms; financing the transfer of technology, including in particular the collection and dissemination of information and financing the introduction of innovations in firms; improved access for firms to the capital market, particularly by the provision of guarantees and equity participation; direct aid to investment, where no aid scheme exists; and the provision of small-scale infrastructure.

Other Assistance

The Fund may assist the financing of two further kinds of investment. Thus it may assist investment contributing to regional development in the field of research and technological development.[125] It may also assist productive investment and investment in infrastructure aimed at environmental protection, according to the principles of sustainable development. Such investment must be linked with regional development.[126]

20.3.6 Forms of Assistance

Assistance from the European Regional Development Fund is to be provided in a variety of forms that reflect the nature of the operations concerned.[127] By a qualified majority and on a proposal from the Commission the Council may introduce other forms of assistance of the same type.[128]

Projects

The Fund may contribute to the financing of projects.[129] The projects may concern investments in infrastructure[130] or productive investments, to enable permanent jobs to be created or maintained.[131]

Regional Aid Schemes

The grant of Fund assistance to regional aid schemes of Member States shall constitute one of the main forms of incentive to investment in firms.[132] To decide the financial participation of the Fund, the Commission shall examine, with the competent authorities designated by the Member State, the characteristics of the aid scheme concerned. Account is to be taken of:

---

[124] Art. 1(c) of Reg. 2083/93 (OJ 1993 L193/34).
[125] *Ibid.*, Art. 1(e). The original Commission proposal of 12 Mar. 1993 (COM(93)67) had envisaged an express reference to the contribution of such measures to the implementation of the Union's multiannual framework programmes.
[126] Art. 1(f) of Reg. 2083/93 (OJ 1993 L193/34).
[127] Art. 5(1) of Reg. 2081/93 (OJ 1993 L193/5).
[128] *Ibid.*, Art. 5(2).   [129] Art. 5 of Reg. 2083/93 (OJ 1993 L193/34).   [130] *Ibid.*, Art. 1(b).
[131] *Ibid.*, Art. 1(a).   [132] *Ibid.*, Art. 4(1).

the relationship between the rate of aid and the socio-economic situation of the regions concerned and the consequent locational disadvantages for firms; the relationship between operating procedures and the types of aid, including rates, and the needs to be met; the priority given to small and medium-sized enterprises and to the encouragement of services supplied to them, such as management advice and market surveys; the economic repercussions of the aid scheme; and the characteristics and impact of any other regional aid scheme in the same region.[133]

Regional Operational Programmes

The Fund may contribute to the financing of regional operational programmes.[134] Such a programme may be undertaken not only on the initiative of the Member States but also on the initiative of the Commission in agreement with the Member State concerned.[135] A programme is defined as a series of consistent multiannual measures implemented through recourse to one or more of the Structural Funds and/or of the other financial instruments and the European Investment Bank.[136]

Global Grants

The Commission[137] may entrust to appropriate intermediaries,[138] including regional development bodies designated by the Member State in agreement with the Commission, the management of global grants.[139] Such grants are used primarily to assist local development initiatives. The intermediaries must be present or represented in the regions concerned, operate in the public interest, and associate adequately the socio-economic interests directly concerned by the implementation measures planned.[140] The procedures for the use of global grants shall be the subject of an agreement, concluded in agreement with the Member State concerned, between the Commission and the intermediary concerned. These procedures shall detail, in particular, the types of measures to be carried out, the criteria for choosing beneficiaries, the conditions and rates of Fund assistance, and the arrangements for monitoring use of the global grants.[141]

---

[133] *Ibid.*, Art. 4(2).   [134] *Ibid.*, Art. 3.

[135] See below, regarding programmes undertaken on the initiative of the Commission.

[136] Art. 5(5) of Reg. 2081/93 (OJ 1993 C193/5).

[137] On the initiative of the Member State or the Commission in agreement with the Member State concerned (Art. 6(3) of Reg. 2083/93 (OJ 1993 L193/34)).

[138] In Ireland, e.g., they are administered by Bord Failte Eireann and the Shannon Free Airport Development Company under the operational programme for tourism and are intended to assist private sector investments in tourism. See Commission Reply to WQ 2285/90 (OJ 1991 C161/9) by Mrs Jackson.

[139] See, regarding the role of such grants in supporting SMEs, Report on the ERDF 1991, COM(93)140, 2.

[140] Art. 6(1) of Reg. 2083/93 (OJ 1993 L193/34).   [141] *Ibid.*, Art. 6(2).

Studies and Pilot Schemes

The Fund may, using up to 1 per cent of its annual budget, contribute to the financing at Union level of studies and pilot schemes.[142]

According to Article 10(1)(a) of Regulation 2083/93,[143] the former should be studies on the Commission's initiative aiming to identify: the spatial consequences of measures planned by the national authorities, particularly major infrastructures, when their effects go beyond national boundaries; measures aiming to correct specific problems of the border regions within and outside the Union; and the elements necessary to establish a prospective outline of the utilisation of Union territory.

Pilot schemes should, according to Article 10(1)(b) of the same Regulation, constitute incentives to the creation of infrastructure, investment in firms, and other specific measures having a marked Union interest,[144] in particular in the border regions within and outside the Union; and encourage the pooling of experience and development co-operation between different Union regions[145] and innovative measures.[146]

Technical Assistance

The Fund may finance, up to a limit of 0.5 per cent. of its annual budget, the preparatory, accompanying, and assessment measures necessary for implementation of Regulation 2083/93.[147] The measures may be carried out by the Commission or by outside experts. They may include studies, such as those of a general nature concerning Union regional action. They may also include technical assistance or information measures, particularly measures to provide information for local and regional development agents.[148] They may be embodied within the sub-programmes of regional operational programmes or added to Community Support Frameworks.[149]

Community Initiatives

Community initiatives may be adopted by the Commission under Article

---

[142] A list of studies and pilot schemes supported under Art. 10 of Reg. 4254/88 (OJ 1988 L374/15) was provided in the Commission Reply to WQ 1866/90 (OJ 1991 C90/24) by Mr J.G. Urizza.

[143] OJ 1993 L193/34.

[144] See, e.g., the Call for proposals for pilot actions aiming at integrating the concept of the information society into regional development policies of less favoured regions pursuant to Art. 10 of the ERDF Reg. and Art. 6 of the ESF Reg. (OJ 1996 C253/27).

[145] See e.g. Call for proposals from networks of regional and local authorities wishing to implement joint pilot inter-regional co-operation projects for economic development in the cultural field under Art. 10 of the ERDF Reg. (OJ 1996 C253/26).

[146] See e.g. Innovative measures: new sources of employment, particularly local employment initiatives – call for proposals (OJ 1996 C253/29).

[147] OJ 1993 L193/34.

[148] *Ibid.*, Art. 7(1).

[149] Annual report of the Court of Auditors for 1993 (OJ 1994 C327/1), para. 7.68. CSFs are designed to programme assistance from the Structural Funds and other financial instruments.

11(1) of Regulation 2082/93,[150] and Article 3(2) of Regulation 2083/93.[151] According to the former provision, the Commission may, on its own initiative, propose to the Member States that they submit applications for assistance in respect of measures of significant interest to the Union which are not covered by regional development plans.[152] Such initiatives may be supported by a maximum of 1.9 per cent. of Structural Fund resources.[153]

For a limited part of the resources available, Article 11(2) of Regulation 2082/93[154] provides that Community initiatives may benefit areas other than those covered by Objectives 1, 2, and 5b. In the view of the Commission, the flexibility entailed will assist it in responding to new economic and social problems as they arise, including unforeseen industrial problems. As the Commission recognises, such problems may not necessarily be limited to areas covered by these Objectives.[155] In other words, effective implementation of Union policy may be found to demand exceptions from basic Union criteria for aid eligibility. However, this aspect of implementation of Community initiatives, given the limited resources available for their implementation, may be a symptom of, rather than a solution to, underlying problems in legislation governing the allocation and use of aid from the Fund.

Such initiatives shall be designed, within the framework of the tasks entrusted to the Fund by Article 3(1) of Regulation 2081/93,[156] to help resolve problems common to certain categories of region; to help resolve serious problems directly associated with the implementation of other Union policies and affecting the socio-economic situation of one or more regions; or to promote the application of Union policies at regional level.[157] These three categories relate, respectively, to regions with common problems, to regions dependent on declining sectors, and to regions which need assistance to implement Union policies.

As for regions with common problems, the Regis initiative[158] concerns Guadeloupe, French Guyana, Martinique, Reunion, the Canary Islands, the Azores, and Madeira. The Leader (*Liaison entre actions de développement de*

---

[150] Amending Reg. 4253/88 laying down provisions for implementing Reg. 2052/88 as regards co-ordination of the activities of the different Structural Funds between themselves and with the operations of the EIB and the other existing financial instruments (OJ 1993 L193/20).

[151] OJ 1993 L193/34.

[152] I.e. plans drawn up by Member States, on which CSFs or SPDs are formulated.

[153] Art. 12(5) of Reg. 2081/93 (OJ 1993 L193/5).

[154] OJ 1993 L193/20.

[155] Difficulties encountered in the implementation of the Interreg initiative (see below 510), where cross-border co-operation between eligible and non-eligible areas was involved, may also be removed. See Community Structural Funds 1994–9, COM(93)67, 22.

[156] OJ 1993 L193/5.

[157] *Ibid.*, Art. 5(5).

[158] Notice laying down guidelines for operational programmes in the framework of a Community initiative concerning the most remote regions, which Member States were invited to establish (OJ 1990 C196/15). See now Regis II, OJ 1994 C180/44.

l'économie rurale) initiative[159] concerns rural areas more generally and seeks to encourage integrated rural development at local level. The Urban initiative[160] concerns urban areas. Finally, the Interreg initiative[161] concerns co-operation between regions. It has been replaced by Interreg II,[162] which covers both cross-border co-operation and completion of energy networks.[163] A third "strand" – transnational co-operation on spatial planning – has now been added to the initiative.[164]

As regards regions dependent on declining industries, Resider II[165] seeks to assist the conversion of steel regions. The Rechar II initiative[166] seeks to assist the conversion of coal-mining regions. The Retex initiative[167] concerns the structural adjustment of the textile industry. The Pesca initiative[168] seeks to address the problems of "crisis" in the fishing industry. Finally, the Konver initiative[169] seeks to assist the diversification of economic activities in regions heavily dependent on the defence industry and to encourage the adjustment of commercially viable businesses in all sectors of industrial activities.

As regards regions needing assistance to implement Union policies, the Telematique initiative[170] concerned the accessibility of advanced telecommu-

---

[159] Notice laying down guidelines for integrated global grants for which Member States are invited to submit proposals in the framework of a Community initiative for rural development (OJ 1991 C73/33).

[160] Notice laying down guidelines for operational programmes which Member States are invited to establish in the framework of a Community initiative concerning urban areas (OJ 1994 C180/6).

[161] Notice laying down guidelines for operational programmes which Member States were invited to establish in the framework of a Community initiative concerning border areas (OJ 1990 C215/4).

[162] OJ 1994 C180/60.

[163] See, earlier, the Regen initiative: Notice laying down guidelines for operational programmes in the framework of a Community initiative concerning transmission and distribution networks for energy which Member States were invited to establish (OJ 1990 C326/7).

[164] Communication laying down guidelines for operational programmes which Member States are invited to establish in the framework of a Community Interreg initiative concerning transnational co-operation on spatial planning (OJ 1996 C200/23).

[165] Notice to Member States laying down guidelines for operational programmes or global grants which they are invited to establish in the framework of a Community initiative concerning the economic conversion of steel areas (OJ 1994 C180/22).

[166] Notice laying down guidelines for operational programmes in the framework of a Community initiative concerning the economic conversion of coal-mining areas, which Member States are invited to establish (OJ 1994 C180/26).

[167] Notice laying down guidelines for operational programmes which Member States are invited to establish within the framework of a Community initiative for regions heavily dependent on the textiles and clothing sector (OJ 1992 C142/5); and Notice to Member States laying down guidelines for the Retex initiative (OJ 1994 C180/17).

[168] Notice laying down guidelines for global grants or integrated operational programmes for which Member States are invited to submit applications for assistance within the framework of a Community initiative concerning the restructuring of the fisheries sector (OJ 1994 C180/1).

[169] Notice laying down guidelines for operational programmes or global grants which Member States are invited to establish in the framework of a Community initiative concerning defence conversion (OJ 1994 C180/18).

[170] Notice to Member States laying down guidelines for operational programmes in the framework of a Community initiative for regional development concerning services and networks related to data communication (OJ 1991 C33/7).

nications services. The Stride initiative[171] aimed to strengthen the research, technological, and innovatory capacity of Objective 1 regions, so that they were better placed to attract or retain technologically advanced activities in the productive sectors of the region and highly qualified personnel. The Prisma initiative[172] sought to assist enterprises in Objective 1 regions to adapt to the completion of the internal market, so that they could benefit fully from the opportunities which arose. The SME initiative, for small and medium-sized enterprises, is designed to take over the tasks of Telematique, Stride, and Prisma. It aims to stimulate such enterprises or service enterprises, particularly in the less-developed regions, to adapt to the single market and to ensure that they become internationally competitive.[173]

Integrated Development Operations

Article 13(1) of Regulation 2082/93[174] provides that at the initiative of a Member State or of the Commission pursuant to Article 11, which concerns Community initiatives, and in agreement with the Member State concerned, assistance may be implemented in the form of an integrated approach. Three conditions must be met. First, financing by more than one fund or at least one fund and one financial instrument other than a loan instrument must be involved.[175] Secondly, the measures to be financed by different funds or financial instruments must be mutually reinforcing, and significant benefits must be likely to accrue from close co-ordination between all the parties involved. Thirdly, the appropriate administrative structures must be provided at national, regional, and local level in the interests of integrated application of these measures.

In the implementation of an integrated approach the Commission shall ensure that Union assistance is provided in the most effective manner taking into account the special coordination effort required.[176] However, the legislation leaves implementation to the administrative practice of the Commission. The latter has been criticised for tending to rely on "multifund operational plans", made up of sub-programmes, each managed by one Fund.[177]

---

[171] Notice C(90)1562/2 (OJ 1990 C196/18) laying down guidelines for operational programmes which Member States were invited to establish, in the framework of a Community initiative concerning regional capacities for research, technology, and innovation.

[172] Notice laying down guidelines for operational programmes which Member States were invited to establish in the framework of a Community initiative concerning the preparation of enterprises for the single market (OJ 1991 C33/9).

[173] Notice to Member States laying down guidelines for operational programmes or global grants which they are invited to propose in the framework of a Community initiative concerning the adaptation of SMEs to the single market (OJ 1994 C180/10).

[174] OJ 1993 L193/20.

[175] E.g., the IDO for Merseyside brought together the ERDF and the ESF to co-finance measures in 1989–91. Details were given in the Reply by Mr Millan to WQ 1776/91 (OJ 1992 C78/24) by Mr Kenneth Stewart.

[176] Art. 13(3) of Reg. 2082/93 (OJ 1993 L193/20).

[177] Report of the Committee on Budgetary Control on the management of the budget of the Structural Funds within the framework of the reform: assessment and outlook, EP Doc. A–0191/92, 12.

20.4 EAGGF, Guidance Section

The tasks of the Guidance Section of the European Agricultural Guidance and Guarantee Fund are, according to Article 3(3) of Regulation 2081/93:[178] strengthening and reorganising agricultural and forestry structures, including those for the marketing and processing of agricultural and forestry products; helping to offset the effects of natural handicaps on agriculture; ensuring the conversion of agricultural production and fostering the development of supplementary activities for farmers; helping to ensure a fair standard of living for farmers; and helping to develop the social fabric of rural areas, to safeguard the environment, and to preserve the countryside, *inter alia*, by securing the conservation of natural agricultural resources. These tasks are to be performed in pursuit of Objective 5a as well as Objectives 1 and 5b. Actions under Objective 5a and Objective 5b are intended to be complementary.[179]

20.4.1 Objective 5a

Objective 5a is promoting rural development by speeding up the adjustment of agricultural structures in the framework of the reform of the common agricultural policy.[180] It is the responsibility of the Guidance Section of the European Agricultural Guidance and Guarantee Fund, though the Financial Instrument for Fisheries Guidance has now become responsible for fisheries.[181]

Eligibility

Where the Guidance Section provides assistance in pursuit of Objective 5a, eligibility depends on the functional requirements of the common measures concerned.[182]

Aid Allocation

Indicative aid allocations by Member State have been made. The indicative allocations are based principally on the need for continuity[183] regarding the use of resources in previous programming periods and the specific structural needs of agriculture.[184]

---

[178] OJ 1993 L193/5.

[179] Fourth periodic report on the social and economic situation and the development of the regions of the Community, COM(90)609, 55. See also Report on the EAGGF Guidance Section 1992, COM(94)261.

[180] See sect. 21.1 below.   [181] Art. 2(1) of Reg. 2080/93 (OJ 1993 L193/1).

[182] Art. 2 of Reg. 2085/93 (OJ 1993 L193/44) amending Reg. 4256/88 laying down provisions for implementing Reg. 2052/88 as regards the EAGGF, Guidance Section.

[183] Art. 12(4) of Reg. 2081/93 (OJ 1993 L193/5).

[184] Dec. 94/279 (OJ 1994 L120/50) establishing the indicative allocation by Member State of the commitment appropriations from the Structural Funds for the agricultural part of Objective 5a except for those fields covered by Objective 1 for 1994–9.

Scope of Assistance

In pursuit of Objective 5a, the Fund may finance "market-policy accompanying measures" contributing to re-establishing balance between production and market capacity; measures to support farm incomes and to maintain viable agricultural communities in mountain, hill, or less-favoured areas by means of agricultural aid, such as compensation for natural handicaps; concrete measures to encourage the installation of young farmers; and measures to encourage assistance to farmers and for the creation of groupings with a view to improving production conditions. Provision for aid to such measures implicitly confirms the rejection of the market mechanism as a resource allocation device implicit in traditional arrangements for the grant of aid by the Guidance Section. Other measures are aimed in part at smoothing natural adjustment processes in a declining sector. They include equally traditional measures to improve the efficiency of the structures of holdings as well as preserving and improving the natural environment; to improve the marketing and processing of agricultural products; and to encourage the establishment of producer groups.[185]

Accordingly, Regulation 950/97[186] provides for aid for investments in agricultural holdings;[187] setting-up aid for young farmers;[188] aid for the introduction of accounting practices;[189] setting up aid for farmers' groups;[190] setting-up aid for farm relief services;[191] aid for farm-management services;[192] aid to farmers in less-favoured agricultural areas;[193] and aid for adjustment of vocational training to the requirements of modern agriculture.[194]

Moreover, Regulation 951/97[195] concerns the improvement and rationalisation of the treatment, processing, and marketing of agricultural products. Aid may be granted for investments helping to guide production in keeping with foreseeable market trends or encouraging the development of new outlets for agricultural products; investments relieving the intervention mechanisms of the market organisations by furthering long-term structural improvement where this is needed; investments in regions which are faced with special problems in adapting to the economic consequences of developments on the agricultural markets and investments of benefit to such regions; investments helping to improve or rationalise marketing channels or processing procedures for agricultural products; investments helping to improve the quality, presentation, and preparation of products or encouraging a better use of by-products particularly by recycling waste; investments

---

[185] Art. 2 of Reg. 2085/93 (OJ 1993 L193/44). See also Reg. 952/97 (OJ 1997 L142/30) on producer groups and associations thereof.

[186] On improving the efficiency of agricultural structures (OJ 1997 L142/1).

[187] *Ibid.*, Arts. 4–9.   [188] *Ibid.*, Arts. 10–11.   [189] *Ibid.*, Art. 13.   [190] *Ibid.*, Art. 14.

[191] *Ibid.*, Art. 15.   [192] *Ibid.*, Art. 16.   [193] *Ibid.*, Arts. 17–25.   [194] *Ibid.*, Arts. 26–28.

[195] On improving the processing and marketing conditions for agricultural products (OJ 1997 L142/22).

contributing to the adjustment of sectors facing new situations as a result of reform of the common agricultural policy; investments helping to facilitate the adoption of new technologies relating to environmental protection; or investments encouraging the improvement and monitoring of quality and of health conditions.[196] More detailed criteria for the grant of aid are provided by Decision 94/173.[197]

Forms of Assistance

Under Regulation 950/97[198] the Guidance Section part finances national aid schemes by reimbursing expenditure incurred by Member States.[199] Under Regulation 951/97[200] it provides assistance through operational programmes and global grants.[201] It may also contribute to technical assistance and information operations and provide support for studies or pilot schemes concerning the adjustment of agricultural structures and the promotion of rural development at Union level.[202]

20.4.2 Objectives 1 and 5b

Within the context of its contribution to achieving Objective 1, Article 3(1) of Regulation 2085/93[203] provides that the Guidance Section of the Fund may finance measures for sustainable development of the rural environment. These measures may aim at developing and strengthening agricultural and forestry structures; or maintaining, enhancing, and restoring the landscape. In particular, they are to tackle the backwardness of agricultural structures.[204]

Eligibility

Where the Guidance Section provides assistance in pursuit of Objective 1 or 5b, regional criteria are applicable.[205]

Aid Allocation

Indicative aid allocations by Member State have been made. The indicative allocations are based principally on the need for continuity[206] regarding the use of resources in previous programming periods and the specific structural needs of agriculture. They may entail higher levels of aid in Objective 1 regions than in Objective 5b regions.[207]

---

[196] *Ibid.*, Art. 1(2).

[197] On the selection criteria to be adopted for investments for improving the processing and marketing conditions for agriculture and forestry products (OJ 1994 L79/29).

[198] OJ 1997 L142/1.   [199] *Ibid.*, Art. 2.   [200] OJ 1997 L142/22.   [201] *Ibid.*, Art. 9.

[202] Art. 8 of Reg. 2085/93 (OJ 1993 L193/44). See, e.g., Call for proposals relating to the adjustment of agricultural structures and the promotion of rural development (OJ 1994 C303/17).

[203] Amending Reg. 4256/88 laying down provisions for implementing Reg. 2052/88 as regards the EAGGF, Guidance Section (OJ 1993 L193/44).

[204] *Ibid.*, Art. 3.   [205] Sect. 20.3 above.   [206] Art. 12(4) of Reg. 2081/93 (OJ 1993 L193/5).

[207] Reg. 223/90 (OJ 1990 L22/62) fixing the rates of Community part financing for the measures referred to in Regs. 797/85, 1096/88, 1360/78, 389/82, and 1696/71.

Scope of Assistance

According to Article 5 of Regulation 2085/93,[208] in pursuit of Objective 1 the Fund may support the conversion, diversification, reorientation, and adjustment of production potential, including the production of non-food agricultural products; promotion of local agricultural and forestry products; development of rural infrastructures; encouragement of diversification; and the renovation and development of villages and the protection and conservation of the rural heritage, to the extent that financing is not provided by the European Regional Development Fund under Regulation 2083/93;[209] reparcelling and associated work; individual or collective land or pasture improvement; irrigation; encouragement for tourist and craft investments; restoration of agricultural and forestry production potential after natural disasters and the introduction of appropriate prevention measures in ultra-peripheral areas particularly at risk from such disasters; development and exploitation of woodlands and protection of the environment; maintenance of the countryside and restoration of landscapes, to the extent that financing is not provided for under measures accompanying reform of the common agricultural policy; development of agricultural and forestry advisory services and the improvement of facilities for agricultural and forestry vocational training; measures in the area of forestry technological research and development; and financial engineering measures for agricultural and agri-food businesses.[210] Such measures may also be adopted in pursuit of Objective 5b.[211]

Forms of Assistance

Intervention pursuant to Objectives 1 and 5b is in the main to take the form of operational programmes, including those using integrated approaches, and global grants.[212] In addition, the Fund can contribute up to 1 per cent of its resources to pilot projects concerning development of rural areas, including forestry development; technical assistance and preparatory studies; evaluation studies; demonstration projects for farmers; and measures necessary for diffusion of results of work and experience regarding improvement of agricultural structures.[213]

20.5 European Social Fund

Article 123 of the EC Treaty provides for the European Social Fund to improve employment opportunities for workers in the common market and to contribute thereby to raising the standard of living. It shall aim to render the employment of workers easier and to increase their geographical and

---

[208] OJ 1993 L193/44.   [209] OJ 1993 L193/34.
[210] Art. 5 of Reg. 2085/93 (OJ 1993 L193/44).
[211] *Ibid.*, Art. 6.   [212] *Ibid.*, Arts. 4 and 6.   [213] *Ibid.*, Art. 8.

occupational mobility within the Union. It shall also aim to facilitate their adaptation to industrial changes and to changes in production systems, in particular through vocational training and retraining. The Fund is responsible for Objectives 3 and 4 and contributes to the other Objectives of the Structural Funds.

20.5.1 Objectives 3 and 4

Objective 3 concerns combating long-term unemployment and facilitating integration into working life of young people and of persons exposed to exclusion from the labour market.[214] Objective 4 concerns facilitating the adaptation of workers of either sex to industrial changes and to changes in production systems.[215] The aim is to forestall the effects of such changes on unemployment.[216] It is envisaged that the Fund will address the underlying causes of problems relating to industrial adaptation and not deal with short-term, market-related symptoms. At the same time, it should meet the general needs of workers resulting from changes in production systems identified or predicted and should not be designed to benefit a single firm or a particular industry.[217]

According to the Commission, Objective 3 supports and strengthens policies which are already well established in Member States. In contrast, Objective 4 "represents a specific approach to the employment, training, and competitiveness problem".[218]

20.5.2 Personal Eligibility

Detailed rules regarding persons eligible for aid from the Fund are contained in Regulation 2084/93.[219]

Objective 3

Under Objective 3 the following persons are eligible: unemployed persons exposed to long-term unemployment; young people in search of employment; persons exposed to exclusion from the labour market; and women not

---

[214] See e.g. the Call for proposals for pilot actions aiming at integrating the concept of the information society into regional development policies of less favoured regions pursuant to Art. 10 of the ERDF Reg. and Art. 6 of the ESF Reg. (OJ 1995 C253/27).

[215] Art. 1(3) and (4) of Reg. 2081/93 (OJ 1993 L193/5). See e.g. the Call for proposals for pilot projects and demonstration projects concerning innovative schemes for women in agricultural areas (OJ 1996 C284/21).

[216] Opinion of the Economic and Social Committee of 30 Apr. 1992 (CES(92)501) on the Commission document "From the Single Act to Maastricht and beyond: the means to match our ambitions", 7. See, more particularly, the Council Resolution of 16 May 1994 (OJ 1994 C149/1) on the automobile industry, para. I.9.

[217] Operation of the Community Structural Funds, COM(93)124, 15.

[218] ESF – the new Objective 4, COM(94)510, 3–4.

[219] OJ 1993 L193/39.

possessing vocational qualifications or returning to the labour market after a period of absence.[220]

Objective 4

Under Objective 4 persons of either sex needing to adapt to changed conditions are eligible. In particular, persons threatened with unemployment or faced with industrial changes and changes in production systems are eligible.[221]

20.5.3 Aid Allocation

At least 80 per cent of the total resources for Objectives 3 and 4 must be allocated to Objective 3, "in view of the seriousness of the unemployment problem".[222] In practice, 35 per cent of spending under Objective 3 is targeted on promoting the occupational integration of young people.[223] Most aid has been allocated to the United Kingdom and France. However, all Member States whose territory is not entirely covered by Objective 1 have been allocated some aid.[224]

20.5.4 Scope of Assistance

In pursuit of Objective 3, the Fund is to assist vocational training; temporary employment aids; and the development of appropriate training, employment, and support structures.[225] In pursuit of Objective 4, assistance is to cover anticipation of labour market trends and vocational qualification requirements; vocational training and retraining, guidance, and counselling; and the improvement and development of appropriate training systems.[226]

Further measures are envisaged in regions covered by Objectives 1, 2, or 5b. In these regions the Fund is to support employment growth and stability, particularly through continuing training and vocational guidance, and is to boost human potential in research, science, and technology.[227] In Objective 1 regions it is also to strengthen and improve education and training systems; and to contribute to development through the training of public officials.[228]

The Fund may grant assistance towards expenditure to cover the income and related costs as well as subsistence and travel costs of people participating in the above actions; support the preparation, operation, management, and evaluation of operations existing in the Member States;[229] and provide technical assistance.[230]

---

[220] *Ibid.*, Art. 1(1).   [221] *Ibid.*, Art. 1(2).

[222] Statement regarding Objective 3 in the Minutes of the meeting between the European Parliament, the Council, and the Commission of 12 July 1993 (OJ 1993 C255/17).

[223] Reply by Mrs Cresson to WQ E–0783/96 (OJ 1996 C297/25) by Amedeo Amadeo.

[224] *EU General Report 1994* (EC Commission, Brussels, 1995), 155.

[225] Art. 1(1) of Reg. 2084/93 (OJ 1993 L193/39).

[226] *Ibid.*, Art. 1(2). Cf. the "incentive measures" envisaged in Art. 129 EC.

[227] Art. 1(3) of Reg. 2084/93 (OJ 1993 L193/39).   [228] *Ibid.*, Art. 1(4).   [229] *Ibid.*, Art. 2(1).

[230] *Ibid.*, Art. 2(2).

20.5.5 Forms of Assistance

Operational programmes and global grants constitute the main forms of assistance.[231] The Fund may also participate, with up to 5 per cent of its resources, in financing innovatory measures; transfer of knowledge between undertakings; guidance and advice for the reintegration of the long-term unemployed; and measures of preparation, accompaniment, and management necessary for implementation of other Fund operations.[232] In addition, Community initiatives, such as the Adapt initiative and the initiative on Employment and Development of Human Resources, may be adopted.

Adapt

The Adapt initiative[233] is intended to serve as a catalyst for Union-wide innovation as well as for the organised transfer of expertise and the dissemination of good practice between Member States. It seeks to accelerate the adaptation of the workforce to industrial change; to increase the competitiveness of industry, services, and commerce; to prevent unemployment by developing the workforce through improving the qualifications of workers and their "internal and external flexibility" and ensuring greater occupational mobility; and to anticipate and accelerate the development of new jobs and new activities, particularly labour-intensive ones, including exploitation of the potential of small and medium-sized enterprises. Attention is to be given to actions aimed at promoting equal opportunities for women.[234] The initiative is applicable to the whole territory of the Union, but particular emphasis is to be placed on the needs of the less favoured regions.[235]

A further "priority" within this initiative – Adapt-bis – (building the information society) has been adopted.[236] It is to facilitate the transition to the information society and minimise the social exclusion effects which can result from it.[237] Eligible measures must have "some specific features". Thus they must encourage a more active and co-ordinated approach at local level. Such an approach is intended to have a greater employment impact by involving in the planning, implementation, and evaluation of the measures all relevant actors designated by the Member State, including local and regional authorities, economic and social partners, and training bodies.[238]

---

[231] *Ibid.*, Art. 5(1).   [232] *Ibid.*, Art. 6(1).

[233] Communication laying down guidelines for operational programmes or global grants which Member States are invited to propose within the framework of the Community initiative, Adaptation of the Workforce to Industrial Change, aimed at promoting employment and the adaptation of the workforce to industrial change (OJ 1994 C180/30).

[234] *Ibid.*, para. 6.   [235] *Ibid.*, para. 8.

[236] Communication laying down amended guidelines for operational programmes or global grants which Member States are invited to propose within the framework of a Community initiative on employment and development of human resources aimed at promoting employment growth mainly through the development of human resources (OJ 1996 C200/7).

[237] *Ibid.*, para. 4.   [238] *Ibid.*, para. 7(d).

Employment and Development of Human Resources

The initiative on Employment and Development of Human Resources[239] aims to contribute to the development of human resources and to improve the working of the labour market. It is intended thereby to enhance employment growth, to promote social solidarity in the Union, and to promote equal opportunities for women on the labour market.[240] It is applicable throughout the Union territory, but particular emphasis is to be given to the needs of less favoured regions. Hence, some measures will be limited to Objective 1, 2, or 5b regions.[241] The allocation of aid among Member States will be based on the relative severity of structural problems, particularly unemployment levels, as well as the quality of proposals submitted.[242]

A further "strand" – Integra – has been added to this initiative. This strand is designed to promote measures to improve the access to the labour market and the employability of vulnerable groups who are excluded from this market or risk being excluded from it.[243]

20.6 Sectoral Instruments

The operations of sectoral instruments entail that Union aid may be allocated by reference to requirements of the relevant sectoral policy. These requirements may be integral elements of common policies for which the EC or ECSC Treaty provides an express basis. They may also reflect responses in Union practice to the needs of "growth" sectors[244] or the problems of declining sectors, such as oil refining[245] or wool production.[246]

Indeed, in October 1978 the Commission presented the Council with a proposal[247] for granting aid to assist industry generally in its restructuring

---

[239] Communication laying down guidelines for operational programmes or global grants which Member States are invited to propose within the framework of the Community initiative on Employment and the Development of Human Resources aimed at promoting employment growth mainly through the development of human resources (OJ 1994 C180/36).

[240] *Ibid.*, para. I.3.　　[241] *Ibid.*, para. III.7.　　[242] *Ibid.*, para. VI.17.

[243] Communication laying down guidelines for operational programmes or global grants which Member States are invited to propose within the framework of the Community initiative on Employment and the Development of Human Resources aimed at promoting employment growth mainly through the development of human resources (OJ 1996 C200/13).

[244] See e.g. Dec. 92/421 (OJ 1992 L231/26) on a Community action plan to assist tourism; the proposal of 6 June 1996 (OJ 1996 C222/9) for a decision on a first multiannual programme to assist European tourism – Philoxenia (1997–2000); and Art. B5–325 "Community measures to assist tourism" in the Budget for 1997 (OJ 1997 L44/3).

[245] Budget for 1979 (OJ 1979 L23/3), Item 3751.

[246] Resolution of the European Parliament of 19 Apr. 1996 (OJ 1996 C141/250) on the need for support measures for producers and processors of European wool.

[247] Proposal of 31 Oct. 1978 (OJ 1978 C272/3) for a Reg. on Community aid for industrial restructuring and conversion; and Item 3750 of the Budget for 1979 (OJ 1979 L23/3).

efforts,[248] the sectors concerned to be determined by the Council.[249] If the employment situation in the region of the undertaking to be restructured was so serious as to justify aid and if jobs had not been found for the labour made redundant, aid could also be granted for conversion to other sectors.[250] The aid envisaged could take the form of investment premiums or interest rebates on loans.[251] However, this proposal was not accepted by the Council.

Article 130(1) of the EC Treaty now provides that the Union and Member States are to aim at speeding up the adjustment of industry to structural changes. The implication is that the Union funds are to play a role in tackling adjustment problems. However, it is stipulated in Article 130(3) of the Treaty that this provision shall not provide a basis for the introduction by the Union of any measures which would lead to a distortion of competition.

20.6.1 Financial Instrument for Fisheries Guidance

Operations in favour of fishery structures are provided for in Regulation 3699/93,[252] fall within Objective 5a,[253] and are funded by the Financial Instrument for Guidance in the Fisheries Sector. Such funding is apparently designed to ensure that specific problems of the fishing industry are taken into account more effectively than in the case of aid from the Guidance Section of the European Agricultural Guidance and Guarantee Fund, which is essentially concerned with farming.

Objectives

The Commission favoured the creation of Objective 6 of the Structural Funds, which would have covered structural measures in the fishing industry.[254] However, the Member States apparently proved unenthusiastic about the idea of creating a new Objective for this purpose, and the idea was dropped by the Commission. Instead, the Commission took note[255] of the conclusion of the Edinburgh European Council that "appropriate attention should be given to the needs of areas dependent on fishing within the relevant Objectives".[256] Hence, Objective 5a was redefined to refer to fishing,[257] with a view to integration of fisheries policy and "the Union's cohesion effort".[258]

---

[248] Art. 1(1) of the proposal of 31 Oct. 1978 (OJ 1978 C272/3). See also the European Parliament Resolution of 22 Apr. 1982 (OJ 1982 C125/119) on the European Parliament's guidelines for the Budget for 1983, para. 20.

[249] Art. 1(2) of the proposal of 31 Oct. 1978 (OJ 1978 C272/3).

[250] *Ibid.*, Art. 2(2).   [251] *Ibid.*, Art. 3.

[252] Laying down the criteria and arrangements regarding Community structural assistance in the fisheries and aquaculture sector and the processing and marketing of its products (OJ 1993 L346/1).

[253] *Ibid.*, Art. 9(1).

[254] Community finances between now and 1997, COM(92)2001, 25.

[255] Community Structural Fund operations 1994–9, COM(93)67, 11.

[256] Conclusions of the Presidency (Bull. EC 12–1992, I.55).

[257] Art. 1(5) of Reg. 2081/93 (OJ 1993 L193/5).

[258] Community Structural Fund operations 1994–9, COM(93)67, 11.

In implementation of Objective 5a the Financial Instrument for Fisheries Guidance is to contribute to achieving a sustainable balance between fishery resources and their management. At the same time, it is to strengthen the competitiveness of structures and the development of economically viable businesses in the fisheries sector. It is also to improve market supply and the value added to fisheries and aquaculture products.[259]

Eligibility

It is recognised that fisheries problems may not be separable from the more general regional problems of areas dependent on fishing. Hence, assistance from the Financial Instrument for Fisheries Guidance may be complemented by assistance from the Structural Funds, notably the European Regional Development Fund. Most areas suffering from decline in fishing and fish processing activities are likely to be covered by Objective 1, 2, or 5b. Restructuring problems in the sector are, therefore, taken into account in the overall assessment of the infrastructure, training, and job-creation needs in these areas.

Moreover, areas which were not already covered by these Objectives may be brought within their scope. Their selection is based on "simple socio-economic parameters such as the relative and absolute number of jobs in the fisheries sector and the contribution to the local economy".[260] The question whether they are included under Objective 2 or 5b depends essentially on whether the redevelopment effort required is based on industrial and urban development or on rural development.

Aid Allocation

Indicative allocations for Objective 5a (fisheries) have been made to Member States.[261] For Objective 1 regions aid allocations are part of the general assistance programmes under this Objective. Elsewhere allocations are based on the importance of the fishing industry in the Member State concerned in comparison with all the regions outside Objective 1 and the structural situation of this industry in that Member State.[262]

Scope of Assistance

Assistance may be granted under Regulation 2080/93[263] for the implementation of measures directly contributing towards ensuring compliance with the requirements of the common fisheries policy in relation to: redeployment

---

[259] Art. 1(2) of Reg. 2081/93 (OJ 1993 L193/5).

[260] Community Structural Fund operations 1994–9, COM(93)67, 12.

[261] Dec. 94/447 (OJ 1994 L183/50) establishing the indicative allocation by Member State of the commitment appropriations from the Structural Funds for Objective 5a (fisheries structures) 1994–9.

[262] Structural Funds, adaptation of fisheries structures (Objective 5a): allocation of financial resources between Member States, COM(94)421, 2.

[263] Laying down provisions for implementing Reg. 2081/93 as regards the FIFG (OJ 1993 L193/1).

operations; temporary joint enterprises; joint ventures; and adjustment of capacities.[264] Assistance may also be granted for: restructuring and renewal of the fishing fleet; modernisation of the fishing fleet; improvement of the conditions under which fishery and agricultural products are processed and marketed; development of aquaculture and structural works in coastal waters; exploratory fishing; facilities at fishing ports; search for new markets; and "specific measures".[265]

It seems from Regulation 3699/93[266] that the last category of measures may include aid to short-term operations of collective interest undertaken by "members of the trade"[267] and aid for the temporary cessation of activities.[268]

In addition, socio-economic measures may be assisted. In particular, aid may be granted to assist: early retirement schemes for fishermen; individual compensatory payments to fishermen whose vessel is permanently withdrawn from fishing or transferred to a third country; and establishment of bad weather unemployment funds and mechanisms for the financial compensation of fishermen, when the market value of products landed fluctuates sharply.[269]

Forms of Assistance

Assistance may take the form of part-financing of operational programmes; part-financing of national aid schemes; provision of global grants; part-financing of projects; and support for technical assistance.[270]

20.6.2 ECSC Assistance

According to Article 5 of the ECSC Treaty, the European Coal and Steel Community is to place financial resources at the disposal of coal and steel undertakings for their investment and to bear part of the cost of readaptation.

Objectives

Article 54 of the ECSC Treaty envisages aid to promote the general objectives referred to in Article 46. The objectives referred to are: modernisation, long-term planning of manufacture, and expansion of productive capacity in the coal and steel industries.

More particularly, Article 56(1) envisages readaptation aid. Such aid is designed to assist adjustment to new processes or equipment which lead to

---

[264] *Ibid.*, Art. 2(1).

[265] *Ibid.*, Art. 3(1). See e.g. Dec. 97/292 (OJ 1997 L121/20) on a specific measure to encourage Italian fishermen to diversify out of certain fishing activities.

[266] Laying down the criteria and arrangements regarding Community structural assistance in the fisheries and aquaculture sector and the processing and marketing of its products (OJ 1993 L346/1).

[267] *Ibid.*, Art. 13.   [268] *Ibid.*, Art. 14.

[269] *Ibid.*, Art. 14a, as introduced by Reg. 2719/95 (OJ 1995 L283/3), amending Reg. 3699/93.

[270] Art. 3(2) of Reg. 3699/93 (OJ 1993 L346/1).

an exceptionally large reduction in labour requirements in the coal or steel industry, making it particularly difficult in one or more areas to re-employ redundant workers. Article 56(2), in turn, recognises that fundamental changes[271] in market conditions for the coal or the steel industry may compel some undertakings permanently to discontinue, curtail, or change their activities. It envisages aid to promote the rationalisation of the market necessitated by such changes.[272] Under both paragraphs the aid is to provide social protection for workers affected by restructuring and to promote the reintegration of these workers into productive life by facilitating their access to new employment.[273]

Eligibility

Basically, only coal and steel undertakings and workers in these industries are eligible for ECSC assistance. However, under Article 54(2) of the Treaty the Commission may, with the unanimous consent of the Council, also provide assistance to other industries, where the coal and steel industries will benefit indirectly.

Aid Allocation

ECSC aid is to be allocated according to sectoral needs. In practice, however, the allocation may be controversial. For example, the lack of geographical balance in the distribution of aid under Article 56(2) of the ECSC Treaty has been criticised.[274]

Scope of Assistance

Under Article 54(1) of the ECSC Treaty the Commission may assist investment programmes of coal[275] or steel undertakings.[276] Under Article 54(2) the Commission may, with the unanimous consent of the Council, go further. It may assist the financing of works and installations which contribute, directly or indirectly, to increasing production, reducing the production costs, or facilitating the marketing of ECSC products. Hence,

[271] I.e. structural rather than conjunctural changes. See R. Quadri, R. Monaco, and A. Trabucchi, *Trattato istitutivo della Comunità europea del carbone e dell'acciaio: comentario* (Guiffré, Milan, 1970), ii, 734.

[272] *Procedure for Amendment Pursuant to Art. 95(3) and (4) ECSC* [1960] ECR 39, 51.

[273] Procedures concerning the social measures in connection with the restructuring of the coal industry (1994–7) (OJ 1994 C108/3). Cf., regarding aid for maintenance of employment during a "crisis", Art. 58(2) ECSC.

[274] Annual report of the Court of Auditors concerning the ECSC (for 1993) (OJ 1994 C346/1), para. 2.27.

[275] Industrial loans carrying interest rebates available to the coal industry from the Commission pursuant to Art. 54(1) ECSC (OJ 1988 C131/2). See, more particularly, Granting of industrial loans at reduced interest rates under Art. 54 ECSC for safety and hygiene purposes and particularly for the prevention of nuisances (OJ 1974 C146/1).

[276] Industrial loans at reduced rates granted by the EC Commission to the iron and steel industry under Art. 54 ECSC (OJ 1980 C99/2).

"consumption of Community coal" loans,[277] "consumption of Community steel" loans,[278] which may benefit major infrastructure projects, and "raw materials" loans may be granted.[279] Loans may also be granted under Article 53b, which envisages making financial arrangements necessary for performance of ECSC tasks, and "equalisation payments" may also be financed.[280]

More particularly, Article 55(2)(b) and (c) provide that aid may be granted to technical and economic research. Such aid must relate to the production and increased use of coal and steel and to occupational safety in the coal and steel industries. The principles of research policy were first laid down in a communication on requests and the grant of financial aid for technical and economic research (coal, iron, and steel).[281] There are now separate guidelines for coal[282] and steel.[283]

At the same time, assistance under Article 53a may be used to facilitate implementation of closure programmes in the steel industry.[284] Moreover, assistance under Article 56(2)(a)[285] may be used to cofinance productive investment projects[286] or programmes[287] which help to create new and economically sound activities, to expand existing activities or to transform enterprises which could be expected to generate additional employment.[288]

Low-interest housing loans may also be made under Article 54(2), though it seems that they could also be granted under Article 54(1).[289] They are designed to facilitate the restructuring of coal and steel industries. They are also designed to prevent the deterioration of industrial areas dominated by

[277] Industrial loans at reduced rates of interest available under Art. 54(2) ECSC for investments aimed at promoting the consumption of Community coal (OJ 1982 C343/2).

[278] Loans which may be granted pursuant to Art. 54(2) ECSC for investment aimed at promoting the consumption of Community steel (OJ 1987 C291/3).

[279] Future of the ECSC Treaty borrowing/lending activity, COM(93)512. Loans are now only granted for large infrastructure projects of particular Union interest. See Adjustment of borrowing and lending policy with a view to the expiry of the ECSC Treaty (23 July 2002) (OJ 1994 C175/5).

[280] Art. 62 ECSC. See, e.g., Dec. 22/54 (JOCECA 1954 286) establishing a financial mechanism to allow for the equal distribution of scrap imported from third countries. In such circumstances the "common interest" may have priority over "certain individual interests". See Case 15/57 *Cie des Hauts Fourneaux de Chasse* v. *ECSC High Authority* [1957–8] ECR 211, 228.

[281] JO 1963 1433.

[282] Medium-term guidelines for technical coal research 1994–9 (OJ 1994 C67/7).

[283] Medium-term guidelines for the ECSC programmes of technical steel research and of steel pilot/demonstration projects (1991–5) (OJ 1990 C252/3).

[284] Intermediate report on the restructuring of the steel industry, COM(94)125, 5. See, e.g., Dec. 94/6 (OJ 1994 L6/30) authorizing common financial arrangements in respect of individual programmes involving the closure of production capacity in the Community steel industry for heavy sections, hot-rolled wide coils and strip, and reversing-mill plate.

[285] Conversion loans granted under Art. 56 ECSC for investments which create alternative employment opportunities for redundant workers in the coal or steel industries (OJ 1983 C191/3).

[286] *Ibid.*, point 7.1.   [287] *Ibid.*, point 7.2(a).

[288] In principle, such loans are no longer to be granted. See Adjustment of borrowing and lending policy with a view to the expiry of the ECSC Treaty (23 July 2002) (OJ 1994 C175/5). Instead, EIB loans are envisaged (ibid., para. 7).

[289] R. Quadri, R. Monaco, and A. Trabucchi, n. 271 above, ii, 711.

the coal and steel industries and affected by the withdrawal or contraction of these industries.[290] Such loans may originally have been seen as increasing production through preserving and increasing manpower.[291] They are increasingly seen as alleviating the social costs of restructuring.[292]

Finally, Article 56(1)(c) provides for: the payment of tideover allowances to workers; the payment of resettlement allowances to workers; and the financing of vocational training for workers having to change their employment. Article 56(2)(b) provides for the grant of the same kind of aid,[293] except that there is an additional category of aid. This category concerns the payment of allowances to undertakings to enable them to continue paying workers temporarily laid off as a result of the undertaking's change of activity. The extension of these arrangements to other industries with similar adaptation problems has been advocated.[294]

Forms of Assistance

Assistance may take the form of loans, including global loans to small and medium-sized enterprises[295] and low-interest housing loans. Interest rebates[296] and guarantees on the loans[297] may be provided. In addition, non-repayable, readaptation aid may be granted.

In practice, a distinction is made between "traditional" and "supplementary" readaptation aid.[298] The former aid is granted according to bilateral agreements with each Member State and covers aid for early retirement, employment, internal transfer, external transfer, and training. The latter also covers aid for early retirement, redeployment, and unemployment. However, it is designed to "enable a more significant part of the costs" of restructuring in the coal[299] and steel industries[300] to be covered.

[290] Guidelines for implementing the twelfth ECSC low-cost housing programme over the period 1993–7 (OJ 1994 C19/14).

[291] Roemer AG in Joined Cases 41 & 50/59 *Hamborner Bergbau AG and Friedrich Thyssen Bergbau AG* v. *ECSC High Authority* [1960] ECR 493, 530.

[292] Resolution of the ECSC Consultative Committee of 4 Oct. 1988 (OJ 1988 C277/7) on the implementation of an 11th ECSC housing programme. See also Future of the ECSC Treaty borrowing/lending activity, COM(93)512, 11.

[293] Following the initial objections of the ECJ in *Procedure for Amendment Pursuant to Art. 95(3) and (4) ECSC* [1959] ECR 259, 272–3, discretion was reduced and a proposed time-limit was removed.

[294] ECSC Consultative Committee, Memorandum on social aspects connected with the expiry of the ECSC Treaty in 2002 (OJ 1996 C334/3), Part IV.

[295] The EIB, the other financial instruments and strengthening economic and social cohesion, COM(88)244, 2.

[296] Interest rebates of up to 3% may be granted. See point 13 of the Guidelines and operational rules for the granting of conversion loans under Art. 56 ECSC (OJ 1990 C188/9).

[297] Art. 54 ECSC.

[298] 1993 Report on the activities of the ECSC readaptation aid for workers, COM(94)247, 3.

[299] Social measures in connection with the restructuring of the coal industry (1998–9/2000) (OJ 1997 C198/6); and Notice to Member States laying down the criteria for the grant of readaptation aid under Art. 56 ECSC available under the Rechar programme (OJ 1990 C185/18).

[300] Implementation of the social measures for the restructuring of the steel industry (1993–5) (OJ 1993 C146/5), para. 2.

20.6.3 Trans-European Networks

Assistance to major infrastructural projects concerning the development of trans-European networks is envisaged in the EC Treaty.

Objectives

Article 129b(1) of the EC Treaty provides that to help achieve economic and social cohesion "and to enable citizens of the Union, economic operators, and regional and local communities to derive full benefit from the setting up of an area without internal frontiers, the Union shall contribute to the establishment and development of trans-European networks in the areas of transport, telecommunications, and energy infrastructures". Within the framework of a system of open and competitive markets, such action shall aim at promoting the interconnection and inter-operability of national networks as well as access to such networks. It shall take account the need to link island, landlocked, and peripheral regions with the central regions of the Union.[301]

More particularly, Decision 1254/96[302] lays down a series of guidelines on trans-European energy networks. Their aim is to help to reduce energy supply costs and thus contribute to a higher rate of economic growth, more employment, and enhanced competitiveness of the European economy. The Union may also provide financial support for such networks.[303]

Eligibility

According to Regulation 2236/95,[304] projects are eligible for Union aid, if they are covered by guidelines[305] adopted by the Council and Parliament under Article 129c(1) of the Treaty.[306] Account is to be taken of the contribution of the project to the smooth running of the internal market and to economic and social cohesion. Particular account is to be taken of the contribution to the connection of island, landlocked and peripheral regions to the central areas of the Union; the importance to development of trade at European level; the contribution to increasing the competitiveness of the European economy; compliance with environmental considerations; and consistency with Union regional planning.

---

[301] Art. 129b(2) EC.   [302] OJ 1996 L161/147.

[303] Dec. 96/391 (OJ 1996 L161/154) laying down a series of measures aimed at creating a more favourable context for the development of trans-European networks in the energy sector, Art. 3.

[304] Laying down general rules for the granting of Community financial aid in the field of trans-European networks (OJ 1995 L228/1).

[305] Dec. 1692/96 (OJ 1996 L228/1) on Community guidelines for the development of the trans-European transport network; and Dec. 1336/97 (OJ 1997 L183/12) on a series of guidelines for trans-European telecommunications networks.

[306] Art. 2(1) of Reg. 2236/95 (OJ 1995 L228/1).

Aid Allocation

The Council rejected the proposal of the European Parliament that priority in the allocation of aid be given to regions eligible under the Structural Funds. The Council felt that the proposal disregarded "the balance apparent in Article 129b(1) of the Treaty, which refers to a multiplicity of objectives".[307] As a result, priority in the allocation of aid depends on the degree of the contribution to: the establishment of trans-European networks, harmonisation of technical standards, interconnection and interoperability of national networks, integration of the various networks, and the reliability and safety of networks.[308]

Scope of Assistance

Assistance may not only be provided for the development of networks within the Union. Provision is also made for assistance to projects ensuring the compatibility of third-country networks with the trans-European networks.[309]

Forms of Assistance

Assistance may take the form of aid to projects; aid for studies related to projects; interest subsidies; contributions to fees for loan guarantees; or any combination of these forms.[310] In addition, the Commission has proposed that the Union should assist feasibility studies and innovative measures.[311]

20.6.4 Euratom Loans and Guarantees

The task of Euratom includes promoting research and facilitating investment and ensuring the establishment of the basic installations necessary for the development of nuclear energy in the Union.[312] Accordingly, under the Euratom Treaty the development of nuclear energy may be supported.[313] Support may take the form of loans for research or investment,[314] particularly for research programmes[315] and joint undertakings.[316] By March 1995 Euratom loans totalling Euro 2,876 million had been granted. All these loans concerned nuclear power stations and industrial installations involved in the

---

[307] Common Position 3/95 (OJ 1995 C130/1).

[308] Art. 6(1) of Reg. 2236/95 (OJ 1995 L228/1).

[309] Art. 6 of Dec. 1692/96 (OJ 1996 L228/1).   [310] *Ibid.*, Art. 4(1).

[311] Art. 4(1) of the proposal of 9 Oct. 1996 (OJ 1996 C343/4) for a reg. concerning the granting of financial assistance for actions to promote combined goods transport.

[312] Art. 2 Euratom, and Dec. 77/270 (OJ 1977 L88/9) empowering the Commission to issue Euratom loans for the purpose of contributing to the financing of nuclear power stations, as amended by Dec. 94/179 (OJ 1994 L84/41).

[313] The proposal for the Euratom Treaty was apparently seen by Germany as an attempt by France to gain subsidies for the development of a nuclear power industry. See S. Weber and H. Wiesmith, "Issue Linkage in the European Community" [1991] *JCMS* 255–67, 256.

[314] Art. 172(4) Euratom.   [315] Art. 6(a) Euratom.   [316] Art. 47(a) Euratom.

fuel cycle within Member States.[317] Guarantees in connection with the loans are financed under Article B0–201 of the budget.[318]

In addition, grants may be provided from the budget.[319] In particular, pursuant to Article 7 of the Euratom Treaty, research and training programmes are supported by such grants.[320] Accordingly, a Framework Programme of Community activities in the field of research and training for Euratom has been established for 1994 to 1998.[321] The Programme is to include all activities concerning research and technological development, demonstration projects, dissemination and optimisation of results, and training in the fields of nuclear fission safety and controlled thermonuclear fusion.[322] The criteria for allocation of the aid include the contribution of the research to the strengthening of cohesion, and its consistency with the pursuit of scientific and technical quality.[323]

Two specific programmes have been adopted. One is to be implemented by the Joint Research Centre.[324] The other concerns research and training in the field of nuclear fission safety.[325]

20.6.5 Measures Accompanying Reform of the CAP

Measures accompanying reform of the common agricultural policy are the responsibility of the Guarantee Section of the European Agricultural Guidance and Guarantee Fund.[326] Thus resources additional to those of the Structural Funds are made available to assist agricultural restructuring.

Environmentally Friendly Farming

Regulation 2078/92[327] provides for aid to encourage agricultural production methods compatible with the protection of the environment and the maintenance of the countryside.[328] The aim is to encourage farmers to serve society as a whole by protecting the environment[329] and to help to adapt agriculture

---

[317] Reply by Mr de Silguy to WQ E–2878/94 (OJ 1995 C103/47) by Undine-Uta Block von Blottnitz.

[318] See e.g. for 1997, OJ 1997 L44/3.   [319] Art. 176 Euratom.

[320] Title B6–3 in the Budget for 1997 (OJ 1997 L44/3).

[321] Dec. 94/268 (OJ 1994 L115/31) concerning a framework programme of Community activities in the field of research and training for Euratom (1994–8).

[322] *Ibid.*, Art. 1(2).   [323] *Ibid.*, Annex II.

[324] Dec. 94/919 (OJ 1994 L361/132) adopting a specific RTD programme, including demonstration, to be implemented by the JRC for Euratom (1995–8).

[325] Dec. 94/920 (OJ 1994 L361/143) adopting a specific RTD programme of research and training in the field of nuclear fission safety (reactor safety, waste management, and radiation protection) (1994–8).

[326] Art. 2(2) of Reg. 2085/93 (OJ 1993 L193/44).

[327] On agricultural production methods compatible with the requirements of the protection of the environment and the maintenance of the countryside (OJ 1992 L215/85).

[328] The requirements of environmental protection are treated as an integral part of the CAP (1st recital in the preamble, *ibid.*).

[329] *Ibid.*, 8th recital.

to market requirements by encouraging less intensive production methods.[330] The aid envisaged is to relate to the use of farming practices which reduce the polluting effects of agriculture; environmentally favourable extensification of crop farming and sheep and cattle farming; ways of using agricultural land which are compatible with protection and improvement of the environment; the upkeep of abandoned farmland and woodlands, where this is necessary for environmental reasons or because of natural hazards and fire risks, thereby averting the dangers associated with depopulation of agricultural areas;[331] long-term set-aside of agricultural land for reasons connected with the environment; land management for public access and leisure activities; or education and training for farmers in types of farming compatible with the requirements of environmental protection and upkeep of the countryside.

Early Retirement

Aid for early retirement is provided for under Regulation 2079/92.[332] The aid is to be granted by Member States within the framework of multiannual programmes drawn up at national or regional level.[333]

Afforestation

Afforestation aid is provided under Regulation 2080/92.[334] According to the Preamble to the Regulation, afforestation is important from the point of view of soil use and the environment. It contributes to reducing the shortage of forestry products in the Union and accompanies the Union's policy of controlling agricultural production.[335] Hence, aid may be provided for afforestation, for the improvement of woodlands by the provision of shelter-belts, firebreaks, waterpoints, and forest roads; and for the improvement of cork oak stands.[336] Aid may also be granted to cover maintenance costs for the first five years and an annual premium per hectare to cover losses of income resulting from the afforestation of agricultural land.[337]

"Transitional Aid"

"Transitional", aid was introduced under Regulation 768/89,[338] to assist family agricultural holdings in adjusting to reforms in the common agricultural policy. The Regulation provided for such aid where overall family income was below a threshold to be fixed by the Member States. The threshold might be no higher than 70 per cent of the national gross domestic product or 90 per cent of the regional gross domestic product per member of

---

[330] *Ibid.*, 9th recital.   [331] *Ibid.*, Art. 2.

[332] Instituting a Community aid scheme for early retirement from farming (OJ 1992 L215/91).

[333] *Ibid.*, Art. 4(1).

[334] Instituting a Community aid scheme for forestry products in agriculture (OJ 1992 L215/96).

[335] *Ibid.*, 5th recital in the preamble.

[336] *Ibid.*, Art. 2.   [337] *Ibid.*, Art. 6.

[338] Establishing a system of transitional aids to agricultural income (OJ 1989 L84/8).

the working population.[339] The aid was originally provided from a special chapter in the budget,[340] but its provision became the responsibility of the Guarantee Section in the 1993 Budget.[341]

20.7 Horizontal Instruments

"Horizontal" instruments provide aid which is not limited to particular regions or sectors. Some such instruments were provided for in the EEC Treaty. Other such instruments emerged in the practice of the Union institutions and were subsequently given an express legal basis through Treaty amendments.

20.7.1 Loans and Guarantees from the European Investment Bank

The Spaak Report envisaged the creation of an investment fund for financing "global aids" to Member States to support conversion efforts and the creation of new activities. During negotiation of the EEC Treaty the preference emerged for a financial institution with the characteristics of a bank,[342] which was established as the European Investment Bank.

According to Article 3(j) of the EEC Treaty, the Bank was intended to facilitate the economic expansion of the Union by opening up fresh resources. It was thereby to assist achievement of objectives set out in Article 2 of the Treaty.[343] More particularly, Article 130 of the Treaty required the Bank to contribute to the balanced and steady "development" of the common market. To this end, it was to grant loans and give guarantees[344] which facilitated the financing of three kinds of projects.

The first kind comprised projects for developing the less developed regions.[345] The regions had to be less developed by Union rather than national standards.[346] The operations of the Bank were intended to counter the tendency of the common market to increase the differences between such regions and the rest of the Union.[347]

---

[339] *Ibid.*, Art. 4(1).   [340] Item 3901 in the Budget for 1989 (OJ 1989 L26/3).

[341] OJ 1993 L31/3, Art. B1–410.

[342] R. Quadri, R. Monaco, and A. Trabucchi, *Trattato istitutivo della Comunità economica europea: commentario* (Giuffré, Milan, 1965), ii, 992.

[343] Mancini AG in Case 85/86 *EC Commission* v. *Board of Governors of the EIB* [1988] ECR 1281, 1305.

[344] Art. 20(2) of the EIB Statute prohibits the Bank, in principle, from participating in risk capital.

[345] Art. 130(a) EEC.

[346] R. Quadri, R. Monaco, and A. Trabucchi, n. 342 above, ii, 1009. During negotiation of the Treaty Germany had favoured an express reference to the objective as being to adjust the economic level of the less developed regions to that of other regions (S. Neri and H. Sperl, *Traité instituant la Communauté économique européenne* (Court of Justice of the European Communities, Luxembourg, 1960), 326).

[347] R. Quadri, R. Monaco, and A. Trabucchi, n.342 above, ii, 1008.

The second kind of projects concerned the modernisation[348] or conversion of undertakings or the development of fresh activities called for by the progressive establishment of the common market. Such projects could be financed, where they were of such a size or nature[349] that they could not be entirely financed by the various means available in the individual Member States.[350] The expression "progressive" was seen as implying that support from the Bank had to be limited to the transitional period for establishment of the common market.[351] It was recognised, however, that such finance could not be limited to problems shown to be caused by the establishment of the common market.[352]

Finally, the Bank could finance projects of common interest to several Member States which were of such a size or nature that they could not be entirely financed by the means available in the individual Member States.[353] Such projects included, in particular, those which would contribute to the integration of the economies of the Member States.[354]

All three kinds of projects were, according to the Statute of the Bank, to "promote the attainment of the common market".[355] Further details were provided in the General Directives for the Credit Policy of the Bank.[356] According to these Directives, the Bank was to participate in financing projects aimed at the modernisation or conversion of enterprises or the creation of new activities furthering the progressive establishment of the common market.[357]

In practice, development of the less developed regions was expected to be the "principal" task of the Bank.[358] The underlying concern was that "mechanical integration" of the Member States could harm such regions.[359]

Originally the Bank made loans for infrastructure projects and specific large industrial projects. However, in 1968 global loans, passed on through sub-loans to small and medium-sized enterprises, were introduced.[360] The bulk of the loans has been allocated to poorer regions, especially in Italy.[361]

---

[348] Germany had argued that modernization should not be covered, because it was a normal and permanent task of undertakings (S. Neri and H. Sperl, n.346 above, 327)

[349] I.e., they were not to be purely local or particular (R. Quadri, R. Monaco, and A. Trabucchi, n.342 above, ii, 1009).

[350] Art. 130(b) EEC. France had proposed a stipulation that the projects be viable (S. Neri and H. Sperl, n.346 above, 326). This stipulation was included in para. 3 of the General Directives of the Bank (*European Investment Bank: Statutes and Other Provisions* (EIB, Luxembourg, 1981), 3–4).

[351] S. Neri and H. Sperl, n.346 above, 327.   [352] *Ibid.*

[353] Art. 130(c) EEC. The German Government considered that "supraregional" projects could be encouraged under this provision (S. Neri and H. Sperl, n.346 above, 325).

[354] *Second EEC General Report* (EEC Commission, Brussels, 1959), 54.

[355] Art. 20(1)(b) of the EIB Statute.   [356] (EIB, Luxembourg, 1981), 32–3.

[357] *Ibid.*, sect. II.   [358] *Second EEC General Report* (n.354 above), 54.

[359] R. Quadri, R. Monaco, and A. Trabucchi, n.342, above, 962.

[360] *Annual Report of the EIB 1968* (EIB, Luxembourg, 1969), 79–80. According to D.A. Pinder, "Small Firms, Regional Development and the European Investment Bank" (1986) 24 *JCMS* 171–86, these loans had only a marginal impact on employment in problem regions.

[361] Between 1958 and 1973 46% of total EIB lending related to projects in Italy.

For example, loans have been made for irrigation and other rural projects in the Mezzogiorno, and numerous transport and industrial rehabilitation schemes have benefited.

Such work is given greater prominence in Article 130 of the EC Treaty, which has replaced Article 130 of the EEC Treaty. The new provision maintains the original tasks of the Bank, but it contains an additional paragraph. According to this paragraph, in carrying out its tasks, the Bank is to facilitate the financing of investment programmes in conjunction with assistance from the Structural Funds and other Union financial instruments. At the same time, according to the Protocol on Economic and Social Cohesion, the Bank must continue to devote the majority of its resources to the promotion of economic and social cohesion.[362] Article 130 of the Treaty and the Protocol are said to establish the Bank as a "real regional development bank".[363]

Accordingly, the preamble to Regulation 2081/93[364] envisages that the Bank "will continue to devote the majority of its resources to promoting economic and social cohesion and in particular to developing further loans in the Member States which benefit from the cohesion financial instrument and in the Community's Objective 1 regions".[365] However, to ensure that the Bank makes the envisaged contribution to cohesion may be problematic, because it is subject to no democratic control.[366]

New Community Instrument

To support the work of the Bank, the New Community Instrument (NCI)[367] was established by Decision 78/870.[368] It was designed to strengthen the link between the European Investment Bank and the implementation of policies demanded by the development of the common market. In particular, it was to make available finance, in the form of loans, for investment projects of small and medium-sized enterprises, especially in connection with innovation, and for infrastructure and energy projects. Its administration and the selection of projects were to be responsibilities of the Bank. However, the

---

[362] Para. 13 of the Protocol.

[363] C. Mestre and Y. Petit, "La Cohesion économique et sociale après le Traité sur l'union européenne" [1995] *RTDE* 207–43, 231.

[364] OJ 1993 L193/5.

[365] *Ibid.,* 19th recital in the preamble. See also the declaration of the European Council meeting in Dec. 1992, regarding the importance of the EIB to cohesion (Bull. EC 12–1992, I.55).

[366] Cf. the European Parliament Resolution on giving discharge to the Commission in respect of the implementation of the Budget for 1994 (OJ 1996 L148/44), para. 53.

[367] C. André, "Le Nouvel instrument communautaire d'emprunts et de prêts (N.I.C.)" [1980] *RMC* 66–71; and L. Battistotti, "I Finanziamenti concessi della banca europea per gli invetimenti ed il nuovo strumento communitario" [1985] *Cronache Economiche* 63–8.

[368] Empowering the Commission to contract loans for the purpose of promoting investment within the Community (OJ 1978 L298/9); and Dec. 83/200 (OJ 1983 L112/26) empowering the Commission to contract loans under the NCI for the purpose of promoting investment within the Community.

Commission was to be responsible for determining the eligibility of projects.[369]

Article 1 of Decision 78/870[370] provided for loans to be granted to finance investment projects which contributed to greater convergence and integration of the economic policies of the Member States. More particularly, the projects were to help attain Union objectives relating to energy, industry, and infrastructures. Account was to be taken, *inter alia*, of the regional impact of the projects and the need to combat unemployment.

More details of the priorities to be pursued were given in Article 3 of Decision 84/383.[371] This provision treated as priorities for support: investment projects, mainly those of small and medium-sized enterprises, in industry and directly allied services, which were designed in particular to promote the dissemination of innovation and new technology and the implementation of which contributed directly or indirectly to job creation; rational use of energy, replacement of oil by other sources of energy in all sectors and infrastructure projects facilitating such replacement; and infrastructure projects associated with the development of productive activities, which contributed to regional development or which were of "Community interest", such as telecommunications, including information technology, and transport, including the transmission of energy.

Article 3 of Decision 87/182[372] now provides for support of investment projects of small and medium-sized enterprises in industry and other productive sectors. Such support is to relate, in particular, to the application of new technologies and innovation and to improving the rational use of energy. The projects of small enterprises have priority. At the same time, the preamble to the Decision refers to the importance of reducing regional disparities.[373] Guarantees on the loans may be financed from the budget.[374]

European Investment Fund

To provide further support for the work of the Bank,[375] its Board of Governors established a European Investment Fund.[376] This Fund is to contribute to the strengthening of the internal market, the promotion of economic recovery in Europe, and the furthering of economic and social cohesion.[377] It provides loans for large infrastructural projects, particularly

---

[369] Art. 5 of Dec. 78/870 (OJ 1978 L298/9).   [370] *Ibid.*

[371] Implementing Dec. 83/200 (OJ 1984 L208/53).

[372] Empowering the Commission to borrow under the NCI for the purpose of promoting investment within the Community (OJ 1987 L71/34).

[373] *Ibid.*, 8th recital in the preamble.

[374] See e.g. Art. B0–202 of the Budget for 1997 (OJ 1997 L44/3).

[375] In response to a declaration of the European Council meeting in Dec. 1992 on promoting economic recovery in Europe, Bull. EC 12–1992, I.30.

[376] Note the Statute of the Fund (OJ 1994 L173/1).

[377] 5th recital in the preamble to Dir. 94/7 (OJ 1994 L89/17) adapting Dir. 89/647 (OJ 1989 L386/14) on a solvency ratio for credit institutions as regards the technical definition of "multilateral development banks"; and Dec. 94/375 (OJ 1994 L173/12) on Community membership of the EIF.

those related to trans-European networks in the areas of transport, telecommunications, and energy. It also provides loans for the development of small and medium-sized enterprises,[378] particularly in Union-assisted areas.[379] At the same time, the Fund may provide guarantees for loans in whatever form is permitted by the rules of law applicable. It may also acquire, hold, and manage equity interests in enterprises.[380]

Temporary Lending Facility

In response to a call from the European Council in December 1992,[381] the Board of Governors of the Bank established a temporary lending facility.[382] This facility is designed to accelerate the financing of infrastructure projects, notably those connected with trans-European networks. Small and medium-sized enterprises which obtain such loans receive interest subsidies from the Union Budget.[383]

20.7.2 Framework Programmes for Research and Technological Development

Union assistance to research and development[384] had its origins in concerns for particular sectors,[385] such as data processing,[386] aerospace,[387] and ceramics.[388] Articles 130f to 130p of the EC Treaty go beyond the traditional approach. They provide the Union with express, general powers in the field of research and technological development.

Objectives

Article 130f(1) of the Treaty establishes the objective of "strengthening the scientific and technological bases of Community industry and encouraging it to become more competitive at international level,[389] while promoting all the

---

[378] Art. 2 of the Statute, n.376 above.   [379] European Investment Fund, COM(93)3, 2.

[380] Art. 3(1) of the Statute, n.376 above.   [381] Bull. EC 12–1992, I.30.

[382] *EIB Annual Report 1993* (EIB, Luxembourg, 1994), 12–3.

[383] Dec. 94/217 (OJ 1994 L107/57) on the provision of Community interest subsidies on loans for SMEs extended by the EIB under its temporary lending facility; and Art. B5–322 of the Budget for 1997 (OJ 1997 L44/3).

[384] See, generally, J. Elizade, "Legal Aspects of Community Policy on Research and Technological Development (RTD)" (1992) 29 *CMLRev.* 309–46.

[385] See, e.g., the Memorandum on industrial policy in the EEC, COM(70)100. See, regarding the oil industry, A. Evans, "The Development of a Community Policy on Oil" (1980) 17 *CMLRev* 371–94

[386] Proposals of 22 Sept. 1975 (OJ 1976 C14/5) for a development project for a common language for real time programming; projects in data-processing concerning software portability; studies in support of the use of data-processing; and projects for applications and studies in the field of data-processing.

[387] Action programme for the European aeronautical sector, COM(75)475.

[388] Proposal of 5 June 1979 (OJ 1979 C155/4) for a decision on the adoption of a programme of technological research in the field of clay minerals and technical ceramics.

[389] Art. 130(1) EC also provides that the Union and the Member States shall foster better exploitation of the industrial potential of policies of innovation and RTD.

research activities deemed necessary by virtue of other chapters of this Treaty."[390]

Eligibility

According to Article 130f(2) of the Treaty, undertakings, research centres, and universities are eligible for assistance.

Aid Allocation

According to Article 130f(2) of the Treaty, aid is to be allocated throughout the Union to "research and technological development activities of high quality".

Scope of Assistance

Pursuit of the objectives is, according to Article 130g of the Treaty, to involve the following "activities": implementation of research, technological development, and demonstration programmes, by promoting co-operation with and between undertakings, research centres, and universities; promotion of co-operation in this field with third states and international organisations; dissemination and optimisation of the results of the activities; and stimulation of the training and mobility of researchers in the Union.

Forms of Assistance

All Union activities in support of research and technological development are to be set out in a multiannual Framework Programme. This Programme shall establish the scientific and technological objectives to be achieved by the activities and fix the relevant priorities and indicate the broad lines of such activities. It shall also fix the maximum overall amount of, and the detailed rules for, Union financial participation in the programme and the respective shares in each of the supported activities.[391] The Fourth Framework Programme in the field of research and technological development and demonstration[392] covers the period 1994 to 1998.

Implementation is to be based on specific programmes developed within each activity. Each specific programme shall define the detailed rules for its implementation, fix its duration, and provide for the financial resources deemed necessary. The sum of the amounts deemed necessary shall not

---

[390] According to Art. 130f(3) EEC, pursuit of this objective had to respect "the establishment of the internal market and the implementation of common policies, particularly as regards competition and trade". See, regarding the kind of reconciliation problems involved, M. van Empel, "Technology and Common Market Law" in Aspen Institute Colloquium on European Law, *Technological Development and Co-operation in Europe – Legal Aspects* (TMC Asser Institute, The Hague, 1986), 57–71; and B. Hawk, "La Recherche et le développement en droit communautaire et en droit antitrust americain" [1987] *Revue Internationale de Droit Economique* 211–69.

[391] Art. 130i(1) EC.

[392] Dec. 94/1110 (OJ 1994 L126/4) concerning the fourth framework programme of the EC activities in the field of research and technological development and demonstration.

exceed the overall maximum amount fixed for the framework programme and each activity.[393]

20.7.3 Financial Instrument for the Environment

Article 130s(4) of the EC Treaty provides that "without prejudice to certain measures of a Community nature, the Member States shall finance and implement the environmental policy". The implication is that the Union may provide certain environmental aid. In the case of the Cohesion Fund,[394] the implication is confirmed by Article 130s(5) of the Treaty. According to this provision, "without prejudice to the principle that the polluter should pay, if a measure involves costs deemed disproportionate for the public authorities of a Member State, the Council shall, in the act adopting that measure, lay down appropriate provisions [for] financial support from the Cohesion Fund".[395]

More particularly, a Financial Instrument for the Environment (LIFE) was established by Regulation 1973/92.[396]

Objectives

The objectives of the Instrument are to strengthen and increase the effectiveness of administrative structures or services designed to ensure the implementation of environmental provisions; to help control and reduce the various forms of pollution; and to help protect sensitive areas and maintain biogenetic diversity.[397]

Eligibility

The Instrument may assist actions of Union interest which contribute significantly to the implementation of Union environmental policy and meet the conditions for implementation of the "polluter pays" principle.[398] According to this principle, polluting may not be subsidised, though action to reduce pollution may be.

Aid Allocation

Assistance provided by the Instrument is to be differentiated in the light of the seriousness of the specific, notably regional, environmental problems to be tackled; the special importance attaching to the measures from a Union viewpoint; and the capacity of the Member State or of the beneficiary to contribute.[399] The European Parliament stresses the need to help the less prosperous Member States to honour their commitments. To this end, it has

---

[393] Art. 130i(3) EC.   [394] Reg. 1164/94 (OJ 1994 L130/1) establishing a Cohesion Fund.
[395] Art. 130r(4) EEC required that in the application of the "polluter pays" principle particular account should be taken of the economic and social development of the Union as a whole.
[396] Establishing a financial instrument for the environment (OJ 1992 L206/1).
[397] *Ibid.*, Art. 2(1).   [398] *Ibid.*, Art. 2(2).   [399] *Ibid.*, Art. 9.

called for a substantial increase in the funds earmarked for the instrument.[400]

Scope of Assistance

The Commission considers that aid from the Instrument should concern "translation" of concepts of environmental responsibility and sustainable development into everyday actions. Hence, the principal tasks of the Instrument relate to: defining and promoting models of production and behaviour which are in line with the principles of sustainable development; practical demonstration of the technical viability and economic efficiency of chosen models and actions;[401] supporting specific demonstrations, pilot projects, "horizontal information", education, and training designed to influence economic actors through practicable examples; and strengthening administrative structures.[402]

The Commission is to assure co-ordination and coherence as between such assistance and actions undertaken by the Structural Funds and by the other Union financial instruments.[403] The Envireg initiative[404] impliedly recognised the difficulties of reconciling assistance provided by the Instrument and cohesion activities. However, this initiative was too limited to overcome problems of reconciling environmental and cohesion policies in Union spending generally[405] and, in any case, has been discontinued.

Such problems are not squarely addressed in the amendments to Regulation 1973/92 introduced by Regulation 1404/96.[406] The amendments are designed to concentrate efforts by specifying more clearly the activities able to benefit from Union aid; to improve the management procedures and define more clearly the selection and evaluation criteria for these activities; and to improve the efficiency and transparency of the application procedures and the procedures for informing the public and potential beneficiaries.[407] Activities eligible for support are nature conservation; other activities designed to implement Union environmental legislation and policy; monitoring and evaluation measures; and dissemination of results.[408]

---

[400] Resolution of 8 Apr. 1992 (OJ 1992 C125/122) on the implementation of EC environmental legislation, paras. 12–13.

[401] Presumably, such action may complement that envisaged in Dec. 94/911 (OJ 1994 L361/1) adopting a specific programme of RTD, including demonstration, in the field of environment and climate (1994–8).

[402] *Towards sustainability*, COM(92)23, ii, 71.

[403] Art. 6 of Reg. 1973/92 (OJ 1992 L206/1).

[404] Notice laying down guidelines for operational programmes, which Member States were invited to establish within the framework of a Community initiative concerning the environment (OJ 1990 C115/3).

[405] See e.g. the Annual report of the Court of Auditors for 1994 (OJ 1995 C303/1), para. 6.42.

[406] OJ 1996 L181/1.   [407] *Ibid.*, 9th and 10th recitals in the preamble.   [408] *Ibid.*, Art. 2.

20.7.4 Cohesion Fund

In accordance with the Protocol on Economic and Social Cohesion to the EC Treaty and Article 130d of this Treaty, a Cohesion Fund has been established.[409] The Fund assists projects in the fields of environment and trans-European networks in Member States with a *per capita* gross domestic product of less than 90 per cent of the Union average which have a programme leading to the fulfilment of the conditions of economic convergence, as set out in Article 104c of the Treaty.[410] In other words, the Fund is designed to assist Ireland, Portugal, Spain, and Greece in meeting the economic convergence requirements for participation in the third stage of monetary union.

20.7.5 Other Budgetary Resources

Other Budgetary resources[411] may be used to support small and medium-sized enterprises, to assist Member States in tackling balance-of-payments problems, and to support the development of the outermost regions.

Programmes for Small and Medium-sized Enterprises

Article 130(1) of the EC Treaty provides for encouragement of an environment favourable to initiative and to the development of undertakings throughout the Union, particularly small and medium-sized enterprises. This provision reflects a long-standing recognition of the desirability of Union assistance for such enterprises.[412] However, Article 130(3) states that this provision shall not provide a basis for the introduction by the Union of any measures which would lead to a distortion of competition.

In Union practice a medium-sized enterprise is defined as an enterprise which

– has no more than 250 employees

and

– has an annual turnover not exceeding 40 million Euro or
– has a balance sheet total not exceeding 27 million Euro

and

    – is not more than 25 per cent owned by one or more companies not falling within this definition, except public investment corporations,

---

[409] Reg. 1164/94 (OJ 1994 L130/1) establishing a Cohesion Fund.

[410] These criteria concern budget deficits, public debt, inflation and exchange rates. See also the Protocol on the convergence criteria, annexed to the EC Treaty.

[411] Cf. the distinction between an "an operating budget" and "a financial policy instrument" in *Opinion 1/94 International Agreements Concerning Services and the Protection of Intellectual Property* [1994] ECR I–5267, I–5395.

[412] See, regarding the "enterprise policy" of the Union, N. Moussis, "Small and Medium Enterprises in the Internal Market" [1992] *ELR* 483–98.

venture capital companies or, provided no control is exercised, institutional investors.

A small enterprise is one which
- has no more than 50 employees

and
- has an annual turnover not exceeding Euro 7 million or
- has a balance sheet total not exceeding Euro 5 million

and
- is not more than 25 per cent owned by one or more companies not falling within this definition, except public investment corporations, venture capital companies or, provided no control is exercised, institutional investors.[413]

A multiannual programme for such enterprises has been established by Decision 93/379.[414] To facilitate co-ordination between the various measures in their favour, an integrated programme has also been established.[415]

More particularly, Business and Innovation Centres are supported.[416] The creation of a network of these bodies, the European Business and Innovation Centre Network, has also been assisted.[417] These centres operate in areas falling within the scope of the European Regional Development Fund, areas covered by Integrated Mediterranean Programmes, ECSC areas, and other areas adversely affected by major industrial decline.[418] They are designed to create innovative activities with growth potential through detecting and selecting entrepreneurs; finding, assessing, and developing technologies; management training; rigorous business planning; and the supply of common premises. In other words, they seek to assist regions in developing their indigenous potential.[419] They follow a Union model, though they depend at local level on agreement between the public and the private sectors. Their work is concentrated on new or existing firms which put forward innovative development projects adding value to the economy of the region.[420]

---

[413] Art. 1 of the Annex to Rec. 96/280 (OJ 1996 L107/4) concerning the definition of SMEs. According to Art. 1(5) (*ibid.*), "micro-enterprises" are those having fewer than 10 employees. Craft enterprises "continue to be defined at national level due to their specific characteristics" (28th recital in the preamble, *ibid.*).

[414] Dec. 93/379 (OJ 1993 L161/68) on a multiannual programme of Community measures to intensify the priority areas and to ensure the continuity and consolidation of policy for enterprise, in particular SMEs, in the Community. See e.g. Assistance in the field of transnational co-operation between small enterprises and the craft sector – call for proposals (OJ 1996 C232/47). Finance is provided under Art. B5–320 of the Budget for 1997 (OJ 1997 L44/3).

[415] Integrated programme in favour of SMEs and the craft sector, COM(94)207. See, more particularly, Interprise (OJ 1997 C329/17).

[416] Explanatory memorandum to the proposal for a decision concerning a Community programme to create and develop BICs and their network, COM(86)785, 3.

[417] Bull. EC 11–1984, 2.1.82.   [418] Art. B2–601 of the Budget for 1997 (OJ 1997 L44/3).

[419] Explanatory memorandum to the proposal for a decision concerning a Community programme to create and develop BICs and their network, COM(86)785, 1.

[420] Reply by Mr Millan to WQ 1939/91 (OJ 1992 C126/16) by Mr François Musso.

Moreover, in accordance with a scheme launched in 1989,[421] the Commission has provided financial assistance for the creation and development of seed-capital funds to acquire equity holdings in new or embryonic companies.[422] Repayable advances may be available from Directorate General XXIII (Enterprise Policy)[423] to meet part of the operating costs of a fund. A capital contribution from Directorate General XVI (Regional Policy) may be made to the Business and Innovation Centre established in the area, if the latter is willing to invest in the fund. These funds have formed themselves into a network.[424] Venture capital may also be available to small and medium-sized enterprises generally through Union-supported arrangements such as "Venture consort" and "Eurotech capital".[425] However, the Union has not gone so far as to create a "Regional Development Company" of the kind proposed by the Commission in 1972[426] and subsequently recommended by the European Parliament.[427]

Balance-of-payments Loans

Balance-of-payments loans were introduced by Regulation 397/75.[428] They were originally designed to assist Member States in tackling balance-of-payments difficulties without disruption of the common market. The difficulties envisaged were those attributable to the increase in oil prices. However, the original arrangements were reformed by Regulation 682/81.[429]

Loans are now provided for in Regulation 1969/88.[430] They seek, more generally, to assist Member States with monetary problems that may hamper investment and growth.[431] For example, a loan to France of 1983 was to

---

[421] Notice of Tender: Pilot action to create and develop seed-capital funds (OJ 1988 C306/12). See also Extension of the seed-capital fund pilot action in the new *Länder* in Germany (OJ 1992 C115/36).

[422] *Twenty-Fifth EC General Report* (EC Commission, Brussels, 1992), 93.

[423] See sect. 2.2.3 regarding Directorates General.   [424] *Ibid.*, 163.

[425] *Twenty-Sixth EC General Report* (EC Commission, Brussels, 1993), 25; and Improvement of the fiscal environment of SMEs, COM(94)206.

[426] Proposal of 19 June 1972 (JO 1972 C94/7) for a Council resolution on instruments of Community regional policy. Note also the idea of creating a European Company for Industrial Parks in *Les Régimes d'aide régionale dans la communauté européenne – étude comparative* (EC Commission, Luxembourg, 1979), 306.

[427] Resolution of 16 Dec. 1976 (OJ 1977 C6/86) on the first annual report on the ERDF, para. 9. See, later, the Resolution of 16 Feb. 1982 (OJ 1982 C66/26) on a "Mediterranean plan" for the benefit of Mediterranean countries belonging to the EC and the applicant countries, Portugal and Spain, para. 7.

[428] Concerning Community loans (OJ 1975 L46/1).

[429] Adjusting the Community loan mechanism designed to support the balance of payments of Member States (OJ 1981 L73/1).

[430] Establishing a single facility providing medium-term financial assistance for Member States' balances of payments (OJ 1988 L178/1). Such aid may be used under Art. 109h EC. See, generally, the Review of the facility providing medium-term financial assistance for Member States' balances of payments, COM(96)545.

[431] The EIB, the other financial instruments and strengthening economic and social cohesion, COM(88)244, 2. See e.g. Dec. 93/67 (OJ 1993 L22/121) concerning a Community loan in favour of Italy.

support national measures to strengthen the competitiveness of firms and to create conditions which would favour recovery of investment in the sectors subject to competition.[432] Loans to Greece have been concerned with more fundamental structural problems.[433] They have been designed to assist the strengthening and modernisation of productive structures. Indeed, use of the latest loan is to have regard to the Community Support Framework for Greece.[434] Guarantees on these loans are financed from the budget.[435]

Poseidom, Poseican, and Poseima Programmes

The Poseidom, Poseican, and Poseima programmes were adopted under Article 235 of the EEC Treaty. According to this provision, if action proves necessary to attain, in the course of the operation of the common market, one of the Treaty objectives and the Treaty has not provided the necessary powers, the Council shall, acting unanimously on a proposal from the Commission and after consulting the European Parliament, take the appropriate measures.

The programmes concern, respectively, the French overseas departments,[436] the Canary Islands,[437] and Madeira and the Azores.[438] The programmes are based on the principle that such regions form an integral part of the Union. However, they recognise "the regional reality", characterised by the features and constraints specific to the regions concerned as distinct from the Union as a whole.[439] Accordingly, structural aid is granted to take account of their handicaps of remoteness and insularity.[440]

Aid for Reconstruction after Natural Disasters

Budgetary resources may be used to assist reconstruction after natural disasters. For example, following earthquakes in Greece in September 1986, the Council provided for the Budget to fund interest rate subsidies on loans granted by the European Investment Bank in the stricken areas.[441] Similar assistance was provided following earthquakes in Italy in May 1976[442] and

---

[432] Dec. 83/298 (OJ 1983 L153/44) concerning a Community loan in favour of France.

[433] Dec. 85/543 (OJ 1985 L341/17) concerning a Community loan in favour of Greece.

[434] 8th recital in, and para. 4 of, the preamble to Dec. 91/136 (OJ 1991 L66/22) concerning a Community loan in favour of Greece.

[435] Art. B0–200 of the Budget for 1997 (OJ 1997 L44/3).

[436] Dec. 89/487 (OJ 1989 L399/39) establishing a programme of options specific to the remote and insular nature of the French overseas departments (Poseidom).

[437] Dec. 91/314 (OJ 1991 L171/5) setting up a programme of options specific to the remote and insular nature of the Canary Islands (Poseican).

[438] Dec. 91/315 (OJ 1991 L171/10) setting up a programme of options specific to the remote and insular nature of Madeira and the Azores (Poseima).

[439] See e.g. para. 1 of the Poseidom Programme (OJ 1989 L399/39).

[440] *Ibid.*, para. 12.2.

[441] Dec. 88/561 (OJ 1988 L309/32) relating to exceptional Community aid for the reconstruction of the areas stricken by earthquakes which took place in Greece in Sept. 1986.

[442] Reg. 1506/76 (OJ 1976 L168/11) on the Community contribution towards repairing the infrastructural damage caused by the earthquake in May 1976 in Friuli/Venezia Giulia. See, more

November 1980,[443] earthquakes in Greece in 1981,[444] and a cyclone in Madeira in 1993.[445]

20.8 Union Aid and Third States

Article 130(1) of the EC Treaty provides that "the conditions necessary for the competitiveness of the Community's industry" are to be ensured.[446] In practice, the grant of some Union aid may be a response to repercussions within the Union of commercial policy decisions. The grant of some other Union aid may be an integral element of the pursuit of fund objectives.

20.8.1 "Internal" Repercussions of the Commercial Policy

Where implementation of the common commercial policy leads to increased liberalisation of trade with third states, the funds may assist Union actors exposed to greater competition with such states.

Prisma

Completion of the internal market implies that national measures of commercial policy will no longer be authorised under Article 115 of the EC Treaty.[447] The Prisma initiative[448] provides for the grant of aid to industries in Objective 1 regions previously benefiting from protection under such measures.

Perifra

Perifra[449] is designed to support regions affected by the opening of Union markets to Central and East European countries. Preference is given to regions covered by Objective 1, 2, or 5b of the Structural Funds.[450]

particularly, Reg. 1505/76 (OJ 1976 L168/9) on the Community contribution towards repairing the damage caused to agriculture by the earthquake in May 1976 in Friuli/Venezia-Giulia.

[443] Dec. 81/19 (OJ 1981 L37/21) on Community aid granted by way of exception for the reconstruction of the regions affected by the Italian earthquake in Nov. 1980.

[444] Dec. 81/1013 (OJ 1981 L367/27) on Community aid granted by way of exception for the reconstruction of the regions affected by the Greek earthquakes in Feb. and Mar. 1981.

[445] Dec. 95/250 (OJ 1995 L159/16) relating to exceptional Community aid for the reconstruction of the areas stricken by the cyclone that hit Madeira in Oct. 1993.

[446] See, more particularly, Art. 130f(1) EC. Cf. the argument that the denial of Union aid for the construction of fishing boats could seriously undermine efforts to make the Union fleet more competitive in the face of "increasingly cut-throat competition from third countries" in the Opinion of the Economic and Social Committee of 21 Dec. 1993 (OJ 1994 C52/35) on the proposal for a regulation laying down detailed rules for implementing Reg. 2080/93 on Community structural assistance in the fisheries and aquaculture sector and the industry processing and marketing its products, para. 1.9.

[447] Sect. 8.5.5 above.

[448] Notice laying down guidelines for operational programmes which Member States are invited to establish in the framework of a Community initiative concerning the preparation of enterprises for the single market (OJ 1991 C33/9).

[449] Budget for 1991 (OJ 1991 L30/3), Item B2–610.

Retex

Adoption of the Retex initiative[451] was influenced by recognition of the problems likely to result for certain regions from liberalisation of trade in textiles with Hungary, Poland, and the then Czechoslovakia. Likewise, GATT liberalisation led to adoption of a special aid programme for Portuguese textiles.[452]

Agricultural Aid

Liberalisation of trade with third states in agricultural products and introduction of aid through measures accompanying reform of the common agricultural policy were apparently linked.[453] More particularly, an aid system was introduced to improve the competitiveness of Union raspberry producers in the face of imports from such states.[454]

20.8.2 Pursuit of Fund Objectives

Pursuit of fund objectives may be seen as requiring the provision of aid to third states. For example, the Financial Instrument for the Environment[455] provides for aid to be granted to third states. Similarly, Union aid may be provided for ensuring the compatibility of third-country networks with trans-European networks.[456]

20.9 Agreements with Third States

Agreements with third states may provide for co-operation involving the use of the Structural Funds and other financial instruments of the Union.

[450] Cf. Dec. 89/10 (OJ 1989 L7/30) on a concerted measure for the grant of a standby indemnity to fishermen from certain Member States who had to suspend their fishing activities in waters under the sovereignty or jurisdiction of Morocco, which was adopted under the 3rd indent of Art. 32 of Reg. 4028/86 (OJ 1986 L376/7) on Community measures to improve and adapt structures in the fisheries and aquaculture sector.

[451] Notice laying down guidelines for operational programmes which Member States are invited to establish within the framework of a Community initiative for regions heavily dependent on the textiles and clothing sector (OJ 1992 C142/5).

[452] Reg. 852/95 (OJ 1995 L86/10) on the grant of financial assistance to Portugal for a specific programme for the modernization of the Portuguese textile and clothing industry. Cf., regarding the possibilities of a Union response to the difficulties implied for the Greek textiles industry by the "new terms of international competition", Council Reply to WQ E–0067/96 (OJ 1996 C280/8) by Yannos Krandiotis.

[453] Reply by Mr Fischler to WQ E–0802/96 (OJ 1996 C297/28) by Sebastiano Musumeci.

[454] Reg. 1991/92 (OJ 1992 L199/1) establishing a special scheme for raspberries intended for processing. This aid was provided by the Guarantee Section of the EAGGF.

[455] Reg. 1973/92 (OJ 1992 L206/1) establishing a financial instrument for the environment, as amended by Reg. 1404/96 (OJ 1996 L181/1).

[456] Art. 6 of Dec. 1692/96 (OJ 1996 L228/1) on Community guidelines for the development of the trans-European transport network.

20.9.1 Free Trade Agreements

Co-operation agreements may be concluded with third states which are party to free trade agreements. For example, EFTA states contributed to the budget for the research programme regarding wood, including cork, as a renewable raw material.[457] The contributions were proportionate to gross domestic product. In the case of the TEDIS Programme, national budget contributions of EFTA states were passed to the EFTA Secretariat, and the latter passed them on to the Union.[458] In either case expenditure by such states was ultimately determined by Commission decisions concerning implementation of the relevant programme.

20.9.2 Association Agreements

Association agreements may provide for "financial co-operation" between the Union and the third states concerned. Of particular importance are the arrangements concerning the European Development Fund and Phare.

EDF

The Fourth Lomé Convention[459] provides for the Union to grant financial assistance to the overseas countries and territories of the Member States and the African, Caribbean, and Pacific countries. This assistance is provided through the European Development Fund. The assistance concerns: national indicative programmes and regional co-operation; structural adjustment; the scheme for mineral projects (Sysmin); venture capital; interest-rate subsidies; emergency aid; and aid for refugees.[460]

Phare

The Europe Agreement with Poland[461] provides for financial co-operation between the Parties.[462] More particularly, an Additional Protocol to the Polish Agreement[463] envisages in Article 2 that the Association Council shall decide the terms and conditions for the participation of Poland in Community framework programmes, specific programmes, projects, or other actions. A central role is played by the Phare programme.[464]

The Phare programme is primarily concerned with economic restructuring in Central and East European countries. Co-operation between border regions in these countries and border regions within the Union is also envisaged within the programme.[465] It is envisaged that this programme and the

---

[457] Annex B to the Co-operation Agreement with Sweden (OJ 1983 L185/20).

[458] Annex C to the Agreement with Sweden on trade electronic data interchange systems (OJ 1989 L400/22).

[459] OJ 1991 L229/1.   [460] Title B7–1 of the Budget for 1997 (OJ 1997 L44/3).

[461] OJ 1993 L348/2.   [462] *Ibid.*, Arts. 96–101.   [463] OJ 1995 L317/35.

[464] Reg. 3906/89 (OJ 1989 L375/11) on economic aid to Hungary and Poland.

[465] Cf. the Jopp Programme (OJ 1991 C46/11) for promoting the establishment of joint ventures

Structural Funds[466] may provide complementary support for such co-operation.[467] At the same time, there is also a special heading in the Union Budget for assistance to border regions in such countries where the assistance is complementary to that provided to border regions within the Union.[468]

Co-ordination of Phare activities with the work of the European Regional Development Fund, notably Interreg,[469] is envisaged.[470] In addition, network support is provided under Ouverture and Ecos. The latter programme is designed to encourage regions and cities, particularly in the less-favoured areas of the Union, to establish links and to co-operate with counterparts in Eastern Europe. To this end, the Union supports the establishment of a co-operation network between various Union cities and their Eastern partners.[471]

20.9.3 EEA Agreement

When the EEA Agreement[472] was concluded, Member States demanded compensation for trade liberalisation with the comparatively developed EFTA states. According to the preamble to the Agreement, the Contracting Parties aim to promote a harmonious development of the European Economic Area. They are also convinced of the need to contribute through the application of this Agreement to the reduction of economic and social disparities between their regions.[473] Article 115 confirms the agreement of the Parties to reduce such disparities. To this end, Article 116 provides for the establishment by the EFTA states of a Financial Mechanism, details of which are set out in Protocol 38 to the Agreement.[474]

The Protocol provides for the Mechanism to provide assistance in the form of grants and interest rebates.[475] Finance is provided by the EFTA states, and operations are administered by the European Investment Bank.[476]

---

in the countries of central and eastern Europe. Cf. also Phare Baltic Sea region cross-border co-operation programme Funding for joint projects with Interreg Call for proposals (OJ 1997 C336/14).

[466] See e.g. the Notice laying down guidelines for operational programmes which Member States are invited to establish in the framework of a Community initiative concerning border development, cross-border co-operation, and selected energy networks (OJ 1994 C180/60), para. 19.

[467] 7th recital in the preamble to Reg. 2082/93 (OJ 1993 L193/20) amending 4253/88 and the 3rd indent of Art. 3(1) thereof.

[468] Art. B7–502, "Transfrontier co-operation in the field of structural operations", in the Budget for 1997 (OJ 1997 L44/3).

[469] Future of Community initiatives under the Structural Funds, COM(93)282, 16.

[470] Reg. 1628/94 (OJ 1994 L171/14) concerning the implementation of a programme for cross-border co-operation between countries in central and eastern Europe and Member States in the framework of the Phare programme.

[471] *European Report* 1728 (11 Dec. 1991).   [472] OJ 1994 L1/3.

[473] *Ibid.*, 6th recital in the Preamble.   [474] Art. 117 EEA.

[475] Art. 1(2) of Prot. 38, on the Financial Mechanism.

[476] *Ibid.* A co-operation agreement has been concluded between the EFTA states and the EIB, and the EFTA Standing Committee has adopted Dec. 4/94 (OJ 1994 L85/79) establishing a financial mechanism committee.

With a view to maintaining consistency between intervention by the Mechanism and Union actions, the financial management of the subsidised loans is entrusted to the European Investment Bank. However, its decisions are subject to approval by EFTA states and to a Commission opinion. Applications for grants have to be approved by the same procedure.[477]

Over the period 1993 to 1997 inclusive the total amount of grants provided was to be 500 million Euro.[478] The total volume of loans to be eligible for interest rebates[479] over the same period was to be 1,500 million Euro.[480] Assistance is limited to projects in Greece, the Island of Ireland, Portugal, and the regions of Spain listed in the Appendix to the Protocol.[481] The shares allocated to each beneficiary region are determined for a five-year period in the light of the region's relative level of economic development and population size and "other relevant factors".[482] Priority is given to projects which place particular emphasis on the environment (including urban development), transport (including transport infrastructure), or education and training. Among projects submitted by private undertakings, special consideration is given to small and medium-sized enterprises. The maximum grant element for any project supported by the Financial Mechanism must be fixed at a level which is not inconsistent with Union policies in this regard.[483]

---

[477] Report of the Committee on External Economic Relations on economic and trade relations between the EC and the EFTA countries in the EEA, EP Doc. A3–306/92.

[478] Art. 3(1) of Prot. 38.

[479] The percentage fixed for the interest rebates was reduced from 3% to 2% by Art. 16 of the Protocol adjusting the EEA Agreement (OJ 1994 L1/572).

[480] Art. 2(5) of Prot. 38.

[481] *Ibid.*, Art. 4(1).

[482] Art. 8(1) of Reg. 2894/94 (OJ 1994 L305/6) concerning arrangements for implementing the EEA Agreement.

[483] Art. 4(2) of Prot. 38. See, e.g., Annual report on the EEA Financial Mechanism, COM(96)653.

21

Common Policies

The common policies constitute substantive frameworks within which legislative harmonisation and harmonisation through financial instruments are to take place. These policies go beyond prohibiting national measures or the conduct of undertakings which may interfere with the common market and seek to harmonise national policies. Most of the common policies are provided for in Part Three of the EC Treaty, though this Part is headed "Community policies" and also covers the "four freedoms". Article 2 of the same Treaty refers to "common policies or activities", and Article A of the Treaty on European Union refers to "policies and forms of co-operation" established by this Treaty. More particularly, Article 130b of the EC Treaty refers to the "Community's policies and actions". Thus the concept of a common policy and its relationship with the law of the common market[1] are ill-defined in the Treaties.

21.1 Agricultural Policy

Articles 38 to 47 of the EC Treaty provide for a common policy for agriculture. According to Article 38(1) of the Treaty, agricultural products are products of the soil, of stockfarming, and of fisheries and products of first-stage processing[2] directly related to these products. The products concerned are listed in Annex II to the Treaty. Article 38(4) requires that the common policy should cover these products. They are subject to the general rules of the common market, unless Articles 39 to 43 stipulate otherwise.[3] Agricultural products not listed in Annex II to the Treaty[4] are fully subject to the general rules.

---

[1] Cf., in connection with social policy, Case 43/75 *Gabrielle Defrenne* v. *SA Belge de Navigation Aérienne (Sabena)* [1976] ECR 455, 472.

[2] "Products of first-stage processing" were defined in Case 185/73 *Offene Handelsgesellschaft in Firma H.C. König* v. *Hauptzollamt Bielefeld* [1974] ECR 607, 618.

[3] Art. 40(2) EC

[4] Joined Cases 2 & 3/62 *EEC Commission* v. *Luxembourg and Belgium: gingerbread* [1962] ECR 425, 434.

21.1.1 Objectives

The objectives of the common agricultural policy are, according to Article 39(1) of the Treaty: to increase agricultural productivity by promoting technical progress and by ensuring the rational development of agricultural production and the optimum utilisation of factors of production, in particular labour; to ensure a fair standard of living for the agricultural community, in particular by increasing the individual earnings of persons engaged in agriculture; to stabilise markets; to assure the availability of supplies; and to ensure that supplies reach consumers at reasonable prices.

In implementation of the policy account is to be taken of the particular nature of agricultural activity, which results from the social structure of agriculture and from structural and natural disparities between the various agricultural regions. Account is also to be taken of the need to effect the appropriate adjustments by degrees and the fact that in the Member States agriculture constitutes a sector linked with the economy as a whole.[5]

The need may be implied for the Union institutions to make a choice between the various objectives. When this need arises, the Union institutions must decide which objective should be given priority, taking account of the principle of "Community preference" in favour of farmers.[6]

21.1.2 Common Organisations

Article 40(1) of the Treaty requires that common organisations of agricultural markets be established. A common organisation may take the form of common rules on competition; compulsory co-ordination of the various national market organisations; or a European market organisation. It may include all measures to attain the objectives set out in Article 39. In particular, it may include: price regulation; aids for the production and marketing of the various products, storage, and carryover arrangements; and common machinery for stabilising imports or exports. A common price policy may be entailed.

Any discrimination between producers or consumers within the Union shall be excluded by the common organisations.[7] Thus, for example, discrimination between producers of the same product is prohibited.[8] The establishment of a common organisation also has the effect of depriving Member States of the power to take any measure which may undermine or create exceptions to it.[9] In short, such an organisation is based on the

---

[5] Art. 39(2) EC.

[6] Case 5/67 *W. Beus GmbH & Co.* v. *Hauptzollamt München* [1968] ECR 83, 98.

[7] Art. 40(2) EC.

[8] Joined Cases 124/76 & 20/77 *SA Moulins et Huileries de Pont-à-Mousson* v. *Office National Interprofessionnel des Céréales* [1977] ECR 1795, 1811.

[9] Case 51/74 *P.J. Van der Hulst's Zonen* v. *Produktschap voor Siergewassen* [1975] ECR 79, 94; and Case 111/76 *Officier van Justitie* v. *Beert van den Hazel* [1977] ECR 901, 909.

concept of the open market to which every purchaser has access and which is regulated solely by the instruments provided for by the organisation.[10]

Implementing measures are adopted under Article 43(2) of the Treaty. Measures adopted under this provision may lay down uniform rules governing the conditions under which products, including those originating from third states, may be marketed.[11] In particular, provision may be made for adoption of protective measures against imports from third states.[12]

Price Regulation

In practice, a "target price", which is usually higher than the world market price, may be established for products covered by a common organisation. To prevent overproduction from threatening this price, Member States intervene when the market price falls to the "intervention price" and purchase excess supplies. Moreover, to prevent the target price from being undercut, levies are imposed on imports from third states to bring them up to the "threshold price". Such levies are intended to protect and stabilise the Union market. In particular, they seek to prevent price fluctuations on the world market from affecting prices within the Union.[13] Conversely, exporters to a third state receive a subsidy, which is equal to the difference between the price within the Union and the world market price.[14]

Reform of such arrangements has proved necessary. In particular, to limit the costs of subsidising over-production, set-asides[15] and stabilisers[16] have been introduced. According to the former, farmers receive financial incentives to take land out of production. According to the latter, the price at which intervention takes place is reduced where production is excessive. In addition, export subsidies have been cut. Further price cuts,[17] accompanied by compensation payments to farmers,[18] are being made.

Fisheries

Particular problems are faced by the fisheries policy, which is pursued through a common organisation for fishery products. This policy seeks to

---

[10] Case 83/78 *Pigs Marketing Board* v. *Redmond* [1978] ECR 2347, 2371.

[11] Case C–131/87 *EC Commission* v. *EC Council: animal glands* [1989] ECR I–3743, I–3771.

[12] See e.g. Art. 37(2) of Reg. 2200/96 (OJ 1996 L297/1) on the common organisation of the market in fruit and vegetables. It was applied by Reg. 903/97 (OJ 1997 L130/6) adopting a protective measure applying to imports of garlic originating in China.

[13] Case 113/75 *Giordano Frecassetti* v. *Amministrazione delle Finanze dello Stato* [1976] ECR 983, 992.

[14] See e.g. Reg. 2727/75 (OJ 1975 L281/1) on the common organisation of the market in cereals.

[15] See e.g. Arts. 21–22 of Reg. 870/85 (OJ 1985 L95/1) amending Reg. 729/70.

[16] See e.g. Reg. 1097/88 (OJ 1988 L110/7) amending Reg. 2727/75. Price cuts were introduced, if maximum guaranteed quantities were exceeded.

[17] Reg. 1766/92 (OJ 1992 L181/21) on the common organisation of the market in cereals, Art. 3.

[18] Reg. 1765/92 (OJ 1992 L181/12) establishing a support system for producers of certain arable crops.

conserve fish stocks and prevent overfishing.[19] Accordingly, total allowable catches have been allocated to individual Member States.[20] At the same time, agreements may be concluded regarding access to the fisheries resources of third states.[21]

21.2 Transport Policy

The importance attached to transport by the authors of the EEC Treaty was reflected in its inclusion, along with agriculture in Part Two of this Treaty. This Part was headed "Foundations of the Community". The transport policy is now provided for in Articles 74 to 84 of the EC Treaty.

21.2.1 Objectives

Article 74 of the EC Treaty states that the objectives of the Treaty are to be pursued in the transport sector "within the framework of a common transport policy". Article 75(1) provides that, for the purpose of implementing Article 74, the Council must lay down common rules applicable to international transport to or from the territory of a Member State or passing across the territory of one or more Member States; the conditions under which non-resident carriers may operate transport services within a Member State; measures to improve transport safety; and any other appropriate provisions. According to Article 75(2) of the EEC Treaty, such rules were to have been laid down during the transitional period for establishment of the common market.[22] However, this deadline was not met.

In *European Parliament* v. *EC Council: transport policy*[23] the European Parliament sought a declaration from the Court of Justice that the Council had unlawfully failed to introduce a common policy for transport. As the Court noted, the obligations imposed on the Council by Article 75 of the EEC Treaty included the introduction of freedom to provide transport services. The scope of the obligation to introduce this freedom was clearly defined by the Treaty.[24] This freedom was to entail the removal of any discrimination against the person providing the services based on his nationality or the fact that he was established in a Member State other than that where the services were to be provided. Discretion was available only as regards the means

---

[19] Reg. 3094/86 (OJ 1986 L288/1) laying down certain technical measures for the conservation of fishery resources; and Dec. 97/413 (OJ 1997 L175/27) concerning the objectives and detailed rules for restructuring the Community fisheries sector for the period 1 Jan. 1997–31 Dec. 2001 with a view to achieving a balance on a sustainable basis between resources and their exploitation.

[20] Art. 8 of Reg. 3760/92 (OJ 1992 L389/1) establishing a Community system for fisheries and aquaculture.

[21] See e.g. the Agreement with the Government of Mauritius on fishing in Mauritian waters (OJ 1989 L159/2).

[22] Art. 8 EEC.   [23] Case 13/83 [1985] ECR 1513.   [24] Arts 59 and 60 EEC.

employed to secure this freedom, bearing in mind, those features which were special to transport.[25] Accordingly, the Court found unlawful the failure of the Council to ensure freedom to provide services in the sphere of international transport and to lay down the conditions under which non-resident carriers might operate transport services in a Member State.[26] However, the claim that the Council had unlawfully failed to introduce a common transport policy could not be upheld, because the claim was too general.[27]

Liberalisation

Apparently, the transport policy is to be inspired partly by the demands of economic liberalism. According to Article 76 of the EC Treaty, no Member State may, without the unanimous approval of the Council, make the provisions governing transport when the Treaty came into force less favourable in their direct or indirect effect on carriers of other Member States as compared with carriers who are nationals of that Member State.

Moreover, according to Article 79(1), in the case of transport within the Union territory, there shall be no discrimination which takes the form of carriers charging different rates and imposing different conditions for the carriage of the same goods over the same transport links on grounds of the country of origin or of the destination of the goods in question. The Commission, acting on its own initiative or on application by a Member State, shall investigate any cases of discrimination contrary to this provision. It shall also take the necessary decisions within the framework of rules to be enacted by the Council.[28]

Again, according to Article 81, charges or dues in respect of the crossing of frontiers which are charged by a carrier in addition to transport rates shall not exceed a reasonable level after taking into account the costs actually incurred thereby. The Member States shall endeavour to reduce these costs progressively. The Commission may make recommendations to Member States for the purposes of this provision.

Intervention

Some intervention is explicitly authorised by the Treaty. Thus Article 75(2) requires that in elaborating the common transport policy, the Council is to take account of the need for adaptation to the economic development which results from establishment of the common market. More particularly, according to Article 77, aid shall be compatible with the Treaty, if it meets the needs of transport co-ordination. It shall also be compatible, if it represents reimbursement for the discharge of certain obligations inherent in the concept of a public service.[29]

---

[25] [1985] ECR 1513, 1599–1600.
[26] *Ibid.*, 1601.   [27] *Ibid.*, 1596–7.   [28] Art. 79(4) EC.
[29] See, regarding the definition of such obligations, Case 36/73 *NV Nederlandse Spoorwegen* v. *Minister van Verkeer en Waterstaat* [1973] ECR 1299.

Objectives of Other Policies

Pursuit of the objective of transport liberalisation may be affected by the objectives of other policies. In particular, according to Article 80(1) of the Treaty, the imposition, in respect of transport operations carried out within the Union, of rates and conditions involving any element of support or protection in the interest of one or more particular undertakings or industries may be authorised by the Commission.[30] The Commission shall, acting on its own initiative or on application by a Member State, examine such rates and conditions. In doing so, it must take particular account of the requirements of an appropriate regional economic policy, the needs of underdeveloped areas, and the problems of areas seriously affected by political circumstances. It must also take account of the effects of such rates and conditions on competition between the different modes of transport. After consulting each Member State concerned, the Commission shall take the necessary decisions under Article 80(2).

21.2.2 Transport Infrastructure

Early arrangements were made for consultation regarding transport infrastructure "of Community interest".[31] It was envisaged that co-ordinated development of transport links and removal of any existing obstacles and breaks in continuity at the Union's internal frontiers would be promoted by such consultation.[32] However, according to a memorandum of 1961,[33] the main concern was to facilitate establishment of the common market.

Consultation arrangements regarding transport infrastructure are said to have proved inadequate[34] and were revised by Decision 78/174.[35] Article 1(2) of the Decision provided that a project was of "Community interest" where it was a major project designed to create new transport links, remove a bottleneck, or appreciably increase the capacity of transport links and concerned cross-frontier routes; had a significant effect on traffic between Member States or with third states; affected a Union policy, particularly the regional policy; or made use of new transport technologies which could be used for long-distance interurban transport.[36]

---

[30] See also, regarding tariffs fixed to meet competition, Art. 76(3) EC.

[31] Dec. 66/161 (JO 1966 583) establishing a consultation procedure in relation to transport investments.

[32] *Ibid.*, 6th recital in the preamble.

[33] *Fourth EEC General Report* (EEC Commission, Brussels, 1961), 138.

[34] *Development of the Common Transport Policy*, Bull. EC, Supp. 8/71, 5.

[35] Instituting a consultation procedure and setting up a committee in the field of transport infrastructure (OJ 1978 L54/16). See, regarding the work of the committee, the Triannual report of the Commission on the work of the Transport Infrastructure Committee (1984–7), COM(88)289.

[36] See, most recently, Clarification of the Commission recommendations on the application of the competition rules to new infrastructure projects (OJ 1997 C298/5).

21.2.3 Transport by Rail, Road, and Inland Waterway

The Treaty provisions concerning transport apply to transport by rail, road, and inland waterway under Article 84(1). Various implementing measures have been enacted concerning these modes of transport.

Rail

Union legislation requires that the transport of passengers and the management of railway networks are handled separately, at least from an accounting point of view. Where there are several users, the body managing the network must charge them non-discriminatory fees.[37] At the same time, the public service obligations of railways are to be performed independently of their commercial activities.[38]

Road

Road transport generally was liberalised by Regulation 881/92.[39] Cabotage, that is, where a non-resident carrier trades in another Member State, was liberalised in the case of passenger transport by Regulation 2454/92[40] and in the case of haulage by Regulation 3118/93.[41]

At the same time, road safety legislation has also been introduced. For example, maximum weights and dimensions of goods vehicles have been harmonised.[42]

Inland Waterway

Inland waterway transport, including transport within a Member State, has been liberalised by Regulation 3921/91.[43]

21.2.4 Sea Transport

General provisions of the Treaty apply to sea transport.[44] More particularly,

---

[37] Reg. 1192/69 (JO 1969 L156/8) on common rules for the normalisation of the accounts of railway undertakings.

[38] Reg. 1191/69 (JO 1969 L156/1) on action by Member States concerning the obligations inherent in the concept of a public service in transport by rail, road, and inland waterway.

[39] On access to the market in the carriage of goods by road within the Community to or from the territory of a Member State or passing across the territory of one or more Member States (OJ 1992 L95/1).

[40] Laying down the conditions under which non-resident carriers may operate national road passenger transport services within a Member State (OJ 1992 L251/1).

[41] Laying down the conditions under which non-resident carriers may operate national road haulage services within a Member State (OJ 1993 L279/1).

[42] Dir. 96/53 (OJ 1996 L235/59) laying down for certain road vehicles within the Community the maximum authorised dimensions in national and international traffic and the maximum authorised weights in international traffic.

[43] Laying down the conditions under which non-resident carriers may transport goods or passengers by inland waterway within a Member State (OJ 1991 L373/1).

[44] Case 167/73 *EC Commission* v. *France: merchant seamen* [1974] ECR 359, 371.

according to Article 84(2) of the Treaty, the Council may decide to what extent and by what procedure appropriate provisions may be laid down for such transport.[45] Certain provisions of this kind have been adopted.

In particular, Regulation 4055/86[46] provides for a free market in the provision of shipping services: by ships flying Member State flags and plying between Member States; by ships flying such flags and plying between Member States and third states; and by other ships between Member States and between them and third states. Moreover, the freedom to provide shipping services within the waters of a Member State other than that in which the vessel is registered was established by Regulation 3577/92.[47] At the same time, Regulation 4056/86[48] determines the application of Articles 85 and 86 of the Treaty to sea transport.

21.2.5 Air Transport

General provisions of the Treaty apply to air transport.[49] More particularly, according to Article 80(2) of the Treaty, the Council may decide to what extent and by what procedure appropriate provisions may be laid down for such transport. Certain provisions of this kind have been adopted.

Access to routes between Member States has been liberalised,[50] as has access to routes within Member States.[51] Fares have also been liberalised.[52] At the same time, competition law has been made applicable to air transport.[53]

---

[45] The requirement that the Council act on a Commission proposal was introduced by the SEA (OJ 1987 L169/1).

[46] Applying the principle of freedom to provide services to maritime transport between Member States and between Member States and third countries (OJ 1986 L378/1).

[47] Applying the principle of freedom to provide services to maritime transport within the Member States (maritime cabotage) (OJ 1992 L364/1). See also Report on the implementation of Reg. 3577/92, COM(97)296.

[48] Laying down detailed rules for the applications of Arts. 85 and 86 of the Treaty to maritime transport (OJ 1986 L378/4).

[49] Case 167/73 *EC Commission* v. *France: merchant seamen* [1974] ECR 359, 371; and Joined Cases 209–213/84 *Ministère Public* v. *Lucas Asjes* [1986] ECR 1425, 1466.

[50] Reg. 2343/90 (OJ 1990 L217/8) on access to air carriers to scheduled intra-Community air service routes and on the sharing of passenger capacity between air carriers on scheduled air services between Member States. See also Reg. 95/93 (OJ 1993 L14/1) on common rules for the allocation of slots at Community airports.

[51] Reg. 2408/92 (OJ 1992 L240/8) on access for Community air carriers to intra-Community air routes. See also Case T–260/94 *Air Inter SA* v. *EC Commission* (19 June 1997).

[52] Reg. 2409/92 (OJ 1992 L240/15) on fares and rates for air services.

[53] Reg. 3975/87 (OJ 1987 L374/1) laying down the procedure for the application of the rules on competition to undertakings in the air transport sector. It only covered flights between airports within the Union. See also Case 66/86 *Ahmed Saeed Flugreisen and Silver Line Reisebüro GmbH* v. *Zentrale zur Bekämpfung Unlauteren Wettbewerbs eV* [1989] ECR 803.

21.2.6 Transport and Third States

Article 75(1)(a) of the Treaty concerns transport to or from third states,[54] to the extent that part of a journey takes place on Union territory. Therefore, the powers of the Union extend to relationships arising from international law and may entail the need for agreements with the third state concerned.[55]

In particular, the Union institutions may, in the common rules laid down by them, prescribe the approach to be taken by the Member States in their "external" dealings or concert action in relation to third states. Thus Regulation 4058/86[56] concerns co-ordinated action to safeguard free access to cargoes in ocean trades. It provides that the Council may decide on co-ordinated action, when action by a third state restricts free access to shipping companies of Member States to the transport of liner cargoes.[57] Again, Regulation 4055/86,[58] applying the principle of freedom to provide services to maritime transport between Member States and third states, requires the phasing-out or adjustment of existing cargo-sharing arrangements.[59] It also subjects cargo-sharing arrangements in any future agreements to a Union authorisation procedure.[60] Moreover, Regulation 4057/86[61] has provided for application of a "redressive duty" to third-country shipowners who engage in unfair pricing.

At the same time, transport to or from third states may be affected by the common foreign and security policy. In particular, embargoes based on Article 228a of the Treaty may involve the suspension of transport services, as in the case of Iraq and Kuwait,[62] Serbia and Montenegro,[63] and Haiti.[64]

21.3 Environmental Policy

Express provision for pursuit of an environmental policy was introduced into the EEC Treaty[65] by the Single European Act.[66] More developed provisions are now contained in Articles 130r to 130t of the EC Treaty.

21.3.1 Objectives

According the Article 130r(1) of the EC Treaty, the environmental policy seeks to preserve, protect, and improve the quality of the environment; to

---

[54] Opinion 1/94 *International Agreements on Services and the Protection of Intellectual Property* [1994] ECR I–5267, I–5410–11.

[55] Case 22/70 *EC Commission* v. *EC Council: ERTA* [1971] ECR 263, 275. See e.g. the Agreement with the former Yugoslav Republic of Macedonia in the field of transport (OJ 1997 L348/178).

[56] OJ 1986 L378/21.   [57] *Ibid.*, Art. 3(3).   [58] OJ 1986 L378/1.   [59] *Ibid.*, Art. 3.

[60] *Ibid.*, Art. 5.   [61] On unfair pricing practices in maritime transport (OJ 1986 L378/14).

[62] Reg. 340/90 (OJ 1990 L213/1) preventing trade by the Community as regards Iraq and Kuwait.

[63] Reg. 990/93 (OJ 1993 L102/14) concerning trade between the EEC and Serbia and Montenegro.

[64] Reg. 1608/93 (OJ 1993 L155/2) introducing an embargo concerning certain trade between the EEC and Haiti.

[65] Arts 130r–130t EEC.   [66] OJ 1987 L169/1.

protect human health; to encourage the prudent and rational utilisation of natural resources; and to promote measures at international level to deal with regional or worldwide environmental problems.[67]

21.3.2 Implementation

Implementing action relating to the environment shall be based on the precautionary principle. It shall also be based on the principles that preventive action should be taken, that environmental damage should as a priority be rectified at source, and that the polluter should pay.[68] Moreover, environmental protection requirements must be integrated[69] into the definition and implementation of other Union policies.[70] The implication is that Union measures should ensure the representation of environmental interests in pursuit of economic goals and not merely their *ex post facto* mediation via public control efforts.[71]

These principles are to be implemented through measures adopted by the Council under Article 130s. According to Article 130t, such measures shall not prevent any Member State from maintaining or introducing more stringent protective measures compatible with the Treaty.

Judicial decision making may play a role in implementation of the same principles. For example, in *EC Commission* v. *Belgium*[72] the Walloon Regional Council had prohibited the storage, tipping, or dumping in Wallonia of waste originating outside the region. Here the Court of Justice invoked the principle that pollution should be rectified at source. According to the Court, this principle implied that it was for each region to act against pollution. Hence, trade restrictions entailed by the Walloon prohibition could be justified by reference to mandatory requirements.[73]

In practice, implementation may be affected by the question whether the "old approach" to environmental policy or the approach envisaged in the current action programme is pursued.

"Old Approach"

The "old approach" to Union environmental policy has concentrated on introduction of harmonised environmental standards in legislative measures,

---

[67] See also sect. 21.16 below, regarding environmental policy and relations with third states.

[68] Art. 130r(2) EC.

[69] Under the version of this provision introduced by the SEA (OJ 1987 L169/1) such requirements merely had to be "a component" of other Union policies.

[70] Art. 3c EC. See also the Declaration on Assessment of the Environmental Impact of Community Measures, adopted along with the TEU. More particularly, in exercising its powers under Arts. 130r–130t EC, the Union is to take account of the specific requirements of nature conservation. See the Declaration on Part Three, Title XVI, of the EC Treaty.

[71] Such efforts may encounter transaction costs which significantly influence policy efficiency. See J. Nicolaisen and P. Hoeller, *Economics and the Environment: A Survey of Issues and Policy Options* (OECD Working Paper No. 82, Paris, 1990), 15.

[72] Case C–2/90 [1992] ECR I–4431.   [73] *Ibid.*, I–4480.

which Member States are required to implement. In terms of "legislative efficiency", this approach may seem to have been successful. A large number of measures has been enacted by the Council.[74] The difficulties often experienced by Member States in complying with these measures may also be taken to suggest that the standards embodied therein are not unduly low.

In policy terms, however, these very difficulties may be viewed as an indication of the inadequacies of this approach.[75] For example, in 1992 the Court of Justice found that the United Kingdom had failed to bring the quality of its water up to the standards specified by a Directive[76] enacted a decade earlier.[77] Judgments of this kind underline that an effective environmental policy depends not simply on embodiment of high standards in Union legislation. It may also be necessary to seek the creation of conditions which promote attainment of the standards in practice. If such conditions are not created, only the minimum improvements necessary to meet the standards may be adopted, and there may be long delays in their adoption.[78]

It is not clear that provision for the imposition of sanctions on a Member State failing to comply with a judgment of the Court in Article 171(2) of the Treaty will substantially affect the situation.[79] According to the Court of Auditors, the relevant legislative measures have become so manifold and complex that the authorities and traders concerned either have no knowledge of them or are not in a position to ensure that they are applied.[80]

Current Action Programme

According to the current Action Programme on the Environment,[81] adopted in 1993, substantial changes in established trends and practices must be

[74] Commission Reply to the Court of Auditors, Special Report 3/92 concerning the environment (OJ 1992 C245/1), introduction, para. 1.

[75] Cf. the distinctions made between legalistic or "technical/expertise" approaches to policy implementation and "policy culture" or "political/interest" approaches in H. Siedentopf and J. Ziller (eds.), *Making European Policies Work: The Implementation of Community Legislation in the Member States* (Sage, London, 1988).

[76] Dir. 80/778 (OJ 1980 L229/11) relating to the quality of water intended for human consumption.

[77] Case C–337/89 *EC Commission v. UK: drinking water* [1992] ECR I–6103. This failure is typical of the inadequate implementation of environmental policy directives by Member States generally. See P. Hagland, 'Environmental Policy' in L. Hurwitz and C. Lequesne (eds.), *The State of the European Community* (Lynne Riener, Boulder, 1991) 259–72.

[78] It is claimed, however, that "the EEC has already gone far in its attempt to make environmental legal rules work in practice". See L. Krämer, "The Implementation of Environmental Laws by the European Economic Communities" [1991] *Jahrbuch für Internationales Recht* 9–53, 53.

[79] Cf. the view that "tightening up the implementation and enforcement of EC environmental legislation in the Member States should . . . become easier" in D. Wilkinson, 'Maastricht and the Environment: the Implications for the EC's Environmental Policy of the Treaty on European Union' (1992) *Journal of Environmental Law* 221–39, 222.

[80] Special Report 3/92 concerning the environment (OJ 1992 C245/1), para. 3.5. See also paras. 4.6–12 (*ibid.*).

[81] Resolution of the Council and the Representatives of the Governments of the Member States, meeting within the Council, of 1 Feb. 1993 (OJ 1993 C138/1) on a Community programme of policy and action in relation to the environment and sustainable development.

effected, and all sectors of society must fully share responsibility for improving the environment. Previous measures have failed to maintain the "quality of the environment". Therefore, a fundamental change of direction, entailing use of a broader mix of policies is considered necessary.[82] As the Commission observes, "it is not feasible to adopt a directive or regulation which says: 'Thou shalt act in a sustainable manner.'"[83]

Hence, the Programme seeks: the prevention of environmental damage by integrating environmental protection in the production process;[84] the sharing of responsibility among all actors (economic forces, government, public authorities at all levels, and the general public);[85] and the broadening of the range of environmental policy instruments, particularly by including economic and tax schemes and incentives.[86]

However, the Commission remains disappointed about lack of progress in the implementation of environmental policy.[87]

21.4 Social Policy, Education, and Vocational Training

Articles 117 to 127 of the EC Treaty deal with social policy, education, and vocational training.

21.4.1 Social Policy

Article 117 of the Treaty establishes the objectives of promotion of employment, improved living and working conditions, proper social protection, dialogue between management and labour, the development of human resources, and the combating of exclusion. It is believed that progress towards these objectives will ensue not only from the functioning of the common market, which will favour the harmonisation of social systems. It will also ensue from the procedures provided for in the Treaty and from the approximation of provisions laid down by law, regulation, or administrative action.

Hence, according to Article 118, Union action is to support and complement the activities of the Member States in the following fields: the working environment;[88] working conditions;[89] the information and consultation of

---

[82] *Ibid.*, para. 31.   [83] *Ibid.*, chap. 7.   [84] *Ibid.*, para. 4 of the introduction.

[85] *Ibid.*, 17th recital in the preamble.

[86] *Ibid.*, 33rd recital in the preamble. See also Environmental taxes and charges in the single market, COM(97)9

[87] See e.g. Progress report on the implementation of "Towards Sustainability", COM(95)624.

[88] Dir. 89/391 (OJ 1989 L183/1) on the introduction of measures to encourage improvements in the safety and health of workers at work; Dir. 93/104 (OJ 1993 L307/18) concerning certain aspects of the organisation of working time; and Dir. 94/33 (OJ 1994 L216/12) on the protection of young people at work.

[89] See, more particularly, regarding conditions of employment of TSNs legally residing in the Union, Art. 118(3) EC.

workers;[90] the integration of persons excluded from the labour market; and equality between men and women with regard to labour market opportunities and treatment at work. Such measures shall not prevent any Member State from maintaining or introducing more stringent protective measures compatible with the Treaty.[91]

Moreover, the Commission is required by Article 118c to promote close co-operation between Member States in the social field. Co-operation is to cover, for example, employment; labour law and working conditions; basic and advanced vocational training; social security; prevention of occupational accidents and diseases; occupational hygiene; and the right of association and collective bargaining between employers and workers.

At the same time, the Commission has the task of promoting the consultation of management and labour at Union level. The Commission shall also take any relevant measure to facilitate their dialogue by ensuring balanced support for the parties.[92] Should management and labour so desire, the dialogue between them at Union level may lead to contractual relations, including agreements.[93] Such agreements may, as in the case of the agreement on parental leave,[94] be embodied in Council enactments.[95]

In practice, the most important legislation has been enacted under Article 100. The legislation concerns the rights of workers in the case of collective redundancies,[96] the transfer of undertakings,[97] and insolvency of employers.[98]

Equal Pay

Article 119 provides that each Member State shall ensure that the principle of equal pay for male and female workers for equal work or for work of equal value is applied.

Such equality means that pay for the same work at piece rates shall be calculated on the basis of the same unit of measurement. It also means that

---

[90] Dir. 94/45 (OJ 1994 L254/64) on the establishment of a European Works Council or a procedure in Community-scale undertakings and Community-scale groups of undertakings for the purposes of informing and consulting employees. It was adopted under the Agreement on Social Policy, which was annexed to the Protocol on Social Policy, adopted with the TEU.

[91] Art. 118(5) EC.   [92] Art. 118a(1) EC.   [93] Art. 118b(1) EC.

[94] Dir. 96/34 (OJ 1996 L145/4) on the framework agreement on parental leave concluded by UNICE and ETUC.

[95] Art. 118b(2) EC.

[96] Dir. 75/129 (OJ 1975 L48/29) on the approximation of the laws of the Member States relating to collective redundancies.

[97] Dir. 77/187 (OJ 1977 L61/27) on the approximation of the laws of the Member States relating to the safeguarding of employees' rights in the event of transfer of undertakings, businesses, or parts of businesses. See also Guidelines on the application of Dir. 77/187, COM(97)85.

[98] Dir. 80/987 (OJ 1980 L283/23) on the approximation of the laws of the Member States relating to the protection of employees in the event of the insolvency of their employer. Cf. also Dir. 91/533 (OJ 1991 L288/32) on an employer's obligation to inform employees of the conditions applicable to the contract or employment relationship.

pay for work at time rates shall be the same for the same job. "Pay" covers the ordinary, basic, or minimum wage or salary and any other consideration, whether in cash or in kind, which the worker receives, directly or indirectly, in respect of his employment, from his employer. It includes, for example, a survivor's pension;[99] employer contributions to a pension scheme;[100] payments to which an employer contributes pursuant to a statutory system, such as sick pay;[101] pensions paid under a contracted out private occupational scheme[102] and any benefits paid by an employer to a worker in connection with his compulsory redundancy;[103] favourable rates for family travel for railway employees;[104] and compensation to members of staff councils or committees attending meetings or training courses.[105] On the other hand, pensions and other benefits received under general state schemes are not covered by Article 119, even if the employer makes a compulsory contribution to a state fund.[106]

This provision has been implemented by directives based on various Treaty provisions.[107] These directives concern equal pay for work of equal value,[108] equal treatment in access to employment and vocational training,[109] equal treatment in social security matters,[110] equal treatment in relation to occupational social security schemes,[111] and equal treatment in self-employed occupations.[112] Legislation on burden-of-proof matters is also proposed.[113]

---

[99] Case C–147/95 *Dimossia Epicheirissi Ilectrismou* v. *Efthimios Evrenopoulos* [1997] ECR I–2057, I–2081.

[100] Case 69/80 *Worringham and Humphreys* v. *Lloyds Bank* [1981] ECR 767, 780.

[101] Case 171/88 *Rinner-Kuhn* v. *FWW Spezial-Gebaudereinigung GmbH* [1989] ECR 493.

[102] Cf. Case 170/84 *Bilka-Kaufhaus GmbH* v. *Karin Weber von Hartz* [1986] ECR 1607.

[103] Case C–262/88 *Douglas Harvey Barber* v. *Guardian Royal Exchange Assurance Group* [1990] ECR I–1889, I–1949.

[104] Case 12/81 *Eileen Garland* v. *British Rail Engineering Ltd* [1982] ECR 359, 369.

[105] Case C–360/90 *Arbeiterwohlfarth der Stadt Berlin eV* v. *Monika Bötel* [1992] ECR I–3589, I–3611–12.

[106] Case 80/70 *Gabrielle Defrenne* v. *Belgium* [1971] ECR 445, 451–2.

[107] Arts. 100, 118a, and 235 EEC and the Agreement on Social Policy.

[108] Dir. 75/117 (OJ 1975 L45/19) on the approximation of the laws of the Member States relating to the application of the principle of equal pay for men and women.

[109] Dir. 76/207 (OJ 1976 L39/40) on the implementation of the principle of equal treatment as regards access to employment, vocational training and promotion, and working conditions. See, more particularly, Dir. 92/85 (OJ 1992 L348/1) on the introduction of measures to encourage improvements in the safety and health at work of pregnant workers and workers who have recently given birth or are breastfeeding.

[110] Dir. 79/7 (OJ 1979 L6/24) on the progressive implementation of the principle of equal treatment in matters of social security.

[111] Dir. 86/378 (OJ 1986 L225/40) on the implementation of the principle of equal treatment in occupational social security schemes.

[112] Dir. 86/613 (OJ 1986 L359/56) on the application of the principle of equal treatment between men and women engaged in an activity, including agriculture, in a self-employed capacity, and on the protection of self-employed women during pregnancy and motherhood.

[113] Amended proposal for a directive on the burden of proof in cases of discrimination based on sex (OJ 1997 C185/21).

At the same time, the case law has also been important for implementation of the principle of equal pay. For example, *Vroege*[114] concerned a pension scheme of which only men and unmarried women working at least 80 per cent of the normal full day could be members. According to the Court of Justice, where a pension scheme was based on an agreement with employees or their representatives and the public authorities were not involved in its funding, benefits under the scheme constituted consideration received by the employees from their employer in respect of their employment within the meaning of Article 119. Given that this provision covered entitlement to such benefits, it necessarily also covered the right to be a member of such a scheme.[115]

Therefore, a pension scheme which excluded married women from membership contravened Article 119. This provision would also be contravened by exclusion of part-time workers from a pension scheme where a much greater number of women than men was affected, unless the employer could provide an objective justification unrelated to any discrimination on sex grounds.[116] The burden of proof is on the employer, who may have to make his remuneration system transparent.[117]

It is stipulated in Article 119(4) that the principle of equal treatment shall not prevent any Member State from maintaining or adopting measures providing for specific advantages in order to make it easier for the underrepresented sex to pursue a vocational activity or to prevent or compensate for disadvantages in professional careers.[118]

Nationals of Third States

Implementation of social policy may be seen as demanding action regarding nationals of third states. In particular, it is feared that discrimination against such persons may lead to "social dumping" within the Union. In other words, some traders and Member States may seek competitive advantages through such discrimination. To avoid this outcome, harmonisation of national law governing the treatment of third-state nationals has been sought.[119]

For example, Decision 85/381,[120] based on Article 118 of the EEC

---

[114] Case C–57/93 *Anna Adriaantje Vroege* v. *NCIV Instituut voor Volkshuisvestering BV and Stichting Pensioenfonds NCIV* [1994] ECR I–4541.

[115] *Ibid.*, I–4573.

[116] *Ibid.*, I–4573–4. Cf. Case C–278/93 *Edith Freers and Hannelore Speckmann* v. *Deutsche Bundespost* [1996] ECR I–1165, I–1192.

[117] Case 109/88 *Handels-og Kontorfunktionærernes Forbund i Danmark* v. *Dansk Arbejdsgiverförening (acting for Danfoss)* [1989] ECR 3199, 3226.

[118] The ECJ had ruled that Art. 119 EEC did not permit "positive discrimination". See, regarding a French ban on night-work by women, Case C–197/96 *EC Commission* v. *France: night work* [1997] ECR I–1489.

[119] Opinion of the Economic and Social Committee of 24 Apr. 1991 (OJ 1991 C159/12) on the status of migrant workers from third countries.

[120] Setting up a prior communication and consultation procedure on migration policies in relation to non-member countries (OJ 1985 L217/25).

Treaty,[121] referred in the Preamble to the importance of ensuring that the migration policies of Member States in relation to third states took into account common policies and actions adopted at Union level. In particular, Union labour market policy was not to be jeopardized.[122] Hence, the Decision established a prior communication and consultation procedure regarding national policies and agreements with third states in this field. The aims of the procedure included ensuring that national policy measures and agreements with third states were in conformity with, and did not compromise, the results of Union policy; examining the possibility of adoption of Union measures harmonising national legislation concerning nationals of third states; promoting the inclusion of a maximum of common provisions in bilateral agreements; and improving the protection of Union Citizens working and living in third states.[123]

In seeking to demonstrate the legality of this Decision before the Court of Justice, the Commission in *Germany, France, Netherlands, Denmark, and the United Kingdom* v. *EC Commission*[124] stressed the need to protect Union social policy.[125] According to the Commission, measures taken by the Member States regarding nationals of third states should not conflict with the social policy pursued by the Union, such as the priority of Union workers[126] with regard to access to employment[127] and the operation of the European Social Fund.[128] However, the Court ruled that the Commission had exceeded its competence under Article 118 of the Treaty. It had done so by requiring in the Decision that Member States participate in a procedure designed to ensure the compatibility of national action in this field with Union policies.[129]

21.4.2 Education

According to Article 126(1) of the Treaty, the Union shall contribute to the development of quality education. The Union shall do so by encouraging

---

[121] According to Art. 121 EEC, the Council might assign to the Commission tasks in connection with the implementation of common measures in the social policy field, particularly as regards social security for the migrant workers referred to in Arts 48 and 51 EEC. However, the first provision was regarded as inapplicable to TSNs because of the narrow interpretation given to the last 2 provisions.

[122] 4th recital in the Preamble (OJ 1985 L217/25). According to Mancini AG in Joined Cases 281, 283–285 & 287/85 *Germany, France, Netherlands, Denmark, and the UK* v. *EC Commission: migration policy* [1987] ECR 3203, 3229, if the Commission had stressed the perspective of the Union labour market, the decision would have been more acceptable to Member States.

[123] See, now, Art. 3 of Dec. 88/384 (OJ 1988 L183/35) setting up a prior communication and consultation procedure in migration policies in relation to non-member countries.

[124] Joined Cases 281, 283–285 & 287/85 [1987] ECR 3203.

[125] *Ibid.*, 3216.

[126] According to AG Mancini, Member States must not take measures regarding TSNs which adversely affect the freedom of movement of Union Citizens (*ibid.*, 3239).

[127] Art. 104 EEC required the Member States "to ensure a high level of employment".

[128] See, regarding ESF activities and TSNs, the Commission Reply to WQ 381/74 by Mr Cousté (OJ 1974 C150/24).

[129] [1987] ECR 3203, 3255.

co-operation between Member States and, if necessary, by supporting and supplementing their action. In taking such action, the Union must fully respect the responsibility of the Member States for the content of teaching and the organisation of education systems and their cultural and linguistic diversity.[130]

Moreover, the Union and the Member States shall, according to Article 126(3), foster co-operation with third states[131] and the competent international organisations in the field of education, particularly the Council of Europe.

21.4.3 Vocational Training

Article 128 of the EEC Treaty provided for implementation of a common vocational training policy capable of contributing to the harmonious development both of the national economies and of the common market. This provision was invoked in *Blaizot*.[132] This ruling concerned French nationals who were in Belgium to study and were charged a supplementary fee by Belgian universities not payable by Belgian students. The Court of Justice ruled that the development of the common vocational policy under Article 128 meant that university studies fell within the scope of the Treaty. Therefore, discrimination regarding university fees was prohibited by the then Article 7,[133] and the supplementary fee could not be imposed on students from other Member States.[134]

Article 127(1) of the EC Treaty now requires implementation of a vocational training policy which shall support and supplement the action of the Member States. However, the responsibility of the Member States for the content and organisation of the policy must be fully respected.

Moreover, the Union and the Member States shall, according to Article 127(3), foster co-operation with third states[135] and the competent international organisations in the sphere of vocational training.

---

[130] See e.g. Dec. 819/95 (OJ 1995 L87/10) establishing the Community action programme "Socrates".

[131] See e.g. the Agreement with the US establishing a co-operation programme in higher education and vocational training (OJ 1995 L279/13).

[132] Case 24/86 *Vincent Blaizot* v. *University of Liège* [1988] ECR 379.

[133] See now Art. 6 EC.

[134] [1988] ECR 379, 402–5. But cf., regarding student grants, Case 197/86 *Steven Malcolm Brown* v. *Secretary of State for Scotland* [1988] ECR 3205, 3243; and Case C–357/89 *V.J.M. Raulin* v. *Minister van Onderwijs en Wetenschappen* [1992] ECR I–1027, I–1063.

[135] See e.g. Dec. 97/739 (OJ 1997 L299/21) concerning the conclusion of bilateral agreements with Cyprus on Cyprus' participation in Community programmes in the fields of education, training, and youth.

21.5 Culture

According to Article 128(1) of the EC Treaty, the Union shall contribute to the flowering of the cultures of the Member States. In doing so, the Union must respect their national and regional diversity and, at the same time, bring the common cultural heritage to the fore.[136] More particularly, Union action concerns: improvement of the knowledge and dissemination of the culture and history of the European peoples; conservation and safeguarding of cultural heritage of European significance; non-commercial cultural exchanges; and artistic and literary creation, including that in the audiovisual sector.

Moreover, the Union and the Member States shall, according to Article 128(3), foster co-operation with third states[137] and the competent international organisations in the field of culture, in particular the Council of Europe.

21.6 Public Health

According to Article 129 (1) of the EC Treaty, a high level of human health protection shall be ensured in the definition and implementation of all Union policies and activities. To this end, the Union is to encourage co-operation between the Member States and, if necessary, lend support to their action. Such action shall be directed towards improving public health, preventing human illnesses and diseases, and obviating sources of danger to human health. Such action shall cover the fight against major health scourges, by promoting research into their causes, their transmission, and their prevention, as well as health information and education.

Moreover, the Union and the Member States shall, according to Article 129(3), foster co-operation with third countries[138] and the competent international organisations in this field.

21.7 Consumer Protection

According to Article 129a(1) of the EC Treaty, the Union is to promote the interests of consumers and ensure a high level of consumer protection.[139] It

---

[136] See e.g. Dec. 2228/97 (OJ 1997 L305/31) establishing a Community action programme in the field of cultural heritage (the Raphael programme).

[137] See e.g. the Council Resolution of 4 Apr. 1995 (OJ 1995 C247/2) concerning co-operation with the associated countries of Central and Eastern Europe in the cultural domain.

[138] See e.g. the Agreement with Bolivia on precursors and chemical substances frequently used in the illicit manufacture of narcotic drugs or psychotropic substances (OJ 1995 L324/3).

[139] Before the TEU, the consumer protection policy was pursued without a specific Treaty basis. See e.g. A. Evans, "European Consumer Protection Law" [1981] *Journal of Business Law* 77–88.

is to seek to protect the health, safety,[140] and economic interests of consumers and to promote their right to information, education, and to organise themselves in order to safeguard their interests. It is to do so through measures adopted pursuant to Article 100a of the Treaty in the context of the completion of the internal market. Such measures have been enacted on, for example, unfair terms in consumer contracts,[141] product liability,[142] misleading advertising,[143] doorstep selling,[144] the protection of consumers in respect of distance contracts,[145] and consumer credit.[146]

The Union is also to adopt specific action which supports, supplements, and monitors the policy pursued by the Member States. This action shall not prevent any Member State from maintaining or introducing more stringent protective measures. Such measures must, however, be compatible with the Treaty, and the Commission is to be notified of them.

No express reference is made to co-operation with third states or international organisations in this area. However, the origins of the consumer protection policy owed much to the work of the Council of Europe.[147]

21.8 Trans-European Networks

Articles 129b to 129d of the EC Treaty deal with Trans-European networks. The Union is to establish a series of guidelines covering the objectives, priorities, and broad lines of measures envisaged in the context of such networks. These guidelines shall identify projects of common interest.[148]

The Union may implement any necessary measures to ensure the interoperability of networks, particularly in the field of technical standardisation. It may also provide financial support for projects of common interest identified by the guidelines, particularly through feasibility studies, loan guarantees, and interest-rate subsidies.[149]

---

[140] Dec. 84/133 (OJ 1984 L70/16) providing for exchange of information relating to dangers arising out of use of consumer products.

[141] Dir. 93/13 (OJ 1993 L95/29) on unfair terms in consumer contracts.

[142] Dir. 85/374 (OJ 1985 L210/29) on the approximation of the laws, regs., and administrative provisions of the Member States concerning liability for defective products.

[143] Dir. 84/450 (OJ 1984 L250/17) relating to the approximation of the laws, regs., and administrative provisions of the Member States concerning misleading advertising.

[144] Dir. 85/577 (OJ 1985 L372/31) to protect the consumer in respect of contracts negotiated away from business premises.

[145] Dir. 97/7 (OJ 1997 L146/31) on the protection of consumers in respect of distance contracts.

[146] Dir. 87/102 (OJ 1987 L42/48) for the approximation of the laws, regulations, and administrative provisions of the Member States concerning consumer credit. See also Report on the operation of Dir. 87/102, COM(97)465.

[147] A. Evans, "Council of Europe: Consumer Protection Initiatives" [1980] *Journal of World Trade Law* 454–61.

[148] Trans-European networks 1997 Report, COM(97)654.

[149] Art. 129c(1) EC. See also sect. 20.6.3.

Moreover, the Union may decide to co-operate with third states to promote projects of mutual interest and to ensure the interoperability of networks.[150]

21.9 Industrial Policy

Industrial policy is provided for in Article 130 of the EC Treaty.

21.9.1 Objectives

Article 130(1) of the Treaty provides that the Union and the Member States shall ensure that the conditions necessary for the competitiveness of Union industry exist. For this purpose, in accordance with a system of open and competitive markets, action shall aim at:

- speeding up the adjustment of industry to structural changes;
- encouraging an environment favourable to initiative and to the development of undertakings throughout the Union, particularly small and medium-sized enterprises;[151]
- encouraging an environment favourable to co-operation between undertakings; and
- fostering better exploitation of the industrial potential of policies of innovation and research and technological development.

21.9.2 Implementation

The Union shall contribute to the achievement of industrial policy objectives through initiatives to co-ordinate the action of Member States[152] and through policies and activities pursued under other Treaty provisions.[153] However, it is stipulated that no basis is provided for the introduction by the Union of any measure which may lead to a distortion of competition.[154]

21.10 RTD Policy

An express basis for research and technological development policy was first introduced into the EEC Treaty[155] by the Single European Act.[156] This policy is now provided for in Articles 130f to 130p of the EC Treaty.

---

[150] Art. 129c(3) EC.
[151] Dec. 97/15 (OJ 1997 L6/25) on a third multiannual programme for SMEs in the EU (1997–2000).
[152] Art. 130(2) EC.   [153] Art. 130(3) EC.   [154] *Ibid.*   [155] Art. 130 EEC.
[156] OJ 1987 L169/1.

21.10.1 Objectives

According to Article 130f(1) of the EC Treaty, the Union shall have the objective of strengthening the scientific and technological bases of Union industry and encouraging it to become more competitive at international level.[157]

21.10.2 Implementation

Implementation of the policy for research and technological development is to be based on multiannual framework programmes and specific programmes.[158] In addition, supplementary programmes may involve the participation of certain Member States only, which shall finance them subject to a possible Union contribution.[159] The Union may also establish joint undertakings or any other structure necessary for the efficient execution of the programmes.[160]

In implementing the multiannual framework programme, the Union may make provision for co-operation in Union research, technological development, and demonstration with third states or international organisations. The detailed arrangements for such co-operation may be the subject of agreements between the Union and the third parties concerned.[161]

21.11 Economic and Monetary Policy

The EC Treaty deals with both economic policy and monetary policy. It goes further in providing for harmonisation in relation to the latter than in relation to the former.

21.11.1 Economic Policy

The "co-ordination" of national economic policies is envisaged in the EC Treaty.[162]

Economic Policy Guidelines

According to Article 102a of the EC Treaty, Member States shall conduct their economic policies with a view to contributing to the achievement of the objectives defined in Article 2 of the Treaty and in the context of the broad guidelines on economic policies to be adopted by the Council.[163] In doing so, the Member States, like the Union, shall act in accordance with the

---

[157] According to Art. 130f(3) EEC, special account was to be taken of the relationship between the common research and development effort, the establishment of the internal market, and the implementation of common policies, particularly as regards competition and trade.

[158] Sect. 20.7.2 above.   [159] Art. 130k EC.   [160] Art. 130n EC.

[161] Art. 130m EC. See e.g. the Framework Agreement for scientific and technical co-operation with Switzerland (OJ 1985 L313/6).

[162] Art. 103 EC.

[163] Art. 103(2) EC. See e.g. Rec. 94/480 (OJ 1994 L200/38) on the broad guidelines of the economic policies of the Member States and of the Union.

principle of an open market economy with free competition, favouring an efficient allocation of resources, and in compliance with the principles set out in Article 3a.[164] If the economic policies of a Member State are inconsistent with the guidelines or risk jeopardizing the proper functioning of economic and monetary union, the Council may make "the necessary recommendations" to the Member State concerned.[165]

Budgetary Discipline

Member States are to avoid excessive government deficits.[166] Moreover, like the Union institutions, they may not borrow from the European Central Bank or national central banks,[167] and privileged access, not based on prudential considerations, to financial institutions is prohibited.[168] At the same time, neither the Union nor the Member States shall be liable for or assume the commitments of central governments, local or other public authorities, or public undertakings of any Member State.[169]

In practice, the Commission monitors the development of the budgetary situation and of the stock of government debt in the Member States with a view to identifying "gross errors". It examines compliance with budgetary discipline on the basis of two criteria: the ratio of planned or actual government deficit to gross domestic product; and the ratio of government debt to gross domestic product.[170]

If there is found to be an excessive deficit, the Council may require the Member State concerned to reduce it. To secure respect for the requirement, the Council may invite the European Investment Bank to reconsider its lending policy towards the Member State concerned; require the Member State concerned to make a non-interest bearing deposit of an appropriate size with the Union until the excessive deficit has, in the view of the Council, been corrected; and impose fines of an appropriate size.[171]

21.11.2 Monetary Policy

Monetary policy is the responsibility of the European System of Central Banks.[172]

---

[164] Chapt. 1.   [165] Art. 103(4) EC.   [166] Art. 104c(1) EC.   [167] Art. 104b EC.
[168] Art. 104a EC. See also Reg. 3604/93 (OJ 1993 L332/4) specifying definitions for the application of the prohibition of privileged access referred to in Art. 104a EC.
[169] Art. 103 EC. See also Reg. 3603/93 (OJ 1993 L332/1) specifying definitions for the application of the prohibitions referred to in Arts. 104 and 104b(1) EC.
[170] Art. 104c(2) EC. See also Reg. 1466/97 (OJ 1997 L209/1) on the strengthening of the surveillance of budgetary positions and the surveillance and co-ordination of economic policies. Stability programmes for participants in EMU and convergence programmes for non-participants are envisaged. See also the European Council Resolution of 17 June 1997 (OJ 1997 C236/1) on the stability and growth pact.
[171] Art. 104c(11) EC. See also Reg. 3605/93 (OJ 1993 L332/7) on the application of the Protocol on the excessive deficit procedure and Reg. 1467/97 (OJ 1997 L209/6) on speeding up and clarifying the implementation of the excessive deficit procedure.
[172] Sect. 6.2.2 above.

Objectives

According to Article 105(1) of the EC Treaty, the primary objective of monetary policy shall be to maintain price stability, though such stability is not defined in the Treaty. Without prejudice to this objective, the European System of Central Banks shall also support the general economic policies within the Union with a view to contributing to the achievement of the objectives laid down in Article 2.[173] In doing so, the System shall act according to the principle of an open market economy with free competition and in compliance with the principles set out in Article 3a.[174]

Implementation

The basic tasks to be carried out through the European System of Central Banks are: to define and implement the monetary policy of the Union; to conduct foreign-exchange operations;[175] to hold and manage the official foreign reserves of the Member States;[176] and to promote the smooth operation of payment systems.[177]

21.12 Common Commercial Policy

The common commercial policy is governed by Articles 110 to 115 of the EC Treaty. This policy often concerns issues similar to those which arise in the operation of the law of the common market. However, the very fact that the former issues are approached within this policy framework may affect their treatment.

21.12.1 Objectives

Article 113(1) of the EC Treaty provides that the common commercial policy shall be based on uniform principles. These principles shall, in particular, concern changes in tariff rates, the conclusion of tariff and trade agreements,[178] the achievement of uniformity in measures of liberalisation, export policy,[179] and measures to protect trade, such as those to be taken in case of dumping or subsidies. The Court of Justice deduces from this provision that establishment of a single trading system with third states constitutes one of the fundamental objectives of the common market.[180] It is thus according to the

---

[173] Chap. 1 above.   [174] *Ibid.*

[175] These operations are to be regulated under Art. 109h EC.

[176] Though the governments may hold and manage foreign-exchange working balances (Art. 105(3) EC).

[177] Art. 105(2) EC.   [178] Art. 113(3) EC.

[179] Art. 112(1) EC provides that without prejudice to obligations undertaken by them within the framework of other international organisations, Member States shall progressively harmonise the systems whereby they grant aid for exports to third states, to the extent necessary to ensure that competition between Union undertakings is not distorted.

[180] See e.g. Case 135/79 *Gedelfi Großeinkauf GmbH & Co. KG v. Hauptzollamt Hamburg-Jonas* [1980] ECR 1713, 1729.

requirements of the common commercial policy that issues arising in trade with third states are supposed to be tackled.[181]

The further implication is apparently drawn that this policy should govern relations between the Union as an independent state-like entity and third states. In practice, this implication is reflected in the way that the Court of Justice treats GATT rules as applying to trade between the Union and third states but not to trade within the Union.[182] It may also be reflected in the "power-oriented, mercantilist perception of the liberal GATT rules as reciprocal concessions"[183] which the Union is said to exhibit in relation to issues of trade with third states.[184]

Such practice may be bound up with differing conceptions of supranationalism. Supranationalism, in the sense of the independence of institutions such as the Commission and European Courts from Member States, may play a vital role in securing liberalisation of trade between Member States. However, conceptions of supranationalism which favour centralisation of decision-making power within the Union may hinder liberalisation of trade with third states.[185]

Liberalisation

The Preamble to the EC Treaty regards the common commercial policy as a means of contributing to the progressive abolition of restrictions on world trade.[186] Moreover, Article 110(1) of the Treaty states that by establishing a customs union between themselves Member States aim to contribute in the common interest to the harmonious development of world trade, the progressive abolition of restrictions on international trade, and the lowering of customs barriers.

Article 110(1) may be interpreted as opposing interference by a Member State with trade with third states.[187] When Union rather than national action is involved, the same provision may have less impact. It is said to imply that the Union adheres to the same aims as the GATT.[188] In practice, however,

---

[181] Case 70/77 *Simmenthal SpA* v. *Amministrazione delle Finanze* [1978] ECR 1453, 1470; and Case 340/87 *EC Commission* v. *Italy: charges for frontier inspections* [1989] ECR 1483, 1513.

[182] Case 10/61 *EC Commission* v. *Italy: radio components* [1962] ECR 1, 10–11; and Case 266/81 *Società Italiana per l'Oleodotto Transalpino (SIOT)* v. *Ministero delle Finanze* [1983] ECR 731, 780.

[183] E.-U. Petersmann, "Strengthening the Domestic Legal Framework of the GATT Multilateral Trade System: Possibilities and Problems of Making GATT Rules Effective in Domestic Legal Systems" in E.-U. Petersmann and M. Hilf (eds.), *The New GATT Round of Multilateral Trade Negotiations* (Kluwer, Deventer, 1991), 33–113, 68–9.

[184] See, most recently, Gulmann AG in Case C–280/93 *Germany* v. *EC Council: bananas* [1994] ECR I–4973, I–5020–6.

[185] Cf., regarding the legal capacity of the Union institutions to prescribe the attitudes to be taken by Member States "in their external dealings", *Opinion 1/94 International Agreements on Services and the Protection of Intellectual Property* [1994] ECR I–5267, I–5411–12.

[186] 6th recital.

[187] Lenz AG in Joined Cases 62 & 72/87 *Exécutif Régional Wallon and Glaverbel* v. *EC Commission* [1988] 1573, 1588.

[188] Joined Cases 21–24/72 *International Fruit Company NV* v. *Produktschap voor Groenten en Fruit*

there is reluctance to treat it as prohibiting Union action which may distort competition in trade with third states.[189] In other words, there is reluctance to treat Article 110(1) as requiring the Union unilaterally to liberalise such trade.

Such practice apparently reflects a concern for reciprocity.[190] In theory, unilateral liberalisation may often increase welfare in the Union,[191] and it is only in "strategic" sectors that such liberalisation may be disadvantageous.[192] Other research suggests that a combination of "internal" and "external" trade liberalisation may generally be a superior strategy to internal liberalisation alone.[193] However, legislative enactments, such as those relating to merger control,[194] public procurement,[195] and protection of semi-conductors,[196] suggest that such theory has not been readily received in Union practice.

Although Union practice of this kind may lack a theoretical justification, a formal legal basis may be suggested by reciprocity concerns in the Treaty.

In particular, Article 238 describes an association agreement as "involving reciprocal rights and obligations, common action, and special procedures". Moreover, in Article 18 of the EEC Treaty Member States declared their readiness to contribute to the development of international trade and the lowering of barriers to trade. This contribution was to involve the conclusion of agreements on a basis of reciprocity and mutual advantage. The agreements were to reduce customs duties below the general level of which Member States could avail themselves as a result of establishment of a

[1972] ECR 1219, 1227. See also Capotorti AG in Case 812/79 *Attorney-General* v. *Juan C. Burgoa* [1980] ECR 2787, 2815.

[189] See e.g. Trabucchi AG in Case 154/73 *Firm of Kurt A. Becher* v. *Hauptzollamt Emden* [1974] ECR 19, 30.

[190] Warner AG in Case 51/75 *EMI Records Ltd* v. *CBS United Kingdom Ltd* [1976] ECR 811, 860 and 862.

[191] R.C. Hine, "Protection in the European Community Before and After 1992" in D. Greenaway, R.C. Hine, A.P. O'Brien, and R.J. Thornton (eds.), *Global Protectionism* (Macmillan, London, 1991) 69–98, 79.

[192] J. Pelkmans, 'Europe – 1992 a Handmaiden to GATT' in F. Laursen (ed.), *Europe 1992: World Partner? the International Market and the World Political Economy* (EIPA, Maastricht, 1991), 125–53, 151.

[193] A. Sapir, *Regional Integration in Europe* (EC Commission Economic Papers No. 94, Brussels, 1992).

[194] Art. 24 of Reg. 4064/89 (OJ 1989 L395/1) on the control of concentration of undertakings.

[195] Art. 29 of Dir. 90/531 (OJ 1990 L297/1) on procurement procedures of entities operating in the water, transport, and telecommunications sectors. This provision was apparently adopted because the US telecommunications market was "closed". See the *Financial Times*, 25 Feb. 1992. However, US opposition led to the watering-down of reciprocity requirements. See the *Financial Times*, 19 June 1992. See now Dec. 93/324 (OJ 1993 L125/54) concerning the extension of the benefit of the provisions of Dir. 90/531 in respect of the US.

[196] Dec. 90/510 (OJ 1990 L285/29) on the extension of the legal protection of topographies of semi-conductor products to persons from certain third states and territories; and Dec. 90/511 (OJ 1990 L285/31) on the extension of the legal protection of topographies of semi-conductor products to persons from certain third states and territories.

customs union between them. Union practice suggests that these references to reciprocity are treated as implying a general need for reciprocity in liberalisation of trade with third states.[197] Implicit support for such treatment may be found in Article 110(1), which refers to the harmonious development of trade with third states. It may be argued that such harmony implicitly depends on reciprocity.

A consequence of seeking reciprocity according to such provisions may be to limit the contribution of the common commercial policy to the liberalisation of trade with third states.

Trade Management

Reciprocity concerns may lead to a preference in the common commercial policy for seeking to manage trade in certain sectors. For example, the adoption of measures in concert with third states is envisaged, as in the GATT Multifibre Arrangement for textiles and the Organisation for Economic Co-operation and Development (OECD) agreement on steel. The latter guarantees "solidarity" between the Union and the other producer countries in restructuring the steel industry.[198]

In effect, implementation of the common commercial policy is sought through achievement of uniformity in the treatment of trade with third states. This is the very kind of approach which was found to be generally unsuitable for securing reduction of obstacles to trade between Member States and led the Commission to adopt its "new approach" to harmonisation.[199] The former approach may be equally unsuitable to liberalisation of trade with third states.

In particular, differences in national policies or national conditions may impede development of the common commercial policy.[200] Such differences may be rendered all the more significant by special ties between some Member States and their colonies or ex-colonies.[201] Problems also used to arise in connection with the division of Germany.[202]

---

[197] Cf. Warner AG in Joined Cases 37 & 38/73 *Sociaal Fonds voor de Diamantarbeiders* v. *NV Indiamex and Association de Fait De Belder* [1973] ECR 1609, 1629, regarding questions of negotiating positions. See, generally, H. Froment Meurice, *La Dimension extérieur du marché intérieur* (Presses universitaires de France, Paris, 1988).

[198] A Community strategy to develop Europe's industry, COM(81)639, 9.

[199] Technical harmonisation and standards: a new approach (COM(85)19). See also the Council Resolution of 7 May 1985 (OJ 1985 C136/1) on a new approach to technical harmonisation and standards.

[200] L. Tsoukalis, *The New European Economy: the Politics and Economics of Integration* (Oxford University Press, Oxford, 1991), 273.

[201] See e.g. the Protocol on the Canary Islands and Ceuta and Melilla, annexed to the Portuguese and Spanish Act of Accession. See, regarding such ties generally, H. Dicke and R.J. Langhammer, *The Institutional Framework and External Dimension of the EC Internal Market* (Kiel Working Paper No. 453, Kiel University, 1990), 27–8.

[202] See the Protocol on German Internal Trade, annexed to the EEC Treaty.

Objectives of Other Policies

The development of the common commercial policy may be affected by the impact of various other common policies. The formulation of the latter may be unfavourable to the liberalisation of trade with third states. For example, the development of the common commercial policy may be affected by requirements of the common agricultural policy. In formulating the latter policy, the Union institutions must take into account, where necessary, the principle of "Community preference" in favour of Union farmers. This is one of the principles of the Treaty and in agricultural matters was laid down in Article 44(2) of the Treaty.[203] This provision referred to the minimum import prices for agricultural products, which Member States might impose during the transitional period for establishment of the common market. It stated that these prices should not be imposed in such a way as to form an obstacle to the development of a natural preference between Member States.

In fact, development of the common commercial policy depends on the interaction of various policies. Sometimes agreements with third states are concluded in execution of a policy fixed in advance. Sometimes that policy is defined by the agreements themselves.[204] In practice, however, while there may be concern to avoid the risk of retaliation,[205] demands of other Union policies are likely to prevail over liberalisation considerations in relation to trade with third states. For example, the Union may enact a measure restricting such trade, where the adoption of the measure is required by the risk of a serious disturbance endangering objectives of the common agricultural policy.[206] The result is said to be that the common commercial policy has become "sectoralised by protectionist trade restrictions for the benefit of agricultural, textiles, steel, and other lobbies".[207]

Implementation of this policy may be sought "autonomously" through establishment of the common customs tariff, common rules for imports and exports, anti-dumping and anti-subsidy rules, and other measures of

---

[203] Case 5/67 *W. Beus GmbH & Co.* v. *Hauptzollamt München* [1968] ECR 83, 98. Although this provision has been repealed by the Amsterdam Treaty (OJ 1997 C340/1), the principle of "Community preference", as defined by the ECJ, has been preserved. See the Declaration on the repeal of Art. 44 EC, adopted along with the Amsterdam Treaty.

[204] *Opinion 1/75 Draft Understanding on a Local Cost Standard* [1975] ECR 1355, 1363; and *Opinion 1/94 International Agreements on Services and the Protection of International Property* [1994] ECR I–5267, I–5398.

[205] Joined Cases 154, 205, 206, 226, 228, 263 & 264/78, 31, 39, 83 & 85/79 *SpA Ferriera Valsabbia* v. *EC Commission* [1980] ECR 907, 1015–16; and Case 258/80 *SpA Metallurgica Rumi* v. *EC Commission* [1982] ECR 487, 505.

[206] Case 112/80 *Firma Anton Dürbeck* v. *Hauptzollamt Frankfurt am Main-Flughafen* [1981] ECR 1095, 1119–20. See also Mayras AG in Case 90/77 *Hellmut Stimming KG* v. *EC Commission* [1978] ECR 995, 1016.

[207] E.-U. Petersmann, "GATT Law as International Legal Framework of the European Free Trade System" in O. Jacot-Guillarmod (ed.), *L'Avenir du libre-échange en Europe: vers un Espace économique européen* (Schulthess, Zürich, 1990), 111–29, 118.

commercial defence. It may also be sought through conclusion of agreements with third states, which are discussed in section 21.17.

21.12.2 Common Customs Tariff

The common customs tariff is provided for in Article 28 of the EC Treaty.[208] According to Article 19(1) of the EEC Treaty, the duties entailed were to be set at the level of the arithmetical average of the duties applied in the customs territories comprised in the Union. In taking decisions relating to the common customs tariff, the Union is now required by Article 29 of the EC Treaty to be guided by the need to promote trade between Member States and third states; developments in conditions of competition within the Union, in so far as they lead to an improvement in the competitive capacity of undertakings; the requirements of the Union as regards the supply of raw materials and semi-finished goods;[209] and the need to avoid serious disturbances in the economies of Member States and to ensure rational development of production and an expansion of consumption within the Union. Thus, for example, the needs of Union user industries may justify suspension of duties.[210]

Tariff Uniformity

A uniform nomenclature for goods subject to the common customs tariff was established by Regulation 950/68,[211] which was replaced by Regulation 2658/87.[212] There are annual reviews, the results of which are published in the Official Journal. Moreover, uniform rules relating to valuation[213] and origin[214] apply.

The uniformity in the treatment of trade with third states sought by this legislation is considered important. Thus, for example, a product may not be classified under different tariff headings in different Member States. In accordance with the demands of the customs union, the elimination of differences in classifications is deemed necessary.[215]

---

[208] See also, regarding customs co-operation between Member States and between Member States and the Commission, Art. 116 EC.

[209] In this connection, the Commission shall take care to avoid distorting conditions of competition between Member States in respect of finished goods.

[210] Case 58/85 *Ethicon* v. *Hauptzollamt Itzehoe* [1986] ECR 1141, 1145. See e.g. Reg. 3640/92 1992 (OJ 1992 L375/9) temporarily suspending the autonomous CCT duties on a number of products intended for the construction, maintenance, and repair of aircraft. See also Reg. 2590/97 (OJ 1997 L355/1) replacing the Annex to Reg. 1255/96 temporarily suspending the autonomous CCT duties on certain industrial and agricultural products. See, generally, the Communication concerning autonomous tariff suspensions (OJ 1989 C235/2).

[211] On the CCT (JO 1968 L172/1).

[212] On the tariff and statistical nomenclature and on the CCT (OJ 1987 L265/1).

[213] Arts. 28–36 of Reg. 2913/92 (OJ 1992 L302/1) establishing the Community Customs Code.

[214] *Ibid.*, Arts. 22–27.

[215] Case 40/84 *Casteels PVBA* v. *EC Commission* [1985] ECR 667, 672.

The underlying concern is not only to counter the risk of trade deflections and distortions of competition, including distortions which favour traders from third states,[216] within the Union.[217] There is also concern to ensure equal tariff treatment for third-country importers.[218] However, it may be a formal equality, based on common customs tariff classifications rather than on real questions of competition, which is entailed.[219]

Moreover, the emphasis is on aligning conditions of competition between user industries in the different Member States.[220] It is not equality between third state traders and Union traders but equality between the former which is entailed.[221] Thus the levels of common customs tariff duties are fixed at such a level as to take account of the position of economic sectors in the Union.[222]

Even so, the approach may be consistent with Article XXIV(8)(a) of GATT. According to this provision, for the establishment of a customs union duties and barriers eliminated in trade between Member States must be accompanied by substantially identical duties and barriers in relation to trade with third states.

Charges Having Equivalent Effect

Introduction of the common customs tariff has been taken to imply a prohibition on the unilateral introduction by Member States of charges having equivalent effect to customs duties and on the raising of existing charges having such an effect.[223] On the other hand, Member States may charge for

---

[216] Case 30/79 *Land of Berlin* v. *Wigei, Wild-Geflügel-Eier-Import GmbH & Co. KG* [1980] ECR 151, 164.

[217] Joined Cases 37 & 38/73 *Sociaal Fonds voor de Diamantarbeiders* v. *NV Indiamex and Association de Fait De Belder* [1973] ECR 1609, 1622; and Case 70/77 *Simmenthal SpA* v. *Amministrazione delle Finanze* [1978] ECR 1453, 1476–7.

[218] Trabucchi AG in Case 8/73 *Hauptzollamt Bremerhaven* v. *Massey-Ferguson GmbH* [1973] ECR 897, 916.

[219] See e.g. Case 168/78 *EC Commission* v. *France: tax arrangements applicable to spirits* [1980] ECR 347, 368.

[220] Joined Cases 267–269/81 *Amministrazione delle Finanze dello Stato* v. *Società Petrolifera Italiana SpA (SPI) and SpA Michelin Italiana (SAMI)* [1983] ECR 801, 828. See, generally, J. Bourrinet and M. Torelli, *Les Relations extérieurs de la CEE* (Presses universitaires de France, Paris, 1980).

[221] Cf. Darmon AG in Case C–432/92 *R.* v. *Minister of Agriculture, Fisheries, and Food, ex parte S.P. Anastasiou (Pissouri) Ltd* [1994] ECR I–3087, I–3111.

[222] Case 248/80 *Kommanditgesellschaft in Firma Gebrüder Glunz* v. *Hauptzollamt Hamburg-Waltershof* [1982] ECR 197, 213.

[223] Joined Cases 37 & 38/73 *Sociaal Fonds voor de Diamantarbeiders* v. *NV Indiamex and Association de Fait De Belder* [1973] ECR 1609, 1623. See also, regarding the importance of allowing speedy checks on customs clearance, Case 317/81 *Howe and Bainbridge BV* v. *Oberfinanzdirektion Frankfurt am Main* [1982] ECR 3257, 3264. On the other hand, application of the CCT is entrusted to Member States, which designate the authorities to undertake tariff classification and decide their training (*ibid.*, 3625). As regards simplifying clearance through customs of goods contained in the personal luggage of travellers coming from third states, see Case 278/82 *Rewe-Handelsgesellschaft Nord mbH and Rewe-Market Herbert Kureit* v. *Hauptzollamter Flensburg Itzehoe and Lübeck-West* [1984] ECR 721, 756.

carrying out customs inspections required in connection with the common customs tariff, whereas they may not do so in the case of products traded between Member States.[224] They may also impose a "consumption tax" on products from third states.[225]

21.12.3 Import and Export Rules

Common rules for imports from third states are laid down in Regulation 3285/94,[226] and common rules for exports to third states are laid down in Regulation 2603/69.[227] These rules prohibit quantitative restrictions on trade between the Union and third states. This prohibition has been found to cover measures having equivalent effect to quantitative restrictions.[228]

However, the liberalisation requirements embodied in such legislation may be interpreted more narrowly than those embodied in EC Treaty provisions. For example, a licensing system applicable to trade between Member States is prohibited by Articles 30 and 34 of the Treaty.[229] In contrast, it is not prohibited by the prohibition of quantitative restrictions on exports to third states in Article 1 of Regulation 2603/69.[230]

21.12.4 Anti-Dumping Rules

Anti-dumping rules applicable to trade with third states are contained in Regulation 384/96.[231] Regulation 2026/97[232] covers unfair subsidies. However, anti-dumping measures are more frequently adopted,[233] even where subsidies may have been granted to undertakings engaged in dumping.

---

[224] Case 340/87 *EC Commission* v. *Italy: charges for frontier inspections* [1989] ECR 1483, 1512–13.

[225] Joined Cases C–228, 234, 339 & 353/90 *Simba SpA* v. *Ministero delle Finanze (Dogane di Savona e della Spezia)* [1992] ECR I–3713.

[226] On common rules for imports and repealing Reg. 518/94 (OJ 1994 L349/53).

[227] Establishing common rules for exports (JO 1969 L324/25).

[228] Case C–83/94 *Peter Leifer* [1995] ECR I–3231, I–3247, regard being had to Art. XI of GATT. See, similarly, Case C–70/94 *Fritz Werner Industrie-Ausrüstungen GmbH* v. *Germany* [1995] ECR I–3189, I–3226.

[229] Joined Cases 51–54/71 *International Fruit Company NV, Kooy Rotterdam NV, Velleman en Tas NV, and Jan Van den Brink's Im-en Exporthandel* v. *Produktschap voor Groenten en Fruit* [1971] ECR 1107, 1116–17.

[230] Jacobs AG in Case C–367/89 *Aimé Richardt and Les Accessoires Scientifiques SNC* [1991] ECR I–4621, I–4640.

[231] On protection against dumped imports from countries not members of the EC (OJ 1996 L56/1). See, more particularly, Reg. 385/96 (OJ 1996 L56/21) on protection against injurious pricing of vessels.

[232] On protection against subsidised imports from countries not members of the EC (OJ 1997 L228/1).

[233] See e.g. Fifteenth annual report on the Community's anti-dumping and anti-subsidy activities, COM(97)428.

Margins

According to Regulation 384/96,[234] dumping occurs when the export price of a product is below the normal value of a like product.[235] The export price may be the actual one charged by the exporter on the Union market[236] or may be constructed.[237] The normal value is, in principle, the price actually charged for a like product in the state of origin or exportation.[238] If the exporter does not sell in his own country in sufficient quantities,[239] or where the domestic price is below the cost of production[240] or otherwise unreliable, the normal value may also be constructed.[241] A like product must be "identical, that is, alike in all respects, to the product under consideration, or, in the absence of such a product, another product which has characteristics closely resembling those of the product under consideration".[242]

Thus a finding of dumping is seen as depending simply on a comparison of prices, and the amount by which the normal value exceeds the export price constitutes the dumping margin. Determination of the normal value, establishment of the export price, and comparison of the two prices are separate operations, for which different methods of calculation may be used.[243]

Where a dumping margin is found, the Union institutions are required to establish whether the dumping causes material injury[244] and whether "the Community interest" calls for intervention.[245]

Injury

The fact that dumping is regarded as wrongful *per se* means that an investigation of injury does not require consideration of possible justifications for dumping. Hence, for example, the possibility that differential pricing may simply reflect different price elasticities in different markets or that below-cost pricing may simply be a response to a recession is not considered, once a dumping margin is found. Article 3(2) of Regulation 384/96[246] merely requires examination of the volume of dumped imports, their prices, and consequent impact on the Union industry concerned, to determine the presence of injury. Where a dumping margin is found in respect of imports

---

[234] OJ 1996 L56/1.　　[235] *Ibid.*, Art. 1(2).　　[236] *Ibid.*, Art. 2(8).

[237] *Ibid.*, Art. 2(9). See e.g. Reg. 1289/87 (OJ 1987 L121/11) imposing a provisional anti-dumping duty on urea from Czechoslovakia, the GDR, Kuwait, Libya, Saudi Arabia, the USSR, Trinidad and Tobago, and Yugoslavia.

[238] Art. 2(1)(a) of Reg. 384/96 (OJ 1996 L56/1).

[239] Reg. 1355/78 (OJ 1978 L165/20) imposing a provisional anti-dumping duty on ferrochromium from South Africa and Sweden.

[240] Export prices below the cost of production in the exporting country were not considered as dumped prices under Reg. 459/68 (JO 1968 L93/1), so long as there was no price discrimination in the exporting country and no "particular market situation".

[241] Art. 2(3)(b)(ii) and 2(4) of Reg. 384/96 (OJ 1996 L56/1).　　[242] *Ibid.*, Art. 1(4).

[243] See e.g. Joined Cases 273/85 & 107/86 *Silver Seiko Ltd* v. *EC Council* [1988] ECR 592.

[244] Art. 3 of Reg. 384/96 (OJ 1996 L56/1).　　[245] *Ibid.*, Art. 21.　　[246] *Ibid.*

from several countries, the effects of these imports may be cumulated to establish injury.[247]

Moreover, the Union institutions only reluctantly accept that market penetration by dumped products may be too low to be injurious. For example, in Regulation 1633/82[248] the Bulgarian share of the hardboard market had varied from 0.7% to 0.2%. Hence, anti-dumping measures were considered unnecessary. The Romanian market share, however, was 0.8% in the first half of 1981, and measures against imports from that country were considered necessary. Injury may be found even where the volume of dumped imports decreases in absolute terms[249] or in percentage terms.[250] The underlying idea is that the market share of dumped products, though small, may be significant enough to cause material injury because of the low prices of these products.[251]

In examining the effects of dumping, the Union institutions may concentrate on the question of price cutting. In other words, they may concentrate on the question whether the prices of dumped products are below those of Union producers. In the absence of price cutting, dumping may be found not to be injurious.[252] To this extent, exporters may be free to align their export prices with Union prices, even though the latter may be lower than their domestic prices or lower than their production costs. Since, however, the prices of Union producers may be affected by the dumping, the Union institutions consider that a "model price" for Union products may have to be adopted in order to establish price cutting. This practice has been accepted by the Court of Justice,[253] though establishment of the model price by adding a profit margin to the costs of Union producers has been criticised.[254]

In exceptional circumstances, price cutting may be found not to be injurious. For example, in Decision 83/9[255] it was found that prices of dumped products in Germany, though below those of German producers,

[247] *Ibid.*, Art. 3(4).

[248] Imposing a provisional anti-dumping duty on fibre building board from Romania and accepting undertakings in connection with the proceeding in respect of fibre building board from Czechoslovakia, Finland, Hungary, Norway, Poland, Spain, Sweden, and the USSR (OJ 1982 L181/19).

[249] Dec. 1958/82 (OJ 1982 L212/32) imposing a provisional anti-dumping duty on photographic enlargers from Poland and the USSR and accepting an undertaking in respect of imports from Czechoslovakia.

[250] See e.g. Reg. 864/87 (OJ 1987 L83/1) imposing a definitive anti-dumping duty on electric motors from Bulgaria, Czechoslovakia, the GDR, Hungary, Poland, and the USSR.

[251] Reg. 2317/85 (OJ 1985 L217/7) imposing a provisional anti-dumping duty on roller chains for cycles from the USSR and China.

[252] See e.g. Dec. 83/493 (OJ 1983 L268/60) terminating the anti-dumping proceeding concerning imports of xanthan gum from the US.

[253] Joined Cases 260/85 & 106/86 *Tokyo Electric Co.* v. *EC Council* [1988] ECR 5855, 5924.

[254] VerLoren van Themaat AG in Case 53/83 *Allied Corporation* v. *EC Council* [1985] ECR 1621, 1631.

[255] Terminating the anti-dumping proceeding concerning codeine and its salts from Czechoslovakia, Hungary, Poland, and Yugoslavia (OJ 1983 L16/30).

were well above the comparable price of the products originating in other Member States. In these circumstances, it was not established that there was material injury to the German complainant.[256]

Generally however, the Union institutions seem reluctant to accept that price cutting may be other than injurious. For example, in Regulation 864/87[257] it was admitted that the prices of products found to be dumped were often undercut by small Italian producers. However, those Union producers whose prices were undercut by the dumped products had made considerable efforts towards automation and relocation of production plants. In these circumstances, injury to Union industry was found.

Such injury may take the form simply of an increase in the market shares of dumped products,[258] a decrease in Union production,[259] a reduction of employment,[260] losses or reduced profits for Union producers,[261] inability of Union producers to recover their full costs,[262] or prevention of price increases that would otherwise have occurred.[263] Often emphasis is placed on secondary effects. Thus injury may be found where profitable investment becomes impossible.[264] It may also be found where dumping leads to increased stocks held by Union producers,[265] exacerbates adjustment problems,[266] leads to dependence on outdated technology[267] or to overcapacity,[268] hinders recovery,[269] increases the burden on Union production

---

[256] See also Dec. 82/808 (OJ 1982 L339/58) terminating the anti-dumping procedure concerning aluminium foil from Austria, the GDR, Hungary, and Israel; and Dec. 86/536 (OJ 1986 L313/20) terminating the anti-dumping proceeding concerning tube and pipe fittings from Brazil, Taiwan, Yugoslavia, and Japan.

[257] OJ 1987 L83/1.

[258] Reg. 1778/77 (OJ 1977 L196/1) concerning the application of the anti-dumping duty on ball-bearings and tapered roller bearings from Japan.

[259] Reg. 789/82 (OJ 1982 L90/1) imposing a provisional anti-dumping duty on cotton yarns from Turkey.

[260] Reg. 1778/77 (OJ 1977 L196/1).

[261] Dec. 81/406 (OJ 1981 L152/44) accepting undertakings in connection with the anti-dumping proceedings concerning ball and tapered roller bearings from Japan, Poland, Romania, and the USSR.

[262] Reg. 1198/88 (OJ 1988 L115/1) imposing a provisional anti-dumping duty on roller chains for cycles from China.

[263] Reg. 1633/82 (OJ 1982 L181/19).

[264] Reg. 407/80 (OJ 1980 L48/1) imposing a provisional anti-dumping duty on sodium carbonate from the USSR.

[265] Reg. 1633/82 (OJ 1982 L181/19).

[266] Dec. 83/248 (OJ 1983 L138/65) accepting undertakings offered in connection with the anti-dumping duty proceeding concerning polyethylene from the USSR, the GDR, Czechoslovakia, and Poland.

[267] Reg. 2681/84 (OJ 1984 L254/5) imposing a provisional anti-dumping duty on pentaerythritol from Canada and accepting an undertaking given in connection with the proceeding concerning pentaerythritol from Sweden.

[268] Reg. 207/83 (OJ 1983 L203/13) imposing a provisional anti-dumping duty on dicumyl peroxide from Japan.

[269] Reg. 2712/79 (OJ 1979 L308/11) imposing a provisional anti-dumping duty on acrylic fibres from the US.

aid,[270] or jeopardizes the willingness of third states not involved in the investigation to respect or renew export restraint agreements.[271]

Such practice may reflect the fact that Union legislation permits the imposition of an anti-dumping duty without the need to show that dumping is the principal cause of the injury.[272] For example, in Decision 82/220[273] there was found to be material injury, though it was admitted that non-dumped products were also a "significant factor" causing injury. The Court of Justice accepts that injury attributable to dumping need only be part of more extensive injury attributable to other factors.[274]

In fact, once a dumping margin is established and Union producers are found to be faced by difficulties of the above kinds, there seems to be a presumption that these difficulties are the result of the dumping concerned.[275] Possible causes of these difficulties other than dumping which may be considered include: reduction of sales to third countries, a fall in Union demand, an increase in imports from other countries,[276] and currency fluctuations.[277] Little consideration is apparently given to the likelihood that at least some of the effects of dumping may reflect the inefficiency of Union producers. Similarly, little account may be taken of the argument that injury should not be found by reference to prices in the importing Member State which are artificially raised by restrictive practices.[278] The Council and Commission have been willing to do no more than accept that an anti-trust finding against Union producers may justify a review of anti-dumping action.[279]

In short, injury will apparently be found, unless the prices of dumped products or their market share are such that there is no real impact on the market position of Union producers.[280] If there is no real impact, the Union

---

[270] Dec. 83/260 (OJ 1983 L196/22) terminating the anti-dumping proceeding in respect of pears in syrup from Australia, China, and South Africa.

[271] Dec. 2247/87 (OJ 1987 L207/21) imposing a provisional anti-dumping duty on sheets and plates, of iron and steel, from Mexico.

[272] The original 1967 version of the GATT Agreement on the Implementation of Art. VI and Reg. 459/68 (JO 1968 L93/1) required dumping to be the principal cause of the injury. See also Art. 2(3)(a) of Reg. 1681/79 (OJ 1979 L196/1). The requirement was removed by Reg. 3017/79 (OJ 1979 L339/1), apparently because the US was unwilling to adopt a similar practice. See Bull. EC 4–1979, 1.2.11.

[273] Terminating an anti-dumping proceeding in respect of upright pianos from Czechoslovakia, the GDR, and Poland (OJ 1982 L101/45).

[274] Joined Cases 277 & 300/85 *Canon Inc.* v. *EC Council* [1988] ECR 5731, 5809.

[275] See e.g. Joined Cases 273/85 & 107/86 *Silver Seiko Ltd* v. *EC Council* [1988] ECR 5927, 5981.

[276] Dec. 87/443 (OJ 1987 L235/22) amending an undertaking and accepting another in connecting with the anti-dumping review investigation concerning copper sulphate from Poland and the USSR, respectively.

[277] Dec. 82/220 (OJ 1982 L101/45).

[278] Verloren van Themaat AG in Joined Cases 239 & 275/82 *Allied Corporation* v. *EC Commission* [1984] ECR 1005, 1047.

[279] Reg. 1361/87 (OJ 1987 L129/5) imposing a provisional anti-dumping duty on ferro-silico-calcium/calcium silicide from Brazil; and Reg. 3687/87 (OJ 1987 L346/27) imposing a definitive anti-dumping duty on mercury from the USSR.

[280] Thus in Dec. 88/125 (OJ 1988 L62/39) terminating the anti-dumping proceeding concerning imports of kraftliner paper and board from Brazil and South Africa, where the prices of dumped

institutions may find that there is no injury and that there is no need to establish whether there is a dumping margin.[281]

"Community Interest"

Regulation 384/96[282] requires that intervention against dumping must be in the "Community interest".[283] According to the *Guide to the European Communities' Anti-Dumping and Countervailing Duty Legislation*,[284] produced by the Commission, the interests of consumers and processors of the imported product are to be considered. Questions concerning the competitiveness of the Union market are also to be taken into account. In practice, however, little apparent consideration is given to the possibility that the injury attributed to dumping may be compensated for by beneficial effects of the kind, for example, which may justify an Article 85(3) exemption from the prohibition of restrictive practices in Article 85(1) of the Treaty.[285] Rather, after establishing the presence of dumping and injury, the Commission may merely assert that in these circumstances the Community interest requires the imposition of a provisional anti-dumping duty.[286] Not only does such practice risk depriving this condition for intervention of effective significance. It is also of doubtful compatibility with the requirement in Article 190 of the Treaty that reasons must be given for Union measures.

Even when more elaborate reasoning is given, attention is focussed on the position of Union producers in competition with undertakings engaged in dumping. For example, in Regulation 3019/86[287] the Commission considered the financial losses of the Union producers concerned. Particular account was also taken of the fact that the production of standardised multi-phase electric motors was central to the Union rotary machines sector. For these reasons, the Commission considered intervention to be in the Community interest.

Consumer interests appear to be given little weight. Union practice in this regard is reflected in a ruling of the Court of Justice that the Council and Commission may reasonably regard the need to protect Union industry as outweighing the "short-term interests of consumers".[288]

---

products had increased and by the end of the investigation period no dumping was discovered, the Commission found no injury.

[281] Case C–121/86 *Anonymos Etaireia Epicheiriseon Metalleftikon Viomichanikon kai Naftiliakon AE* v. *EC Council* [1989] ECR 3919.

[282] OJ 1996 L56/1.　　[283] *Ibid.*, Art. 21.　　[284] Para. 12.　　[285] Sect. 13.5.1.

[286] Reg. 724/82 (OJ 1982 L85/9) imposing a provisional anti-dumping duty on imports of standardised multiphase electric motors having an output of more than 0.75 kW but not more than 75 kW originating in Bulgaria, Czechoslovakia, the GDR, Poland, Romania, and the USSR and terminating the proceeding in respect of imports of said products originating in Hungary. See also Reg. 3648/83 (OJ 1983 L361/6) imposing a definitive anti-dumping duty on imports of hardboard originating in Sweden.

[287] Imposing a provisional anti-dumping duty on imports of standardised multi-phase electric motors having an output of more than 0.75 kW but not more than 75 kW, originating in Bulgaria, Czechoslovakia, the GDR, Hungary, Poland, Romania, and the USSR (OJ 1986 L280/68).

[288] Case C–156/87 *Gestetner Holdings plc* v. *EC Council and EC Commission* [1990] ECR I–781, I–843.

For example, in Decision 83/248[289] Union processors of polyethylene argued that the introduction of anti-dumping measures would prejudice their competitive position, which would not be in the Community interest. However, in view of the particularly difficult position of the polyethylene producers in the Union,[290] the Commission considered that the Community interest did require the imposition of a provisional anti-dumping duty on polyethylene imports.

Again, in Decision 84/406[291] consumers had argued that the introduction of anti-dumping measures against horticultural glass imports would lead to an increase in the costs of the horticultural industry. Hence, they maintained, such measures would not be in the Community interest. However, the Commission stressed the serious difficulties facing Union producers and the minimal effect of a price increase of horticultural glass on the costs of the horticultural industry. On these grounds, the Commission concluded that it was in the Community interest for it to intervene.

Often consumer interests are interpreted as positively favouring intervention. For example, in Regulation 551/83[292] the Commission considered that if Union producers were to disappear from the market, the Union would become dependent upon external suppliers of this product. It seemed to be in the interests of users to have access to both sources of supply. Therefore, the Community interest required adoption of anti-dumping measures. Similarly, in Regulation 541/91[293] the Council considered that ensuring the survival of the Union firms would be beneficial for competition on the Union market. At the same time, the disappearance of a major part of Union production of barium chloride would pose a threat to the supplies of Union consumers. The Community interest was, therefore, held to call for intervention.

The result of such concentration on the effects of dumping on Union manufacturers of competing products is that Union intervention against dumping found to be injurious is likely to be considered to be in the Community interest, unless such intervention is unnecessary for, or incapable of, protecting such manufacturers. For example, in Decision

---

[289] Imposing a definite anti-dumping duty on kraftliner paper and board originating in the USA and accepting undertakings given in connection with the review of the anti-dumping proceeding on kraftliner paper and board originating in Austria, Canada, Finland, Portugal, the Soviet Union and Sweden (OJ 1983 L138/65).

[290] See similarly, Reg. 2908/84 (OJ 1984 L275/12) imposing a provisional anti-dumping duty on imports of copper sulphate originating in Poland; and Dec. 87/443 (OJ 1987 L235/22), where account was taken, more particularly, of the fact that 2 Union producers had ceased production since 1983.

[291] Accepting undertakings given in connection with the anti-dumping proceeding concerning imports of horticultural glass and certain drawn glass originating in Czechoslovakia, the GDR, Hungary, Poland, Romania, and the USSR and terminating that proceeding (OJ 1984 L224/26).

[292] OJ 1983 L64/25.

[293] Imposing a definitive anti-dumping duty on imports of barium chloride originating in China (OJ 1991 L60/1).

84/103[294] the Commission decided that intervention against injurious dumping would not at the time be in the Community interest because prices for the products concerned had begun to increase. Again, in Decision 83/9[295] it was felt that the Community interest did not call for intervention against the imports found to have been dumped. It was so felt, because other Member States, while maintaining import restrictions, continued to export low-priced codeine to Germany. Generally, however, the Community interest is regarded as requiring intervention against dumping found to be injurious.

The fact that the conditions for intervention against dumping are undemanding adds to the potential significance of the methods of intervention. These methods comprise price undertakings and anti-dumping duties.

Price Undertakings

In the course of anti-dumping proceedings the Commission may accept an undertaking[296] from the exporter concerned to the effect that the dumping or its injurious effects will cease.[297] It appears that such undertakings may also be used to deter exporters from concentrating their sales on more vulnerable Member States.[298] Undertakings may, however, be rejected on the basis of general considerations, such as "the present trade relations with Japan".[299]

Few details of the undertakings obtained by the Commission are usually given.[300] They may involve an agreement by the exporter concerned[301] or the country concerned[302] to limit sales within the Union, but they normally require price increases. They may require price increases sufficient to remove the whole dumping margin.[303] Sometimes, however, a smaller price increase, such as one which entails a cessation of "price-cutting",[304] may be regarded

[294] Terminating the anti-dumping proceeding concerning imports of non-alloyed unwrought aluminium originating in Norway, Surinam, the Soviet Union, and Yugoslavia (OJ 1984 L57/19).

[295] OJ 1983 L16/30.

[296] Undertakings had a more central role in Commission practice before the judgment of the ECJ in Case 113/77 *NTN Toyo Bearing Co Ltd* v. *EC Council* [1979] ECR 1185, which resulted in increased legalisation of such practice.

[297] Art. 8 of Reg. 384/96 (OJ 1996 L56/1).

[298] Dec. 229/88 (OJ 1988 L23/13) imposing a provisional anti-dumping duty on imports of certain sheets and plates, of iron and steel, originating in Yugoslavia.

[299] Reg. 1877/85 (OJ 1985 L176/1) imposing a definitive anti-dumping duty on imports of certain hydraulic excavators originating in Japan.

[300] Confidentiality obligations are imposed on the Commission by Art. 19 of Reg. 384/96 (OJ 1996 L56/1) and Art. 214 EC. See also Case 264/82 *Timex Corporation* v. *EC Council* [1985] ECR 849, 861.

[301] See e.g. Dec. 229/88 (OJ 1988 L23/13).

[302] See e.g. Dec. 83/126 (OJ 1983 L86/23) terminating the anti-dumping proceeding concerning imports of television image and sound recorders or reproducers originating in Japan.

[303] Art. 8(1) of Reg. 384/96 (OJ 1996 L56/1). See e.g. Reg. 1958/82 (OJ 1982 L212/32) and Reg. 2908/84 (OJ 1984 L275/12).

[304] Dec. 90/196 (OJ 1990 L104/14) terminating the anti-dumping proceeding concerning imports of methenamine originating in Hungary and Yugoslavia and accepting undertakings offered in connection with the proceeding concerning imports of methenamine originating in Bulgaria, Czechoslovakia, Poland and Romania.

as sufficient to eliminate injury.[305] Occasionally, a rather more elaborate indication of the function of the undertaking may be given. Thus an undertaking may be required having regard to "on the one hand, the selling price necessary to provide an adequate return to Union producers and, on the other hand, the purchase price of the Union importers and their costs and profit margins".[306]

While such a form of intervention may be attractive to the Commission in terms of initial administrative convenience, there may be subsequent problems of securing enforcement. There is also the disadvantage that the economic rent from Union intervention is transferred to the exporting countries. In other words, their traders benefit from the higher prices. At the same time, conduct distorting competition which may otherwise be prohibited by Article 85 or 86 of the Treaty[307] may apparently be legitimated.

Anti-dumping Duties

If no satisfactory undertaking can be secured, anti-dumping duties may be imposed on the products of the exporter. These duties must be no higher than necessary to remove the injury.[308] Article 11(8) of Regulation 384/96[309] provides for the refunding of any duty collected in excess of the margin. On the other hand, Article 13(11) provides that where the exporter bears the anti-dumping duty, an additional anti-dumping duty may be imposed to compensate for the amount borne by the exporter.

Even if an undertaking has been accepted, a change of circumstances may apparently justify the re-opening of proceedings, repeal of the decision accepting the undertaking, and imposition of anti-dumping duties. Article 8(9) of Regulation 384/96[310] only refers to such action where the undertaking has been withdrawn or where the Commission "has reason to believe that it has been violated". However, in Regulation 3019/86[311] the Commission accepted that the undertakings had generally been respected, but provisional anti-dumping duties were imposed, because dumping and injury continued.[312] Duties may also be imposed, because the undertakings previously accepted have "not been passed on to the market in such a way as to remove the injury suffered by the producers".[313]

Duties are provisionally imposed by the Commission,[314] and definitive

---

[305] See e.g. Dec. 81/406 (OJ 1981 L152/44) accepting undertakings in connection with the anti-dumping proceedings concerning ball and tapered roller bearings from Japan, Poland, Romania, and the USSR; and Dec. 83/248 (OJ 1983 L138/65) accepting undertakings offered in connection with the anti-dumping duty proceeding concerning polyethylene from the USSR, the GDR, Czechoslovakia, and Poland.

[306] Dec. 84/406 (OJ 1984 L224/26) and Dec. 87/443 (OJ 1987 L235/22).

[307] See, regarding price-fixing, sects 13.3 and 14.2 above.

[308] Art. 7(2) of Reg. 384/96 (OJ 1996 L56/1).

[309] Ibid.   [310] Ibid.   [311] OJ 1986 L280/68.

[312] Cf. regarding the raising of duties, Reg. 541/91 (OJ 1991 L60/1).

[313] See e.g. Reg. 864/87 (OJ 1987 L83/1).   [314] Art. 8 of Reg. 384/96 (OJ 1996 L56/1).

duties may be imposed by the Council.[315] These duties may be *ad valorem*;[316] variable based on a minimum price;[317] a combination of the two;[318] or a fixed amount per unit, weight, or measure.[319]

While the duty may simply be imposed at a rate equivalent to the dumping margin established by the Commission,[320] a lower rate may often be fixed. The method used to determine the lower rate may not be fully explained. In Regulation 2667/82[321] the Commission simply said that to determine the amount of duty necessary to eliminate the injury, it compared the Union producers' weighted average prices, costs, and profit and loss conditions with the individual importers' costs and special marketing conditions. Sometimes the rate may be equivalent to the difference between a minimum price fixed by the Commission and the import price to the first independent buyer.[322] There may, however, be little explanation of the method used to determine the former price.[323] Occasionally some account may be taken of the impact of the duty on competition within the Union. Thus in Regulation 2322/85[324] the duty was fixed at a lower level than that needed to eliminate injury because of the adverse impact which a higher duty would have had on the competitive structure of the Union market.[325] Basically, however, the Union institutions concentrate on questions of the costs and profit needs of Union industry.

Such costs may be the average costs of Union producers,[326] their weighted average costs,[327] or the costs of the most efficient industrial producers within the Union. For example, in Regulation 864/87[328] the Council took account of the intra-Union competition in the standardised multi-phase motor sector and the need to maintain as far as possible the competitiveness of the downstream industries. For these reasons, the Council considered it appropriate to determine the level of the duty on the basis of the cost prices of the most efficient manufacturers.

The profit needs of Union industry may be assessed by reference to various

---

[315] *Ibid.*, Art. 9(4).

[316] Reg. 1695/88 (OJ 1988 L151/39) imposing a provisional anti-dumping duty on imports of polyester yarn originating in Mexico, South Korea, Taiwan, and Turkey.

[317] Reg. 864/87 (OJ 1987 L83/1).   [318] Reg. 1198/88 (OJ 1988 L115/1).

[319] Dec. 2247/87 (OJ 1987 L207/21).

[320] See e.g. Reg. 1958/82 (OJ 1982 L212/32); and Reg. 2908/84 (OJ 1984 L275/12).

[321] OJ 1982 L283/9.   [322] Reg. 3019/86 (OJ 1986 L280/68).

[323] See e.g. Reg. 724/82 (OJ 1982 L85/9).

[324] Imposing a definitive anti-dumping duty on imports of glycene originating in Japan (OJ 1985 L218/1). See also Reg. 997/85 (OJ 1985 L107/8) imposing a provisional anti-dumping duty on imports of glycene originating in Japan.

[325] Apparently the influence of DG IV, the Directorate General for Competition, was decisive in this case.

[326] Reg. 3019/86 (JO 1986 L280/68).

[327] Reg. 1306/89 (OJ 1989 L131/4) imposing a definitive anti-dumping duty on imports of light sodium carbonate originating in Bulgaria, the GDR, Poland, and Romania.

[328] OJ 1987 L83/1.

factors. For example, in Regulation 1306/89[329] the Council considered that there should be a reasonable profit sufficient to finance the necessary level of investment. In the light of the capital invested by Union producers, the normal rate of return, and the risk involved, a profit margin of 8 per cent was fixed. In Regulation 3019/86[330] the Commission took account of the stiff competition between Union manufacturers and the financial results obtained in the Union "standardised motors" sector for many years. Accordingly, a gross profit margin of 5 per cent was considered appropriate.[331] In Regulation 541/91[332] the profit margin was calculated on the basis of the profit margin of the most efficient producer before increased penetration of dumped exports.[333]

Sometimes, therefore, anti-dumping duties may offer average Union producers protection against serious price competition from dumped products and may virtually be treated as an instrument of industrial policy. For example, in Regulation 2684/88[334] anti-dumping duties were imposed on videocassette recorders from Japan and the Republic of Korea. These duties were designed to safeguard employment in the Union and to maintain for Union industry a foothold in an important technological sector. It is recognised that application of such duties alone is an inadequate industrial policy instrument.[335] However, little attempt is apparently made to link the protection provided by the duties with a requirement of restructuring of the relevant Union industry. In particular, consideration has not apparently been given to the possibility that revenue raised from anti-dumping duties may be used to assist such restructuring.

Where, however, the rate of duty is fixed having regard to the costs and profit margins of the most efficient producers in the Union, some stimulus towards restructuring may be entailed. An approach comparable in certain respects may sometimes be adopted by the Commission when, in accordance with Articles 92 and 93 of the Treaty, it seeks to control the grant of aid by Member States to sectors in crisis. For example, Directive 90/684[336] on aid to shipbuilding provided for the Commission to fix a ceiling for operating aid to shipbuilders throughout the Union.[337] This ceiling was to be fixed by reference to the difference between the prices of major international competitors and the costs of the most competitive producers within the Union and was to be progressively reduced. However, in the case of anti-dumping duties, even where their level is such as to provide some stimulus towards the restructuring of Union industry, there is no requirement that

---

[329] OJ 1989 L131/4.   [330] OJ 1986 L280/68.

[331] A profit margin of only 4% was subsequently employed in Reg. 864/87 (OJ 1987 L83/1) as a basis for calculation of the level of definitive duties to be imposed.

[332] OJ 1991 L60/1.   [333] See also Reg. 864/87 (OJ 1987 L83/1).   [334] OJ 1988 L240/5.

[335] Thus, e.g., the Commission may seek to secure an opening-up of the Japanese domestic market rather than relying on anti-dumping actions. See the *Financial Times*, 15 Oct. 1990.

[336] OJ 1990 L380/2.   [337] *Ibid.*, Art. 4(1).

this level be progressively reduced.[338] Hence, the costs of such restructuring tend to be imposed on third states and on Union consumers rather than on Member States and Union producers.

21.12.5 Commercial Defence

Regulation 2641/84[339] provided for adoption of "commercial defence" measures by the Union. For example, proceedings were opened against United States restrictions on imports of aramid fibres;[340] unauthorised reproduction of sound recordings in Indonesia;[341] and Japanese harbour charges.[342] "Illicit" commercial practices, such as the piracy of sound recordings in Thailand[343] and the use by the United States of the Antidumping Act 1919,[344] may now be tackled under Regulation 3286/94.[345]

21.13 Development Co-operation Policy

Article 130u of the EC Treaty provides for a development co-operation policy. Union policy in this sphere shall be complementary to the policies pursued by the Member States.

21.13.1 Objectives

The objectives of development co-operation policy are:

– the sustainable economic and social development of the developing countries, and more particularly the most disadvantaged among them;

---

[338] Cf. the arrangements for progressive liberalisation in the 1991 agreement with Japan concerning the limitation of sales of Japanese vehicles in the Union (*Financial Times*, 5 Aug. 1991).

[339] On the strengthening of the common commercial policy with regard in particular to protection against illicit commercial practices (OJ 1984 L252/1).

[340] Dec. 87/251 (OJ 1987 L117/18) on the initiation of an international consultation and disputes settlement procedure concerning a US measure excluding imports of certain aramid fibres into the US.

[341] Notice of initiation of an illicit commercial practice procedure concerning the unauthorised reproduction of sound recordings in Indonesia (OJ 1987 C136/3).

[342] Dec. 92/169 (OJ 1992 L74/47) suspending the examination procedure concerning illicit practices within the meaning of Reg. 2641/84 consisting of the imposition in Japan of a port charge or fee used for the creation of a Harbour Management Fund.

[343] Dec. 96/40 (OJ 1996 L11/7) suspending the proceeding under Reg. 3286/94 on trade barriers, concerning piracy of Community sound recordings in Thailand and its effects on Community trade in sound recordings.

[344] Notice of initiation of an examination procedure concerning an obstacle to trade within the meaning of Reg. 3286/94 (OJ 1997 C58/14).

[345] Laying down Community procedures in the field of the common commercial policy in order to ensure the exercise of the Community's rights under international trade rules, in particular those established under the auspices of the WTO (OJ 1994 L349/71).

- the smooth and gradual integration of the developing countries into the world economy; and
- the reduction of poverty in the developing countries.[346]

The policy shall contribute to the general objective of developing and consolidating democracy and the rule of law and to that of respecting human rights and fundamental freedoms.[347] These objectives are to be taken into account in other Union policies that are likely to affect developing countries.[348] At the same time, the Union and the Member States shall comply with the commitments and take account of the objectives they have approved in the context of the United Nations and other competent international organisations.[349]

21.13.2 Implementation

The Union and the Member States shall co-ordinate their policies on development co-operation. Accordingly, they shall consult each other on their aid programmes, including in international organisations and during international conferences. They may go further and take joint action. If necessary, Member States shall contribute to the implementation of Union aid programmes.[350]

More particularly, within their respective spheres of competence, the Union and the Member States shall co-operate with third states and with the competent international organisations. The arrangements for Union co-operation may be the subject of agreements between the Union and the third parties concerned. The competence of Member States to negotiate in international bodies and to conclude international agreements is not prejudiced.[351]

21.14 CFSP

Arrangements for development of the common foreign and security policy (CFSP) are made in Articles J.1 to J.18 of the Treaty on European Union. This provision seeks to provide a more developed basis for what used to be called European political co-operation and was provided for by Article 30 of the Single European Act.[352]

Even before the Single European Act,[353] various principles of foreign policy were developed.[354] According to these principles, for example, the

---

[346] Art. 130u(1) EC. See e.g. Reg. 1484/97 (OJ 1997 L202/1) on aid for population policies and programmes in the developing countries; and Reg. 2046/97 (OJ 1997 L287/1) on north-south co-operation in the campaign against drugs and drug addiction.

[347] Art. 130u(2) EC.   [348] Art. 130v EC.   [349] Art. 130u(3) EC.
[350] Art. 130x(1) EC.   [351] Art. 130y EC.   [352] OJ 1987 L169/1.

[353] In practice, foreign ministers had begun in 1959 to meet to discuss "European political co-operation".

[354] J.-L. Dewost, "La Communauté, les dix et les 'sanctions' économiques: de la crise iranienne à la crise des Malouines" [1982] *AFDC* 215–32.

peaceful settlement of disputes was to be encouraged,[355] and the territorial integrity of states and the right of self-determination of peoples were to be respected.[356]

Joint action might be taken according to such principles, in the form of the denial of military supplies to belligerents. For example, use of chemical weapons in the Iran–Iraq war was condemned,[357] and measures were taken to control exports of chemicals which might be used to produce such weapons by warring countries. These measures were implemented in accordance with Article 224 of the EEC Treaty.[358] More generally, guidelines were introduced for export of nuclear materials, equipment, and technology.[359]

Imposition of economic sanctions might be entailed. For example, following the Argentine invasion of the Falkland Islands, the other Member States expressed solidarity with the United Kingdom in a statement of 2 April 1982.[360] That solidarity subsequently took practical shape with the adoption of sanctions against Argentina.[361] Again, sanctions were adopted against South Africa partly because of the internal situation in that country and partly in response to South African use of military force against neighbouring states.[362]

21.14.1 Objectives

According to Article J.1 of the Treaty on European Union, the Union is to define and implement the common foreign and security policy. The common policy is to cover all areas of foreign and security policy,[363] "including the progressive framing of a common defence policy . . . which might lead to a common defence".[364] The objectives are: safeguarding common values, interests, independence, and integrity of the Union; strengthening the security of the Union in all ways; preserving peace and strengthening international security; promoting international co-operation; and developing and consolidating democracy, the rule of law, and respect for human rights and fundamental freedoms.[365] They are to be pursued according to principles and general guidelines[366] adopted by the European Council.

The Member States shall support this policy actively and unreservedly in a spirit of loyalty and mutual solidarity. Thus they shall work together to enhance and develop their mutual political solidarity. They shall also refrain from any action which is contrary to the interests of the Union or likely to impair its effectiveness as a cohesive force in international relations. The

---

[355] Bull. EC 3–1983, 1.5.9. [356] Bull. EC 4–1984, 2.4.1. [357] Bull. EC 3–1984, 2.4.3.
[358] Bull. EC 5–1984, 2.4.2. [359] Bull. EC 11–1984, 1.3.7 and 2.4.3.
[360] Bull. EC 4–1982, 1.1.1–8; and Bull. EC 5–1982, 1.1.5.
[361] Reg. 877/82 (OJ 1982 L102/1) suspending imports of all products originating in Argentina.
[362] Bull. EC 6–1985, 2.5.1; Bull. 9–1985, 2.5.4; and Bull. EC 9–1986, 2.5.11.
[363] Art. J.1(1) TEU. [364] Art. J.7(1) TEU. [365] Art. J.1(1) TEU. [366] Art. J.3(1) TEU.

Council of the Union shall ensure compliance with these principles.[367]

However, the "specific character of the security and defence policy of certain Member States" is not to be prejudiced.[368] At the same time, provisions concerning the common commercial policy must be respected.[369]

21.14.2 Implementation

The Council of the Union is to take the decisions necessary for implementing the common foreign and security policy.[370] The Council is, in principle, to act by a qualified majority.[371] Implementation may take the form of common strategies, joint actions, common positions, and co-operation.

Implementation may also be sought through the involvement of Member States in the Western European Union, the North Atlantic Treaty Organisation, and the United Nations and through the conclusion of agreements with third states and international organisations.[372]

Limited arrangements are made for European Parliamentary supervision of the implementation of this policy.[373] However, there is no provision for judicial review by the European Courts.[374]

Common Strategies

Common strategies are adopted by the European Council in areas where the Member States have important interests in common. The strategies set out their objectives, duration, and the means to be made available by the Union and the Member States. They are to be implemented by the Member States.[375]

Joint Actions

Joint actions are adopted by the Council of the Union. They address specific situations where operational action by the Union is deemed to be required. They lay down their objectives, scope, the means to be made available to the Union, if necessary their duration, and the conditions for their implementation.[376] They commit the Member States in the positions they adopt and in the conduct of their activity.[377]

Joint actions may entail participation in peace efforts.[378] Joint actions may also lead to the imposition of sanctions. A basis for their imposition used to be provided by Article 113 of the EC Treaty. On the basis of this provision,

---

[367] Art. J.1(2) TEU.   [368] Art. J.7(1) TEU.

[369] Case C–124/95 R. v. *HM Treasury and the Bank of England, ex p. Centro-Com srl* [1997] ECR I–81, I–123.

[370] Art. J.3(3) TEU.   [371] Art. J.13(2) TEU.   [372] Art. J.14 TEU.   [373] Art. J.11 TEU.

[374] Art. L TEU.   [375] Art. J.3(2) TEU.   [376] Art. J.4(1) TEU.   [377] Art. J.4(3) TEU.

[378] See e.g. Dec. 94/276 (OJ 1994 L119/1) on a joint action in support of the Middle East peace process; and Joint Action 96/676 (OJ 1996 L315/1) in relation to the nomination of an EU special envoy for the Middle East peace process.

trade boycotts might be imposed on third states in implementation of decisions reached within the context of European political co-operation.[379] Article 228a of the EC Treaty now refers specifically to common positions or joint actions adopted within the context of the common foreign and security policy requiring that the Union interrupt or reduce, in part or completely, economic relations with one or more third states. It provides for enactment of the necessary measures under the EC Treaty.

Common Positions

Common positions are adopted by the Council of the Union. They define the approach of the Union to a particular matter of a geographical or thematic nature. Member States shall ensure that their national policies conform to the common positions.[380]

Co-operation

Systematic co-operation between Member States in the conduct of policy is to be strengthened. Accordingly, consultations take place within the Council on any common foreign and security policy matter of general interest. Such consultations are designed to ensure that the combined influence of Member States is exerted as effectively as possible by means of concerted and convergent action.[381]

WEU

The Western European Union, to which ten Member States belong, is an integral part of the development of the European Union.[382] The latter "will avail itself of the WEU to elaborate and implement decisions and actions of the Union which have defence implications". The Council shall, in agreement with the Western European Union institutions, adopt the necessary practical arrangements.[383]

NATO

The common foreign and security policy shall respect the obligations of certain Member States under the North Atlantic Treaty and be compatible with the common security and defence policy established within that framework.[384] Equally, the development of closer co-operation between two or more Member States on a bilateral level, in the framework of the Western

---

[379] See e.g. Reg. 945/92 (OJ 1992 L101/53) preventing the supply of certain goods and services to Libya; and Reg. 1432/92 (OJ 1992 L151/4) prohibiting trade between the Community and Serbia and Montenegro.

[380] Art. J.5 TEU.   [381] Art. J.6 TEU.   [382] Art. J.7(1) TEU.

[383] Art. J.7(3) TEU. See also the Declaration on the WEU, adopted with the TEU; the Protocol on Art. J TEU, which was annexed to the TEU by the Amsterdam Treaty (OJ 1997 C340/1); and the Declaration on the role of the WEU and its relations with the EU and with the Atlantic Alliance, adopted with the Treaty of Amsterdam.

[384] Art. J.7(1) TEU.

European Union and the Atlantic Alliance is not prejudiced. However, such co-operation must not run counter to or impede that provided for in Articles J.1 to J.18 of the Treaty on European Union.[385]

United Nations

Member States represented in international organisations or international conferences where not all the Member States participate shall keep the latter informed of any matter of common interest.[386] In particular, Member States which are members of the United Nations Security Council will concert and keep the other Member States fully informed. Moreover, Member States which are permanent members of the Security Council[387] will, in the execution of their functions, ensure the defence of the positions and the interests of the Union. Their responsibilities under the United Nations Charter are not to be prejudiced.[388]

21.15 Police and Judicial Co-operation

Articles K.1 to K.14 of the Treaty on European Union provide for police and judicial co-operation in criminal matters.[389]

21.15.1 Objectives

The objectives of police and judicial co-operation in criminal matters are outlined in Article K.1. Such co-operation seeks to provide citizens with a high level of safety within an area of freedom, security, and justice. It is to be achieved through closer co-operation between police forces, customs authorities,[390] and other competent authorities in the Member States, both directly and through the European Police Office (Europol).[391] At the same time, closer co-operation is envisaged between judicial and other competent authorities of the Member States. Where necessary, approximation of rules on criminal matters in the Member States is to take place.

21.15.2 Implementation

Article K.1(1) provides that Member States shall inform and consult one another within the Council concerning matters covered by Articles K.1 to

---

[385] Art. J.7(4) TEU.   [386] Art. J.9(2) TEU.
[387] I.e., France and the UK.   [388] Art. J.9(2) TEU.
[389] Arts. K.15–K.17 TEU also allow for "closer co-operation" in unspecified fields. See also the Protocol integrating the Schengen *acquis* into the framework of the EU.
[390] See e.g. Joint Action 96/698 (OJ 1996 L322/3) on co-operation between customs authorities and business organisations in combating drug trafficking. See also, regarding customs co-operation, Art 116 EC.
[391] See e.g. Joint Action 96/748 (OJ 1996 L342/4) extending the mandate given to the Europol Drugs Unit.

K.14 with a view to co-ordinating their action. To that end, they shall establish collaboration between the relevant departments of their administrations.
Furthermore, Article K.6(2) provides that the Council may adopt common
positions, framework decisions, other decisions, and establish conventions
which it shall recommend to the Member States for adoption.[392]

Within international organisations and at international conferences in
which they take part Member States shall defend these common positions.[393]
Agreements may also be concluded with third states and international organisations.[394]

However, the exercise of the responsibilities incumbent upon Member
States concerning the maintenance of law and order and the safeguarding of
internal security is unaffected.[395]

21.16 Common Policies and Third States

Formally, the EC Treaty and the Treaty on European Union recognise that
common policies generally need to be implemented in co-operation with
third states. However, the very formulation of policy may, as in the case for
example of agricultural policy and commercial policy, jeopardize such co-
operation.

Even where the formulation of a policy seems more "internationalist", its
implementation may be less so. In practice, the tendency may be to seek the
alignment of policy in third states with that of the "internal" policy of the
Union.[396] This tendency may reinforce, and be reinforced by, the dominant
role that commercial policy considerations may play in relations with third
states.

The problems may be controversial in the field of environmental policy.
Article 130r(1) of the EC Treaty requires that Union environmental policy
must contribute to promoting measures at international level to deal with
worldwide environmental problems. Consistently with this provision, the
Action Programme on the Environment[397] advocates developing the role of
the Union in policies and programmes to promote environmental protection
worldwide.[398]

More particularly, Article 130r(4) of the Treaty provides that within their
respective spheres of competence, the Union and the Member States shall

---

[392] Art. K.7 TEU deals with the jurisdiction of the ECJ.

[393] Art. K.9 TEU.   [394] Art K.10 TEU.   [395] Art. K.5 TEU.

[396] E.g., according to Art. 19 of Reg. 1210/90 (OJ 1990 L120/1) establishing the European
Environment Agency and the European Information and Observation Network, third states involved
in the Agency are expected to participate in implementing Union policy.

[397] Resolution of the Council and the Representatives of the Governments of the Member States,
meeting within the Council, of 1 Feb. 1993 (OJ 1993 C138/1) on a Community programme of policy
and action in relation to the environment and sustainable development.

[398] *Ibid.*, introduction.

co-operate with third states and the competent international organisations.[399] The arrangements for Union co-operation may be the subject of
agreements between the Union and the third parties concerned.

In practice, however, the Commission tends to adopt a balancing
approach to trade liberalisation and environmental requirements in
relations with third states. Such an approach may reflect the search for
reciprocity in international trade but may produce problems where a third
state imposes environmental requirements different from those prevailing
in the Union.[400]

For example, the desirability of EU–EFTA co-operation in relation to
environmental protection was recognised in the 1984 Luxembourg
Declaration.[401] Various areas for co-operation were considered at a High
Level Contact Group meeting in October 1985.[402] In practice, the co-operation was affected by trading concerns. In the case of vehicle exhaust
emissions, the Commission stressed the need for a harmonised approach to
avoid the creation of obstacles to trade between the Union and EFTA states.
However, Sweden,[403] Switzerland, and Austria decided to introduce
standards similar to those established in the United States. Their decision
was criticised by the Union. In particular, the Committee on External
Relations of the European Parliament insisted that EFTA states had to "apply
real reciprocity and not take the attitude of '*Alleingang*' they took under
Sweden's guidance in the affair of exhaust gases".[404]

21.17 Agreements with Third States

Many EC Treaty provisions governing common policies expressly provide for
the conclusion of agreements with third states. They are to be negotiated and
concluded under Article 228 of the Treaty. However, the relationship
between the common policies and such agreements may be problematic.

For example, the Council may formulate general orientations for
exchange-rate policy in relation to non-Union currencies. Moreover, "formal

---

[399] See also the Reply by Mr Andriessen to WQ 3186/91 (OJ 1992 C269/22) by Mrs Maartje van
Putten.

[400] Cf. the preference of the European Parliament for removing distortions of competition in
international trade through the establishment of international minimum standards for environmental protection (Resolution of 11 Oct. 1995 (OJ 1995 C287/118) on the Commission communication on economic growth and the environment: some implications for economic policy making,
para. 22).

[401] EFTA Bull. 2/1984, 6–7, point 5.

[402] *Sverige – EG 1985* (Utrikesdepartementets handelsavdelning, Stockholm, 1986) 46.

[403] Reg. on car exhaust gases (SFS 1987:586).

[404] Report on economic and trade relations between the EEC and EFTA countries, EP Doc.
2–32/89/B, 12.

agreements"[405] may be concluded with third states or international organisations on an exchange-rate system for the Euro in relation to such currencies[406] or on other monetary or foreign-exchange regime matters.[407] However, the orientations, and by implication the agreements, shall be without prejudice to the primary objective of the European System of Central Banks to maintain price stability.[408] In other words, agreements inconsistent with the common policy may not lawfully be concluded.

On the other hand, agreements with third states may be concluded where they are consistent with a common policy. For example, reforms of the agricultural policy involve reduced subsidies and protectionism for Union farmers.[409] Consistently with these reforms, the Agreement establishing the World Trade Organisation[410] requires further reductions in farm support and in export subsidies.[411] In addition, import levies are to be converted to tariffs or tariff equivalents.[412]

The problems entailed by the relationship between Union policies and agreements with third states may be acute in the case of free trade agreements and association agreements.

21.17.1 Free Trade Agreements

Free trade agreements may be expected to affect the development of Union policies in relations between the parties.

Preamble Recitals

In the third recital in the Preamble to the Swedish Free Trade Agreement[413] the Parties declared their readiness to examine, in the light of any relevant factor, and in particular of developments in the Union, the possibility of developing and deepening their relations. They would do so, where it would appear to be useful in the interests of their economies to extend them to fields not covered by the Agreement. This recital may be regarded simply as having contemplated extension of liberalisation provisions to fields other than trade in manufactured goods, such as the supply of services. However, the idea of "deepening" the relations between the Parties may be regarded as

---

[405] This expression is not intended to create a new category of international agreement within the meaning of Union law. See the Declaration on Art. 109 EC, adopted with the TEU.

[406] Art. 109(1) EC.

[407] Art. 109(3) EC. See also the Declaration on monetary co-operation with non-Community countries, adopted along with the TEU.

[408] Art. 109(2) EC.   [409] Sect. 21.1.2 above.

[410] Agreement on Agriculture (Annex 1a to the WTO Agreement, OJ 1994 C336/3).

[411] Note Reg. 3290/94 (OJ 1994 L349/105) on the adjustments and transitional arrangements required in the agricultural sector in order to implement the agreements concluded during the Uruguay Round of multilateral trade negotiations.

[412] *Ibid.*

[413] JO 1972 L300/96.

having envisaged the possibility of a qualitative change in their relations going beyond simply the removal of trade obstacles.[414]

"Evolutionary Clauses"

Article 32 of the Swedish Free Trade Agreement,[415] which was discussed in Chapter 19, constituted an "evolutionary clause".[416] This provision did not mention the "deepening" of relations between the Parties. However, its terms seemed broad enough to be interpreted, particularly in the light of the Preamble, as providing a framework for the development of common policies between the Parties.

In the Swedish Agreement, as in the Norwegian Agreement,[417] Article 32 was to be activated on the basis of the "common interest" of the Parties. In contrast, the Austrian,[418] Icelandic,[419] and Swiss Agreements[420] required that resort to the procedure be based on the "interests of the economies" of the Parties.[421] This contrast implies that considerations other than exclusively economic ones could be taken into account within the framework of the Norwegian and Swedish Agreements. The implication becomes stronger when Article 32 of the Swedish Agreement is taken together with the reference in the first recital in the Preamble to the Agreement to the desire of the Parties to contribute "to the work of constructing Europe".

Certainly, the Swedish Government considered that use could be made of Article 32 in relation to questions of public procurement, energy policy, transport policy, environmental policy, and research and development. To this extent, Article 32 was said to compensate for the fact that the Agreement did not itself provide for co-operation in many of the areas of interest to Sweden. During negotiation of the Agreement the Commission accepted that such questions could at least be considered in the future as Union policies began to emerge.[422]

Practice

In practice, limited use was made of Article 32 of the Swedish Free Trade Agreement.[423] Its limited use may have been an inevitable consequence of the fact that the Agreement was simply a commercial policy instrument adopted under Article 113 of the EC Treaty.[424] The real issues arising in relations between the Parties were often the same as those which arose within

---

[414] It was presumably because any such change was regarded in Finland as unacceptable at the time that the recital was omitted from the Preamble to the Finnish Free Trade Agreement (OJ 1973 L328/2).

[415] JO 1972 L300/96.   [416] Sect. 19.6.1 above.   [417] OJ 1973 L171/2.
[418] JO 1972 L300/2.   [419] JO 1972 L301/2.   [420] JO 1972 L300/189.
[421] See, similarly, the Free Trade Agreement with Israel (OJ 1975 L136/2).
[422] AiH 4/1972, 22.   [423] JO 1972 L300/96.

[424] This consideration was taken as justifying an approach to trading problems between parties to such an agreement different from that applied to such problems within the Union. See Capotorti AG in Case 225/78 *Procureur de la République, Besançon* v. *Bouhelier* [1979] ECR 3151, 3165.

the Union and were tackled within the framework of other Union policies. Hence, the treatment of the former issues could not be satisfactorily contained within the framework of such an instrument.

21.17.2 Association Agreements

Association agreements contain provisions regarding common policies, such as agricultural and commercial policies.[425]

Agricultural Policy

Association agreements may refer to agricultural matters, though there is concern to maintain the integrity of the common agricultural policy. This concern is reflected in the case law. For example, *Haegeman*[426] concerned a countervailing charge imposed pursuant to the common organisation of the wine market on imports of Greek wine into Belgium. Here the Court of Justice characterised the imposition of the charge on Greek wine imports as a stabilisation measure essential to the common organisation of the wine market. As such, the measure was permissible under Protocol 12 to the Greek Association Agreement.[427] It did not have to be adopted as a safeguard measure under Article 41 or 43 of the Agreement itself.[428] Thus the Court accepted the legality of Commission action based on the needs of the common agricultural policy.

It is uncertain whether such problems are resolved in the Europe Agreements. For example, Article 25(3) of the Europe Agreement with Poland[429] deals with agricultural policy. It refers to the "standstill" clauses on customs duties and charges having equivalent effect[430] and quantitative restrictions and measures having equivalent effect on trade between the Parties.[431] These clauses, it is stipulated, shall not restrict in any way the pursuit of the respective agricultural policies of Poland and the Union or the taking of any measures under such policies.[432] However, Article 20(6) takes account of the need for an increased harmony between the agricultural policies in the Union and Poland, as well as Poland's objective of becoming a member of the Union. It provides that both Parties will have regular consultations in the Association Council on the strategy and practical modalities of their respective agricultural policies.

---

[425] Arrangements may also be made for participation by associated states in Union framework programmes, specific programmes, projects, or other actions in fields relevant to "economic and cultural co-operation". See e.g. the Additional Protocol to the Europe Agreement with Poland (OJ 1995 L317/35).

[426] Case 181/73 *R. & V. Haegeman* v. *Belgium* [1974] ECR 449.   [427] JO 1963 293.

[428] [1974] ECR 449, 463.   [429] OJ 1993 L348/2.   [430] *Ibid.*, Art. 25(1).

[431] *Ibid.*, Art. 25(2).

[432] Art. 25(3) (*ibid.*) provides that this stipulation is without prejudice to concessions granted under Art. 20 (*ibid.*).

Commercial Policy

Article 27(1) of the Europe Agreement with Poland[433] provides that the Agreement shall not preclude the maintenance or establishment of customs unions, free trade areas, or arrangements for frontier trade, unless they alter the trade arrangements provided for in this Agreement. However, Article 27(2) provides that consultations between the Parties shall take place within the Association Council concerning agreements establishing customs unions or free trade areas. Where requested, consultations shall also take place between the Parties on other major issues related to their respective trade policies with third states. In particular, if a third state accedes to the Union, such consultations shall take place to ensure that account can be taken of the mutual interests of the Union and Poland stated in this Agreement.

21.17.3 EEA Agreement

The EEA Agreement[434] makes comparatively sophisticated arrangements for the development of common policies between the Parties. Even so, there may be concern for the integrity of the policies of the Parties.

Co-operation outside the "Four Freedoms"

Articles 78 to 88 of the EEA Agreement provide for "co-operation outside the four freedoms". To this end, Article 79 of the Agreement requires that the Parties shall strengthen the dialogue between them by all appropriate means, in particular, through the procedures provided for in Part VII.[435] They are thus to identify areas and activities where closer co-operation outside the four freedoms can contribute to the attainment of their common objectives in the fields referred to in Article 78. These fields are: research and techno-logical development, information services, the environment, education, training and youth, social policy, consumer protection, small and medium-sized enterprises, tourism, the audiovisual sector, and civil protection. However, Article 88 states that nothing in these provisions shall preclude the possibility for any Party to prepare, adopt, and implement measures independently.

Monetary Policy

Concern for the integrity of the policies of the Parties to the EEA Agreement may be more manifest in certain provisions than in others. For example, Article 46 of the Agreement provides for consultations between the Parties regarding monetary policy. However, it is stipulated that exchange of views and information "shall take place on a non-binding basis".

---

[433] OJ 1993 L348/2.   [434] OJ 1994 L1/3.
[435] See sect. 19.6.3 above, regarding these procedures.

Bibliography

Abrams, R.K., P.K. Cornelius, P.L. Hedfors and G. Tersman, *The Impact of the European Community's Internal Market on the EFTA* (International Monetary Fund, Washington, DC, 1990)

Addison, J.T., and W.S. Siebert, "The Social Charter of the European Community: Evolution and Controversies" [1991] *Industrial and Labor Relations Review* 597–625

Ahnlid, A., "Free or Forced Riders? Small States in the International Political Economy: the Example of Sweden" [1992] *Cooperation and Conflict* 241–76

Alexander, W., "Free Movement of Non-EC Nationals: A Review of the Case-Law of the Court of Justice" [1992] *European Journal of International Law* 53–64

Alting van Geusau, F.A.M., "Problèmes institutionnels des Communautés européennes" [1966] *Cahiers de Droit Européen* 227–50

Anderson, J.J., "Skeptical Reflections on a Europe of Regions: Britain, Germany, and the ERDF" [1990] *Journal of Public Policy* 417–45

André, C., "Le Nouvel instrument communautaire d'emprunts et de prêts (N.I.C.)" [1980] *Revue du Marché Commun* 66–71

Andriessen, F.H.J.J., "The Role of Anti-Trust in the Face of Economic Recession: State Aids in the EEC" [1983] *European Competition Law Review* 340–50

Antunes, L.M.P., "L'Article 90 du Traité CEE: obligations des états membres et pouvoirs de la Commission" [1991] *Revue Trimestrielle de Droit Européen* 187–209

Audretsch, H.A.H., *Supervision in European Community Law: Observance by the Member States of their Treaty Obligations* (2nd edn., North-Holland, Amsterdam, 1986)

Ayral, M., "Essai de classification des groupes et comités" [1975] *Revue du Marché Commun* 330–42

Bael, I. van, "EEC Anti-Dumping Law and Procedure Revisited" [1990] *Journal of World Trade* 5–23

—— "Public Procurement and the Completion of the Internal Market: Law and Practice" [1989] *Legal Issues of European Integration* 21–48

Baldi, M., "Direct Applicability of Free Trade Agreements between the EEC and the EFTA Countries from a Swiss Perspective" [1985] *Swiss Review of International Competition Law* 30–8

Baldwin, R. E., "Assessing the Fair Trade and Safeguards Laws in Terms of Modern Trade and Political Economy Analysis" [1992] *The World Economy* 185–202

—— "The Case against Infant-Industry Tariff Protection" [1969] *Journal of Political Economy* 295–305

—— "Rent-Seeking and Trade Policy: An Industry Approach" [1984] *Weltwirtschaftliches Archiv* 662–76

Baragiola, P., *North-South: the EC Development Policy* (Club de Bruxelles, Brussels, 1991)

Barents, R., "New Developments in Measures Having an Equivalent Effect" (1981) 18 *Common Market Law Review* 271–308

Barnard, C., and E. Sharpston, "The Changing Face of Article 177 References" (1997) 34 *Common Market Law Review* 1113–1137

Barr, F., "The New Commission Notice on Agreements of Minor Importance: Is Appreciability a Useful Measure" [1997] *European Competition Law Review* 202–13
—— "Recente ontwikkelingen in de rechtspraak over steunmaatn" [1988] *Sociaal-Economische Wetgeving* 352–64
Battistotti, L., "I Finanziamenti concessi della banca europea per gli invetimenti ed il nuovo strumento communitario" [1985] *Cronache Economiche* 63–8
Bellis, J.-F., "Further Changes in the EEC Anti-Dumping Regulation: a Codification of Controversial Methodologies" [1989] *Journal of World Trade Law* 21–34
Bello, J.H., "Midterm Report on Binational Dispute Settlement Under the United States-Canada Free-Trade Agreement" [1991] *The International Lawyer* 489–516
Bernard, N., *Le Comité Economique et Social* (ESC, Brussels, 1972)
Bernitz, U., "The EEC–EFTA Free Trade Agreements with Special Reference to the Position of Sweden and the Other Scandinavian EFTA Countries" [1986] 23 *Common Market Law Review* 567–90
Biancarelli, P., "Le Contrôle de la Cour de justice des Communautés européennes en matière d'aides publiques" [1993] *Actualité Juridique de Droit Administratif* 412–36
Bianchi, P., "La Réorientation des politiques structurelles de la CEE" [1991] *Revue du Marché Commun* 599–603
Bieber, R., R. Dehousse, J. Pinder and J.H.H. Weiler (eds.), *1992: One European Market* (Nomos, Baden-Baden, 1988)
Blumann, C., "Régime des aides d'état: jurisprudence recente de la Cour de justice" [1992] *Revue du Marché Commun* 721–39
Boltuck, R.D., "An Economic Analysis of Dumping" [1987] *Journal of World Trade Law* 45–54
Bondi, A., "The Merchant, the Thief and the Citizen: the Circulation of Works of Art within the European Union" (1997) 34 *Common Market Law Review* 1173–95
Boudant, J., *L'Anti-Dumping Communautaire* (Economica, Paris, 1991)
Bourgeois, J.H.J., "The EC in the WTO and Advisory Opinion 1/94: An Echternach Procession" (1995) 32 *Common Market Law Review* 763–87
—— "EEC Control over International Mergers" [1990] *Yearbook of European Law* 103–32
—— "The EFTA Countries and EC Legal Systems: is Integration Possible? Comment" in J. Jamar and H. Wallace (eds.), *EEC–EFTA: More Than Just Good Friends?* (De Tempel, Bruges, 1988) 299–304
Bourrinet, J. and M. Torelli, *Les Relations Extérieurs de la CEE* (Presses universitaires de France, Paris, 1980)
Brander, J.A. and B.J. Spencer, "Export Subsidies and International Market Share Rivalry" [1985] *Journal of International Economics* 83–100
Brandtner, B., "The Drama of the EEA: Comments on Opinions 1/91 and 1/92" in O. Jacot-Guillarmod (ed.), *Accord EEE: Commentaires et réflexions* (Schulthess, Bern, 1992) 300–28
Bredima-Savopoulou, A. and J. Tzoannos, *The Common Shipping Policy of the EEC* (North-Holland, Amsterdam, 1990)
Breibart, E., "The Wood Pulp Case: the Application of EEC Competition Law to Foreign-Based Undertakings" (1989) 19 *Georgia Journal of International and Comparative Law* 149–73
Bressand, A., "Beyond Interdependence: 1992 as a Global Challenge" [1990] *International Affairs* 47–65
Bronckers, M., "Business Strategies for a Unified Market. Comment" in J. Jamar and H. Wallace (eds.), *EEC–EFTA: More Than Just Good Friends?* (De Tempel, Bruges, 1988) 61–7

—— and R. Quick, "What Is A Countervailable Subsidy Under EEC Trade Law" [1989] *Journal of World Trade Law* 5–31

Brouwers, G., "Free Movement of Foodstuffs and Quality Requirements: Has the Commission Got it Wrong?" (1988) 25 *Common Market Law Review* 237–62

Brunner, H.E., "Die Ursprungsregeln im europäischen Freihandelsraum" [1977] *Aussenwirtschaft* 55–63

Brzezinski, C., "The EC–Poland Association Agreement: Harmonization of an Aspiring Member State's Company Law" (1993) 34 *Harvard International Law Journal* 105–48

Buess, T., "Perspektiven für eine engere Zussammenarbeit zwischen der Europäischen Gemeinschaft und den EFTA-Mitgliedstaaten" [1985] *Aussenwirtschaft* 341–87

Bulmer, S., "The European Council's First Decade: Between Interdependence and Domestic Politics" (1985) 23 *Journal of Common Market Studies* 89–104

Camagni, R. and R. Cappellin, "Policies for Full Employment and More Efficient Utilization of Resources and New Trends in European Regional Development" [1981] *Lo Spettatore Internazionale* 99–135

Capelli, F., "Les Relations CE/Etats-Unis et la réalisation du marché intérieur" in J. Schwarze (ed.), *The External Relations of the European Community, in Particular EC-US Relations* (Nomos, Baden-Baden, 1989) 139–43

Carter, B.E., "A Code of Conduct for EC-US Relations" in J. Schwarze (ed.), *The External Relations of the European Community, in Particular EC-US Relations* (Nomos, Baden-Baden, 1989) 131–39

Cassese, A., A. Clapham and J.H.H. Weiler (eds.), *Fundamental Rights and the European Community: Methods of Protection* (Nomos, Baden-Baden, 1991)

Catalano, M., "I Poteri dell'Assemblea parlamentare europea" [1971] *Rivista di Diritto Europeo* 31–47

Caves, R.E., "Industrial Policy and Trade Policy: The Connections" in H. Kierzkowski (ed.), *Protection and Competition in International Trade* (Blackwell, Oxford, 1987) 68–85

Chalmers, D., "Repackaging the Internal Market – The Ramifications of the *Keck* Judgment" [1994] *European Law Review* 385–403

Chard, J. S. and M.J. Macmillan, "Sectoral Aids and Community Competition Rules: the Case of Textiles" [1979] *Journal of World Trade Law* 132–57

Close, G., "External Relations in the Air Transport Sector: Air Transport Policy or the Common Commercial Policy?" (1990) 27 *Common Market Law Review* 107–27

Cocks, B., *The European Parliament* (HMSO, London, 1973)

Collins, L., *European Community Law in the United Kingdom* (4th edn., Butterworths, London, 1990)

Collins, P. and M. Hutchings, "Articles 101 and 102 of the EEC Treaty: Completing the Internal Market" [1986] *European Law Review* 191–9

Corbett, R., "Testing the New Procedures" (1989) 27 *Journal of Common Market Studies* 359–72

Cottier, T., "Constitutional Trade Regulation in National and International Law: Structure-Substance Pairings in the EFTA Experience" in M. Hilf and E-U. Petersmann (eds.), *National Constitutions and International Economic Law* (Kluwer, Deventer, 1993) 409–42

Cramér, P., "Funderingar kring permanent neutralitet och integration i västeuropa" in U. Nordlöf-Lagerkranz (ed.), *Svensk Neutralitet, Europa, och EG* (Foreign Policy Institute, Stockholm, 1990) 27–51

Curzon Price, V., *1992: Europe's Last Chance? From Common Market to Single Market*

Bibliography

(Institute of Economic Affairs, London, 1988)

—— "Industrial Trade Policy in a Period of Rapid Industrial Change" [1986] *Aussenwirtschaft* 201–23

—— "La Suisse et le marché unique de 1992: une comparaison entre les scénarios 'First best' et 'Least best'" [1990] *Schweizerische Zeitschrift für Volkswirtschaft und Statistik* 215–29

—— "The Threat of 'Fortress Europe' from the Development of Social and Industrial Policies at a European Level" [1991] *Aussenwirtschaft* 119–38

Dam, K.W., "The Economics and Law of Price Discrimination: herein of three Regulatory Schemes" (1963) 30 *University of Chicago Law Review* 1–62

Daniele, L., "Non-Discriminatory Restrictions to the Free Movement of Persons" [1997] *European Law Review* 191–200

Davenport, M., *The Charybdis of Antidumping: A New Form of EC Industrial Policy?* (Discussion Paper 22, Royal Institute of International Affairs, London, 1989)

—— "The Economics of Antidumping and the Uruguay Round" [1990] *Intereconomics* 267–73

Davidson, I., "Sovereignty in the European Economic Community: The Case of France" [1975] *The Round Table* 235–42

Davies, P., "Posted Workers: Single Market or Protection of National Labour Law Systems" (1997) 34 *Common Market Law Review* 571–602

Davignon, E., "The Future of the European Steel Industry" [1980] *Annals of Public and Cooperative Economy* 507–19

Deen, A. and D.A. Westbrook, "Return to Europe: Integrating Eastern European Economies into the European Market through Alliance with the European Community" (1990) 30 *Harvard International Law Journal* 660–70

Dehousse R. (ed.), *Europe After Maastricht An Ever Closer Union?* (Beck, Munich, 1994)

Denton, R., "The Non-Market Economy Rules of the European Community's Anti-Dumping and Countervailing Duties Legislation" [1987] *International and Comparative Law Quarterly* 198–239

Desterbecq-Fobelets, H., "Le Contrôle externe de l'octroi des aides étatiques aux entreprises privées en Belgique" [1979] *Administration Publique* 277–301

Devroe W., "Privatizations and Community Law: Neutrality versus Policy" (1997) 34 *Common Market Law Review* 267–306

Dewost, J.L., "La Présidence dans le cadre institutionnel des Communautés européennes" [1984] *Revue du Marché Commun* 31–4

Dicke, H. and R.J. Langhammer, *The Institutional Framework and External Dimension of the EC Internal Market* (Kiel Working Paper No. 453, University of Kiel, 1990)

Didier, P., "EEC Anti-Dumping Rules and Practices" (1980) 17 *Common Market Law Review* 349–69

Dixit, A., "International Trade Policy for Oligopolistic Industries" [1984] *Economic Journal* 1–16

Duff, A.M., "The Report of the Three Wise Men" (1981) 19 *Journal of Common Market Studies* 237–54

Dunlop, J. and R.N. King, "Regional Economic Integration and GATT: the Effects of the EEC-EFTA Agreements on International Trade" [1974] *Law and Policy in International Business* 207–35

Dyson (ed.), K., *Local Authorities and New Technologies: the European Dimension* (Croom Helm, London, 1988)

Edwards, G., "The Relevance of Theory to Group-to-Group Dialogue" in G. Edwards and E. Regelsberger (eds.), *Europe's Global Links* (Pinter, London, 1990) 201–18

Edwards, S., *On the Sequencing of Structural Reforms* (OECD Working Paper No. 70, Paris, 1989)

Eek, H., "Neutralitet, neutralitetspolitik och EEC" [1971] *Svensk Juristtidning* 1–21

Ehlermann, C.-D. and G. Campogrande, "Rules on Services in the EEC: a model for Negotiating World-Wide Rules?" in E-U. Petersmann and M. Hilf (eds.), *The New GATT Round of Multilateral Trade Negotiations* (Kluwer, Deventer, 1991) 481–98

—— "The Financing of the Community: the Distinction between Financial Contributions and Own Resources" (1982) 19 *Common Market Law Review* 371–92

—— "State Aid Control in the European Union: Success or Failure?" (1995) 18 *Fordham International Law Journal* 1212–29

—— "State Aids under European Community Law" (1994) 18 *Fordham International Law Journal* 410–36

Elizade, J., "Legal Aspects of Community Policy on Research and Technological Development (RTD)" (1992) 29 *Common Market Law Review* 309–46

Epiney, A., "La Cour de justice des Communautés européennes et l'Espace économique européen" [1992] *Revue Suisse de Droit International et de Droit Européen* 275–304

Ethier, W.J., "Dumping" [1982] *Journal of Political Economy* 487–506

Evans, A., "Article 85(3) Exemption: 'Allowing Consumers a Fair Share of the Resulting Benefit'" in M. Goyens (ed.), *EC Competition Policy and Consumers* (Bruylant, Brussels, 1985) 99–120

—— *EC Law of State Aid* (Oxford Series in EC Law, Clarendon Press, Oxford, 1997)

—— "Economic Policy and the Free Movement of Goods in EEC Law" [1983] *International and Comparative Law Quarterly* 577–99

—— "The Enforcement Procedure of Article 169 EEC: Commission Discretion" [1979] *European Law Review* 442–56

—— "Freedom of Trade under the Common Law and European Community Law: The Case of the Football Bans" (1986) 102 *Law Quarterly Review* 510–48

—— "Institutions of the European Communities Other Than The Court of Justice" in *Stair Memorial Encyclopaedia of the Laws of Scotland*, (Butterworths, London, 1990) x, 132–262

—— *The Integration of the European Community and Third States in Europe: A Legal Analysis* (Clarendon Press, Oxford, 1996)

—— *The Law of EU Regional Policy* (Kluwer, Deventer, 1995)

—— "Nationality Law and European Integration" [1991] *European Law Review* 190–215

—— "Participation of National Parliaments in the European Community Legislative Process" [1981] *Public Law* 388–98

—— "Privatization and State Aid Control in EC Law" [1997] *European Competition Law Review* 259–64

—— "Secondary Immigration Control and EEC Law" (1984) 134 *New Law Journal* 965–7

—— "Treaties and United Kingdom Legislation: the Scottish Dimension" [1984] *Juridical Review* 41–62

Fagerberg, J., "The Process of Economic Integration in Europe: Consequences for EFTA Countries and Firms" [1991] *Cooperation and Conflict* 197–215

Fidler, D.P., "Competition Law and International Relations" [1992] *International and Comparative Law Quarterly* 563–89

Flaesch-Mougin, C., "Les Accords externes de la CEE (1 juillet 1986/31 octobre 1989)" [1990] *Revue Trimestrielle de Droit Européen* 457–518

Flam, H., *Reverse Dumping* (Institute for International Economic Studies, Stockholm, 1985)

Forest, P., "Il Mecanismo decisionale comunitari visto attraverso il Consiglio dei Ministri delle Comunità europea" [1982] *Diritto Comparato e degli Scambi Internazionale* 755–85

Frazer, T., "Competition Policy after 1992: the Next Step" (1990) 53 *Modern Law Review* 609–23

Froment Meurice, H., *La Dimension extérieur du marché intérieur* (Presses universitaires de France, Paris, 1988)

Gadbin, D., "Le Droit communautaire des structures agricoles: organisation ou dilution?" [1991] *Revue du Marché Commun* 218–30

Gaisford, J.D. and D.L. McLachlan, "Domestic Subsidies and Countervail: The Treacherous Ground of the Level Playing Field" [1990] *Journal of World Trade* 55–77

Gaja, G., "Instruments for Legal Integration in the European Community – A Review" in M. Cappelletti, M. Seccombe, R.M. Buxbaum, K.J. Hopt, T. Daintith, S.F. Williams, T. Bourgoignie, and D. Trubek (eds.), *Integration Through Law* (de Gruyter, Berlin, 1986) 113–60

Ganshof van der Meersch, W.G., *Organisations européennes: les institutions* (Larcier, Brussels, 1963)

Gerbet, P., "La Genèse du Plan Schuman" [1956] *Revue Française de Science Public* 525–53

Gold, M., "Managing Dumping in a Global Economy" (1988) 21 *George Washington Journal of International Law and Economics* 503–38

Gormley, L., *Prohibiting Restrictions on Trade Within the EEC* (North-Holland, Amsterdam, 1985)

Grabitz, E., *Kommentar zum Europäische Union* (Beck, Munich, 1992)

Greenaway, D. and P. Tharakan, *Imperfect Competition and International Trade: The Policy Aspects of Intra-Industry Trade* (Wheatsheaf Books, Brighton, 1986)

Greenwald, J., "Negotiating Strategy" in G.C. Hufbauer (ed.), *Europe 1992: An American Perspective* (Brookings Institution, Washington, DC, 1990) 345–88

Greenwood J., (ed.), *Organized Interests and the European Community* (Pinter, London, 1992)

Grieco, J.M., *Cooperation among Nations* (Cornell University Press, Ithaca, NY, 1990)

Groeben, H. von der, H. von Boeckh, J. Thiesing and C.-D. Ehlermann (eds.), *Kommentar zum EWG Vertrag* (Nomos, Baden-Baden, 1983)

Grolig, O. and P. Bogaert, "The Newly-Amended EEC Anti-Dumping Regulation: Black Holes in the Common Market" [1987] *Journal of World Trade Law* 79–87

Gruszecki, T. and J. Winiecki, "Privatisation in East-Central Europe: A Comparative Perspective" [1991] *Aussenwirtschaft* 67–100

Guggenheim, P., "Organisations économiques supranationales, indépendance et neutralité de la Suisse" [1962] *Zeitschrift für Schweizerisches Recht* 221–343

Haas, E.B., *The Uniting of Europe: Political, Social, and Economic Forces 1950–1957* (Stanford University Press, Cal., 1968)

Hagland, P., "Environmental Policy" in L. Hurwitz and C. Lequesne (eds.), *The State of the European Community* (Lynne Riener, Boulder, Colo., 1991) 259–72

Hailbronner, K., "Legal Aspects of the Unification of the Two German States" [1991] *European Journal of International Law* 18–41

Hancher, L., T., Ottervanger and P.J. Slot, *EC State Aids* (Chancery Publishing, London, 1993)

Harden (ed.), I., *State Aid: Community Law and Policy* (Bundesanzeiger, Trier, 1993) 52–60

Harlow, C., "A Community of Interests? Making the Most of European Law" (1992) 55

Modern Law Review 331–50

Hart, J.A., "The Effects of State-Societal Arrangements on International Competitiveness: Steel, Motor Vehicles, and Semiconductors in the United States, Japan, and Western Europe" [1992] *British Journal of Political Science* 255–300

Hawk, B., "The American (Anti-trust) Revolution: Lessons for the EEC?" [1988] *European Competition Law Review* 53–87

—— "La Recherche et le développement en droit communautaire et en droit antitrust americain" [1987] *Revue Internationale de Droit Economique* 211–69

Hay, P., *Federalism and Supranational Organizations* (University of Illinois Press, Chicago, Ill., 1966)

Hayder, R., "Neue Wege der europäischen Rechtsangleichung?" [1989] *Rabels Zeitschrift für Ausländisches und Internationales Privatrecht* 622–98

Hayes-Renshaw, F., C. Lequesne, and P.M. Lopez, "The Permanent Representatives of the Member States to the European Communities" (1989) 27 *Journal of Common Market Studies* 119–37

Haymann, M., "Joint Ventures and Mergers as a Test-Mark for a European Competition Law Between EEC and EFTA: Switzerland as an Example" [1990] *World Competition* 5–29

Hellingman, K., "State Participation as State Aid under Article 92 of the EEC Treaty: the Commission Guidelines" (1986) 23 *Common Market Law Review* 111–31

Helpman E. and P. Krugman, *Market Structure and Foreign Trade* (Wheatsheaf Books, Brighton, 1985)

Henig, S., "The Institutional Structure of the European Community" (1973) 11 *Journal of Common Market Studies* 373–409

—— "New Institutions for European Integration" (1973) 11 *Journal of Common Market Studies* 129–38

Hesse, J.J., (ed.), *Local Government and Urban Affairs in International Perspective* (Nomos, Baden-Baden, 1991)

Hilf, M., "Settlement of Disputes in International Economic Organisations: Comparative Analysis and Proposals for Strengthening the GATT Dispute Settlement Procedures" in E.-U. Petersmann and M. Hilf (eds.), *The New GATT Round of Multilateral Trade Negotiations* (Kluwer, Deventer, 1991) 285–322

Himsworth, C.M.G., "Things Fall Apart: the Harmonization of Community Judicial Procedural Protection Revisited" [1997] *European Law Review* 291–311

Hindley, B., "The Economics of Dumping and Anti-Dumping Action: Is there a Baby in the Bathwater?" in P.K.M. Tharakan (ed.), *Policy Implications of Antidumping Measures* (North-Holland, Amsterdam, 1991) 25–43

Hine, R.C., "Protection in the European Community Before and After 1992" in D. Greenaway, R.C. Hine, A.P. O'Brien, and R.J. Thornton (eds.), *Global Protectionism* (Macmillan, London, 1991) 69–98

Hoogenboom, T., "Integration into Society and Free Movement of Non-EC Nationals" [1992] *European Journal of International Law* 36–52

Horlick, G.N. and S. Shuman, "Non-Market Economy Trade and US Anti-Dumping/Countervailing Duty Laws" [1984] *The International Lawyer* 807–40

Hornsby, S.B., "Competition Policy in the 80's: More Policy Less Competition?" [1987] *European Law Review* 79–101

Horovitz, D., "Dealing with Dumping in the EEC-EFTA Free Trade Areas" [1989] *European Competition Law Review* 540–56

—— "EC–Central/East European Relations: New Principles for a New Era" (1990) 27 *Common Market Law Review* 259–84

—— "The Impending "Second Generation" Agreements between the European Community and Eastern Europe – Some Practical Considerations" [1991] *Journal of World Trade* 55–80

Hösli, M., "Decision-making in the EEA and EFTA State's Sovereignty" [1990] *Aussenwirtschaft* 463–94

Hufbauer, G.C., *Procedures for Monitoring and Disciplining Government Aids* (EFTA Occasional Paper No. 30, Geneva, 1989)

—— and J.J. Schott, *Trading for Growth: the Next Round of Trade Negotiations* (Institute for International Economics, Washington, DC, 1985)

Hughes, G. and P. Hare, "Competitiveness and Industrial Restructuring in Czechoslovakia, Hungary and Poland" in *European Economy* (Special Edition No. 2, The Path of Reform in Central and Eastern Europe) 83–105

Hummer, W. and M. Schweitzer, "Möglichkeiten und Grenzen der Dynamisierung der Beziehungen Österreichs zu den Europäischen Gemeinschaften" [1987] *Europa-Archiv* 343–50

Hurni, B., "EFTA-EC Relations: Aftermath of the Luxembourg Declaration" [1986] *Journal of World Trade Law* 497–506

Hurtig, S., "The European Common Market" [1958] *International Conciliation* 317–81

Isaacs, G., "La Rénovation des institutions financiers des Communautés européennes depuis 1970" [1977] *Revue Trimestrielle de Droit Européen* 736–810

Jackson, J.H., "EC "92 and Beyond: Comments from a U.S. Perspective" [1991] *Aussenwirtschaft* 341–48

Jacobs, F.G., "Isoglucose Resurgent: Two Powers of the European Parliament Upheld by the Court" (1981) 18 *Common Market Law Review* 219–26

Jacot-Guillarmod, O. (ed.), *Accord EEE: commentaires et reflexions* (Schulthess, Bern, 1992)

—— *L'Avenir du libre-échange en Europe: vers un Espace économique européen* (Schulthess, Zürich, 1990) 111–29

Jacqué, J-P, "The Draft Treaty Establishing the European Union" (1985) 22 *Common Market Law Review* 19–42

Jäger, M. "Die sogenannte Entwicklungsklauseln in den Abkommen der EWG mit den Rest-EFTA-Staaten, inbesondere der Schweiz" [1972] *Aussenwirtschaft* 323–39

Jenny, F. Y., "Competition and State Aid Policy in the European Community" (1994) 18 *Fordham Int. Law J.* 525–54

Joliet, R., "Droit des marques et libre circulation des marchandises: l'abandon de l'arrêt Hag I" [1991] *Revue Trimestrielle de Droit Européen* 169–85

Keeling, D.T., "The Free Movement of Goods in EEC Law: Basic Principles and Recent Developments in the Case Law of the Court of Justice of the European Communities" [1992] *International Lawyer* 467–83

Kelly, M., N. Kirmani, M. Xaja, C. Boonekamp, and P. Winglee, *Issues and Developments in International Trade Policy* (International Monetary Fund, Washington, DC, 1988)

Kennedy, D. and L. Specht, "Austria and the European Communities" (1989) 28 *Common Market Law Review* 615–41

—— "Austrian Membership in the European Communities" (1990) 31 *Harvard International Law Journal* 407–61

Kennedy, D. and D.E. Webb, "The Limits of Integration: Eastern Europe and the European Communities" (1993) 30 *Common Market Law Review* 1095–117

Keohane, R.O. and S. Hoffmann, "Institutional Change in the 1980s" in R.O. Keohane and S. Hoffmann (eds.), *The New European Community* (Westview Press, Boulder, Colo., 1991) 1–39

Kierzkowski H. (ed.), *Protection and Competition in International Trade* (Blackwell, Oxford, 1987)

Kirgis, F.L., *International Organisations in Their Legal Setting* (West Publishing, St. Paul, Minn., 1977)

Koopman, G. and H.-E. Scharrer, *Scenarios of a Common External Trade Policy for the EC after 1992* (Institut für Wirtschaftsforschung Report No. 84, Hamburg, 1990)

Korah, V., "The Exhaustion of Patents by Sale in a Member State when a Monopoly Profit Could not be Earned" [1997] *European Competition Law Review* 265–72

—— "Interpretation and Application of Article 86 of the Treaty of Rome: Abuse of a Dominant Position Within the Common Market" (1978) 53 *Notre Dame Lawyer* 768–98

—— *An Introductory Guide to EC Competition Law and Practice* (Hart Publishing, Oxford, 1997)

Korte, J., *Primus Inter Pares: the European Court and National Courts* (Nomos, Baden-Baden, 1991)

Kovar, R., "Les Prises de participation publiques et le régime communautaire des aides d'état" [1992] *Revue Trimestrielle de Droit Européen* 109–57

Kramer, H,. "The EC and the Stabilisation of Eastern Europe" [1992] *Aussenpolitik* 12–21

Krämer, L., "Environmental Protection and Article 30 EEC Treaty" (1993) 30 *Common Market Law Review* 111–43

—— "The Implementation of Environmental Laws by the European Economic Communities" [1991] *Jahrbuch für Internationales Recht* 9–53

Krenzler, H.G., "The Dialogue between the European Community and the United States of America: Present Form and Future Prospects" in J. Schwarze (ed.), *The External Relations of the European Community, in Particular EC-US Relations* (Nomos, Baden-Baden, 1989) 91–103

—— "Die Rolle der Kabinette in der Kommission der Europäischen Gemeinschaften" [1974] *Europa Recht* 75–9

—— "Zwischen Protektionismus und Liberalismus: Europäischer Binnenmarkt und Drittlandsbeziehungen" [1988] *Europa-Archiv* 241–48

Krueger, A.O., "The Political Economy of the Rent-Seeking Society" [1974] *The American Economic Review* 291–303

Krugman, P., *EFTA and 1992* (EFTA Occasional Paper No. 23, Geneva, 1988)

Kulms, R., "Competition, Trade Policy and Competition Policy in the EEC: The Example of Antidumping" (1990) 27 *Common Market Law Review* 285–313

Kuyper, P.J., "The European Communities and Arbitration" in A.H.A. Soons (ed.), *International Arbitration: Past and Prospects* (Kluwer, Dordrecht, 1989) 181–8

Ladeur, K.-H., "European Community Institutional Reforms: Extra-National Management as an Alternative Model to Federalism" (1990/2) *Legal Issues of European Integration* 1–21

Lagrange, M., "The Theory of the *Acte Clair*: a Bone of Contention or a Source of Unity?" (1971) 8 *Common Market Law Review* 313–24

Laird, S. and A. Yeats, "Trends in Non-tariff Barriers of Developed Countries, 1966–1986" [1990] *Weltwirtschaftliches Archiv* 299–325

Lanneaux, Y.S., "International Trade: Joint Report of the United States-Japan Working Group on the Structural Impediments Initiative" (1991) 32 *Harvard International Law Journal* 245–54

Laprat, G., "Les Groupes politiques en le Parlement européen" [1975] *Revue du Marché Commun* 22–30

Lary H. de, "Libre circulation et immigrés à l'horizon 1993" [1989] *Revue Française des*

Affaires Sociales 93–117

Lasok D. and J.W. Bridge, *Law and Institutions of the European Communities* (5th edn., Butterworths, London, 1991)

Lauwaars, R.H., "The European Council" (1977) 14 *Common Market Law Review* 25–44

Lazar, F. "Structural/Strategic Dumping: a Comment on Richard Boltuck's 'An Economic Analysis of Dumping'" [1988] *Journal of World Trade Law* 91–3

Leborgne, D. and A. Lipietz, "How to Avoid a Two-Tier Europe" [1990] *Labour and Society* 177–99

Legrand-Lane, R., "Vers une relance institutionnelle de la Communauté européenne" [1985] *Etudes* 293–305

Lehner S. and R. Meiklejohn, "Fair Competition in the Internal Market" (*European Economy* No. 48, EC Commission, Brussels, 1991) 7–114

Leman, C., "Patterns of Policy Development: Social Security in the United States and Canada" [1977] *Public Policy* 261–91

Lenaerts, K., "Regulating the Regulatory Process: 'Delegation of Powers' in the European Community" [1993] *European Law Review* 23–49

—— "Some Reflections on the Separation of Powers in the European Community" (1991) 28 *Common Market Law Review* 11–28

Leopold, P.M., "Community Law-Making: Opinions of the European Parliament" [1982] *Oxford Journal of Legal Studies* 454–59

Letteron, R., "Les Aides des collectivités territoriales aux services publics" [1993] *Actualité Juridique de Droit Administratif* 437–43

Lidgard, H., "Sverige – EEG och konkurrensen" [1974] *Svensk Juristtidning* 18–33

—— "Tre års frihandelssamarbete med EEC" [1976] *Svensk Juristtidning* 689–714

Lindberg, L. and S.A. Scheingold, *Europe's Would-be Polity* (Prentice Hall, Englewood Cliffs, New Jersey, 1970)

Lipsey, R.G. and K. Lancaster, "The General Theory of the Second Best" [1956] *Review of Economic Studies* 11–32

LLavero, M.V., "The Possible Direct Effect of the Provisions on Competition in the EEC-EFTA Free Trade Agreements in the Light of the Kupferberg Decision" (1984/2) *Legal Issues of European Integration* 83–101

Lowe, P., "The Reform of the Community's Structural Funds" (1988) 25 *Common Market Law Review* 503–21

Luif, P., "Decision Structures and Decision-Making Processes in the European Communities" Relations to the EFTA Countries: A Case Study of Austria" [1983] *Österreichisches Zeitschrift für Aussenpolitik* 139–60

Lysén, G., "Some Views on Neutrality and Membership of the European Communities: The Case of Sweden" (1992) 29 *Common Market Law Review* 229–55

—— "Varumärken som konkurrensbegränsande medel – en komparativ betraktelse utifrån frihandelsavtalet mellan Sverige och EEC" [1982] *Svensk Juristtidning* 461–90

Majone, G., *Evidence, Argument and Persuasion in the Policy Process* (Yale University Press, New Haven, Conn., 1989)

—— "Regulating Europe" [1989] *Jahrbuch zur Staats-und Verwaltungswissenschaft* 159–77

Mancini, C.F., "L'Incorporazione del diritto comunitario nel diritto interno degli stati membri delle Comunità europee" [1988] *Rivista di Diritto Europeo* 87–100

March Hunnings, N., "Enforceability of the EEC-EFTA Free Trade Agreements" [1977] *European Law Review* 163–89

Marsden, P.B., "Inducing Member State Enforcement of European Competition Law: a

Competition Policy Approach to 'Antitrust Federalism'" [1997] *European Competition Law Review* 234–41

Martin, A.M., "Le Comité des représentants permanents" [1980] *Cahiers de Droit Européen* 25–53

Martin, S. (ed.), *The Construction of Europe: Essays in Honour of Emile Noel* (Kluwer, Deventer, 1994)

Mattera, A., "De l'Arrêt 'Dassonville' à l'arrêt 'Keck': l'obscure clarté d'une jurisprudence riche en principes novateurs et en contradictions" [1994] *Revue du Marché Unique Européen* 117–60

Mattioni, A., "Lo Sviluppo democratico delle Comunità e il ruolo del Parlamento europeo" [1982] *Diritto Comunitario e degli Scambi Internazionali* 431–49

McGee, A. and S. Weatherill, "The Evolution of the Single Market-Harmonisation or Liberalisation" (1990) 53 *Modern Law Review* 578–96

McLaughlin, D., "The Work and Aims of the Economic and Social Committee of the EEC and Euratom" (1976–7) 14 *Journal of Common Market Studies* 9–28

Mégret, J., J.V. Louis, D. Vignes, M. Waelbroeck, J-L. Dewost, P. Brueckner and A. Sacchettini, *Le Droit de la Communauté économique européenne* (University of Brussels, Brussels, 1980)

Meij, A.W.H. and J.A. Winter, "Measures Having an Equivalent Effect to Quantitative Restrictions" (1976) 13 *Common Market Law Review* 79–104

Melchior, M., "Les Communications de la Commission" in *Mélanges en honneur de Fernand Dehousse* (Labor, Brussels, 1979), ii, 243–58

Merciai, P., "Safeguard Measures in GATT" [1985] *Journal of World Trade Law* 41–66

Messerlin, P.A., "The EC Antidumping Regulations: A First Economic Appraisal, 1980–83" [1989] *Weltwirtschaftliches Archiv* 563–87

—— "Nonborder Measures to Assist Industry" in J.M. Finger and A. Olechowski, *The Uruguay Round* (World Bank, Washington, DC, 1987) 127–36

Mestre, C. and Y. Petit, "La Cohesion économique et sociale après le Traité sur l'union européenne" [1995] *Revue Trimestrielle de Droit Européen* 207–43

Meyring, B., "Intergovernmentalism and Supranationality: Two Stereotypes for a Complex Reality" [1997] *European Law Review* 221–47

Miert, K. van, "The Appointment of the President and Members of the European Commission" (1973) 10 *Common Market Law Review* 257–73

Milas, R., "Les Relations entre la Communauté européenne et les pays nordiques" [1984] *Revue du Marché Commun* 534–43

Minneci, F. "Le Partecipazioni pubbliche al capitale di imprese" [1991] *Diritto Comunitario e degli Scambi Internazionali* 365–72

Mitchell, J.D.B., "The Tindemans Report – Retrospect and Prospect" (1976) 13 *Common Market Law Review* 455–70

Moller, J.O., "Financing European Integration: the European Communities and the Proposed European Union" in R. Bieber, R. Dehousse, J. Pinder, and J.H.H. Weiler (eds.), *1992: One European Market* (Nomos, Baden-Baden, 1988) 73–102

Mortelmans, K., "Article 30 of the EEC Treaty and Legislation Relating to Market Circumstances: A Time to Consider a New Definition?" (1991) 28 *Common Market Law Review* 115–36

—— "The Compensatory Justification Criterion in the Practice of the Commission in Decisions on State Aids" (1984) 21 *Common Market Law Review* 405–34

Moussis, N., "Small and Medium Enterprises in the Internal Market" [1992] *European Law Review* 483–98

Munch, F., "Prolégomènes à une théorie constitutionnelle des Communautés européennes" [1961] *Rivista di Diritto Europeo* 127–37

Muoser, T., *Finnlands Neutralität und die Europäische Wirtschaftsintegration* (Nomos, Baden-Baden, 1986)

Musgrave, R.A,. *The Theory of Public Finance* (McGraw-Hill, New York, 1959)

Nell, P. G., "EFTA in the 1990s: the Search for a New Identity" (1990) 28 *Journal of Common Market Studies* 327–58

Nene, C., "1992 et la Clause de l'article 115: à quand une politique commerciale commune?" [1988] *Revue du Marché Commun* 578–83

Neri, S. and H. Sperl, *Traité instituant la Communauté économique européenne* (Court of Justice of the European Communities, Luxembourg, 1960)

Neunreither, K., "Subsidiarity as a Guiding Principle for European Community Activities" [1993] *Government and Opposition* 206–20

Nicholl, W., "Historique de la composition de la majorité qualifiée dans Conseil en vertu des Traités" [1986] *Revue du Marché Commun* 135–37

—— "La Procedure de concertation entre le Parlement européen et le Conseil" [1986] *Revue du Marché Commun* 11–5

Nicolaides, P., "How Fair is Fair Trade?" [1986] *Journal of World Trade Law* 148–62.

—— "The Antidumping Policy of the European Communities" [1990] *Intereconomics* 273–79

Nicolaisen J. and P. Hoeller, *Economics and the Environment: A Survey of Issues and Policy Options* (OECD Working Paper No. 82, Paris, 1990)

North, D.C., *Institutions, Institutional Change and Economic Performance* (Cambridge University Press, Cambridge, 1990)

Nuttall, S., "The Commission: Protagonists of Inter-regional Cooperation" in G. Edwards and E. Regelsberger (eds.), *Europe's Global Links* (Pinter, London, 1990) 143–57

O'Cléireacáin, S., "Europe 1992 and Gaps in the EC's Common Commercial Policy" (1990) *Journal of Common Market Studies* 201–17

O'Leary, S., "Nationality Law and Community Citizenship: A Tale of Two Uneasy Bedfellows" [1992] *Yearbook of European Law* 353–84

Oliver, P., "Measures of Equivalent Effect: A Reappraisal" (1982) 19 *Common Market Law Review* 217–44

—— *The Free Movement of Goods in the EEC* (European Law Centre, London, 1988)

Ophuls, C.F., "La Rélance européenne" [1958] *European Yearbook* 3–15

Palmer, M. *The European Parliament* (Pergamon Press, Oxford, 1981)

Pålsson, L., *EG-rätt* (Studentlitteratur, Lund, 1976)

Peers, S., "An Ever Closer Waiting Room? The Case for Eastern European Accession to the European Economic Area" (1995) 32 *Common Market Law Review* 187–213

Pelkmans, J., "Europe – 1992 a Handmaiden to GATT" in F. Laursen (ed.), *Europe 1992: World Partner? the International Market and the World Political Economy* (EIPA, Maastricht, 1991) 125–53

—— "The European Community and the Newly Industrializing Countries" in W. Maihofer (ed.), *Noi si Mura* (EUI, Florence, 1986) 510–39

—— and M. Egan, *Fixing European Standards: Moving Beyond the Green Paper* (CEPS Working Document No. 65, Brussels 1992)

—— and A. Murphy, "Catapulted into Leadership: the Community's Trade and Aid Policies vis-à-vis Eastern Europe" [1991] *Revue d'Intégration Européenne* 125–51

Petersmann, E-U., "Constitutionalism, Constitutional Law and European Integration" [1991] *Aussenwirtschaft* 247–80

—— "GATT Law as International Legal Framework of the European Free Trade System" in O. Jacot-Guillarmod (ed.), *L'Avenir du libre-échange en Europe: vers un Espace économique européen* (Schulthess, Zürich, 1990) 111–29

—— "Strengthening the Domestic Legal Framework of the GATT Multilateral Trade System: Possibilities and Problems of Making GATT Rules Effective in Domestic Legal Systems" in E-U. Petersmann and M. Hilf (eds.), *The New GATT Round of Multilateral Trade Negotiations* (Kluwer, Deventer, 1991) 33–113

Phlips, L., *The Economics of Price Discrimination* (Cambridge University Press, Cambridge, 1983)

Pinder, D.A., "Small Firms, Regional Development and the European Investment Bank" (1986) 24 *Journal of Common Market Studies* 171–86

Pinder, J., "Positive Integration and Negative Integration: Some Problems of Economic Union in the EEC" [1968] *The World Today* 88–110

Porro, G., *L'Integrazione giuridica nell'Associazione europea di libero scambio* (Giuffré, Milan, 1983)

Priebe, R., "Le Droit communautaire des structures agricoles" [1988] *Cahiers de Droit Européen* 3–38

Priess, H.-J., "Recovery of Illegal State Aid: an Overview of Recent Developments in the Case Law" (1996) 33 *Common Market Law Review* 69–91

Pryce, R., *The Political Future of the European Community* (Marshbank, London, 1973)

Quadri, R., R. Monaco and A. Trabucchi, *Trattato istitutivo della Comunità economica europea* (Giuffré, Milan, 1965)

—— *Trattato istitutivo della Comunità europea del carbone e dell'acciaio: comentario* (Giuffré, Milan, 1970)

Quigley, C., "The Notion of State Aid in the EEC" [1988] *European Competition Law Review* 242–56

Regelsberger, E., "The Dialogue of the EC/Twelve with Other Regional Groups: A New European Identity in the International System" in G. Edwards and E. Regelsberger (eds.), *Europe's Global Links* (Pinter, London, 1990) 3–26

Reich, N., "The 'November Revolution' of the European Court of Justice: Keck, Meng and Audi Revisited" (1994) 31 *Common Market Law Review* 459–92

—— "Protection of Diffuse Interests in the EEC and the Perspective of "Progressively Establishing" an Internal Market [1988] *Journal of Consumer Policy* 395–417

Reuter, P., "Le Plan Schuman" (1952–II) *Revue des Cours* 523–640

Ringstedt, N., *Europa och Konsumentpolitiken* (Konsumentverket, Rapport 1989/90:7, Stockholm, 1990)

Rivello, R., "Il Ruolo delle regioni nel diritto comunitario e nel diritto internazionale: considerazioni sulla normativa vigente e sui progetti di revisione costituzionale" [1995] *Diritto Comunitario e degli Scambi Internazionali* 255–308

Roberti, G.M., "Le Contrôle de la Commission des Communautés européennes sur les aides nationales" [1993] *Actualité Juridique de Droit Administratif* 397–411

Robson, P. and I. Wooton, "The Transnational Enterprise and Regional Economic Integration" (1993) 31 *Journal of Common Market Studies* 71–89

Rosenthal, D.E., "Competition Policy" in G.C. Hufbauer (ed), *Europe 1992: an American Perspective* (Brookings Institution, Washington, DC, 1990) 293–343

Ross, M., "A Review of Developments in State Aids 1987–8" (1989) 26 *Common Market Law Review* 167–92

Sacchettini, A., "La Coopération européenne dans le domaine de la recherche scientifique et technique (COST)" [1974] *Revue Trimestrielle de Droit Européen* 445–63

Sadurska, R., "Reshaping Europe – or 'How to Keep Poor Cousins in (their) Home': A Comment on *The Transformation of Europe*" (1991) 100 *Yale Law Journal* 2501–10

Sahm, Y., "Die Verfassung der Europäischen Gemeinschaft für Kohle und Stahl" [1951]

Europa-Archiv 3977–85

Sandholtz, W. and J. Zysman, "1992: Recasting the European Bargain" (1989/90) 42 *World Politics* 94–128

Santiago, M.G., "Las 'Comunicaciones interpretativas' de la Comission: concepto y valor normativo" [1992] *Revista de Instituciones Europeas* 933–49

Sapir, A., "Les Aspects extérieurs du grand marché européen" [1989] *Revue d'Économie Politique* 692–719

—— *Regional Integration in Europe* (EC Commission Economic Papers No. 94, Brussels, 1992)

Scharpf, F.W., "The Joint-Decision Trap: Lessons from German Federalism and European Integration" [1988] *Public Administration* 239–78

Schermers, H.G., "Comment on Weiler's *The Transformation of Europe*" (1991) 100 *Yale Law Journal* 2525–36

Schricke, C. "La CEE et l'OCDE à l'heure de l'Acte Unique" [1989] *Revue Générale de Droit International Public* 801–30

Schricker, G., "European Harmonisation of Unfair Competition Law – a Futile Venture?" [1991] *International Review of Industrial Property and Copyright Law* 788–801

Schütte, M. and J.-P. Hix, "The Application of the EC State Aid Rules to Privatizations: The East German Example" (1995) 32 *Common Market Law Review* 215–48

Schwarze, J. (ed.), *The External Relations of the European Community, in Particular EC-US Relations* (Nomos, Baden-Baden, 1989)

Schwartz, W.F. and E.W. Harper, "The Regulation of Subsidies Affecting International Trade" (1972) 70 *Michigan Law Review* 831–58

Schwed, J.J., "Les Questions écrites du Parlement européen à la Commission" [1970] *Revue du Marché Commun* 365–8

Scott, A., J. Peterson, and D. Millar, "Subsidiarity: a Europe of the Regions v. the British Constitution" (1994) 32 *Journal of Common Market Studies* 47–68

Seeler, H.-J., "Vertrag zur Gründung der Europäischen Union" [1984] *Europa Recht* 41–53

Senti, R., *EG EFTA Binnenmarkt* (edn., Schulthess, Zurich, 2nd 1992)

—— "Ein EFTA-EG-Freihandelsvertrag für Dienstleistungen: Vorschlag eines Konzeptes" [1988] *Aussenwirtschaft* 367–84

Shigehara, K., "External Dimension of Europe 1992: Its Effects on the Relationship between Europe, the United States and Japan" [1991] *Bank of Japan Monetary and Economic Studies* 87–102

Sidjanski, D., "L'Originalité des Communautés européennes et la repartition de leurs pouvoirs" [1961] *Revue Générale de Droit International Public* 40–61

Siebert, H., *The New Economic Landscape in Europe* (Blackwell, Oxford, 1991)

—— and M. J. Koop, "Institutional Competition. A Concept for Europe" [1990] *Aussenwirtschaft* 439–62

Siedentopf, H. and J. Ziller (eds.), *Making European Policies Work: The Implementation of Community Legislation in the Member States* (Sage, London, 1988)

Silver, D.B. and G.L. Bustin, "Settlement of EEC Antidumping Proceedings" [1985] *The International Lawyer* 1273–87

Silvia, S.J., "The Social Charter of the European Community: A Defeat for European Labor" [1991] *Industrial and Labor Relations Review* 626–43

Simon, D., "Ordre public et libertés publiques dans les Communautés européennes" [1976] *Revue du Marché Commun* 201–23

Simon, H.A., *Models of Man* (John Wiley, New York, 1957)

—— "Rational Decision Making in Business Organizations" [1979] *American Economic*

Review 493–513

Sjöstedt, G., "Nordic and World Economic-Political Cooperation: Competition, Adaptation or Participation?" [1987] *Cooperation and Conflict* 209–26

Sloot, T. and P. Verschuren, "Decision-Making Speed in the European Community" (1990) 28 *Journal of Common Market Studies* 75–85

Slotboom, M.M., "State Aid in Community Law: Broad or Narrow Definition?" [1995] *European Law Review* 289–301

Smit, H. and P. Herzog, *The Law of the European Economic Community* (Matthew Bender, New York, 1976)

Smith, H., *The Power Game* (Ballantine, New York, 1993)

Snape, R.H., "International Regulation of Subsidies" (1991) 14 *The World Economy* 139–63

Snyder, F., "The Effectiveness of European Community Law: Institutions, Processes, Tools, and Techniques" (1993) 56 *Modern Law Review* 19–55

—— "Ideologies of Competition in European Community Law" (1989) 52 *Modern Law Review* 149–78

Spinelli, A., "Riflessioni sul Trattato-Costituzione per l'Unione Europea" [1984] *Annuario di Diritto Comparato e di Studi Legislativi* 27–52

Springer, U., "Meeting Competition: Justification of Price Discrimination under EC and US Antitrust Law" [1997] *European Competition Law Review* 251–8

Staker, C., "Free Movement of Goods in the EEC and Australia: A Comparative Study" [1990] *Yearbook of European Law* 209–42

Stechow, A. von, "The Council of Ministers: The Constraint on Action" in G. Edwards and E. Regelsberger (eds.), *Europe's Global Links* (Pinter, London, 1990) 161–8

Stegmann, K., "Anti-Dumping Policy and the Consumer" [1985] *Journal of World Trade Law* 466–84

—— "EC Anti-Dumping Policy: Are Price Undertakings a Legal Substitute for Illegal Price Fixing?" [1990] *Weltwirtschaftliches Archiv* 268–98

Steiner, J.M., "Drawing the Line: Uses and Abuses of Article 30 EEC" (1992) 29 *Common Market Law Review* 749–74

Stenberg, H., "Sweden and the Internal Market – Situating Some Problems" [1989] *Legal Issues of European Integration* 89–107

Stigler, G.J., *The Citizen and the State* (University of Chicago Press, Chicago, Ill., 1975)

Strange, S., "The Persistence of the Problems in EC-US Relations: Conflicts of Perception" in J. Schwarze (ed.), *The External Relations of the European Community, in Particular EC-US Relations* (Nomos, Baden-Baden, 1989) 109–18

Streeck, W. and P.C. Schmitter, "From National Corporatism to Transnational Pluralism: Organised Interests in the Single European Market" [1991] *Politics and Society* 133–64

Sun, J-M. and J. Pelkmans, "Regulatory Competition in the Single Market" (1995) 33 *Journal of Common Market Studies* 567–89

Techini, I., "Il Contributo delle regioni al processo d'integrazione europea" [1990] *Rivista di Diritto Europeo* 267–77

Thomasis, G. de, "Project d'Union européenne à la veille de la campagne pour les deuxième elections européennes"[1984] *Revue du Marché Commun* 212–14

Timmermans, C.W.A., "Common Commercial Policy (Article 113 EEC) and International Trade in Services" in F. Capotorti, C.-D. Ehlermann, J.A. Fröwein, F. Jacobs, R. Joliet, T. Koopmans, and R. Kovar (eds.), *Du Droit international au droit de l'intégration, Liber Amicorum Pierre Pescatore* (Nomos, Baden-Baden, 1987) 675–89

—— "How Can One Improve the Quality of Community Legislation" (1997) 34 *Common Market Law Review* 1229–57

Tinbergen, J., *International Economic Integration* (2nd edn, Elsevier, Amsterdam, 1965)

Torre, A. de la and M.R. Kelly, *Regional Trade Arrangements* (International Monetary Fund, Occasional Paper No. 93, Washington, DC, 1992)

Torrelli, M., "La Neutralité en question" [1992] *Revue Générale de Droit International Public* 5–43

Traxler, F., "Interests, Politics and European Integration" [1992] *European Journal of Political Research* 193–217

Tsoukalis, L., *The New European Economy: the Politics and Economics of Integration* (Oxford University Press, Oxford, 1991)

Urban, S. and S. Vendemini, *European Strategic Alliances* (Blackwell, Oxford, 1992)

Verhoeven, J., "Les Citoyens de l'Europe" [1993] *Annales de Droit de Louvain* 165–91

Verloren van Themaat, P., "The Contribution of the Establishment of the Internal Market by the Case Law of the Court of Justice of the European Communities" in R. Bieber, R. Dehousse, J. Pinder, and J.H.H. Weiler (eds.), *1992: One European Market* (Nomos, Baden-Baden, 1988) 109–20

—— "Some Preliminary Observations on the Intergovernmental Conferences: the Relations between the Concepts of a Common Market, a Monetary Union, an Economic Union, a Political Union, and Sovereignty" (1991) 28 *Common Market Law Review* 291–318

Vermulst, E. and P. Waer, "European Community Rules of Origin as Commercial Policy Instruments" [1990] *Journal of World Trade* 55–100

Verrill, C.O., "Non-market Economy Dumping: New Directions in Fair Value Analysis" (1988) 21 *George Washington Journal of International Law and Economics* 427–37

Verschueren,, H. "EC Social Security Coordination Excluding Third Country Nationals: Still in Line with Fundamental Rights after the Gaygusuz Judgment?" (1997) 34 *Common Market Law Review* 991–1017

Vignes, D., *Communauté européenne du charbon et de l'acier* (Thone, Liège, 1956)

Viner, J., *Dumping: a Problem in International Trade* (Chicago University Press, Chicago, Ill., 1923)

Vogel, L., *Droit de concurrence et concentration économique* (Economica, Paris, 1988)

Waelbroeck, M., "Les Effets internes des accords internationaux conclus par la Communauté économique européenne" in *Le Droit des peuples à disposer d'eux-mêmes, Mélanges offerts à Charles Chaumont* (Pedone, Paris, 1984) 579–91

Wallace, H., "The Best is the Enemy of the 'Could': Bargaining in the European Community" in S. Tarditi, K.J. Thompson, P. Pierani, and L. Croci-Angelini (eds.), *Agricultural Trade Liberalization and the European Community* (Clarendon Press, Oxford, 1989) 193–206

—— "The Council and the Commission after the Single European Act" in L. Hurwitz and C. Lequesne (eds.), *The State of the European Community* (Lynne Rienner, Boulder, Colo., 1991) 19–31

Wallace, W., *The Transformation of Western Europe* (Pinter, London, 1990)

Weber S. and H. Wiesmith, "Issue Linkage in the European Community" (1991) 29 *Journal of Common Market Studies* 255–67

Weidemann, R. "The Anti-Dumping Policy of the European Communities" [1990] *Intereconomics* 28–35

Weiler, J., "Thou Shalt Not Oppress a Stranger: on the Judicial Protection of the Human Rights of Non-EC Nationals – A Critique" [1992] *European Journal of International Law* 65–91

—— "The Transformation of Europe" (1991) 100 *Yale Law Journal* 2403–83

Weiss, F., "The European Free Trade Association After Twenty-five Years" [1985] *Yearbook of European Law* 287–323

Wellens, K.C. and G.M. Borchardt, "Soft Law in European Community Law" [1989] *European Law Review* 267–321

Wellenstein, E.P., "The Free Trade Agreements Between the Enlarged European Communities and the EFTA-States" (1973) 10 *Common Market Law Review* 137–49

Wetter, T., "Trade Policy Developments in the Steel Sector" [1985] *Journal of World Trade Law* 485–96

Wettig, G., "Security in Europe: A Challenging Task" [1992] *Aussenpolitik* 3–11

White, E.L., "In Search of the Limits to Article 30 of the EEC Treaty" (1989) 26 *Community Market Law Review* 235–80

Wijkman, M., *Patterns of Production and Trade in Western Europe: Looking Forward After Thirty Years* (EFTA Occasional Paper No. 32, Geneva, 1990)

Wilke, H. and H. Wallace, *Subsidiarity: Approaches to Power-Sharing in the European Community* (RIIA Discussion Paper 27, London, 1990)

Wilkinson, D., "Maastricht and the Environment: the Implications for the EC's Environmental Policy of the Treaty on European Union" [1992] *Journal of Environmental Law* 221–39

Wille, E., "The Conciliation Procedure and the European Parliament's Pursuit of Legislative Power" [1984] *Il Politico* 489–500

Wils, G., "The Concept of Reciprocity in EEC Law: An Exploration into these Realms" (1991) 28 *Common Market Law Review* 245–74

Wils, W.P.J., "The Search for the Rule in Article 30EEC Much Ado About Nothing?" [1993] *European Law Review* 475–92

Winter, J.A., "Supervision of State Aid: Article 93 in the Court of Justice" (1993) 30 *Common Market Law Review* 311–29

—— "The ERDF and the Principle of Additionality" in *In Orde, Liber Amicorum Pieter Verloren van Themaat* (Kluwer, Deventer, 1982), 365–80

Winters, A., "Goals and Own Goals in European Trade Policy" (1992) 15 *The World Economy* 557–74

Wohlfarth, E., U. Everling, H.J. Glaesner, and R. Sprung, *Die Europäische Wirtschaftsgemeinschaft* (Vahlen, Berlin, 1960)

Woodland, P., "Le Processus legislatif dans la Communauté économique européenne" [1985] *Revue du Marché Commun* 503–11

Wyatt, D. and A. Dashwood, *The Substantive Law of the EEC* (3rd edn., Sweet & Maxwell, London, 1993)

Yannopoulos, G.N., "Trade Policy Issues on the Completion of the Internal Market" in G.N. Yannopoulos (ed.), *Europe and America, 1992* (Manchester University Press, Manchester, 1991), 9–23

Zellentin, G., "The Economic and Social Committee" (1962–3) 1 *Journal of Common Market Studies* 22–8

Index